AFRICA 2050
REALIZING THE CONTINENT'S FULL POTENTIAL

AFRICA 2050
REALIZING THE CONTINENT'S FULL POTENTIAL

Editors

Theodore Ahlers
Hiroshi Kato
Harinder S. Kohli
Callisto Madavo
Anil Sood

OXFORD UNIVERSITY PRESS

OXFORD
UNIVERSITY PRESS

Oxford University Press is a department of the University of Oxford.
It furthers the University's objective of excellence in research, scholarship,
and education by publishing worldwide. Oxford is a registered trademark of
Oxford University Press in the UK and in certain other countries

Published in India by
Oxford University Press
YMCA Library Building, 1 Jai Singh Road, New Delhi 110001, India

© Centennial Group International 2014

Centennial Group International
2600 Virginia Avenue NW,
Suite 201, Washington, DC 20037

Japan International Cooperation Agency Research Institute
10-5 Ichigaya Honmura-cho Shinjuku-ku
Tokyo 162-8433, Japan

The moral rights of the authors have been asserted

First edition published in 2014

All rights reserved. No part of this publication may be reproduced, stored in
a retrieval system, or transmitted, in any form or by any means, without the
prior permission in writing of Oxford University Press, or as expressly permitted
by law, by licence, or under terms agreed with the appropriate reprographics
rights organization. Enquiries concerning reproduction outside the scope of the
above should be sent to the Rights Department, Oxford University Press, at the
address above

You must not circulate this work in any other form
and you must impose this same condition on any acquirer

ISBN-13: 978-0-19-945040-4
ISBN-10: 0-19-945040-4

Printed in India at Lustra Print Process Pvt Ltd., New Delhi

This report is part of a study commissioned by 5th Joint Annual Meetings of the AU
and ECA Conference of Ministers.

The findings and recommendations of the report are solely the responsibility of the
Centennial Group International.

Table of Contents

xi	**List of Appendixes, Boxes, Figures, and Tables**
xxi	**List of Abbreviations**
xxiii	**Foreword**
xxv	**Preface**
xxvii	**Acknowledgments**
1	**Introduction**
1	Background
2	Rising Aspirations
3	A Highly Diverse and Heterogeneous Region
4	What Is Unique about This Book?
5	Assumptions and Organization
9	**Part 1: Realizing the Continent's Full Potential**
11	**Chapter 1: A 2050 Vision to Meet African Aspirations**
11	The Big Picture
12	People, Economies, and the Continent
15	Alternative Scenarios: Enormous Cost of Failure
25	**Chapter 2: Historical Perspectives and Drivers of Future Change**
25	Past Performance
27	Lessons from Asia and Latin America
30	Drivers of Change: Global and Africa-Specific

41	Major Risks — Need to be Actively Managed

51	**Chapter 3: Action Agenda — Jobs for People, Economies, and the Continent**
51	Prosperous People and Cohesive Societies — Jobs to Transform Lives
59	Diverse, Competitive Economies — Private Investment to Create Jobs
67	Integrated Africa — Bigger Markets to Foster Investment and Higher Productivity Jobs

73	**Chapter 4: Better Governance to Deliver Results**
73	Capable States
77	Pragmatic Leadership
78	Concluding Note: Africa's Future Is in Its Own Hands

81	**Part II: People, Economies, and the Continent**

81	**Section A: Prosperous People and Cohesive Societies — Jobs to Transform Lives**

83	**Chapter 5: Accelerating the Demographic Transition**
85	Components of the Demographic Transition
94	Implications for the Future
99	Action Agenda

105	**Chapter 6: Eliminating Fragility and Conflict**
105	Africa in 2013: Success, Diversity, and Fragility
106	Fragile, Conflict-Affected, and Failed States — The Underlying Realities
117	Future Shocks May Either Destroy or Force Change on Fragile States
122	Action Agenda

137	**Chapter 7: Ensuring Equity and Inclusion**
138	Evolution of Poverty and Inequality in Africa
143	Access to Education
144	Access to Health
147	Access to Water and Sanitation
150	Prospects for 2050
150	Action Agenda

159 Chapter 8: Breaking the Human Capital Barrier
- 161 Key Drivers of Change in Education and Health
- 167 Key Messages
- 172 Action Agenda

193 Section B: Diverse, Competitive Economies – Private Investments to Create Jobs

195 Chapter 9: Maintaining Macroeconomic Stability and Increasing Resilience
- 196 Broad Trends in Africa's Economic Performance (1960 – 2011)
- 216 Investment and Savings Needs for Sustained High Growth
- 223 Action Agenda

233 Chapter 10: Enhancing Growth, Competitiveness, and Job Creation
- 234 Current Status: Economic Structure, Employment, Competitiveness, and Productivity
- 240 Factors Underlying Africa's Competitiveness, Productivity, and Growth
- 256 Vision Africa 2050
- 258 Action Agenda

267 Chapter 11: Transforming African Agriculture
- 267 The Challenges
- 268 Economic Growth and Agriculture
- 270 African Agriculture in 2010
- 273 Agriculture Paths to 2050
- 291 Action Agenda

309 Chapter 12: Harnessing Natural Resources for Diversification
- 311 Historical Context
- 324 A Vision for Africa's Extractive Industries in 2050
- 324 Action Agenda

339 Chapter 13: Managing Urbanization for Growth
- 340 Urban Transition
- 346 Urban Policy Challenges
- 349 Vision for 2050
- 350 Action Agenda

Section C: Integrated Continent—Bigger Markets to Foster Investment and Higher Productivity Jobs — 359

Chapter 14: Enhancing Regional Cooperation and Integration on the Continent — 361
- 361 Why Africa Should Strive for Regional Cooperation and Integration
- 362 Economic Imperatives for Regional Cooperation
- 365 Past Efforts on Regional Cooperation and Integration
- 368 Status of Regional Trade and Investment Flows
- 369 Lessons from Other Regions
- 372 Action Agenda

Chapter 15: Mitigating and Adapting to Climate Change — 379
- 380 Dealing with Climate Change
- 381 Africa and Climate Change
- 384 Mitigation Measures
- 386 Adaptation Plans
- 390 Funding, Technology, and Market Mechanisms Associated with Climate Change Measures
- 392 Action Agenda

Chapter 16: Repositioning Africa in the World — 399
- 400 Evolution of Old and New Partnerships
- 410 The Trade Dimension
- 413 Investment in Africa: Growing Rapidly but Concentrated
- 414 Conflict and Climate Change Have Risen on the Agenda
- 416 What is Likely to Happen Next
- 420 Action Agenda

Annex 1: Commodity Terms of Trade in Africa: A Fragile Blessing — 429

Annex 2: Model of Global Economy — 453

References — 459

About the Editors and Contributors — 475
- 475 Editors
- 477 Contributors

483 **Index**

489 **Photo Credits**

List of Appendixes, Boxes, Figures, and Tables

List of Appendixes

Chapter 11

298	Appendix 1: Cropped Areas by Path in IFPRI IMPACT
301	Appendix 2: Crop Yields by Path in IFPRI IMPACT
303	Appendix 3: Value by Path in Transformation Scenario

Chapter 14

375	Appendix 1: Active Regional Economic Communities

Annex 1

446	Appendix 1: Measurement of Trading Gains and Losses
448	Appendix 2: Classification of African Countries

List of Boxes

Chapter 2

28	2.1	The different lessons from East Asia and Latin America
31	2.2	Managing natural resources: The example of Chile
39	2.3	Africa's commodity terms of trade — A fragile blessing
46	2.4	Are some African economies mired in the middle-income trap?

Chapter 3

56	3.1	Agenda for education
58	3.2	Agenda for reducing conflict and fragility
60	3.3	Agenda for competition, private sector development, and productivity

61	3.4	Agenda for jobs
64	3.5	Agenda for agriculture
65	3.6	Agenda for extractive industries
66	3.7	Agenda for cities

Chapter 4
| 74 | 4.1 | Rule of law |
| 76 | 4.2 | Governance |

Chapter 6
| 108 | 6.1 | Declining number of armed conflicts in Africa |
| 126 | 6.2 | Building institutions that are inclusive and legitimate in the eyes of local people |

Chapter 7
| 139 | 7.1 | Current situation and future challenges for achieving the MDGs |

Chapter 8
| 173 | 8.1 | The imperative to sharply increase SSA's investment in young children |
| 176 | 8.2 | Health in Africa — big gains…and big challenges |

Chapter 11
| 271 | 11.1 | African agriculture performance |

Chapter 12
321	12.1	Mining ownership in Zimbabwe and South Africa
323	12.2	Botswana – Diamond Sorting Initiative
327	12.3	Global transparency initiatives for resource-rich countries
330	12.4	African countries with stabilization or wealth funds
332	12.5	Chile's structural overall balance rule and wealth funds

Chapter 14
| 374 | 14.1 | East African Community — Ahead of the rest |

List of Figures

Introduction

1	I	African economies have turned around since 1995
4	II	Africa is largely made up of low- and lower-middle-income countries

Chapter 1

16	1.1	African GDP growth has greatly increased since 1995
17	1.2	There is a high opportunity cost for not achieving the convergence scenario
20	1.3	Raising future income levels depends on achieving the convergence scenario

Chapter 2

26	2.1	Africa's share of world population has risen since 1900, but its share of GDP continued to decline until 1995
26	2.2	Africa's GDP per capita growth lagged the world's until 2000
30	2.3	TFP in African countries has grown at a low rate compared to China and India
36	2.4	The number of children and working age adults depends critically on fertility
38	2.5	Africa's GDP per capita growth rate has generally followed the growth rate of commodity prices
42	2.6	Poverty has declined more quickly in Asia than in Africa
43	2.7	Sub-Saharan Africa has the highest disparities after Latin America
43	2.8	South Africa has the highest inequality in Africa
44	2.9	African GDP per capita relative to global GDP per capita is lower today than at independence
46	2.i	GDP per capita

Chapter 3

52	3.1	Framework for achieving the 2050 vision
54	3.2	A virtuous circle of inclusion, demographic transition, and human capital
57	3.3	A significant portion of Africa is considered fragile

Chapter 4

74	4.i	Most African countries fair poorly on the rule of law scale

Chapter 5

86	5.1	Most countries in Africa have had their 2005-2010 fertility revised upwards
87	5.2	Countries across the continent are at very different stages in their fertility transition

88	5.3	Many other emerging markets have seen greater demographic progress since 1960
89	5.4	Total fertility and life expectancy are inversely related
91	5.5	Contraception adoption in Sub-Saharan Africa has been very slow
92	5.6	In much of Africa, modern contraception is rare
98	5.7	Much of Africa will rapidly urbanize between 2010 and 2050

Chapter 6
| 108 | 6.i | Conflict in Africa has become less frequent since the late 1990s |
| 108 | 6.ii | ...following the global downward trend since the early 1990s |

Chapter 7
138	7.1	Poverty has declined much faster in Asia than in the rest of the developing world
140	7.2	Rural poverty is more prevalent than urban poverty in Africa
142	7.3	Inequality varies significantly throughout Africa
145	7.4	In much of Africa, far more girls are out of school than boys
147	7.5	Infant mortality varies widely for rich and poor families
148	7.6	An increasing percentage of Africans have access to safe drinking water
149	7.7	Access to improved sanitation remains a serious problem
151	7.8	Millions of Africans would be lifted out of poverty in the convergence scenario
152	7.9	The emergence of an African middle class would be a hallmark of convergence

Chapter 8
163	8.1	Africans are spending more time in school, but the continent still lags well behind the rest of the world
163	8.2	Africa's young population will boom in the next decade, making its educational institutions critically important
166	8.3	Infectious diseases are still central in Africa, but non-communicable ailments are becoming more important
176	8.i	Average annual rate of reduction for under-five mortality
176	8.ii	Average annual rate of reduction for maternal mortality

Chapter 9
197	9.1	After declining over two decades Africa's growth has averaged above 4 percent since the mid-1990s
198	9.2	High growth in the 1960s and 1970s was accompanied by volatility
200	9.3	Investment has generally outpaced savings in Africa

200	9.4	After a surge in the 1990s, inflation has largely been brought down to more manageable levels
201	9.5	Inflation in Africa has historically been tied closely to monetary expansion
203	9.6	Both Sub-Saharan Africa and North Africa ran large deficits during the 1980s and early 1990s
204	9.7	External current account deficits were large relative to exports
205	9.8	Debt sustainability became a central issue in the early 1990s
206	9.9	Debt relief efforts helped Africa to begin accumulating foreign reserves
207	9.10	In spite of recent global headwinds, Africa has grown steadily in the past 15 years
208	9.11	Long plagued by volatility, African economies have recently become much more resilient
210	9.12	Even Africa's fragile countries have had recent success managing inflation
211	9.13	Africa's public finances deteriorated after the financial crisis
212	9.14	Government revenues dropped, more than in other regions, during the crisis
212	9.15	Government expenditures in Africa have remained relatively stable since 2007
213	9.16	Public finances have varied greatly across the continent
214	9.17	Government revenues are larger in fragile states and early convergers
214	9.18	Increases in government spending have mirrored increases in government revenues
215	9.19	Since the crisis, public debt has slowly increased in Africa
216	9.20	The increase in African debt has been driven by the early convergers
217	9.21	In spite of the crisis, Africa has managed its current account balance well
217	9.22	Early convergers have tended to run larger deficits than other African economies
219	9.23	African investment trails behind many emerging economies
219	9.24	Although late convergers have seen a recent rise in investment, the meager performance of Africa's early convergers is worrisome
220	9.25	African savings rates trails those in Developing Asia
220	9.26	Late convergers have had higher rates of savings than early convergers

Chapter 10

234	10.1	Africa is growing faster and GDP per capita growth has kept pace with the world since 1995
239	10.2	Africa scores low on global competitiveness
240	10.3	Africa's share of global exports is negligible, except in fuels and minerals
241	10.4	Starting from a very low base….
241	10.5	…African economies have been catching up
242	10.6	TFP contributes over a third of Africa's growth
243	10.7	Savings rates have risen but need to be increased further together with investment

245	10.8	African intraregional trade is below that of other regions
246	10.9	Africa faces competition in export markets mostly with respect to commodities
247	10.10	Africa ranks poorly in terms of "Doing Business," but there are significant differences between countries
248	10.11	Africa is average in terms of starting a business, with early convergers ranking relatively high
248	10.12	Most African countries rate poorly on rule of law
249	10.13	Africa scores lower on infrastructure than all other regions
252	10.14	African economies rank poorly in innovation…
252	10.15	…but some African economies rate higher for innovation than others
253	10.16	Entrepreneurship is strongly correlated with TFP
254	10.17	African economies rank poorly for entrepreneurship
255	10.18	Africa was an attractive destination for FDI in the early 1970s
255	10.19	Absolute levels of FDI into Africa rose sharply between 2000 and 2011

Chapter 11

| 271 | 11.i | Increases in African agricultural output have largely come from increased harvested areas, not higher yields |
| 272 | 11.ii | The trade deficit in cereals has widened for Sub-Saharan Africa over the past 40 years |

Chapter 12

| 313 | 12.1 | Resource rents and GDP growth are not strongly correlated in Africa |
| 315 | 12.2 | Commodity prices fluctuate in a boom-bust cycle |

Chapter 13

| 341 | 13.1 | African cities will explode in size over the next decade |
| 342 | 13.2 | Africa's population will be largely urban by 2050 |

Chapter 15

382	15.1	African emits less GHG than any region
382	15.2	Some African states exceed the global average for GHG emission
391	15.3	The flow of external funding to Africa has increased in the past decade

Chapter 16

| 402 | 16.1 | ODA as a percentage of GNI has varied throughout the past 50 years |
| 410 | 16.2 | African trade with emerging partners more than doubled between 1992 and 2009 |

Annex 1

433	A1.1	Rising world demand for raw materials since 2000 has helped push commodity prices up
433	A1.2	The terms of trade of the developing world are highly volatile
435	A1.3	Africa's terms of trade move closely in line with commodity prices
437	A1.4	Imports in Africa and Latin America track the purchasing power of the region's exports
438	A1.5	A large portion of GDP growth in the past decade has been tied to terms of trade increases, especially in Africa
442	A1.6	Without the terms of trade effect, Africa's past decade would have been far less successful
444	A1.7	Even minor drops in African terms of trade would dampen future growth prospects
445	A1.8	Policymakers need to take into account the impact of a plateauing of Africa's terms of trade

List of Tables

Chapter 2
39	2.i	Africa GDI, GDP, and terms of trade

Chapter 5
95	5.1	The medium-fertility scenario paints an optimistic demographic picture

Chapter 7
141	7.1	Many African nations struggle with gender equality
142	7.2	Africa's top quintile spends significantly more per capita than its bottom quintile
143	7.3	Primary completion rates have increased dramatically since 1991, especially for girls
146	7.4	The impact of HIV/AIDS has led to differing health outcomes across the continent

Chapter 8
168	8.1	Ambitious education target would help drive Africa toward convergence

Chapter 9
209	9.1	Resilience Index

Chapter 10

236	10.1	Africa is still undergoing its sectoral transformation
237	10.2	Participation rates are low and unemployment high for females in North Africa
237	10.3	Three-quarters of employment in SSA is vulnerable employment
238	10.4	The share of industry and services in employment remains very low in SSA
244	10.5	Lack of competition is a serious concern for African economies
244	10.6	Cost of trading across borders is high
246	10.7	Africa's exports are concentrated in a small number of products and a small number of trading partners
250	10.8	Africa's infrastructure costs are also higher

Chapter 11

269	11.1	Incomes in 2050 depend crucially on productivity growth assumptions
270	11.2	African incomes can grow faster than population in the convergence scenario
275	11.3	Agricultural production would grow dramatically in the transformation scenario

Chapter 12

311	12.1	Africa contains modest portions of many of the world's most valuable resources
312	12.2	Several African nations have vast stocks of hydrocarbons
317	12.3	Some African nations are heavily reliant on resource rents, while others lack them entirely
318	12.4	The same framework applies to most resource deposits, although it depends on a country's legal complexities

Chapter 13

345	13.1	Cities will require much more land in the coming decades

Chapter 14

363	14.1	No African nation reaches the top rankings of the world's largest economies
364	14.2	Most African economies are relatively small
368	14.3	African intraregional trade is low by global standards
374	14.i	The EAC has done relatively well moving toward integrated reform

Chapter 15

383	15.1	The changing climate is a serious risk factor for much of Africa

Chapter 16

404	16.1	ODA, FDI, and remittances are all key sources of external financing for Africa
411	16.2	China has become more and more important for Africa in the past decade
413	16.3	Traditional partners remain the key source of FDI, but emerging markets are becoming increasingly important
414	16.4	FDI flows vary greatly throughout the continent

Annex 1

434	A1.1	Terms of trade changes
439	A1.2	The terms of trade effect has fueled growth but will not last forever
440	A1.3	Terms of trade have a powerful impact on Africa's economic activity
443	A1.4	A decline in the developing world's terms of trade would significantly impact their domestic economies

List of Abbreviations

ACP	African, Caribbean, and the Pacific
AfDB	African Development Bank
AMU	Arab Maghreb Union
AQIM	Al-Qaeda in the Islamic Maghreb
AU	African Union
BRIC	Brazil, Russia, India, China
CAR	Central African Republic
CEMAC	Central African Economic and Monetary Union (Communauté Économique et Monétaire de l'Afrique Centrale)
CESs	city enabling systems
CET	common external tariff
COMESA	Common Market for Eastern and Southern Africa
CPR	contraceptive prevalence rates
DAC	Development Assistance Committee
DHS	Demographic and Health Surveys
DRC	Democratic Republic of the Congo
EAC	East African Community
ECCE	early childhood care and education
ECOWAS	Economic Community of West African States
EITI	Extractive Industries Transparency Initiative
ESSF	Economic and Social Stabilization Fund (Chile)
FAO	Food and Agriculture Organization
FDI	foreign direct investment
GER	gross enrollment ratio
GHG	greenhouse gases
GNI	gross national income
GSPC	Salafist Group for Preaching and Combat
HIPC	heavily indebted poor countries

ICT	information and communications technology
IFPRI	International Food Policy Research Institute
IPCC	Intergovernmental Panel on Climate Change
LAM	lactational amenorrhea method
MDG	Millennium Development Goal
MDRI	Multilateral Debt Relief Initiative
MFN	most favored nation
MSME	micro, small, and medium enterprises
MUJOA	Movement for Oneness and Jihad in West Africa
NAMA	Nationally Appropriate Mitigation Actions
NAP	National Adaption Plan
NIC	newly industrialized country
ODA	official development assistance
OECD	Organisation for Economic Co-operation and Development
PIU	project implementation unit
PPP	purchasing power parity
PPP	public-private partnership
REC	Regional Economic Community
REDD	Reduced Emissions from Deforestation and Forest Degradation
SACU	Southern African Customs Union
SADC	Southern African Development Community
SME	small and medium enterprises
SSA	Sub-Saharan Africa
STI	science, technology, and innovation
TICAD	Tokyo International Conference on African Development
TFP	total factor productivity
TFR	total fertility rate
TVSD	technical and vocational skills development
UNDP	UN Development Programme
UNECA	UN Economic Commission for Africa
WAEMU	West African Economic and Monetary Union

Note: Unless otherwise specified, all currency is given in US dollars.

Foreword

Africa is on the march again. In the past ten years the continent has dramatically turned around its fortunes after two decades of social turmoil and disappointing economic performance. Vast numbers of countries in the region are enjoying macroeconomic stability, and economic growth has risen to satisfactory levels; indeed, in the last decade, six of the world's ten fastest-growing economies were in Africa. Millions of Africans have escaped absolute poverty. Literacy rates for both men and women have risen, and other human development indicators have started to exhibit similar improvements. The curse of HIV/AIDS and other diseases like malaria and tuberculosis is finally being curbed, though their incidence remains much too high. We Africans have also intensified our joint efforts to reduce civil strife in our midst. Democracy is starting to take hold in more and more countries; we finally have a growing number of examples of peaceful and constitutional transitions of power through open and credible elections. This process is bringing to power a new generation of leaders.

Despite this solid progress, we cannot rest on our laurels. While our successes are real, our journey is by no means complete. And while our successes are hard-earned, our recent economic growth has been facilitated by a favorable global economic environment, including high prices for our main exports. We must stand ready to face potential headwinds in the future from a changing world economy. Overcoming the scourge of poverty — we still suffer from the highest incidence of absolute poverty — will take many more decades of high economic growth. More inclusive growth is necessary to eliminate the widespread inequities. Our economies are still too heavily dependent on the vicissitudes of commodity markets. Too many of our young are without meaningful jobs, and they are getting restless. Indeed, our recent economic successes combined with the communications revolution have raised people's expectations even higher.

Our recent progress provides a solid basis to propel our region to even higher levels of performance and bolster our people's well-being. What we need is a clear common vision of where our continent should be headed over the longer term and a broad strategy for getting there. This common vision can then guide our actions at the regional level as well as provide the basis for specific plans and actions at the individual country level.

I had the privilege of hosting and chairing the Fourth Africa Emerging Markets Forum in Abidjan in June 2013 at which the Emerging Markets Forum presented the main findings of its study on Africa 2050 commissioned by the Joint Ministerial Meeting of the UN Economic Commission for Africa (UNECA) and the African Union (AU) in Addis Ababa in March 2012. The Africa 2050 Vision presented in the study is inspirational and ambitious, yet eminently plausible.

This study presents exactly the kind of vision and strategy Africa urgently needs and must agree on in order to build on its recent successes and realize the full potential of the continent.

I congratulate the Emerging Markets Forum for taking on this challenging project and the editors for producing an excellent book so soon after the Forum in Abidjan. I believe that this book is a must-read for all African leaders — whether in politics, business, or civil society — and all top policymakers, academics, senior officers of international development institutions, and opinion leaders interested in our continent's long-term economic and social development.

Alassane Ouattara

President
Côte d'Ivoire

Preface

Africa is a huge and highly diverse region. It has the second largest population and also the second largest land mass (after Asia) of all regions. Comprising 54 countries of different sizes and with widely different history, culture, resource endowment, institutional and human capacity, and level of per capita income, the continent offers both a daunting challenge and a major opportunity for economic and social development. What happens in the countries during the next two generations will have a decisive impact not only on the well-being of the more than 2 billion Africans who will inhabit the continent but also on the rest of humanity.

Since 1995, Africa's social and economic performance has been strong. It became the second fastest growing region of world. Its per capita income grew at 2.2 percent annually, and the poverty rate fell by a total of 10 percentage points, by far the best performance in the last 40 years. Simultaneously, the continent has made major progress in many, though not all, social indicators including childhood mortality and primary school enrollment.

Africans and their international development partners should derive much satisfaction from the economic and social turnaround since 1995; still, they should neither take this progress for granted nor become complacent. Over the longer term, though Africa has made some welcome progress since independence in the 1950s and 1960s, its progress has been slow compared to Southeast Asia. Yet this recent progress does provide an excellent foundation for Africa to do even better in the future and catch up with the faster-growing emerging economies, particularly in Asia. Then, by 2050 the continent could occupy a place in the global economy that is more representative of its size, population, and resource endowment. To get there, Africa must embrace a more ambitious vision and then work hard to realize it.

We commend the Emerging Markets Forum for developing such a vision in response to a request by the 5th Joint Annual Meetings of the AU and ECA Conference of Ministers held in March 2012 in Addis Ababa. In our view, such an ambitious vision and related strategies are necessary to effectively marshal Africa's vast resources — human, physical, and political — and lift an average African's well-being to the level she or he aspires to and deserves.

In our view, the vision portrayed in this book is ambitious but plausible. African leaders and people must embrace it and do their utmost to achieve it. Failure to do so could put the social and political fabric of the continent at risk.

The biggest danger is that Africans may feel satisfied with the current pace of change. Only if Africans — and their international partners, both public and private — raise their ambitions still further will the continent achieve its full potential.

We congratulate the authors for presenting such a compelling inspirational vision and for discussing some very sensitive topics with professionalism and, at the same time, due respect. The report deserves close attention from all Africans and their partners. We hope that it will lead to urgent action.

Benjamin Mkapa
Co-chair, Emerging Market Forum
Former President, Tanzania

Horst Koehler
Co-chair, Emerging Markets Forum
Former President, Germany

Michel Camdessus
Co-chair, Emerging Markets Forum
Former Managing Director, IMF

Acknowledgments

This book originates from a study commissioned by the 5th Joint Annual Meetings of the AU and ECA Conference of Ministers in March 2012 and conducted by the Emerging Markets Forum and Centennial Group International.

The study was directed by a core team led by Callisto Madavo and composed of Theodore Ahlers, Harinder S. Kohli, Praful Patel, and Anil Sood. The book benefited greatly from the discussion of the study's findings and proposals at a JICA-sponsored seminar at the 5th TICAD meeting in Yokohama in June 2013 and at the Africa Emerging Markets Forum held in Abidjan also in June 2013.

The chapters are based on the study overview prepared by Theodore Ahlers, Harinder S. Kohli, and Anil Sood and background papers prepared by (in alphabetical order): Emmanuel Akpa, Mahmood Ayub, Anupam Basu, James Bond, Fantu Cheru, David DeGroot, Jose Fajgenbaum, Herve Ferhani, Birger Fredriksen, Jean-Pierre Guengant, Ruth Kagia, Harinder S. Kohli, Harpaul A. Kohli, Brian Levy, Claudio M. Loser, John May, John Murray McIntire, Serge Michailof, Letitia Obeng, Praful Patel, Jeffrey Racki, Anil Sood, and Graham Stegmann.

The book has also benefited from the inputs of Naohiro Kitano of the Japanese International Cooperation Agency (JICA) and his colleagues Koji Makino, Ryutaro Murotani, Tomonori Sudo, Ikuo Takizawa, Ippei Tsuruga, and Kei Yoshizawa in Tokyo as well as Hiroto Kamishi and Miki Inaoka at JICA's office in Washington, DC. Drew Arnold, Katy Grober, Michael Lopesciolo, Alex Tate, and Ieva Vilkelyte provided valuable research and production support.

The study was made possible by generous support from JICA, Deutsche Gesellschaft für Internationale Zusammenarbeit (GIZ), and others.

The editors are indebted to Michel Camdessus, Abdoulie Janneh, Gautam Kaji, and Hiroto Arakawa for their valuable insights, guidance, and suggestions throughout the study. They are grateful for the inspiration and encouragement provided by former Presidents Benjamin Mkapa of Tanzania and Horst Koehler of Germany. They also thank Albert Toikeusse Mabri for moderating the Forum discussions in Abidjan and for agreeing to share the study results with his fellow AU and ECA ministers.

Finally, the editors and the Emerging Markets Forum would like to express their gratitude to President Alassane Ouatarra for his strong support for the study, for hosting the Emerging Markets Forum in Abidjan, and for his continuing advocacy of the study's findings to his fellow heads of state and other leading policymakers in Africa.

Editors

Theodore Ahlers   Hiroshi Kato   Harinder S. Kohli   Callisto Madavo   Anil Sood

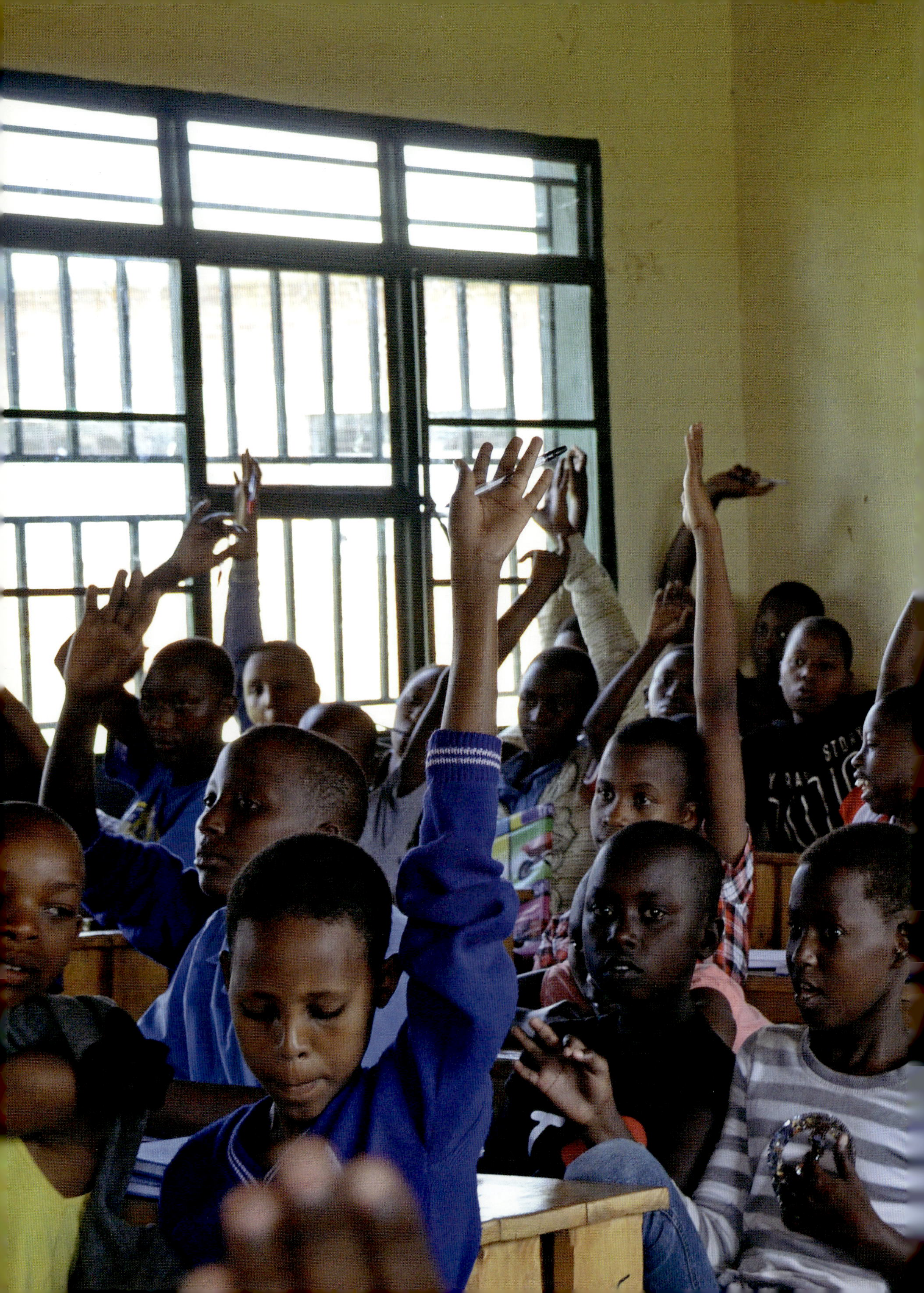

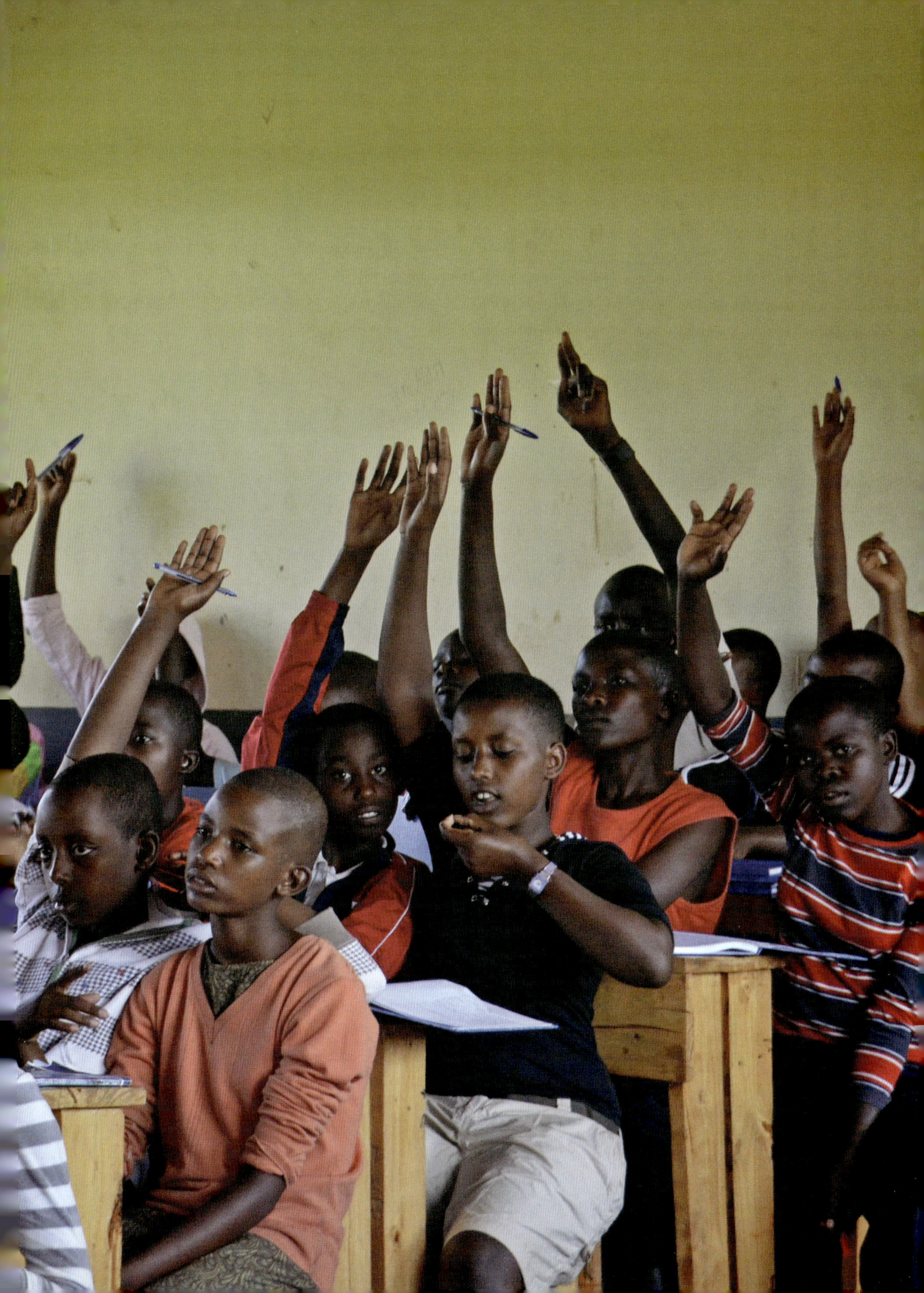

Introduction

Theodore Ahlers, Harinder S. Kohli, Callisto Madavo, and Anil Sood

Background

Africa is at a critical point. What the continent and its leaders do now will determine whether the rising aspirations of Africans are met and, consequently, whether the future promises a cohesive society, prosperous people, competitive economies, and strong regional and global integration.

After a turnaround in the mid-1990s, Africa's economic and social performance over the last decade has been strong (see Figure I). This achievement provides the foundation for a concerted and broad-based effort to capitalize on this success with a comprehensive program to meet the aspirations of the continent's peoples.

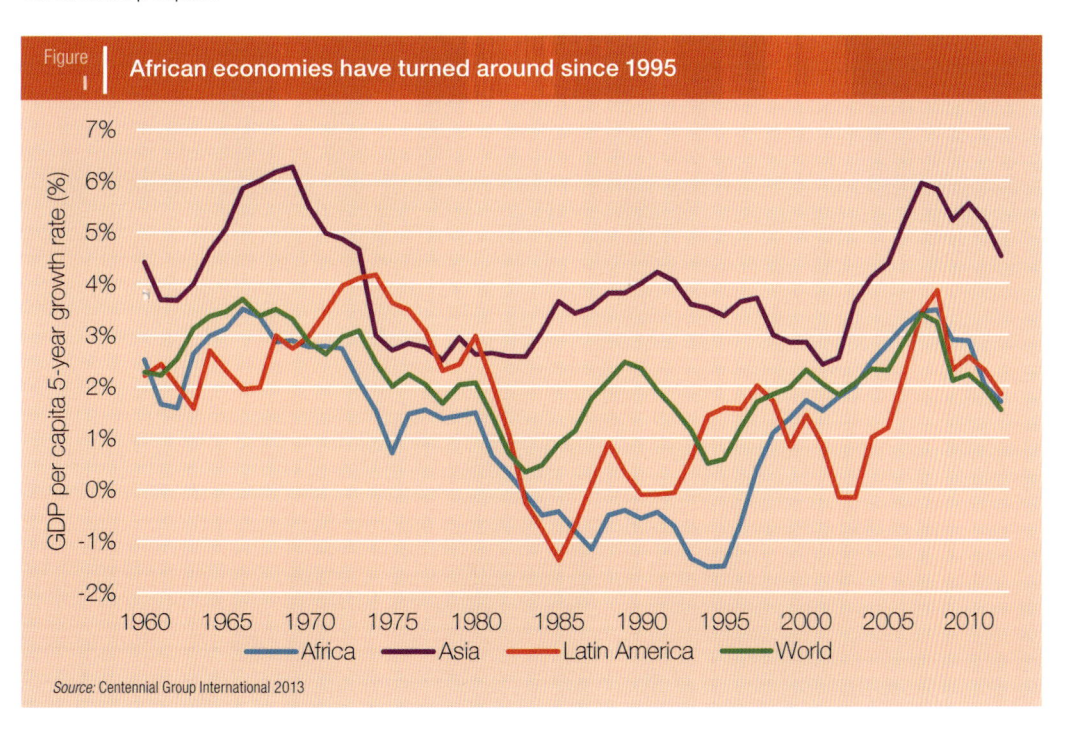

Figure I — African economies have turned around since 1995

Source: Centennial Group International 2013

Africa has been the second fastest growing region in the world since the mid-1990s, behind Asia but ahead of Latin America, Europe, and North America. GDP grew by 4.5 percent and per capita incomes by 2.2 percent annually; the median poverty rate fell by a total of about 10 percentage points to near 43 percent. Over the same period, median under-five mortality declined from 135 deaths per thousand to 93, and gross primary school enrollment increased by 35 percentage points to 110 percent.

Rising Aspirations

Since 1995 African economies have exhibited impressive economic growth. This success brings with it new challenges. Two in particular stand out. First, economic history teaches that very few countries have successfully sustained uninterrupted high economic growth over a generation or more. The continent will face daunting challenges to sustain over the next forty years the economic momentum gained since the turnaround started in 1995. Second, Africa's recent success has led to rising aspirations among its people (and expectations worldwide) to see even better performance in the future. However, as recent events in North Africa and the Middle East have demonstrated so vividly, people — especially the young — can become frustrated unless their aspirations are met.

The rising aspirations have rekindled both hope for a better life and the desire to make it happen. Aspirations are also fed by a communications revolution that has made it easy for people to see what is happening elsewhere. For an increasing number of Africans, it is no longer adequate to be a bit better off than last year or than one's neighbor. The relevant comparison is global.

Such aspirations can be described in shorthand as calls for decent jobs and dignity. The continent's human and natural resource wealth combined with some 50 years of post-independence institution-building for most of its 54 countries can potentially provide the foundation for satisfying these aspirations.

Over the last decade, Africa's economic growth, while better than that of the 1970s, has not been sufficient to allow it to catch up with the rest of the world or with faster-growing emerging economies, such as China, India, Indonesia, or Turkey. Africans are aware of these experiences and want their countries to become more like the successful emerging economies in East Asia and Latin America. They also frequently see growing inequality at home — sometimes driven by corruption, entrenched vested interests, and state capture — which has led to intensified frustration from unmet aspirations.

The biggest threats to meeting current aspirations are complacency and inadequate political resolve to tackle the big problems: poor access to quality education, misuse of natural resource rents, entrenched vested interests, unattractive investment climate, growing inequality, and weak governance. Complacency spreads because, after a decade of strong performance, it is easy for leaders to succumb to the illusion that strong performance is a trend that will continue quasi-automatically. Inadequate resolve results from underestimating the challenge. Even a continuation of the past decade's performance will neither meet people's aspirations nor allow Africa to catch up with the rest of the world. The challenges to be overcome are big and politically complex.

What needs to be done is in large measure known, but how to do it is less obvious, and the political resolve and leadership to do whatever it takes to get the job done will be seriously tested.

A Highly Diverse and Heterogeneous Region

Africa is arguably the most diverse and heterogeneous region of the world. Continental Africa, with its 54 countries, is the second largest continent in both area and population. Given its size and number of countries, it is also exceptionally diverse. Its history ranges from ancient kingdoms to colonially determined states that became independent in the middle of the 20th century. Its geography runs the gamut from deserts to tropical forests. Its natural resource endowments vary by country from extensive oil and mineral wealth to little more than poor soils. Its countries vary in size: six have populations under one million, while three (Egypt, Ethiopia, and Nigeria) have populations over 80 million. At the national level, this diversity is further complicated in much of the continent by borders drawn by colonial authorities that frequently divided ethnic, geographic, or historical identities.

The economic diversity is as striking as the geographic, historic, or cultural (see Figure II). The continent has 27 middle-income countries,[1] including upper middle-income countries such as Algeria, Botswana, South Africa, and Tunisia that have been solidly middle-income for decades. Of the 21 African countries that were middle-income countries 25 years ago, however, none are high-income today. Africa also has 27 low-income countries[2] with a total population of 490 million (47 percent of Africans), including eight (with a total population of 207 million) where the average per capita income is below $1.25 a day. Many of the low-income countries are landlocked, fragile, or conflict-affected.

There is thus no "one Africa" but rather several that share a single land mass, borders, and a history of exchanges among rich kingdoms centuries ago and foreign control through much of the 19th and early 20th centuries. Today the continent has a number of shared pan-African institutions such as the African Union (AU), the UN Economic Commission for Africa (UNECA), and the African Development Bank (AfDB). The region's political leaders now regularly meet to discuss issues of common interest and to forge common approaches and strategies to advance regional economic and social progress. The joint request of the AU and UNECA to the Emerging Markets Forum to prepare the study underlying this book is an illustration of such initiatives.

Such region-wide studies have both value and limitations. They are excellent vehicles for developing and debating a broad vision for the region as a whole, identifying common opportunities and challenges, and agreeing on a general framework for realizing the vision. But beyond this, the specific strategies as

---

1. Algeria, Angola, Botswana, Cameroon, Cape Verde, Republic of Congo, Côte d'Ivoire, Djibouti, Egypt, Equatorial Guinea, Gabon, Ghana, Lesotho, Libya, Mauritania, Mauritius, Morocco, Namibia, Nigeria, Sao Tome and Principe, Senegal, Seychelles, South Africa, Sudan, Swaziland, Tunisia, and Zambia.
2. Benin, Burkina Faso, Burundi, Central African Republic, Chad, Comoros, Democratic Republic of the Congo, Eritrea, Ethiopia, The Gambia, Guinea, Guinea-Bissau, Kenya, Liberia, Madagascar, Malawi, Mali, Mozambique, Niger, Rwanda, Sierra Leone, Somalia, South Sudan, Tanzania, Togo, Uganda, and Zimbabwe.

well as the action agenda and its timetable must be developed at the level of each economy depending on its unique circumstances, including its economic and political history, aspirations of its people, stage of development, resource endowment, and sophistication of institutions and governance.

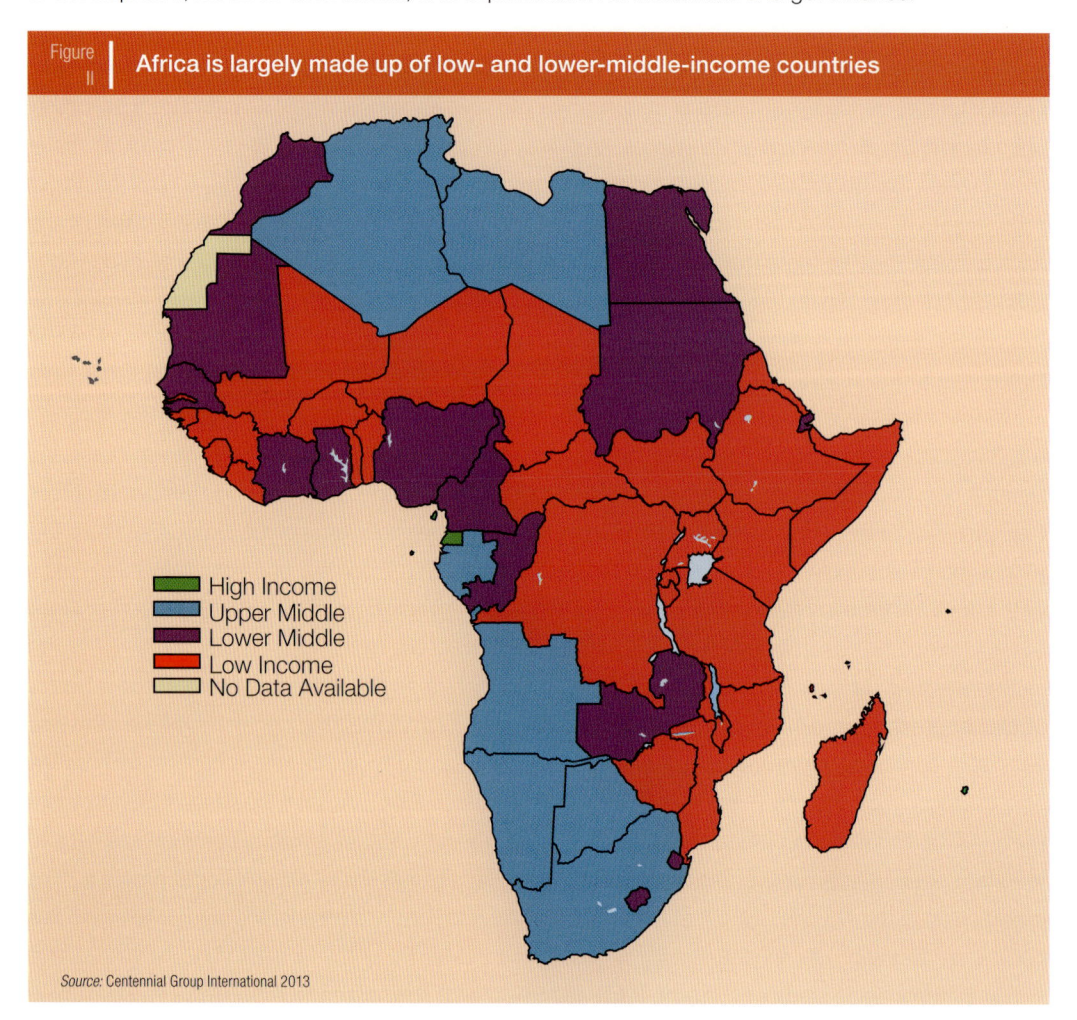

Figure II. Africa is largely made up of low- and lower-middle-income countries

Legend:
- High Income
- Upper Middle
- Lower Middle
- Low Income
- No Data Available

Source: Centennial Group International 2013

What Is Unique about This Book?

The point of departure of this book is a vision of where Africa can be 40 years — or two generations — from now. The vision is deliberately based on stretch goals in key social and economic areas. While clearly ambitious, the vision is certainly plausible. The book goes on to identify the key multigenerational and cross-cutting issues, challenges, and risks that must be tackled starting now in order to realize the vision. The intent is to inspire and lift the ambitions of all Africans and their leaders.

Other distinguishing features of the book are:
- It results from the efforts of a highly experienced international team that has no institutional or ideological agenda;
- It combines analytical work on the lessons from other regions, particularly from Asia and Latin America, with the best existing work on Africa;
- It puts forth a framework that transcends the traditional ideological debates and gives equal priority to three overarching prerequisites for realizing the vision: putting greater focus on people, inclusion, and social cohesion; continuously enhancing the competitiveness of African economies; and achieving greater cooperation, trade, and capital flows within the continent and with the rest of the world; and
- The book focuses on multi-generational issues that require long lead times and are critical for Africa to address to meet the rising aspirations of its people.

Assumptions and Organization

The work underlying this book is based on a number of assumptions about the global economy. First, it is assumed that overall the world will remain peaceful and there will be neither a widespread military conflict nor a natural or man-made calamity (e.g., nuclear war) effecting a wide swath of humanity. Second, that like the past fifty years, the ongoing historic shift in the balance of the global economy from North America and Europe to emerging markets will continue peacefully. Third, that the global financial and trading systems will remain stable and continue to drive further globalization, though with the usual ups and downs associated with business cycles. Fourth, that changes in the global climate will remain within the range currently anticipated by the scientific community. And finally that the pace of technological progress and improvements in the productivity frontier will be similar to that over the past century. If one or more of these assumptions fail to hold then the outcomes for the world economy as a whole, including Africa, could well be outside the scenarios portrayed in the book.

The book is intentionally not comprehensive. Instead it covers a limited number of topics that will have a decisive impact on African economies over the next forty years. Other criteria for selecting the topics included: intergenerational nature of the issues, horizontal interplay between the issues, and availability of data for all or the vast majority of countries. In addition, given the limited resources and time available, the book does not cover certain important topics covered in recent work elsewhere. These subjects are recognized in the book, but detailed analysis and the related action agendas are not developed here.

Part I of the book includes four chapters that lay out the 2050 vision (Chapter 1), provide a historical perspective and discuss drivers of future change (Chapter 2), lay out an action agenda to realize the 2050 vision (Chapter 3), and discuss the cross-cutting themes of governance and leadership focused on results (Chapter 4). Part II is organized in sections corresponding to the three dimensions of the 2050 vision: prosperous people (Chapters 5-8 covering demographics, fragility, inclusion, and human capital), competitive economies (Chapters 9-13 covering macroeconomics, competitiveness, agriculture, natural resources, and urbanization), and an integrated continent (Chapters 14-16 covering regional cooperation, climate change, and global integration).

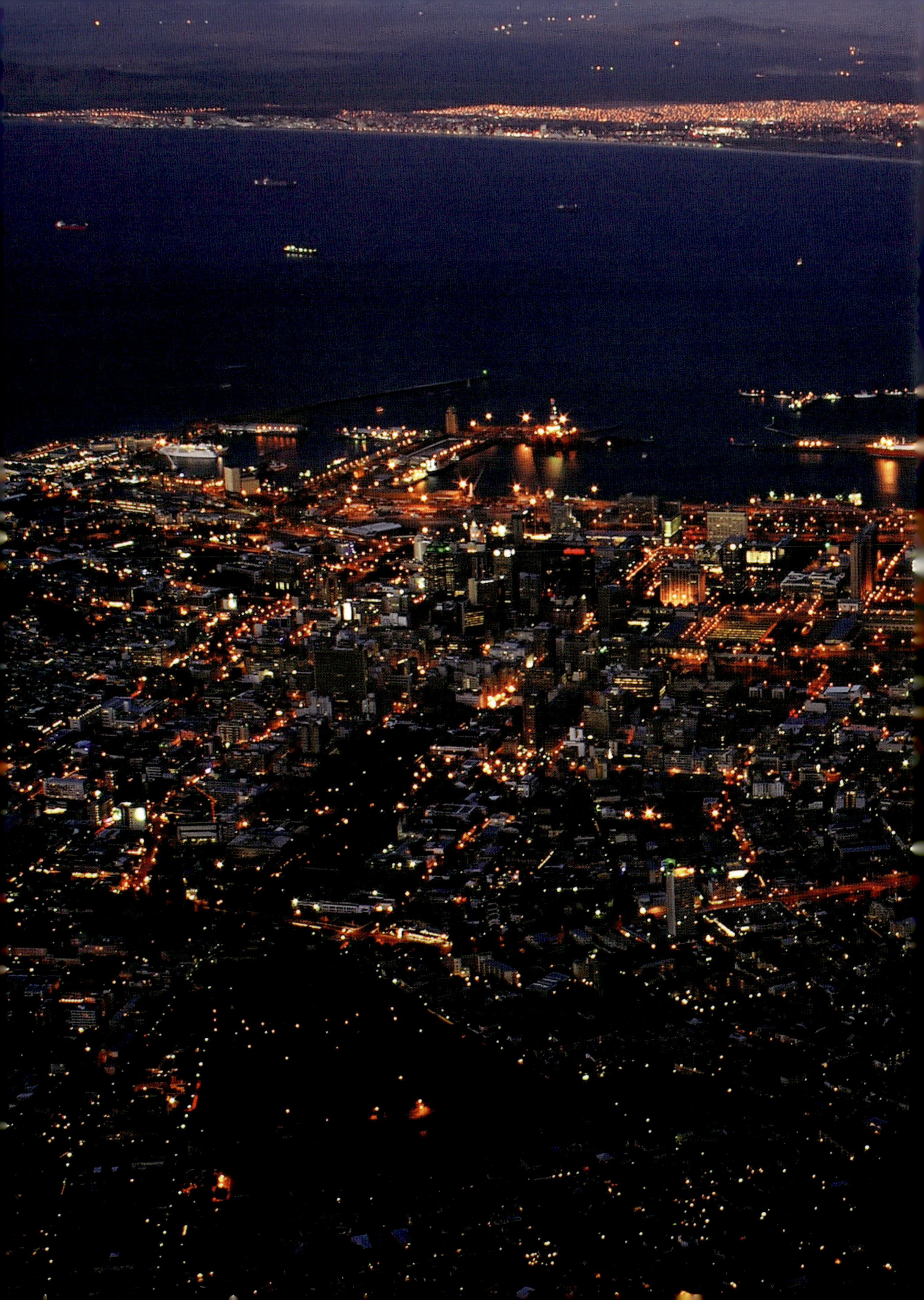

PART I: REALIZING THE CONTINENT'S FULL POTENTIAL

A 2050 Vision to Meet African Aspirations

Chapter 1

Theodore Ahlers, Harinder S. Kohli, Callisto Madavo, and Anil Sood

If action is taken to sustain and accelerate recent growth by Africa's best performers and to spread that performance to Africa's less successful economies, the rising aspirations of the continent's people can be met, and the Africa of 2050 will be a transformed continent. Such growth implies much-enriched human capital and higher investment rates but, even more so, accelerated growth in productivity from rapid adoption of modern technologies, economy-wide reallocation of resources, and fundamental improvements in institutions and governance. Jobs are the key to achieving such transformation, the most powerful vehicle to improve people's lives, and perhaps the single most important instrument for meeting the aspirations of Africans.

The vision of Africa in 2050 described below is not a prediction. It is just one of many possible scenarios — the convergence scenario modeled in a subsequent section — in which convergence in standards of living across countries is driven by free trade that increases wages in labor-abundant countries, capital deepening in countries with lower capital/labor ratios, and most importantly accelerated productivity growth to catch up with productivity levels in advanced economies. It is the stretch vision of what could be: an Africa that meets the expectations of its people and is catching up (converging) with the rest of the world in productivity and incomes on a sustainable path.

The Big Picture

In 2050 Africa will be home to some 2.1 billion people, with a productive and skilled workforce of 1.1 billion.[1] It will be the youngest region in the world, with a labor force larger than that of China or India. The majority of people will live in cities and towns rather than rural areas.

Under the convergence scenario, a rapid decline in total fertility rates would have allowed the continent to moderate population growth and allowed the economies to provide quality education and training to youth and create a more productive workforce employed in good jobs. Most notably the economies would generate more stable and better paid jobs in a rapidly growing private sector. The continent would thus reap the benefits of a demographic dividend as East Asia has done in the past 30 to 40 years.

---

1. Low-fertility variant scenario (United Nations 2013)

The average African would enjoy a nearly six-fold increase in per capita income to $17,500 from $2,900 today (in 2010 US dollars PPP), bringing the average per capita income to half of the global average (up from one-fourth today). An additional 1.4 billion Africans would have joined the middle class, the number in poverty would have fallen by more than 300 million, an 85 percent decline, and extreme poverty would have been eliminated. The vast majority of countries would have achieved a noticeable reduction in disparities and inequities by promoting inclusive growth.

In parallel to this sustained higher economic growth, countries would have achieved major improvements in the quality of life and social indicators. The continent would have universal access (99 percent) to reliable electric power, clean water and basic sanitation, basic and secondary education, and health care. The vast majority of Africans would live without fear of conflict, violence, and crime.

By sustaining an average annual growth rate of 6.6 percent between 2012 and 2050 (compared to 4.5 percent in the past fifteen years), Africa's share of global GDP would more than triple and reach 9 percent in 2050 compared to 2.7 percent in 2011.

People, Economies, and the Continent

The big picture outcome of Africa's economic success would be reflected in the quality of life of its people, the dynamism of its economies, and an enhanced role for a more integrated continent on the global stage.

People and society — inclusion and jobs to transform lives

The most telling transformation of the continent would be sharply *reduced poverty and inequality — based on jobs.* Able-bodied men and women interested in working would not only have jobs but also would have moved to higher productivity jobs permitting a significant rise in incomes and job security. The majority of Africans would be middle class. This combination would help meet African aspirations for much higher living standards and greater dignity.

The specifics would vary by country, but in aggregate, the shares of employment in services and manufacturing would have increased, with the fastest growth in wage-paying jobs. Employment in household enterprises would still be large, but even here, productivity would have increased because of a more highly skilled workforce, higher investment, and the higher quality goods and services sought by the large more demanding middle class. By 2050 African countries would have developed the *human capital* needed to foster rapid, inclusive, and job-creating growth, cohesive societies, and accountable governments.

An accelerated demographic transition to lower fertility and lower mortality would have permitted the necessary level of per capita investment in human capital. A well-educated, skilled, and healthy labor force would have reinforced economic transformation in multiple ways. It would have raised productivity, enhanced adaptive and innovative capacity, and provided the managerial and technical skills required to run increasingly complex socioeconomic systems. These developments would not only raise per capita income levels many-fold but also sharply narrow the inequities in income and participation in political processes.

Like the rest of the world, Africa would have become urbanized. Sixty percent of Africans would live in *cities,* large and small. The continent would have undergone a transformative shift from rural to urban societies, with almost 90 percent of economic activity (GDP) taking place in the burgeoning cities and towns.

The rapidly growing middle class would, in turn, drive much *improved governance* throughout the continent. By 2050, the continent would have capable governments accountable to their citizens for delivering security, the rule of law, and key social services. A variety of political systems would all embody sufficient accountability to give citizens the confidence to invest in their future and to prevent state capture by well-connected families or those close to power. As a result, people would see their own future in their country. Visas to emigrate and schemes to get money out of the country would no longer dominate people's aspirations.

The continent's people would finally have rid themselves of the curse of conflicts and violence emanating from the initial *fragility* of many African states. The improvement in physical security would contribute to increased productivity and to a greater confidence in the future that would, in turn, mobilize investment.

Economies — private investment to create jobs

Jobs and a skilled workforce would have transformed the continent based on *increased competitiveness and productivity* of Africa's economies. The private sector would have become the leading engine for creating jobs on the scale required. Lower costs and increased productivity, combined with larger markets through trade, would have led to a large increase in private investment that spurred diversification and job creation. Firms across Africa would serve larger sub-regional markets and would have both grown and become more competitive in response to the strong competition fostered by trade and to lower costs of inputs, transport, logistics, and other infrastructure services. As a result, productivity levels would have continued to catch up with global best practice.

A fundamental transformation and breakthrough in the *productivity of African agriculture* would have allowed the rural population to enjoy a many-fold increase in incomes while also making farms — both large and small — profitable. The share of agriculture in employment would have fallen but much higher productivity would lead to increased agricultural production in response to export demand for grains and specialized crops and strong urban demand for higher-value products such as fruit, vegetables, dairy products, and meat. The continent would have become a major supplier of agricultural products to the rest of world.

Africa would continue to *supply global markets with oil, gas, and minerals.* It would, however, capture a larger share of the associated rents and have used these resources to invest in human capital and physical infrastructure, avoid the boom and bust cycles associated with commodity price fluctuations, and establish savings and sustainable extraction mechanisms to ensure benefits for future generations even as resources are eventually depleted.

Most economies would boast a *thriving enterprise sector* with a mix of companies of different sizes. Some 20 to 30 African companies would rank among the top 500 global companies, investing across Africa and the globe. Many smaller enterprises, with origins as informal enterprises, would be integrated into global supply chains. Businesses of all sizes would have access to needed technology, communication services, and know-how, as well as finance from a deeper financial sector including non-bank financial institutions. Most importantly, firms of all sizes would have access to reliable electricity, water, sanitation, and transport infrastructure. Public-private partnerships would be common, particularly in building infrastructure and low-cost housing.

Well-managed *cities* (large and small), operating through transparent and accountable governance structures at the local level, would be driving economic growth, delivering key services at international standards and attracting investment through private sector-friendly environments. Cities would serve as incubators for innovation and small- and medium-sized business development. They would be the primary loci for job creation and for sustaining gains in living standards and the absorption of the emerging, educated labor force.

African continent — bigger markets to foster investment and higher productivity jobs

A pragmatic and *results-focused approach to regional economic integration* would have produced seamless sub-regional markets where goods, capital, and people move easily across borders. This would have significantly increased the size of the markets for firms based in Africa and thus allowed them to achieve economies of scale necessary to compete in world markets. Intraregional trade would have increased from 11 percent of total trade to some 25 percent.

Africa's *relations with the rest of the world* would be on a more equal footing based primarily on trade, investment, and the exchange of technology and knowledge. Africa would have seized the opportunities offered by the convergence of OECD and emerging markets and the shift of global economic weight toward the latter. It would be self-reliant and a respected and active participant in global councils, with a voice in setting the global agenda. Relations with the rest of the world would be based on trade and investment rather than aid, based on agreements negotiated on a regional as well as continental level. Africa would be an attractive consumer market and become a magnet and preferred destination for global foreign direct investment (FDI).

Alternative Scenarios: Enormous Cost of Failure

Africa can realize the vision sketched above, but it will not be automatic. It will require aggressive and sustained action by African leaders (see Chapter 3).

Three scenarios — convergence, business-as-usual, and downside — are outlined here to illustrate the broad range of outcomes possible. These scenarios are based on a model of the global economy and methodology prepared by Centennial Group International, which projects long term evolution of GDP of 186 countries as a function of labor force, capital stock, and total factor productivity (TFP) (see Annex 2).[2]

Convergence vs. business-as-usual

Africa's recent improved performance (Figure 1.1) forms the basis for the convergence scenario, in which convergence in standards of living is driven by trade that reduces factor price differences between rich and poor countries, capital deepening in countries with lower capital/labor ratios, and accelerated TFP growth to catch up with TFP levels in advanced economies. The scenario assumes that 19 African countries are "early convergers"[3] whose TFP growth begins to converge with that of advanced countries this decade, that 15 are "late convergers"[4] whose TFP growth begins to converge in the following decade, and that the remaining 20 countries currently considered "fragile"[5] transition out of fragility over the next 30 years.

Under the convergence scenario, per capita incomes in Africa could grow by 4.6 percent annually over the next 40 years and exceed $17,000 (2010 PPP US dollars) in 2050 (Figure 1.2). Africa-wide per capita income would be higher than that of Russia, Malaysia, Mexico, or Turkey today. Under such a scenario African per capita incomes would begin to converge with the rest of the world, moving from 27 percent of the world average today to 52 percent in 2050.

Such sustained growth would set in motion many changes that would transform the lives of Africans and Africa's role in the world. On the individual front, the size of the middle class[6] would increase more than ten-fold to 68 percent of the population, up from 12 percent today. The number of poor would decline to 50 million (or under 3 percent of the population) from 380 million (or 37 percent) today. Africa's share of world GDP would more than triple from less than 3 percent today to 9 percent in 2050.

The charts in Figure 1.2 compare these outcomes of the convergence scenario with those under the business-as-usual and downside scenarios. The business-as-usual scenario assumes that Africa's higher investment rates of recent years continue, its labor force continues to grow, commodity prices remain high, and the generally improved policies of the last 10 to 15 years are maintained — but that there is

---

2. The Centennial growth model is explained in Kohli, Szyf, and Arnold (2012) and its results are reflected in numerous studies including *Mexico 2042 — Achieving Prosperity for All* (Loser, Fajgenbaum, and Kohli 2012), *Asia 2050 — Realizing the Asian Century* (Kohli, Sharma, and Sood 2011), *India 2039 — An Affluent Society in One Generation* (Kohli et al. 2009), *Latin America 2040 — Breaking Away from Complacency* (Arnold et al. 2013), and *Kazakhstan 2050 — Towards a Modern Society for All* (Aitzhanova et al. forthcoming).
3. Four countries (Botswana, Cape Verde, Mauritius, and Mozambique) with 25 years of per capita GDP growth greater than 3.5 percent plus 15 countries with annual TFP growth over the last decade greater than 1 percent.
4. Fifteen non-fragile countries with annual TFP growth over the last decade of less than one percent
5. The 20 countries classified by the African Development Bank and the World Bank as being in "fragile situations"
6. Middle class defined as per capita income greater than $10.80 and less than $100 a day (2010 PPP US dollars)

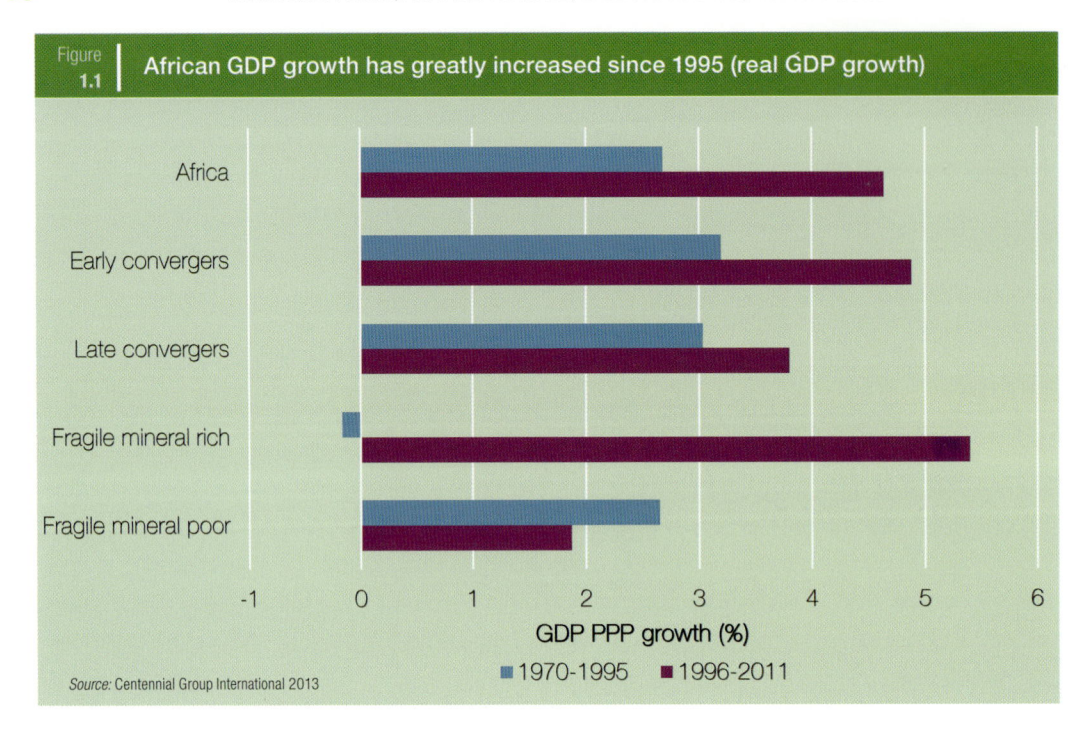

Figure 1.1 African GDP growth has greatly increased since 1995 (real GDP growth)

Source: Centennial Group International 2013

■ 1970-1995 ■ 1996-2011

no sustained action on the policy agenda described in Chapter 3. As a result, unlike the convergence scenario, productivity growth does not accelerate. Four countries with consistently high growth for the last 25 years[7] continue to converge, but the other 30 non-fragile countries do not converge,[8] and the fragile countries stay fragile.

Under the business-as-usual scenario per capita incomes continue to rise at 1.9 percent annually and reach more than $6,000 (2010 US dollars PPP) by 2050 (Figure 1.2). Given faster growth in other regions, however, Africa's per capita incomes would actually diverge further from those in the rest of the world, falling to 20 percent of the world average by 2050. The size of the middle-class would increase but after 40 years would still be only 27 percent of the population. Nearly one in five Africans would, correspondingly, still live in poverty. Finally, given growth elsewhere in the world, Africa's share of global GDP would stagnate at around 3 percent.

The lightly shaded area in the charts indicates the enormous opportunity cost to Africans if Africa follows the business-as-usual scenario and fails to realize the convergence scenario. Per capita income would be lower by more than $10,000, some 40 percent of the population (900 million) would be unable to reach middle-class status, and an additional 15 percent of the population (325 million) would be left in poverty. With most African countries approaching 100 years of independence, a continent with a

---

7. Botswana, Cape Verde, Mauritius, and Mozambique
8. Their TFP growth matches long-run TFP growth of the advanced economies (1 percent).

A 2050 VISION TO MEET AFRICAN ASPIRATIONS 17

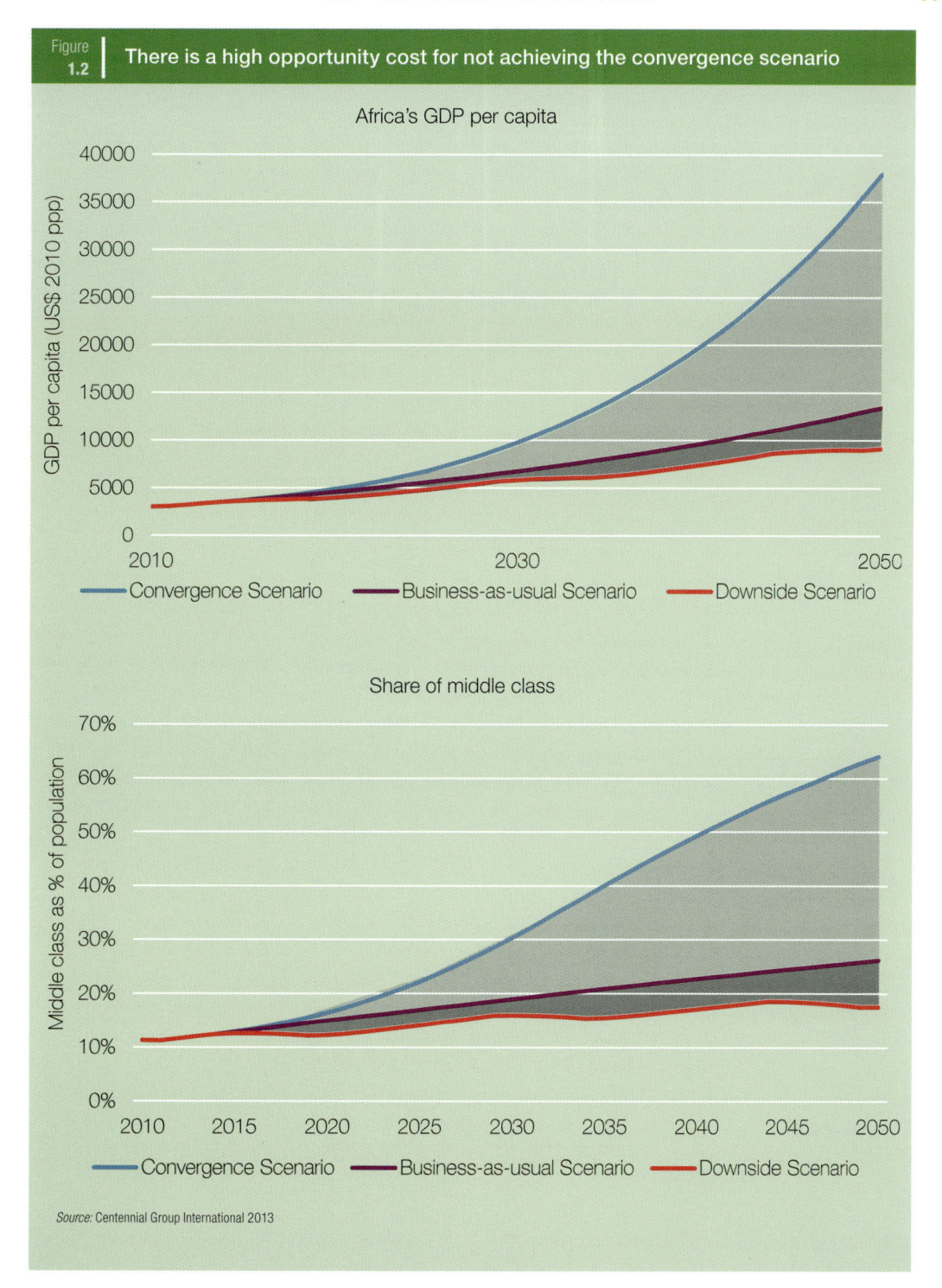

Figure 1.2 | There is a high opportunity cost for not achieving the convergence scenario

Africa's GDP per capita

— Convergence Scenario   — Business-as-usual Scenario   — Downside Scenario

Share of middle class

— Convergence Scenario   — Business-as-usual Scenario   — Downside Scenario

Source: Centennial Group International 2013

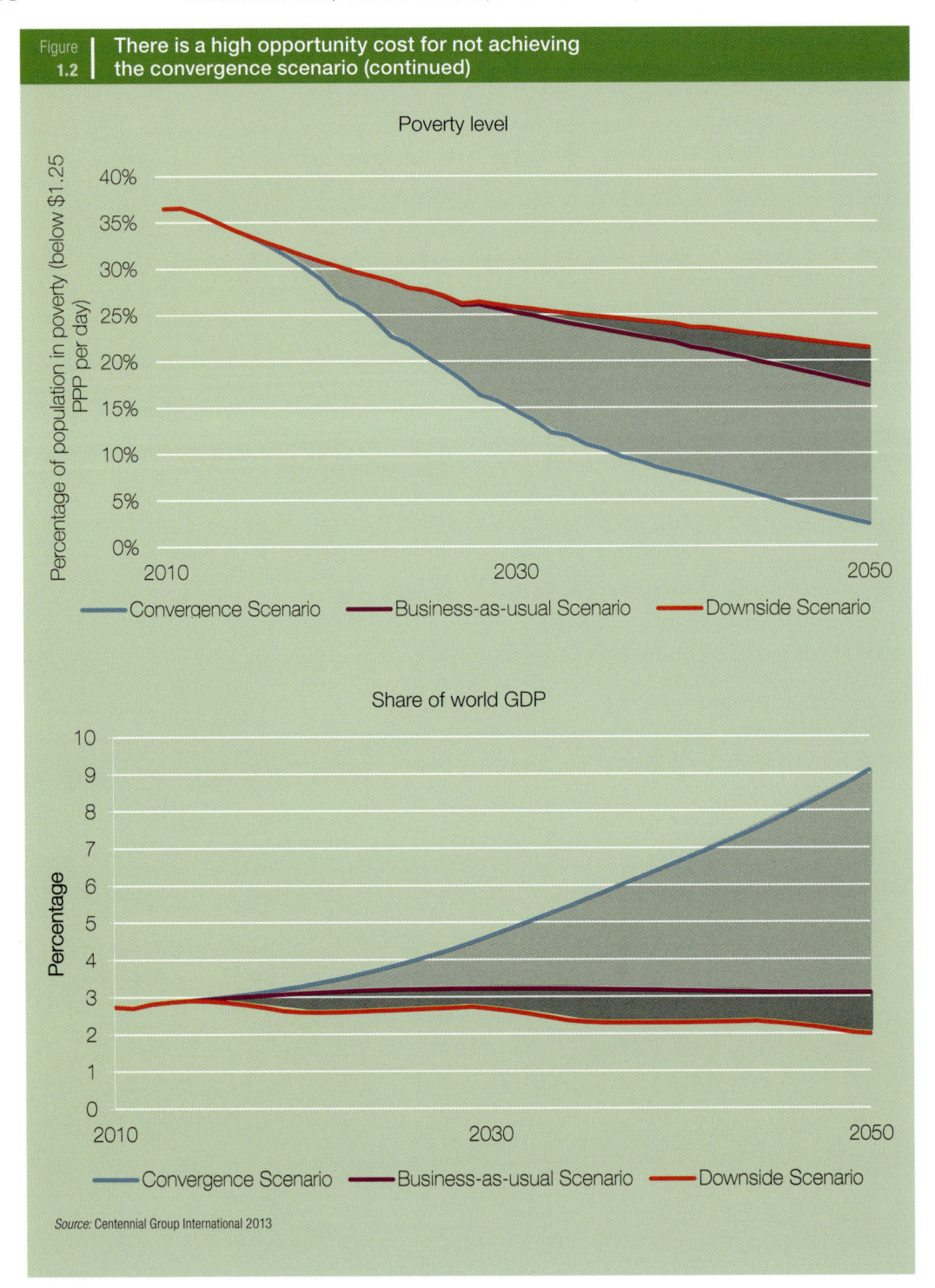

Figure 1.2 | There is a high opportunity cost for not achieving the convergence scenario (continued)

Poverty level

Percentage of population in poverty (below $1.25 PPP per day)

— Convergence Scenario   — Business-as-usual Scenario   — Downside Scenario

Share of world GDP

Percentage

— Convergence Scenario   — Business-as-usual Scenario   — Downside Scenario

Source: Centennial Group International 2013

quarter of the world's population but only 3 percent of its economic activity is not only highly undesirable but poses serious threats to social and political stability. The threat is acute because such an outcome diverges so far from the aspirations of Africans.

Downside scenario

The business-as-usual scenario is, however, by no means the pessimistic scenario. A much more worrisome downside scenario could arise, for example, if Africa's terms of trade were to deteriorate because of commodity price changes and if fragility and conflict were to spread to more countries. It is difficult to model such a scenario because of the variety of forms it could take. The downside scenario shown in Figure 1.2 is just one possibility and assumes that, as a result of commodity price fluctuations, Africa's terms of trade cyclically fall by 15 percent over five years and then recover 15 percent over the following decade (hardly dramatic when seen in the perspective of the last 40 years), that an additional five countries slip into fragility and conflict, and that all the middle-income countries are stuck in the middle-income trap and do not converge with today's advanced economies.

In such a scenario per capita income would grow by less than one percent a year and would in 2050 be only around $4,000 (2010 US dollars PPP). Given faster growth in the rest of the world, Africa's per capita income would have fallen to only 14 percent or one-seventh of the world average, its lowest level ever. One in three Africans, some 690 million people, would still be in poverty and the middle class would have grown to only 18 percent of the population. Africa would still have many low-income countries and few high-income ones (Figure 1.3). On the global stage Africa would be marginalized with only 2 percent of world GDP. Under such a scenario the aspirations of Africans would be crushed.

The downside and the business-as-usual scenarios paint a very unattractive future. The convergence scenario is feasible but will be realized only if there is vigorous and sustained implementation of the action agenda outlined in Chapter 3. This scenario requires sustained, higher productivity growth for most countries over the next 40 years. Countries in other regions have achieved such sustained productivity growth, but not many. Success with a 40-year agenda depends most on institutional development and political resolve for sustained implementation.

Such a strategy would be a clear break with the past and requires a cultural change; African leaders would have to focus on realizing the convergence scenario and be willing to be judged on their success in delivering results. To be able to do so, however, they need to have established a new social contract with their citizens — one that cuts across political, ethnic, and religious lines and that promises the Africa in 2050 described above but recognizes that delivering it depends on an unrelenting focus on the action agenda set out in Chapter 3.

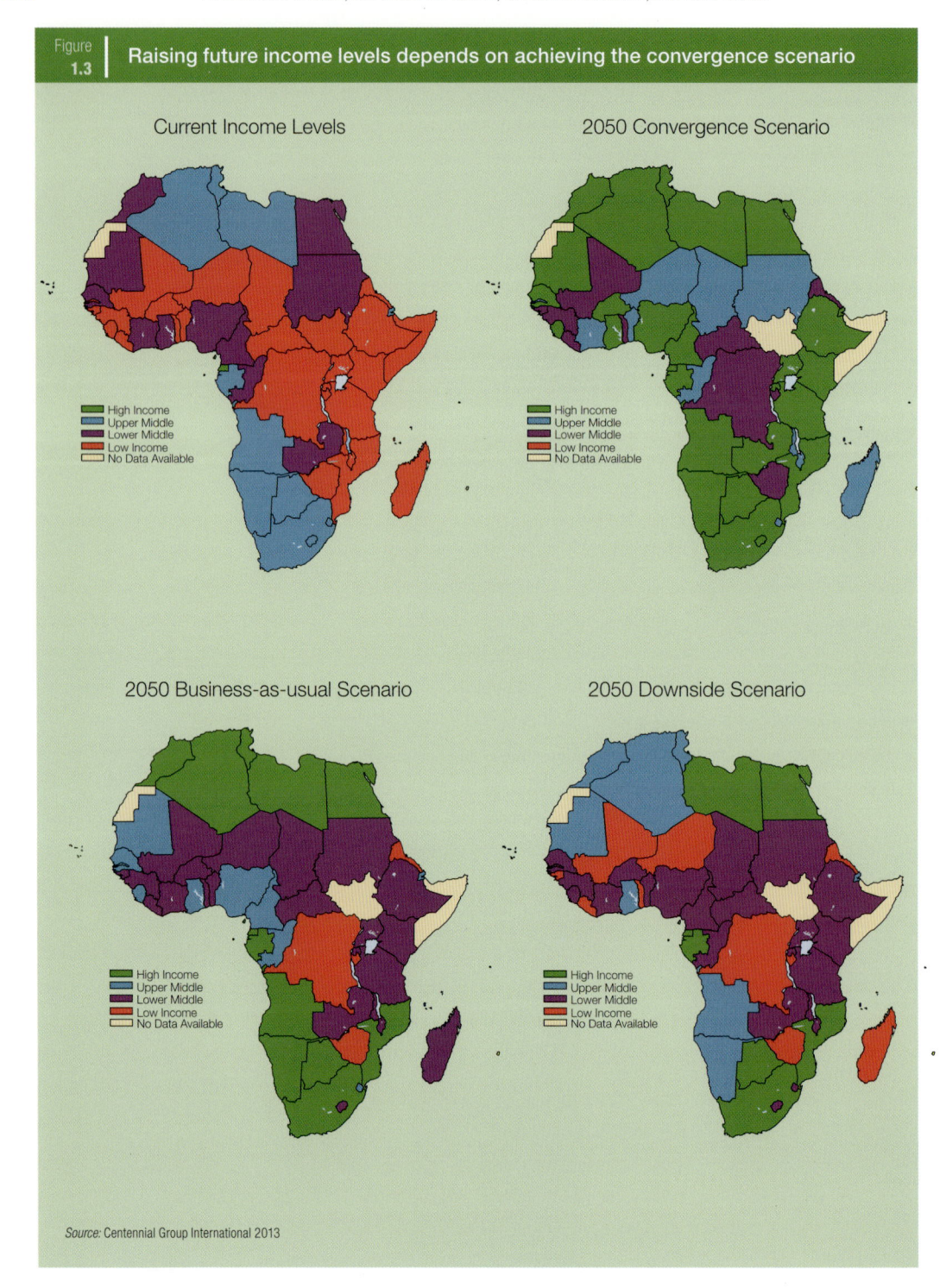

Figure 1.3 Raising future income levels depends on achieving the convergence scenario

Current Income Levels

- High Income
- Upper Middle
- Lower Middle
- Low Income
- No Data Available

2050 Convergence Scenario

- High Income
- Upper Middle
- Lower Middle
- Low Income
- No Data Available

2050 Business-as-usual Scenario

- High Income
- Upper Middle
- Lower Middle
- Low Income
- No Data Available

2050 Downside Scenario

- High Income
- Upper Middle
- Lower Middle
- Low Income
- No Data Available

Source: Centennial Group International 2013

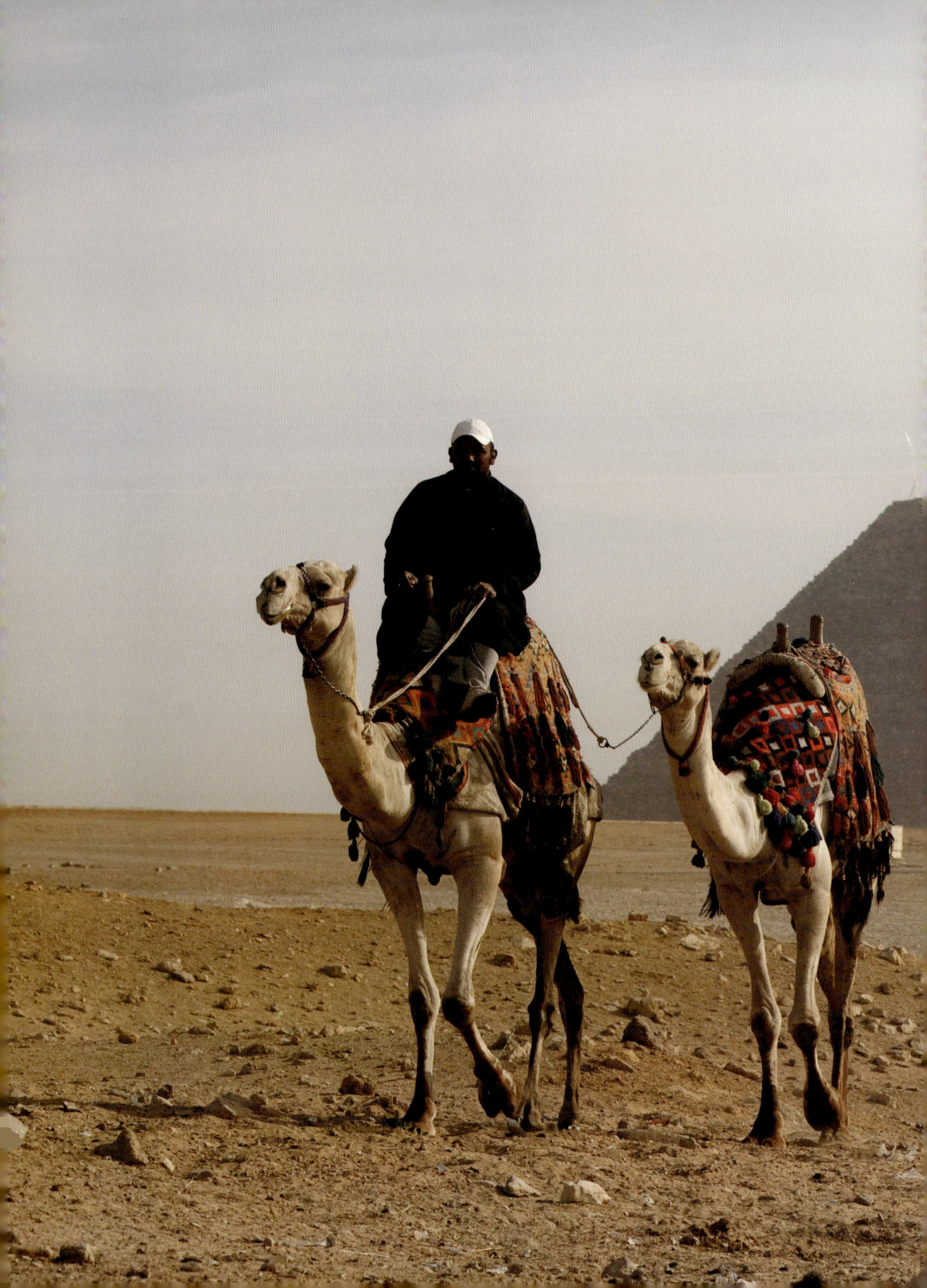

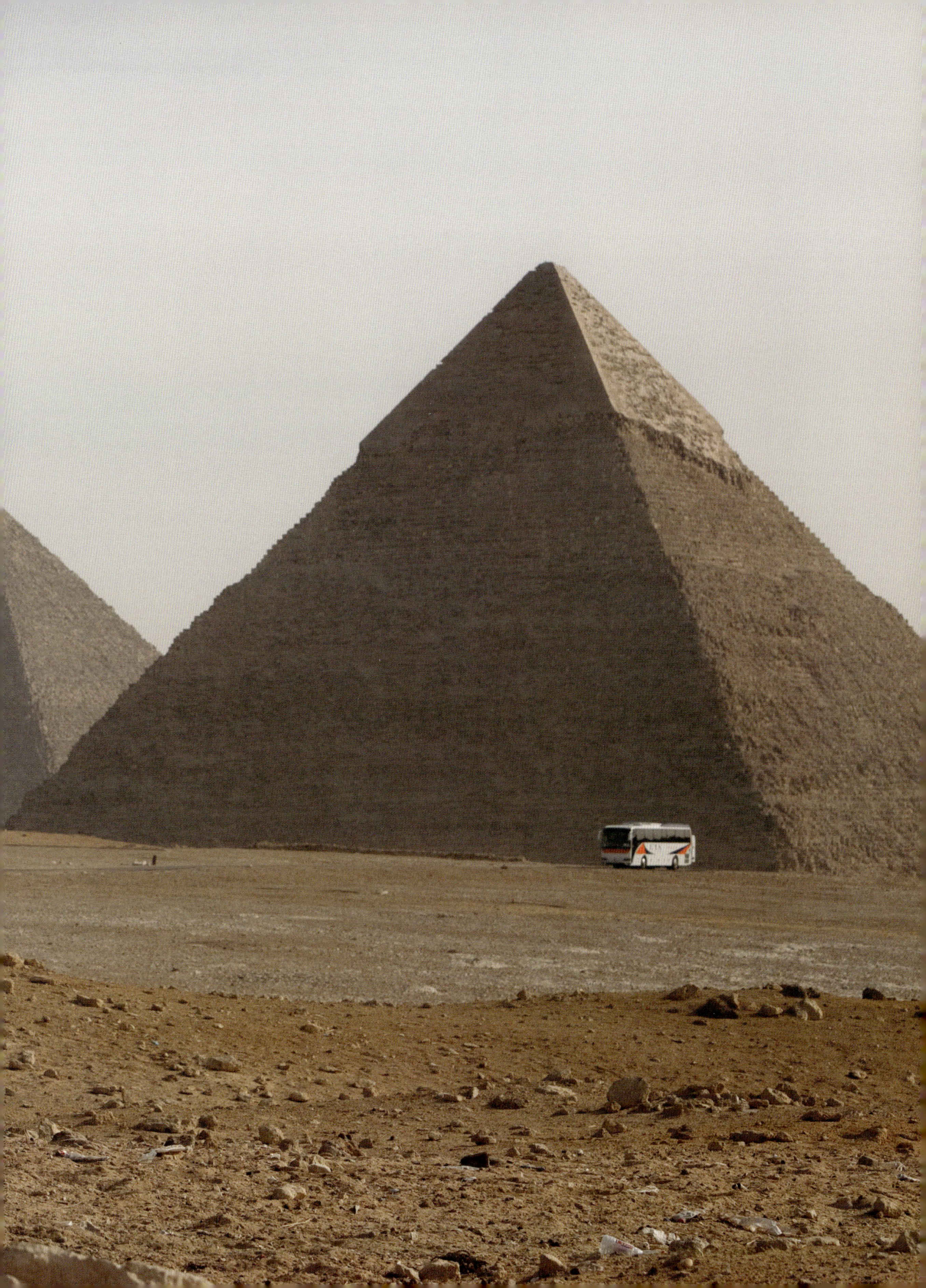

Historical Perspectives and Drivers of Future Change

Chapter 2

Theodore Ahlers, Harinder S. Kohli, Callisto Madavo, and Anil Sood

Past Performance

Knowing both where one has been and where one currently stands is essential for getting to where one wants to go. Understanding the past is in itself a challenge for Africa because it is so diverse. But with a more open but interlinked continent, the very diversity of experience and endowments would represent an opportunity. Africa has much to learn from the experience of other emerging economies, but it need not always look outside its borders for solutions. If the "best African practice" — whether in maternal/child care, teacher accountability to parents, fiscal management, natural resource revenue management, or rule of law — were generalized throughout the continent, Africa would be transformed and well along the way of closing the gap with other regions.

Long-term divergence

Economically, Africa has diverged from the rest of the world for three centuries. Whatever the reasons — foreign conquest, societal disruption from the slave trade, extractive economic institutions of colonial rule — Africa did not benefit from the surge in productivity and, hence, in per capita incomes of the 18th, 19th, and early 20th centuries. As a result, its share of world GDP in 2012 was less than half of what it was in 1700 (see Figure 2.1). Its share of world population declined in the 18th and 19th centuries but grew rapidly in the 20th century. Consequently, Africa's per capita income, despite some growth in the last century, is substantially lower as a share of world per capita income today than in 1700 (see Figure 2.2).

The gap in economic performance between Africa and the rest of the world can be turned into an enormous opportunity, if tackled aggressively. Asia provides a clear example; its share of world GDP also plummeted in the 19th century and much of the first half of the 20th century but has rebounded dramatically in the last 50 years. Much of the rest of the world has already benefited from the big productivity boosters since the industrial revolution in the 18th century, such as clean water and sanitation, better health care, dramatically lower transport costs, widespread access to electricity, and, most recently, the revolution in information technology. Much of Africa has not. Catching up will not be easy, but it is

Figure 2.1 — Africa's share of world population has risen since 1900, but its share of GDP continued to decline until 1995

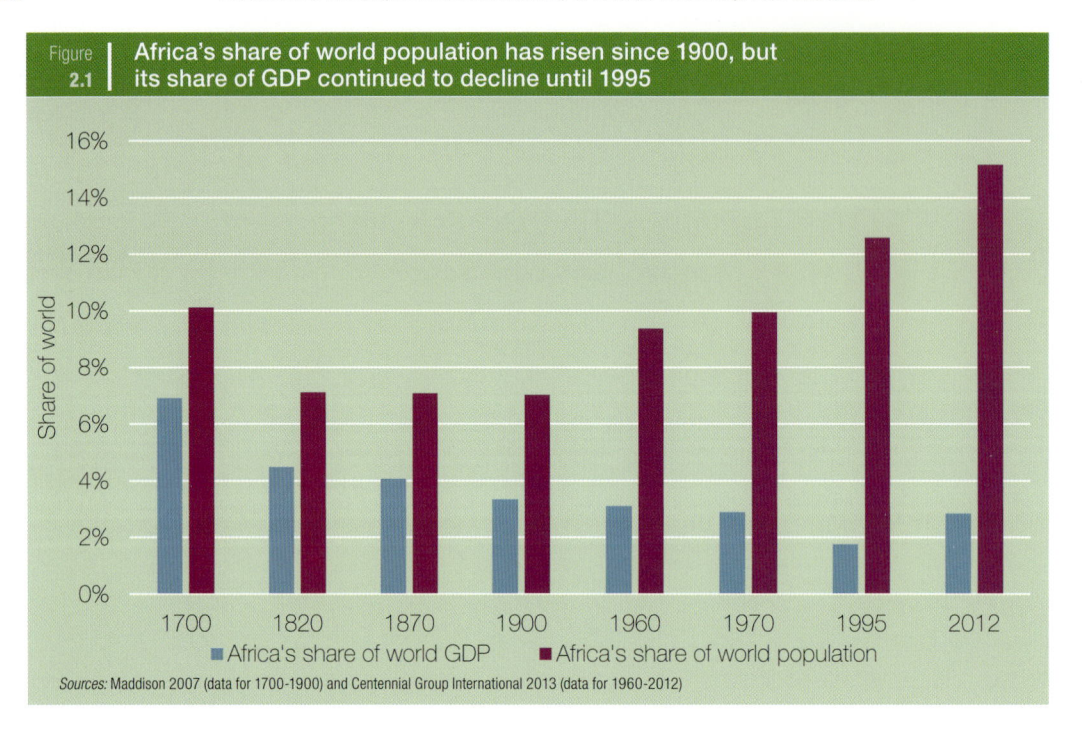

- Africa's share of world GDP
- Africa's share of world population

Sources: Maddison 2007 (data for 1700–1900) and Centennial Group International 2013 (data for 1960–2012).

Figure 2.2 — Africa's GDP per capita growth lagged the world's until 2000

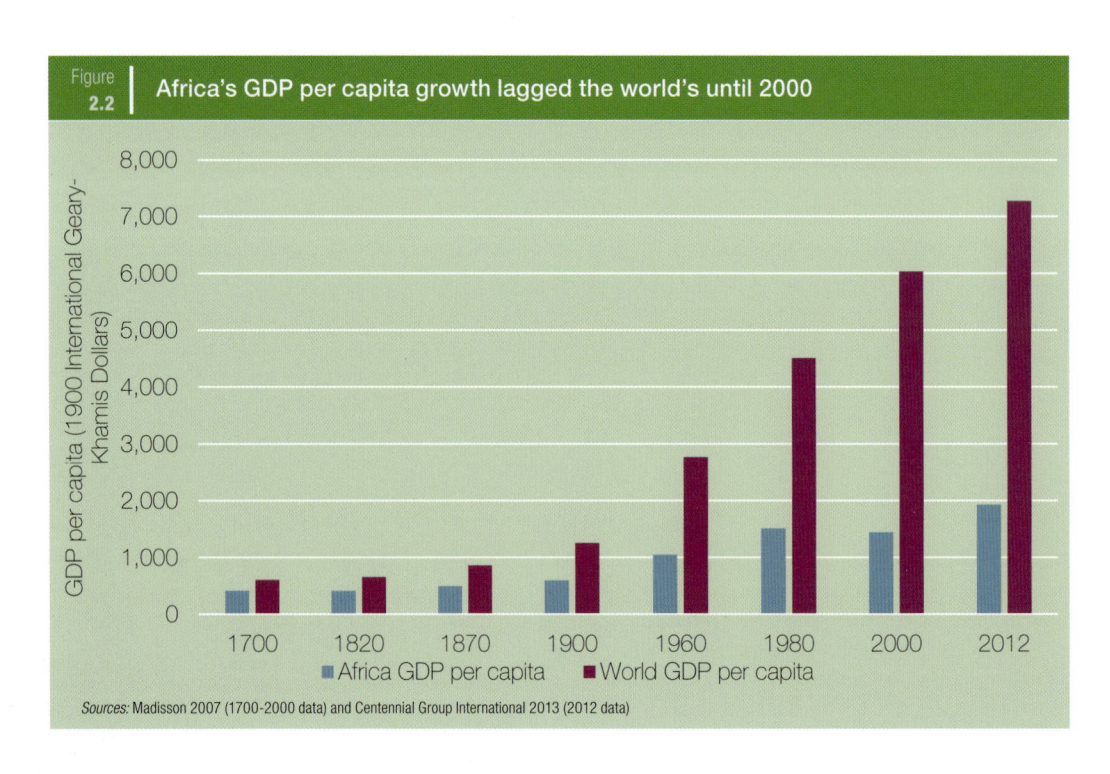

- Africa GDP per capita
- World GDP per capita

GDP per capita (1900 International Geary-Khamis Dollars)

Sources: Maddisson 2007 (1700–2000 data) and Centennial Group International 2013 (2012 data).

surely possible and is likely to lead to large one-off gains in productivity. In particularly, the potential to leapfrog to newer technology, as is already occurring in several countries of the region, presents an important opportunity.

The last 50 years

Africa's economic performance since the 1960s, when most of the continent's countries gained independence, is, of course, not uniform across countries and is more correctly assessed according to many sub-periods. But in the broadest terms, three distinct periods emerge at the continent-wide level. The first decade after independence showed a strong but short-lived rebound in growth rates. From the early 1970s to the mid-1990s, a combination of unsustainable economic policies, external shocks, failure to adjust to changing economic conditions, and increasingly exclusionary politics produced 25 years of decelerating growth; the result was stagnation of progress in most social indicators. Since about 1995, several factors — painful economic adjustment, stronger macroeconomic management, greater openness to trade and private sector activity, and improved governance — have led to a steady acceleration of per capita growth rates as seen in Figure I. In addition, a dramatic improvement in commodity prices in the last decade and a major reduction in the foreign debt burden contributed to faster growth.

In addition to growing faster over the last decade, most African economies were also relatively resilient to the 2008 global financial crisis: some because of large external reserves generated by natural resource exports; others because of little integration with the global economy (which also makes them poor); and a leading few because of strong macroeconomic management, banking reforms, and export diversification (see Chapter 9).

Over the same 50 years, many other developing regions — especially Asia — showed uninterrupted, higher economic growth and slowing population growth. As a result, Asia's per capita GDP has soared relative to the world average while Africa's has stagnated. The Asian performance demonstrates that sustained high growth is possible. In an increasingly interconnected world, such growth has, moreover, been a driver of the aspirations (and hence social, political, and economic expectations) of Africans. The sustained high growth of Japan, followed by that of the newly industrialized "Asian tigers," and now of China and India, shows that growth is possible even in countries that are strikingly different in size, resource endowment, initial human capital, culture, and political regimes.

Lessons from Asia and Latin America

Africa and Latin America share many of the same characteristics: rich endowments of natural resources, economies heavily dependent on commodity exports, levels of economic activity tightly linked to global commodity markets, sparsely populated large land masses, heavy reliance on developed market economies in North America and Europe until recently, large internal inequities, large informal sectors, and relatively underdeveloped manufacturing. There are, however, also many important differences between the two regions, not least of which is the big difference in per capita incomes. Africa can draw lessons from the development performance of Latin America and, importantly, from an analysis of the factors that explain Latin America's very different performance compared to that of East Asia and in particular the so-called newly industrialized countries (NICs).

The main policy lessons for Africa from the comparisons between East Asia and Latin America are presented in Box 2.1 are:

Box 2.1 | The different lessons from East Asia and Latin America

Between 1965 and 2009, the per capita income of the NICs grew at an average annual rate of 5.8 percent, while Latin America recorded a growth rate of only 1.8 percent. As a result, in terms of per capita income, the NICs — that lagged well behind Latin America in 1965 ($1,794 vs. $3,918, constant 2011 US dollars) — had leapfrogged over Latin America by 2011 ($23,554 vs. $8,776). These statistics illustrate how the most dynamic economies in Asia, now joined by China and India, have continued to converge with advanced economies, while most Latin American economies have become stuck in the middle-income trap. The striking differences between East Asia and Latin America include:

- Political leaders in East Asia were intensely focused on economic issues and not preoccupied with geo-political issues or ideological debates, in sharp contrast to Latin America
- All successful East Asian countries, as well as China and India, have achieved major gains in total factor productivity (TFP), while Latin American countries have remained stagnant
- East Asian countries have much higher savings and investment rates than those in Latin America (51 percent vs. 23 percent of GDP)
- Asia has placed much greater emphasis on human development and a high premium on meritocracy in its education system; it has much higher educational standards and graduates a significantly higher number of engineers, scientists, and doctors
- Asia has made much higher investment, both public and private, in infrastructure, and it has deeper financial markets, particularly non-bank financial institutions
- NICs have much more open economies than does Latin America, with total trade to GDP ratios of 196 percent vs. 45 percent for Latin America
- East Asia has dramatically restructured production in the past forty years to become the manufacturing hub of the world, while Latin American economies remain highly dependent on commodities and agricultural products
- Regional trade (over 55 percent) and investments (FDI) flows in East Asia are much higher and approach European Union levels; these flows are market-driven thanks to extensive production networks — scarcely visible in Latin America — developed by private businesses
- Even as East Asian economies have moved from low-income to middle-income and finally to upper middle-income status, their income distribution and other social indicators have remained much more equitable than Latin America, which continues to suffer from the highest disparities of any region in the world
- East Asia's more equitable distribution of incomes and assets allowed it to more rapidly develop a larger middle class, which gradually became an engine of innovation, entrepreneurship, and domestic consumption that fueled further economic growth

Source: Centennial Group International 2013

Be pragmatic, not dogmatic. Asian countries — and successful economies worldwide — got the fundamentals right. They maintained macroeconomic stability, fully exploited opportunities offered by the world economy, mustered high rates of savings and investment (including in human capital), allowed markets to allocate resources, and had committed, credible, and capable governments with strong leadership. These fundamentals are necessary but not sufficient. Asian countries supplemented them with many other policy initiatives to promote faster growth. One key to success was making decisions on these supplemental policies based on extreme pragmatism and with a focus on results rather than adherence to a particular ideology. Policies and actions that worked were expanded and, most importantly, those that did not deliver results were stopped quickly.

Educate everyone. Already at independence, human capital was one of the key differences between much of Africa and other regions. Since the end of the colonial era, however, the difference has widened in the case of most African countries. Africa cannot duplicate the performance of Asian or Latin American emerging markets without a much greater effort to educate its entire population (with a premium on meritocracy, particularly in higher education) and build the skills demanded by a transformed continent.

Compete in export markets to drive increases in productive investment and raise productivity. East Asian economies are much more open than African economies, with total trade-to-GDP ratios of 70 percent in emerging East Asia compared to 36 percent in Africa. Trade openness and, in particular, an explicit export orientation provide (i) competition and the resulting market discipline needed to weed out crony capitalism, maintain pressure for competitive infrastructure services, and avoid the protection of inefficient (public or private) companies, (ii) the bigger markets needed for private investment and job creation, and (iii) a channel through which to learn about and adopt new technology and management know-how.

Africa's competitiveness has been constrained by low investment rates and slow growth in productivity. Savings and investment rates in Asia are both nearly double those in Africa. In some instances, the higher savings in Asia are forced from compressed consumption, and most African countries neither could nor would want to replicate this. Still, the difference in rates is very large and compounded further by capital flight, which is rampant in Africa. The Asian experience points to the value of establishing confidence in the rule of law and security of property. This confidence, in turn, is also the best calling card for the increased FDI in Africa that is so necessary for future growth of the region.

The performance of all successful Asian economies, including China and India, illustrates the importance of major gains in TFP. In contrast, most African countries have seen their TFP stagnate or even decline (see Figure 2.3) until recently. Productivity changes in Asia were based on improving the skills of the workforce, creating jobs to allow people to move out of lower productivity activities (such as from traditional agriculture to higher productivity manufacturing and services), technological adoption, and institutions that encourage and reward innovation.

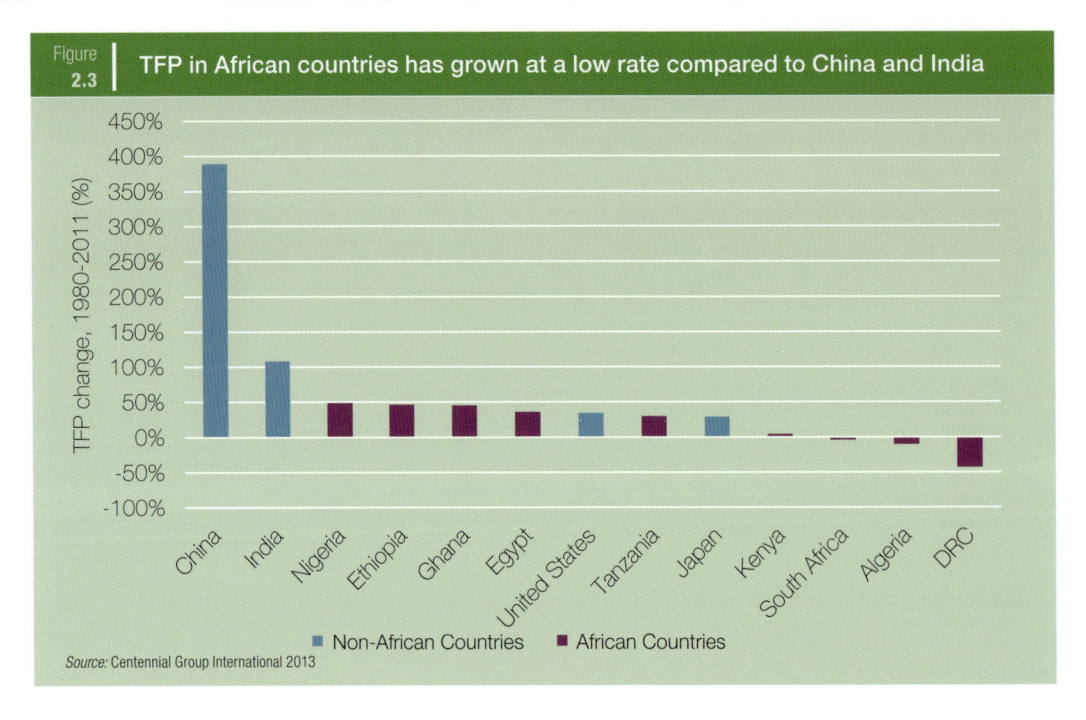

Figure 2.3 TFP in African countries has grown at a low rate compared to China and India

Source: Centennial Group International 2013

Manage natural resource rents to diversify and to avoid boom-and-bust cycles. One of the central challenges faced by all African countries rich in natural resources is managing the resulting rents (see Chapter 12). The main lesson from resource-rich Latin American (and Persian Gulf) countries is that it is very hard to break the past strong links between the vagaries of global commodity markets and the countries' economic performance. When a large proportion of exports and GDP is generated by extractive industries, other segments of the economy have historically found it very difficult to improve productivity and compete in global markets, partly due to appreciation of their currencies. In addition, without strong institutions, natural resource rents can easily lead to increased corruption rather than economic development.

The task before African countries of diversifying the economy and developing new competitive activities will not be easy. One example of success in this context is Chile, which has successfully diversified and become globally competitive in a number of areas (see Box 2.2).

Drivers of Change: Global and Africa-Specific

The aspirational vision portrays an Africa that could be. It is a plausible scenario but by no means guaranteed. Formulating a strategy to realize this vision requires, first of all, a clear assessment of the drivers of change — the trends and opportunities facing the continent. Some of these are global; Africa can affect them very little but must leverage them for its benefit. Others are regional and can be altered by the actions of governments, businesses, and individuals.

> **Box 2.2 | Managing natural resources: The example of Chile**
>
> Chile has marshaled its natural resource wealth to successfully diversify its economy and become globally competitive in a number of areas. Four key actions stand out from its experience and explain its success.
> - First, in order to open its internal markets to international competition and diversify its export markets, Chile has focused on Asian markets for many years and, more recently, on Korea and China. As a result, these fast-growing Asian economies have become major trade partners. This approach required a long-term vision and strategy by the government and aggressive follow-up by Chilean companies.
> - Second, the country opened the mineral sector to the private sector and managed public companies on a strictly commercial basis. As a result, all Chilean companies engaged in the sector have become more efficient and competitive. In addition, they have spawned services companies that now serve not only domestic but also international mining companies.
> - Third, the country's central bank has discouraged excessive inflows of "hot" money, which has prevented excessive currency appreciation and permitted other sectors to remain globally competitive.
> - Finally, the country has skillfully managed revenues from commodity exports during price booms, stabilizing public expenditure across cycles, saving part for future generations, and using part to increase infrastructure investments to boost its long-term competitiveness.
>
> *Source:* Centennial Group International 2013

Global Drivers — Need to be Leveraged

The world is changing and all countries will be affected by a number of global phenomena — an increasingly multipolar global economy, tightening competition for resources, aging societies, technological development, and climate change.

Multipolar global economy

Major shifts are taking place in the global economy that will affect Africa's future (World Bank 2011a). The global economy no longer depends on the North American or European consumer but increasingly on the Asian investor. Structural growth in developing countries has partly decoupled from high-income countries, but global financial markets and trading systems bind major economies more tightly than ever. Business cycles have become more synchronized and developing countries' contribution to global investment growth is now higher than that of high-income countries. At the same time, cyclical upswings and downswings in growth in developing and high-income countries remain highly synchronized.

Developing countries already drive global growth. Historically they have accounted for around 20 percent of the growth in global GDP; in 2011 they accounted for more than half. This trend will be accompanied by major sectoral shifts, such as a rising share of services in GDP within developing countries. Shifts in the labor supply will be particularly striking. Over the next 40 years, labor supply will decline everywhere except in Africa and South Asia.

The trade, investment, and consumption shifts associated with growth in a multipolar world will create opportunities, such as growing global trade, new sources of investment, and fast-growing consumption in emerging markets. African economies must seize these opportunities. At the same time, they must avoid the risk that the fast-growing emerging economies converge with today's advanced economies while developing countries with low productivity growth stagnate and remain marginal to the global economy.

Competition for finite natural resources

Intense competition for scarce natural resources (energy, minerals, water, and fertile land) could be unleashed with growth and the increasing affluence of Asians, Latin Americans, and Africans, especially if they emulate current Western lifestyles. Global supply may not readily accommodate changes in demand of this magnitude, especially for non-renewable raw materials, thus constraining growth. Concerns about the sustainability of economic growth date back to Malthus and re-emerge whenever growth is rapid. Today there is a backdrop of recent rises in prices for food, fuel, and other raw materials. The new equilibrium will surely be found in a combination of adjustments: price increases to reduce demand and increase supply; new technologies to reduce unit consumption and/or substitute with more plentiful, renewable resources; and recycling to minimize waste.

Commodity prices have also become more synchronized and have been on a steep upward trend, though they remain volatile. The post-2005 boom is one of the largest on record, and the movements of energy, metal, and agriculture prices are much more tightly linked than in the past. Given increased synchronization of business cycles, commodity price fluctuation will continue. Commodity demand is high, but technological progress continues to increase the efficiency of resource use, and energy use per unit of global GDP continues to decline. Metals, important for many African countries, are the exception, where use per unit of GDP has increased over the last decade. Real commodity prices may stay high, but they are unlikely to continue to increase at current rates over the long run and periodic downswings are possible.

For Africa, these trends present two important opportunities. First, as a continent rich in oil and minerals, Africa will remain a major supplier of energy and other minerals to the rest of the world for an extended period, generating financial resources to invest in the future. Second, based on its endowment of other natural resources (including underutilized arable land and water), it could become a major exporter of agricultural products to the world.

Aging world

Over the last two decades, the world has benefited from a demographic dividend. The number of people aged 20 to 64, traditionally taken as the potential labor force, has been growing. About 560 million people were added to the global labor force in the 1990s, and almost 640 million more between 2000 and 2010. Globally, that dividend is now slowing and will lose steam by 2035.

Over the following decades, an even smaller absolute number of workers will enter the global labor force, largely due to lower population growth rates in advanced and (some) emerging economies. By 2050, the global labor force will be essentially flat, growing perhaps by 0.4 percent annually. Three offsetting trends are in play beyond the overall aging of the population. In some countries, especially emerging markets, a far higher proportion of youth will go on to complete secondary school and get some tertiary education, thus entering the labor market later. In countries such as India and Indonesia, the current large gap in the labor participation rates of males and females could narrow, increasing the total number of workers. And, in advanced countries, more of the elderly could remain in the labor force. Despite some uncertainty driven by these trends, it seems clear that the rate of increase of workers that has helped power the global economy forward is set to decline.

Asia provides a powerful illustration of an aging world. Its labor force has been growing at 2 percent a year over the past two decades (1991–2010). In the next twenty years (2011–2030), Asia's labor force growth will have been halved to 0.9 percent a year. And in the following two decades (2031–2050), its labor force will not grow at all. Similar developments are expected in Latin America. Total population in Japan and Europe is expected to decline, and the Chinese population will have peaked by around 2030.

In this global context, Africa stands out as the region with a still-growing population and an even faster growing labor force. Indeed, between 2031 and 2050, Africa could account for as much as 75 percent of total growth in the global labor force. Africa's growing labor force both moderates the global trend and offers the continent an opportunity to converge with the rest of the world.

Innovation and technological advances

Innovation is widely recognized as a key source of growth for all economies irrespective of their income level. While there is considerable debate on the pace of future change, it is clear that the technological frontier will continue to expand. Knowledge and innovation will drive the performance of some countries, and a lack of it will lead to disappointing results in others. The big opportunity for Africa is the possibility of catching up rapidly. At the country level, progress may often mean leapfrogging to existing technologies that are new to Africa. Africa has high-productivity firms as well, and a second source of productivity growth will be bringing its lowest-productivity firms to the level of its highest. Knowledge will also affect performance beyond pure technological advances. Innovation that meets the needs of the poorer segments of the population — so-called inclusive innovation — is important for broad-based growth and social development.

Information and communication technology will make communication easier and cheaper. This advance has clear economic dimensions but also political ones. Mobile phones in Kenya, for example, have not only opened banking to millions who were previously excluded but also accelerated communication that can crystallize political aspirations or inflame ethnic rivalry. As a result of advances in communications technology, Africans' aspirations are shaped by what is going on not only within their country but throughout the world, and they are increasingly able to force accountability — as exemplified by the Arab Spring.

Climate change

Global warming is leading to climate changes that are difficult to quantify but are certain to have a major impact on all countries. The implications of increased water scarcity, more frequent severe weather events, and increased coastal flooding are probably manageable over the next 10 to 20 years. Beyond 2030, however, there is much greater uncertainty and clear risks of catastrophic developments. This book recognizes, but does not attempt to assess, such risks. Beyond the immediate needs for investment in climate-resilient infrastructure and adaptive agricultural research, the development of strong, flexible institutions emphasized in this book will be key to dealing with the evolving challenges of climate change (see Chapter 15).

African drivers — Need to be steered to positive outcomes

Trends in demographics, natural resource development, and urbanization will inevitably lead to change in Africa. The actions of its political, business, and civil society leaders will, however, determine the outcome of that change.

Demographics — dividend or social time bomb?

Over the next 40 years, Africa's population is likely to more than double, reaching 2.1 to 2.7 billion,[1] and the number of youth will increase from 260 million today to between 375 and 500 million.[2] These demographic shifts can lead to higher productivity and per capita incomes or to unmanageable social tensions, violence, and conflict (see Chapter 5).

The potential for a demographic dividend is clear. Africa's share of the world labor force will steadily grow. By 2050, Africa will be the only region in the world where the number of working-age adults will be rising and the dependency ratio falling (see Figure 2.4). This population shift creates the potential for a rapid rise in per capita incomes — a demographic dividend — provided that more jobs are created and worker productivity improved. In the simplest terms, *realizing the potential depends on people finding higher productivity jobs*.

How many people will need such jobs? Under the UN's low-fertility variant, Africa's working age population[3] would increase by around 700 million — from 0.5 billion today to 1.2 billion by 2050 — and its dependency ratio[4] would fall from 122 today to 80 in 2050 (see Figure 2.4). Even with no change

---

1. 2.1 billion under the UN 2012 low-fertility variant and 2.7 billion under its high-fertility variant
2. Population aged 15–24
3. Population aged 20–64, recognizing that an increasing share of 15–19 year olds need to be in school
4. Population aged 0–19 plus 65+ per 100 of working age population (20–64). This differs slightly from the UN calculation (0-15 plus 65+ per 100 15-64), due to the altered definition of the working age population explained in the previous footnote.

in productivity, the greater number of workers for every child or elderly person would yield nearly a 25 percent increase in per capita incomes, and make possible a virtuous circle of increased income to increased savings to increased investment to even higher income.

In sharp contrast, under the UN's high-fertility variant, the working age population would increase by 870 million by 2050 and the dependency ratio would fall from 122 today only to 102. With no other changes, the result would be only around a 10 percent increase in per capita incomes. Under the high-fertility variant, which already assumes a decline in fertility from today's levels, it is highly unlikely that Africa would be able to increase jobs and productivity enough to raise per capita incomes substantially.

The population will continue to increase, but the pace of fertility decline is a key determinant of the number of children to be educated, the number of jobs needed, and the number of very young and old supported by each working adult. As Figure 2.4 illustrates, the differences in these numbers between fertility scenarios is very large. If fertility were to stay at today's level or even decrease to the UN's high-fertility variant, it is very unlikely that Africa could produce either the required access to quality education or jobs.

How many jobs, and what kind of jobs? Job creation is both more uncertain and more amenable to big changes than population growth. Even the low-fertility scenario implies a need for 12 to 15 million new jobs every year just to absorb the increase in the working age population. Big increases in jobs will have to come from the private sector. Given rudimentary social protection systems, unemployment is not an option for most, and household enterprises are likely to stay the residual source of employment. It is very likely that people will be employed; the question is whether they will be employed in low-productivity traditional agriculture and household enterprises (survival jobs) or in higher-productivity agriculture, manufacturing, and services jobs that are transformational. The answer depends on whether workers have the needed skills and private investors have the confidence to invest.

Oil and minerals — blessing or curse?

Africa is well-endowed with mineral resources. The continent accounts for more than 5 percent of both production and reserves of oil, gas, bauxite, titanium, copper, and gold (see Chapter 12). In addition, many of its reserves are of particularly high quality. Furthermore, the region has had less exploration than elsewhere and has good prospects for additional discoveries, as seen recently in East Africa.

As a result, natural resources play a big part in the regional economy. Hydrocarbons and metals account for more than 50 percent of exports in 14 African countries that are home to 39 percent of the continent's total population. Similarly, resource extraction rents represent more than 2 percent of GDP in 27 countries with 72 percent of the population. Commodity prices have historically played a big role in growth, as illustrated in Figure 2.5. One-quarter of African GDP growth over the last decade is estimated to be attributable to commodity price increases (see Box 2.3).

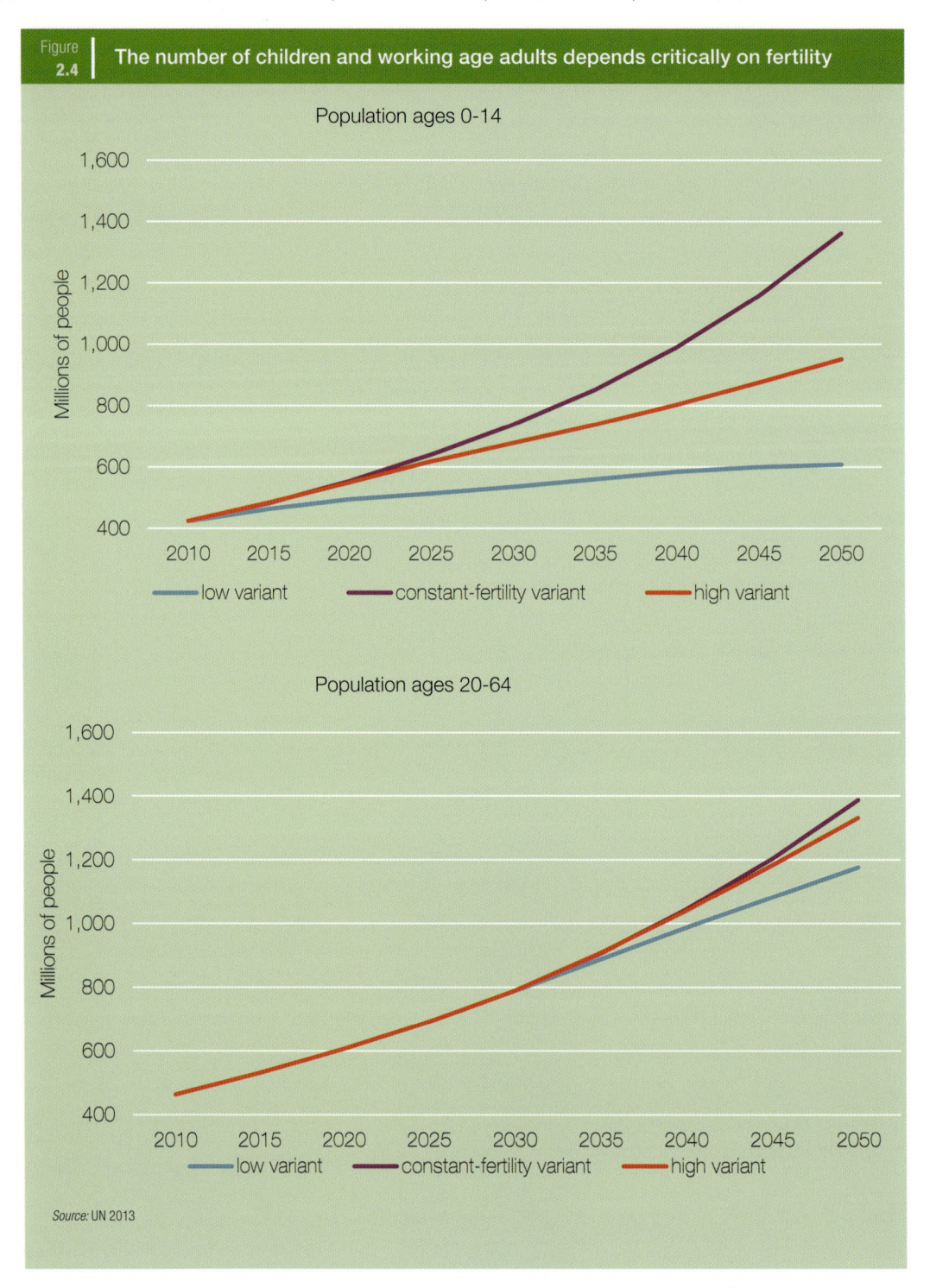

Figure 2.4 | The number of children and working age adults depends critically on fertility

Population ages 0-14

— low variant — constant-fertility variant — high variant

Population ages 20-64

— low variant — constant-fertility variant — high variant

Source: UN 2013

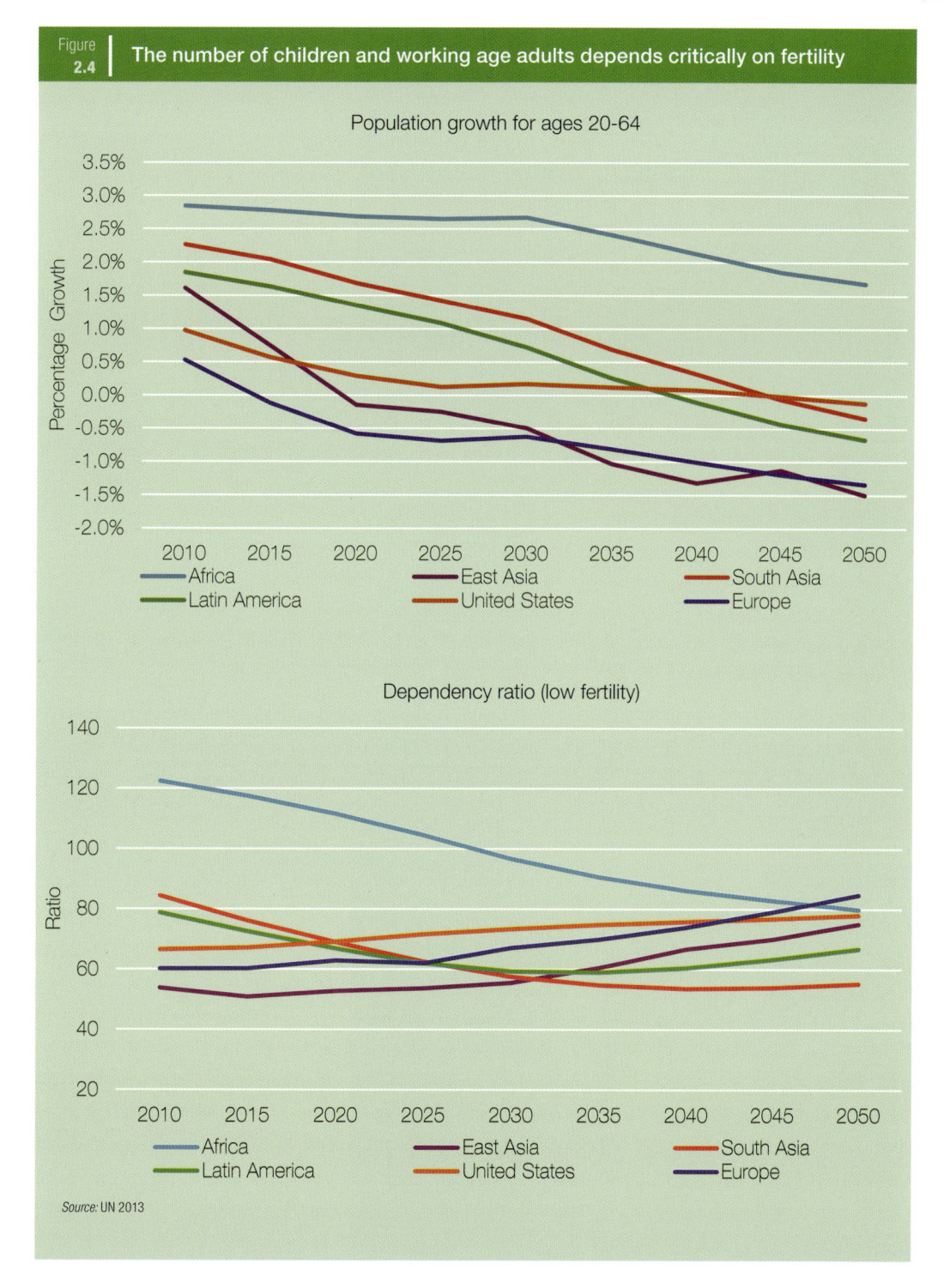

HISTORICAL PERSPECTIVES AND DRIVERS OF FUTURE CHANGE

Figure 2.4 | The number of children and working age adults depends critically on fertility

Population growth for ages 20-64

Dependency ratio (low fertility)

Source: UN 2013

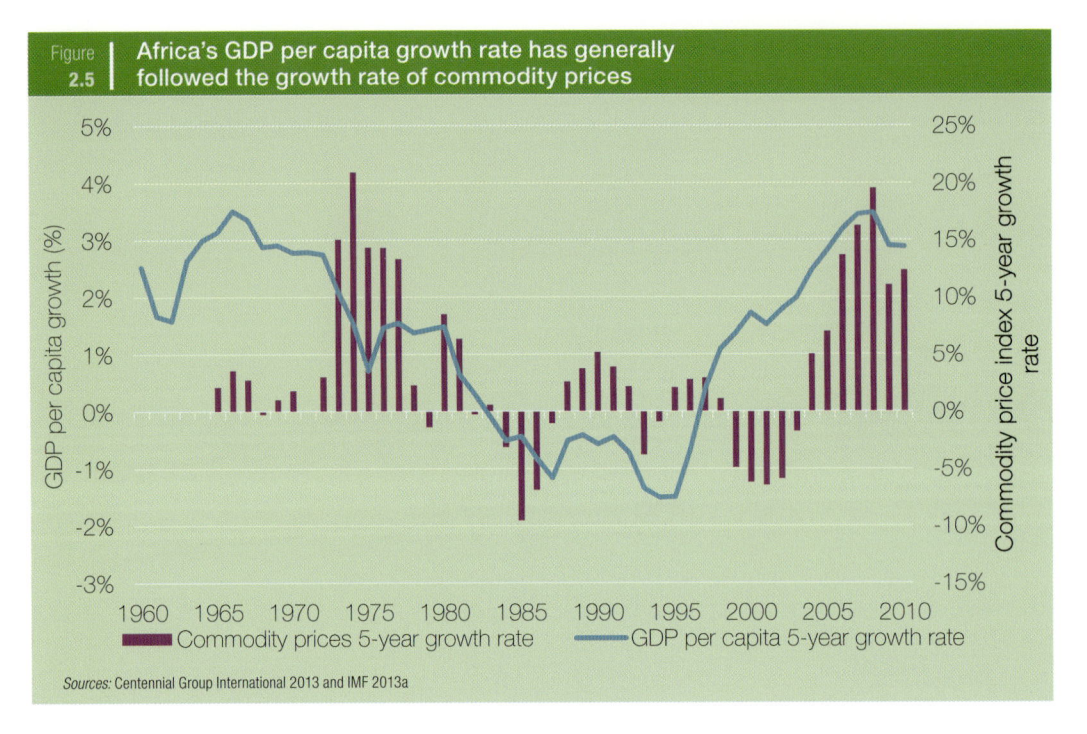

Figure 2.5 Africa's GDP per capita growth rate has generally followed the growth rate of commodity prices

Sources: Centennial Group International 2013 and IMF 2013a

Hydrocarbon and mineral wealth is intrinsically a blessing but can easily become a curse. Africa has examples of such resources being managed efficiently and thus contributing to dramatic improvements in well-being, as in Botswana. But there are also examples where these resources have fueled wars, as in Sierra Leone or the Democratic Republic of the Congo (DRC), or led to widespread corruption and poverty, as in Nigeria.

Extracting non-renewable resources is, by definition, not a sustainable source of growth over the long run, and it creates few jobs. The source of either the blessing or the curse is that natural resource extraction generates revenues that are much greater than the cost of extraction, what economists refer to as "rents." Everything depends on who gets the rents and how they are used. They can be stolen (and frequently sent abroad), consumed, or invested.

Countries can get more (or less) of the rents depending on the risks and costs of doing business in their country, the extent of transparency to reduce corruption, and the expertise they mobilize in contract and taxation matters. The risk is that such rents can lead to boom-and-bust cycles in the economy linked to fluctuations in commodity prices, to an overvalued exchange rate that makes diversification and the associated job creation difficult, or to unsustainable consumption that ends when the resources are depleted. The opportunity is to use these rents effectively to convert mineral assets into human, physical, and financial capital that could in turn transform not only individual economies and their people but also the continent as a whole.

Box 2.3 | Africa's commodity terms of trade — A fragile blessing

Africa has developed its commercial links with the rest of the world on the basis of commodity exports. Despite export diversification in a few countries, the share of commodities in African exports has risen to about 82 percent in 2011 from 71 percent in 1995, as commodity prices and output have gone up sharply. The increase in commodity prices, well in excess of the increase in prices of Africa's imports, has resulted in 70 percent improvement in terms of trade since 2000.

African countries are estimated to have gained purchasing power equivalent to 27 percent of 2000-level GDP as a result of the terms of trade improvements since 2000. However, gains from improvement in the terms of trade are not fully captured in changes in GDP since the latter reflects only changes in output quantities. As a result, gross domestic income (GDI) has risen faster than GDP. Estimates of GDI, actual GDP, and GDP net of the impact of terms of trade changes (see Table 2.i) reveal that, in addition, one-quarter of the increase in GDP since 2000 is attributable to the multiplier effect of improved terms of trade on GDP. The combined direct and multiplier effect of terms of trade changes on GDI in the period 2000–12 is estimated at about 3.6 percent per year. In summary, the impact of terms of trade explains nearly half of the total increase in disposable income.

On the basis of these estimates, if terms of trade in the future were to stabilize at the current high levels, GDP growth rates would tend to fall to the trend growth rate of 3.4 percent, as the multiplier effect would disappear and the purchasing power of exports would stabilize (see Annex 1). A decline in the terms of trade of 10 percent would entail a decline of 2 percent in GDP and of 4.4 percent in disposable income, yielding a total decline in GDI of about 6.4 percent. A decline of this size, while steep, is not unusual. A 10 percent fall in commodity prices is possible, as prices would still be almost 50 percent higher than in 2003 and certainly within the range of the long-term cycle of commodity prices.

The decade-long improvement in Africa's terms of trade has led to a degree of complacency among policy-makers and economic agents that is not warranted. The impact of lower terms of trade would be staggering. Since commodity prices will fluctuate and could even show a secular downward trend, it is essential for African countries to prepare for the contingency of lower prices. Establishment of structural fiscal rules is of the essence. Without such action, there is a high risk that volatility will increase, hindering growth and hurting the most vulnerable groups in African society.

Table 2.i: Africa GDI, GDP, and terms of trade (average annual and cummulative growth 2000-2012)

	Average annual rate of growth	Cummulative growth (%)
Terms of trade	5.0	63.7
GDI	6.3	108.5
Direct effect of terms of trade	1.1	27.0*
GDP	5.1	81.5
Multiplier effect of terms of trade	1.2	20.6*
Trend GDP	3.9	60.9

Note: *Residual cumulative rate 2000-2013
Sources: IMF 2012b; Centennial Group International 2013

Urbanization — agglomeration benefits or explosive slums?

Africa's cities will triple in size from a population of 400 million today to at least 1.2 billion in 2050[5] and will be the loci of much job creation. The size of urban markets, rising income of urban residents, and concentration of economic activity could make cities dynamic centers for higher productivity jobs — offering the prospects of a better life to more than 1 billion people (see Chapter 13).

This positive outcome would be realized if people have skills, cities function well, and economies are open to competition. In contrast, if people are illiterate and unskilled, cities dysfunctional, and economies trapped in extractive activities and crony capitalism, urban areas will be poor and violent — offering only the desperation of hopelessness to residents. All the prospective health gains, all the potential for a dramatically expanded and enhanced skills base, and the possibilities for generating jobs and attracting investment in Africa will depend on how effectively cities function since it is the urban areas where most of the future population will live and where the jobs will have to be created.

African cities are already the fastest growing in the world. Today there are only three cities in Africa (Cairo, Kinshasa, and Lagos) with population greater than 5 million, but by 2050 there could be 35 such cities in 21 countries. Moreover, by 2050 the continent could be home to as many as 15 mega-cities of more than 10 million inhabitants; Cairo, Kinshasa, Lagos, and Luanda could all be mega-cities as early as 2030.

The extent to which the cities fulfill their prospective role as drivers of economic growth will depend on delivering services to their residents and creating an environment where private sector activity flourishes. The latter will make the difference between productive and parasitic cities. Cities' success will depend on a variety of attributes. First is the level, quality, and competitiveness of their services, as well as the efficiency and sustainability with which these services are delivered. Second is the predictability of their governance and accountability functions and the reliability of their regulatory implementation and business environment. Third is the efficiency of their land, housing, and transport markets, and their ability to strategically plan and implement initiatives that address environmental challenges. Fourth is enhanced livability derived from high-standard infrastructure linkages to attractive hinterlands. These attributes are necessary to make African cities globally competitive, attract international investment, open up local capital markets and local investment, and encourage businesses to locate there. Such cities would also foster dynamic new business initiatives and a thriving start-up/innovation culture as well as a nurturing environment for micro and small enterprise development.

Larger urban populations mean that cities will occupy more land to accommodate businesses, housing, public spaces, and circulation. Physical expansion will require increased capacities of the associated water and sewerage systems, sanitation and solid waste management, roads and drainage, parks and recreation, electricity supply, and urban transport — all of which are to be provided on a massive scale by cities which, for the most part, have failed to meet much less pressing service demands to date. Recent studies have shown that despite the economic gains made by Africa over the past decade,

---

5. UN 2012 low-fertility variant and projected 58 percent urban population

there has been a significant increase in urban slums and a worsening of urban poverty levels, both to a much greater extent than in Asia. Innovation and managerial capacity will be key to providing services in these conditions.

Major Risks — Need to be Actively Managed

In addition to leveraging global drivers of change and steering regional drivers to positive outcomes, realization of a vision that meets the aspirations of Africans will require managing three specific risks — the threats of conflict, growing disparities, and the middle-income trap.

Fragility — Growing security or contagious conflict?

Many countries have an element of latent fragility given their often ethnically heterogeneous populations, relatively recent process of modern state formation, and the weakness of many sovereign state institutions that are sometimes controlled by a small political or ethnic group or family. Other elements of fragility are religious divides, fast-growing populations, lack of job opportunities for the young, and the challenge of controlling large territories with low population densities and difficult topography that are vulnerable to criminal and external threats. Finally, a critical element of fragility in some countries is non-inclusive political systems that fuel frustration and resentment. Some elements of latent fragility, such as ethnic and religious divides, will persist for a long time. But they need not lead to conflict if other elements, particularly the institutional weakness and political inclusiveness, are addressed. Inaction, on the other hand, is likely to lead to conflict that spills over borders and creates sub-regional insecurity that is highly detrimental to investment and growth (see Chapter 6).

Disparities — Inclusive growth or growing inequality?

Huge disparities between the rich and poor; inequality in access to education, health, and other social services; and a large proportion of the population still living in poverty constitute a time bomb under much of Africa. Unless these disparities are overcome, and overcome soon, Africa's ability to realize the aspirational vision outlined in Chapter 1 will be severely compromised (see Chapter 7).

As mentioned above, poverty rates have declined over the last decade in much of Africa; still, the absolute number of poor (defined here as those with income less than $1.25/day) has almost doubled in the past 30 years, from about 205 million in 1981 to 386 million in 2008. Almost half of all Sub-Saharan Africans still live below the poverty line.

More fundamental is the issue of huge inequities and disparities between the rich and the poor. Unfortunately, despite the recent improvement in economic growth, the disparities are still growing nationally, regionally, and with respect to the rest of the world (see Figure 2.6). At the national level, inequality, as measured by Gini coefficients, increased over the last decade in two-thirds of the African countries for which data are available. As a result, income inequality in Africa is now higher than in any other region

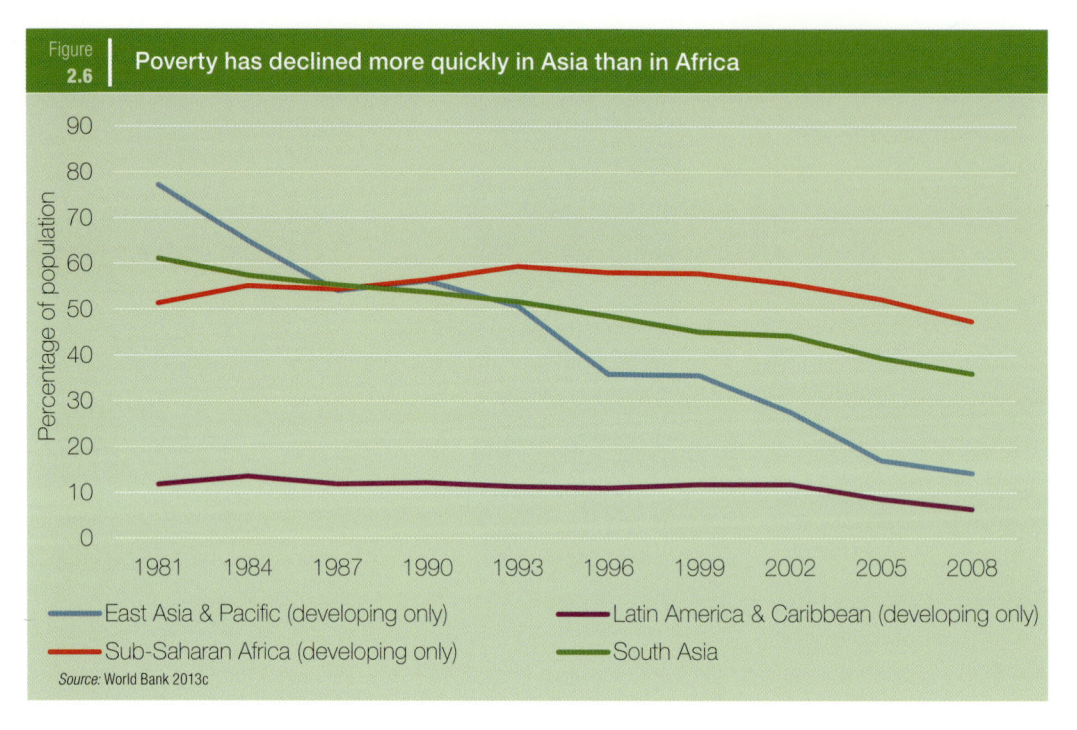

Figure 2.6 | **Poverty has declined more quickly in Asia than in Africa**

[Line chart showing percentage of population from 1981 to 2008 for East Asia & Pacific (developing only), Latin America & Caribbean (developing only), Sub-Saharan Africa (developing only), and South Asia.]

Source: World Bank 2013c

of the world except Latin America (where income inequality is declining) (see Figures 2.7 and 2.8). The earnings of the richest 20 percent of the population are 11 times those of the poorest 20 percent in Africa compared to only 7 times greater in Asia.

At the regional level, per capita incomes in the five richest African countries are 30 times those of the poorest five countries today, compared to 16 times greater 20 years ago. There is a major risk that landlocked and conflict-affected countries will be left behind and eventually threaten the entire continent's progress. Thus, even as the percentage of people living in absolute poverty declines over time, inequities and disparities must remain a major concern of economic policymakers and political leaders alike throughout Africa. At the global level, African per capita incomes are a smaller share of the world average than they were at independence, and this share has remained stagnant over the last decade (see Figure 2.9).

Access to basic services, such as education, health, and water supply, has also improved considerably over the last decade. Like reductions in poverty, however, the overall improvement in access masks large and sometimes growing disparities based on gender, rural or urban location, and family income level. They deserve much greater attention.

HISTORICAL PERSPECTIVES AND DRIVERS OF FUTURE CHANGE

Figure 2.7 Sub-Saharan Africa has the highest disparities after Latin America

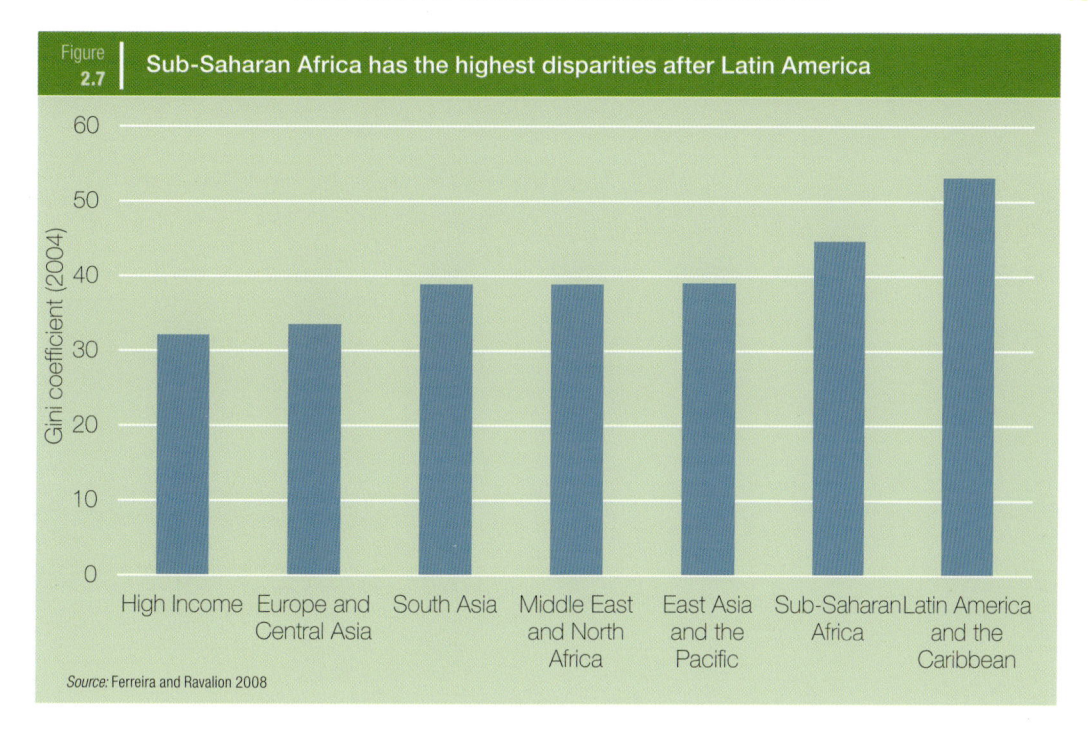

Source: Ferreira and Ravalion 2008

Figure 2.8 South Africa has the highest inequality in Africa

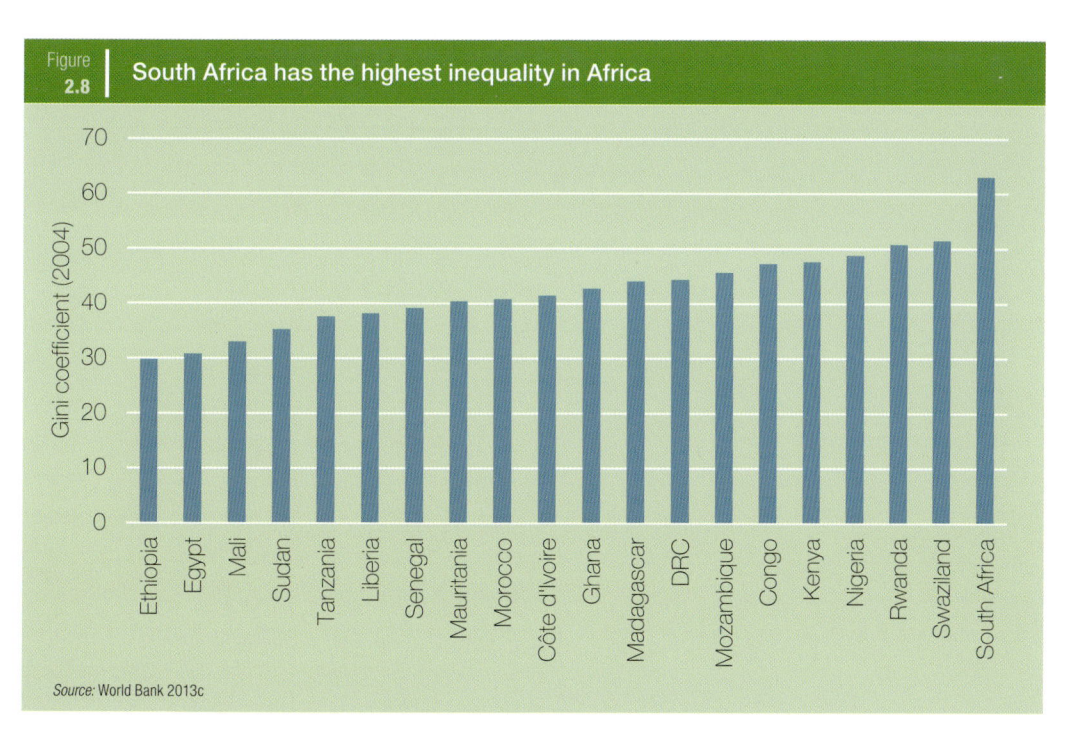

Source: World Bank 2013c

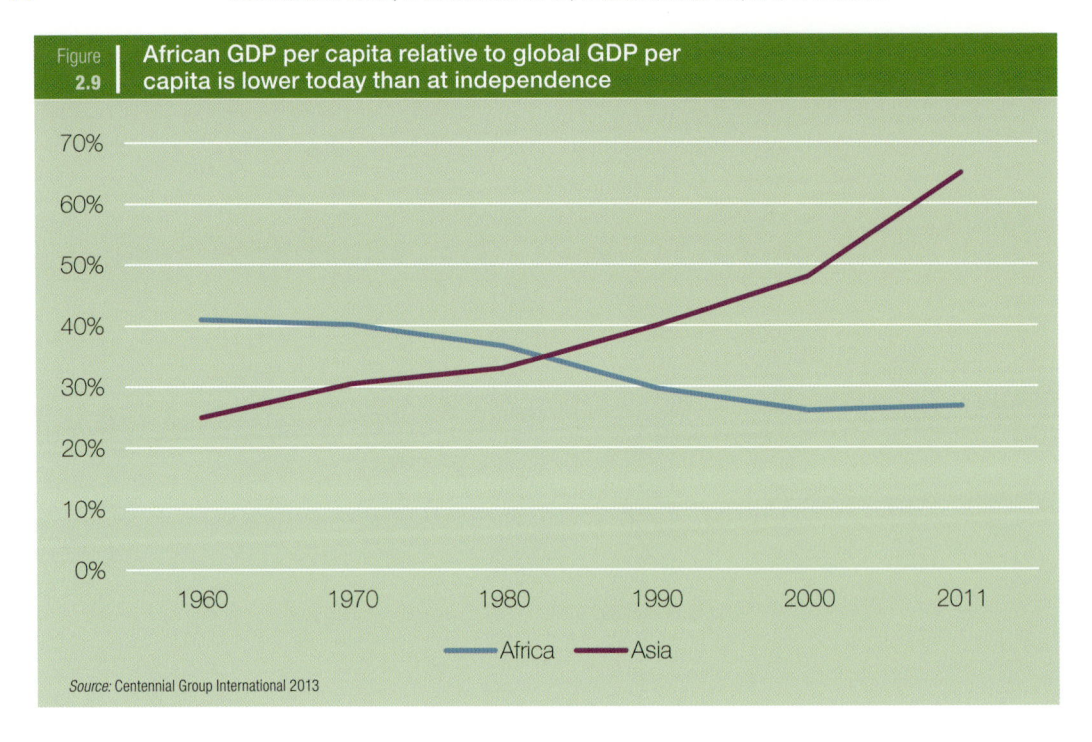

Figure 2.9 African GDP per capita relative to global GDP per capita is lower today than at independence

Source: Centennial Group International 2013

The Africa Progress Panel has clearly stated the implications of inequities and disparities:

> "Not all inequalities are unjust, but the levels of inequality across much of Africa are unjustified and profoundly unfair. Extreme disparities in income are slowing the pace of poverty reduction and hampering the development of broad-based economic growth. Disparities in basic life-chances — for health, education and participation in society — are preventing millions of Africans from realizing their potential, holding back social and economic development in the process" (Africa Progress Panel 2012).

Any further growth in inequities would likely spur social unrest, ranging from possible collapse in fragile countries, to increased social tension in more stable countries, to large population movements across borders.

There are also strong positive reasons for reducing disparities. As the recent experience in Brazil and Mexico has demonstrated, programs to reduce disparities and facilitate the access of all citizens to the opportunities offered by economic growth are also pro-growth. Earlier longer-term experience in countries like Korea has demonstrated that, for a given level of per capita income, lower inequality creates a larger middle class, which in turn expands domestic savings and consumption and opens new possibilities for growth and job creation. Socially, the middle class strives for better education of the next generation, creates a new work ethic, and drives entrepreneurship. Over time it also becomes a strong advocate for improvements in governance. All these attributes are essential for Africa's longer-term prosperity and social cohesion. Given the dimensions of the problem, increasing the opportunities for the most vulnerable is the only way to both sustain overall growth and reduce disparities.

Middle-income stage — Road to prosperity or trap?

African countries were for many years thought of as poor. This has changed rapidly. Africa is increasingly a middle-income continent, but with many poor people. Half of the continent's countries are now middle-income and the majority of its population lives in middle-income countries. The inability of most middle-income African countries to further reduce the productivity and income gaps with advanced economies suggests that many countries in the region find themselves in the middle-income trap (see Box 2.4). Of the 21 African countries that had per capita GDP above $1,000 (constant 2011 US dollars) in 1985, none are high-income today. Three of these countries (Botswana, Cape Verde, and Mauritius) did achieve per capita growth rates above 4 percent over the subsequent 25 years and show that convergence with the rest of the world is possible. Most, however, remain middle-income, including two of Africa's largest middle-income countries (Algeria and South Africa), which averaged per capita growth below 1 percent over the last 25 years. More ominous yet, no less than six of these countries regressed, and had negative per capita growth over the last 25 years.

Few countries sustain high growth for more than a generation, and even fewer continue high growth rates once they reach middle-income status. Yet this is what African economies must do if they are to avoid the middle-income trap. The Commission on Growth and Development identified five common characteristics among the countries (mainly East Asian) that have done so successfully (Commission on Growth and Development 2008):

- Openness to the global economy in knowledge and trade
- Macroeconomic stability
- A "future orientation," exemplified by high rates of saving and investment
- A reliance on markets and market-based prices to allocate resources
- Leadership committed to growth and inclusion with a reasonable capacity for administration.

Box 2.4 | Are some African economies mired in the middle-income trap?

The middle-income trap refers to countries stagnating in middle-income status and not growing to high-income levels. This is illustrated in Figure 2.i, which plots the income per capita of six middle-income countries between 1975 and 2011. In a steadily growing economy, the line would rise steadily over time toward higher income levels, as is the experience of South Korea. But many middle-income countries, including Brazil, Mexico, and Africa's biggest middle-income countries, do not follow this pattern. Instead, they have short periods of growth largely offset by periods of decline. Rather than steadily moving up over time, their GDP per capita moves up and down but rises only very slowly over time. That stalled trajectory defines the middle-income trap — unable to compete with low-income, low-wage economies in manufacturing exports, yet unable to compete with advanced economies in high-skill innovations.

Productivity growth in low-income economies can be characterized as moving people out of low-productivity activities such as traditional agriculture to higher productivity activities such as labor-intensive manufacturing and modern services. Productivity growth in affluent societies is driven by innovation. Some middle-income countries lose their low-cost advantage but do not have the institutions — property rights, capital markets, successful venture capital — or critical mass of highly skilled people to grow through innovation. Caught between these two groups, middle-income countries may be unable to find a viable high-growth strategy. This seems to be what has happened to middle-income African economies such as South Africa, Egypt, and Algeria.

Income distribution can also play an important role in sustaining growth. In many countries, domestic consumption typically becomes an important source of demand growth when incomes per capita reach around US$6,000 in purchasing power parity (PPP) terms. For the most part, this has not happened in Africa, perhaps because of the highly unequal distribution of income. Compare South Africa with South Korea, for example. South Africa's growth started to slow after 1975, when it had reached a per capita income level of about US$9,000 (PPP). At that time, its middle class (defined as households with incomes of between US$10 and US$100 per capita per day) was just 38 percent of the population, largely as a result of apartheid and the resulting divided society, which was inadequate to drive further growth. In contrast, by the time South Korea's income per capita reached US$9,500 (PPP) in 1987, the country's evenly distributed growth had produced a sizeable middle class, which accounted for 69 percent of the population. The demand from this large middle class fueled growth of the country's service industries and created the building blocks for a knowledge economy.

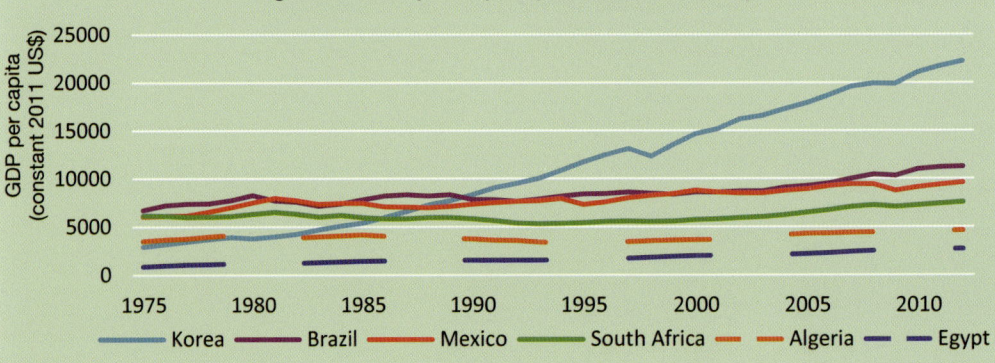

Figure 2.i GDP per capita (constant 2011 US$)

Source: Centennial Group International 2013

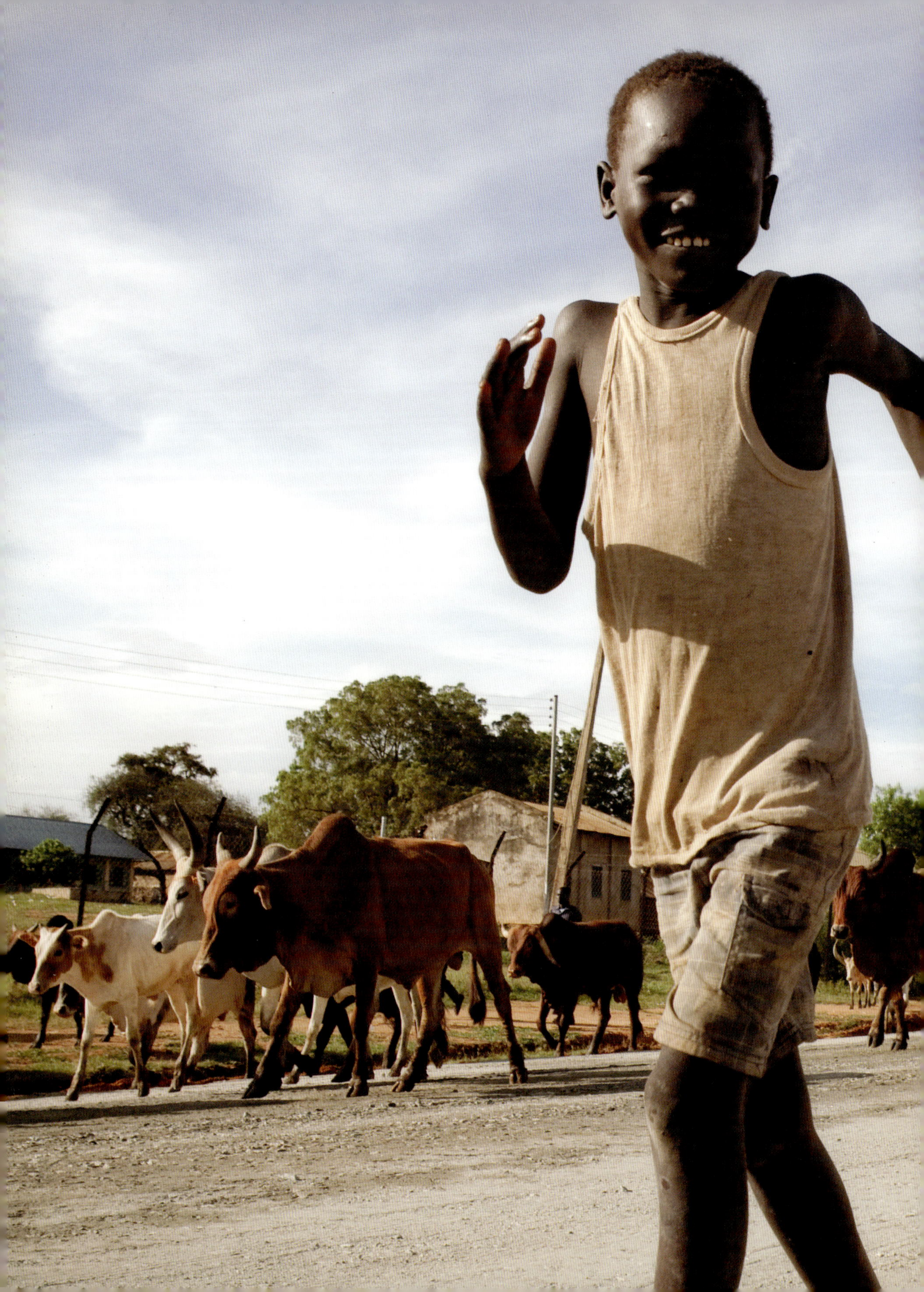

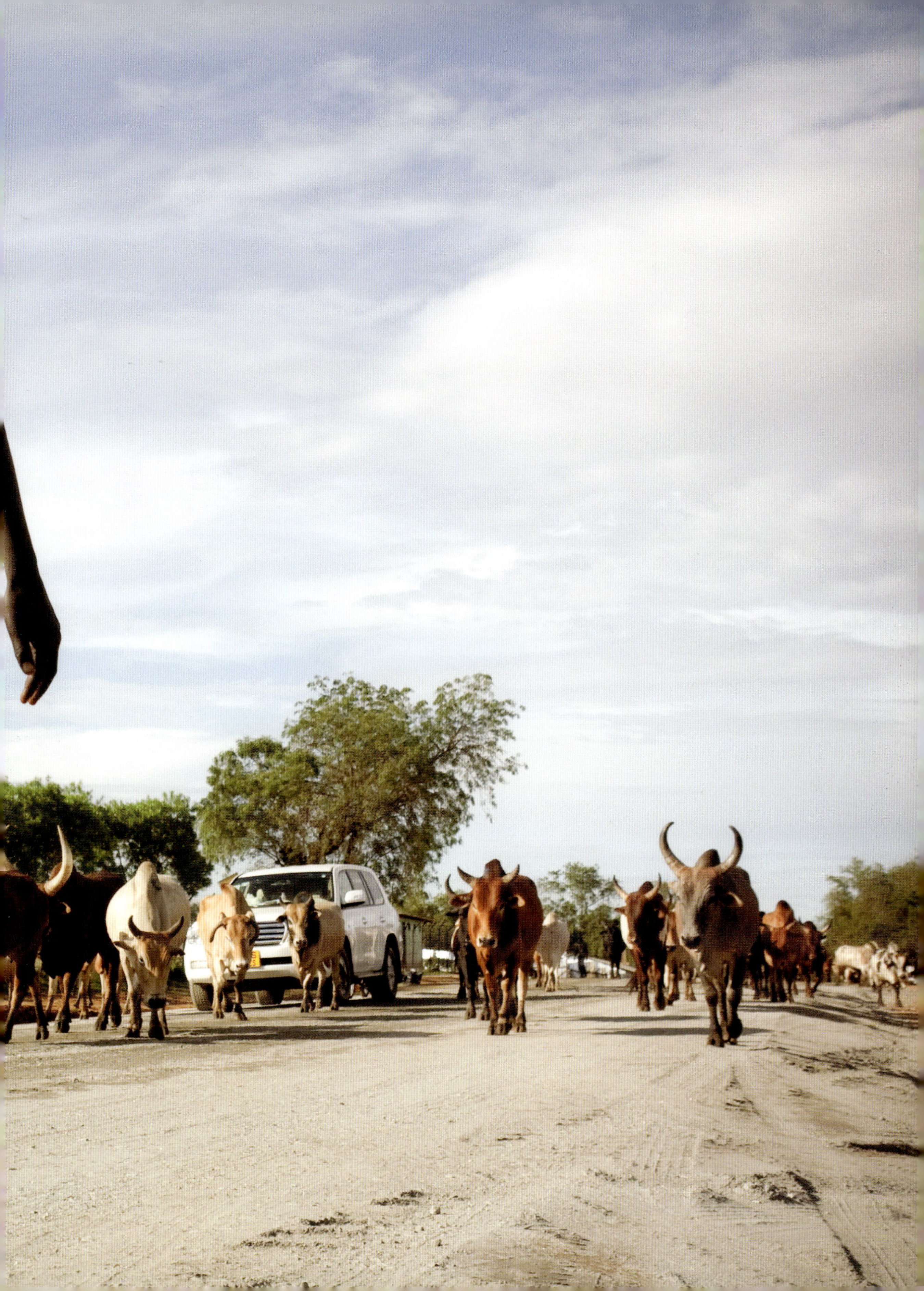

Chapter 3

Action Agenda — Jobs for People, Economies, and the Continent

Theodore Ahlers, Harinder S. Kohli, Callisto Madavo, and Anil Sood

Africa must grow both more rapidly and more inclusively than it has in the past if it is to meet the aspirations of its people and realize the 2050 vision traced in Chapter 1. Given Africa's broad diversity, strategies to achieve this vision will necessarily be country-specific. Even for individual countries, the strategies will evolve over time: as immediate challenges are met new ones will arise, ranging from restoring basic institutions following conflict to avoiding the middle-income trap. The framework set out here attempts to identify the big issues that all countries in the region must address, even if the specifics vary between countries and over time.

Higher sustained growth requires more investment, particularly in Africa's lower-income countries. Most importantly, it requires increases in productivity, since today's low productivity robs the continent of the full benefit of even its existing human and physical resources, and convergence of incomes with the rest of the world depends on a rapid convergence in productivity levels.

The 2050 vision will be realized (or not) through jobs — jobs that move people from lower to higher productivity activities. Jobs are in large measure the vehicle to build an Africa of prosperous people, competitive economies, and global integration. These three dimensions — people, economies, and the continent — are interrelated and directly affect each other. They also serve to identify ten key areas for action if the global and regional drivers of change are to be leveraged and steered effectively. The three dimensions and the ten key action areas are illustrated in Figure 3.1.

Prosperous People and Cohesive Societies — Jobs to Transform Lives

At its most basic level, the vision is about the prosperity of people and the cohesiveness of their societies. The dimensions of the vision imply different things for different countries. Cutting across all countries, however, are four areas of strategic importance on which action is required now: inclusion, demographic transition, human capital, and fragility and conflict.

Promote inclusion

Prosperity for people implies greater inclusion, and in Africa this largely means equalizing opportunity, particularly the opportunity for the social mobility offered by higher productivity jobs (see Chapter 7). Beyond moral considerations, equalizing opportunity is key to mobilizing all of a society's human

Figure 3.1 | Framework for achieving the 2050 vision

Pragmatic Leadership with Focus on Results

- Promote Inclusion
- Build Human Capital
- Accelerate Demographic Transition
- Reduce Conflict and Fragility
- Foster Competition/PSD
- Transform Agriculture
- Manage Urbanization for Growth
- Mobilize and Invest Natural Resource Rents
- Promote Regional Cooperation and Markets
- Reposition Globally (Trade & FDI, Not Aid)

Prosperous People, Cohesive Societies · Competitive Economies · Integrated Africa

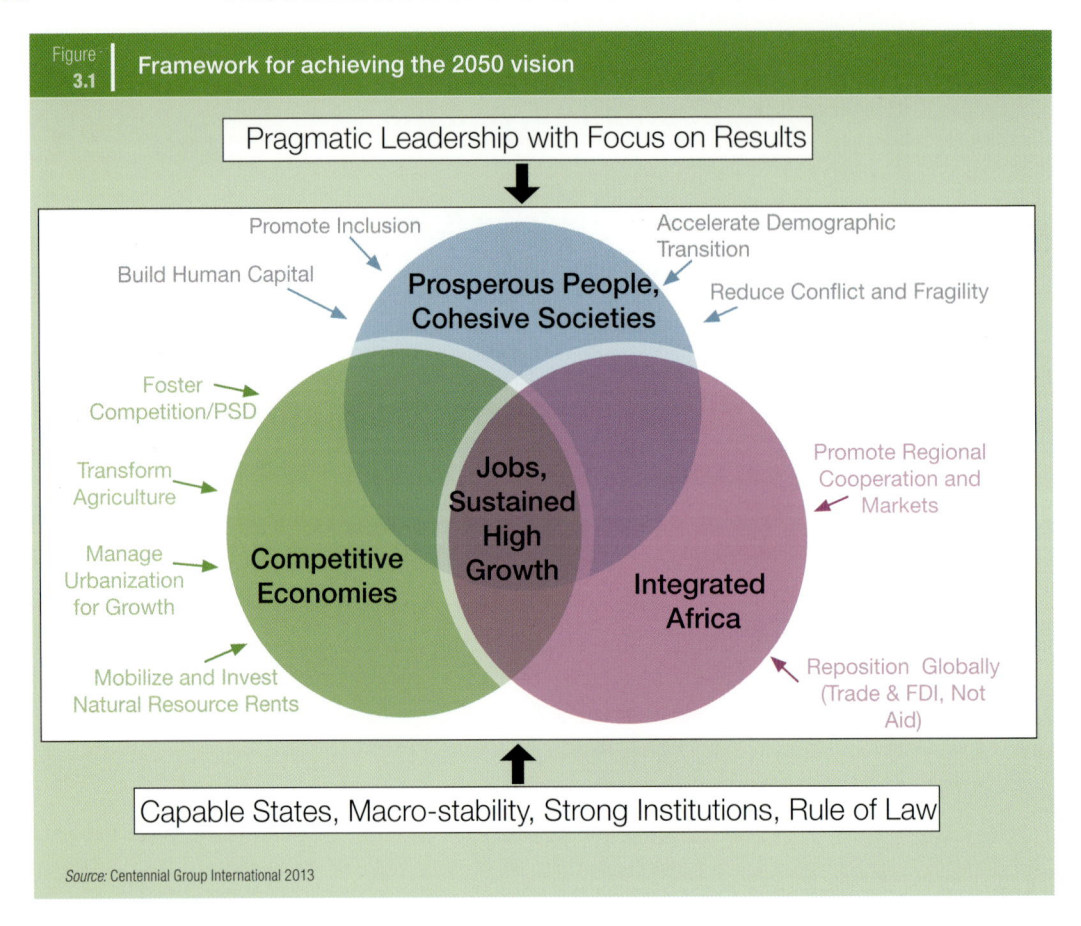

Jobs, Sustained High Growth

Capable States, Macro-stability, Strong Institutions, Rule of Law

Source: Centennial Group International 2013

resources and giving everyone the stake in the future on which investment, innovation, and risk-taking are based. Without equalizing opportunity, growth will be both slower — because human potential is squandered — and more unequal, which may undermine its future. Inclusion, in turn, has many aspects. In some countries, it will mean assuring that university degrees are earned not bought and, in others, providing better access to quality education in rural areas. In some countries it will mean removing legal restrictions on women's activities; in others, making sure it is safe for girls to attend school. In most it will mean merit-based education and job selection; in others, greater political openness and inclusion of groups traditionally marginalized for ethnic, religious, or other reasons. In all, it means assuring that those at the bottom of the income distribution have access to quality basic services comparable to those on the top. These include provision of infrastructure services, such as electricity in rural areas, as well as social services, particularly early childhood interventions and quality basic education.

Inclusive growth is more than an outcome — it is also a process. The ability of citizens to express and exercise their views is an important part of inclusive growth, as is the participation of citizens in decisions that influence their well-being. Empowering citizens can thus be key to effective inclusion. Governments need to include citizens directly in monitoring and assessing programs, re-target general subsidies to demand-side subsidies (such as conditional cash transfers) to increase access for the poor and, where possible, make provision of resources dependent on beneficiary choice (such as education financing that follows students).

Accelerate demographic transition

Educating and creating jobs for 700 million more working age adults by 2050 in a context of fewer dependents per working age adult is a challenge. Doing so for 900 million more with a growing number of dependents per working age adult could be a nightmare. The pace of total fertility decline is the key difference between these two fundamentally different outcomes (see Chapter 5). It is not a question of whether the population should continue to grow. The current age structure means that even if fertility fell immediately to replacement levels (around 2.1 births per woman), the population of Africa would still double. It is rather a question of how fast the population grows and countries' ability to educate people and give them productive livelihoods. Educating girls and giving couples access to modern contraceptives is essential for a future with prosperous people and cohesive societies.

Under the UN's (2013) low-fertility projections, Africa would have 610 million children under age 15 in 2050 up from 420 million in 2010. Under the high-fertility scenario it would have 950 million in 2050 (UN 2013). Providing quality health and education services for 190 million more children than today appears eminently feasible, but providing it for 530 million more probably is not. Reducing both child mortality and fertility in order to increase life expectancy but slow population growth constitutes a crucial strategic choice. In the 40 counties in Africa that are still far from completing their demographic transition (more than four children per woman), it is urgent to set programmatic objectives to accelerate the fertility transition. Contraceptive prevalence rates must increase rapidly from 10 to 20 percent today to around 60 percent by 2050. This is feasible — Egypt is already at this level of contraceptive use and Ethiopia, starting from a very low level, would achieve it in 15 years if the current rate of increase continues.

Promoting inclusion and the demographic transition offers the prospect of a virtuous circle involving both better education outcomes and higher incomes (see Figure 3.2). Fostering inclusive service provision — including girls' education and access to modern contraceptives — could help accelerate a demographic transition that, in turn, would lead to a lower dependency ratio and higher per capita incomes, more resources per capita for investment, wider access to improved services, and even broader inclusion.

Figure 3.2 A virtuous circle of inclusion, demographic transition, and human capital

- Foster inclusion/equity
- Better girls' education
- Accelerated demographic transition
- Higher per capita income, lower dependency ratio
- More resources to invest in human capital, infrastructure, and jobs
- Wider access to improved services

Source: Centennial Group International 2013

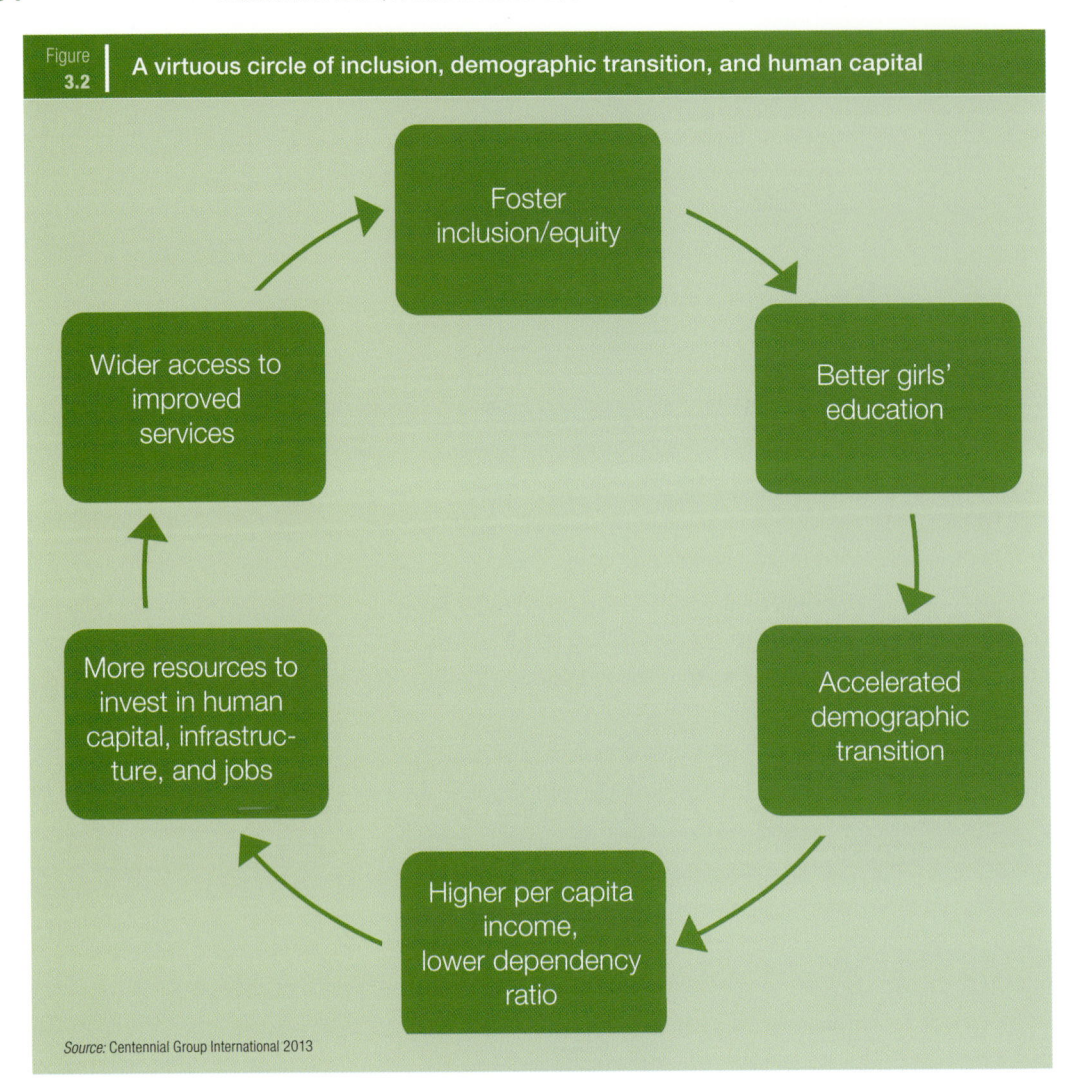

Build human capital

Beyond equalizing opportunities, building human capital is the cornerstone of Africa's future economic growth (see Chapter 8). Education, in particular, is the most powerful tool to accelerate growth, improve competitiveness, and foster inclusion. Recent efforts to measure the wealth of countries (UNU-IHDP and UNEP 2012) show that the world's richest countries hold most of their wealth as human capital, rather than physical capital or natural resources. In a 40-year perspective, Africa must transform its depletable natural resource wealth into the human capital wealth required to grow and remain competitive in a dynamic world.

This transformation requires Africa-specific action on five fronts, even though the emphasis will be different across countries and time. First, early childhood interventions have been shown to be one of the highest return investments a country can make, yet they are rare in Africa. Too many children will be handicapped for life because of inadequate early childhood nutrition, health care, or school preparedness. Second, adult literacy programs and "second-chance" options for school-leavers are urgently needed. Third, even though school access has improved, unless quality is addressed aggressively now, countries will continue to waste education resources and undermine their futures. Fourth, both vocational and tertiary educational institutions must be much more attuned to the needs of the labor market to produce graduates with the skills for higher productivity jobs — rather than unemployable graduates increasingly frustrated with their lack of future prospects. Finally, despite recent advances, malaria and HIV/AIDS remain big killers that must be tamed.

For many countries this is a question of urgent catch-up over the next decade to correct the fact that their young children and youth fare much worse in terms of basic health and education than those of other regions. This stage cannot be leapfrogged: high-quality basic education and health care are the foundation for development in all other areas. Children that are born today will be leading and managing the economy in 2050. Investing heavily in their human capital today will pay large dividends by 2050.

The main constraint on catch-up is implementation. Most of what must be done to provide basic education and health care is known (see Box 3.1). The main constraint is poor capacity to translate this knowledge into interventions and, especially, effective implementation of these interventions. Countries' ability to build institutions for leadership, accountability, and innovation will be crucial to universalizing good quality service delivery, and pressure from citizens for increased accountability is likely to become an increasingly important driver of progress in this domain.

Regional cooperation will also be necessary to provide a common set of educational standards across the continent to favor trade in services and labor mobility. Increasingly, national decisions in these areas have implications beyond national borders, including the decision to promote needed cross-border movements of education and health workers and trade in education and health services.

Reduce conflict and fragility

Conflict affects people's lives very directly. It is not just their economic prospects that are affected. Armed conflict, people fleeing their homes, and overall insecurity destroy people's lives. Today 25 percent of Africans live in countries classified as "fragile situations" by the AfDB and World Bank and that are either in active conflicts or trying to manage post-conflict challenges[1] (see Figure 3.3). In addition, many of their neighbors are worried about spillover effects. Reducing conflict and managing its aftermath are imperative for more than one-quarter of Africans. Most of these countries must move out of conflict and fragility if the 2050 vision for Africa as a whole is to become a reality (see Chapter 6).

---

1. "Fragile situations" have either (a) an AfDB/World Bank-harmonized Country Performance Indicator Assessment of 3.2 or less, or (b) the presence of a UN and/or regional peacekeeping or peacebuilding mission during the past three years.

Box 3.1 | Agenda for education

- Build critical foundation capacities for all children:
    - Broaden access to early childhood interventions to reduce child mortality, improve nutrition, and expand coverage of pre-primary education
    - Erase the legacy of slow progress to universal primary education through "second-chance" programs, including adult literacy training
    - Extend the duration of basic education to nine years
    - Raise the educational attainment and achievement levels of girls in order to harness the intergenerational virtuous cycle of educating girls and women
    - Enhance the quality of learning by improving the support for and the deployment, management, and accountability of teachers.
- Revitalize technical and vocational skills development (TVSD) particularly for the youth:
    - Improve the governance of TVSD by strengthening the regulatory role of government and the coordination of public-private training programs
    - Raise the quality of TVSD through a skills-based approach to training, upgrading the skills of master craftsmen, and modernizing traditional apprenticeship systems
    - Establish national certification frameworks for validating the qualifications acquired through TVSD programs
    - Develop national skills inventory and labor market information systems that analyze the supply and demand of labor and track the growth sectors of the economy
    - Foster the development of partnerships between schools, training providers and employers to increase the relevance of training and lifelong learning.
- Build knowledge- and innovation-driven economies:
    - Broaden access to quality upper secondary education as the critical link between basic and higher education and the bridge between the school system and the labor market
    - Increase tertiary enrollments from the current 6 percent to 30 percent, and channel expansion toward the development of innovative capacity and scientific and technical knowledge
    - Invest at least 2 percent of GDP in R&D and provide incentives for tertiary institutions and industry to collaborate in applied research in strategic areas.
- Reinforce training and skill development through regional cooperation and pooling of resources:
    - Increase support for regional networks and centers of excellence to strengthen joint research, deepen national capacity, leverage economies of scale, and reduce the time needed to develop the skilled workforce needed in select priority areas
    - Establish common educational standards and certification systems to increase the flexibility and mobility of labor across the continent
    - Strengthen inter-country and inter-university exchanges of staff, students, research, and partnerships with the private sector.

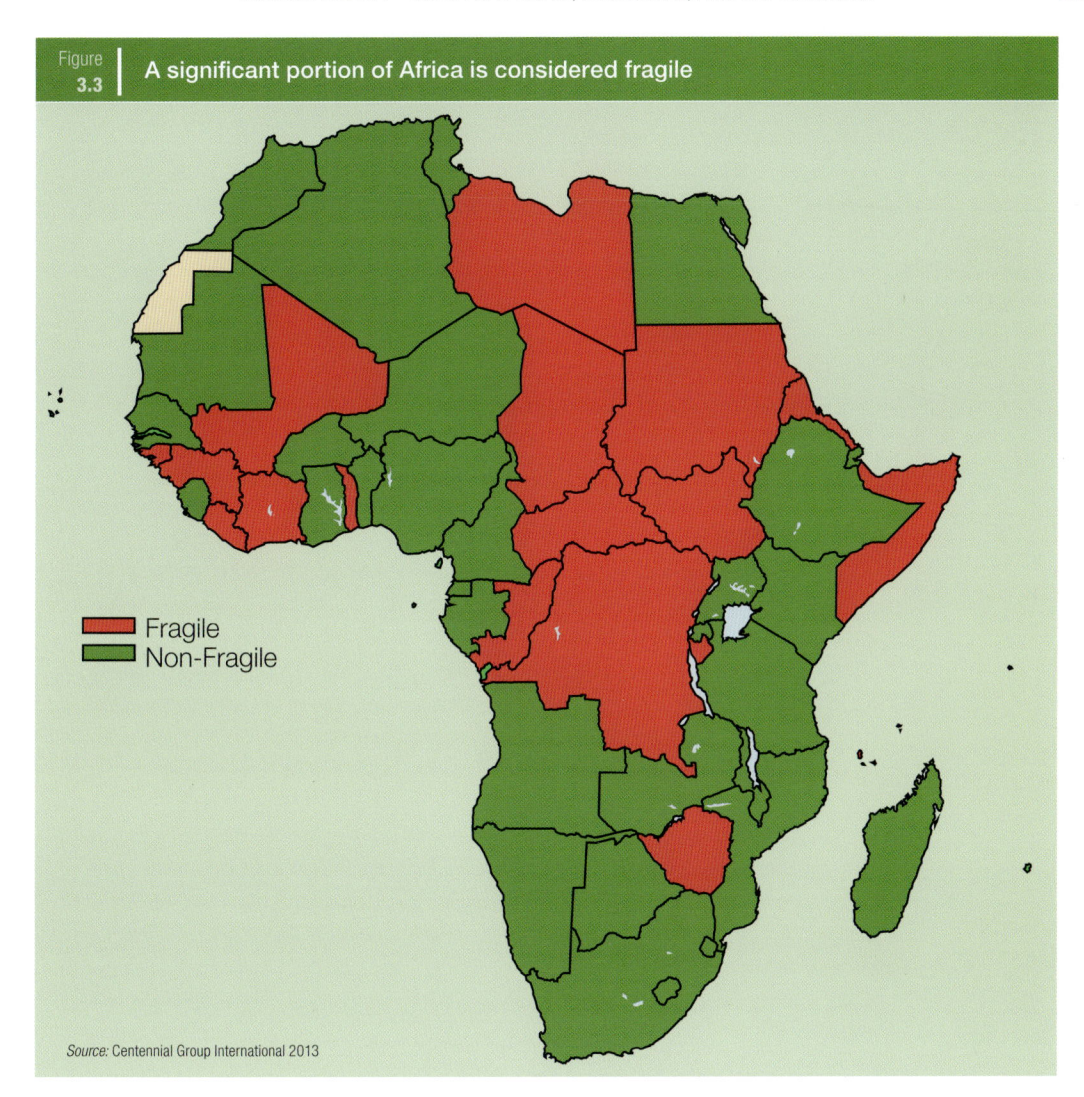

Figure 3.3 | A significant portion of Africa is considered fragile

Source: Centennial Group International 2013

While the origins of conflicts are region- or country-specific, moving forward depends on three things. First, the pre-conflict mediation role of regional organizations needs to be strengthened. Second, regional intervention capacity to halt conflict must be strengthened for cases where mediation fails. Finally, strengthening state institutions needs to proceed step-by-step, should focus on key sovereign and economic institutions, and must combine sound technical approaches with smart politics (see Box 3.2).

> **Box 3.2 | Agenda for reducing conflict and fragility**
>
> While the origins of internal conflicts are extremely diverse, the risks of conflict are always heightened by two key factors: non-inclusive politics and state fragility. In societies fragmented along ethnic or religious lines, inclusive political systems represent the first available "insurance" against spiraling violence that can easily get out of control. However, conflicts are also often the consequence of deep fragilities in a state apparatus that proves unable to provide basic services, including security and justice, to all of its population. Finally, if state fragility heightens conflict risks, conflicts in turn tend to additionally weaken state apparatuses up to a point where they may finally collapse. On the basis of this diagnosis, a three-point agenda is proposed:
>
> - *Strengthen the pre-conflict mediation role of regional organizations*. Conflicts are a regional public bad due to their spillover effects. Regional organizations should no longer hesitate to exercise pressure and even impose sanctions to push reluctant neighbors for greater political inclusion whenever social and political tensions are seriously building up and putting peace at risk. Such pressures may, of course, be viewed by some as infringing on a country's sovereignty, but they may also represent a necessary step to avoid a regionally damaging conflict or prevent its resumption after a ceasefire.
> - *Strengthen the intervention capacity of regional coalitions to halt conflicts*. If regional mediation pressures have failed and conflict has erupted, regional organizations or ad hoc regional coalitions need to be able to intervene with adequate military means to halt it, whenever the political and military context offers serious chances for the success of such interventions. This will require the buildup of adequate military forces and establishment of regional arrangements to authorize military intervention under a UN or eventually a regional mandate. Specific rules of engagement should go beyond the standard and often ineffective UN peacebuilding mandates. An example is provided by the multi-country force deployed in eastern DRC in 2013.
> - *Strengthen state institutions, particularly sovereign and economic institutions*. Fragile states have very fragile state agencies and institutions. Hence, reinforcing institutions should become a key priority. Particular focus should be put in this respect on sovereign institutions (local government, justice, and security services) and key economic ministries (finance, economy, agriculture, and infrastructure). Development of long-term institutional capacity should take precedence over the usual short-term project-based approaches that tend to further weaken the state apparatus. Implementation of this agenda requires combining sound technical approaches with clever politics to build modern, efficient state apparatuses. Across-the-board public administration reforms frequently fail to deliver the expected benefits and can get bogged down in bureaucracy. Creating a critical mass of managerial and technical capacity in key state agencies in a reasonable timeframe requires mobilizing special expertise to take over core functions in a dilapidated public administration. One option is merit-based recruitment of experienced teams of managers and professionals from the private sector or the diaspora, followed by progressive introduction of modern human resource management techniques. Since such approaches usually meet with considerable resistance from entrenched vested interests, a step-by-step, institution-by-institution approach may be needed to progressively build on successful experience.

Diverse, Competitive Economies — Private Investment to Create Jobs

Jobs will transform people's lives, or alternatively, leave them stuck with little income and less hope. Some 90 percent of jobs in Africa are already in the private sector, and jobs on the scale needed can only come from increased private sector investment, both domestic and foreign. Investors, whether neighborhood seamstresses or multinationals, invest to make money. To do so they need macroeconomic stability, a business environment that promotes growth of the private sector, adequate infrastructure and access to needed inputs and services, and the skilled workforce discussed above. Although the actions required are again country-specific, four broad areas for action cut across all African economies: competition, agricultural transformation, management of natural resource rents, and urbanization.

Macroeconomic stability is a prerequisite for private sector competitiveness and job creation (see Chapter 9). Africa's macroeconomic management has strengthened dramatically over the last 15 years. The fiscal and monetary policies of the past that generated rampant inflation, collapsing currencies, and unsustainable debt are for the most part vanquished. The new threat, particularly if Africa is to take advantage of greater global integration, is that of volatility. Fortunately, better policies over the last decade have been accompanied by a boom in the prices of Africa's commodity exports and the resulting improvement in the terms of trade accounts for a quarter of the continent's GDP growth in the last decade (see Box 2.3). Whether one thinks that commodity prices will trend higher because of relative scarcity or eventually decline as technology both increases supply and introduces alternatives, it is clear that prices will remain volatile. Having enjoyed a decade of continuously improving terms of trade, very few countries have prepared themselves to dampen future volatility in their own economies. All commodity exporters need to look to strong fiscal rules and savings mechanisms to protect themselves from such volatility in coming decades.

Foster competition to promote economic competitiveness

Fostering competition, including through entry and growth of enterprises (see Box 3.3), a key challenge for most African economies, entails actions to put in place pro-competition policies and, on the other hand, *curb anti-competitive behavior* demonstrated by state or private monopolies, strong vested interests, and instances of state capture (see Chapter 10). The burden of regulatory requirements (the number of procedures, the time required to comply with them, and the costs of complying with them) need to be reduced to allow domestic firms to become competitive in a global setting. Reduction of unnecessary regulations relating to the entry and exit of firms, which directly affect the process of resource allocation from firms with low productivity to firms with high productivity, is especially necessary.

Dealing with the bureaucracy is a significant cost in most African countries. Cross a land border, start a business, get something through customs, or even pay taxes, and the cost imposed on individuals and firms in everyday economic activity is immediately visible. It is easy to improve some of the commonly measured indicators by adopting new laws or regulations, but this frequently changes nothing. Bureaucratic habits die hard and rent collection opportunities are valuable to those who administer rules.

> **Box 3.3 | Agenda for competition, private sector development, and productivity**
>
> - Adopt an unrelentingly pragmatic approach to improving the investment climate to increase private investment, both domestic and foreign
> - Implement pro-competition policies and measures to curb anti-competitive practices
> - Reduce transport costs through competitive trucking and efficient ports
> - Implement the Yamoussoukro (open skies) Decision
> - Expand markets by lowering non-tariff barriers and behind-the-border costs
> - Open trade in services
> - Facilitate intra-African trade
> - Promote technology adoption and foster "catch-up," inclusive innovation
> - Improve the business environment and streamline regulation to promote entrepreneurship, entry, and growth of enterprises.

Thus, such costs will not be eliminated overnight; unless there is sustained political leadership to see that they are dramatically reduced, African enterprises, big and small, cannot be competitive, grow, and create jobs.

Governments need to introduce competition in shipping and port services and break the collusion between public and private actors that benefits both but precludes new entrants, dismantle transport cartels, and implement the Yamoussoukro (open skies) Decision. The small size of markets in most African economies makes it hard to generate competition among firms, putting a premium on access to export markets and the domestic competition from imports.

African economies need to promote entrepreneurship — supported by education and management training, access to finance, and needed professional services. Ending state capture by families or insider groups is an essential prerequisite. India and China offer good examples for African economies to follow in encouraging innovation, with a focus on "catch-up" (vs. pioneering) inclusive innovation. Research and development (R&D) expenditures, directed largely at adapting technology, need to be raised from a negligible less than 0.5 percent of GDP to some 2 to 3 percent — mostly by the private sector, supported by building world-class universities with productive links between universities/research centers and industry.

The fundamentals required for competition and private sector development, and thus for investment and growth, are also the primary enablers of job creation. Additionally, African economies must ensure that the broad agenda of promoting labor-intensive diversification is successfully implemented. The second element of the job agenda would be that of addressing the most visible problems of job creation that arise in a variety of country situations in Africa: rural-urban migration; worker productivity, particularly in the informal sector; women's entry into higher productivity activities; and education and vocational training (see Box 3.4).

> **Box 3.4 | Agenda for jobs**
>
> Elements of the Agenda for jobs that are specific to country situations in Africa include:
> - Extending adequate health and education services in both rural and urban areas to better prepare rural migrants for entry into the urban job market and facilitate rural-urban migration, and promote rural sector opportunities for absorbing labor in productive off-farm activities
> - Taking measures to improve worker productivity and prospects of better paying jobs in both the formal and informal sectors, including efforts to improve the informal sector's access to inputs, finance, markets, and opportunities to link up with formal sector firms
> - Facilitating women's entry into high productivity market activities by removing obstacles to their access to productive assets such as education, capital, and land to support entrepreneurship, and eliminate regulations that disadvantage women in the labor market
> - Improving the education system — including vocational training — to provide youth with the education and skills that respond better to the needs of the private sector; on-the-job training and apprenticeships can help youth adapt better to the work environment of the private sector
> - Ensuring that public sector hiring and wage policies also take into account the realities of the macroeconomic situation and the need to avoid maintaining wages and non-wage benefits more generous than in the private sector.

Economic agents require competitive costs in order to sell anything. As with other issues, the strategies for reducing costs and becoming competitive will be largely country-specific. In particular, poor infrastructure services must be addressed at the country level to enhance competitiveness and the ability to trade, as well as to support domestic agricultural, education, and health needs in rural and urban space. Two areas of infrastructure services stand out, however, for continent-wide action: transport logistics and energy. For costs to be competitive enough to make doing business attractive, logistics need to be smooth, regulations need to be limited but enforced, and barriers to efficiency in all infrastructure areas need to be removed.

Trade — whether within countries, with neighbors, or global — means moving goods, people, and data. The *cost of transport and logistics* is thus a key element in being competitive. Africa is, unfortunately, notorious for high transport costs, related in part to inadequate infrastructure but mostly attributable to polices and how infrastructure is managed. Logistics performance — where Africa has three countries in the global top 50 (South Africa, Tunisia, and Morocco) but 27 in the bottom 50 — is one indicator of such performance (World Bank 2012e). Port performance (the number of days to get a container out) is one clear area for action. International norms are 3 to 4 days from arrival. Durban, Casablanca, and Tunis approach such performance, but the average for Africa's other large ports is 16 days or 4 to 5 times the global norm. Land transport costs are another area where transport cartels in much of the continent lead to high costs. Finally, air transport services and costs are particularly important for tourism, high-value products, global supply chains, and many services. Africa has only three countries (Algeria, Morocco, and Tunisia) in the top 50 worldwide for air connectivity but 31 countries in the bottom 50 (Arvis and Shepherd 2011). Opening access and eliminating ownership restrictions would increase the number of flights, reduce fares, and improve service, as Morocco's open sky policy has demonstrated.

Enterprises, whether single-person household enterprises or large firms, that do not have access to *reliable electric power*, cannot possibly be competitive and will not create the jobs for 2050. Widespread access to reliable electricity is often cited as one of the technological developments that drove productivity growth a century ago in the currently developed countries. With the exception of those in North Africa, most African firms still do not have such access. Providing reliable and affordable power 7 days a week, 24 hours a day would be the single biggest productivity booster for African firms. Without it, the potential in agro-processing, light manufacturing, and most services will remain an illusion.

Africa needs to invest in the transmission grids for electricity distribution, in addition to a significant boost in power production. Thermal production can be private sector-financed but developing Africa's enormous and cost-effective hydropower potential will require new public-private partnerships in order to mobilize the massive financial sums needed. Most countries are too small to have even a single optimum-sized plant and thus regional investments will be required. Investment in regional transmission grids and in the continent's biggest under-exploited resource — hydropower — are urgent.

Africa has the advantage of a growing labor force in an aging world and many people stuck in low productivity jobs. The division of tasks across global supply chains and their geographic mobility gives Africa the possibility of joining such chains. It must do so if it is to create the jobs that are the vehicle for employing its labor and increasing its productivity. Countries have differing potential to do so and will require country-specific strategies but, as discussed above, two actions remain central to progress across most of the continent: reducing transport and logistics costs and providing reliable 24/7 power.

Transform agriculture

Agriculture employs more people in Africa than any other sector, but many of these people are poor. In addition, food security remains an issue for many Africans. Even if growth in manufacturing and services is expected to outpace that in agriculture, productivity increases in agriculture are essential to raise the incomes of farmers, enhance food security, and realize Africa's agricultural export potential. Given the diversity of the continent, raising agricultural productivity depends on evolution across seven distinct agricultural paths (see Chapter 11):

1. Extensive, mechanized, rainfed farming producing exportable grains and fibers across semi-arid and sub-humid areas with suitable soils
2. Intensive export-crop farming producing beverage crops, spices, and other tree crops in humid areas
3. Intensive peri-urban farming producing for urban populations

4. Low productivity subsistence crop and livestock farming in low rainfall areas with poor market access
5. Reserves and game ranching
6. Irrigated production of high-value crops north of the Sahara
7. Rainfed farming north of the Sahara

Realizing Africa's export potential, raising farm incomes, and increasing food security implies a declining share of the labor force working in agriculture and a shift of resources out of subsistence farming to the other paths set out above. The extent of this shift will depend in part on governments' success in addressing land rights, water availability, and the use of new technology (see Box 3.5).

Land issues are sensitive everywhere and even more so in Africa given its colonial history. Clarifying land rights, titling land, and creating land markets is the biggest agricultural challenge for African governments over the next 40 years and will be critical for realizing the benefits from Africa's currently uncultivated arable land. The private sector can play a major role in addressing other constraints, but defining land rights is a role for the state. Land titling is particularly important in areas of high export potential both to secure land rights needed for investment and to protect against "land grabs" whether initiated by foreigners or nationals.

Water availability will become an even more critical issue with climate change and global warming. In addition to many country-specific constraints, two big water issues cut across the continent. First, the major rivers in Africa invariably cover many countries, and riparian cooperation on river basin management for irrigation and hydropower development has been too slow. Second, irrigation development costs need to be lowered through greater private competition and private sector involvement.

African agriculture faces the technological challenge of catching up with the rest of the world in fertilizer use and in benefiting from genetically modified organisms (GMOs). The primary constraints on fertilizer use have been economic. Governments need to reexamine agriculture pricing and tax policies that have historically distorted incentives against agriculture and reduced the incentives for using fertilizer or other modern inputs even as monopolistic supply arrangements have kept input prices high or fertilizers unavailable. Contract farming could facilitate huge technological leaps by providing access to guaranteed markets and prices and well-organized credit and input delivery systems. The trend of global farm technology will be to use more GMOs to raise crop yields, develop new products, and adapt to stresses, notably those caused by global warming. Governments need to provide the framework for African agriculture to catch up in GMO use in two respects. The first is to take advantage of global research to produce higher productive potential, e.g., maize that tolerates higher temperatures, pest-resistant cotton, or disease-resistant coffee trees. The second is to apply these technologies in the field.

The challenge for Africa is to develop public and private institutions that contribute at levels of both productive potential and field application. Africa must foster scientific institutions — public, private, and public-private partnerships — that contribute to global technology generation through national and sub-regional scientific infrastructure; continental broadband connectivity that facilitates knowledge

> **Box 3.5 | Agenda for agriculture**
>
> - Promote irrigation
>   - Pursue riparian agreements on river basin management
>   - Reduce the cost of irrigation equipment
>   - Extend modern energy supplies, including off-grid electricity and renewables, so that the variable costs of lifting water decline
>   - Promote competition in irrigation investment
>   - Increase irrigation efficiency
> - Improve land access
>   - Accelerate land titling
>   - Establish a sound framework for land leasing, including by foreigners
> - Promote fertilizer use
>   - Remove distortions (overvalued exchange rates and suppressed producer prices) that reduce incentives to use fertilizer
>   - Address access through private sector delivery
> - Harness global science and technology
>   - Use more genetically modified organisms (GMOs) to raise yields, develop new products, and adapt to new stresses (such as global warming)
>   - Rebuild regional agricultural research institutions
> - Lower cost of market participation
>   - Improve and reduce cost of communications, essential for market discovery
>   - Reduce transport costs by both infrastructure improvements and more competition in the transport sector
> - Ensure better access to regional and world markets
>   - Facilitate trade
>   - Improve logistics

generation and sharing; and governments that let economic incentives reach producers by, among other actions, opening trade channels. Commercial farmers, whether small or large, would thus be able to respond to profits by adopting new biological technology.

Mobilize and invest natural resource rents

Africa is rich in hydrocarbon and mineral resources. But extraction of these resources creates few jobs and requires even higher productivity gains for other industries to remain competitive. For this wealth to help drive the Africa 2050 vision, African countries must mobilize a larger share of the resource rents created by extracting these resources; transform them into human, physical, and financial wealth; and foster economic diversification, including the development of world-class ancillary service industries (see Box 3.6 and Chapter 12).

> **Box 3.6 | Agenda for extractive industries**
>
> All African countries with natural resource exports will need to implement the following measures to get onto the convergence path:
> - Obtain a greater share of resource rents
>   - Ensure greater transparency in their extractive industries by requiring public disclosure of the terms of resource extraction contracts
>   - Employ world-class expertise when negotiating new contracts
> - Manage resource rents effectively
>   - Lock in application of revenue management rules (Non-Resource Primary Fiscal Balance Target or Structural Primary Fiscal Target) to remove cyclicality of resource and non-resource revenues
>   - Consider the creation of stabilization and wealth management funds, managed independently and domiciled in an external bank of international standing
> - Transform natural resource wealth into human capital and infrastructure wealth

Capturing a larger share of the rents requires both greater transparency through public disclosure of the terms of resource extraction contracts and mobilization of world-class expertise when negotiating new contracts. Investing the resources well requires clear priorities and performance-based public finance management in general, and the adoption of countercyclical fiscal rules and externally-domiciled stability and wealth funds in particular. Growing the ancillary industries requires a skilled workforce, joint ventures initially, and policies that support service exports.

Manage urbanization for growth

The success of cities in meeting the service delivery challenge confronting them will determine countries' effectiveness in capitalizing on their natural resource endowments, gains in health and education, governance improvements, and trade and regional development initiatives, as well as overall efficiency enhancements (see Chapter 13). It will be crucial for policymakers to avoid the trap of characterizing the urban challenge only as a massive capital investment program in service supply.

Cities may be the locus of most economic activity but it is private sector firms that will drive growth and job creation. Cities must not only provide traditional urban services to their residents but must also focus on creating the environment required to attract and grow private businesses whether micro-enterprises, small and medium enterprises (SMEs), or large firms. Policymakers must give explicit attention to business-friendly policies, spatial planning, and facilitating the links between industry and universities. Physical security and low crime are special concerns for both people and businesses. Provision of this "security infrastructure" will be as important as building the physical infrastructure.

Huge infrastructure and service-related capital investments will be required for cities to establish the platforms necessary for driving economic growth. However, the lessons of the past 50 years have shown that a "projectized" approach fails to produce sustainable infrastructure networks and services. On the contrary, much of such investment is lost to inadequate operation and maintenance practices. Consequently, urban development strategies need to ensure that cities have the capability to lead and sustain the investment initiatives in service provision.

Moreover, experience worldwide has shown that urban service demands cannot be sustainably delivered from the center but have to be driven and managed by city government. This is a significant challenge in Africa where most political environments do not provide the enabling policy, fiscal frameworks, and legal and regulatory regimes necessary for cities to function effectively. In addition, city governments only operate effectively if there are clear lines of accountability between them and their constituents.

The most critical area for action over the next ten years will be institutional — introducing and making operational key systems of local government that are essential to effective city management (see Box 3.7). These systems, taken together, represent an enabling environment for sound urban development. The pressure for investment has to be measured against the extent to which the systems have been solidly grounded, and the progress individual cities are making in implementing them. In this context, capital investment needs, however pressing, would be carefully calibrated against progress in the development of effective urban local governments in an iterative process, with investments expanding as cities demonstrate greater capabilities.

Box 3.7 | Agenda for cities

The essential ingredients of an urban action plan for the next decade are to:
- Review existing local governance legal structures in order to ensure that a minimum set of enabling laws/decrees/regulations are in place to permit cities to deliver selected local services without competing with parallel central government structures
- Introduce fiscal transfer systems that are predictable and allow for effective planning (e.g., five-year time horizons), and that have performance incentives built into them. Cities that perform well against predetermined indicators would be rewarded with significant increments in capital transfers (with independent annual assessments of performance being undertaken to ensure the legitimacy and credibility of the incentive system)
- Increase the size of annual transfers over time as cities demonstrate growing capacity, with expanded capability being aggressively supported by on-the-job training linked to more formal but tailored classroom-based skills development

Establishing effective urban local governments requires action on three broad fronts. First, *sound political and fiscal enabling frameworks* need to be established. Legislation and regulation must unambiguously allocate functional assignments to cities for the delivery of services and create reliable fiscal systems that ensure adequate, predictable flows to city governments to meet their responsibilities within effective oversight structures. Second, *effective social contracts between elected urban local government officials and their communities* must be built. Governance systems, as measured in tangible areas of management such as budgeting, investment decisions, and operational performance, need to follow transparent procedures, routinely meet satisfactory audit standards, and deliver services to standards that address citizen expectations. Finally, *urban local government capacity* needs to be strengthened through a process of "learning-by-doing" whereby cities, in implementing their mandates for service delivery, build capacity to manage these responsibilities and are assisted during this transitional period with targeted training support programs. Capital development resource transfers to local governments would be scaled up in relation to demonstrated capacity to perform.

Most countries in Africa now have some form of enabling urban legal structure and some form of elected representation at the local level that can serve as a legitimate framework for introducing more robust accountability practices. While some countries have well-advanced local governance structures (with South Africa representing African best practice in this regard), in most instances little has been done to implement programs building on these frameworks, and local fiscal capacity and national fiscal transfer structures are weak and unreliable at best. Consequently, little capacity has been developed at the local level, and accountability and confidence building between elected officials and their constituents has eroded badly. Inadequate and unpredictable flows of funds have contributed to these failures and created a self-fulfilling cycle of poor performance by local governments and reluctance by central governments to transfer funds to institutions they consider incompetent. This cycle has to be broken if cities are to be able to meet the challenges they face.

Integrated Africa — Bigger Markets to Foster Investment and Higher Productivity Jobs

Most African countries are small. Africa must integrate both sub-regionally and globally if it is to have markets that are large enough for firms to grow and create jobs and if it is to have a voice in global forums where rules affecting its future will be set. Two areas for action are particularly important: opening regional markets and basing relations with the rest of the world on trade and investment rather than aid.

Promote regional cooperation and trade

There is little prospect for firms in small markets to grow, specialize, and increase productivity — and thus create jobs — without access to larger markets both sub-regionally and globally (see Chapter 14). Actions need to go beyond lowering tariffs to genuinely opening up, reducing non-tariff and "behind the border" barriers, and improving connectivity. Opening economies in order to both enlarge markets and introduce competition also offers opportunities for "policy leapfrogging." Much may be said about improving the physical links between countries, but certainly the simplest and highest return activity is to take down the "roadblocks" (both literal and figurative).

Intra-African trade is minimal (11 percent of exports) not because there are no opportunities but because it so costly to overcome the obstacles, whether they are physical or bureaucratic (see Chapter 14). That Morocco trades little with Mozambique or Kenya with Cameroon is not surprising, given geography. That members of the Economic Community of West African States (ECOWAS) or the East African Community (EAC) do so little with each other is self-defeating. Africa's diversity is a plus in this regard since trade, and the investment flows which frequently follow, have particularly big payoffs for countries with differing endowments. Landlocked countries need access to coastal ones. A small Benin could one day be a "Hong Kong" provider of services to a giant Nigeria. And North African countries already integrated in European supply chains, like Morocco and Tunisia, could extend them southward as they move up the value chain.

The first priority of the key regional economic organizations and their member states should be to pragmatically identify and then aggressively remove the obstacles to people and goods crossing borders. These range from warlord bandits or freelance bureaucrats who collect tolls for passage, to agriculture export prohibitions and bureaucratic procedures that serve no purpose beyond confirming the power (and rent collection ability) of those who administer them, to the simple lack of harmonized standards. Whatever their manifestation, these obstacles exist across the continent — and will only be removed if there is an unconditional and pragmatic commitment by political leaders to do so.

If these roadblocks come down, then regional transport infrastructure investments will be critical to open markets but most particularly to lower transport costs. A continent-wide strategy for regional infrastructure has been endorsed by African leaders but implementation is lagging. Major challenges are to ensure adequate financial resources and effective implementing capacity. Experience from other regions suggests that Africa will need to significantly increase spending on infrastructure from 2–3 percent of GDP currently to at least 5 percent. Infrastructure (energy and electricity, transport, information and communication technology, water management) and related services underpin regional cooperation and trade.

Reposition Africa globally — replace aid with trade and FDI

Many countries have opened their economies by removing barriers to trade in goods but only much later (or not at all) in services. It has become increasingly apparent that opening services to foreign direct investment and trade increases productivity and jobs in both the services and manufacturing sectors (Duggan, Rahardja, and Varela 2013).

If Africa wants to catch up fast, it needs to leapfrog to opening trade and FDI in both goods and services. A pragmatic focus on identifying and aggressively lifting barriers to export will be key and will involve actions both with global partners and domestically to improve access in target markets and to remove barriers. The political economy of such opening must be explicitly recognized — opening trade will create opportunity but it will also destroy uncompetitive firms and mobilize their vested interests in opposition.

Fifty years after independence, aid is already diminishing as a resource for most African countries. By 2050, traditional and donor-driven development aid should have disappeared, replaced by cooperation between equals, in pursuit of joint interests (see Chapter 16). In the interim, one focus of aid should be fragile states, recognizing that conflict spills across borders and fragility can be a slippery slope leading to conflict.

The broader movement away from aid requires active management of relations with both today's "old" and "new" partners and, in the short term a more strategic use by Africa of aid and export credits. Going forward, domestic and foreign investment, trade, and remittances will be the source of economic development, with Africa able to make informed choices in its own interests.

Most economic exchange will be determined by markets, by the private sector, and not directed by governments. As discussed above, Africa can only converge with the rest of the world if it has the bigger markets and market discipline offered by global trade and it can only mobilize the needed technology, knowhow, and increased investment if it increases FDI. Market access and joining supply chains through FDI need to be the focus of future relations.

Asia and Latin America will represent more than 60 percent of global GDP by 2050 and should represent a corresponding share of Africa's trade.[2] Increasing trade with these regions implies attracting FDI outside of resource extraction industries (where shared rents make it attractive even in investment-unfriendly contexts) into manufacturing, agriculture, and services. Given their large share of world manufacturing and rising labor costs, integration into the supply chains of "emerging" partners is particularly important.

A shift from aid to trade and investment will position Africa well to reshape its relations with the rest of the world and place it on more equal footing than in the past. African countries should strive to move from relations with emerging market countries that are centered on government-to-government dialogue to a broader, more inclusive relationship with the engagement of the private sector, local government authorities, and other relevant non-state actors on both sides of the partnership.

The evolution of Africa's partnership with the OECD countries must reflect a more considered and proactive African position based on a compelling longer-term vision rooted in what Africa itself will do. Africa has to try to speak, wherever possible, with one voice, and to ensure that the issues of interest to it are addressed. Africa has to move from being a passive onlooker to global debates and rule-making to becoming an active participant. To participate actively in setting the global agenda and be more influential, Africa needs to have additional full participants in the G20 and allied bodies dealing with banking and finance.

---

2. Based on the convergence scenario described in Chapter 1.

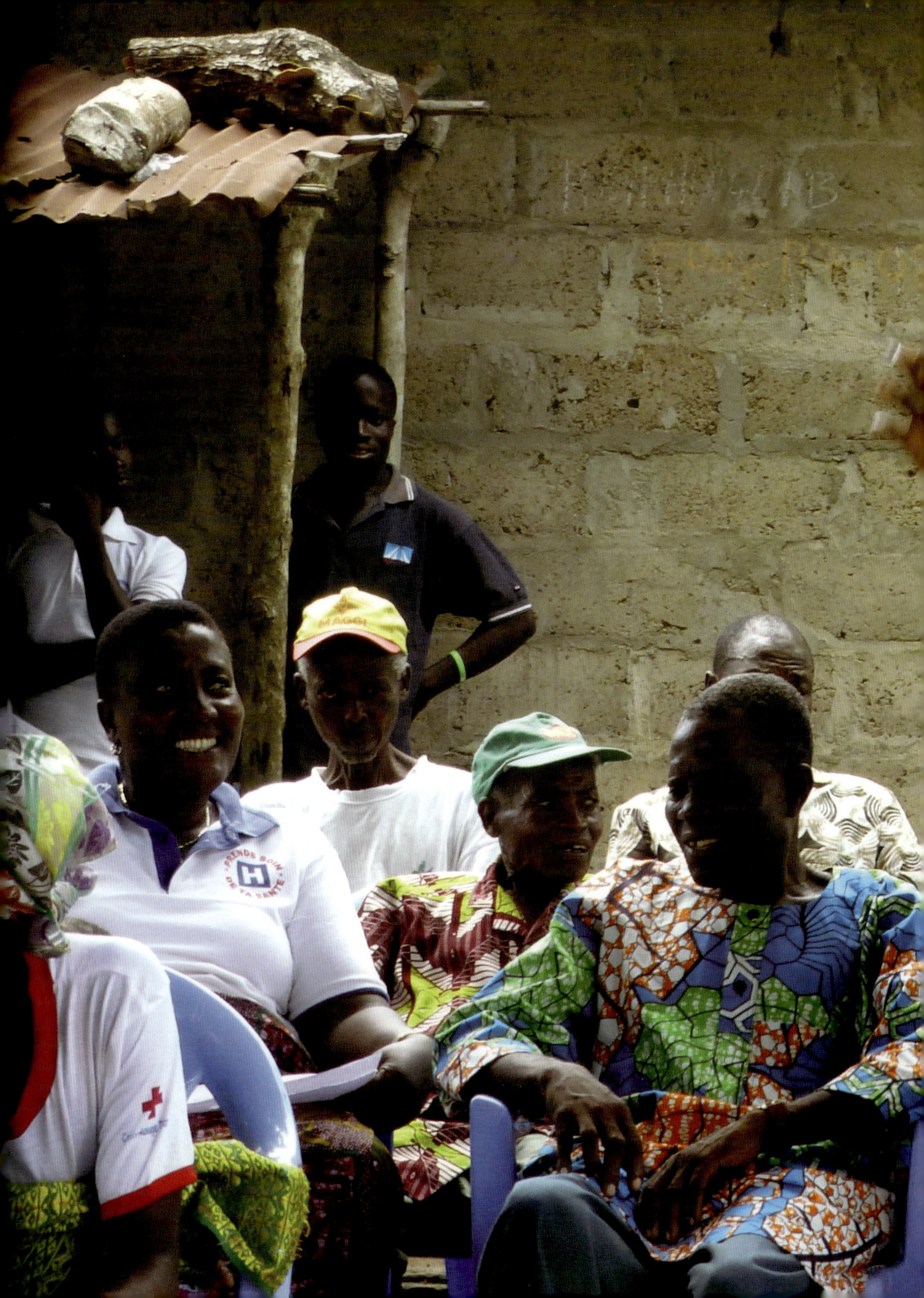

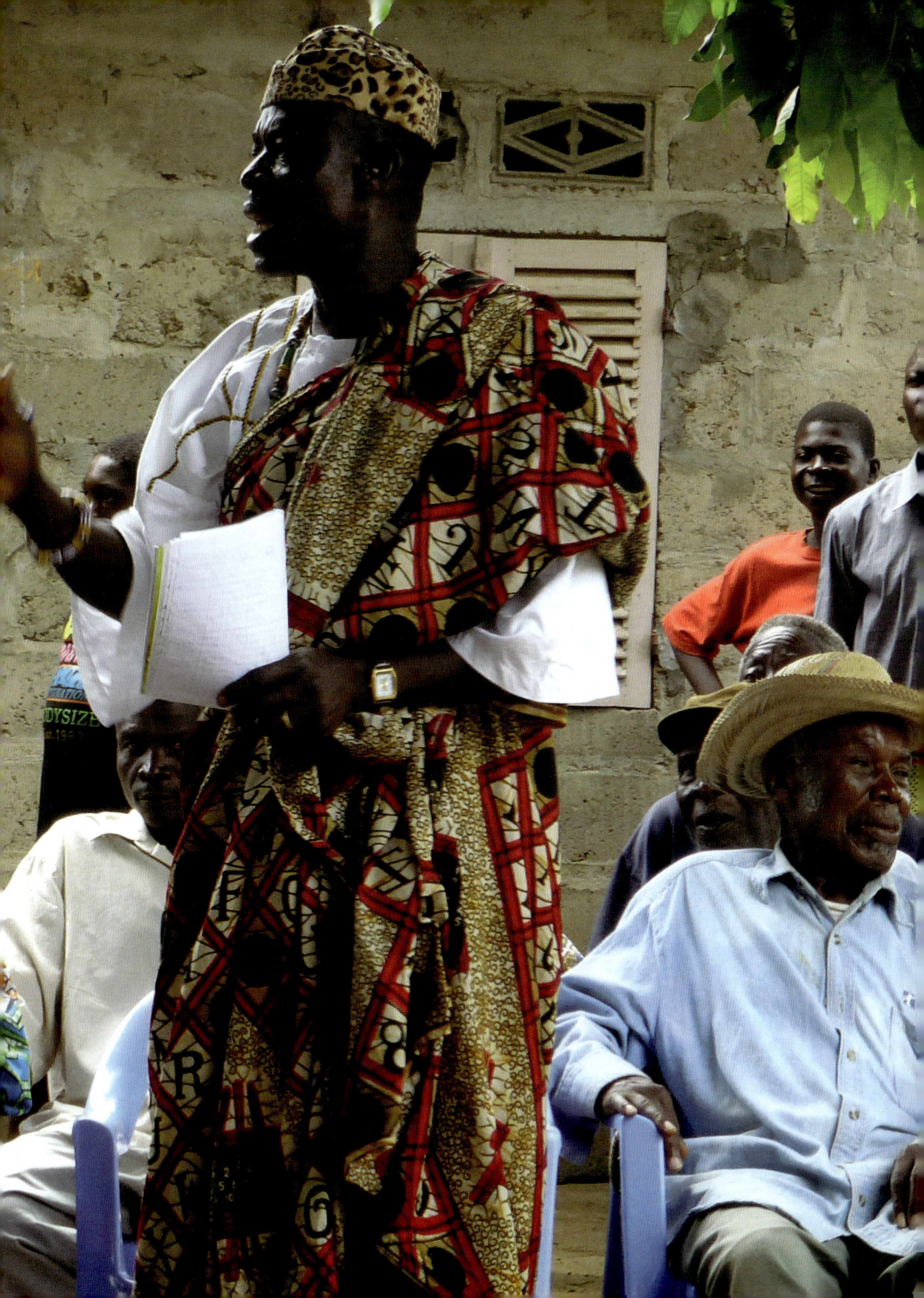

Chapter 4
Better Governance to Deliver Results

Theodore Ahlers, Harinder S. Kohli, Callisto Madavo, and Anil Sood

Among the many issues facing African governments, the ten issues in the action agenda of Chapter 3 are highlighted because they are particularly important for meeting the aspirations of Africans over a 40-year time horizon. Most, however, are not new. There are two overarching issues that cut across all the action items and are likely to ultimately determine the success or failure of the overall agenda.

The first is capable states that can deliver security, rule of law, and key social services to all their citizens. Capability is largely a question of governance, of how institutions work. Capable states can encompass a variety of political systems, but ultimately they need to be accountable to their citizens for delivering results. The second is strong, pragmatic leadership. Both capable states and pragmatic leadership are necessary to avoid two of the biggest threats to meeting the aspirations of Africans — complacency and inadequate political resolve to tackle the big problems. As noted in the introduction, the challenge is not so much what to do, but how to implement the chosen course of action and how to sustain a "do whatever it takes" mentality to get results.

Capable States[1]

A thriving 2050 Africa will need to have institutions capable of delivering, on a sustained basis, individual and property rights security to all citizens, assuring that successful people are able to reap the fruits of their efforts rather than have them appropriated by politically well-connected groups; access to quality education, health, and infrastructure services; and a business environment that fosters competition and supports innovation.

There is considerable consensus on the characteristics of a well-functioning state capable of delivering such public goods:

- Strong rule of law (see Box 4.1)
- Capable merit-based bureaucracies
- Well-functioning public expenditure and financial management systems
- Limited corruption — and strong sanctions when it is discovered
- Accountability of public officials and governments to their people
- Broad acceptance of the legitimacy of governance arrangements

---

1. This section is based on a background paper prepared by Brian Levy for Centennial Group International.

> **Box 4.1** | **Rule of law**
>
> Most African countries score poorly on the rule of law by international standards (see figure below). Most have reasonable legal frameworks, but enforcement is weak. In some countries, even the physical security of individuals is not assured. In others, successful investors, whether individuals, small companies, or large ones, risk losing their gains to the politically well-connected. In others, simple contract enforcement is a challenge and court decisions can be easily bought. In all cases, these deviations from the rule of law are fatal for investment, innovation, and private initiative — without which there will be no job creation. Quite perversely, these problems are frequently more acute for domestic investors than for foreign ones; the latter are often large enough to strike deals with vested interests or are less vulnerable because of their visibility. If the Africa 2050 vision is to be realized, African countries need guaranteed individual and property rights and a fair judiciary to enforce them.
>
> **Figure 4.i: Most African countries fair poorly on the rule of law scale**
>
> *Source:* World Bank 2012b

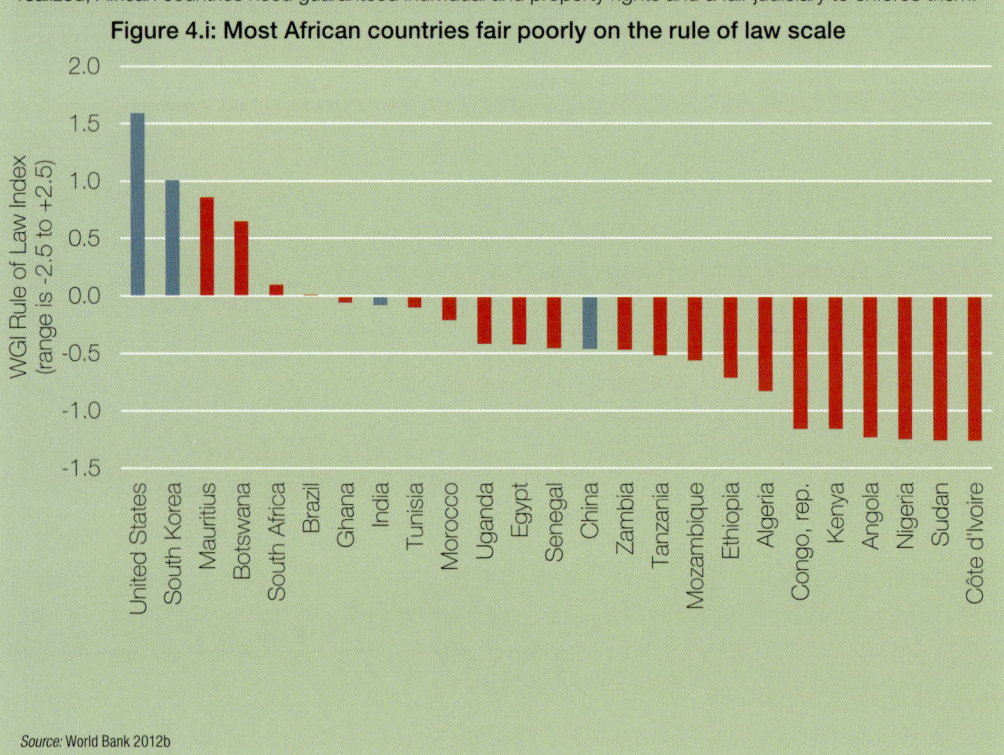

Most countries that approach such norms have long, country-specific histories of institutional and political development. Many analysts suggest, moreover, that inclusive economic and political institutions are key to such an evolution (Acemoglu and Robinson 2012).

Defining the characteristics, however, offers little guidance about how to realize them. The challenge for most African leaders is indeed how to get from a starting point of relatively weak institutions to stronger institutions that deliver results. The long timeframe required to solidify institutional changes creates both urgency to start and concern about what steps to take first. The answers are, of course, country-specific, but all countries will need to strengthen capacity and build credibility and accountability.

Strengthening capacity

Capacity refers to the extent to which a country's public sector has the skills and organizational competencies needed for good policymaking and implementation. Fifty years ago when many African countries became independent, capacity was extraordinarily weak because many colonial administrations had had no interest in building national human capital. Given limited attention to education, there were simply very few people with the necessary skills.

The problem today is different. There are large numbers of highly skilled Africans working in many capacities all around the world. With few exceptions, the big capacity constraint today is using the skills that exist both within and outside the countries. Taking advantage of existing professional capacity is a matter of insuring that institutional arrangements offer sufficient stability and adequate remuneration as well as sufficient professionalism, meritocracy, and influence in policy implementation to attract skilled individuals.

Lack of institutional capacity applies across the income spectrum of Africa. Sierra Leone, Liberia, and DRC have begun to attract their trained and experienced nationals to important positions in the public administration, something that was unthinkable when they were embroiled in wars. For more than a decade, Morocco has succeeded in attracting highly-trained Moroccans both to stay in the country and to work in the public sector. Tunisia, over the same period, did not. Most would say the most important difference was a political ethos that valued technical skills in top positions in Morocco and one where state capture by the politically well-connected undermined the upper echelons of a once well-regarded civil service in Tunisia.

Whether it is restoring basic financial management in a post-conflict country or creating an agile administration to face the challenges of the middle-income trap in a highly globalized world, African governments need to mobilize high-quality, focused technical capacity in areas that can show results and harness stakeholders with a strong incentive to see reforms succeed.

Building a capable public sector is a long-term endeavor, but there are some areas where results can be achieved, rapidly even in settings where the initial platform is weak, as Box 4.2 details. A step-by-step approach initially focused on such areas will in most situations offer the best prospects for the rapid spread of technical and managerial capacity throughout the public sector. The initial opportunities will of course be country-specific, but range from creating capable central banks and ministries of finance to mobilizing the best expertise for planning tomorrow's cities and devising smart public-private partnerships.

> **Box 4.2 — Governance**
>
> The journey from weak to good governance is long. The key to realizing the Africa 2050 vision is to begin with actions which can support development results in the short-term and provide a platform for more far-reaching gains over time. High-potential actions along these lines include:
>
> - Strengthening public sector capacity with a focus on actions which can be directly linked to specific development results:
>   - Build high-capacity units in central macro policy and budget agencies
>   - Assure that public budgets deliver resources to managers in a predictable manner
>   - Pursue quick wins to binding development constraints
>   - Initiate results-driven institutional reform in a few sectors
> - Building credible commitment capability and clearly signal that government is committed to results and respects the rules of the game:
>   - Legislate credible institutional framework for domestic and foreign investment
>   - Framework for local participation
>   - Transparent taxation
>   - Credible dispute resolution, including extraterritorial disputes
>   - Utilize global and regional commitment mechanisms to lock-in reforms
>   - Initiate programs to strengthen high-level auditing mechanisms
>
> There is one additional challenge for the long-term which needs to be given top priority early on: namely, nurturing a culture of citizenship, of civic expectations that government should deliver on its promises and that politicians should be held to account:
>
> - Support for press freedom and media capacity building, and the introduction of service delivery scorecards and other demand-side monitoring mechanisms

Enhancing credibility and accountability

Credibility refers to the extent to which citizens and firms (domestic and foreign) have confidence that government commitments will be honored. Credibility is built on results — articulating what is being sought and delivering it — and on accountability. Prerequisites for credibility are a state strong enough to enforce its decisions within its territory and consistent enough to convey what it wants to achieve.

Credibility can be damaged by incompetence but its deadliest enemy is the use of state power by political leaders or well-connected groups to extract for themselves as much as they can in as short a time as possible. Development requires leadership that is committed to investing for the benefit of all of the country's citizens and for the long-term. A minimum threshold for credibility is demonstrating enough control and reliability so that private investors, whether domestic or foreign, are willing to invest their money in activities other than resource extraction.[2]

Increasing accountability is critical for moving beyond this minimum credibility. Accountability arrangements can both directly improve service provision (for example, when parents have a say in running schools and can block pay to absent teachers) and create the confidence necessary for individuals to invest, take risks, and innovate.

Even more so than for other issues, what is required to maintain or restore credibility will vary between countries and over time. Some actions can make an early difference by sending clear, strong signals that government is committed to results and will respect the rules of the game (see Box 4.2). Restoring order and security may be sufficient following a chaotic civil conflict. Success at restoring order will, however, quickly engender expectations for minimum service delivery.

The biggest credibility/accountability challenge facing many African governments over a 40-year horizon will be meeting the expectations of a growing middle class. An expanding middle class can be an important driver of economic growth both in demand for goods and services and in a virtuous circle of increased income, increased saving, increased investment, and further increased income. Most importantly, a growing middle class will also demand more accountability, and thus improved governance, from its leaders and governments.

Credibility and accountability are possible under diverse political arrangements provided there is a clear social contract that engages all of society. The nature of that contract must evolve as standards of living rise, communications improve, and expectations change otherwise credibility will suffer.

To meet the aspirations of its people, Africa needs leaders and governments with a single-minded focus on results, sufficient foresight to evolve to face tomorrow's challenges, and willingness to be held accountable.

Pragmatic Leadership

As important as the inter-generational issues highlighted above are, there are overriding non-tangibles related to leadership that will be critical to sustain Africa's newfound momentum for another 40 years and ultimately shape Africa's long-term destiny:

- First, the ability of its leaders to persevere during the inevitable ups and downs, to maintain a sharp focus on the long-term, and to make continuous adjustments in strategy and policies to respond to changing circumstances within and outside the continent — despite the relentless pressures of day-to-day concerns;
- Second, the willingness to adopt and pursue pragmatic — rather than ideological or geopolitical — approaches to policymaking and thus keep a strict focus on results;

---

2. Some investment in resource extraction can be possible even with low government credibility because all that is required is an agreement on how to share the rents.

- Third, building much greater mutual trust and confidence between the major economies of the region as the basis for effective regional cooperation and collaboration; and
- Fourth, the commitment and ability of Africa's leadership to modernize governance and institutions on a continuous basis, while enhancing transparency and accountability throughout.

Concluding Note: Africa's Future Is in Its Own Hands

In an era of increasing globalization, the continent will clearly be affected by developments elsewhere, including in commodity markets, but the basic direction of its future economic and social trajectory will be determined by actions of African governments, public and private institutions, the business community, and civil society themselves. In this context, what African leaders choose and manage to do in the next few years to start implementing the agenda outlined in Chapter 3 will make an enormous difference.

Almost all important changes — in policies, institutions, investments, relations with others within the region and its partners in the rest world — require a long-term perspective, strategy, and action agenda. Reforms in the most crucial areas are inter-generational issues that take decades to initiate, pilot, adapt as lessons are learned, and ultimately scale up to the national or regional level. If they are not initiated early, the reforms will not be mature enough to yield results by the time the problems they address become binding constraints.

Africa is at a critical juncture. It faces a window of opportunity to break away from the historical ups and downs in its economic performance and to embrace an ambitious vision of a transformed continent by 2050. An unwavering focus on realizing this vision will allow Africa to meet the rising aspirations of both its people and the rest of the world, and to stand on its own feet in the global community. This path will not be easy. But Africans deserve and require nothing less from their leaders, and progress is essential in order to avoid scenarios that could result in social turmoil and global marginalization.

In human terms, the stakes for the next two generations of Africans are staggering. Under the vision outlined in Chapter 1, over 2 billion Africans living in 2050 would enjoy the fruits of affluent societies similar to countries such as Malaysia, Mexico, or Turkey today and be free of the violence and insecurity that currently afflict almost one in three Africans. Poverty, illiteracy, and disease would have been practically eliminated. But under a business-as-usual scenario, the continent's standard of living would in 2050 still be lower than that of Egypt or South Africa today and almost 20 percent of the population, some 380 million people, would still be poor. Even more socially and politically unacceptable would be the downside scenario, which would be, simply put, a nightmare.

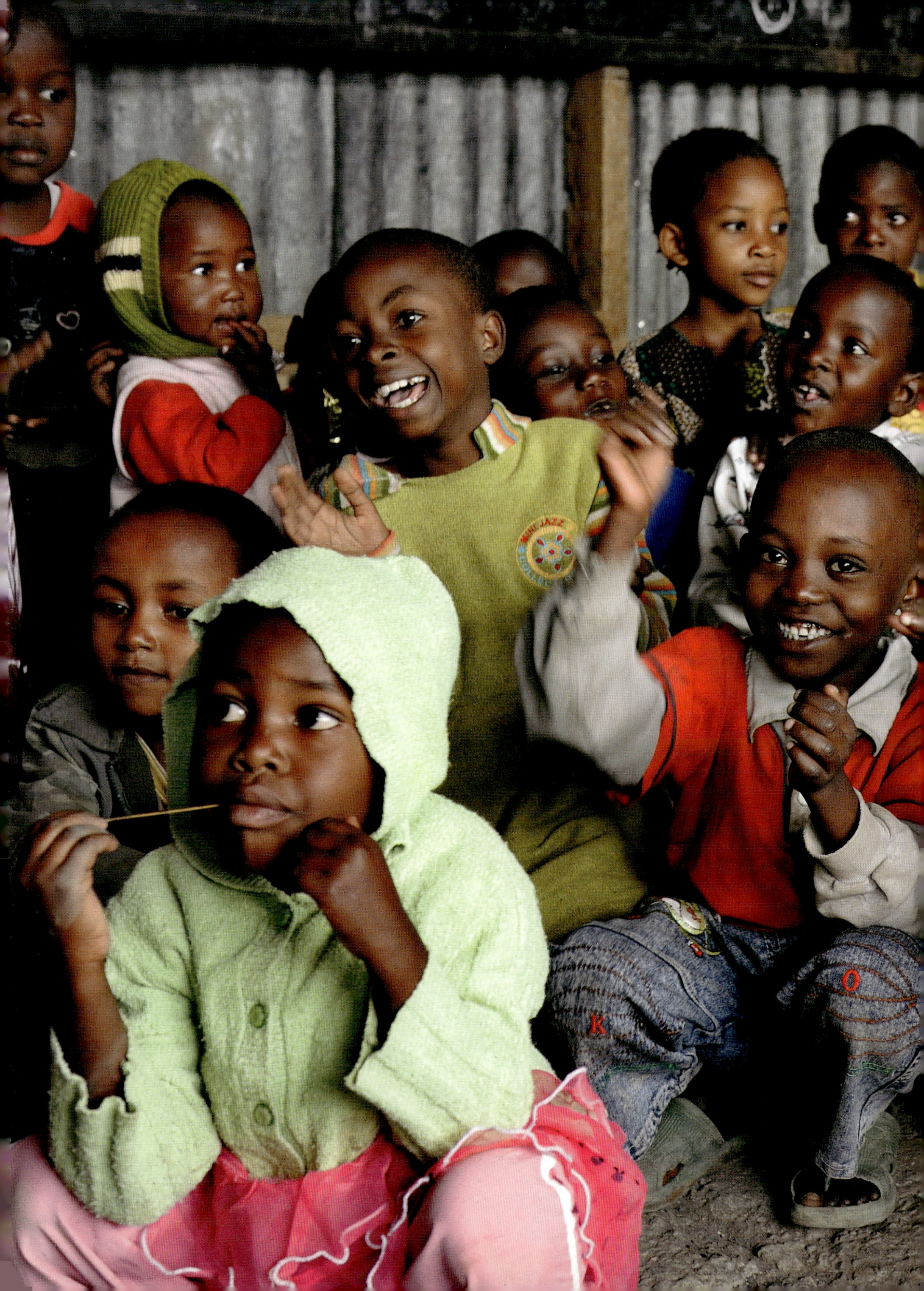

PART II: PEOPLE, ECONOMIES, AND THE CONTINENT

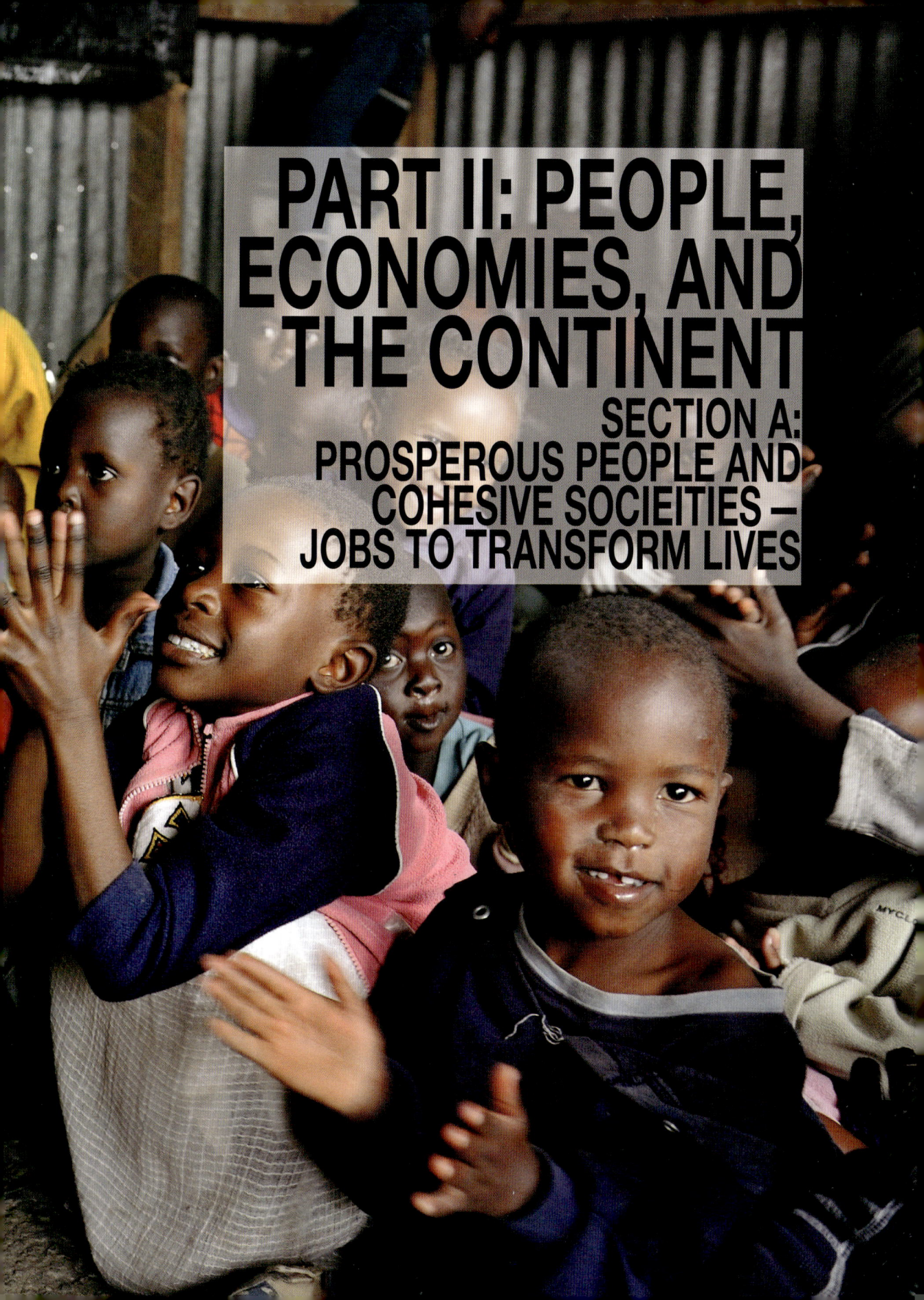

SECTION A: PROSPEROUS PEOPLE AND COHESIVE SOCIEITIES – JOBS TO TRANSFORM LIVES

Accelerating the Demographic Transition

Chapter 5

Jean-Pierre Guengant and John F. May

The story of the demographic transition in Africa is one of immense growth. According to some estimates, Africa's population has the potential to *double* over the next 35 years, which would mean roughly an additional 1.5 *billion* people. Policymakers in Africa need to take a closer look at the demographic processes at hand in order to understand the burden this growth will pose and the impact it will have on society and the economy. Using geographic regions as a framework, we will discuss the demographic transition, defined here as the shift from a traditional regime characterized by high mortality and high fertility to a modern regime of low mortality and low fertility.

The speed of demographic transition can be slower or faster, and it can both influence and be influenced by various socioeconomic factors. The transition can be accelerated by the design and implementation of adequate population and health policies. The 1986 report of the US National Academy of Sciences had claimed that the population factor was neutral in the development process (National Research Council 1986). Empirical evidence, however, and new research findings today make it unmistakably clear that population matters and attention to the demographic transition is imperative in formulating socioeconomic policy goals.

Conceptually, this chapter relies on the empirical evidence of the two-way relationship between socioeconomic conditions and demographic outcomes. The chapter posits that socioeconomic advances help foster demographic transformations and that improvements in demographic indicators also help trigger socioeconomic advances (World Bank 2007). However, improvements in socioeconomic conditions alone will not bring demographic changes nor will demographic transformations alone bring socioeconomic changes. Public authorities need to intervene on mortality and particularly on fertility for the demographic changes to occur rapidly.

Note: The authors want to acknowledge the contribution of Jamie Mullaney, Research Assistant, Georgetown University, who helped draft this chapter.

Demographic trends are not an independent variable. On the contrary, public policies influence demographic outcomes and may do so even in a relatively short timeframe due to their rapid impact on the annual number of births (May 2012; Guengant 2012). Realizing the Africa 2050 vision of prosperity and inclusive growth set out in Chapter 1 is intrinsically linked to the attainment of a modern demographic regime. Reaching such a regime in the next 40 years requires that most African countries continue their efforts to reduce mortality levels, while simultaneously implementing public policies to initiate, accelerate, and complete their fertility transition. This is a daunting challenge.

Analysis of past demographic trends suggests that most African countries will find it necessary to adopt policies to encourage and stimulate economic growth in order to accommodate the likely doubling or even tripling of the working age population. The impending growth of the working age population is the direct result of high fertility levels since the 1960s, a consequence of the neglect of demographic trends by public authorities, civil society, and international donors. This unprecedented increase in the working age population is an inescapable phenomenon–a demographic heritage of the past. Most African countries have a youth bulge (where 40 percent or more of the population above age 15 is between the ages of 15 and 29) and must address the widespread implications. These young people will be increasingly concentrated in urban areas, and the major source of job creation may very well remain in the informal sector. Discontent among this sizeable group could translate into major social disruptions similar to those that have been observed recently in several Northern African countries during the Arab Spring.

Creating the conditions needed to bring a better future for Africa's generations of tomorrow is crucial. Future development and prosperity depend on a rapid decline in the currently high dependency ratios (the number of dependents aged less than 20 or more than 65 divided by the population aged 20 to 64). Such a decline would allow important resources, which are now devoted to the health and education of large numbers of children below age 15, to be reallocated to enhance secondary and tertiary education of young adults as well as to create essential jobs. African countries are confronted today with the pressing need to expand the coverage of health and education services, while still allotting appropriate resources to maintain adequate infrastructure, equipment, and economic investments.

Simultaneously lowering mortality and fertility will in turn create an auspicious environment for lower dependency ratios and a relatively smaller but more productive labor force. To summarize, the dual challenge of most African countries will be to deal with the demographic situation inherited from the past (i.e., the irreversible results of past inattention to the consequences of demographic trends), while at the same time preparing for a better future for the upcoming generations. This challenge can be managed through the design and implementation of sound population, health, education, and economic policies. These policies, however, *must* be put in place as soon as possible in order to capture the demographic dividend, trigger inclusive growth, reduce poverty levels, and eventually achieve economic convergence.

Components of the Demographic Transition

One of the reasons for the rapid population growth of most African countries since the 1960s is that they have experienced late and slower demographic transitions than other countries of the world (Bongaarts and Casterline 2012; Guengant 2007; Guengant 2012; and Guengant and May 2011). Demographic transition is usually accompanied by other major changes, namely an epidemiological transition characterized by a shift in health patterns from communicable to non-communicable diseases (May 2012) and other broad-based socioeconomic changes. There are also associated migratory movements (from rural to urban areas) that can have an important economic impact.

Mortality levels and trends since 1960

In the early 1960s, mortality levels were high in most African countries, and life expectancies at birth were low. Life expectancy is the average number of years that a newborn would be expected to live. Indeed 20 of the 54 countries in Africa had life expectancies below 40 years. Only six countries had life expectancies above 50 years, and only two (Mauritius and Seychelles) had life expectancies above 60 years. Since the 1960s, life expectancy at birth has increased in most African countries despite slow progress in some. According to 2012 UN estimates, life expectancies at birth in 2005-2010 were above 50 years in all but 11 countries but greater than 70 years in only 6 countries (Algeria Seychelles, Mauritius, Cape Verde, Libya, and Tunisia). For some countries life expectancy increases have been modest, stagnant, and, in some cases, even reversed since the 1990s. Southern and Eastern African countries have been hit especially hard, specifically in the countries most affected by HIV/AIDS and civil strife.

Although adult mortality estimates are less reliable than child mortality estimates—mostly due to scarce data availability—it remains important to understand adult mortality numbers in order to envision the big picture of the demographic dividend. In terms of adult mortality, estimates in the 1960s put the chance of dying between the ages of 15 and 60 at about one in two or three. That was, at best, a 66 percent chance of seeing a 60th birthday. In about half of African countries in 2005-2010, the probability of dying between 15 and 60 was still estimated at more than one in three and in some cases in Southern and Eastern African more than one in two. In many African countries these numbers illustrate little improvement, and odds like these provide little incentive for individuals or governments to plan for or invest in an adult's future.

Fertility levels and trends since 1960

As observed with mortality, fertility declines have been slow and uneven in most African countries. In many countries, the 2010 World Population Projections Revision of the United Nations underestimated the Total Fertility Rate (the average number of births per woman, or TFR) as revealed when they are compared with estimates from survey data published since the revision (see Figure 5.1).

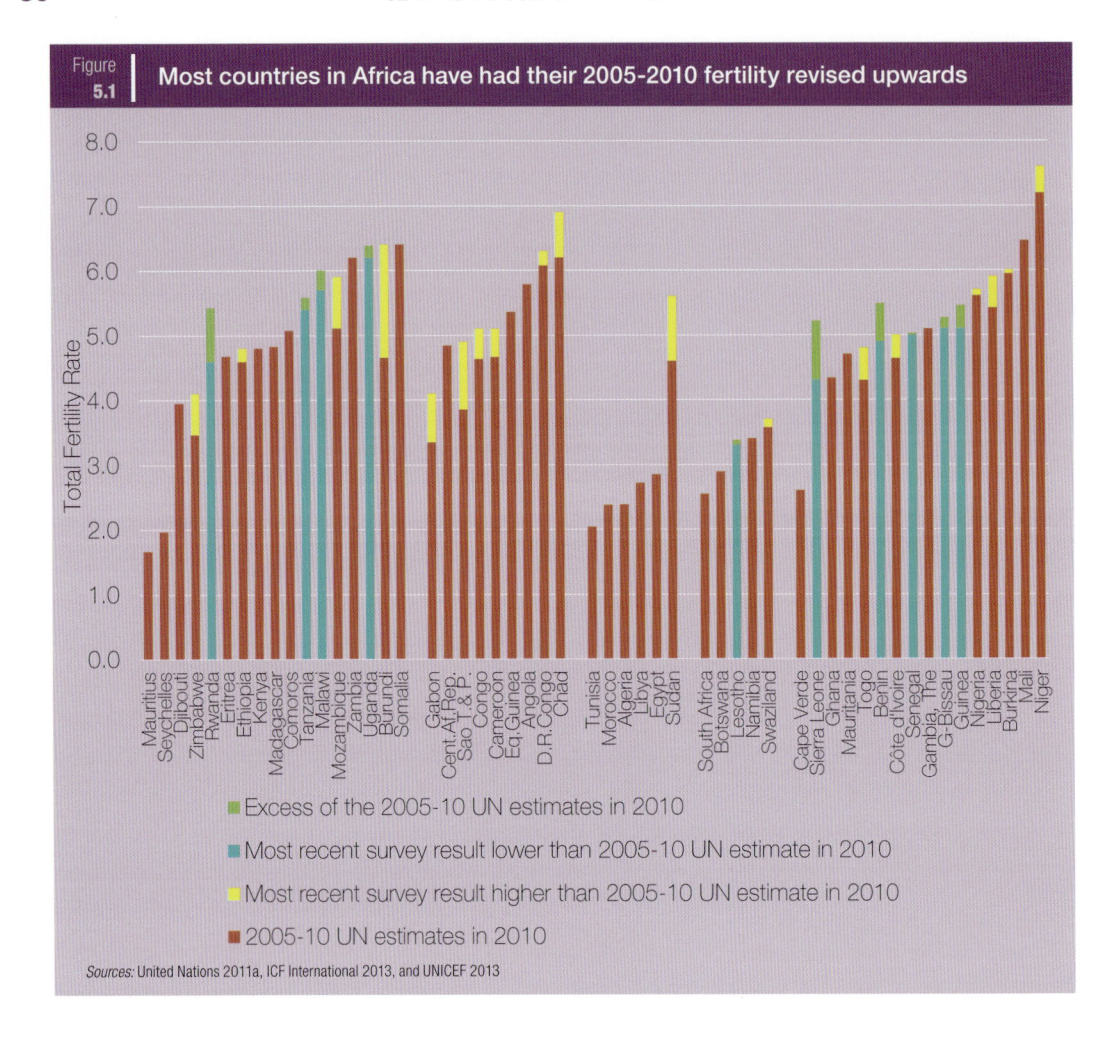

Figure 5.1: Most countries in Africa have had their 2005-2010 fertility revised upwards

- Excess of the 2005-10 UN estimates in 2010
- Most recent survey result lower than 2005-10 UN estimate in 2010
- Most recent survey result higher than 2005-10 UN estimate in 2010
- 2005-10 UN estimates in 2010

Sources: United Nations 2011a, ICF International 2013, and UNICEF 2013

Using the 2012 UN World Population Prospects, which corrected the earlier estimates and was released in June 2013, we have established an updated typology of fertility transition in Africa (see Figure 5.2). A first group, "fertility transition completed or close to completion," comprises countries where the TFR is now less than four children per woman. These 15 countries, which have completed or are close to completing the fertility transition, account for 23 percent of the total population of the continent. They generally have more advanced economies and the majority is early convergers, according to the typology developed in Chapter 1.

ACCELERATING THE DEMOGRAPHIC TRANSITION

The remaining countries, where the fertility transition is far from completion, account for three quarters of the continent's population and can be divided into three groups, as follows:

- Transition in progress: Ten countries (Ghana, Gabon, Sao Tome and Principe, Kenya, Madagascar, Sudan, Central African Republic, Togo, Côte d'Ivoire, and Mauritania) with a TFR between 4 and 5 children per woman, accounting for 15 percent of the population of Africa. These are generally coastal countries with high urbanization and, in some cases, political commitment, albeit uneven and irregular, to lower fertility. Their economic situations also vary.
- Slow and irregular transition: Nineteen countries with a TFR between 5 and 6 children per women (Comoros, Congo, Senegal, Rwanda, Sierra Leone, Eritrea, Cameroon, Liberia, Ethiopia, Guinea-Bissau, Benin, Equatorial Guinea, Guinea, South Sudan, Mozambique, Tanzania, the Gambia,

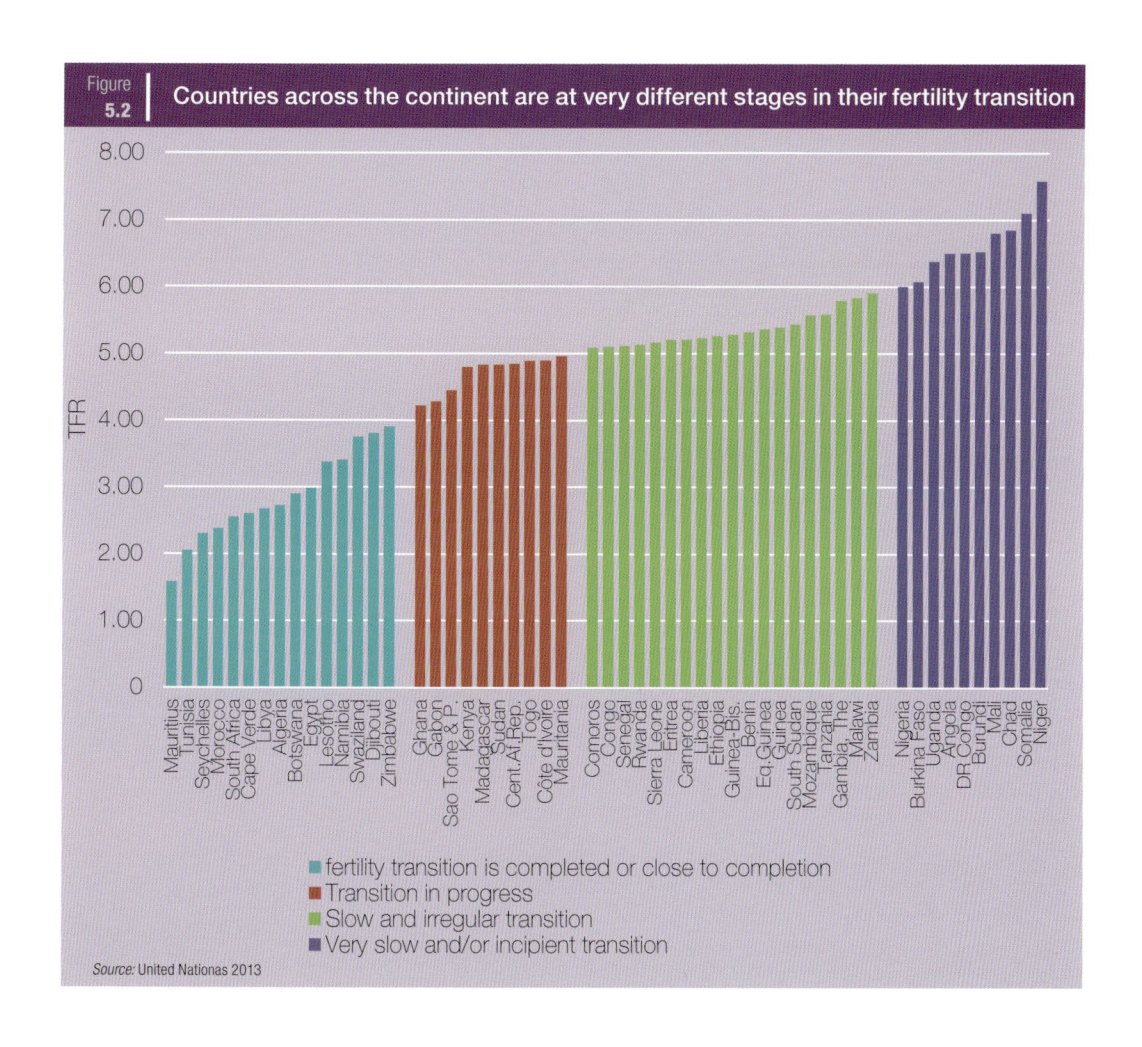

Figure 5.2 | Countries across the continent are at very different stages in their fertility transition

- fertility transition is completed or close to completion
- Transition in progress
- Slow and irregular transition
- Very slow and/or incipient transition

Source: United Nationas 2013

Malawi, and Zambia), accounting for 28 percent of the African population. These countries have mixed urbanization rates and, with the notable exceptions of Rwanda and Ethiopia, a weak political commitment to lower fertility.

- Very slow and/or incipient transition: 10 countries where the TFR is greater than 6 children per woman (Nigeria, Burkina Faso, Uganda, Angola, DRC, Burundi, Mali, Chad, Somalia, and Niger), accounting for 34 percent of the total African population. These countries have low levels of urbanization and a lack of strong political commitment to lower fertility.

This pattern of persisting high levels of fertility in the majority of African countries differs markedly from what has been observed in other developing countries since the 1960s, as can be seen in Figure 5.3.

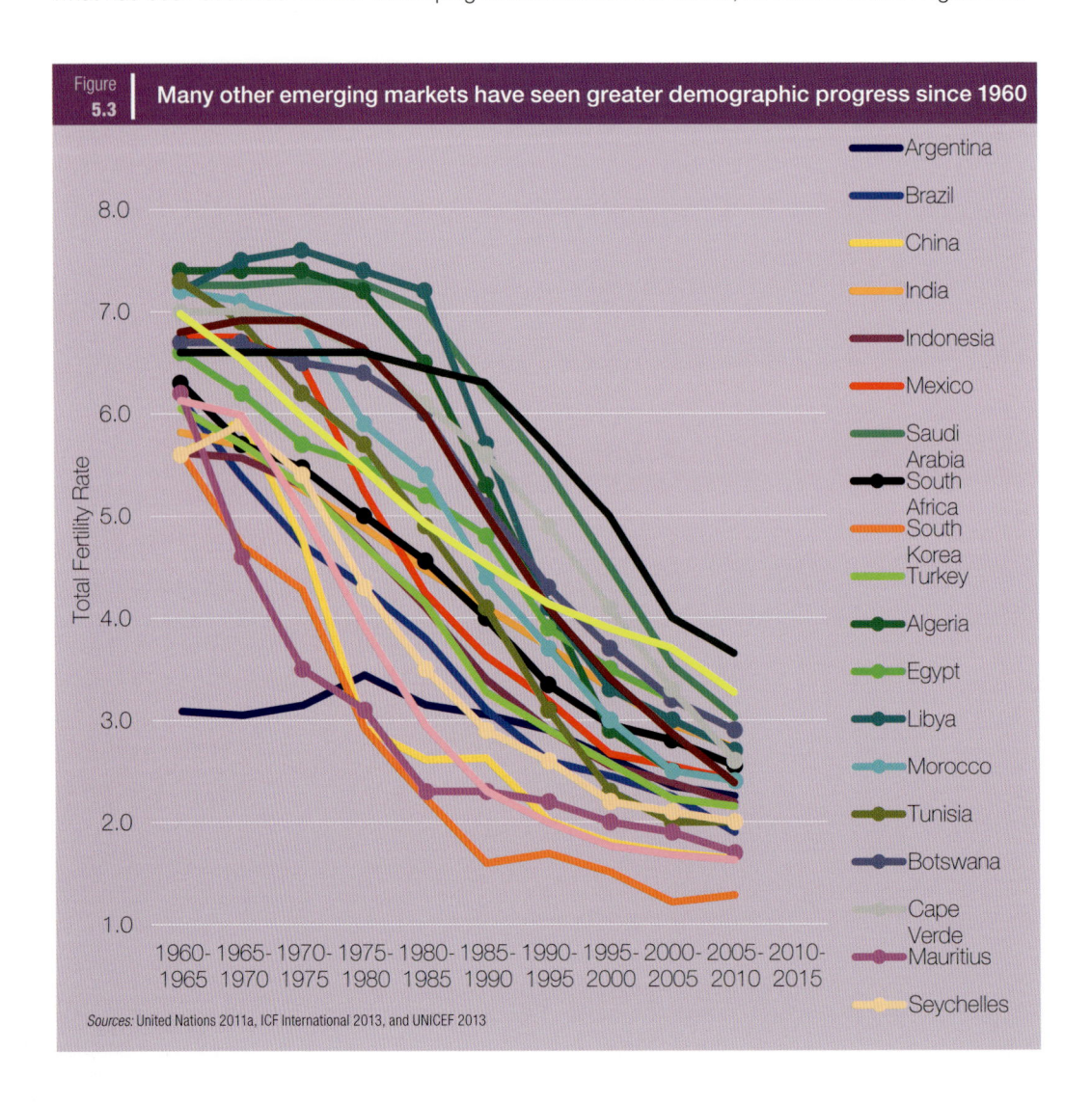

Figure 5.3 Many other emerging markets have seen greater demographic progress since 1960

Sources: United Nations 2011a, ICF International 2013, and UNICEF 2013

Of the 39 SSA countries where fertility transition is far from completed, the average number of children per women (unweighted) was 5.5. Some of these countries experienced a fertility decline in the 1980s or even in the 1970s, but in recent years, fertility decline has stalled. If recent trends were to continue, a majority of these countries would still have fertility levels above 4 children per woman in 2045-2050.

The TFR is inversely correlated with life expectancy at birth, as seen in Figure 5.4. This pattern does not necessarily indicate causality but may suggest that there are socioeconomic factors that are affecting both fertility and mortality, as discussed below.

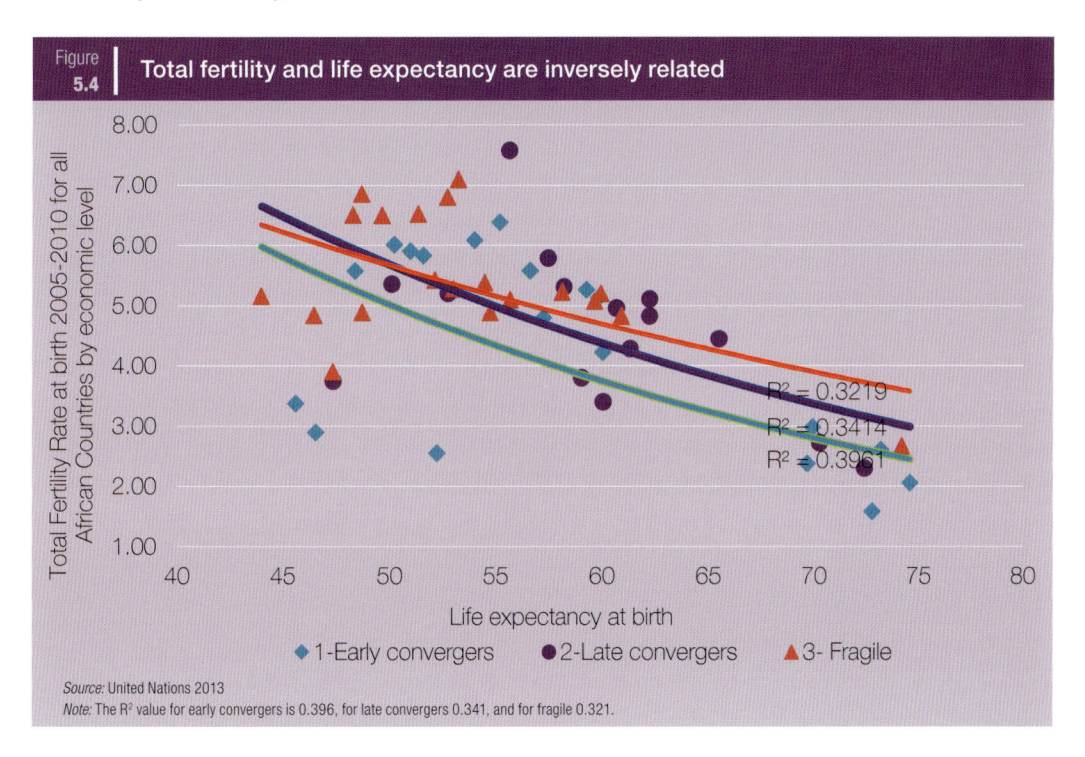

Figure 5.4 | Total fertility and life expectancy are inversely related

$R^2 = 0.3219$
$R^2 = 0.3414$
$R^2 = 0.3961$

◆ 1-Early convergers   ● 2-Late convergers   ▲ 3- Fragile

Source: United Nations 2013
Note: The R^2 value for early convergers is 0.396, for late convergers 0.341, and for fragile 0.321.

Fertility determinants and contraceptive prevalence

Fertility outcomes are shaped by two sets of determinants, which are either intermediate or proximate. The intermediate determinants of fertility are essentially socioeconomic in nature, and they influence fertility *indirectly*. Higher levels of education, health status, employment in the formal sector, and income, as well as urban or rural residence are all *intermediate determinants*. Policy interventions in these fields generally do not appear to affect fertility rates immediately, and their impacts can vary from one country to another depending on other variables. Family norms, social networks, and cultural values can and will change a country's reaction to changes in public policies. Raising education levels for girls — especially increasing secondary education levels, reducing maternal and child mortality, increasing female labor participation in the formal sector, and achieving a more inclusive economic growth are policy objectives in themselves and not just proxy policy interventions aimed at accelerating the fertility transition. In African countries, as in other developing countries, fertility levels are generally lower among the most educated and urban women (see Bongaarts 2010). However, the effect on national fertility levels is limited because in most African countries relatively few women of reproductive age have post-primary education levels, and urbanization rates remain generally low.

Wealthier households also have generally lower fertility levels than poorer ones. A proxy wealth index constructed using easy-to-collect data on a household's ownership of selected assets (such as televisions and bicycles, housing materials, and types of water access and sanitation facilities) permits categorization of households into quintiles and assessment of the impact of wealth on the health and well-being of the population. TFRs by wealth index quintiles have been calculated for 40 African countries and, not surprisingly, the wealthiest households—the 20 percent with the highest wealth index—have fewer children (TFR of 3.4) than the poorest 20 percent (TFR of 6.4). Although this difference cannot be applied universally to all African countries, TFRs of the poorest households are above 5 children per woman in 37 out of the 40 countries, and they range from 6 to more than 8 children per woman in 28 countries. Family norms favoring large families (expressed by the ideal number of children in the Demographic and Health Surveys (DHS)) are still dominant among the poorest households but can also be found among the wealthiest households in several countries.

Women from the wealthiest households can afford good prenatal care and adequate delivery conditions while women from the poorest households generally cannot. According to DHS, in 35 countries more than 80 percent of women from the wealthiest households who had given birth in the three years preceding the survey benefited from the assistance of a doctor and/or health professional during delivery. By contrast, in more than half of the countries, less than a third of the women from the poorest households benefited from any such assistance. These less than ideal birthing environments mean that poorer women are at higher risk of maternal death and/or infant mortality.

Let us turn now to the *proximate determinants* of fertility. Proximate determinants are biological and/or behavioral in nature. Some of these determinants include marriage (unions), induced abortion, temporary postpartum infecundability (insusceptibility), and sterility. Traditional and modern contraceptive methods also belong to the proximate determinants. Modern methods are hormonal (the pill, implants, and injectables), chemical (spermicides), mechanical (IUDs and barrier methods such as condoms), or surgical (male and female sterilization). Some of these determinants are more amenable to policy interventions than others, especially when results are needed in short time periods (May 2012). For this reason, in high fertility countries, access to contraception has long stood at the top of the list of preferred population policy interventions. However, one should not underestimate the importance of the less publicized determinants of fertility, namely postpartum infecundability (which is essentially linked to the duration of breastfeeding), increasing age at marriage, and recourse to induced abortion because of limited access to family planning services.

It appears that the high fertility levels observed today in most African countries are largely the result of persisting low contraceptive prevalence rates (CPR). Conversely, the lower fertility levels observed in most emerging market countries, as well as some of the 15 African countries in the group "fertility transition completed or close to completion" can be traced to a rapid increase in the use of modern contraceptive methods over the past 40 years — a process that has been called the contraceptive revolution. Globally, contraceptive prevalence rates have increased rapidly to 60 percent or more in some countries. Much of Sub-Saharan Africa, however, has not taken part in contraceptive revolution, and contraceptive prevalence rates for modern methods have not reached 20 percent in a majority of SSA countries.

Figure 5.5 reveals the striking gap in the use of modern contraception since 1970 between emerging economies and most SSA countries. Most emerging market countries shown in Figure 5.5 had a CPR of greater than 20 percent by the 1990s. But many of the SSA countries had barely reached a CPR of 20 percent in 2010.[1]

Figure 5.5 | Contraception adoption in Sub-Saharan Africa has been very slow

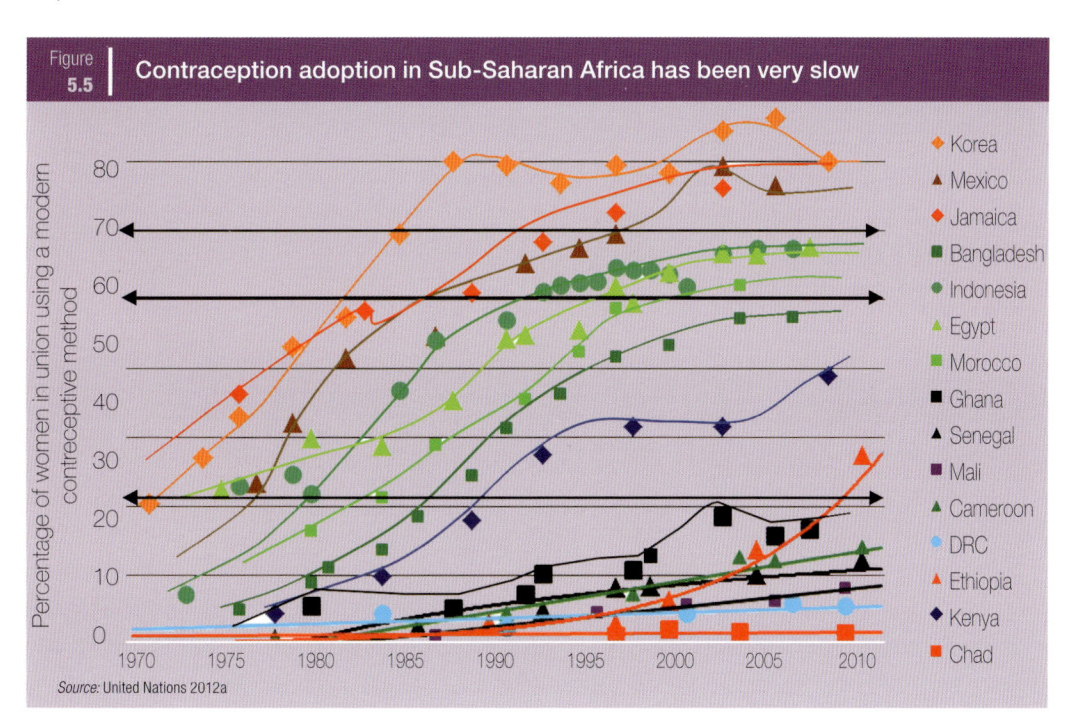

Source: United Nations 2012a

Figure 5.6 presents recent CPR for all methods for 52 African countries (there is no data for the Seychelles and South Sudan). In some countries modern contraceptive coverage is just a small fraction of total contraceptive use and traditional methods remain important.

---

1. However, according to the 2011 Ghana MICS survey the CPR for modern methods has increased to 25.4%.

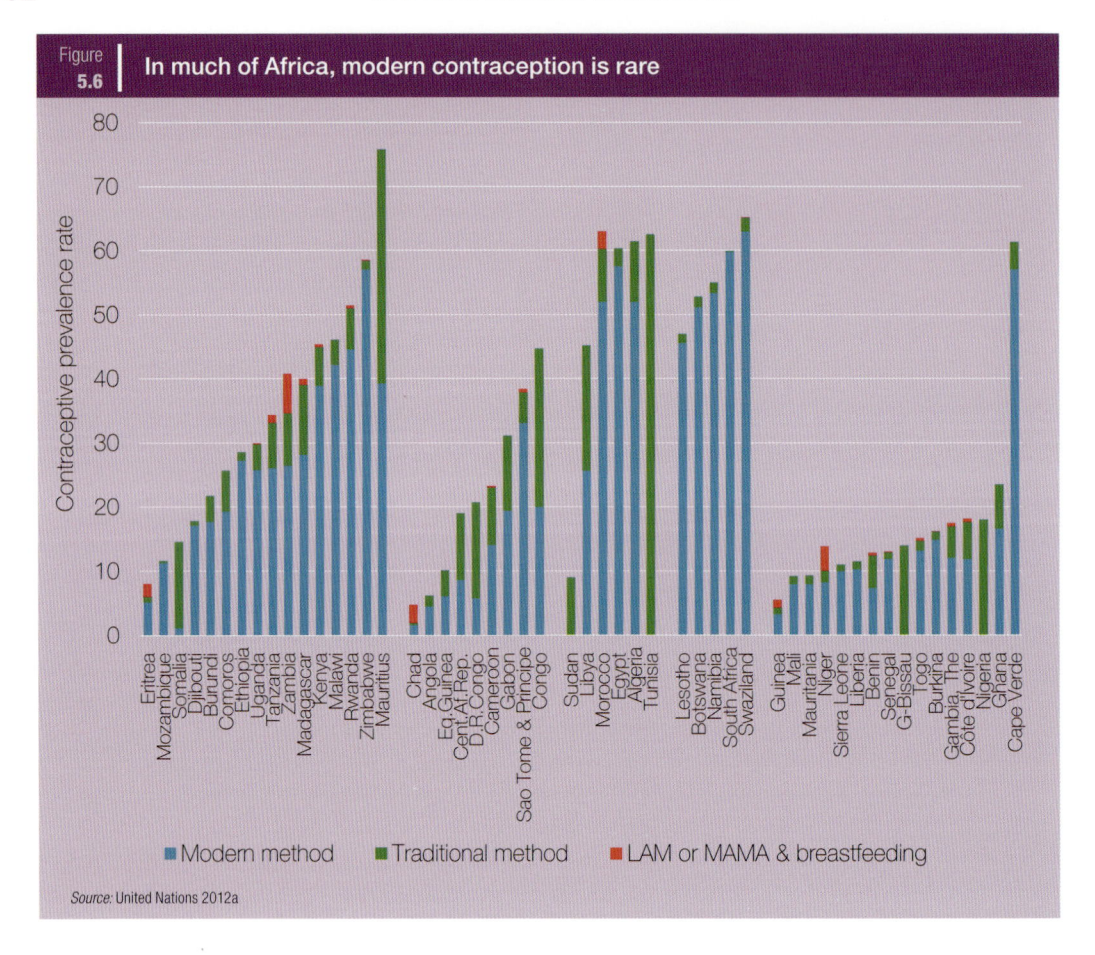

Figure 5.6 — In much of Africa, modern contraception is rare

Contraceptive prevalence rate by country, with breakdown by Modern method, Traditional method, and LAM or MAMA & breastfeeding.

Source: United Nations 2012a

Only 7 countries, accounting for 13 percent of the continent's population, had a recent contraceptive rate above 60 percent (Morocco, Egypt, Cape Verde, Algeria, Tunisia, Swaziland, and Mauritius). At the other end of the spectrum, 30 countries, accounting for 62 percent of the continent's total population, have a contraceptive rate below 30 percent. The minimum CPR required for achieving the contraceptive revolution and fertility transition is about 70 to 80 percent. All Western African countries but one (Cape Verde) have CPR below 30 percent. In Sub-Saharan Africa, 78 percent of the population lives in a country where less than 30 percent of the women in union are using any method of contraception.

For some countries in Figure 5.6, contraceptive prevalence rates include the LAM (lactational amenorrhea method, or postpartum contraception) which is now often regarded as a modern method of contraception, as well as breastfeeding which is generally considered a traditional method. The effectiveness of LAM is based on three conditions that must be met simultaneously: 1) the baby must be less than 6 months old, 2) the mother must be amenorrheic (not having her periods), and 3) breastfeeding must be practiced day and night, on demand. LAM is often equated with breastfeeding, and data regarding the percentages of LAM users is generally low and unreliable. For comparison purposes, therefore, the percentages of users of LAM or breastfeeding have been displayed separately from the percentages of users of other methods. In addition, the most recent data given for Sudan, Tunisia, Guinea-Bissau, and Nigeria are for all methods.

Why might an African woman not be using any methods of contraception? There may be a reluctance to use modern methods rooted in traditional culture, attitudes, norms, and family structures, but it may also be that the woman is unaware of her options. Lack of knowledge is a key obstacle that family planning programs urgently need to address. Although in most SSA countries the total demand for family planning remains rather weak, a portion of this demand results in high levels of unmet needs. Total demand includes all women in need but not using any method plus those in union currently using contraception; unmet needs for family planning refers to the condition of wanting to avoid or postpone childbearing but not using any method of contraception. A weak demand for family planning translates into low use of any contraceptive.

Both the lack of information on and the lack of access to contraceptives have hindered the rapid expansion of contraceptive coverage in SSA. At the onset of the fertility transition, not only the application of contraceptive methods, but also the very idea that it is possible and legitimate to control one's fertility is limited to a small group of couples and women. As the concept of family planning spreads within a society, demand can increase more rapidly than the availability of modern methods, especially in countries where counseling and health services are insufficient. The result may be higher demand but also higher levels of unmet needs.

The leading group of contraceptive users is generally made of more educated and urbanized women as well as women from the wealthiest households. The data on contraceptive use by wealth quintiles from the DHS surveys confirm this pattern. The use of contraceptive methods is two times more frequent among women from the wealthiest households (41 percent) than among women from the poorest households (20 percent). However, modern methods account for only about half of contraceptive use among women from the wealthiest households, and unmet needs remain quite high at around 21 percent. Not surprisingly, the situation is worse among women from the poorest households where modern methods account for only a quarter of contraceptive use and unmet needs are slightly higher (28 percent). Finally, the total demand for family planning among women from the wealthiest households appears moderately high at 62 percent, while demand among women from the poorest households remains at less than half (48 percent). Although some countries have a total demand between 60 and 80 percent in the poorest households, others (specifically Chad) have a total demand of only around 35 percent even in the wealthiest households. This finding reinforces the idea that the social context can play a major role in family planning desires and practices.

Desired fertility in SSA (i.e., the ideal number of children) indeed remains high among younger women, even young women with secondary levels of education. In addition, marriage at young ages (and sometimes child marriage) should be included as an explanatory factor for the high fertility levels observed.

To a large extent, this situation is the consequence of lukewarm commitment or lack of engagement vis-à-vis family planning on the part of governments and donors alike. So far, only two governments in Sub-Saharan Africa (Rwanda and Ethiopia) appear to have organized successful, large-scale campaigns in support of family planning. Additionally, a survey of eight countries in Western Africa found that only half had a government budget-line item for the procurement of contraceptives (USAID 2011).

Finally, persistent high fertility levels in most African countries often result in high-risk pregnancies, i.e., pregnancies that are too early, too frequent, too close, or too late. High-risk pregnancies translate into very high maternal mortality ratios, high under-five mortality rates, and high proportions of stunted children among the children who do survive. Moreover, the future of these children is compromised because they are less resistant to diseases and have more difficulties learning in school (World Bank 2010a). These outcomes have the greatest impact on the poorest households and jeopardize countries' chances of achieving more inclusive growth and fulfilling their development objectives. The low levels of contraceptive use, the rather weak demand for family planning, the high percentage of unmet needs at the national level, and the inequalities between women with respect to these variables can be partially explained by the pervasive family norms favoring large families (Romaniuk 2011).

Implications for the Future

Future population growth

Africa's population reached one billion people in 2009, and the entire continent is expected to have a population ranging from 2.1 billion to 2.7 billion people by 2050, according to the latest United Nations World Population Prospects (United Nations 2013). The UN World Population Prospects combine several assumptions, including keeping country-specific estimates for mortality, international migration, and urbanization identical across all projection scenarios—with three different scenarios of fertility decline: medium, high, and low plus a constant-fertility scenario that indicates what would happen if TFR remained at current 2005-2010 levels. In the World Population Prospects, future fertility levels for the medium fertility variant converge in a more or less distant future toward fertility replacement levels, depending on the country's pattern of fertility transitions Under the high variant, fertility is projected to remain 0.5 children above the medium fertility assumption over most of the projection period, and the low fertility variant assumes fertility to remain 0.5 children below the medium variant. The United Nations also produces a "World Urbanization Prospects" report every two years using the results of the preceding years' WPP (United Nations 2012b). For purposes of simplicity, this chapter will reflect estimates based on the medium fertility variant.

Table 5.1 shows the 2012 UN WPP assumptions for TFR, life expectancy at birth, international migration, and fertility decline, as well as the 2011 UN World Urbanization Prospects' assumptions for urbanization. They are grouped into values for the five subregions of the continent based on the aggregation of the country-level assumptions.

Table 5.1 — The medium-fertility scenario paints an optimistic demographic picture

	2005-2010	2045-2050 (medium fertility variant)
Total Fertility Rate (number of children per woman)		
Africa	4.88	3.09
Sub-Saharan Africa	5.39	3.22
Eastern Africa	5.38	2.99
Middle Africa	6.17	3.16
Northern Africa	3.07	2.20
Southern Africa	2.64	1.89
Western Africa	5.73	3.64
Life expectancy at birth, both sexes combined (years)		
Africa	55.6	68.9
Sub-Saharan Africa	52.9	67.8
Eastern Africa	55.9	71.6
Middle Africa	49.5	63.5
Northern Africa	68.3	74.7
Southern Africa	51.9	68.1
Western Africa	52.3	65.8
Net annual migration, (thousands)		
Africa	-356	-498
Sub-Saharan Africa	-37	-353
Eastern Africa	-176	-150
Middle Africa	4	-28
Northern Africa	-319	-146
Southern Africa	268	17
Western Africa	-133	-191
Percentage of population residing in urban areas		
Africa	39.2	57.7
Sub-Saharan Africa	36.3	56.5
Eastern Africa	23.3	44.7
Middle Africa	40.9	61.5
Northern Africa	51.2	65.3
Southern Africa	58.5	74.0
Western Africa	44.3	65.7

Sources: United Nations 2013 and 2012b

In the medium fertility variant, the TFR decreases by 1.9 children by 2050 for Africa as a whole and by 2.2 children for Sub-Saharan Africa. The most rapid decline (3.0 fewer children) is projected for Middle Africa, and Northern and Southern Africa are projected to have a TFR decline of 0.9 and 0.8, respectively. According to these estimates, 40 percent of the countries have projected TFRs remaining above 3 children per women in 2045-2050. These fertility declines appear rather optimistic for some countries given the recent fertility trends observed and the persistent low levels of contraceptive use. Based on this evidence, in several countries fertility might decline more slowly than anticipated under the 2012 UN medium variant. If fertility declines are slower than those projected, the dependency ratios will remain high and will prevent many countries from achieving the demographic prerequisites needed to capture a demographic dividend.

Projected total population

Under the medium fertility variant, Africa would have 2.4 billion people in 2050 (up from 1 billion in 2010) with 87 percent of these people in Sub-Saharan Africa. In 2010, there were 424 million children aged 0-14 years in Africa, and by 2050 there would be some 771 million (according to the medium fertility variant). As this population ages, African countries will face the daunting challenge of providing health and education services to the school-age population and jobs for youth entering the labor force. The adoption of policies and programs aimed at slowing down future population growth constitutes a crucial strategic choice both at a regional and national level.

In about half of all African countries, youth aged 15-29 are projected to still represent more than 40 percent of the adult population in 2050, a phenomenon known as the youth bulge. The youth bulge occurs when child mortality falls but fertility remains high. The implications of an enormous young population are manifold. It is also important to realize that irrespective of population policies introduced now, the number of youth entering the labor force will continue to grow rapidly since most future workers are already born. If most youth enter the labor market between ages 15 and 24 and the participation rate remains around 70 percent, about 14 million jobs will need to be created each year in this decade, and 31 million will need to be created each year by 2050. Providing jobs to all the youth entering the labor market will prove very difficult. In its *African Economic Outlook 2012* report the African Development Bank notes that only one-quarter of young African men and 10 percent of young African women are presently able to get secure jobs in the formal or modern sector when they reach the age of 30 (African Development Bank 2012a). This is not likely to change rapidly

In 2010, the number of persons aged 65 years and older was estimated at 35 million. By 2050, the 65+ age group will represent 140 million people. These exceptional and unprecedented increases are the result of medical advances lengthening life expectancy at all ages but also the consequence of the unrelenting increase of the African young population since the end of World War II. Despite this rapid increase, the total elderly population will represent only 6.6 percent of the total population of Africa in 2050, compared to 15.9 percent in developed countries.

The combined effect of the increase in the working age population and the relatively modest increases in the proportion of the 65+ age group will be a rapidly changing dependency ratio. In 2010 Africa's dependency ratio was 1.22 compared to 0.7 in Asia. In Eastern, Middle, and Western Africa the dependency ration was even higher at above 1.3. The dramatic long-term impact of the speed of population growth is shown by the projected dependency ratios under different fertility assumptions. If fertility were to remain constant at today's level, the dependency ratio in Africa in 2050 would actually increase to 1.31. Under the UN's medium fertility variant, Africa's dependency ratio would fall to 0.91. A declining dependency ratio offers the opportunity for per capita incomes to rise much faster and for more resources per capita to be devoted to quality education of children.

Urbanization and mega-cities

The urban population of Africa has grown from 53 million in 1960 to 404 million in 2010. Despite this increase, the level of urbanization in Africa remains low compared to other regions of the world. In 2010, it was estimated that about 40 percent of Africans resided in urban areas. Rapid urbanization has led to 50 cities with more than a million inhabitants in 2010, two of which (Cairo and Lagos) had populations of more than 10 million inhabitants. Estimates of the urbanization rate in 2010 and projections to 2050 are presented in Figure 5.7 (United Nations 2012a).

Given the relatively low levels of urbanization of many African countries in 2010, the projected percentage increases are important. The increases range from 20 to 30 percentage points in 21 countries to between 10 and 20 percentage points in 28 countries. As a result, whereas only one in three countries had a majority of its populations living in urban areas in 2010, in 2050 there will be potentially 43 countries out of 54 with a majority of their population living in urban areas.

At the continental level, the urban population will increase from 404 million in 2010 to about 1.4 billion by 2050 or nearly 60 percent of the total projected population. This rapid increase will be associated with the advent of about 35 cities of more than 5 million people, and 15 cities with more than 10 million people. These 15 mega-cities could represent about 20 percent of the African urban population and 10 percent of the total population of the continent. One out of five Africans living in an urban area in 2050 would live in a mega-city, compared with one out of 50 in 2010. As discussed in Chapter 13, the rapid urbanization of Africa and the emergence of vast urban areas will present both major opportunities and problems. African cities are now more and more a place of exclusion, especially from the modern labor market (Dubresson et al. 2013). This exclusion process fosters the growing criminalization of many African urban economies.

Prospects (population projections)

Mortality levels, which are still high, are expected to continue to decrease. Since 1980, infant and child mortality levels have declined by roughly 50 percent. This progress can be attributed to interventions such as vaccination campaigns, oral-rehydration therapy programs, large-scale distributions of

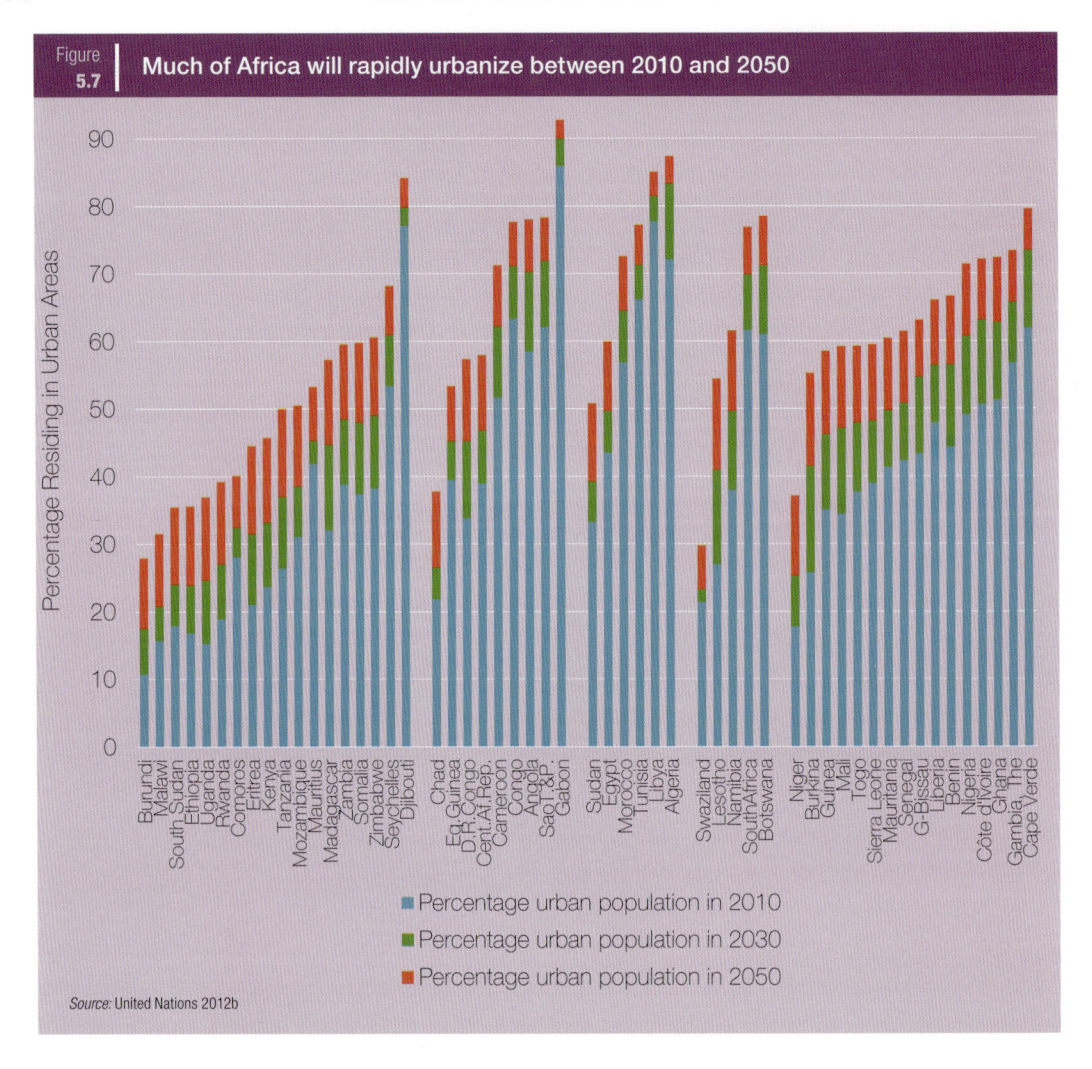

Figure 5.7 Much of Africa will rapidly urbanize between 2010 and 2050

- Percentage urban population in 2010
- Percentage urban population in 2030
- Percentage urban population in 2050

Source: United Nations 2012b

anti-malarial impregnated bed nets, the provision of nutritional supplements, and comprehensive sanitation programs. However, despite the recent progress, there is still much room for improvement. Moreover, progress on adult mortality has been less spectacular, and many SSA countries must now confront the dual burden of communicable and non-communicable diseases. It is important to note that an aging population will contribute to increasing the prevalence of non-communicable diseases. Actions to prevent the spread of HIV/AIDS and programs geared at reducing adult mortality must continue. Decreasing mortality levels will foster continued population growth in most countries. However, mortality rates could stop declining or even increase if major climatic catastrophes, widespread famines, or severe political disruptions occur.

Fertility levels are still high in most African countries and are only declining gradually, as discussed above. The future dynamic of the total population growth of each country will be largely determined by future levels of fertility. Initial levels of TFR will determine future trends of population growth – higher initial levels of fertility resulting in higher potential population growth. Rates of increase in the contraceptive prevalence rate, especially for modern methods, will largely determine the future pace of fertility decline. Population growth in the forthcoming decades will also depend on the percentage of youth in the population and on the pace of demographic growth in this age group (known as population momentum). This phenomenon considers the *additional* population growth factor resulting from a youthful age structure. The population momentum is positive when the age structure is young and there are disproportionate numbers of people in childbearing age groups. It is a powerful and inexorable factor for future demographic growth.

Internal migration and urbanization are important factors in population growth. Future expansion of the urban population will be driven by both natural increase and rural-to-urban migration patterns. Although many *mega-cities* have now reached such sizes and youthfulness that their natural increase exceeds the increase from rural-urban migration, such migration will continue to remain high as TFRs in rural settings remain high. In essence, future urban growth is not independent of rural population growth.

Action Agenda

Fulfilling a vision of prosperity and inclusive growth for Africa by 2050 is intrinsically linked to the attainment of a modern demographic regime. Reaching such a regime will require most African countries to continue their efforts to reduce mortality levels in conjunction with implementing public policies to initiate, accelerate, and complete their fertility transition. Fertility levels would need to drop to somewhere between two or three children per woman, and contraceptive prevalence rates would need to rise to between 50 and 65 percent (compared to 10 to 30 percent in about most countries today). Unfortunately, the 2012 UN projections of fertility decline may still be optimistic for many countries, particularly the 39 countries (representing nearly 80 percent of the continent's total population) with TFR above 4. If fertility declines are slower than anticipated, the dependency ratios will continue to remain high and prevent many countries from achieving the demographic conditions needed to capture the demographic dividend.

In this context, and based on the analysis of past and present demographic characteristics as well as future population trends from the 2012 and 2011 UN World Population and Urbanization Prospects, our demographic vision for African in 2050 can be summarized as follows:

- For all countries, reduce infant and child mortality rates and increase survival prospects for adults.
- For the countries in the group "fertility transition far from completion," trigger a much more rapid decline in the total fertility rates along with a much more rapid increase in the contraceptive prevalence rate, ultimately reaching total fertility rates of less than three children per woman in all African countries.

- For all countries, attain favorable dependency ratios to better allocate resources and enable human capital investments.

In order to achieve this demographic vision for 2050, sound policies and programs will be of the utmost importance. The role of policies and leadership commitment is crucial (May 2012). In particular, two major policy shifts that should translate quickly into a vigorous, broad-based, and far-reaching interventions have been identified:

- A stronger commitment to population and family planning issues from public authorities, civil society organizations, and international donors is required. The commitment must be based on the recognition of the benefits of family planning not only for improving maternal and child health but also for improving economic outcomes. It must be based on the unambiguous recognition of everyone's rights of access to sexual and reproductive education and health services. It requires establishing explicit programmatic objectives for family planning programs.

- A stronger drive toward the empowerment of women is also required implying, among other things, legislative changes increasing the age at which a girl can legally be married. Countries should adopt inheritance laws and/or practices that do not disadvantage women, adopt new *family codes* to guarantee equal rights and duties for males and females, and remove the need for husband's, parents', and/or in-laws' consent for access to family planning services. Reproductive rights need to be promoted and women enabled to exert their reproductive choices freely and without coercion.

Broad-based and far-reaching interventions are urgently needed to accelerate the demographic transition in Africa. Ushered in by rapid declines in mortality and fertility, favorable dependency ratios would allow for increased human capital investment and socioeconomic growth and development.

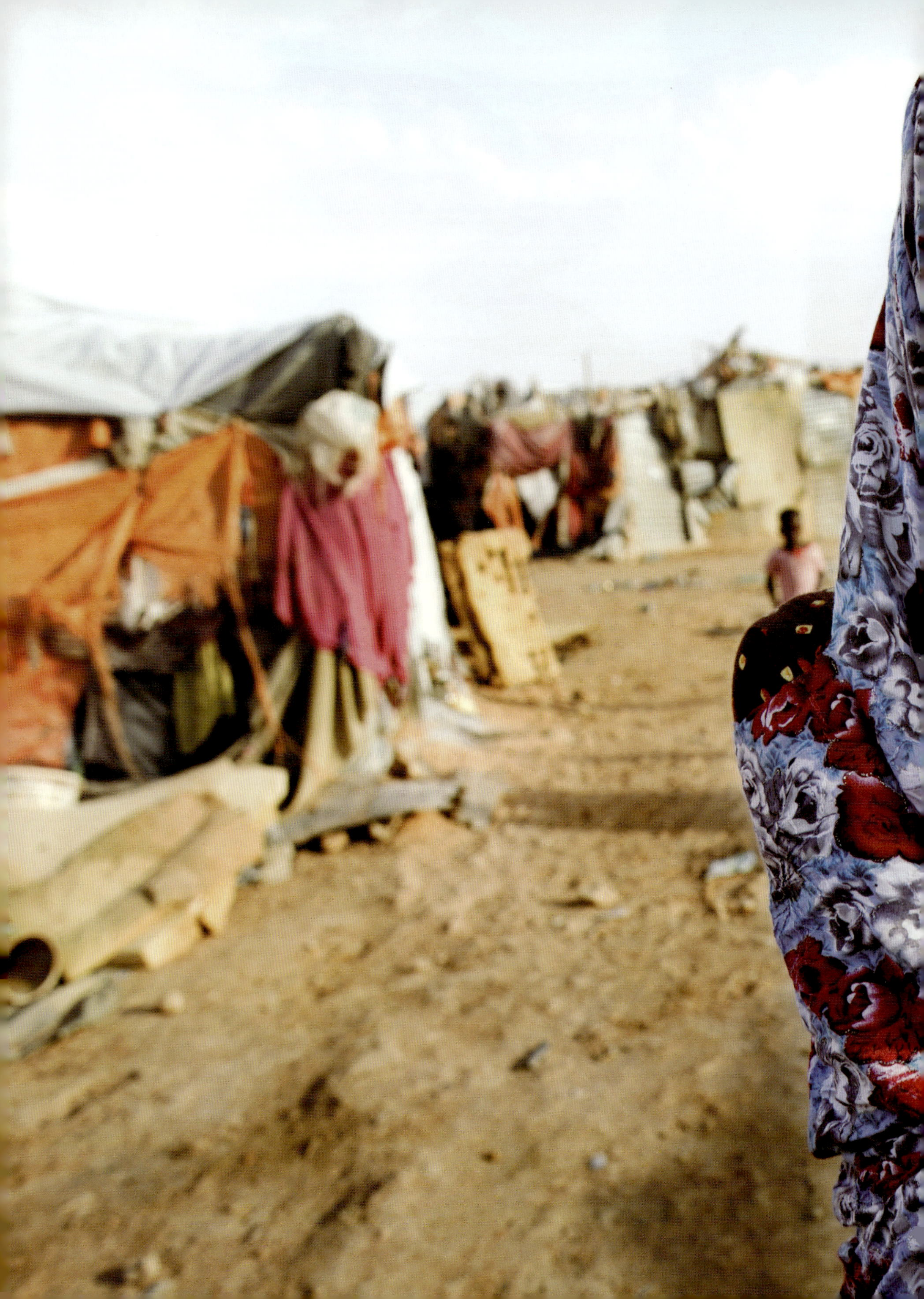

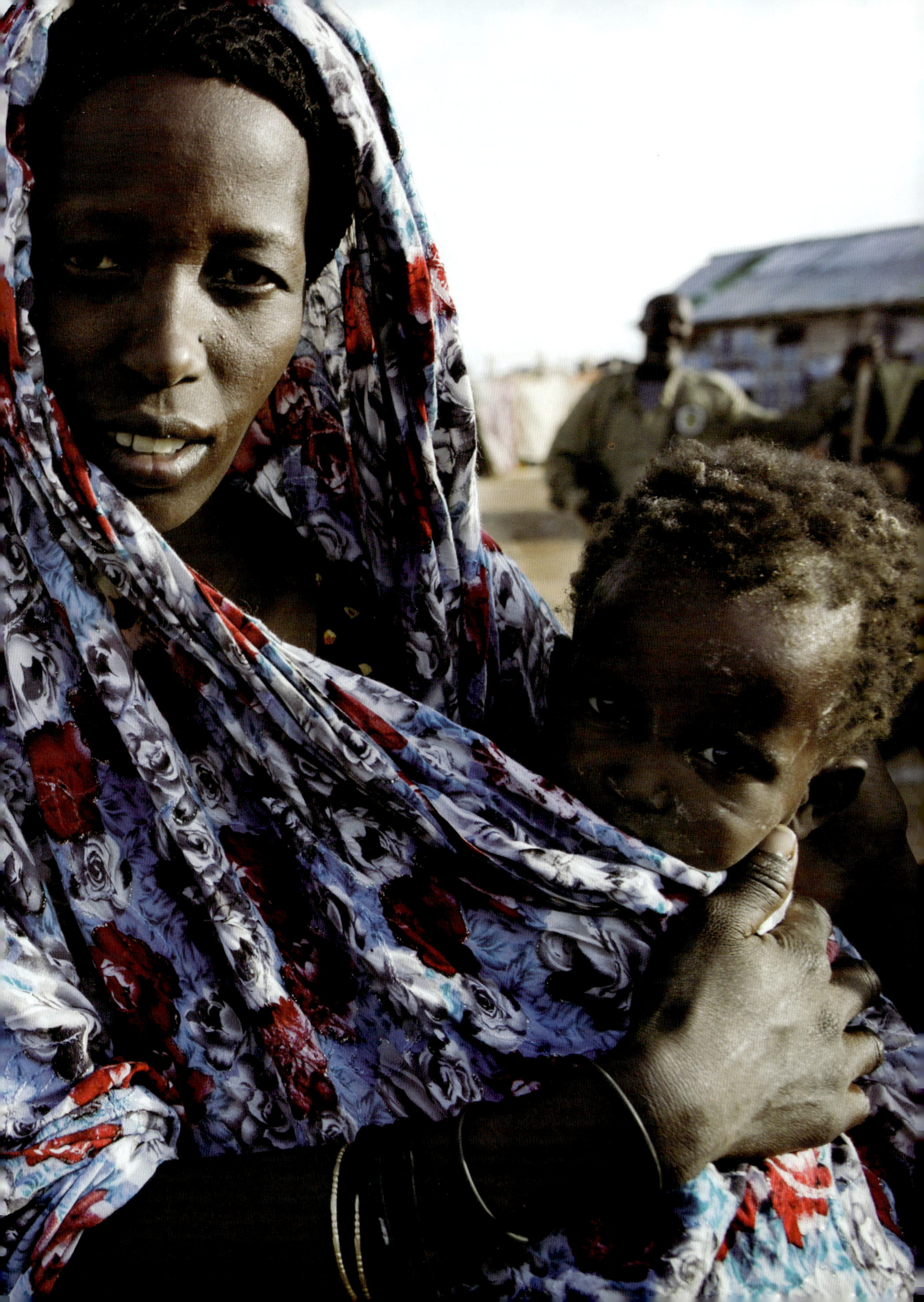

Chapter 6
Eliminating Fragility and Conflict
Serge Michailof

Africa in 2013: Success, Diversity, and Fragility

Thanks to recent progress, Africa is perceived as a new frontier with enormous potential. Nevertheless, the continent is best characterized in 2013 by its diversity and the contrasting trajectories of its individual countries. While 27 countries have already reached middle-income status, others are still prey to economic mismanagement and unresolved political tensions. Some are even left behind, adrift, and caught in conflict traps. Facing economic stagnation, intractable poverty, and civil strife, these countries are usually classified as "fragile." Contrary to expectations, growth alone is not sufficient to cure fragility, and many African countries with strong economic and social performance also have elements of significant fragility.

This chapter tries to go beyond easy categorizations and identifies sources of latent fragility in many African states. The analysis helps identify future constraints to growth and sources of instability in the continent, as well as why some countries seem unable to move out of fragility, failure, and violence. The overall objective is to assess whether and under what conditions these countries can successfully emerge out of such "fragility traps" and allow the continent to decisively move away from fragility and conflict.

The chapter first identifies key characteristics of latent fragility that relate to the social and political organization of many African countries and their specific history. This analysis suggests that latent state fragility is more widespread in Africa than one might think from just looking at broad economic and governance indicators. The chapter then highlights a number of tensions, stresses, and shocks threatening the stability of many African countries, particularly latently fragile ones. It argues that although some challenges may destroy fragile states, they may also force change upon them. It highlights an aggressive agenda for action based on greater political inclusiveness and institution building, and argues that change is not always linear and incremental. Rapid "explosive" types of institutional change may indeed offer new perspectives to fragile countries. The chapter concludes with a vision of an Africa in 2050 that has risen to the challenges and moved out of fragility and associated conflicts. The 2050 vision highlights a clear three-pillar agenda for African leaders: strengthen fragile and conflict-affected countries, diversify the economies to meet the job challenge, and address the specific plight of resource-poor landlocked countries.

Fragile, Conflict-Affected, and Failed States — The Underlying Realities

Process of state formation

Modern states are supposed to exercise a monopoly on the use of force within their territory, perform certain minimal functions for the security and well-being of their citizens, entertain working relations with the international system, and provide law and political order. When such minimal functions are either no longer performed, or imperiled by internal or external shocks, a whole range of state situations can be characterized as "at risk," "fragile," "poorly performing," and, in extreme cases such as Somalia, "failed" or "collapsed." They may also be "conflict-affected" by ongoing or recent, internal or neighboring violent conflicts (Di John 2010).

State formation is a historical process subject to reversal, and fragility, state failures, and civil wars need to be studied in both historical and political perspective. Some states, such as Afghanistan, never consolidated and have never graduated from fragility. Others, such as Côte d'Ivoire, where considerable state- and even nation-building took place in the 1960s and 1970s, "backtracked" and are now in a fragile situation. The history of a state's formation explains its relative position on a theoretical continuum from a chaotic non-state status, such as the feudal system in Europe, to the modern Weberian state. Some states are located at an intermediate "fragile situation" where state institutions have not yet established deep roots. Fragility may also be a deviation from such a continuum and the outcome of specific historical events, leading in the worst circumstances to state collapse.

When nation states have been built over centuries, developed strong institutions, and erased most ethnic, religious, and regional divisions, they have clearly moved out of fragility. When in addition they have over time built political systems recognized as legitimate and a shared identity with a common vision that commands wide internal consensus within the population, their resilience to shocks is considerable. This resilience is lacking in recently established states, where institutions are still shaky, the legitimacy of political systems is subject to controversy, and ethnicity remains an unresolved issue. Most newer states thus retain a latent fragility that can only be reduced over time. Such latent fragility occurs throughout the world but is particularly widespread in Africa because of its colonial history and the relatively recent formation of many states.

In Africa, the historical process of large kingdom and state formation began in Ethiopia in AD 800 and later in West Africa with the kingdom of ancient Ghana (located in present-day Mali) in the 11th century, the Empire of Mali in the 13th century, and the fairly centralized Songhai Empire in the 15th century. Other centralized states also developed in other parts of the continent during the 14th and 15th centuries, such as the Kongo Kingdom in Central Africa (Shillington 1995). However, the process of state formation remained embryonic in most regions.

Beginning in the 16th century, the few centralized kingdoms were either dismantled or their structure was distorted by the slave trade. This chaotic period of constant wars further disorganized local economies and social organization, destroying whatever state authority existed beyond coastal areas.

In the second part of the 19th century, most remaining centralized kingdoms and miniature states were conquered by European powers and organized as colonies. Colonial states developed according to different exploitative and organizational logics, but none tried to attract adhesion from their population in order to build a modern nation state. Most were organized around the export of tropical commodities with the state as "gatekeeper" and the key issue was development and control of export communication lines such as ports, railways, and road networks (Cooper 2002).

The elementary state system was quickly replaced at independence by a supposedly modern state system. However, most borders had been determined by colonial powers and often cut across ethnic and religious boundaries. It should thus be no surprise that state fragility is so common in Africa, since state formation is recent and ethnic and religious diversity remains important. Moreover, state structures have clearly not been devised to build Weberian-type nation states or to command adhesion of the population.

Geographic challenges

Geography has sometimes been an obstacle to the process of state formation. The topography of some countries is too mountainous, remote, or otherwise difficult to penetrate for a state authority to entirely control its territory. Governments, unable to develop or maintain costly road infrastructure in low population density areas such as deep forests and wide deserts, find these areas difficult to control (Herbst 2000). In many colonies, the use of forced labor even pushed populations toward remote areas beyond the control of colonial authorities (Hochschild 1999).

This context helps explain the recent drama in Mali, as no central authority in Bamako has ever been able to control the vast desert expanses of the northern part of the country. Illicit traffic has historically been the norm. Recently, local warlords have developed criminal activities based on drug trafficking and kidnapping. Geography and difficulty in controlling huge and almost empty territories hence explain in part why most Sahelian countries could be considered as latently fragile, whatever their present and expected economic performance.

Effect of wars and conflicts

Conflict can be considered as "development in reverse." For example, after a 10-year conflict Democratc Republic of Congo (DRC) has backtracked to pre-independence levels of GDP per capita and overall well-being for a good part of its population (Prunier 2009; Stearns 2011; Van Reybroucke 2012). However, wars have also been an integral part of the process of state-building, as seen in Europe. State rivalries and almost perpetual conflicts indeed forced European states to develop efficient state organizations and institutions, starting with permanent standing armies and well-organized fiscal and financial systems to fund them. England's early ability in fiscal and debt management explains its successes in the 18th century wars (Reinhart and Rogoff 2009).

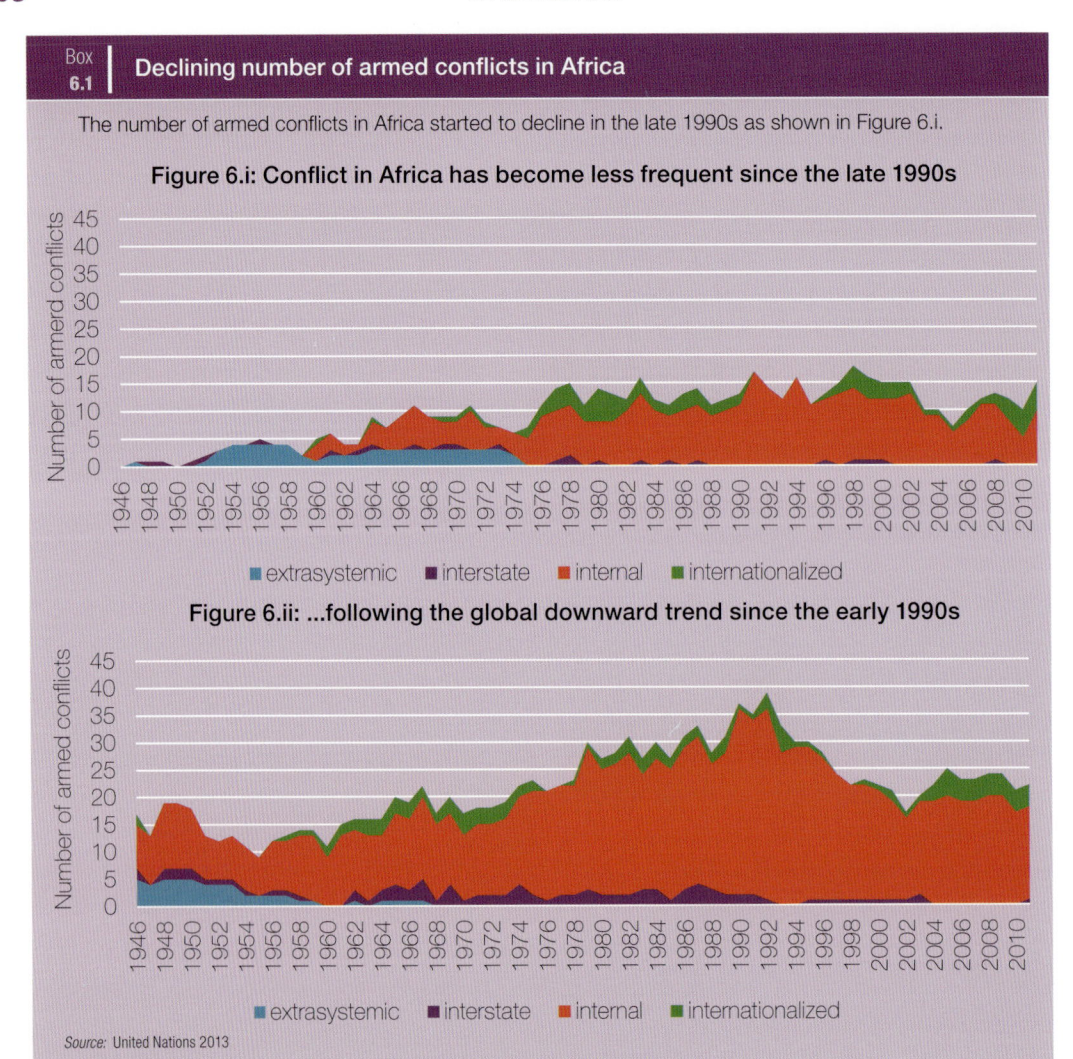

Box 6.1 | Declining number of armed conflicts in Africa

The number of armed conflicts in Africa started to decline in the late 1990s as shown in Figure 6.i.

Figure 6.i: Conflict in Africa has become less frequent since the late 1990s

extrasystemic ▪ interstate ▪ internal ▪ internationalized

Figure 6.ii: ...following the global downward trend since the early 1990s

extrasystemic ▪ interstate ▪ internal ▪ internationalized

Source: United Nations 2013

This is good news for Africa, but three caveats require continued attention:
- The recurrence of conflict in a transition period is a major risk, particularly in Africa where only 15 countries have gone through the last three decades without any armed conflict.
- A new type of conflict with trans-national non-state actors, such as al-Shabaab and al-Qaeda in the Islamic Maghreb, is on the rise in recent years. Capable state institutions that provide basic public services, including public safety, in remote areas are a significant element in preventing such conflicts.
- The decline in the number of conflicts in the rest of the world has been even faster than in Africa (see Figure 6.ii), so Africa's global share of the number of armed conflicts has actually increased.

Building capable and legitimate state institutions, which look after both public safety and livelihood improvement, is essential to address these problems and establish long-term stability.

A key difference during the second part of the 20th century was the shift from interstate wars to the so called "new wars," which are basically civil wars (Van Creveld 1991). Such internal conflicts indeed tend to weaken or break apart states that are still undergoing consolidation instead of strengthening them. In fact, the types of conflicts that have developed in Africa since the 1970s resemble much more the Thirty Years' War in Europe, which wreaked havoc in Central Europe for most of the 17th century, than the 18th and 19th century interstate wars that finally forced European states to consolidate. Just as in Europe before the consolidation of the nation state, in Africa today the distinction between war and organized looting and crime is sometimes blurred, and violence often has primarily predatory objectives. Such conflict may well force some fragile African states to either consolidate or explode and thereby may represent a step in a highly complicated and bloody process of state and nation-building. This may well be the dilemma now confronting the DRC.

Hierarchy of state functions

Indicators of state weakness include the growth of criminal violence, inability to provide basic security, related emergence of warlords, and inability to control borders or significant portions of territory (Rotberg 2003, Ellis 2009). Rotberg suggests a hierarchy of state functions from security; proper institutions to ensure the rule of law, regulate conflicts, and secure property rights; to political participation and political legitimacy; to the provision of basic infrastructure and social services. Others have emphasized both the role of poor economic performance in state breakdown and the role of conflict in destroying economies (Collier and Sambanis 2005; Bannon and Collier 2003). These authors have highlighted the role of poorly managed oil and mineral windfalls and the "resource curse" in state weakness and risks of conflicts.

A country may be weak or even fail in a given dimension of state functions and be strong in others. Some countries, such as Uganda, may have satisfactory economic management and performance, a wide range of public services, strong political participation, and reasonable regime legitimacy, but yet be unable to control some of their territory and provide security in all border areas. Identifying a tipping point when a country's particular weakness leads to serious overall fragility or when such fragility becomes state failure is often hard to determine, impossible to accurately translate into an aggregate "failure index," and largely a matter of judgment.

Despite a lingering conflict in the north with the Lord's Resistance Army, Uganda is definitely not a fragile state. Niger, in contrast, demonstrates strong (mining-driven) growth, fairly sound macro management, a legitimate government, and much progress regarding social service delivery; however, it risks fragility due to its uncontrolled north and to specific stresses and risks such as the unresolved Tuareg issue, extremely rapid demographic growth, a lack of cultivable land, sensitivity to drought, environmental degradation, and proximity to the fragile states of Mali and Libya.

Fragmentation and fragility

Many African states have a wide variety of ethnic groups and sometimes many religions (traditional and modern), in part a result of their artificially built borders. A recognized fault line, which separates Muslim and Christian populations in West, Central, and East Africa, from Senegal and Côte d'Ivoire to Nigeria and Sudan, is now a permanent zone of tension and latent violence. Even though ethnicity sometimes has no clear racial or biological roots, it has often become a social reality, reinforced in the past by deliberate actions of colonial authorities and still today by some African politicians who build their power on fear and ethnic hatred.

States composed of ethnically heterogeneous populations demonstrate greater fragility than states composed of homogeneous populations. This explains, for instance, why ethnically heterogeneous states (such as Yugoslavia) or heterogeneous empires (such as the Austro-Hungarian and Ottoman empires) broke apart so easily. Multiple religions within a given state also create challenges and can complicate the process of state building, as described by Fromkin (1989) for Mesopotamia (now Iraq) in the 1920s. Ethnic, religious, and even cultural heterogeneity clearly create challenges to building resilient states.

In societies fragmented along ethnic or religious lines, particularly when the process of state formation is recent, the first loyalty of an individual beyond one's own family usually goes to the extended family and more broadly to the tribal, ethnic, or religious group. This is true in many African countries, as well as in Afghanistan, Syria, Lebanon, Iraq, and in many countries in the Caucasus. In such contexts, the state and its authority are sometimes viewed with suspicion and even mistrust, which weakens the state's authority and legitimacy and facilitates non-cooperative behavior or even rebellions against centralized political power.

In France, for instance, until the early 20th century, the process of state-building involved an active policy of destruction of all elements of cultural and ethnic diversity, including the deliberate destruction of the Occitan, Breton, and Basque languages. In this context it is interesting to note that Botswana, one of Africa's fastest growing countries, is one of the few African countries that pursued an active policy of nation-building, involving a deliberate policy of reducing ethnic and linguistic differences to strengthen its society's homogeneity.

Despite successive generations of African leaders' efforts since the 1960s and 1970s to build nations and develop a shared societal adhesion, progress in Africa has been uneven. In most ethnically heterogeneous African countries, political affiliations still tend to follow ethnic or religious lines, with Côte d'Ivoire providing a telling illustration. Countries with a more homogeneous society, such as Burkina Faso and Botswana, or with leaders more committed to nation-building, such as Tanzania, have made the most progress. But in many other countries, fragmentation remains the rule, which creates elements of state fragility.

Extractive economic and political institutions

Acemoglu and Robinson (2012) have recently developed a comprehensive theory of state fragility and eventual failure to explain why some nations are prosperous and others remain poor and fail. First, they differentiate between extractive economic institutions, which extract resources from the many for the benefit of a small elite, and inclusive economic institutions, which allow a broad sharing of resources and benefits. Second, they establish a link between economic and political institutions: extractive economic institutions support and are supported by extractive political institutions that reinforce the power of a small elite, while inclusive economic institutions facilitate and are nurtured by inclusive political institutions that distribute political power in a pluralistic manner.

Inclusive political institutions require a certain level of state organization and centralization, which may explain why Sub-Saharan Africa is weak in this regard. Synergies between economic and political institutions create either vicious or virtuous circles. In vicious circles extractive institutions tend to persist. They hamper development and create internal tensions, which lead to political instability as groups excluded from economic and political power fight to obtain access. In virtuous circles, inclusive economic and political institutions create both political stability and an environment conducive to development and the creative destruction that goes along with fast diversified growth.

Acemoglu and Robinson's analysis emphasizes that virtuous and vicious circles are products of history but are not historically determined. Chance, leaders' decisions, and major events ("critical junctures") that disrupt existing political and economic balance may tip a state's destiny one way or the other. However, in their view, there is no clear recipe to trigger such a shift. They provide many compelling analyses of dramatic African spirals leading to state failures due to a combination of extractive economic and political institutions. They emphasize that states that failed in Africa did so because the process of state-building and consolidation began very late in the continent and because the legacy of extractive institutions, which concentrate power and wealth in the hands of a small group that controls the state, opened the way to unrest, strife, and civil war.

Acemoglu and Robinson fully recognize that extractive institutions allow for periods of fast growth but note that such growth is unlikely to be sustained over the long term. They emphasize the unstable nature of regimes that systematically exclude an important fraction of the population from political and economic power and so underline the latent fragility of some African states despite their impressive economic performance.

"Politics of the belly" and "Potemkin" states

State control in post-independence Africa has long been perceived as the fastest and most efficient way to accumulate wealth, and such wealth accumulation is seen as the best way to access or strengthen political power. This process was first described by Bayart (1985) under the generic name of "the politics of the belly." In such states, most state institutions look like standard modern institutions, but behind the façade lies another reality.

This other reality is evident in the presence of deep networks of loyalty. The key purpose of these networks is to use control of the state and its key institutions to extract rents and channel them toward their own group. This tension between loyalty to the group and loyalty to the state is at the heart of what is usually called high-level corruption and explains much of the weakness and inefficiency of African state organizations. Heterogeneous societies exacerbate the resulting inefficiencies, and the weaknesses go a long way toward explaining states' latent fragilities. Many modern African states are hybrid social constructions that retain traditional social structures under modern features (Jacquemot 2013).

In fragmented societies where clans, tribes, ethnic groups, or political parties jockey for control of rents and power, institutions cannot spontaneously become the impersonal social constructions that are common in affluent developed societies. They are highly personalized structures where the representative of a clan, tribe, ethnic group, or political party rules over a clientele. Rules are determined according to one's links with the clan, tribe, ethnic group, or party. Such personalized "rules" have a direct negative impact on the performance of institutions (North 1990). But these mechanisms just reflect the overall state of a society. Hence the "poor governance" or the "neo-patrimonialism"[1] that are associated with these contexts should not be judged on the basis of ethics but on the basis of history and efficiency.

What we usually call corruption is often the rent extraction mechanism from an institution controlled by a specific social group. It is part of a social mechanism. It may even be needed for social stability to "buy" social peace. For the participants, the corrupt one is the individual who diverts part of the rents for his own benefit. In fact, behind the "good governance" concept we tend to project an idealized vision of present-day impersonalized institutions and societies in "advanced" countries. We should be reminded, however, how poor governance was in today's advanced countries just a century ago, and how corrupt were such democracies.

In most heterogeneous, fragile countries, state institutions have a Potemkin dimension. For instance, customs services, ministries of finance, ministries of commerce, energy companies, or port authorities look like ordinary state institutions. They are supposed to collect customs duties, manage public finances, facilitate trade, produce and distribute energy, handle maritime traffic, and, generally speaking, render specific services in the most efficient way to the population at large. If they do not, we tend to believe that their inefficiency is due to management failure or a lack of technical capacity that adequate training and technical assistance will solve. Unfortunately, experience shows that such remedies usually do not work.

Weak state institutions and state fragility

In fragile, heterogeneous states, loyalty to the group is not related to efficiency at delivering public goods to the population at large. Rather, it first requires facilitating preferential access to jobs to one's faction, provision of free services to its clients, money transfers to friends, and award of contracts to cronies. This situation is not specific to Africa. It can be found in many socially heterogeneous societies and explains the gross inefficiency of many state institutions in such contexts.

---

1. Neo-patrimonialism is a concept that emphasizes the confusion between the private and public domains in African states.

In the worst cases, such as Mobutu's Zaire, the state could completely forget the population's expectations as long as rents were extracted and channeled to the right group. Hence the state airline ended up without any aircraft able to fly due to illicit sales of spare parts. The inefficiencies of states' basic institutions induce fragility as they prove unable to provide the basic services expected by their populations — security, law and order, electricity, road maintenance, and basic education. Ineffective states cannot command respect and loyalty from their citizens. Citizens end up relying upon their tribal, ethnic, or religious groups to meet such basic needs, triggering a vicious circle, which requires more loyalty to the group to compensate for the inefficiency of the state. This process has been dramatically evident in Afghanistan since 2002 and largely explains the coalition's failure as described in General McChrystal's 2009 sober assessment.

Unless political leaders are determined to fight against such tendencies and to create a nation going beyond tribal or religious affiliations, which inter alia requires establishing "modern" institutions refusing the tribal or clan logic, the fragmentation of a society along ethnic, tribal, or religious lines translates into global inefficiency of its state institutions and, finally, high state fragility. The fragmentation of most African societies makes state institutions particularly prone to fragility, which in turn has a direct impact on overall state fragility.

Inclusive political systems

Inclusive political systems and broad coalitions may sometimes provide satisfactory answers to state fragility but not always. Inclusive systems can be democratic, as in today's Ghana, or autocratic, as in yesterday's Côte d'Ivoire, where President Houphouët-Boigny took care to personally redistribute the smallest rents and positions among all ethnic groups. Inclusion clearly brings political stability, while exclusion requires repression to provide (usually temporary) stability. It is also useful to distinguish inclusive systems that give everyone a stake and induce investment and innovation from those that distribute just some of the rent to everyone in order to stay in power. The former clearly provides more stability than the latter.

In political systems based on systematic exclusion of specific groups and associated repression, a lack of transparency can easily lead to processes of criminalization of the state, as highlighted by Bayart, Ellis, and Hibou (1999). In these circumstances, all state institutions may be controlled by a particular minority (or even a majority group in a winner-takes-all philosophy), and the associated rents are channeled in total opacity for the leader of the group's benefit. Such states have an inherent institutional inefficiency and overall fragility, and are only sustained by the capacity of their security apparatus, which is controlled by the commanding group. When the security apparatus fails, the regime and the state can collapse under any unexpected shock. If the security apparatus is fairly strong, as was the case in Syria, a shock may lead to a lengthy full-scale civil war.

Should one believe that democratic inclusive political systems are necessarily more efficient, more stable, and less prone to fragility? This is not necessarily the case in heterogeneous societies. Contrary to expectations, standard (superficial) democratic processes, such as those quickly introduced in the 1990s, do not solve such problems. Once elected, the faction in power may quickly learn how to rig elections to remain in control. In such cases, inclusion remains superficial and elusive (Collier 2009). However, even when elections are conducted under a fair process, in a multi-ethnic context with political parties organized along ethnic lines, experience shows that superficial democracy may make matters worse. While a clever dictator may be able to redistribute part of the rents to all ethnic and social groups in order to consolidate his power, an elected president cannot redistribute "his" rents as such redistribution would strengthen his opposition.[2] Thus, elections may exacerbate exclusion instead of fostering inclusion.

Inclusive politics and state fragility

Even in inclusive coalition governments, inclusion may only be a redistribution of rents through a sharing of state institutions as booty for each group to exploit. The same inefficiencies would occur, driving the state into the same fragilities. This situation frequently arises in post-conflict situations in which no clear winner has emerged, and the leading political or ethnic group may try to buy allegiance from other factions by distributing state institutions and positions. In doing so, the group ethnicizes and politicizes key state institutions, from the most financially rewarding (ministry of finance, customs, port authority, key parastatals) to the smallest organizations where only a few per diems can be expected. Again, Potemkin institutions flourish under such circumstances, despite democratic appearances and attempts at inclusiveness.

This process runs contrary to all elementary management rules governing modern institutional efficiency, including the selection of managers based on merit, human resource management based on results, systematic controls requiring transparency, and principles of management for state institutions largely dissociated from ethnic, family, partisan, or religious logic. By "modern" institutions, we mean institutions that are not based on personal relationships and cronyism, but require impersonalized relations. Of course, the merit-based, result-oriented system is to some extent an ideal, and countries may be located on a continuum that goes from this ideal to the worst cronyism.

In heterogeneous countries where factional, ethnic, or religious groups fight for control, obstacles arise to building efficient institutions. During the long period when ethnicity or tribalism permeates the society, selection of leaders and promotion of key managers cannot be dissociated from social and political constraints. Hence countries must manage a complex dual system where both merit and ethnicity (or religious affiliation) need to be taken into account. Their situation and constraints are similar to those faced by multilateral institutions or private multinational companies, but in a context where the requirement for efficiency is usually much weaker and ethnicity much stronger.

---

2. Hence the motto from the Ivorian opposition in the mid-1990s: "Bedié ne partage pas" ("Bedie does not share") is not related to his character but to the shift to an elected system of government where money buys votes.

Clearly not all heterogeneous societies fit this description, but rather they fall along a continuum ranging from a modern, merit-based, efficiency-determined logic, as found in Sweden, to a completely closed, opaque, clan-determined system, as found in today's Guinea-Bissau. Elections may help put efficiency higher on the priority list, but are not a guarantee for engineering modernization process that will move state institutions out of personalized relations and cronyism. This is particularly the case if a regime is weak due to a difficult exit from conflict that requires building complex political alliances and rewarding allies, if perceived lack of government legitimacy will force the commanding group to considerable compromises, or if the state leader still only understands his political role as being a mediator among factions with corruption and rent distribution as his key instrument, as in Afghanistan. Finally, specific constitutional arrangements may also impose an explicit sharing of state responsibilities and institutions among political, ethnic, or religious groups, as in present day Lebanon since the Taief Accord, which ended the civil war.[3]

Preliminary conclusions on state fragility

- *Many African states are unfortunately prone to some level of latent fragility* because they have had little time to develop the deep roots needed to establish a state's resilience, particularly a sense of nationhood and common destiny; inclusive political systems offering political and economic opportunities to all segments of the population; and modern, efficient state institutions free from the cronyism characteristic of non-inclusive political systems. Latent fragility is enhanced by the frequent fragmentation and heterogeneity of societies and the strength of ethnic, tribal, or religious links that permeate social and political life. Heterogeneous societies are especially at risk of fragility if the logic that governs the state is biased by partisan, ethnic, or religious factors and drifts toward cronyism.
- *Key issues are the level of government inclusiveness and legitimacy,* which democracies limited to periodic presidential and legislative elections do not necessarily address, and *the quality of the main state institutions*. Fragile states have fragile state institutions, and the level of a state's fragility may depend on the relative efficiency/inefficiency of its state institutions, particularly its sovereign institutions (army, police, justice, and local government), which are supposed to provide security and law and order, and financial institutions, which are supposed to fund these basic functions. Also critical are the key economic institutions that regulate trade, transport, and access to food; the key social service institutions that provide education and health; and the institutions that provide basic infrastructure services such as water and energy, access to housing, and key urban services.
- *The most fragile states clearly have weak and inefficient sovereign institutions* and may easily collapse under minor shocks, as demonstrated in Mali in 2012. In non-inclusive political systems, particularly in heterogeneous societies, if a specific group has little legitimacy but total control

---

3. Switzerland, paradoxically, is in fact a similar case; its constitution historically developed in a conflict context in the early 19th century provides detailed specific responsibilities and privileges to its different ethnic/linguistic groups which tends to reduce state institution's efficiency. A strong democratic pressure fortunately makes up for the related loss in efficiency!

over the political system, the state apparatus, and all the rent-generating activities, then the state is inherently very fragile regardless of its its short term economic performance. If a regime proves unwilling to share a significant part of its political and economic power with other factions/parties/ethnic groups, trouble is to be expected. In such circumstances, stability depends on the strength of the security apparatus or exceptional oil or mineral wealth, which allows some redistribution without weakening the faction in power, such as in Angola.

- *Inclusive political systems may lower the latent fragility* linked to a society's heterogeneity, but democracy and political inclusiveness do not guarantee state institution's efficiency and hence state resilience. An element of deep fragility is always present if the rules governing changes in leadership are unclear or prone to changes at the will of the head of state. This explains, for instance, the uncertainty and even anxiety of investors and the population at-large in usually stable countries as election deadlines approach. In post-conflict countries where no clear winner has emerged, even in supposedly democratic contexts, whenever state institutions are distributed among factions as booty in order to buy allegiances and hopefully build peace, institutions remain inefficient empty shells. They are prey to rent-seeking mechanisms that cannot support economic growth, but rather act as an impediment. High state fragility is the rule in all such cases and moving out of such fragility traps is always a challenge.

- *The deeply ingrained character of a state's latent fragility explains why moving out of fragility is so difficult* (Michailof 2011a). Fragility indeed goes to the heart of the social, ethnic, and religious structure of a society: its history and its political system. External exhortations and pressures are unlikely to help. A society's ethnic or religious heterogeneity is a given, resistant to any international prescription, and may require careful political management for centuries, as in Spain with the still unresolved Basque and Catalan problems. A society's political system is the product of history and the local balance of power. Reforming state institutions in such contexts requires going beyond usual public sector reforms or the rather ineffectual provision of technical assistance. A deliberate political decision to move away from cronyism in order to drastically improve state institutions' efficiency and to improve the state's capacity to weather external shocks is needed. It is not an easy decision given that it impacts internal political equilibriums. In this context, the fragility rankings, which emphasize only weak policies and governance or low growth rates, tend to focus on symptoms and so miss the essential historical and political dimensions.

- *Times of crisis, the "critical junctures"* described by Acemoglu and Robinson (2012) — such as changes of regimes, arrival of a new generation of leaders, external threats, or a combination of such factors — *are usually necessary to move out of latent fragility* and build resilient states. Building a resilient state also requires a strong will and clear perception by the political leadership of the road ahead and the objectives to be met. Mustafa Kemal's reformation of the collapsed state that emerged out of the ruins of the Ottoman Empire after the First World War may be one of the best historical examples of a fast exit out of a failed state situation. In Africa, the way Museveni led a collapsed post-Idi Amin Uganda out of fragility may also be considered as a model.

- *The type of latent state fragility described is not incompatible with basic economic reforms and strong growth.* Strong growth may over time help reduce the most obvious elements of a state's fragility since economic growth usually triggers the type of interaction with a strengthened civil society and private sector that will require a strengthened bureaucracy, as described by Levy (2012). A good example is Cambodia, which inherited a collapsed state from the Khmer Rouge and put together afterwards a poorly performing state system riddled with cronyism. Nevertheless, Cambodia is now trying to reform some of its faulty state institutions to meet the demands of a dynamic economy driven by Chinese investments. It is only in the most extreme situations of cronyism and abysmal governance, as in former Zaire or today's Zimbabwe, that the economy is plundered to the point that growth is impossible and fragility may turn to failure.

- *Latent state fragility may only come to light when states are confronted by specific tensions, stresses, and shocks.* The main challenge confronting many African countries in the coming decades will be how states with elements of latent fragility react to future tensions, stresses, and shocks. These tensions will be generated by exceptional demography, increasing demand for jobs, environmental degradation of agricultural land and associated deforestation, and huge expected and unexpected changes in the world economy. Will these still fragile states adapt quickly enough? Will they modernize their state institutions fast enough to meet these coming shocks? Some of the upcoming stresses linked to demography are easy to identify. But mitigation measures require vision that goes well beyond the usual short-term political horizon. Will such challenges force reforms and adaptations or will they swamp these countries, driving them backward into crisis and conflict? Most African states will indeed soon be confronted by the kind of challenges that according to Toynbee (1972) could either strengthen or destroy civilizations.

Future Shocks May Either Destroy or Force Change on Fragile States

Chapter 2 identifies a number of drivers of change — demographics, oil and mineral wealth, rapid urbanization, and climate change affecting agriculture — which already affect, for good or ill, many African countries and whose impact will increase in the coming decades. Other chapters address the threats of imbalanced population and job growth, corruption-inducing oil and mineral wealth, poorly managed urban areas, and failed agricultural transformation. It will be particularly challenging to address these challenges in fragile and conflict-affected states. This section identifies an agenda for action based upon a typology of fragile states, including innovative approaches to modernize state institutions. It concludes that, in the next decades, many factors will force change upon even reluctant reformers, and this change can help the continent move out of fragility and conflict.

Success stories may easily unravel

A number of worrying internal and external factors will most likely increase in intensity over the coming decades. In the recent past, some of these factors led countries that were previously perceived as stable and good performers into internal strife and conflict. A good example is Côte d'Ivoire, a success story for 20 years, where a benevolent dictatorship hid flawed political institutions and lack of consensus, while massive foreign technical assistance hid deep institutional weaknesses. Economic success increased massive internal migration and immigration from neighboring countries in a context of already high demographic growth and exacerbated land issues among heterogeneous communities.[4] An inadequate macro answer to a commodity shock led to a long period of economic stagnation that exacerbated urban unemployment. The combination of these stresses and shocks finally threw the country into 10 years of civil conflict (Michailof 2005). Deep scars left by the conflict and the cumulative unresolved problems due to this lost decade put the country at risk despite its recent economic successes.

The demographic dynamic that was critical in Côte d'Ivoire's crisis raises serious challenges for many African countries. The poorest states will be confronted by huge education and social infrastructure problems related to the high ratio of young-to-total population. Two specific critical problems linked to demography are the uncontrolled development of very large cities and the environmental degradation of fragile rural areas. Urban environments as emphasized in Chapter 13 have indeed already become highly flammable due to a combination of lack of jobs, poor urban management, and food price instability. This situation may further deteriorate. Tensions are also rising in many rural areas as described in Chapter 11. Demography and urban bias indeed often lead to widespread land degradation rather than agricultural intensification. Controlling land degradation will require massive investment in knowledge and appropriate policies that are commonly lacking in most countries. In such contexts stagnant agriculture is likely to exacerbate ethnic tensions (National Intelligence Council 2012). In the worst cases, such as in the northern parts of the Sahel, agricultural systems may progressively collapse.

Daunting challenges in the Sahel

The recent collapse of Mali highlighted the magnitude of the challenges confronting Sahelian countries which, from Mauritania to Chad, cover an area about 10 times the size of France. In most Sahelian countries, years of accumulated neglect regarding rural development, an issue that has been regularly highlighted since the early 1980s (Giri 1983; Giri 1989; Belloncle 1985; Bonfils 1987), have now become a huge problem in a context of land scarcity, deforestation, and land degradation (Billaz 2013). Unresolved ethnic and political problems add to the present and future challenges (Michailof 2011b).

Behind its façade of superficial democracy and Potemkin institutions, Mali was already vulnerable because of deeply ingrained corruption and the involvement of some of its elite in illicit trafficking. The return from Libya of a few hundred disgruntled Malian mercenaries of Tuareg origin after the collapse of

---

4. Between 1950 and 2010 the population in Côte d'Ivoire was multiplied by a factor of 7. The same ratio applied to France would put the French population at 360 million.

the Qaddafi regime brought additional instability to an already uncontrolled north. This was enough to topple the regime and send a shock wave throughout the whole of Sahel. This unexpected shock wave is now a marker which highlights deep latent fragilities throughout the region.

Although agricultural potential is not fully realized in the south, the situation is worse in the north where the traditional economy based upon extensive agriculture, small-scale irrigation, and herding is collapsing due to the recurrence of droughts, land degradation, and lack of off-farm activities (Dayak 1992; Thebaud 1988). The ongoing rural crisis is compounded by unresolved ethnic prejudices and a weakening of local state institutions: local police, governments, and justice are often so weak, corrupt, and mismanaged that resentment against state authority is growing. Ethnic clashes have already multiplied between farmers and herders. In what were until recently easy-to-control neighborhoods, quarrels where a few spears were drawn have now become bloody confrontations as the price of Kalashnikovs falls thanks to the Libyan "weapons supermarket."

The young now prefer emigrating or turning to trans-Saharan traffic: stolen cars, cigarettes, and petroleum products coming from Algeria. Customers can even order the brand and color of their cars (stolen in Europe). Nowadays, more and more drugs, mostly cocaine, transit from Latin America through Guinea-Bissau, Benin, or Nigeria and then through the Sahara toward European markets. At the same time as state legitimacy tends to collapse, migration and new communications technology make abysmal poverty and increased inequality unacceptable to younger rural generations, exacerbate frustrations, and make religious extremism attractive (Jacquemot and Michailof 2013).

Northern Mali, covering an area the size of France, was, until the French military intervention, entirely controlled by four main groups of insurgents who had defeated the Malian army. Two of them, Al-Qaeda in the Islamic Maghreb (AQIM) and Movement for Oneness and Jihad in West Africa (MUJOA), are openly connected to al-Qaeda and heavily involved in organized crime, drug trafficking, and kidnapping. They maintain contacts with other rebel groups that operate in Mauritania and the north of Niger, the terrorist Boko Haram sect in Nigeria, and remnants from AQIM's Algerian predecessor, the Salafist Group for Preaching and Combat (GSPC), and benefit from safe havens in the Libyan Fezzan.

In the northern part of Niger, most of the Central African Republic (CAR), north of Cameroon, and parts of Chad and Mauritania, "road robbers" (*coupeurs de routes*) hamper trade and are a constant source of insecurity. Until now, the standard response to such rural insecurity has been ill-conceived and poorly planned military actions. As a result, huge regions in the northern part of the Sahel have now become grey areas where the state's authority is disintegrating as officials can no longer reside or travel safely (Ngoupande 1997).

The parallel between the northern parts of the Sahel with Afghanistan is striking in this respect and has been highlighted, for instance, in the Algerian press as early as September 2010, long before the collapse of Mali (Tlemcani 2010). Despite obvious cultural differences, the two regions are confronted with a similar demographic impasse: 3 percent population growth in a context of severe land and environmental constraints. Their rural populations are confronted with similar issues of land degradation, migration, weak local governments, and lack of support for agriculture and livestock development. Wide Sahelian regions can drift toward a state of anarchy. Such scenarios are now seriously debated among worried national and international intelligence and security circles as no one can predict how the global Sahelian situation will evolve after the French military intervention in Mali (Chevenement and Larcher 2013).

Taking a long-term perspective, the situation of the whole sub-region is worrying. The cumulative population of Niger, Burkina Faso, Mali, and Chad was 49 million in 2005 and will be about 154 million by 2050 (Ferry 2007). Will the ongoing development of oil and mining resources and the expected surge in export services and information technology (IT) provide the millions of urban jobs needed for an exceptionally young population by 2050? Will booming coastal countries, such as Côte d'Ivoire, Ghana, Nigeria, and Cameroon accept new massive inflows of Sahelian immigrants after they already expelled them by the tens of thousands several times over the last decades?

Beware of unexpected shocks

It is clear that African countries are following highly diverse paths. Average per capita income currently varies in a ratio of 1 to almost 100 between the DRC and Equatorial Guinea. Tensions and stresses are unlikely to lessen and will mostly affect fragile countries over the coming decades, and no African country will be completely immune. This risk is demonstrated by Tunisia, which was fairly ethnically homogeneous and had strong state institutions, and which enjoyed political stability, good "doing-business" indicators, and a diversified economy already entering world value chains. It unfortunately also had a corrupt and non-inclusive regime, state capture by those close to power, a high level of unemployment, and a fragile agricultural sector.

Even growth can create tension, as seen in China and other fast-growing countries. The magnitude of expected tensions due to a widening gap in income and wealth in the next 40 years in the African continent (see Chapter 7) should be a source of major concern in the light of the widespread latent fragility. All capital cities in Africa have been thoroughly transformed during the last decades. However, beyond the vibrant urban centers where business is booming, tensions are also building up. They are building up in sprawling slums that no visitor can discover since no road reaches them. They are building up in poorly controlled rural areas where agriculture has been neglected and security is deteriorating. In the past, no one cared much about these regions. The widespread circulation of AK-47s and rampaging jihadist militants have now changed the context (International and Development Studies 2009). Controlling such tensions and their spillover effects over the coming decades will be one of the major challenges confronting the continent. The collapse of the Libyan regime contributed to the unexpected collapse of latently fragile Mali. Will Mali stabilize and recover its balance? Or will latently fragile Niger be the next to fall? Will still-politically-fragile neighboring Côte d'Ivoire be affected?

The weakness of key sovereign state institutions is also creating opportunities for organized crime and facilitating a worrying integration of local criminal networks with international crime. Piracy has become a highly profitable business along the Horn of Africa and evolved into a sophisticated high-tech activity mobilizing financing from the Gulf. A similar development is now taking place in the Gulf of Guinea and is becoming a serious concern for both international maritime traffic and neighboring countries from Togo to Cameroon (International Crisis Group 2012). West Africa, as already noted, has become the main zone of transit for cocaine between Latin America and Western Europe. The Niger Delta is a lawless area where organized gangs ransom oil companies and kidnap wealthy individuals.

Addressing these new challenges will require fixing some of the states' weaknesses in their security apparatuses and addressing the opaque links between organized crime and influential political networks. In a continent going through the stresses of major demographic and economic changes, the magnitude of criminal events should not come as a surprise. Over the coming decades, it will be critical to address these challenges and not allow them to swamp the concerned governments' will and capacity to reform.

Fragility: Subjective concept but widespread commodity in Africa

Assessing fragility implies subjective judgments on likely outcomes, such as the expected resilience of a given political system and the likely efficiency of its state institutions when confronted with stress or shocks. These matters are obviously not easy to quantify despite recent attempts by experienced economists (Guillaumont and Guillaumont Jeanneney 2009). Scholars and professionals alike accept that political and economic governance factors are crucial (Gnessoto and Grevi 2006). The preferred option may still be to use the best judgment of political scientists on selective subjective criteria. These criteria can be organized around three main issues: politics, institutions and governance, and the magnitude of ongoing and expected challenges and likely ability to address them.

Regarding politics, key criteria are the country's history and its past and present leaders' success at building a nation with shared values and a common vision; the level of ethnic, religious, and cultural homogeneity of the society and the persistence of deep ethnic, religious, or cultural tensions; the degree of control of sovereign institutions over the country's entire territory; the level of inclusiveness of the political system; and the degree of consensus among the population regarding the regime.

Regarding institutions and governance, key criteria are the magnitude of high-level corruption and the connection of the political elite with local organized crime and international criminal networks; the impact of cronyism in key state institutions; the magnitude of internal rent-extracting mechanisms; and the related impact on institutions' efficiency at delivering services.

Regarding the magnitude of expected challenges and ability to address them, key criteria are the likely resilience of sovereign institutions to shocks such as spillovers from neighboring conflicts; the magnitude of the urban slum issue and government capacity to address this problem; the government's capacity in delivering basic services, from health to electricity; the unemployment situation; the fragility or resilience of the agricultural sector and the quality of agricultural policies and institutions; and the ability of the agricultural sector to provide efficient support to farmers, address land degradation and environmental destruction, and promote an orderly modernization and intensification process.

A clear lesson is that latent fragility in Africa is much more widespread than a superficial GDP growth-centered analysis would lead one to believe. Mali had an annual per capita GDP growth of 2.2 percent from 2000 until 2011 and an internationally acclaimed multiparty democracy. Unfortunately, it also had red flags for most of the other listed criteria. Such latent fragility explains why it collapsed under the shock of a few thousand jihadists.

Action Agenda

Many African countries suffer from some kind of latent fragility. The agenda for action will differ across countries depending on the nature and depth of each country's fragility. Hence a typology is useful for framing the agenda for action. Five main categories of fragile countries emerge from the above discussion:

1. Countries with unresolved political problems;
2. Landlocked countries with a low agricultural resource base or an inadequate use of it;
3. Conflict-affected countries;
4. Countries suffering from deep governance issues and non-inclusive political systems; and
5. Failed states and countries at war.

Political challenge in Category 1: Change the system, not just the elites in power

In the first category, in which growth potential is held back by unresolved political problems, the political agenda needs to be the priority. Any major political change should thus aim not only at replacing existing political elites but also at changing systems based on cronyism and exclusion. In this context, the standard exhortation to democracy is insufficient. Democracy certainly, but what type of democracy? Democracy in socially and ethnically fragmented countries has to take into account the specific needs of all minority groups and to keep in mind the need for a fair sharing of resources and political power among all segments of the society. Mechanisms need to be devised so that one faction does not misuse democratic processes to monopolize political power and rents, as was successfully done in Switzerland in the early 19th century.

African political scientists should now focus on how to build inclusive democratic systems in socially heterogeneous and fragmented societies. For example, restoring a centralized Malian state but refusing to take into account the specific concerns of the Tuareg and Arab populations could lead to a "Thirty Years' War." Grassroots democracy at village or district levels, decentralization, administrative de-concentration, the buildup of transparent checks and balances, appropriate selection processes for managerial positions in the bureaucracy, and many other subjects should be at the core of such research. The research should also take into account non-African experiences. Many non-African ethnically fragmented societies have been confronted with similar challenges. Why has Afghanistan largely failed in this respect?

What are the lessons to be drawn from a fairly successful Georgia? The key challenge will be to combine administrative efficiency and a fair sharing of power among ethnic and religious groups, an area where Lebanon, for instance, has largely failed.

Another issue will be the role of regional and continent-wide bodies to seriously press for political reforms. Political instability is a regional public bad, one that crosses borders due to refugees and arms smuggling. In the future regional bodies such as Economic Community of West African States (ECOWAS) or Southern African Development Company (SADC) cannot ignore the threat to regional political stability posed by exclusion and cronyism in one of their member countries. Peer pressure, soft power through the media, and economic, as well as political sanctions will have to be used in order to force political reform and changes in behavior in neighboring countries that put regional stability at risk. Such pressures will need to be much more aggressive than in the past when tolerance and non-intervention were the rule despite blatant corruption, mismanagement, and misbehavior.

Economic challenge in Category 2: Using natural resource rents wisely

Landlocked countries with weak agricultural resource bases cover wide expanses where considerable oil and mineral resources are already exploited, as in Chad and Niger, or have been identified. The expected mining bonanza can be perceived as an easy way out of present budget constraints and economic hardships. However, due to their exceptional demography, the critical problem for these countries is job creation (Herderschee, Mukoko, and Tschimenga 2012). As these sectors provide very few jobs, the high growth rates associated with oil or mining will not automatically lead to political stability.

The risk for these countries is to follow the path of least resistance and let oil or mining income play its usual role, leading to debilitating Dutch disease and high-level corruption. Oil and mining income will of course drive high investment in infrastructure and some social expenditure, but no level of oil-driven public investment in infrastructure can sustain the needed level of job creation. The challenge has many facets. Dutch disease is likely to destroy agriculture and small and medium enterprises (SMEs) where the potential for job creation is the highest. Being landlocked, these countries will find it difficult to significantly integrate with international industrial value chains. Finally, the weak or poorly managed agricultural resource base will require sophisticated approaches due to soil fragility and lack of water in a context of global warming. In such heavily constrained contexts, the agenda for action will require an emphasis on agriculture and services.

Regarding agriculture, it will be critical to reconstruct the dilapidated state institutions in charge of overall agricultural policy, agricultural research, extension, and community development. A key issue will be to reconnect farming systems with their urban markets through appropriate rural road networks and price policies. Appropriate exchange rate policies will be needed to counteract the usual appreciation of the real effective exchange rate. These countries need to refuse the early Algerian model based upon neglect of both agriculture and private SMEs that contributed to the Algerian civil war in the 1990s. More broadly, the oil bonanza needs to also fund appropriate social expenditure in rural areas including access to safe water and electricity, to help retain an important fraction of the young in rural areas.

In the service sector, in the coming 40 years, the potential for revolutionary change is considerable. Progress in IT already allows Sahelian countries to compete in the international call center service market. But these countries could learn much in the coming decade from the Indian approach in the IT sector. They also need to carefully study the Philippine labor export model to prepare an ambitious emigration strategy of skilled and highly skilled personnel. Just as the Philippines correctly identified global job opportunities for skilled personnel and developed specific training programs to meet this demand, similar strategies will be needed for Sahelian countries to benefit from the opportunities offered by an aging Europe. Already many nurses and medical doctors in European hospitals are Africans, which may be just the beginning of a wide transfer of skilled labor from the Sahel to Europe.

Political challenge in Category 3: Build strong and efficient state institutions focusing on sovereign institutions and security

Fragile states have fragile state apparatuses. Fragile states coming out of long internal conflicts and mismanagement are frequently confronted with a huge reconstruction agenda. Unless they can considerably strengthen their institutions or rebuild them from scratch, little progress is to be expected. Weak finance ministries will be unable to raise the taxes needed to fund the state apparatus and channel resources toward line ministries and other state bodies. Weak police and judicial systems will be unable to restore security, thus hampering private investment. Weak technical ministries will be unable to maintain infrastructure, devise proper sector policies, and implement or supervise development programs. Weak social ministries will be unable to provide or organize the type of quality services in health and education expected by the population. Weak armies will, finally, be tempted by coups.

While the financial and technical aspects of modernizing state institutions may be tricky, the core issue is political will. Cronyism is incompatible with modern, efficient state institutions. Change will be resisted by existing political forces but is likely to be forced upon them by the magnitude of inefficiencies and strong demand from a more educated population. Information technology has already transformed most of the world into a village. In the next 40 years, the present mismanagement of state institutions will no longer be tolerated. A specific issue in these countries will be the reform of the security sector. Along with access to food, water, and shelter, security is by far the first request of populations regularly confronted with looting, kidnapping, assaults, rape, and murder. In this context, modernizing key sovereign institutions, including the police, the local judicial system, the prison system, local government and civil administration, and finally the army, is badly needed.

International political challenge in Category 4: Support internal agents of change

Countries suffering from deep governance issues and non-inclusive political systems will soon become regional problems and so challenge the principle of non-interference in other countries' internal affairs that has been at the core of international law since the 17th century. Since outright military intervention is ruled out for political and ethical reasons and unlikely to help much in this respect, regional and continent wide-institutions such as ECOWAS, SADC, or the African Union (AU) will have to use soft power to press for change in these countries. The strategy followed by the Soros Foundation in Eastern Europe to support local civil society organizations, local universities, and think tanks provides interesting examples for consideration. Development of pan-African media along the lines of the Al Jazeera model would also help disseminate common values across borders. Specific African strategies should be devised by Africans to avoid clumsy interference of outside actors.

The challenge will be to create a continent-wide environment where non-inclusive political systems will be denounced and misbehaviour in governance will be systematically and internationally reported. In the past, corrupt African dictators supported each other just as royal families supported each other in the aftermath of the Congress of Vienna in 1815 Europe. Expansion of democracy in Africa is expected to produce a regional environment hostile to both dictatorship and gross misbehaviour in governance. The European construction in this regard should be considered a possible model where a mix of peer pressure, public opinion pressure, and political sanctions have succeeded in countering attempts at restoring dictatorial regimes. The pressure of international bodies, including a more aggressive stance regarding transparency in oil and mining contracts and revenues, and support to initiatives such as the Extractive Industries Transparency Initiative (EITI) and the Natural Resource Charter would greatly help. The attitude of China will be critical and its long term interests will hopefully lead to support for such transparency.

Complex global challenge in Category 5: Reconstruct failed or collapsed states

There are neither quick fixes nor common rules to reconstruct failed or collapsed states and each case is specific. However, benign neglect from regional institutions and the international community will not help. The Mali case tends to show that some type of regional and/or international military intervention based on ad hoc alliances may be necessary, taking into account that, beyond military action, success is linked to a proper build-up of a new political consensus and the construction of a modern and efficient state apparatus.

The weakness of many UN peacekeeping missions, as illustrated in 2012 by the UN Organization Stabilization Mission in the Democratic Republic of the Congo (MONUSCO) in the Kivu when confronted by the M23 rebellion, should be seriously addressed. Clearer and more aggressive rules of engagement and a greater focus on effective military capacity are required. Permanent stand-by African military forces may need to be established under an AU umbrella in order to confront the type of threat that caused the collapse of Mali. Logistics and air support will have to be provided for some time by external powers. Finally, there is much to learn about state-building from the mistakes made in Afghanistan (Michailof 2010a; Michailof 2010b), where the efforts to reconstruct a proper state apparatus did not start seriously before 2008, which was much too late given the deterioration in overall security.

Building efficient state institutions

Out of the previous typology and associated agenda for action, it is easy to see that, despite their diversity, fragile countries are all confronted with common challenges. Some challenges have long been identified, such as the urgent need to provide jobs and address the governance problem. This section will focus on a specific and complex issue: how to build modern, efficient state institutions, including modern efficient sovereign institutions to reassert control over uncontrolled territory. This crucial starting step will, in turn, facilitate other tasks. With efficient state institutions, sound policies will be easier to define and implement, talents and resources will be easier to attract, and fragile countries can decisively move out of their fragile situation.

Building efficient state institutions is a difficult and controversial issue, but an issue on which an energetic government can act (see Box 6.2). It is a difficult subject because we cannot just "engineer" institutions according to a standard blueprint as Brian Levy (2012) has reminded us, referring to North, Wallis and Weingast (2009).

> **Box 6.2 | Building institutions that are inclusive and legitimate in the eyes of local people (by Ryutaro Murotani)**
>
> Successful state-building implies strengthening both state capacity and legitimacy. Building legitimacy is an especially difficult task because it is deeply affected by perceptions. Inclusive institutions are therefore important to foster a sense of fairness among the population (Takeuchi, Murotani, and Tsunekawa 2011). Building formal institutions, however, does not automatically nurture people's trust. Three key considerations are important for connecting institution building to people's everyday lives: horizontal inequalities, protection and empowerment, and local perceptions:
> - Horizontal inequalities, the inequalities between different identity groups, are one of the major causes of violent conflicts. They can create political instability, particularly when a group is simultaneously disadvantaged in political, economic, and social terms (Mine et al. 2013). Inclusive institutions, by helping foster compromise among contending forces, are key to consolidating state legitimacy based on stable state-society relations.
> - Human security perspective: protection and empowerment. Legitimacy is strengthened when people perceive state institutions to be acting fairly. Human security integrates top-down measures to protect people and bottom-up measures to empower them. Capable institutions to protect people and empowered communities to hold the state accountable are essential to build legitimacy and a stable state.
> - Local context sensitivity is essential, since perceptions within and between groups may be very different from statistical data. Horizontal inequities need to be reduced but the perceptions of all groups also need to be managed. It is essential, for example, that efforts to assist a disadvantaged group are not perceived as an alliance of external actors to undermine a more advantaged group. Information sharing and communications are important to avoid such outcomes (Mine et al. 2013; Mine and Katayanagi 2012).
>
> Institution building has to be led by the people of each country, while external actors can only foster their state-building efforts. To effectively build institutions, coordination and mutual learning among local stakeholders and international partners will be essential.

According to the 2011 World Development Report (World Bank 2011c), creating legitimate and efficient institutions in fragile states is by necessity a very long (15 to 30 years) process. Many fragile countries cannot, however, wait for the slow "natural" build-up of efficient institutions that the emergence of an ideal democracy may require. Though based on accurate global historical data, assessments of the time required for institutional strengthening send a desperate message to fragile African states that cannot afford to lose another generation. Although a society cannot jump overnight from highly personalized institutions to impersonalized rule-based institutions, slow incremental changes will not do the trick in this time-constrained continent confronted with so many challenges. If DRC has to wait 30 years to reach a Ghanaian level of bureaucratic quality and overall government effectiveness, DRC is unlikely to still be a country in 2050. It is likely to either be a number of different independent countries just exiting a long drawn-out civil war or a zone of chaos like Somalia in the last decade. Demographic pressure may simply make most fragile countries unravel, unless more drastic and immediate action is taken.

Successful experiences in other fragile and mismanaged countries demonstrate that setting up either some modern "island-type" efficient institutions along the Afghan model or a core effective bureaucracy as was done in Albania is feasible in very short time spans (3 to 5 years). Success in this area requires a good understanding of the constraints. It all begins, however, with politics and the absolute need to aggressively eradicate the "politics of the belly" and its associated cronyism.

From innovative technical approaches to politically clever strategies

Innovative approaches are first needed at a technical level to either transform dilapidated state institutions into modern efficient organizations or to build them from scratch. A paradox and a crucial problem is that the actions of donors in fragile countries are often an obstacle to implementing this approach. Confronted with short-term objectives imposed upon them by their political authorities, terrified by the risks of corruption and blatant failure, and discouraged by the prospect of seriously addressing the cause of state institution inefficiencies, donors generally bypass existing state institutions to establish ad hoc structures such as project implementation units (PIUs). By carefully selecting their personnel and providing them with attractive salaries, they meet their disbursement targets and implement their projects.

With this standard and prudent approach adopted since the mid-1960s, if everything goes well, donors may be more likely to reach their project objectives. However, by doing so, they also give the kiss of death to existing state institutions and significantly aggravate state weakness and fragility. In the most fragile countries, which benefit from high aid levels (outside Africa, Afghanistan and Cambodia are typical examples), the number of personnel employed by donors in PIUs or similar schemes exceeds 100,000, i.e., many times the number of technical and managerial staff present in the whole state apparatus. By providing highly attractive salaries, often multiples of existing civil service salaries, they disrupt the labor market and attract the most qualified personnel who rush from state institutions to PIUs to get higher pay.

This situation sometimes reaches a point where PIUs need to be established within the state apparatus to avoid its complete collapse and even ministers are paid by PIUs.[5] In such cases, donors collectively fund what is usually called a second or parallel civil service. But this approach is generally purely project-oriented and does not allow for an orderly buildup of lasting institutional capacity. The corresponding projects have a short lifespan and technical teams are regularly disbanded following project completion. By draining the state apparatus of its most competent staff, donors contribute to its deep weakness, thus perpetuating the need to use PIUs to get meaningful project results. Unless foreign donors continue funding it, the second civil service in Afghanistan will collapse sometime between 2014 and 2016, leaving the country almost as weak as it was in 2002. Unless this vicious circle is deliberately broken, fragile African states will remain as weak as present day Afghanistan.

There is, however, much to learn in this respect from a different experience in Afghanistan, namely building from scratch a small number of highly efficient state institutions between 2002 and 2007. The best example is the Ministry of Rural Rehabilitation and Development under the leadership of an energetic minister, Anif Atmar. Atmar's recipe was fairly simple but somewhat revolutionary in Afghanistan. He asked a consulting firm to help him clarify his ministry's objectives and define the needed organizational structure, staffing, and technical and managerial requirements. On that basis, he secured donor funding and, instead of filling positions with friends and ethnic chums, he set up a transparent recruiting process to select on a merit basis a team to help him establish the ministry and fill the managerial and technical positions. To attract highly qualified staff, he deliberately bypassed the obsolete state salary structure, making good use of a pilot program aimed at rehabilitating state institutions by inter alia introducing premiums to counterbalance the distorting impact of the PIUs salary structure. He established control and audit mechanisms to secure money flows and set up a modern human resource management system based on performance. He then immediately started field work. In three years, the results were impressive. By 2006, despite impassable roads and destroyed infrastructure, the institution was able to transparently manage 17,000 small grants provided to rural communities throughout the huge country. Despite donors' fears, corruption was negligible.

The Ministry of Rural Rehabilitation and Development's approach was not an isolated success and during the same period a new Ministry of Finance, Central Bank, and military intelligence apparatus were established along similar lines with the same success. Atmar's approach summarizes very well the *keys to success* at a technical level in establishing a modern efficient institution in a weak environment — the presence of an energetic leader, clear objectives and organizational structure, merit-based recruitment, market-based salary structures, strong control and auditing mechanisms and modern human resource management rules based on performance. This approach is not simple in a fragile country where modern management rules based on merit and performance would contradict appointment systems based on ethnic or political loyalty and where transparency confronts entrenched rent-seeking mechanisms. In

---

5. Use of technical assistance is also a requirement in such contexts to alleviate extreme inefficiencies. Cost of such technical assitance, which may reach in some countries up to 30 percent of official development assitance (ODA), leads to a financial and political dead end.

fact, strong internal forces systematically tend to oppose the modernization processes. The successful implementation of such an approach beyond a few isolated experiments requires both the full backing of the highest political authorities and a clever implementation strategy.

The requirements to implement this sound approach show that applying such principles at the level of the whole state apparatus would be a great challenge. Fragile countries are unlikely to be able to simultaneously mobilize 40 or 50 energetic ministers and heads of parastatals with the needed charisma and managerial ability. If such talents were available, they might simply be an assembly of technocratic talent not representative of the existing local political forces. Even in today's Italy there have been limits to the duration of a technocratic government whatever its merits. In addition, mobilizing 50 consulting firms to support such a process would be extremely costly and a managerial nightmare. The brutal alignment of government salaries with market salaries would jeopardize macro balances. The process of permanent trial and experiment in human resource management would, finally, be unmanageable at a government-wide level.

A preliminary conclusion is that the idea of a "big bang" government-wide administrative shakeup is doomed to fail. It is indeed already a challenge to build a modern merit-based institution in a dysfunctional patrimonial society. It would be utopian to believe that this is feasible at the level of a whole government.[6] At the same time, building three or four islands of isolated effectiveness, as was done in Afghanistan, is not enough, as they collectively would not significantly affect overall government effectiveness and would be unable to support each other in the inevitable fight against cronyism. Hence a step-by-step approach is likely to be needed to build a critical mass of key modern merit-based state institutions able to support each other both technically and politically. Building on the successes of the pilot institutions, modernization could then progressively expand within government.

A sound technical approach at the level of each institution thus needs be accompanied by a politically clever approach at a country level. The presence, for instance, of a technocratic prime minister, as in DRC today or in Albania in 1998, does not change internal political equilibriums based upon fragile ethnic balance of power and complex rent-sharing agreements. A politically clever approach will require that, first, a small group of state institutions be modernized. These institutions should not be isolated islands of administrative effectiveness swamped in an ocean of corruption, cronyism, and inefficiency as in Afghanistan in the mid-2000s. Rather they must constitute a critical mass of administrative effectiveness within the state apparatus and be part of a coherent plan to expand. Key sovereign institutions should be targeted first (ministry of finance, police, local justice) as well as critical technical ministries such as infrastructure, transport, and agriculture. Their success will be linked to the potentially explosive increase in effectiveness following a proper modernization process as demonstrated by the initial success of the Ministry of Rural Rehabilitation and Development in Afghanistan. Success will allow them to grow beyond isolated technocratic experiments and progressively expand to most, if not all, state institutions.

---

6. An exception may be Georgia in the early 2000s in an exceptional political context.

It is, however, important to underline that a precondition to success in implementing the politically clever strategy is getting the full backing of the highest political authorities. Getting high-level backing remains an unresolved issue in Afghanistan, where the president never really understood the importance of the challenge and balked at the idea of removing key political power players, usually former warlords, from key ministerial positions in order to expand the Ministry of Rural Rehabilitation and Development's approach. Heads of state need to understand that cronyism is a major source of inefficiency leading to instability and fragility. They must understand that it may well be in their long-term interest to accept the short-term political cost entailed by launching such major reforms — sacrificing useful political allies, managing during an interim period a two-speed civil service and institutional system — in order to realize the clear long-term associated benefits — strengthening the state apparatus, meeting peoples' needs, and moving out of fragility. This approach offers a way out of fragility and perhaps the only fast way out.[7] The key message is: fix the flawed institutions and stability will follow.

An explosive improvement in state institutions' efficiency is possible and can take place in a very short time span, as illustrated by the recent Rwandan experience. Without such drastic changes in state institutions' efficiency, many African countries will be unable to meet the upcoming tensions, stresses, and shocks. Only reconstructed or strengthened state institutions will be able to implement the needed agenda to eradicate slums, fix the business environment, and launch the type of job creating industrial development that is needed for these countries' stability. Only modern, merit-based, efficient state institutions will be able to rehabilitate agriculture and restore security. Even more importantly, only with such reforms will the state be able to mobilize the gigantic pool of talent available but currently unused across the continent. Once the faulty politics and flawed institutions have been fixed, then development and stability will follow, and fragility will largely be a relic of the past.

Many pressures are likely to force change

There are too many unmet challenges for latently fragile countries to maintain their illusory stability for much longer. They are on a razor's edge. Unless they change track their elites are just as doomed. These elites are neither blind nor deaf to the current situation but are already taking note. Like Mali's neighbors, they know that unless they upgrade their dilapidated state institutions and fix their faulty politics, new leaders will move in. These new leaders will soon be confronted with the same dilemma. They will either follow the line of least resistance until their countries fall into a downward spiral and end up like Mali in 2012, or they will decide to lead the type of reform and institutional development that triggered an explosive increase in government effectiveness in Rwanda.

---

7. An alternative way out would be to improve institutional efficiency by working on some critical functions such as finance or personnel simultaneously in a large number of state institutions. This approach, usually preferred by donors as it raises fewer problems at a political level (the need to change corrupt leaders is less acute), quickly runs into major obstacles, since it is almost impossible to drastically improve an institution's efficiency by just improving bits and pieces of it.

Other factors will come into play. First, fast growth in successful stable, convergent neighbors will offer attractive African models, just as the success of post-war Japan contributed to the Asian dragons' own models. Second, the collapse of unsuccessful neighbors may lead many to ponder what has gone wrong in their own backyards. Elites in the Sahel are already reflecting on the incredible speed of the Malian collapse. Most have made a correct diagnosis of the role of faulty politics, cronyism, dilapidated state institutions, and high-level corruption. Neighboring leaders are already aware that unless they quickly fix major weaknesses in their sovereign institutions (army, rural police, and local administration) they risk following the Mali experience. Finally, economic growth at the regional level will also put significant pressure on regimes to reform. The private sector will have a greater say in politics and will require greater efficiency from state institutions. Even in oil and mining economies, a middle class will emerge and be more vocal about reform. Regional entities will add to internal pressures.

Will spontaneous changes in the behavior of ruling elites' when confronted with internal and external pressures, lead to a major upgrading of their countries' state apparatus and allow these countries to move out of fragility? Or will state failure push new leaders to the forefront? Perhaps the quick upgrading of state institutions will trigger a whole wave of changes toward more inclusive growth and inclusive politics.

The fear factor is also an important element. Japan would never have modernized during the Meiji era without the fear of becoming an irrelevant US colony. Would South Korea and Taiwan have engaged in their accelerated modernization process without the threat of external aggression? The risks in Africa are largely internal: unemployment, uncontrolled migration, riots, famines, security breakdowns, and regime collapses. In this respect, the Mali collapse, by frightening its neighbors, may bring wisdom.

Countries seldom reform without strong reasons and pressures. The deplorable conditions in post-Idi Amin Uganda allowed Museveni to take over and engage in a thorough reform program. Professor Botchwey once remarked that Ghanaian elites in 1983 had to fear being forced to eat the roadside grass in order to accept reforms. As Toynbee (1972) once predicted, in order to progress, civilizations need challenges, but excessive challenges may destroy them. The fragile African states are confronted with big challenges. Will they be able to rise to these challenges, or will the magnitude of the challenges swamp them? History will tell. But clearly, the line of least resistance will quickly lead fragile states to an impasse. The action agenda based on the urgent need to fix faulty politics and drastically improve the performance of their state apparatus is clear.

Moving decisively out of fragility and conflict by 2050

Africa 2050 vision

Realization of the Africa vision set out in Chapter 1 of prosperous people in cohesive societies, competitive economies, and an integrated continent implies resolution of the conflict and fragility challenges discussed in this chapter. Alternative scenarios leading to increased instability among the most fragile of its 54 states are simply unacceptable for Africa. In 2050, a continent that had once been perceived as hopeless, marred by permanent instability, coups, and civil wars, needs to be a haven of peace and stability, far from the constant European bickering, the Central Asian and Middle Eastern conflicts, and the Asian geopolitical tensions.

Regional security arrangements would enforce peace and common norms regarding inclusive politics, respect of minority rights, and systematic checks and balances. Failed states such as Somalia would have recovered their unity thanks to a mix of successful regional mediations and African military interventions. Criminal networks would have been dismantled. The last surviving warlords would be in prison. Fragile institutions based on neo-patrimonial logic and feeding corruption networks would have been replaced by accountable, modern, merit-based organizations. A remaining unresolved problem would be how to stem the flow of illegal immigrants from a stagnant Europe attracted by the job opportunities offered by fast-growing African metropolises.

Jobs and fragility

As discussed throughout this book, jobs to transform lives, private investment to create jobs, and bigger markets for higher productivity jobs are the keys to realizing the Africa 2050 vision. Fragility and conflict is one of the ten areas for action identified in Chapter 3 but it is highly interdependent with the other nine areas — reducing conflict and fragility may be necessary to create jobs, but jobs are also the vehicle to reducing fragility. Beyond this interdependence, two areas stand out for reducing fragility and conflict:

- Strengthening or, if needed, rebuilding from scratch fragile and conflict-affected states; and
- Addressing the specific plight of resource-poor, landlocked countries.

A first critical issue in *fragile and conflict-affected countries* is to address the "politics of the belly" where "big men" feed their clientele via elaborate corruption networks that penetrate all state institutions and render them dramatically inefficient. A new generation of leaders, some of whom are technocrats, needs to progressively take over the levers of power in most fragile and conflict-affected countries. Deliberately moving out of neo-patrimonialism, this new generation of African leaders would begin developing successful, merit-based state organizations, starting with the critical state institutions providing law and order. They need to refuse the lessons of history, which teach that serious improvement in state institutions in emerging economies will require generations, and devise short cuts to drastically improve performance. The progressive emergence of modern state apparatuses and the first positive economic results brought by restoring security would facilitate an acceleration of such processes as the most fragile countries, often competing regionally for influence, cannot afford to be left behind.

In parallel, this new generation of African leaders would realize that security needs require moving toward more inclusive political and economic systems despite long-standing ethnic rivalries and suspicions. Restoring broad security and justice also requires limiting the power of the state and progressively introducing proper checks and balances as well as transparency in formerly autocratic and opaque political systems. Macroeconomic and fiscal stability would help bring political support to the new elites. Improved transparency in natural resources income and overall growth would provide the resources to restore state authority over uncontrolled territory, provide basic services even in remote areas, and transform mining and oil wealth into human capital and better infrastructure, thus reinforcing a virtuous circle. Transparency in the management of natural resources would also foster a greater sense of fairness among the population and allow old grievances to die out.

Complex regional security issues would be addressed by devising pragmatic responses to cross-border problems and practical approaches to the management of security and conflict at regional levels. Common norms regarding inclusive politics and political legitimacy would be progressively enforced at regional levels, mostly through peer pressure. However, regional security arrangements would need to be established and backed by continent-wide commitments and African standby security forces. Restoration of state authority would help dismantle the main criminal networks and the internationally-connected criminal economy. The last complex challenges would be implementing the vast ambition of transforming multiethnic societies sometimes fragmented along religious fault lines into cohesive nations with common purposes and visions.

Addressing the plight of *resource-poor landlocked countries* confronted with a fragile agriculture, global warming, lack of jobs, and a huge demographic shock is the second critical issue. Making the best of marginal agriculture will require huge investments in land improvement and water management, in agricultural research, as well as in the systematic search for alternative rural incomes. Fortunately, in the main cities, a vibrant, modern IT-based export service sector could provide some relief. A better integration of such landlocked countries with coastal urban growth poles is needed but must overcome the resentment of coastal populations already struggling with their own challenges. Specific training programs need to be developed to upgrade the technical skills of migrants and adapt them to the demands of more affluent economies; in the future, one may envision African medical doctors and surgeons running health centers in most of aging Europe. Remittances from skilled migrants would help fund a vibrant service sector fully integrated with world business centers. Resource transfers would come from affluent emerging African countries to these landlocked regions, and a new sense of common interest in regional stability would take precedence over charity. Formerly fragile Africa would then be out of risk. This is not a dream. It is an agenda for action.

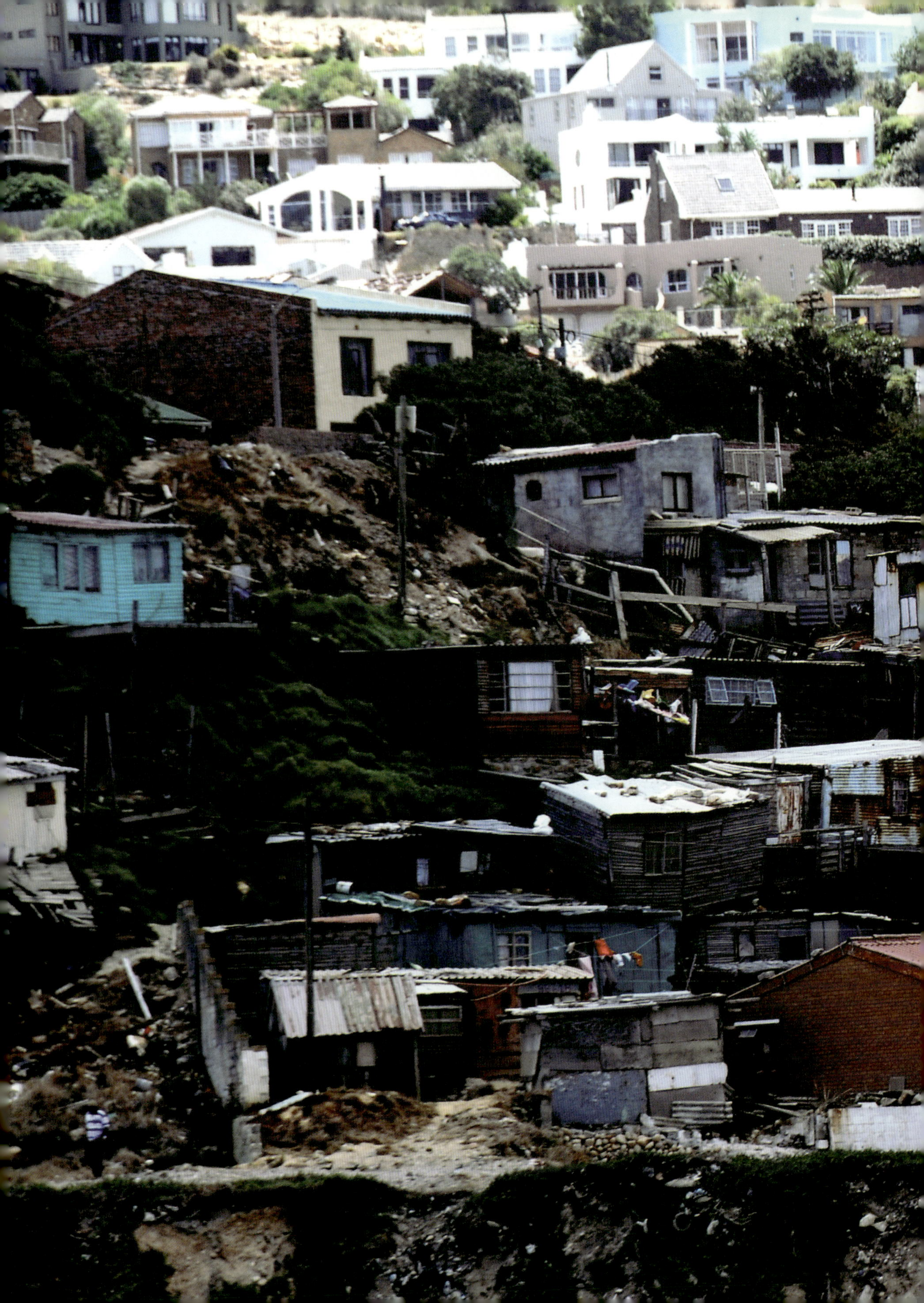

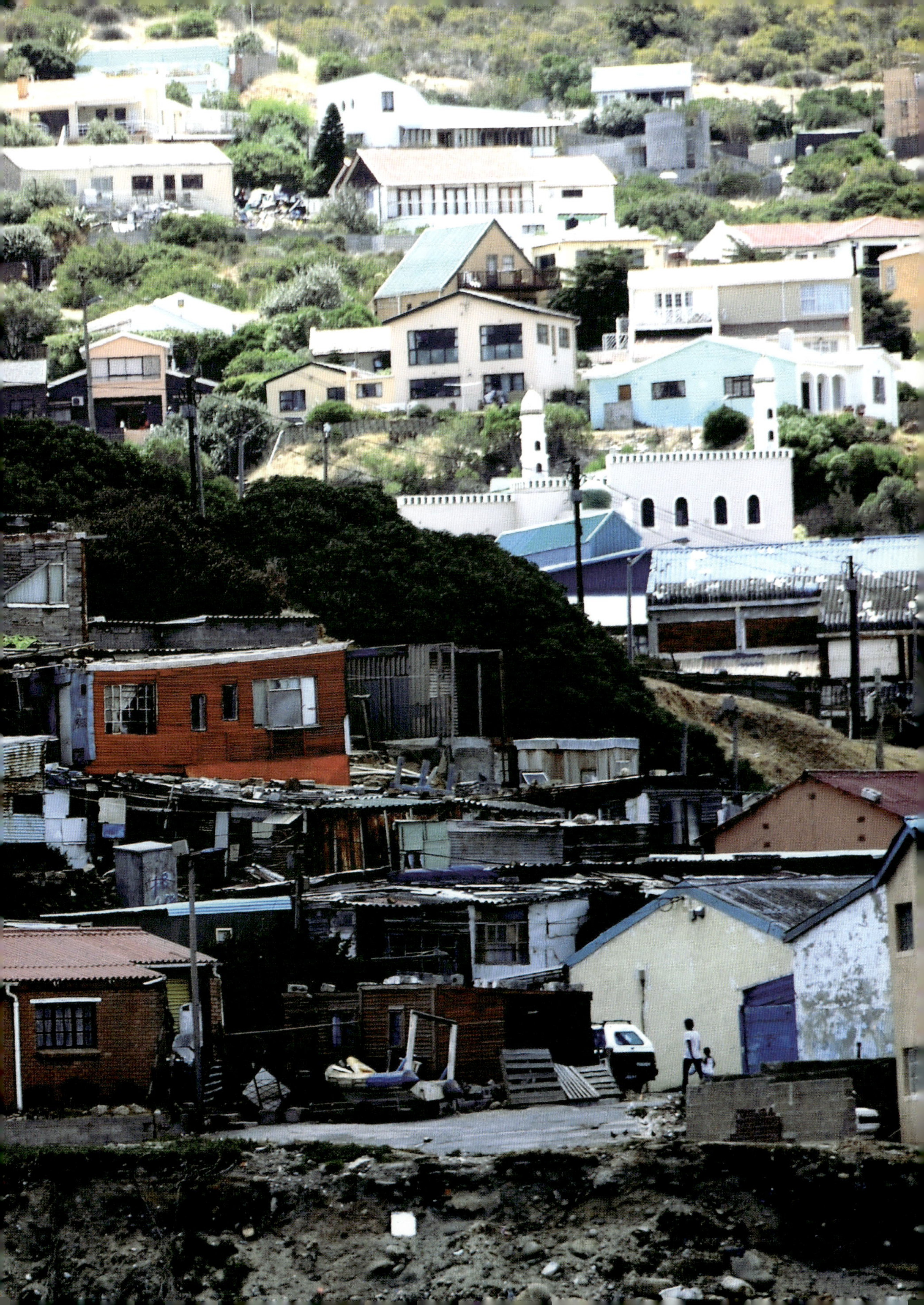

Ensuring Equity and Inclusion

Chapter 7 — Mahmood Ayub and Anil Sood

There is broad consensus that the key determinants of sustained growth are effective political and economic institutions, an outward orientation, macroeconomic stability, and human capital accumulation. However, it is increasingly recognized that income inequality can also, independently, be an important constraint on sustained growth. While some inequality is a result of market economy incentives for investment and growth, too much inequality can be destructive.

Asian experience indicates that even in countries like China and India, where absolute poverty has been reduced on a sizeable scale, income inequality has increased and access to basic services remains spotty. Deep rethinking is taking place in these countries on how to ensure more inclusive growth. Research on growth without equity indicates that growth strategies are less likely to be successful without a commitment to equality of opportunity, including giving citizens a fair chance to participate in the growth process and share the benefits of growth. Inequalities can (i) dampen the anti-poverty impact of growth; (ii) lower the growth rate itself; (iii) hollow out the middle class; (iv) degrade the capacity of a country's institutions, thereby nurturing corruption and rent-seeking; (v) increase crime and violence; and (vi) undermine social stability. Even "converging" African countries (see Chapter 1) could see their growth progress halted and even reversed if policymakers ignore inclusiveness in policies and actions.

Inequality also reduces the length of growth spells. Even the weakest African economies may succeed in initiating growth spurts for a few years. What is rare is the ability to sustain growth over a long period. Growth spells in developed countries and emerging Asia are much more likely than those in Africa to last at least ten years or more.

This chapter summarizes the status of African countries' experiences in alleviating poverty, minimizing inequalities, and increasing access to opportunities. While progress has been achieved in selected aspects of inequality reduction in some countries during the past decade, a large portion of Africa continues to live in poverty and has experienced high levels of inequality of income and opportunities during much of the last two decades.

Following a brief discussion of poverty and inequality, this chapter focuses on the trends in inequality. This discussion is divided into four dimensions of inequality — those related to income, access to education, access to health, and access to water and sanitation services. It then addresses the range of future outcomes related to poverty and inequality. The chapter concludes with an action agenda.

Evolution of Poverty and Inequality in Africa

Africa's economic growth during the last decade was more robust than during the 1990s, even taking into account the negative impact of the global financial and economic crisis. Still, the number of poor (defined here as those with income less than $1.25/day) increased from about 205 million in 1981 to 386 million in 2008, an increase of about 180 million. This is in contrast to East Asia and the Pacific and South Asia, where there was an appreciable decline in the incidence of poverty over the same period (Figure 7.1). Of the total number of poor in Africa in 2008, roughly 220 million (57 percent) lived in one of five countries: the Democratic Republic of the Congo (DRC), Ethiopia, Madagascar, Nigeria, and Tanzania. As discussed in Box 7.1, it is highly unlikely that most African countries will meet their poverty reduction Millennium Development Goal (MDG) by 2015.

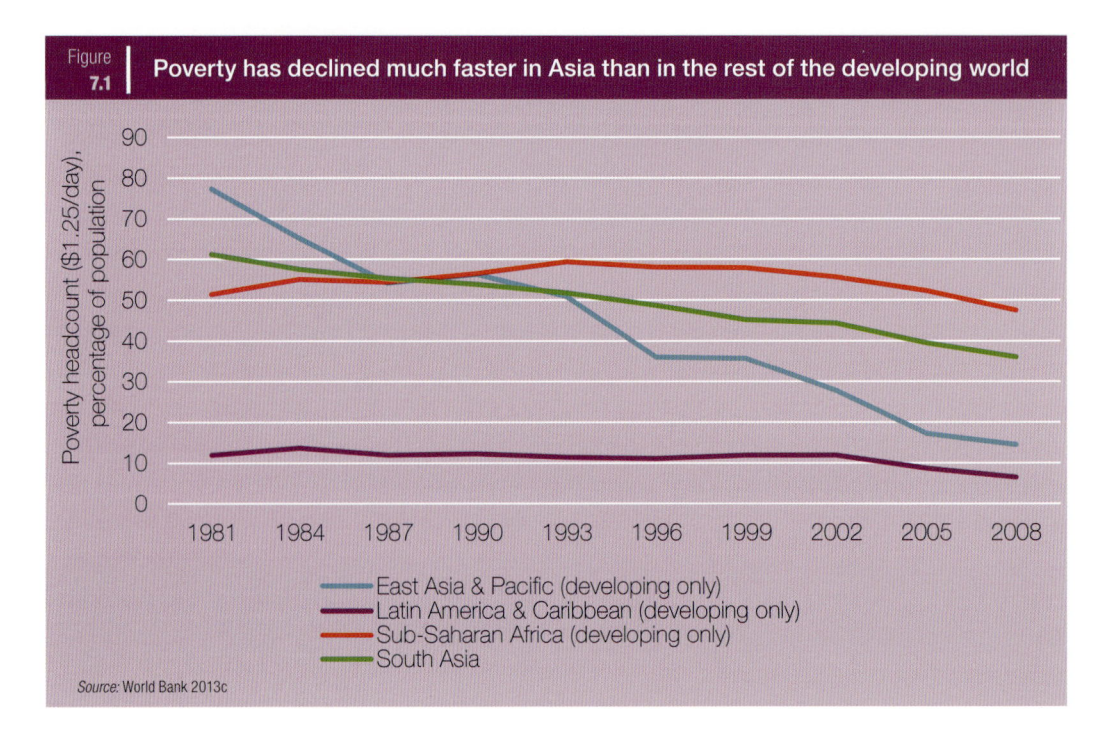

Figure 7.1 | Poverty has declined much faster in Asia than in the rest of the developing world

Source: World Bank 2013c

While data are not available for most African countries, it is possible to obtain a rural-urban breakdown for the larger countries for the 2000s (see Figure 7.2). In all cases, rural poverty incidence exceeds that of urban poverty, indicating that poverty in these African countries is predominately a rural phenomenon.

> **Box 7.1 | Current situation and future challenges for achieving the MDGs (by Kei Yoshizawa)**
>
> Assessment of the progress toward meeting the MDGs in Africa (UNECA et al. 2011) reveals that Africa has recorded remarkable gains in the areas of education (including gender equality in primary education), women's participation in political decision making, immunization for children, prevention of the spread of tuberculosis and HIV/AIDS, and the decrease in the malaria mortality rate. An important decrease has also been observed in the under-five child mortality rate in post-conflict countries.
>
> However, progress is slow in other areas: halving the poverty rate, creating productive employment and decent work, and reducing hunger and malnutrition. Youth unemployment is also high. Although the primary education enrollment rate has risen, the primary education completion rate has not risen enough to match the enrollment rate progress. Gender equality in secondary and higher education is off track. Despite a substantial improvement, access to safe drinking water target is unlikely to be achieved by 2015. Progress in improving access to sanitation is extremely slow.
>
> Progress on MDGs varies by goal and by country, and it is difficult to make sweeping statements about the development goals and policies for Africa beyond 2015. However, major challenges remaining in the post-2015 era include the following:
> - acceleration of poverty-reducing policies or implementation of adequate policies (in areas such as for job creation, agriculture, and rural development) toward inclusive growth
> - initiatives to address the quality of education and to upgrade the curriculum to meet society's needs, while maintaining momentum toward the quantitative improvement toward universal basic education
> - expansion of access to health services in the field of infectious disease control and maternal and child health
> - further expansion of access to safe drinking water and sanitation facilities
> - continuation of support for achieving the MDGs in countries that will not have achieved them by 2015, with diversification of programs and approaches to adapt to conditions of different countries and regions.

Inequality of outcomes and opportunities

A review of inequality needs to distinguish between inequality of outcomes and inequality of opportunities. Citizens use the resources at their disposal to maximize their well-being subject to constraints on their options. In assessing inequality, income and expenditure are commonly used as proxies for the outcome of the process. In addition, non-income dimensions like education and health provide a multi-dimensional and inter-generational perspective on poverty and inequality (Kanbur and Zhuang 2012). Inequality of opportunity is the portion of inequality of outcome that can be attributed to differences in individual circumstances, related to race, region of birth, parental income, mother's education, and the like (Roemer 1998). While some income inequality may be inevitable and part of the growth process, inequities of opportunities violate a sense of fairness, particularly when the individuals affected can do little to change their situation.

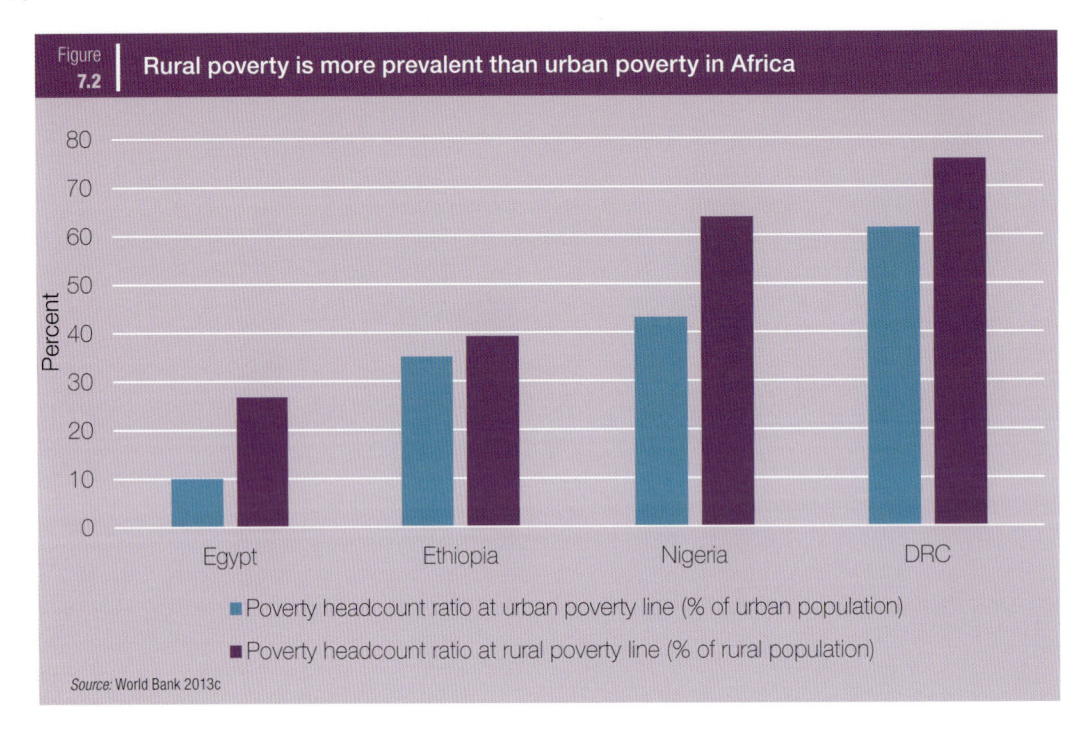

Figure 7.2 Rural poverty is more prevalent than urban poverty in Africa

- Poverty headcount ratio at urban poverty line (% of urban population)
- Poverty headcount ratio at rural poverty line (% of rural population)

Source: World Bank 2013c

Gender-specific indicators are an important measure of inclusiveness. The gender inequality index is a composite measure developed by UNDP reflecting inequality in achievements between women and men in three dimensions: reproductive health, empowerment, and the labor market. The index varies between 0 (when women and men fare equally) and 1 (where one gender fares as poorly as possible in all measured dimensions). Table 7.1 provides the data for selected African countries. Apart from Algeria, Mauritius, and Tunisia, most African countries score poorly compared to countries in other regions.

Recent trends of income inequality in Africa[1]

Of the 22 African economies with data available from the 2000s, 16 had a Gini coefficient greater than 40, which is generally regarded as a threshold for "high inequality."[2] The highest inequality was for South Africa, with a Gini of 63.2, followed by Swaziland, Rwanda and Nigeria. At the other end of the spectrum, the country with the lowest inequality was Ethiopia, with its Gini coefficient slightly under 30, followed by Egypt and Mali (Figure 7.3).

---

1. Inequality can be estimated for per capita income or per capita expenditure. The former measure is generally higher than the per capita expenditure measure. For most African countries, as for most developing Asian countries, estimates are based on expenditure data, unlike those for Latin American and countries for Organisation for Economic Co-operation and Development (OECD), which are based on income data. It is therefore more accurate to compare Africa's inequality measures to those of developing Asia.
2. For convenience, the Gini coefficient is used here as a percentage rather than as a number between 0 and 1.

Table 7.1 | Many African nations struggle with gender equality

	Rank	Value
Tunisia	45	0.293
Mauritius	63	0.353
Algeria	71	0.412
South Africa	94	0.490
Botswana	102	0.507
Morocco	104	0.510
Senegal	114	0.566
Uganda	116	0.577
Zimbabwe	118	0.583
Tanzania	119	0.590
Malawi	120	0.594
Ghana	122	0.598
Mozambique	125	0.602
Kenya	130	0.627
Cameroon	134	0.639
Côte d'Ivoire	136	0.655
DRC	142	0.710

Source: UNDP 2011

Comparing Gini coefficients in Africa with those of developing countries in Asia, Africa's coefficients are on average higher. Africa's range of Gini coefficients of 29 to 63 is also greater than that of developing Asia's 28 to 51. Africa's inequality is second only to that of Latin America, and the latter's inequality has been generally declining over the past decade.

Regarding changes in measured inequality during the 2000s, 14 out of the 22 African countries (accounting for almost half of Africa's population in 2010) experienced increases in their Gini coefficients. By contrast, in Asia only 11 of 25 countries with comparable data experienced increases in inequality.

As an aggregate measure, the Gini coefficient may hide detailed patterns of differences across levels of expenditures. Table 7.2 presents a different measure of inequality, quintile ratios — the ratio of the per capita expenditure of the top 20 percent of the income distribution to that of the bottom 20 percent.

During the 2000s, in 15 out of the 45 African countries for which data are available, the top 20 percent of households earned more than ten times that of the bottom 20 percent (quintile ratio > 10). The mean quintile ratio for the 45 African countries was 10.6. This compares to a mean of 7.1 for the 32 Asian countries for which data are available over the same period.

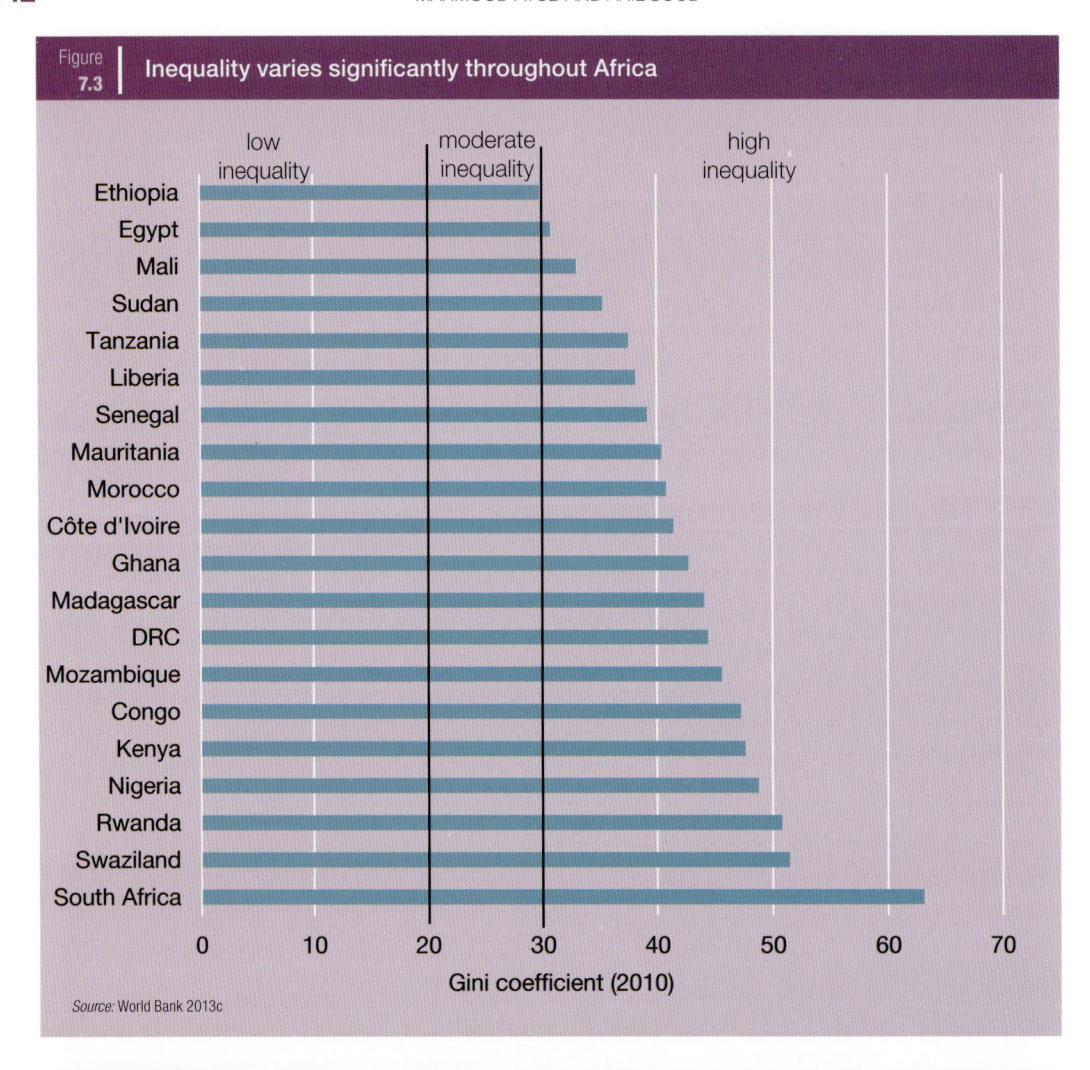

Figure 7.3 | Inequality varies significantly throughout Africa

Country	Gini coefficient (2010)
Ethiopia	~30
Egypt	~30
Mali	~33
Sudan	~35
Tanzania	~37
Liberia	~38
Senegal	~39
Mauritania	~40
Morocco	~40
Côte d'Ivoire	~41
Ghana	~42
Madagascar	~43
DRC	~44
Mozambique	~45
Congo	~47
Kenya	~47
Nigeria	~48
Rwanda	~50
Swaziland	~51
South Africa	~63

Low inequality: <20; moderate inequality: 20–30; high inequality: >30.

Source: World Bank 2013c

Table 7.2 | Africa's top quintile spends significantly more per capita than its bottom quintile

Top 20% / Bottom 20%	Countries
Above 20	Angola, Comoros, Namibia, South Africa
10 to 20	Cape Verde, Central African Republic, Republic of Congo, The Gambia, Kenya, Lesotho, Nigeria, Rwanda, Seychelles, Swaziland, Zambia
5 to 10	Benin, Burkina Faso, Cameroon, Chad, DRC, Côte d'Ivoire, Djibouti, Gabon, Ghana, Guinea, Guinea-Bissau, Liberia, Madagascar, Malawi, Mali, Mauritania, Morocco, Mozambique, Niger, Sao Tome, Sierra Leone, Sudan, Tanzania, Togo, Tunisia, Uganda
Below 5	Burundi, Egypt, Ethiopia

Source: World Bank 2013c

Significantly, South Africa exhibits one of the highest levels of inequality in Africa as measured by both its Gini coefficient and the quintile comparison, its ratio on the latter being above 20. The ratio of the top decile to the bottom decile shows even starker inequality: the top 10 percent in South Africa earn about 44 times as much as the bottom 10 percent, only marginally better than famously unequal Brazil.

Measured income inequality has been worsening over time. Between 1990 and 2010, the Gini coefficient for Africa as a whole increased (worsened) from 45 to 46. This level of inequality is well above the average for Asia's developing economies. During the 2000s, inequality grew markedly in Kenya, Nigeria, South Africa, and Tanzania (Gini coefficients increased by at least 8 percent). It declined for Egypt, Côte d'Ivoire, Mali, and Senegal.

Access to Education

Education is a critically important element in non-income inequality (see Chapter 8). Its importance is magnified because it is a self-perpetuating type of inequality: poor education generally leads to lower income, and lower income in turn leads to poor education of children.

Africa has made significant strides in improving average achievements in education. Over 30 African countries are on track to achieve universal primary education by 2015 (Africa Progress Panel 2010). Table 7.3 provides data for ten African countries with the lowest primary completion rates in 1991. By 2010, all of these countries showed significant improvement, moving on average from 17 percent to 55 percent primary completion rates. This improvement has been even more dramatic for girls, who saw a four-fold increase in the primary completion rates during the last two decades. Female students in Guinea-Bissau and Mali in particular made dramatic gains.

Table 7.3 Primary completion rates have increased dramatically since 1991, especially for girls

	Total (%) 1991	Total (%) 2010	Male (%) 1991	Male (%) 2010	Female (%) 1991	Female (%) 2010
Benin	22	63	30	74	14	53
Burkina Faso	20	45	25	48	15	42
Chad	18	33	29	41	7	24
Eritrea	18	40	21	43	15	36
Ethiopia	23	72	28	75	18	69
Guinea	17	64	24	75	9	53
Guinea-Bissau	5	68	7	75	3	60
Mali	9	55	12	61	7	50
Mozambique	26	61	32	66	21	55
Niger	17	46	21	52	13	40
Average	17	55	23	61	12	48

Source: World Bank 2013c

Nonetheless, enormous challenges remain. Some 50 million African children — especially girls — from poor backgrounds and rural areas still do not have access to primary education. In many cases, the issue is not one of lack of public expenditure allocated to education. With the exception of the Central African Republic (CAR), Chad, Guinea, and Liberia, most African countries allocated between 3 and 8 percent of GDP to education in 2010; Burundi and Lesotho set aside 9 percent and 13 percent, respectively. Costs to families, such as school fees, continue to discourage school attendance. Enrollment-inducing practices, such as the provision of meals and sanitary pads at school, are still not widespread enough. These circumstances may suggest that conditional cash transfer schemes like Brazil's *Bolsa Familia* and Mexico's *Oportunidades* may be warranted in some African countries. However, studies of South Africa's Child Support Grant, under which the state awards unconditional means-tested cash transfers to caregivers of poor children, indicate that it is preferable to address the structural problems of the supply side of education and health rather than to consider conditional transfers that could further exclude poor children and their caregivers (Lund et al. 2002).

Deep-rooted inequalities are a barrier to universal primary education. Disparities linked to wealth, gender, and location (especially rural versus urban) are holding back progress in many African countries. While the gender gaps are narrowing somewhat, they persist in the continent. In many African countries, there are still fewer than nine girls in school for every ten boys.

While enrollment rates are rising, millions of African primary school children drop out before completing a full primary cycle. Some 28 million pupils in Sub-Saharan Africa drop out each year. Girls are more likely than boys to drop out. In 2010, inequality in the ratio of out-of-school children by gender was very wide in Africa. For example, the number of out-of-school girls was more than three times greater for girls as for boys in Angola and Egypt, and about twice as high in the CAR and Mozambique (Figure 7.4).

Access to education gets increasingly difficult as children get older. Secondary and tertiary intake rates in Africa remain as low as 32 percent and 5 percent, respectively. Moreover, the quality of education in almost all African countries is a concern. Teacher absenteeism in, for example, Uganda is around 35 percent, and African scores on global standardized tests are extremely low, even in South Africa. These issues need to be addressed urgently if African labor is to be internationally competitive.

Access to Health

Like education, health is also a self-perpetuating inequality. Poor health affects the ability of the poor to increase their incomes. Even when children from poor families survive preventable diseases such as dysentery, malaria, and respiratory infections, as adults they are likely to give birth to another generation of low-birth weight babies, reinforcing the vicious cycle of low human development. Africa has generally made good progress on life expectancy; average life expectancy has increased by five years from 52 years in 1990 to 57 years in 2010 (Table 7.3). North African countries and Mauritius demonstrate not only relatively high life expectancy — about 72 years — but also improvement since 1990.

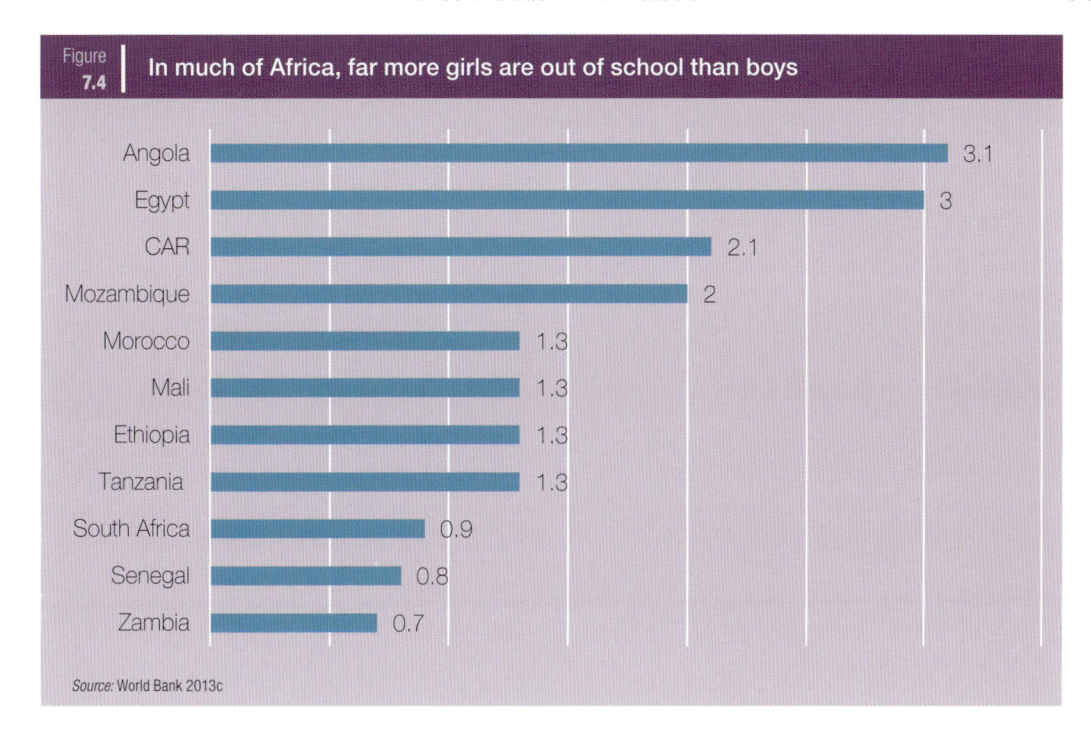

Figure 7.4 | In much of Africa, far more girls are out of school than boys

Country	Value
Angola	3.1
Egypt	3
CAR	2.1
Mozambique	2
Morocco	1.3
Mali	1.3
Ethiopia	1.3
Tanzania	1.3
South Africa	0.9
Senegal	0.8
Zambia	0.7

Source: World Bank 2013c

There are, however, significant differences among countries. For example, a person from Sierra Leone is likely to die 28 years before his Tunisian counterpart. Moreover, there are eight countries (Cameroon, CAR, Chad, Kenya, Lesotho, South Africa, Swaziland, and Zimbabwe) that saw declines in their citizens' life expectancy over the past two decades. The drop was particularly steep for Lesotho, South Africa, Swaziland, and Zimbabwe, where the decline was around ten years. This large decline reflects the devastating impact of HIV/AIDS, although there are recent signs that life expectancy in these countries is starting to increase again.

Inter-country inequalities are also evident in infant mortality rates. Three countries (Libya, Mauritius, and Tunisia) have low levels of around 13 per 1,000 live births compared to Angola, the CAR, Chad, the DRC, Mali, and Sierra Leone, where rates are near or above 100 per 1,000 (Table 7.4).

There are major inequities in access to health by income. Infant mortality rates differ dramatically between the poorest quintile of the population and the richest quintile. In countries like Egypt and Côte d'Ivoire, for example, the chance of a poor infant dying is more than twice that of an infant born to a rich family (Figure 7.5).

Table 7.4 The impact of HIV/AIDS has led to differing health outcomes across the continent

	Life Expectancy at Birth (years)		Infant Mortality Rate (per 1,000 live births)	
	1990	2010	1990	2010
Algeria	67	73	55	31
Angola	41	51	144	98
Botswana	64	53	46	36
Burkina Faso	48	55	103	93
Cameroon	53	51	85	84
CAR	49	48	110	106
Chad	51	49	113	99
DRC	47	48	117	112
Côte d'Ivoire	53	55	105	86
Egypt	62	73	68	18
Ethiopia	47	59	111	68
The Gambia	53	58	78	57
Ghana	57	64	77	50
Kenya	59	56	64	55
Lesotho	59	47	72	65
Libya	68	75	33	13
Mali	44	51	131	99
Mauritania	56	58	80	75
Mauritius	69	73	21	13
Morocco	64	72	67	30
Mozambique	43	50	146	92
Nigeria	46	51	126	88
Rwanda	33	55	99	59
Senegal	53	59	70	50
Sierra Leone	39	47	162	114
Somalia	45	51	108	108
South Africa	62	52	47	41
Sudan	53	61	78	66
Swaziland	59	48	70	55
Tanzania	51	57	95	60
Togo	53	57	87	66
Tunisia	70	75	39	14
Uganda	47	54	106	63
Zambia	47	48	109	69
Zimbabwe	61	50	52	51
Average	52	57	92	65

Source: World Bank 2013c

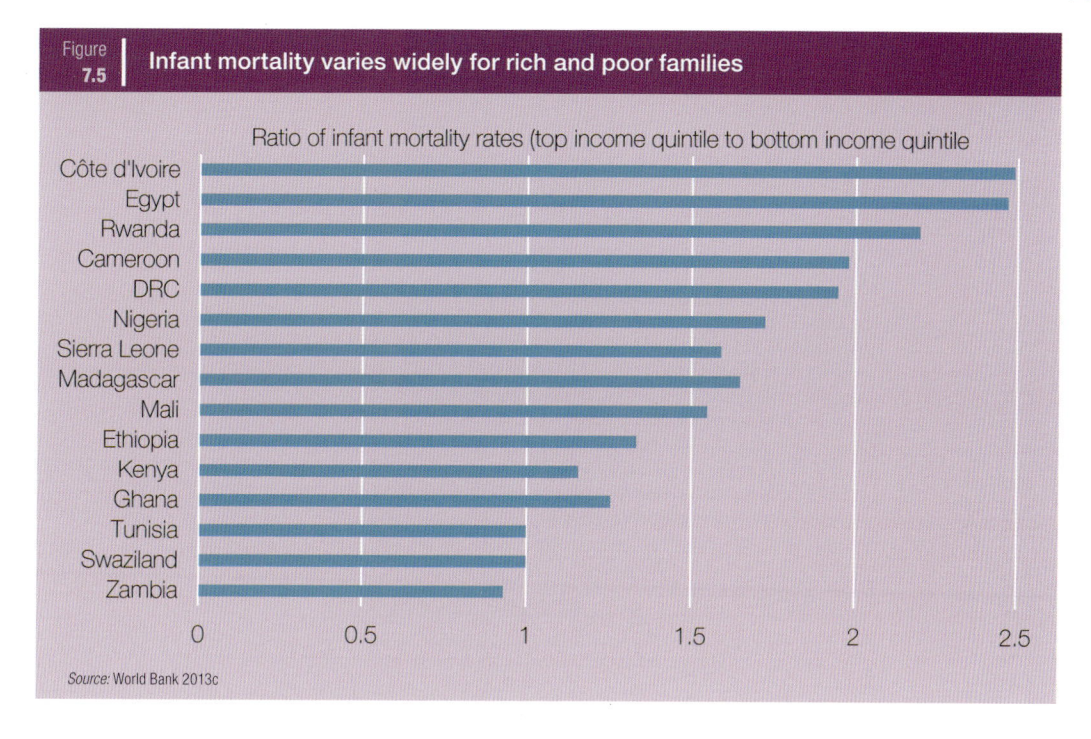

Figure 7.5 | Infant mortality varies widely for rich and poor families

Ratio of infant mortality rates (top income quintile to bottom income quintile)

- Côte d'Ivoire
- Egypt
- Rwanda
- Cameroon
- DRC
- Nigeria
- Sierra Leone
- Madagascar
- Mali
- Ethiopia
- Kenya
- Ghana
- Tunisia
- Swaziland
- Zambia

Source: World Bank 2013c

Access to Water and Sanitation

Overall, the news for Africa (and the rest of the world) on access to improved source of drinking water is positive (see Figure 7.6). The proportion of Africa's population with better access increased from 61 percent in 1990 to 66 percent in 2010 (from 55 percent to 61 percent for Sub-Saharan Africa and from 89 percent to 92 percent for North Africa). Progress has been particularly impressive for six countries (Burkina Faso, Ghana, Liberia, Mali, Namibia, and Uganda) where more than 40 percent of their 2010 population has gained access to improved water sources since 1995. There are, however, several African countries, notably the DRC, Ethiopia, and Madagascar, where about 55 percent of the population still lacks access to safe drinking water.

Progress in access to improved sanitation facilities, however, has been less positive. Much of Africa is off-track to meet the Millenium Development Goals (MDGs) sanitation target by 2015. In 2010, 60 percent of Africa's population (70 percent in Sub-Saharan Africa and 10 percent in North Africa) was without access to improved sanitation facilities, compared to the world average of 37 percent. Access varies considerably by income and location (rural-urban). Countries such as Niger, Tanzania, Sierra Leone, Chad, and Ghana are particularly low in coverage of sanitation facilities (Figure 7.7).

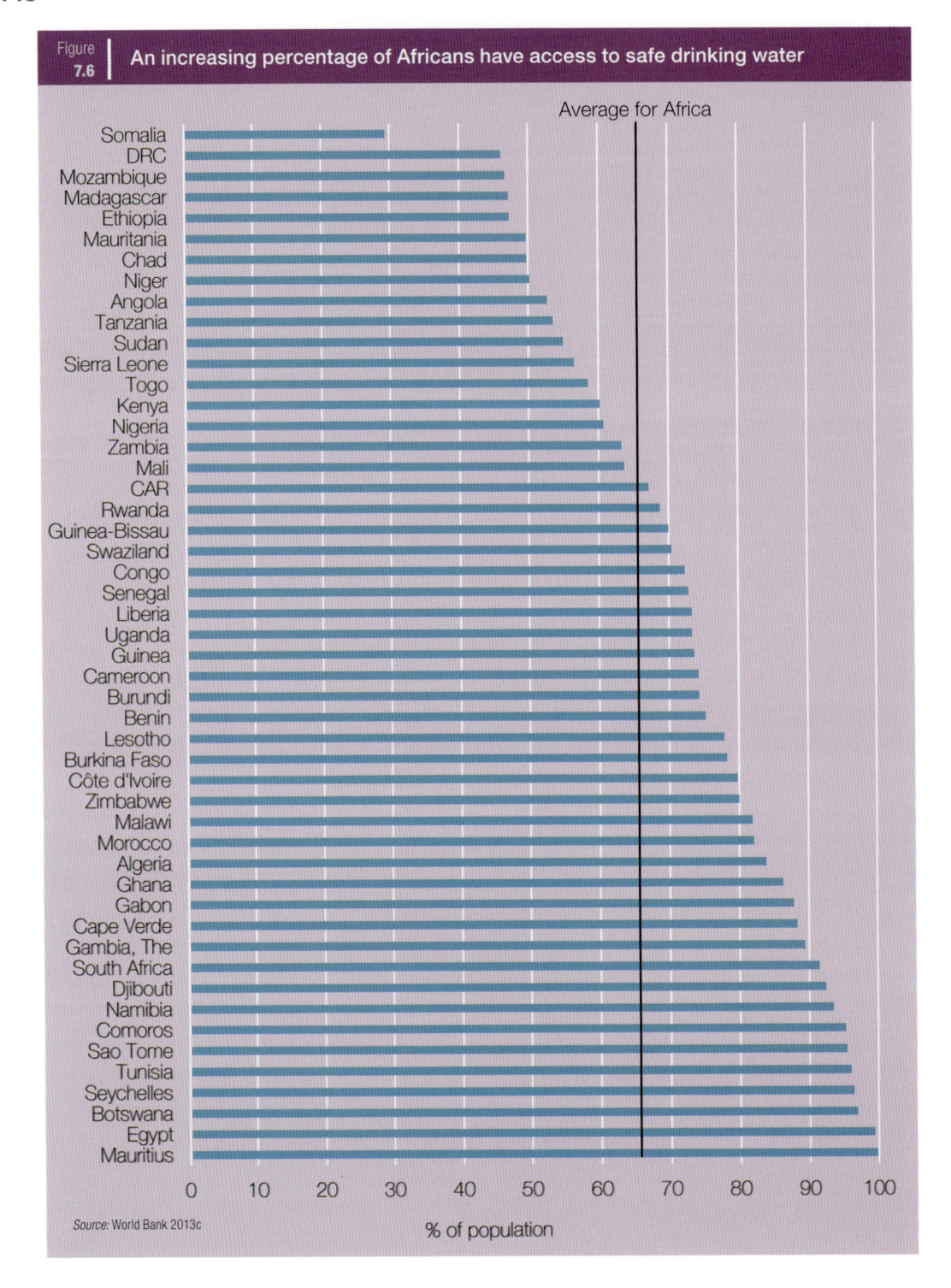

Figure 7.6 An increasing percentage of Africans have access to safe drinking water

Average for Africa

Somalia
DRC
Mozambique
Madagascar
Ethiopia
Mauritania
Chad
Niger
Angola
Tanzania
Sudan
Sierra Leone
Togo
Kenya
Nigeria
Zambia
Mali
CAR
Rwanda
Guinea-Bissau
Swaziland
Congo
Senegal
Liberia
Uganda
Guinea
Cameroon
Burundi
Benin
Lesotho
Burkina Faso
Côte d'Ivoire
Zimbabwe
Malawi
Morocco
Algeria
Ghana
Gabon
Cape Verde
Gambia, The
South Africa
Djibouti
Namibia
Comoros
Sao Tome
Tunisia
Seychelles
Botswana
Egypt
Mauritius

% of population

Source: World Bank 2013c

ENSURING EQUITY AND INCLUSION

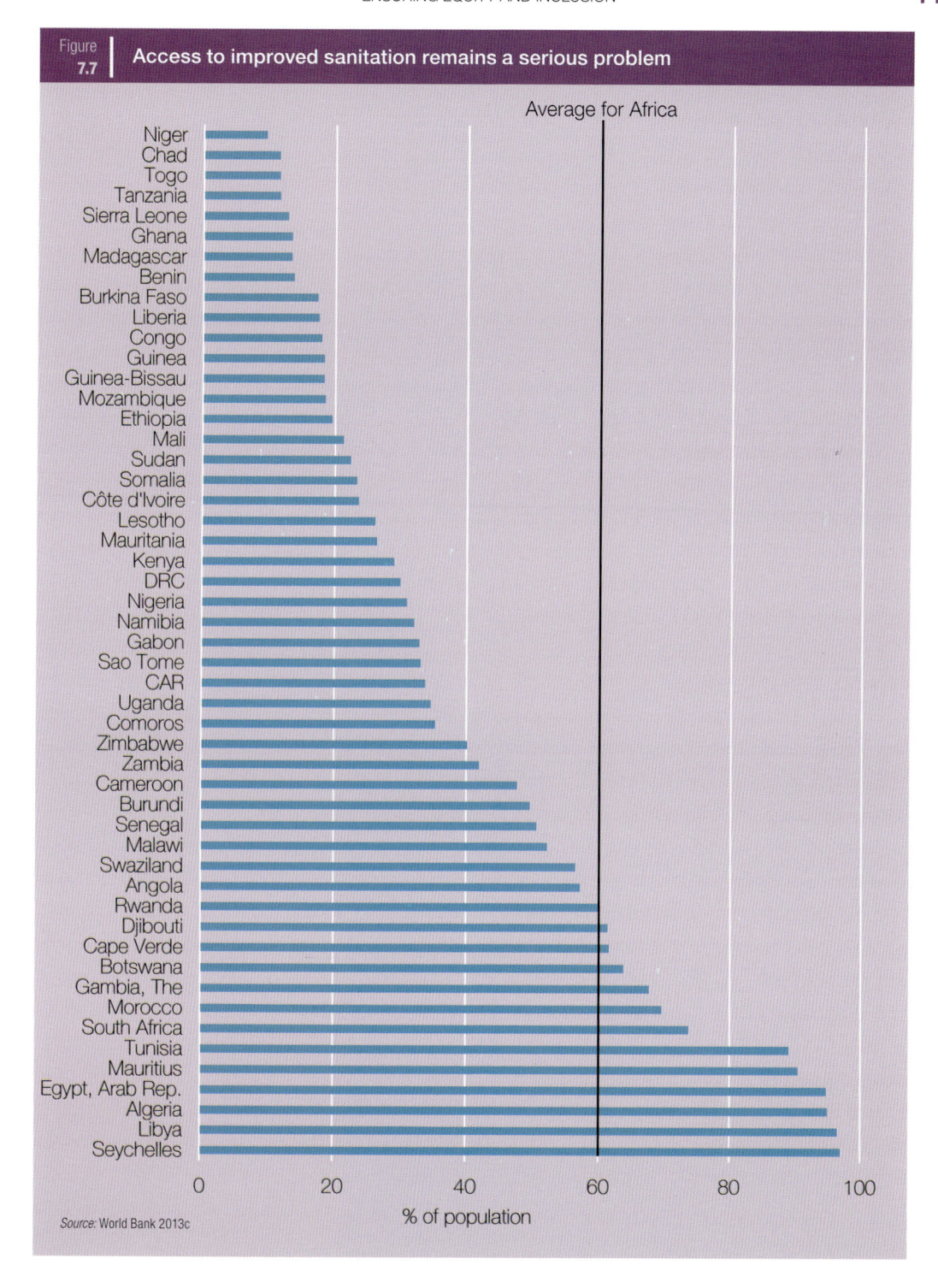

Figure 7.7 Access to improved sanitation remains a serious problem

Source: World Bank 2013c

% of population

Prospects for 2050

Sustained high growth as envisioned in the convergence scenario for 2050 discussed in Chapter 1 would make a significant impact on poverty and the share of Africa's population moving into the middle class.

Poverty under different scenarios

Figure 7.8 shows the poverty rate and the number of Africans in poverty through 2050 under the three scenarios presented in Chapter 1. In the convergence scenario, Africa's poverty rate declines below 5 percent, and, even more strikingly, the poverty rate for fragile countries declines below 10 percent. In the business-as-usual scenario, the poverty rates decline in a linear fashion, with African poverty falling to around 17 percent in 2050. In the downside scenario, the poverty rate declines very little, dropping about 5 percentage points to around 32 percent.

The change in the absolute number of people in poverty in Africa is a slightly different story, due to population growth. Only the convergence scenario reduces the number of people in poverty in Africa, to about 50 million in 2050. In the business-as-usual scenario, the number of people in poverty actually increases to 378 million in 2050. In the downside scenario, the number nearly doubles, increasing to 690 million. Given population growth, reductions in poverty rates will need to be accelerated in order to reduce the number of Africans living in poverty.

Growth of the middle class

Figure 7.9 shows the size of the middle class in Africa through 2050. In the convergence scenario, about 65 percent of Africa's population would be in the middle class. The business-as-usual scenario and downside scenario would yield a middle class of about 30 percent and 20 percent of the population, respectively. The convergence scenario produces a middle class that is twice the size of that in the business-as-usual scenario, and three times the size of that in by the downside scenario.

In the convergence scenario, the total number of people in the middle class would exceed 1.4 billion in 2050, up from 125 million in 2012. The business-as-usual scenario and downside scenario only yield a middle class of about 600 million and 400 million, respectively. The convergence scenario represents a huge opportunity for Africa, not just by raising incomes but also by making Africa a significant region of middle class consumers on the global stage.

Action Agenda

The recent impressive economic growth in Africa has not been accompanied by a reduction in the number of poor or in income inequality. The actual number of poor in the continent has increased and in the last decade, two-thirds of the countries had a Gini coefficient above 40, a threshold for high inequality.

ENSURING EQUITY AND INCLUSION 151

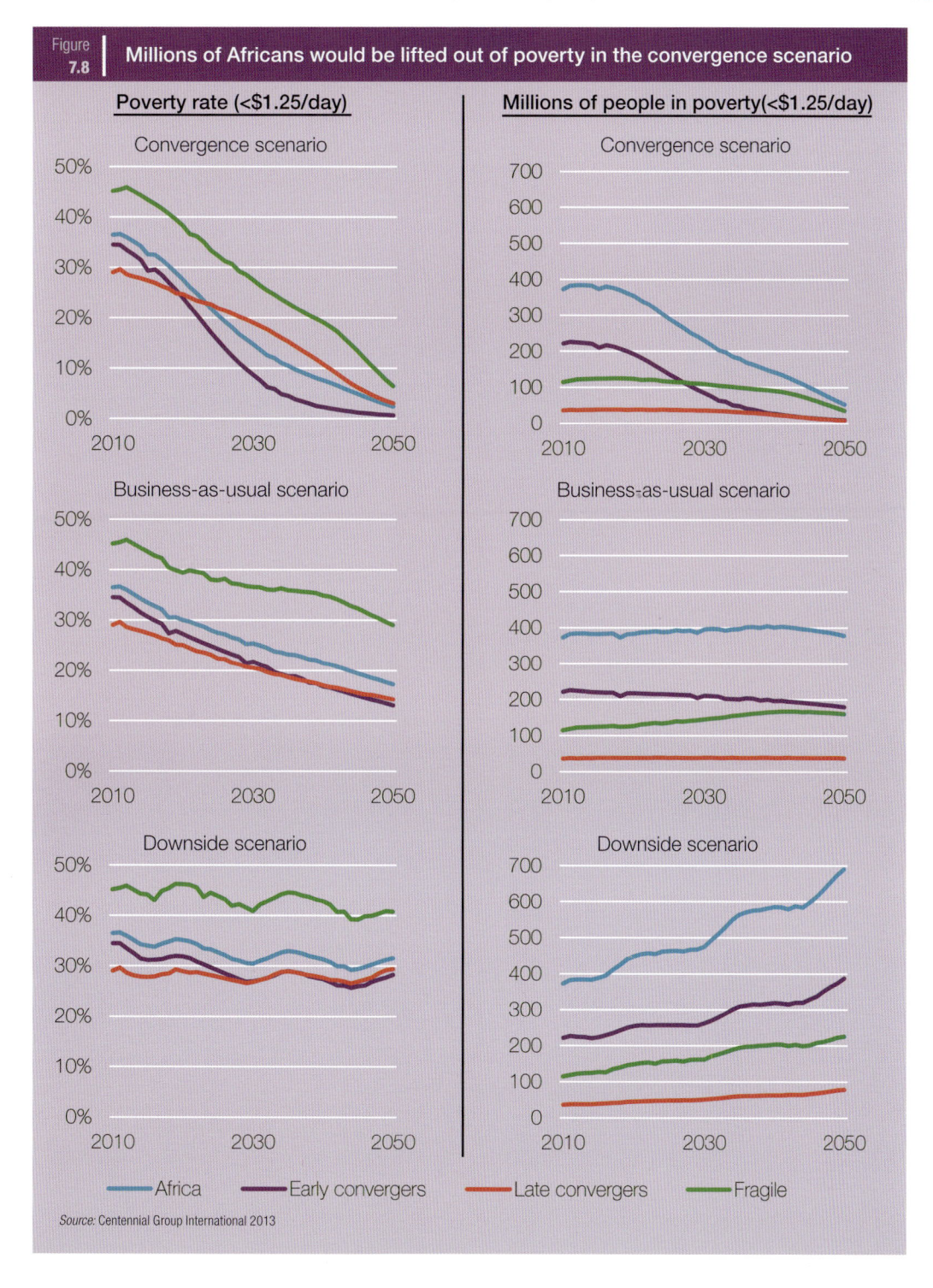

Figure 7.8 | Millions of Africans would be lifted out of poverty in the convergence scenario

Poverty rate (<$1.25/day)
- Convergence scenario
- Business-as-usual scenario
- Downside scenario

Millions of people in poverty (<$1.25/day)
- Convergence scenario
- Business-as-usual scenario
- Downside scenario

— Africa — Early convergers — Late convergers — Fragile

Source: Centennial Group International 2013

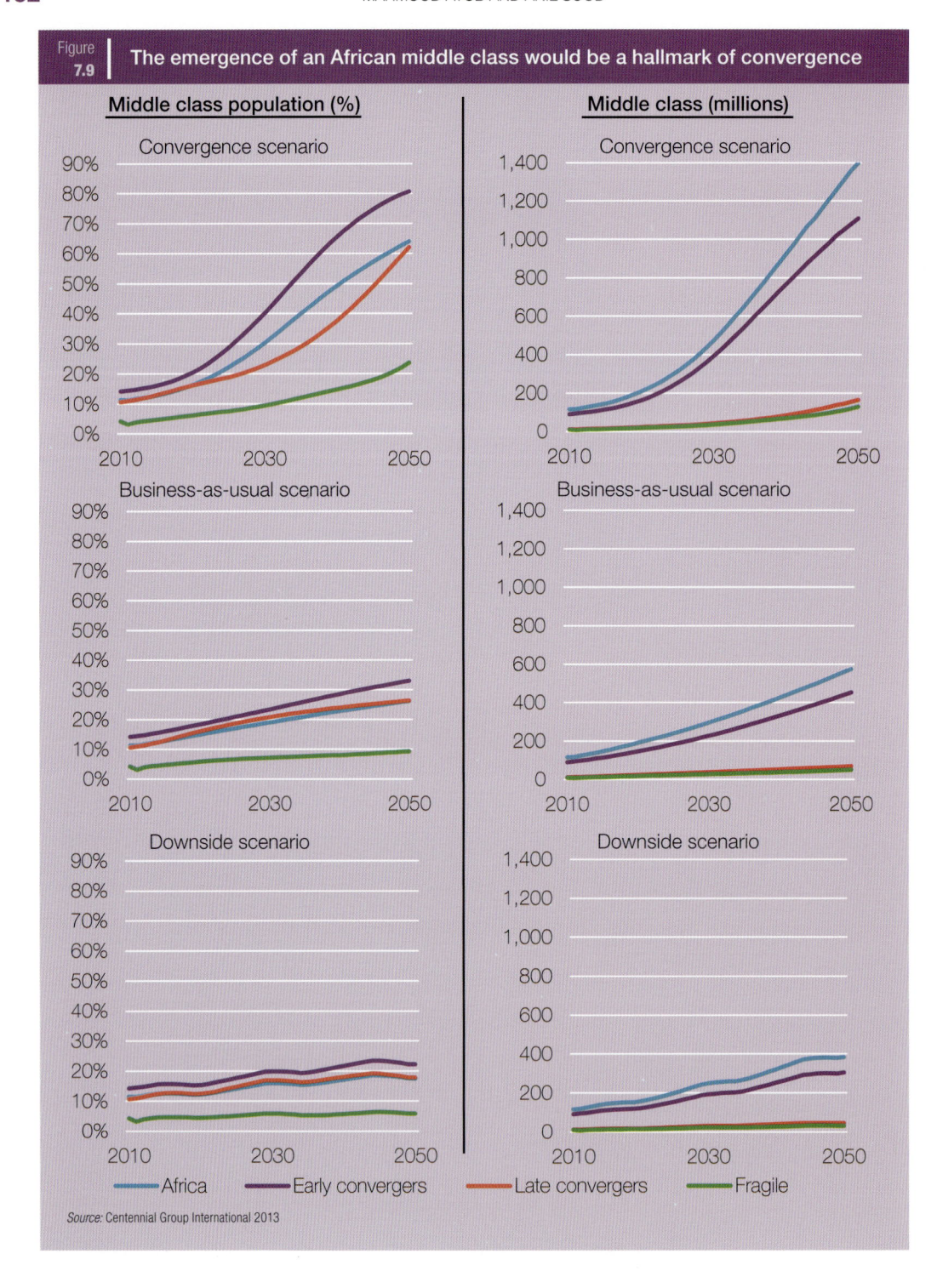

Figure 7.9 | The emergence of an African middle class would be a hallmark of convergence

Middle class population (%)

Convergence scenario

Business-as-usual scenario

Downside scenario

Middle class (millions)

Convergence scenario

Business-as-usual scenario

Downside scenario

— Africa — Early convergers — Late convergers — Fragile

Source: Centennial Group International 2013

Not only has inequality been high, it has increased over time, with two-thirds of the 22 countries for which data are available experiencing increased inequality. Similar results are seen when a comparison of income of quintiles is undertaken.

Africa's economy will need to grow by some 5 percent a year at least to keep the number of poor constant. Growth during the past decade has been higher than during the 1980s and 1990s, and yet the number of poor has increased. Part of the explanation may be that many of the most rapidly growing countries are resource-rich countries, and growth has not translated into widespread improvements in living standards (see Chapter 12). Part of the solution would be to reduce constraints on small businesses to facilitate productivity growth and employment. Access to finance, especially for small and medium enterprises (SMEs), is an important determinant of sustained growth. Access to electricity is a very serious constraint to business in spite of Africa's large natural gas reserves and great hydropower potential (issues related to the business environment are discussed in Chapter 10).

Africa has been more successful in improving average achievements in education (especially of girls), access to health services, and access to improved sources of drinking water. But even in these areas there is still some way to go. Some 50 million African children — especially girls — from poor backgrounds and rural areas still do not have access to primary education. And access to education becomes more difficult as children get older, with secondary and tertiary intake rates falling dramatically. Inter-country inequalities are large both in life expectancy and infant mortality rates. There are countries where more than 55 percent of the population is still without access to safe drinking water. Finally, much of Africa is unlikely to meet the MDG target for access to improved sanitation facilities by 2015.

Reducing inequalities in Africa would entail leveling the playing field through more equitable and broad-based basic education (early childhood development and girls education in particular) which has been a distinguishing feature of education in much of Asia. Brazil proactively used education to help reduce inequality. Other options are increasing income-earning opportunities, increasing access to basic health services and to water and sanitation facilities, and strengthening institutions that promote transparency and fairness.

Inclusive growth is more than just an outcome; it is also a process. Citizens' ability to express and exercise their views is an important part of inclusive growth, as is citizens' participation in decisions that influence their well-being. Active involvement of beneficiaries in anti-poverty programs may lower the informational costs associated with these interventions and offer the potential for the design and implementation of interventions that are in line with the preferences of the population they are designed to assist. Examination of several public works interventions undertaken in the Western Cape province of South Africa supports the benefits of inclusion (Hoddinnot et al. 2001).

Absence of the poor in decisions about their well-being can distort priorities. In many African countries, governments devote about one-third of their budgets to education and health, but they allocate little of it to the poor. For example, even though clean water is critical to health outcomes, in Morocco only 11 percent of the poorest quintile of the population has access to safe water, while everyone in the richest quintile does.

More public spending alone is not enough. Between 1980s and 1990s, total public spending on education in both Ethiopia and Malawi increased by $8 per child of primary school age. In Ethiopia the primary school completion stagnated, going from 22 percent in 1990 to only 24 percent in 1999. In contrast, in Malawi it rose from 30 percent to 50 percent.

When communities are not involved in establishing, supporting, and overseeing a school, it is frequently seen as something alien. A study of schooling in rural Nigeria found that villagers often stopped expecting anything from government schools, instead taking the responsibility for education themselves (Francis et al. 1998). One of the most powerful means of increasing the voice of poor citizens in policymaking is better information, which can serve as a stimulant for public action and a catalyst for change. When the government of Uganda learned that only 13 percent of recurrent spending for primary education was arriving in primary schools, it launched a monthly newspaper campaign on the transfer of funds. That campaign galvanized the population, inducing the government to increase the share going to primary schools (now over 80 percent) and compelling school principals to post the entire budget on school room doors. Similarly, an in-depth study of the Iringa district, a poor rural area in Tanzania, showed that patients bypassed low-quality facilities in favor of those offering higher quality consultations and prescriptions staffed by more knowledgeable physicians and better stocked with basic supplies (Leonard, Mliga, and Mariam 2002).

To increase the quality of education and other public services, reforms should concentrate on increasing the voice and participation of beneficiaries but not neglect the importance of central government oversight. In practical terms, there should be more community management of facilities and demand-side subsidies to the poor, but with continuing stress on nationally determined standards, such as curricula and certification. Decentralizing delivery responsibilities for public services is prominent on the reform agenda of many countries, including Nigeria and South Africa (World Bank 2004). A key objective, usually linked to political motivation for decentralization, is to strengthen citizens' voices by bringing services and elected politicians closer to the beneficiaries.

In short, there are ways to use beneficiary power to improve outcomes. One is to involve citizens directly in the assessment and operation of local service delivery institutions. Another is to use demand-side subsidies to increase access for poor people. A third is to make provider resources depend on client choice: to have money follow students or patients, for example. None is a panacea, but each can be a part of a strategy for public service improvement.

With this overall picture of disparities in Africa, the key message for African policymakers is to confront inequality through efficient interventions that equalize access to basic services such as education, health, water, and sanitation, and to reduce inequality in three areas: (i) access to quality human capital services; (ii) gender and spatial disparities (e.g., rural-urban); and (iii) untargeted subsidies.

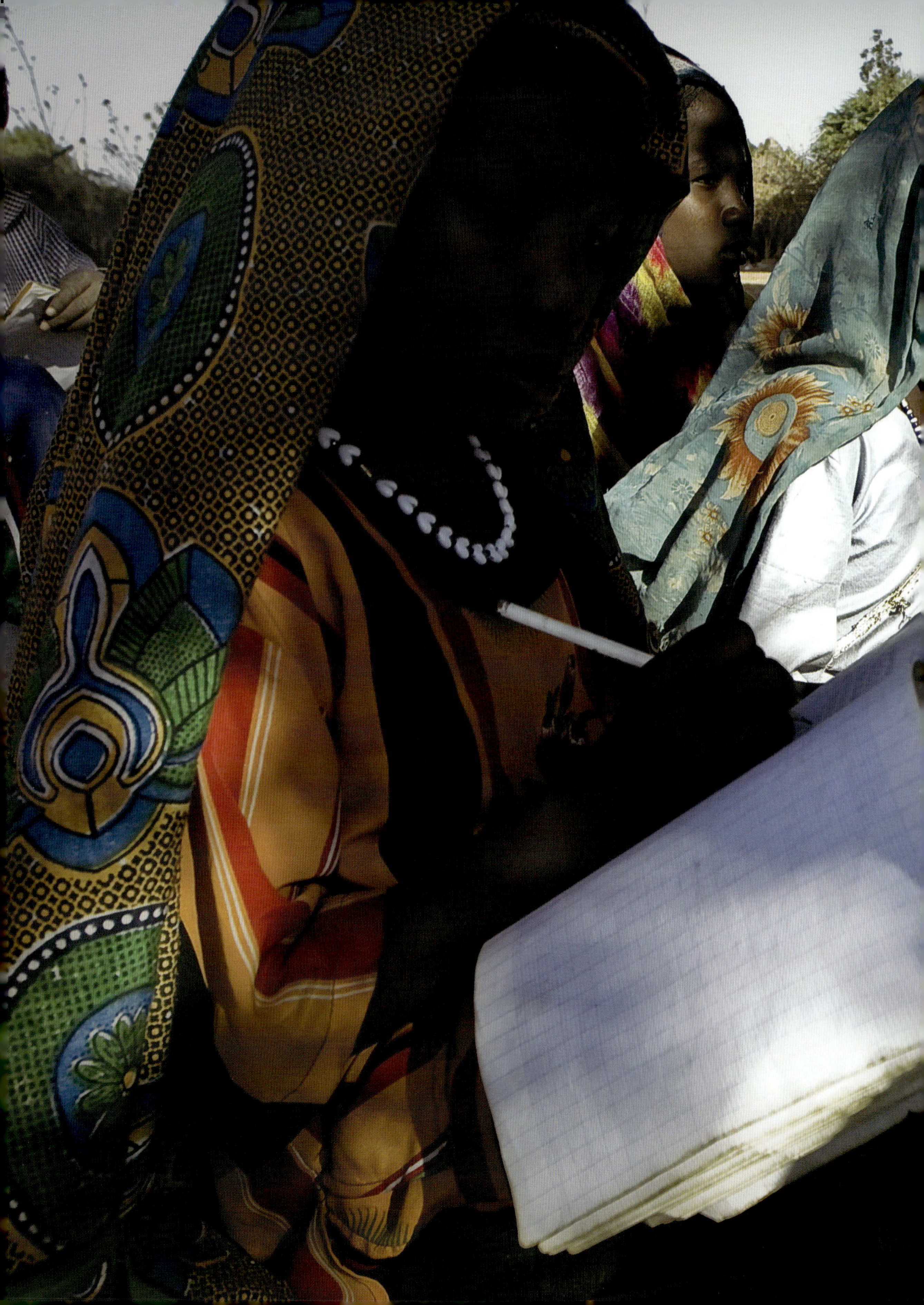

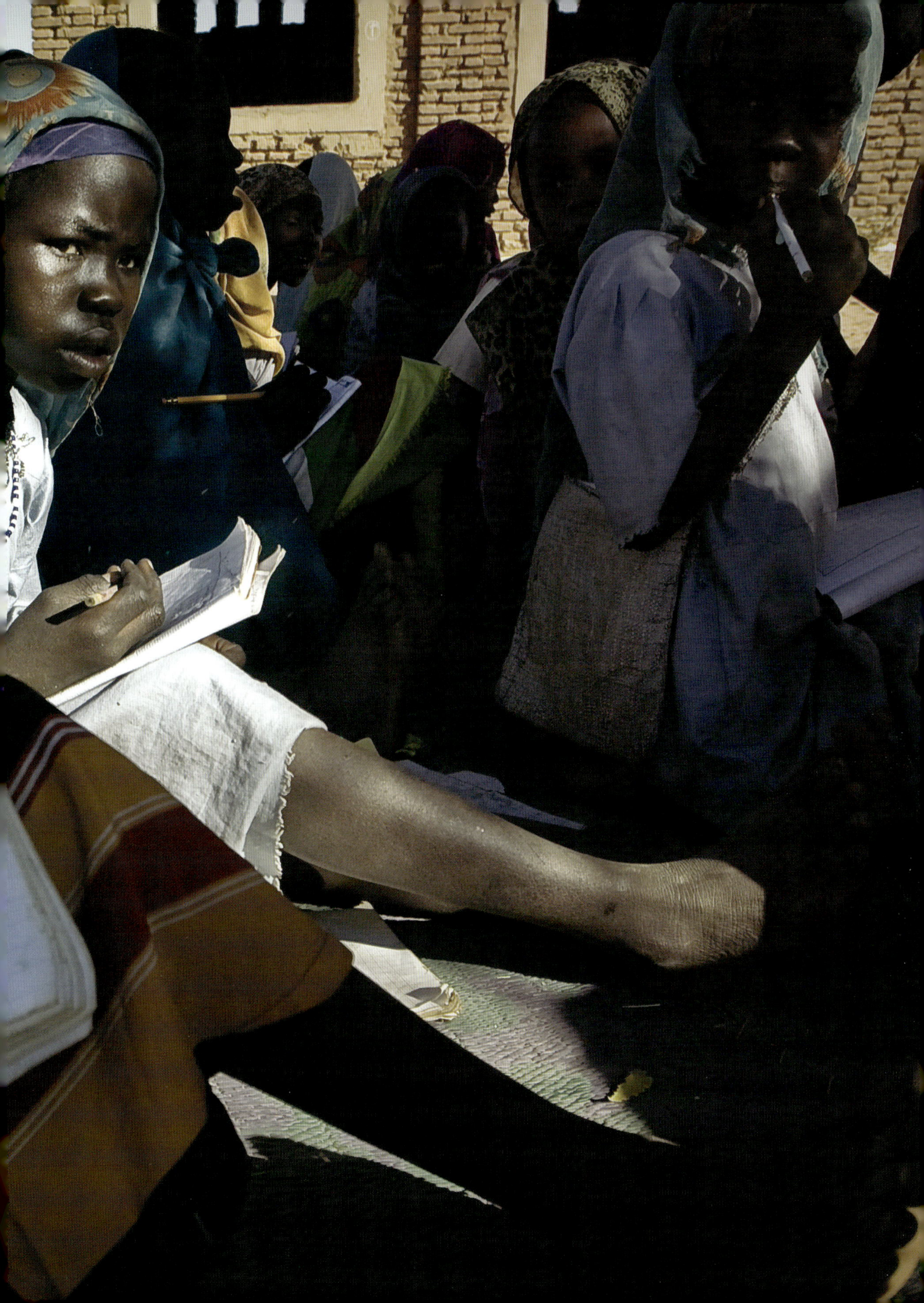

Chapter 8
Breaking the Human Capital Barrier

Birger Fredriksen and Ruth Kagia

Vision: By 2050 African countries would have developed the human capital — through national, regional, and global cooperation in education, health, science, and technology — needed to foster rapid, inclusive, and job-creating growth; cohesive societies; and accountable governments as a basis for catalyzing and supporting sustainable convergence in living standards between African countries and the rest of the world.

It is imperative to scale up human capital in Africa as a prerequisite for economic transformation. This chapter highlights the opportunities and challenges that African countries face in making what would for most countries amount to a quantum leap in raising levels of human capital and outlines some promising approaches toward achieving that objective. Over the next decade, African countries must lay the foundations for unleashing the full potential of their people to enable them to lead healthy and productive lives. Achieving this is crucial for accelerating the economic transition from low to higher productivity sectors and for enhancing Africa's competitiveness in a knowledge-based global economy. The issues covered in the chapter have pan-African relevance, but most of the discussion focuses on Sub-Saharan Africa (SSA) where the challenges are most pronounced.

In the convergence scenario laid out in Chapter 1, by 2050 Africa would be home to 2 billion people with a per capita income of $17,500 and a skilled and productive workforce. Basic education would be universal and free for the first nine years, and enrollment would have exceeded 80 percent at the senior secondary level and 35 percent in higher education. African universities would have become leading global research centers of excellence in fields such as extractive industries, agribusiness, and biotechnology. Africans would be healthier and living longer as a result of better nutrition and health care, higher incomes, and sharply reduced poverty, underpinned by a well-educated middle class.

We have suggested a set of education targets that would need to be met by 2050 to achieve this vision. They include a doubling of the completion rate for an eight- to nine-year basic education cycle, a five-fold expansion in enrollments at the tertiary and pre-school level, and an almost three-fold increase at the upper secondary level. The proposed annual growth rates, while challenging, are not as high as those that African countries achieved in the recent past. During the period 1970-2010, there was more than a twenty-fold expansion of tertiary education, a twelve-fold increase in enrollment in secondary schools, and primary enrollment increased by about 350 percent. In the health sector, we have underscored the imperative for a sharp acceleration in efforts to reduce the burden of disease through an integrated set of multi-sectoral actions, rather than a series of vertical programs. Key among the actions are broadening access to potable water, sanitation, and rural infrastructure; empowering women; improving nutrition; and removing social and financial barriers to basic services. Achieving the 2050 targets will require a major effort because education and health systems are becoming larger and more complex and because reaching the under-served populations will often be more difficult and costly.

Most education indicators in SSA would remain below those of other regions, but expanding education to the proposed levels would provide the labor force with sufficient skills and capacity to support economic transformation. China has become an economic powerhouse, and its education indicators are no higher than those proposed here.[1] Improvements in education coverage, however, must be accompanied by a major improvement in education quality.

Achieving the 2050 vision for human capital development in Africa is important and urgent. Much of the economic growth registered in the last decade has been enabled by improved macro-economic policies, greater political stability, an improved business climate, and growing global interest in Africa primarily driven by commodities. These are important drivers for jump-starting economic growth, but they are insufficient to sustain or expand it without parallel improvements in key fundamentals of growth — human capital, knowledge, and infrastructure.

By raising the quality of human capital, the region would build critical capacities, increase the volume and quality of skills, and deepen the institutional base for harnessing new job, industrial, and technological opportunities that will open up as the economies become more globally connected. In addition, a healthier, better educated, and trained population will produce more, accelerate the demographic transition and contribute to poverty reduction. If, on the other hand, progress in reducing the disease burden and raising the education and skill levels of the population falters, the large reservoir of young people could become a disruptive force and slow or reverse economic growth. The window of opportunity to make the massive investment required is no more than 10 to 15 years, after which a weak human capital base would become a drag on further economic growth.

The rest of this chapter (i) reviews key factors that are likely to drive change in education and health between now and 2050, (ii) highlights the key messages about the urgency and options for responding to these drivers, and (iii) suggests elements of a strategic agenda for attaining the 2050 vision. While the discussion on education covers the entire sector, the focus in health is on the heavy disease burden and its impact on the development of human capital and the labor force.

---

1. In 2009, China's enrollment ratio in tertiary education was 24 percent (up from 3 percent in the early 1980s) and below 70 percent in upper secondary education with only 20 percent coverage in the rural areas (World Bank 2013a).

Key Drivers of Change in Education and Health

Change in education and health is driven by a mixture of factors originating from *inside* these systems as well as from national, regional, and global developments *outside* the systems. Often these two sets of factors are mutually dependent. For example, demography affects education in many important ways, and education, in turn, affects key demographic factors such as fertility, mortality, and migration. Similar mutual dependencies exist between education and economic growth, education and technology, education and health, and education and globalization. Some of the most important and urgent reasons for accelerating human development in Africa are the persistence of longstanding challenges *within* education and health systems. Most notable, there is the legacy of low educational attainment levels that resulted from low education coverage at independence and the education stagnation during most of the 1980s and 1990s. In the health sector, there is the persistence of parasitic and infectious diseases that have been largely brought under control in much of the rest of the world. Others issues, such as the increasing pressure for post-primary education, arise from the major success of rapid primary school enrollment growth over the last decade.

Compared to the past, future pressure for change *will increasingly come from outside the education and health systems* and will be driven by unprecedented economic, demographic, social, and technological change that is reshaping national societies, the global economy, and interaction among nations. Seven *forces outside the system*, discussed below, will be among the most important drivers of education and health policies over the next decades. Their relative importance will depend on the country: Africa is a very diverse continent, including with regard to current developments and future challenges in the education and health sectors. Some of these forces require urgent attention over the next decade to build the human capital foundation for attaining the 2050 Africa vision. Others will increase in importance throughout the period up to 2050.

Growing role of human capital

By 2050 the world will have undergone unprecedented change in most areas affecting the human condition. Countries' ability to manage the change processes in ways that allow them to seize the opportunities while minimizing risks will increasingly depend on the quality of their human capital. The importance of human capital is reinforced by the dramatic rise over the last decades of the *role knowledge and innovation play in development.*

Education's role in creating human capital is as indispensable as it is multiple. It ranges from enhancing productivity and peoples' ability to sustain a livelihood, adopt new technologies, and be better parents and citizens to building the attitudes, skills, and partnerships needed to tackle regional and global development challenges. Historically, public policy to advance basic literacy and numeracy has done more to advance human conditions than perhaps any other single policy. Literacy and numeracy are not only core competencies but are also prerequisites for most forms and levels of lifelong learning. Laying this foundation is a development stage that *cannot be leapfrogged*. Thus, there is a real urgency for the countries that have not yet built this foundation to accelerate the provision of basic education to all.

Countries at all income levels are retooling their education systems to better address their evolving human capital needs. Because most African countries, particularly those in SSA, start from very low levels, the challenge is particularly daunting for them. Figure 8.1 shows that SSA's level of adult educational attainment — a proxy for a country's level of human capital — in 2010 was similar to that of the advanced economies in 1950. Furthermore, SSA's low average hides wide variations across countries.

Barro and Lee (2010) use information on educational attainment for 146 countries for the period 1950-2010 to estimate the relationship between education and output. The key finding is that schooling has a significantly positive effect on output with estimated rates of return for an additional year of schooling ranging from 5 to 12 percent. Rates of return are even higher at the secondary and tertiary levels than in primary education. More importantly, the data demonstrate the symbiotic relationship between education and economic growth — the two expanded in tandem during that 60 year period.

SSA's educational attainment will improve as the large number of students who entered school in the last decade progress up the educational system and into adulthood. However, sustaining this trend requires continued bold corrective measures. In 2010, SSA's coverage of pre-primary education — a critical pillar of human development — was only 17 percent compared to 48 percent in South Asia, 57 percent in East Asia, and 70 percent in Latin America. Similarly, the number of primary school-age children who are out-of-school (31 million in 2010) in SSA has started to increase again, and the region now accounts for 51 percent of the world's total. In the absence of second-chance programs and without reduction in early dropout (30 percent prior to Grade 5), the illiteracy rate for the 15-24 age-group risks stagnating at its current high level of 28 percent, with huge negative impacts on labor productivity, family welfare, women's empowerment, and the speed of the demographic transition.

SSA's slow demographic transition will profoundly affect education over the next decades, significantly adding to the challenge of catching up on human capital formation (see Chapter 5). The SSA countries will need to continue to massively expand their school systems just to meet population growth while other developing regions can start shifting resources to expanding post-basic education and to quality improvements at all levels. Africa's population aged 5-14 is projected to increase by 71 percent (181 million) between 2010 and 2050; an 83 percent increase is projected for SSA but only 6 percent for North Africa. The increase will be especially rapid during the current decade (Figure 8.2). As a result, Africa has the world's youngest labor force, and this youth bulge creates tremendous pressure on skills development and employment creation. At the same time, if countries succeed in providing good quality education and health care and generating sufficient employment, the youth bulge could become a major demographic dividend by progressively adding cohorts of young people with higher productivity to the labor force.

BREAKING THE HUMAN CAPITAL BARRIER 163

Figure 8.1 | Africans are spending more time in school, but the continent still lags well behind the rest of the world

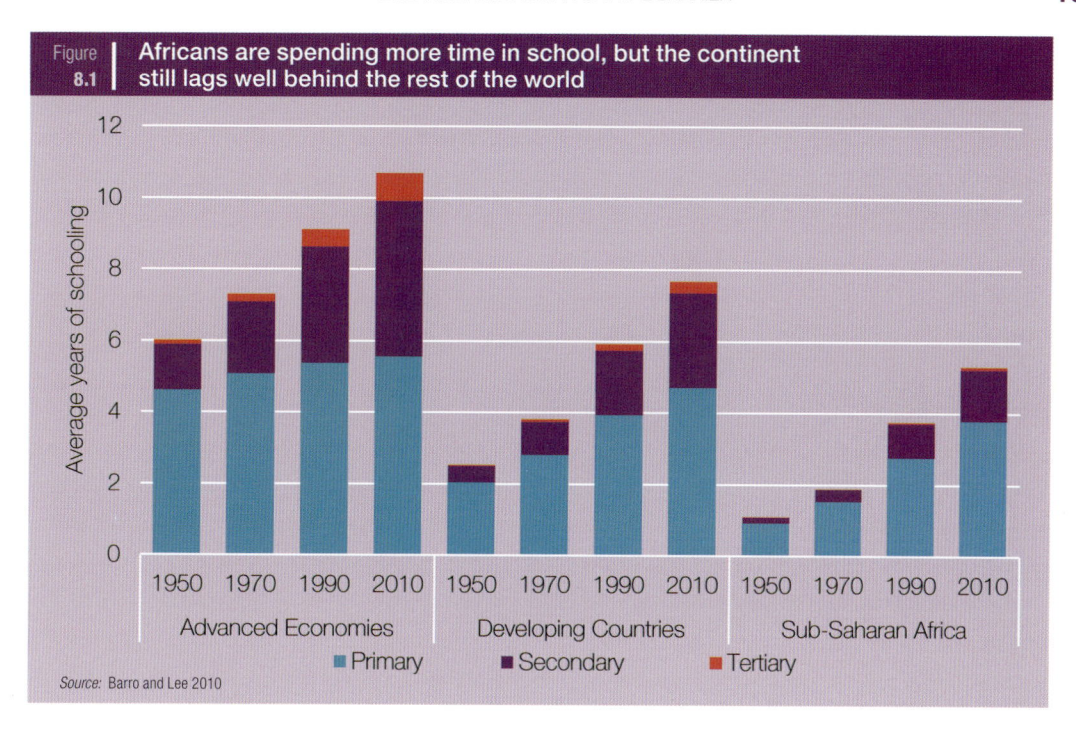

Average years of schooling — Primary, Secondary, Tertiary, across Advanced Economies, Developing Countries, and Sub-Saharan Africa for 1950, 1970, 1990, and 2010.

Source: Barro and Lee 2010

Figure 8.2 | Africa's young population will boom in the next decade, making its educational institutions critically important

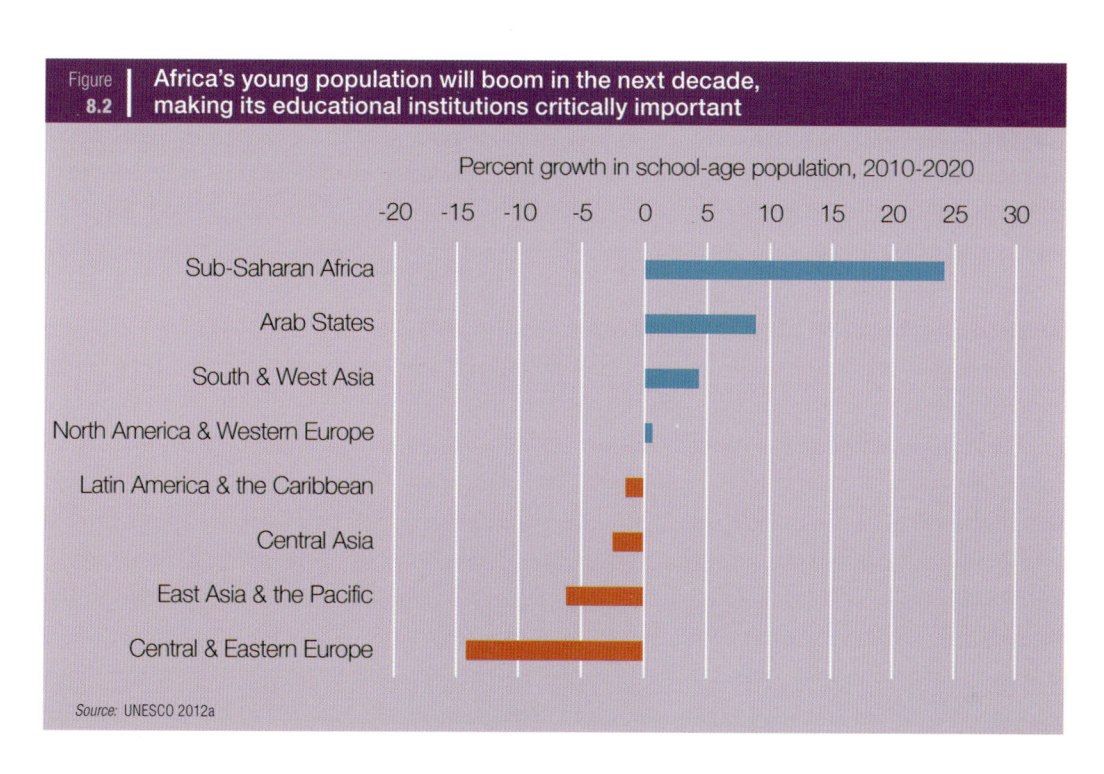

Percent growth in school-age population, 2010–2020

Sub-Saharan Africa	~25
Arab States	~9
South & West Asia	~5
North America & Western Europe	~1
Latin America & the Caribbean	~-2
Central Asia	~-3
East Asia & the Pacific	~-8
Central & Eastern Europe	~-15

Source: UNESCO 2012a

The impact of population growth on education will be reinforced by accelerated urbanization and likely rising regional and global migration. Rapid urbanization will increase pressure on education access but could also reduce unit cost. Further, regional migration will increase in step with progress toward regional integration, offering significant opportunities for economies of scale in the supply of, especially, higher education. Migration between Africa and other regions could also change considerably, depending on policies in the Organisation for Economic Co-operation and Development (OECD) and emerging economies as well as African countries' ability to achieve the economic growth needed to retain their talent at home and foster "brain gain."

Economic growth and structural transformation

Rapid economic growth and labor force transition to more productive sectors will provide new opportunities for countries to achieve better health for their people. It will also sharply increase the demand for education systems to deliver the skills, knowledge, and change agility required to both transform the countries' largely non-formal economies and help the modern sector compete in an increasingly globalized and knowledge-based economy. The skills required will be determined by both global and national trends. The former include more open trade and a growing share of services in such trade, Africa's rising share of global FDI, growing regional integration, and the increasing role of knowledge and innovation as determinants of growth. Skill needs driven by national trends include technological catch-up, countries' efforts to specialize in areas where they have comparative advantage, and efforts to address national priorities in areas such as energy, water, and food security. Progress in such areas will put pressure on education, training, and research systems to promote innovation, entrepreneurship, and knowledge generation, adaptation, and application. It will also call for developing lifelong education systems to support such society-wide change processes. This focus on the long term will be a daunting challenge in countries where education simultaneously must serve the production modes of pre-industrial, industrial, and post-industrial societies and where the solid, basic human capital foundations have not yet been built.

Advances in information and communication technologies

Advances in information and communication technologies (ICT) advances have great potential for facilitating African countries' catch-up growth in basic education, to leap-frog stages in the development of post-basic education, and to generate scale economies through regional cooperation. The opportunities offered by ICT are many, ranging from enhancing the effectiveness of learning, to improving education management and accountability processes, to developing less costly delivery modes through various types of web-based approaches. Even in industrialized countries, the effect of ICT in education is only beginning to take off. The effects on cost, equity in access, quality, and employment are likely to be profound. In particular, web-based learning has the potential to revolutionize the delivery of tertiary education in Africa and make rapid expansion more financially sustainable through, for example, Open Education Resources such as free Massive Open Online Courses (MOOCs). ICT also has the potential to alleviate skill shortages in health care delivery through telemedicine, where nurses and clinicians are able to obtain expert clinical diagnosis online. While not yet widespread in Africa, e-health's takeoff has been swift where it has been piloted, for example, in Tanzania, Lesotho, and Kenya.

Changing disease patterns

Currently, the most frequent causes of death in Africa are infectious and parasitic diseases even though in the rest of the world morbidity and mortality from these diseases has declined over the past twenty years (Figure 8.3). The WHO has predicted that by 2030 there will be a major increase in the number of deaths in Africa from cardiovascular and respiratory diseases, such as asthma and chronic obstructive pulmonary disease, both of which are related to smoking and fuel-burning for cooking. In North Africa, this epidemiological transition has already taken place, and non-communicable diseases are more prominent given comparably wealthier populations and the eradication of many communicable diseases. The increase in the incidence of chronic conditions and the increase in populations living for longer periods with diseases such as HIV/AIDS are already driving a new approach to primary health care. The new focus is on preventive care and a systemic approach to health care delivery, which calls for fundamental changes in the structure and training of health personnel.

Globalization

Globalization will affect education in multiple ways. The advance of the knowledge economy and the strong internationalization trends in higher education and research are leading to greatly increased mobility of students and academic staff. National decisions in the education sector thus increasingly have implications beyond national borders. The globalization effect applies to Africa's interaction with the rest of the world but, especially, among African countries. Globalization is not only shaking up most sectors of the economy; it is also opening up opportunities for cooperation in education and scientific research across borders and continents and making it possible to establish twinning and other arrangements that can enhance the capacity and contribution of African researchers. The global production landscape has also changed in that money follows ideas and/or cheap but well-educated labor. China and India have become attractive as outsourcing hubs because of skilled workforces. Africa, too, has the potential to become a major contributor to the pool of global skills.

Better governance and increased accountability for service delivery

As people become more educated and politically engaged, pressure will build for better governance and increased accountability for service delivery as discussed in Chapter 4. Countries' ability to build institutions for leadership, accountability, and innovation will be crucial to sound management of education change processes. Civil society pressure could be a major positive force in improving the quality and equity of service delivery as well as the effectiveness of resource use (Devarajan, Khemani, and Walton 2011). It could also strengthen education's role in forming more cohesive and equitable societies thereby

Figure 8.3 Infectious diseases are still central in Africa, but non-communicable ailments are becoming more important

Global burden of disease 2010 (with change from 1990)

	West Africa	Central Africa	Eastern Africa	Southern Africa	North Africa and Middle East	Global
1	Malaria +1	Malaria +1	HIV/AIDS +4	HIV/AIDS +4	Ischemic heart diseases ==	Ischemic heart diseases ==
2	Lower respiratory infection +1	Diarrheal disease -1	Lower respiratory infections -1	Lower respiratory infections -2	Stroke ==	Stroke ==
3	HIV/AIDS +10	Lower respiratory infections ==	Malaria ==	Stroke ==	Lower respiratory infections ==	COPD +1
4	Diarrheal diseases -3	Protein energy malnutrition ==	Diarrheal diseases -2	Tuberculosis ==	Road injury +4	Lower respiratory infections +1
5	Protein energy malnutrition -1	HIV/AIDS +6	Stroke +3	Diarrheal disease +3	Diabetes ++	Lower respiratory infetions +1
6	Neonatal sepsis +1	Tuberculosis ==	Tuberculosis ==	Diabetes +2	Other cardio and circulatory +1	HIV/AIDS ++
7	Stroke +3	Stroke ==	Protein energy malnutrition -3	Ischemic heart disease -1	Hypertensive heart disease +3	Diarrheal diseases -2
8	Road injury ++	Ischemic heart disease +2	Preterm birth complications +2	Interpersonal violence ++	Cirrhosis +1	Road injury +2
9	Meningitis -3	Preterm birth complications -1	Road injury ++	Hypertensive heart disease +2	Congenital anomalies -4	Diabetes ++
10	Preterm birth complications -2	Meningitis +2	Ischemic heart disease ++	COPD ==	Preterm birth complications -4	Tuberculosis -4
11	Measles -24	Measles -45	Measles -21		Diarrheal diseases -12	

Legend: Increased since 1990 | Decreased since 1990 | No change since 1990 | +/-n Number of positions changed since 1990 | ++ Not within the top ten in 1990 | Font size corresponds to number of places gained or lost since 1990

Source: Wang et al. 2012

enhancing national viability (Collier 2009). Moreover, as education and health systems develop, they grow more diverse. In particular, governments' role as the sole provider of publicly-financed services tends to decline while its role tends to increase in areas such as standard-setting, quality assurance, certification, and other supportive services to enhance the quality of human capital. The public sector's changing role, in turn, calls for the development of stronger capacity to support these new functions.

In summary, education and health systems throughout the world will both face and help shape unprecedented global change during the next decades. The challenges will be particularly daunting for many African countries because of their weak human capital base. In the absence of vigorous action, there is a very real risk that some of the weakest countries will fall further behind. As discussed in Chapter 6, conflict and instability in one country can have very serious negative neighborhood effects. But, as discussed below, there are also important opportunities for rapid catch-up growth. Choices made over the next decade will determine the extent to which countries can grasp this opportunity.

Key Messages

Responding to the drivers of change highlighted above requires both urgent action and a clear-headed examination of options and priorities. Six key messages for doing so are set out below.

It is urgent to rapidly catch-up in building basic human capital

The best long-term investment most African countries can make over the next decade is to correct the fact that their young children and youth fare much worse in basic health and education status than those of other regions. This development stage *cannot be leapfrogged*: good quality basic education and health care provide the foundation for development in other areas. In education, establishing this foundation means rapidly overcoming the legacy of high levels of illiteracy and out-of-school youth caused by past slow progress toward universal primary education. Since a large segment of youth currently either has incomplete primary education or no formal education, governments must develop a *two-pronged labor force development strategy* — combining efforts to *provide cutting-edge skills for the modern sector* with much stronger efforts than are currently being made to *improve basic education skills for the whole labor force*. Not only will this approach help improve labor productivity, it will also help accelerate progress toward other goals such as improved health, family welfare, and women empowerment; shared growth that will enhance equity; and social cohesion and faster demographic transition.

...and ambitious catch-up goals need to be set

Table 8.1 presents a development vision for the key education indicators for 2030 and 2050. The numbers are not predictions but represent a vision of what is possible and would bring Africa more closely in line with East and South Asia and Latin America. The vision implies that, by 2030, African countries would have achieved (a) 35 percent coverage of a three-year cycle of pre-school education (corresponding to one year for all); (b) 85 to 90 percent completion of 8 to 9 years of basic education;

and (c) cutting in half the 2010 illiteracy rate of 28 percent for the age group 15-24 years. If these goals cannot be reached in the 2030s and 2040s, at least one-third of SSA's prime working age population would be illiterate and more than one-third of children could be born to illiterate mothers. Both outcomes would have severe negative impacts on attaining other key development goals.

Table 8.1 | Ambitious education target would help drive Africa toward convergence

	2010	2030	2050
GER* in three-year cycle of pre-school education	17	35	80
Completion rate for 9 year cycle of basic education	50**	85-90	90-95
Literacy rate age group 15-24	72***	85	95
GER Upper Secondary	31	50	80
GER Higher Education	7	17	35

Note: *GER = Gross Enrollment Ratio, **Based on data for 2010: 62% of the pupils entering primary education completing the cycle and 80% of those entering lower secondary education completing the cycle, *** Actual data for 2005-2010
Source: UNESCO (2012b) for 2010. Authors' illustrative targets for 2030 and 2050

The main constraint to rapid catch-up is implementation

Most of what must be done to provide basic education and health care is known. The main constraint is poor capacity to translate this knowledge into effective implementation and interventions that better serve the poor. This constraint reflects in part serious political leadership and governance weaknesses, which limit the ability to handle effectively the political economy of implementing reforms. The most difficult reforms will be those that require making trade-offs that favor the groups with little political clout who would benefit most from basic education and health services. During the last two decades of the 20th century, such constraints were reinforced by stagnating economies that provided little fiscal space for reform. In the first decade of the 21st century, concerted national and global action helped overcome many of these constraints, leading to a major acceleration in human capital formation. Provided countries can (a) reach the level of growth assumed by the convergence scenario laid out in Chapter 1 (6.6 percent average annual GDP growth between 2012 and 2050) and (b) accelerate the building of institutions for leadership, accountability, and innovation, *Africa should be well placed to achieve rapid catch-up growth*.

…but Africa has shown that rapid catch-up growth is possible when conditions are right

SSA's Gross Enrollment Ratio (GER) for primary education grew by an impressive 18 percentage points between 2000 and 2010 when it reached 101 percent. Enrollment grew by 4.4 percent annually, adding 46 million students, compared to 3.4 percent during the 1990s (25 million) and 2.5 percent during the 1980s (14 million). Growth also picked up in secondary and higher education where enrollments doubled between 2000 and 2010. It is noteworthy that these gains reflect rapid catch-up growth by most of the countries that had very low enrollments. For example, Burkina Faso, Ethiopia, Niger, and

Mali — which all had GERs for primary education of less than 10 percent in 1960 and which even in 1990 only had GERs of between 23 percent (Mali) and 33 percent (Ethiopia) — reached GERs in 2010 ranging from 71 percent (Niger) to 107 percent (Ethiopia). Similarly, in the health sector, while the average level of child mortality declined more slowly in SSA than in other regions, countries such as Rwanda and Senegal achieved spectacular improvements, reducing child mortality rates between 2005 and 2011 by more than 50 percent.

It is imperative to enhance learning outcomes and relevance

The worldwide challenge to improve learning outcomes is more daunting for SSA than for other regions because countries start from very low levels and have systems poorly equipped to address it. Teachers constitute the single-most important determinant of quality, and handling teacher issues may pose the single-most important education challenge. The need to expand the stock of teachers will far exceed that of other regions for several reasons: SSA's population aged 5-14 years is projected to increase by 83 percent between 2010 and 2050; 24 percent of SSA's children of primary school age were out of school in 2010; the provision of pre- and post-basic education as well as of second-chance programs for school leavers must grow rapidly; and primary school pupil-teacher ratios are high (43 in SSA in 2010 compared to 18 in East Asia and 22 in Latin America). In addition, attention must be paid to retraining as well as training since the quality of existing teachers is poor.

... and to mobilize sustainable financing through economic growth

The investments required by SSA countries to address the above challenges will be well above those of other regions, particularly while they fund essential catch-up growth and respond to high population growth over the next decade. Funding teacher salaries will be the single most important challenge. Over the next two decades SSA countries need to massively increase their teaching force at all levels of education, even assuming major progress in using existing teachers more effectively. For example, to reach a GER of 100 percent in a nine-grade basic education cycle by 2030, SSA must almost double the current number of teachers in primary and lower secondary education even at current high pupil-teacher ratios.[2] In constant prices and salaries, an annual increase in the salary budget of 3.3 percent would be required. Taking into account even modest improvement in teaching conditions (e.g., lower pupil-teacher ratio and higher salaries) and the increased needs for teachers in post-basic education brings the annual salary budget increase to at least 4 to 6 percent. But, again, if the 6.6 percent annual economic growth of the convergence scenario is attained, this addition to the budget should be feasible: SSA had an annual increase of 5 percent in public education spending between 1999 and 2010.

---

2. In 2010, SSA had about 3.1 million teachers in primary and 1.0 million in lower secondary education. The pupil-teacher ratio was 43:1 in primary and 28:1 in lower secondary education.

In addition to teachers, there will be a huge need for increased investment in school infrastructure. For example, based on an average class size of 40 pupils, meeting the enrollment increase of 146 million between 2010 and 2030 to reach 100 percent enrollment of the 5-14 age group would require 3.7 million new classrooms. Additional investment would be required for replacement costs of the existing stock, which is generally in poor condition. Theunynck (2009) presents a detailed analysis of unit costs for new construction and replacement needs in primary education in SSA.[3] Based on the study's parameters, the number of new classrooms needed is 6.1 million, for a total cost of $71 billion, or $3.6 billion annually between 2010 and 2030. This represents about 12 to 15 percent of SSA's 2010 total public education expenditures. The infrastructure costs of post-basic secondary education (estimated using the same class size, unit, and classroom replacement costs as for primary education, which likely underestimates the costs) would add about $1 billion annually, which corresponds to another 3 to 4 percent of the total public expenditures in 2010. The infrastructure costs for post-secondary education are likely to be even larger.

Both the financing needs and the scope for resource mobilization vary greatly among countries. However, based on the experience of successful countries in Africa and elsewhere, countries achieving the average 6.6 percent annual GDP growth assumed by the convergence scenario should be well placed to meet the financing challenge. Thus, *attaining high, sustainable economic growth is the single-most important condition for sustainable education financing*. But additional efforts will be required.

First, while the median SSA country spends a higher share of its budget (17.6 percent) and GDP (4.7 percent) on education than other developing regions, some countries spend far less and must increase education's priority. For example, in 2010, the Democratic Republic of the Congo (DRC) — SSA's third most populous country, with enormous education needs — spent only 8.9 percent of the government budget on education (2.7 percent of GDP), relying heavily on school fees to fund even primary education.[4]

Second, there is greater scope for using existing resources more effectively, especially through more strategic deployment and management of teachers, better accountability mechanisms for teachers and heads of schools, more training materials, and reduction of repetition and dropout rates.

Third, education policies must cover the full range of learning opportunities whether they are financed or provided by the public sector or non-public entities. Increasingly, delivering pre-primary education, adult literacy, vocational training, and higher education must include public-private partnerships.

Fourth, it is likely that the future pressure to expand education will result in greater pressure to increase private spending. Governments must, therefore, make public expenditure trade-offs that will enhance education's role in equalizing opportunity. Specifically, government will need to give high priority to good quality basic education for all including, as discussed below, extending the duration of the

---

3. The low-cost scenario is based on community-managed programs. The construction cost per classroom including furniture, latrines, water supply, and some office and storage space, is $11,665. In addition, the replacements need for sub-standard and run down classrooms is estimated at 40% of the total construction need.
4. Parents in DRC have shown remarkable resilience in supporting education despite an almost complete neglect by the government during most of the 1980s and 1990s. DRC's GER in primary education declined from 95% in 1970 to 70% in 1990 and 48% in 1999 and back to its 1970 level in 2010 (94%).

basic-education cycle and using more public resources for second-chance programs and for pre-primary education. Developing financially sustainable strategies for expanding and improving the quality of upper secondary and higher education will be a major challenge for most countries. Often, there will need to be an increase in private funding as many countries in East Asia and Latin America have done. A shift in higher education financing from public to private sources is a common 21st century trend experienced throughout the world (Varghese 2013). To ensure equal opportunities for access for the poor in this context is a major challenge.

Regarding the prospect for mobilizing non-public resources, remittances from migrant workers play a role in funding education in some countries, and some funds from private multinational firms and foundations benefit education. The magnitude of private support is, however, small compared to that of governments, parents, and official development assistance (ODA).[5] UNESCO estimates private support to be equivalent to 5 percent of ODA for education by Development Assistance Committee (DAC) donors (2012b). About 20 percent comes from private foundations. It is not known how much of this support is directed to Africa. However, while small at present, these and other types of innovative financing are likely to increase in the future (Burnett and Bermingham 2010).

Finally, while *external aid* is likely to become insignificant for most countries by 2050, during the next decade aid can play a very helpful role if used more strategically to help countries use their own resources more effectively (Fredriksen 2011). Over time, closer regional cooperation will likely *replace most aid-based cooperation arrangements to generate economies of scale in service delivery, stimulate R&D targeting African priorities and needs, and harness benefits and manage risks related to brain drain/brain gain/brain circulation.* With the advance of the knowledge economy and the growing internationalization of education and research, national decisions in the education sector increasingly have implications beyond national borders. The internationalization trend goes well beyond higher education and research to cover aspects such as lifelong learning, curriculum, quality assurance, open education resources, training materials, and use of ICT. Cooperation will offer economies of scale in many areas of financing, especially for Africa's many small countries (a dozen have two million inhabitants or less), which will find it very costly to develop specialized national training capacity in areas that are essential but where the labor market is very limited.

In summary, rapid economic growth, coupled with peace and stability, are key conditions for SSA to bridge the human capital gap with the rest of the world. Most of the basic health and education problems common to developing countries 40 to 50 years ago — high levels of child mortality, infection, and malnutrition; low levels of enrollment and literacy, especially for women; high birth rates — are increasingly becoming the problems of non-converging and fragile SSA countries, which also have to deal with new

---

5. Health benefits much more from such support than does education. For example UNESCO (2012b) refers to one estimate showing that US foundations give 8 percent of their grants to education and 53 percent to health. As much as 90 percent of corporate contributions are from pharmaceutical companies.

challenges, such as HIV/AIDS and climate change. Still, experience shows that rapid catch-up growth can transform societies in one generation. History also shows that achieving such growth is far from automatic; *it takes good policies and strong political leadership*.

Action Agenda

Good outcomes in nutrition, health, and education are development goals in themselves because they directly improve people's lives. But they also equip people for productive employment and job opportunities and, through this channel, human capital drives economic and social advances (World Bank 2012a). Despite good progress in the last decade, SSA's basic education and health indicators lag seriously behind those of other regions, and the gap has been increasing in many areas. Therefore, achieving good outcomes will require *transformative changes* in the education and health sectors of most Africa countries, at a scale beyond that achieved over the past 40 years. Focusing on *education and skills development*, the following elements need to be part of most African countries' strategic agenda to achieve the 2050 vision:

Invest in all young children: A moral imperative and a smart investment

Arguably the highest-return investment most African countries can make in any sector is in the well-being of the next generation. They need to rapidly address the fact that their young children fare worse in most areas than children in other parts of the world.

Priority actions, described in more detail below, to improve the education and health status of Africa's children include:

- *Increase significantly the investment in Early Childhood Care and Education (ECCE):* Because of strong interdependence, improving the health and education status of young children requires an integrated strategy. For example, nutrition is a key determinant of a child's capacity to learn, and a mother' education plays a key role in lowering mortality and fertility rates. And high child mortality causes higher birth rates as a risk mitigation strategy against childhood deaths.
- *Target vulnerable groups:* Because children's education and health status differ widely depending on family income, urban/rural residence, and gender, an *effective strategy must target those most in need* in order to break the intergenerational vicious cycle where different aspects of inequalities reinforce each other to stifle children's life chances.

SSA has the highest levels of child poverty, and children suffer from "severe deprivation of food, safe drinking water, sanitation, health, shelter, education, information, and basic social services" (Garcia, Pence, and Evens 2008). Box 8.1 shows that, despite recent improvements, SSA's basic child indicators not only lag far behind other developing regions, but, in many cases, the gap is increasing, both with other regions and among SSA countries. Failure to rapidly ramp up investment in young children would be a strategic mistake for African countries that would impact negatively their long-term development prospects.

> **Box 8.1 — The imperative to sharply increase SSA's investment in young children**
>
> - **Under-five mortality:** At 121 per 1000 (2010), SSA's rate is double that of South Asia (67) and five times that of East Asia (24) and Latin America (23). It exceeds the rate achieved by East Asia and Latin America in 1970 and by South Asia in 1990. In 1970, 19 percent of the 16.6 million children worldwide dying before age five were in SSA. In 2010, the worldwide number declined to 6.6 million but SSA's share increased to 49 percent.
> - **Malnutrition:** SSA is the only region where the number of stunted children increased between 1990 and 2010 (from 38 to 55 million). SSA's share of global stunting increased from 15 to 32 percent and is projected to reach 42 percent by 2020. In 2010, SSA had 16 of the 24 countries with stunting of 40 percent or more.
> - **Pre-primary education:** In 2010, SSA's enrollment ratio was 17 percent compared to 48 in South Asia, 57 in East Asia, and 70 in Latin America. While SSA's GER grew by seven percentage points between 1999 and 2010, the growth was much faster in other regions that started from a much higher initial level.
> - **Combined impact:** UNESCO's ECCE index combining the three above indicators covers 68 developing countries. SSA accounts for 19 of the 25 lowest ranked countries, including the ten ranked lowest.
>
> *Sources:* UNICEF 2012a and UNESCO 2012b

Recent research shows that investing in ECCE yields high social and economic returns and the poor benefit the most. Heckman (2006) concludes that the first six years of life are critical for brain pathways and processes to develop and that it is possible to compensate for adverse family environments if action is taken in the early years. Naudeau et al. (2011), summarizing global research in this area, concludes that ECCE interventions (i) enhance school readiness and education outcomes; (ii) improve physical and mental health and reduce reliance on the health care system; (iii) reduce high-risk behavior such as smoking, risky sexual behavior, substance abuse, and criminal and violent activities in adulthood; (iv) have positive externalities because child care increases schooling of older female siblings and raises mothers' labor force participation; and (v) are more cost-effective than remedial interventions even in areas where such interventions are possible. For example, severe malnutrition in the first two years is irreversible, as it causes permanent negative effects on the physical and intellectual capabilities of a child. Save the Children (2012) refers to this effect as a "life sentence for children."

In order to catch up with the rest of the world in the education and health status of their children, SSA countries must give ECCE drastically higher priority, often through partnerships with various non-government entities. In an extensive review of strategies for reducing inequalities and improving developmental outcomes for young children in low- and middle-income countries, Engle et al. (2011) conclude that unless governments allocate more resources to quality ECCE programs for the poorest people in the population "economic disparities will continue to widen."

Because of the wide variety of content and coverage, comparative data on ECCE funding are very scarce worldwide. Naudeau et al. (2011) quote estimates showing that in 2005 OECD governments spent on average 2.36 percent of GDP on a broad range of services to families and young children, including 0.50 percent of GDP on pre-primary education for three-to-six year olds, of which 0.43 percent was public funding. The study ranks 57 countries according to the pre-primary share of public education budgets. The median share was 6.5 percent, ranging from above 10 percent in eight countries to less than 1 percent in five, including three of the seven SSA countries covered.

Calculations based on the cost of primary education indicates that achieving a GER of 80 percent in 2050 would require spending 1.27 percent of GDP on pre-primary education[6] up from about 0.1 percent in 2010. Clearly, it would be difficult to achieve an 80 percent GER for 2050 through public funding alone: 1.27 percent of GDP would correspond to about 27 percent of the total education budget, up from about 2 percent now.[7] Also, SSA's pre-primary age population is projected to increase by 60 percent between 2010 and 2050. The current 17 percent GER is achieved through 55 percent of private provision (compared with 15 percent in the OECD), largely for better-off families in urban areas. To ensure that the poor — who can benefit the most — receive services, public funding must increase and be well-targeted. Thus, even to double the GER by 2030 is likely to mean a substantial increase in the share of public budgets allocated to pre-primary education and success in building public/private partnerships where communities, NGOs, and other stakeholders, provide both financial and in-kind support.[8] With strong investment progress can be rapid: Ghana increased its pre-primary enrollment ratio from 31 percent in 1999 to 69 percent by 2009.

Reduce the burden of disease

The high burden of disease is putting a brake on growth in many economies, especially in SSA. The region has 12 percent of the world's population but 25 percent of the world's burden of disease, Seventy percent of the people living with HIV, and 50 percent of the deaths of children under five years of age. The heavy disease burden lowers labor productivity through missed work days and general debilitation, undermines future capabilities of tomorrow's workers through its heavy toll on children (including missed school days), and necessitates using a high share of scarce resources on care and treatment rather than investment in economic growth.

---

6. In 2010, SSA's GER in primary education was 101 percent, and public spending equaled 2.2 percent of GDP. The average duration was 6.2 years. Thus, the cost of providing one grade of the average 6.2 grade cycle was about 0.35 percent of GDP. Because of (i) higher unit costs in pre-primary than in primary education (largely because of a lower pupil-teacher ratio), and (ii) larger age-cohorts (due to population growth), the cost of one year of pre-primary education is roughly 1.5 times that of primary education, i.e., 0.53 percent of GDP. This GDP per capita cost of providing one grade roughly equals the cost quoted in the text for OECD countries of providing the whole pre-primary cycle (mostly 3-year) because the pre-primary age group in a SSA country is more than 2.5 times that of an OECD country and, measured in GDP per capita terms, teacher salaries in SSA are about twice those of OECD countries. The impact of the latter factor is partly compensated for by higher pupil/teacher pupil ratio in SSA (27 versus 15). The average official duration of the pre-primary cycle in SSA is three years.

7. SSA's 2010 GER of 17 percent equaled 11.9 million pupils of whom 2/3 were in 7 countries totaling 40 percent of SSA's 5-year olds. The 2010 GER 2010 corresponds to enrolling about half of SSA's five-year olds. The GER of 35 percent in 2030 means providing one-year for a whole age-cohort; the 2050 target means providing for 80 percent of the three age-cohorts 3-6 years.

8. Data for Cape Verde, Guinea, Guinea-Bissau, and Senegal suggest that, for these countries, public spending was on average more than three times higher in public than in community run programs (Jaramillo and Mingat 2008).

Priority actions, described in more detail below, to reduce the disease burden include:
- *Accelerate the momentum to lower the high levels of communicable and parasitic diseases* through a multi-pronged approach targeting in particular malaria, pneumonia, diarrhea, and malnutrition, which are key drivers of the high child morbidity and mortality in Africa.
- *Step up measures to prevent the rise in chronic conditions* such as obesity and heart disease through a focus on preventive care and health education.
- *Address the causes of poor health* by improving nutrition; access to water, sanitation and rural infrastructure; empowering women; and removing social and financial barriers to services.
- *Strengthen the health system's management capacity* through greater use of technology, stronger public-private partnerships, and increased quality and quantity of health workers.
- *Develop sustainable financing strategies* to provide universal basic health care coverage through a mix of internal and external funding.
- *Lower catastrophic out-of-pocket expenditures by pooling risks.*

Of the 26 countries worldwide with under-five mortality rates above 100 deaths per 1,000 live births 24 were in Africa in 2012 (UNICEF 2012b). In recent years, SSA has made significant but uneven progress in reducing child mortality: if progress could be sustained and expanded to more countries, then SSA could close the gap with the rest of the developing world well before 2050. This would require urgent scaled-up actions in countries that are doing less well (see Box 8.2). For example, countries such as Burkina Faso, Cameroon, Chad, DRC, Mali, and Somalia saw an increase in the total number of deaths of children under five (WHO 2012a).

Countries that have been successful in reducing child deaths, such as Rwanda, have undertaken a multi-pronged program focused on the top three causes of under-five mortality (i.e., malaria, pneumonia, and diarrhea), or improved nutritional levels of children including the addition of micronutrient supplements such as Vitamin A, such as in Tanzania, where child mortality was reduced by 20 percent. Diarrheal diseases, which account for 11 percent of child deaths, can be prevented by improving access to clean water and sanitation. Improving antenatal care and rural infrastructure would reduce the number of birth-related complications, which cause about 23 percent of child deaths, and reduce the number of maternal deaths. Significant expansion of malaria interventions in Kenya and Uganda has played a major role in reducing malaria deaths, which contribute to about 16 percent of child deaths in Africa (Demombynes and Trommlerova 2012). Similarly, increasing coverage of services to prevent mother-to-child transmission of HIV in about 60 percent in SSA reduced the number of children newly infected with HIV in 2011 by 24 percent overall and by 40 to 59 percent in six countries — Burundi, Kenya, Namibia, South Africa, Togo, and Zambia (UNAIDS 2012).

Addressing the causes of poor health would help to reduce maternal mortality, which has remained stubbornly high. In SSA, in 2008, the chance that a woman would die as a result of complications from pregnancy or childbirth was one in 31 — seven times the rate in South Asia, 19 times higher than in East Asia, and 139 times higher than in advanced economies. Underlying causes of high maternal mortality

Box 8.2 | Health in Africa — big gains...and big challenges (by Ikuo Takizawa)

Many African countries have accelerated health improvements over the last decade. In SSA the annual rate of reduction in under-five mortality (for which 4.4 percent or more is required to achieve the MDG target) more than doubled from 1.5 percent in 1990-2000 to 3.1 percent in 2000-11. The rate of reduction of maternal mortality (5.5 percent is required to meet the MDG target) increased even more, from 1.4 percent to 3.9 percent over the same period. Progress was also made on infectious disease control, where the number of deaths from malaria and HIV/AIDS has been declining.

The improvements are based on strengthening health systems in order to ensure access to essential services. The Community-based Health Planning and Service program in Ghana, Health Extension Program in Ethiopia, and Health Surveillance Assistance in Malawi are good examples of initiatives to improve physical access to essential health services. The Community-based Health Insurance Scheme in Rwanda and the National Health Insurance Scheme in Ghana are examples of public financial protection programs which achieved high population coverage in low income settings.

The remaining health challenges are, however, still daunting. Africa still has a disproportionate share of the global disease burden. It has one-tenth of the global population but accounts for half of the world's child and maternal deaths, two-thirds of deaths due to AIDS, and 90 percent of deaths from malaria.

As in other areas, there is a large disparity in the pace of progress across the continent with many countries in SSA still struggling to ensure physical access to essential health services. Ensuring financial protection especially for the poor is a common challenge across both North Africa and Sub-Saharan Africa. Such disparity is clearly illustrated by the pace of progress toward meeting the health MDGs. One-quarter of African countries (shown in green in Figure 8.i) are likely to meet the MDG child mortality target but another quarter (shown in red) has made very little progress. The prospect for achieving the MDG for maternal mortality is more challenging (Figure 8.ii).

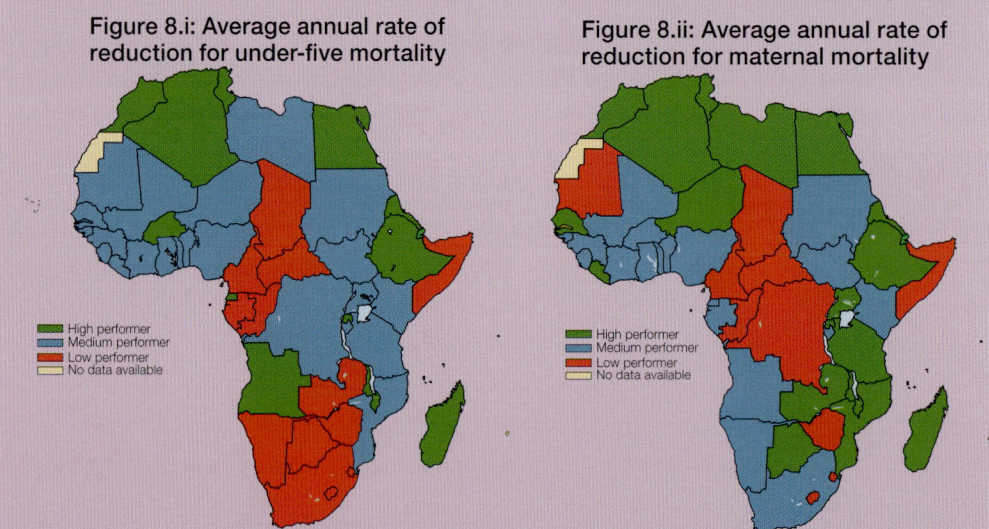

Figure 8.i: Average annual rate of reduction for under-five mortality

Figure 8.ii: Average annual rate of reduction for maternal mortality

Increased disparity in health status and health service utilization within countries another equity challenge. In SSA 76 percent of births in urban areas are attended by skilled birth attendants compared to only 40 percent in rural areas. Disparity across income groups is also striking with 85 percent of births among the richest quintile of the population attended by skilled birth attendants but only 27 percent for the lowest quintile.

include too few health services and providers, poor infrastructure and transport, and low empowerment of women. In high-mortality countries, 70 percent of women have no contact with health personnel following childbirth, only 42 percent of births are attended by skilled health workers, and 28 percent of women never receive prenatal care. As in the case of child mortality, most causes of maternal mortality are preventable through a coordinated set of multi-sectoral actions to provide basic pre- and post-natal services. In addition, education helps to empower women, increase contraceptive use, lower the number of births, and increase child spacing; it also helps increase the use of pre- and post-natal services and their delivery by skilled health workers.

Greater health system capacity for management would help to reduce *HIV/AIDS, tuberculosis (TB), and malaria*. In addition, a high proportion of resources that could be invested in productive sectors is spent on care and treatment.

HIV/AIDS: About 23.5 million (70 percent) of HIV infections worldwide are in SSA. The disease has reached hyper-epidemic proportions primarily in Southern Africa but is a major threat in more than half of SSA countries. HIV/AIDS was ranked the 33rd cause of the disease burden in 1990, but moved to 6th position by 2011 (Figure 8.3). The disease has contributed to the single greatest reversal in human development in modern history. It has orphaned nearly 12 million children under the age of 18 in Africa (UNAIDS 2011), reduced life expectancy at birth in high epidemic countries by more than 10 years, slowed economic growth, and deepened household poverty because of the costs associated with treatment and the loss of income. AIDS has also had a devastating impact on the building of human capital through loss of trained personnel and reduced productivity. Wider access to *antiretroviral treatment* is saving lives and has changed the way in which HIV is viewed, from a death sentence to a chronic illness. The cost of first-line antiretroviral regimens has come down from around $10,000 to under $100 per person per year due in part to availability of low-cost generic medicines. By 2010 more than 6 million people were on antiretroviral therapy. There has also been a major breakthrough in *preventing mother-to-child transmission* and, more recently, in *reducing the risk of transmitting HIV between partners*. Moreover, rapidly scaling up *voluntary medical male circumcision* has the potential to prevent infection for an estimated 1 in 5 of the people who would have acquired HIV infection.

TB: New cases of TB have been declining for several years, and the TB mortality rate has decreased by 41 percent since 1990 (WHO 2012b). TB is one of the top killers of women, causing half a million deaths in 2011. People living with HIV are particularly vulnerable to developing TB because of their increased susceptibility to infection, and AIDS continues to be a leading cause of death in this population group. In South Africa, some 60 percent of new TB cases tested for HIV are seropositive; in Nigeria that figure is 25 percent. Lesotho and Swaziland have high HIV prevalence rates, and the TB co-infection rates are 77 percent and 82 percent, respectively. There has been a rapid increase in screening for TB among people living with HIV, especially in South Africa, but more needs to be done to ensure that all patients are tested for HIV and all TB patients living with HIV receive treatment.

Malaria: There were an estimated 216 million episodes of malaria around the world in 2010, 81 percent of which were in Africa. Malaria accounts for 655,000 deaths worldwide, 86 percent of which are in Africa. Six countries — Nigeria, DRC, Burkina Faso, Mozambique, Cote d'Ivoire, and Mali — account for 60 percent of malaria deaths. Nigeria and DRC have the highest prevalence rates. Within the last decade, malaria deaths have been cut by a third in Africa, bringing the levels back to the levels of the 1960s when malaria had been successfully reduced. The disease is being defeated by the simple and cheap promotion of insecticide-treated bed nets, indoor spraying, and effective rapid diagnosis and treatment. A vaccine is currently being trialed and might be available for use within five years.

Most health care systems in Africa are underfunded. Fifty-three African countries signed the Abuja Declaration pledging 15 percent of their national budgets to health, but most remain far below that target, and some seven countries have actually cut their health spending over the past decade. A WHO taskforce on innovative financing for health systems suggests that the 49 low-income countries surveyed would need to spend about $44 per capita on average (unweighted) in 2009, rising to a little more than $60 per capita by 2015, to meet the costs of delivering the specified mix of interventions to meet the key health goals (WHO 2010). Only eight of the countries could raise the funds needed, and the rest would require external funding ranging from $2 to $41 per capita by 2015. Treatment of HIV/AIDS, malaria, and TB has been largely externally funded (26 SSA countries obtained more than 50 percent of their HIV funding from external sources).

In 2007, 50 percent of total health expenditure came from private sources (of which 71 percent was from households), about 30 percent from governments, and 20 percent from donors. Only about 5 to 10 percent of people in SSA are protected against catastrophic risk. Several approaches are being implemented in Africa to extend health insurance and coverage to the poor. They include (i) *government health insurance*, which offers insurance to formal sector workers (e.g., the Ghanaian national health insurance scheme); (ii) *micro and community health insurance*, which are pro-poor, private insurance schemes, allowing employers, various organized groups, and families to buy health insurance at low rates (e.g., Rwanda uses low cost community-based health insurance coverage to provide health care; in Nigeria, the Dutch government, through PharmAccess, provided a grant for insurance premium subsidies for market women, and other countries are emulating this approach to supporting insurance for workers in the informal sector); and (iii) *vouchers* to help the poor access reproductive and maternal and child health care services.

Build critical foundation skills for all

No country has been able to achieve sustained economic growth without first achieving universal primary education. SSA's coverage of primary education more than doubled between 1960 and 1980 to reach 80 percent. It then declined to 73 percent in 1990 and only returned to its 1980 level around 2000. The slow progress in attaining universal primary education has left a heavy legacy of low educational attainment. The basic cognitive and non-cognitive skills imparted by universal primary education are a prerequisite to building the broad-based 21st century human capital needed for countries to be able to respond to, and help shape, increasingly complex, rapid and unpredictable national, regional, and global developments. During the last decade, most SSA countries resumed rapid growth in building basic human capital. It is crucial that this growth be sustained.

Priority actions, described in more detail below, to achieve this include:[9]

- *Accelerate efforts to achieve admission of all children and reduce late entry.*
- *Reduce dropout.*
- *Provide "second-chance" programs*, addressing the needs of people who never entered school, dropped out, or otherwise did not complete their schooling.
- *Make curricula more relevant* to provide the non-cognitive skills (learning to learn, problem solving, communicating) demanded by employers, in addition to solid cognitive skills (language, math, science) of the basic education cycle.
- *Extend the duration of basic education to 8-9 years* to insure that the population has the skills required to be effective citizens in 21st century societies.

Late entry into the first grade is a major factor in dropout rates in later grades. A study covering 16 SSA countries showed that 41 percent of those who entered primary school over the period 2005-2010 were two years or more above the official entry age. Since the mid-1970s, the dropout rate prior to Grade 5 in SSA has remained stubbornly high, at about 30 percent. A successful strategy to achieve basic education for all must give high priority to eliminating early dropout. To achieve this will require an integrated strategy designed both to improve quality of learning (see below) and address the multiple causes of early dropout related to factors such as poverty, poor health and nutrition, and direct and opportunity cost of attending school.

Second-chance programs must in particular address the needs of three different groups:

Illiterate adults: In 2015, Africa is projected to have 209 million adult illiterates. Of this total, 176 million (84 percent) would be in SSA and 33 million (16 percent) in North Africa. SSA's adult illiteracy rate would be 41 percent for women and 27 percent for men.

Illiterate youth: Youth represent a large proportion of the illiterate population. In 2015, the share of the age group 15-24 years in the total number of illiterate individuals would be 25 percent in SSA and 8 percent in North Africa. SSA's illiteracy rate for this age group would be 24 percent (44 million) and 11 percent in North Africa (3 million) as compared with 12 percent for South Asia, 2 percent for Latin America, and 1 percent for East Asia. SSA's share of the number of illiterate youth worldwide would be 46 percent in 2015, up from 37 percent in the period 2005-2010 and 20 percent for the period 1985-1994.

Out-of-school children: In 2010, 31 million (24 percent) of SSA's children of primary school age were out of school compared with only 3 percent in North Africa. SSA accounted for 51 percent of the world's out-of-school children, up from 39 percent in 1999. About three quarters of these are not expected to enter school. Thus, in the absence of second-chance programs, these children will start their adult life

---

9. The data quoted below are largely derived from (UNESCO 2012b).

illiterate. These children disproportionally live in conflict-affected countries (40 percent); are from poor families (children from the poorest quintile are four times more likely to be out of school than those from the richest quintile); live in rural areas (twice as likely to be out of school as urban children), and are girls (53 percent of total) (UNESCO 2012a).

The neglect of youth and adult literacy over the last two to three decades is partly due to a misconception that, because of the past mixed experience, cost-effective adult literacy programs are not available. They are (Lauglo 2001; Oxenham 2008). And such programs play an important role in promoting equity because they target populations that have a history of marginalization. Second-chance programs for young adults have been tested in many SSA countries; these can be adapted and scaled up.[10] A second misconception is that literacy programs are unaffordable. They are not. First, available information shows high returns (Oxenham 2003). UNESCO (2005) notes that: "the returns to investment in adult literacy programs are generally comparable to, and compare favorably with, those from investments in primary education." Second, regarding costs, UNESCO (2005) refers to a survey of 29 literacy programs in which the average cost per learner having *completed* the program was $68 in SSA, $32 in Asia, and $83 in Latin America.

Lack of vigorous action over the next decade would likely cause youth illiteracy in SSA to stagnate at a high level, with serious negative implications for the attainment of other development goals. First, people aged 15-24 in 2015 (with 25 percent illiteracy) will be in the labor force beyond 2050. Even if all children were to enter primary school in future years, if 30 percent of each cohort continues to drop out prior to Grade 5, at least *a quarter of the population of prime working age would remain illiterate up to 2050 and beyond*.[11] Second, given that both youth illiteracy and dropout rates are higher for females than for males and that the birth rate diminishes with a woman's level of education, maintaining the illiteracy status quo would mean that more than a third of births would be to illiterate mothers.[12] Low maternal literacy reinforces the intergenerational vicious cycle of poverty, low health and education status, and marginalization. It would also have global implications given that the UN population projections (median variant) estimate that, by 2050, SSA will account for 38 percent of all children born worldwide.

The skills required to be effective citizens in 21st century societies go beyond those provided through the six or seven grades of primary education provided by most SSA countries (with only about two-thirds of those entering completing the cycle). Most middle and high-income countries have nine or ten years of compulsory basic education covering the lower secondary cycle. In 2010, SSA's enrollment in

---

10. Examples include: Tanzania's abolition of school fees was accompanied with complementary basic education programs for out-of-school children aged 11-17, including child laborers. In Uganda, evening schools and mobile schools are part of the Complementary Opportunities for Primary Education (COPE) program, and a specific project has been designed for the urban poor. Liberia is providing a three-year Accelerated Learning Program, covering the six-grade primary education curriculum, for ex-combatants and for those who missed out on primary schooling during the civil strife.
11. Traditionally, completing Grade 4 is assumed necessary to gain and retain literacy. But given the low learning outcomes in SSA, a high share of those reaching higher grades may also not have gained permanent literacy and numeracy.
12. Based on data for 36 SSA countries, Majgaard and Mingat (2012) found that the number of births by age 30 was 3.3 for mothers with no formal education and 2.2 for women with secondary education.

lower secondary education (47 percent) was well below that of South Asia (75 percent), East Asia (90 percent), Latin America (102 percent), and North Africa (with around 100 percent for all countries apart from Morocco at 82 percent).

For *cost, equity,* and *labor market* reasons, the most effective strategy for most SSA countries to provide longer basic education would be to merge primary and lower secondary education into a new basic education cycle. Making lower secondary schools accessible to all rural children would not be feasible for most countries over the next decade because of cost. Adding classrooms to existing primary schools would be much less costly, and the recurrent cost per pupil in primary education is only half that of lower secondary education. Also, an eight- or nine-year basic education cycle would be a year or two shorter than the present primary plus lower secondary education cycle. In addition, providing two to three years of education beyond primary school to everyone would be more *equitable* than gradually universalizing lower secondary education over the next couple of decades.

Many studies have shown that expanding secondary education may well be one of the highest return investments in the labor market available to countries.[13] In particular, as shown by East Asian countries, secondary education plays a key role in facilitating the transition of labor from low- to high- productivity sectors.[14] Despite SSA's strong progress the last decade, secondary school coverage in 2010 (combined lower and upper cycle) was below that of East Asia and Latin America in 1980 and South Asia in 1990. Given the poor quality of primary education and the fact that the overwhelming majority of the labor force in SSA over the next couple of decades will continue to be engaged in the non-formal sectors, rapid expansion of *lower* secondary education is particularly important: the skills imparted by that cycle are an integral part of the basic education foundation required to operate effectively in 21st century societies and facilitate the transition from largely subsistence farming to higher-productivity activities. Thus, public education spending on secondary education must give high priority to ensuring that efforts to provide *cutting-edge skills for the modern sector* are combined with efforts to improve *basic education skills for the whole labor force.*

A recent report (OECD 2012) argues that curricula worldwide are overdue for a major redesign similar to that made in the late 1800s in response to the Industrial Revolution. How best to adjust curricula to the extensive changes in the nature and content of jobs is a worldwide concern. The 21st century economies require skills that are very different from those of the 19th century, yet the content of education programs worldwide has remained relatively unchanged.

The core basic skills essential for employment are generally recognized as follows: (i) the 3Rs (reading, writing and arithmetic); (ii) life and career skills/non-cognitive skills including communication, attitude, and ability and willingness to learn on the job; (iii) learning and innovation skills such as problem-solving and creative thinking; and (iv) 21st century skills such as information, media, and technology skills. There is less understanding of how best to transmit these skills to prospective workers or how to align skills development with the rapidly evolving needs of the labor force. The issue has taken center stage in both rich

---

13. See Lewin and Caillods (2001), World Bank (2005), di Gropello (2006), Verspoor (2008), Mingat et al. (2010).
14. See McKinsey (2012) for China and Fredriksen and Tan (2008) for Korea and Thailand.

and poor nations. Key emerging lessons from the United States and the EU include the need to increase the talent pool by vastly improving primary and secondary education in mathematics and science and to provide focused training in science, technology, engineering, and math (STEM); focusing on transversal and basic skills especially in entrepreneurial and IT skills; investing world-class technical and vocational skills development (TVSD) systems and work-based learning; and creating public-private partnerships to boost innovation and increase cross-fertilization between academia and business.

The Association for Development of Education in Africa recently outlined the core skills needed for Africa to remain on a path of sustainable development (ADEA 2012), namely:
- Build critical capacities and a common core of basic skills;
- Raise training and qualification levels through a modernized technical and vocational skills development programs;
- Strengthen science innovation and technology; and
- Foster regional innovation systems.

Skills to increase the productivity of informal sector employment pose a particular problem. A recent survey (Pina et al. 2012) shows that school-based programs seldom penetrate the informal economy, resulting in weak cognitive skills among most informal workers. To the extent that job training in the informal economy exists, it is most often outside of school, primarily in the form of traditional apprenticeships, which are themselves often limited by master teachers' own limited training, overreliance on outdated technologies, and poor working conditions. Governments and NGOs have launched pilot programs in many countries to address the shortfalls of current education and training models; however, these programs have not yet undergone systematic, rigorous, and quantitative impact evaluation.

Reap the intergenerational virtuous cycle of educating girls and women

Gender equity is both a human right and a core development goal. Gains for women translate into gains in family and child welfare that benefit the entire society.

Priority actions, described in more detail below, to achieve this goal include:[15]
- *Close the gender gap in secondary and, especially, in higher education.*
- *Improve women's labor force participation.*

Take actions at multiple levels to promote gender equity including strengthening women's endowments, both tangible and intangible; giving them voice and control over their decisions; and increasing returns to their economic activities.

By 2010, SSA had close to gender parity in primary education but lagged in secondary and, especially, in higher education. In addition, only 54 percent of adult women were literate as compared to 71 percent of men. And about 25 percent (16 million) girls of primary school age were out of school, feeding the large pool of illiterate women. In addition, many girls drop out of school because of pregnancy or early marriage. The high level of female illiteracy represents a *huge missed growth potential and family welfare*

---
15. The data quoted below are largely derived from (UNESCO 2012b).

loss, given women's dominant role in the rural and informal economy and the fact that their income is more likely than men's to benefit the family through provision of children's food, clothing, health services, and education. Low female literacy also *slows down the demographic transition* and limits *children's life chances* since both are closely linked to women's education. For example, of the 8.2 million fewer deaths of children under age 5 worldwide between 1970 and 2009, half can be attributed to more education of women of reproductive age (Gakidou et al. 2010). Moreover, the progress of future generations is directly related to the physical and intellectual condition of today's girls and young women since they will bear and rear the children of the next decades (Levine et al. 2009).

Women's labor force participation needs to be improved. The employment prospects of young women vary considerably across countries. Out of 15 countries analyzed by the AfDB, the female youth unemployment rate was higher than that for males in eight (2012). North African countries have much lower female labor force participation rates than the global or SSA averages. The survey also found that in 8 out of 12 SSA countries (and in all North African countries) young females are more likely to be unemployed than their male counterparts. In SSA gender inequalities manifest themselves primarily in the much higher share of women than men in vulnerable employment. In North Africa, women who seek employment tend to face much poorer employment prospects than men with equivalent qualifications, and female working poverty rates exceed male rates in 22 out of 27 SSA countries with available data (ILO 2011).

A World Bank study proposes three sets of actions to enhance women's labor force participation (2012a):

- Strengthen women's endowments, in particular, education, health, land, and other such assets that individuals accumulate over time.
- Empower them to have voice and control over their decisions.
- Increase returns to economic activities.

Education is both a means to achieving these objectives and an end in itself. To improve girls' education, experience shows that the most successful efforts are those that are comprehensive and integrated, for example, combining actions that alleviate constraints to attendance by reducing distance to school, providing sanitation facilities, bringing water closer to homes, and providing child care for younger siblings. Well-trained female teachers can act as role models for girls, thus helping to change social attitudes toward extra-domestic roles for women. On average in SSA, 43 percent of teachers are female at the primary level, but only 29 percent at the secondary level and below 20 percent at the tertiary level.

Enhance the quality of learning

The quality of learning is crucial in determining how well education can fulfill its multiple roles. In particular, research shows that differences in learning achievements matter more in explaining cross-country differences in productivity growth than do differences in the average number of years of schooling (Hanushek and Wößmann 2007). Improving the poor quality of education at all levels should be a national priority issue in most SSA countries.

Priority actions, described in more detail below, to improve the quality of learning include:

- *Teachers must be turned into a more effective resource.*
- *Issues in making affordable teaching and learning materials available to all students must be addressed.*
- *Institutions for leadership, accountability, and innovation must be built.*

Only a handful of African countries participate in international student assessments. Morocco, Botswana, and South Africa have participated in the Progress in Reading Literacy Survey, and they scored at or near the lowest level. Three regional assessments for African countries reveal a worrisome trend that underscores the fact that the remarkable increase in access over the last decade has not been matched by comparable progress in learning outcomes.[16] Assessment results show that some 40 percent of primary school leavers cannot read. The percentage of 6th graders who are able to read at least at the basic level ranges from 52 percent in Zambia to 98 percent in Swaziland and from less than 30 percent in Cote d'Ivoire to 45 percent in Madagascar. A recent assessment, covering some 350,000 children in Kenya, Uganda, and Tanzania tested children on their ability to perform basic numeracy and literacy tasks at the Standard 2 level. It shows that the children only acquire Standard 2 skills when they reach Standard 4 or 5. In Standard 4, only half of the students were able to pass the Standard 2 Kiswahili test and even fewer could pass the numeracy and English tests (Hoogeveen and Andrews 2012).

Poor education quality limits the opportunity for economic growth and the redistributive effects of education, thus reinforcing social and income inequalities and sustaining inter-generational poverty and marginalization. It raises levels of school drop-out, reversing the gains made over the last decade in increasing access. Poor quality also causes higher repetition rates and increased failure to acquire core skills and competencies, which has a negative impact on labor productivity, as well as on education costs.

Partly because wealthier parents send their children to private schools and colleges at home or abroad, there are not enough influential voices to advocate for quality in public institutions. The main constraint on improving quality is not a lack of knowledge about what to do, nor is action necessarily primarily constrained by shortage of resources. Rather, quality improvement is often hampered by weak institutional and political capacity to turn available knowledge and funding into successful implementation.

---

16. The "Southern and Eastern Africa Consortium for Monitoring Educational Quality" (SACMEQ) comprises 15 Ministries of Education in Southern and Eastern Africa, and the "Program on the Analysis of Education Systems"(PASEC) covers Francophone countries. MLA (Measurement of Learning Achievement) is sponsored by UNESCO. MLA tests students in Grade 4, PASEC in Grade 5 and SACMEQ in Grade 6. The data cover the period 1996-2009.

Priority actions include:
- Improving the training, support, deployment, management, and accountability of teachers.
- Addressing the factors causing the high costs and low availability of basic training materials.
- Strengthening the education sector's capacity for leadership, accountability, and innovation.

Priority issues in these three areas include:

Teachers are the single most important education input in determining learning outcomes, education costs, and success of education reforms. A review of the world's best performing education systems concludes that "studies that take into account all the available evidence on teacher effectiveness suggest that students placed with high-performing teachers will progress three times as fast as those placed with low-performing teachers" (McKinsey 2007). The report points out that high-performing systems consistently get the right people to become teachers, develop them into effective instructors, and put in place systems and targeted support to ensure that every child is able to benefit from excellent instruction. Yet, education strategies often pay little attention to factors affecting teacher effectiveness, such as their training, deployment, management, incentives, supervision, and accountability for learning outcomes. Interventions in these areas are likely to be the most cost-effective actions for African countries over the next decade to improve learning outcomes. The teachers are largely in place; the challenge is to make this valuable resource more effective.

Other aspects of teachers' working conditions also remain poor in most SSA countries: large class sizes (average pupil-teacher ratio of 43 in 2010 compared with 39 in South Asia, 22 in Latin America, and 18 in East Asia), low qualifications (a high share of teachers with only primary or junior secondary education), limited availability of teaching materials (see below), and little access to in-service training and other professional support.[17] For example, much of the remarkable progress in primary school enrollment between 1999 and 2010 in Burkina Faso, Mali, and Niger noted earlier was achieved by recruiting contract teachers paid by the governments or communities but at a much lower rate than civil servant teachers.[18] In general, these teachers received very little professional training.

Countries at all income levels are struggling with how best to use their teachers more effectively. Many developing countries are introducing a variety of reforms to increase teachers' incentives and accountability for education outcomes. These include generating and disseminating information about schooling rights and responsibilities, resources received, and outcomes; decentralizing school-level decisions to various school-level bodies; and developing student assessment systems and policies that link pay or regular recruitment to performance (Bruns, Filmer, and Patrinos 2011).

---

17. SACMEQ data for 2000-2002 show that more than half of 6th grade students in Lesotho were taught reading by teachers with only primary education, and 97 percent of 6th grade students in Tanzania were taught reading by teachers with lower secondary or less. In Malawi, Mozambique and Tanzania, more than two-third of 6th grade reading teachers had not received any in-service training over the previous three years (UNESCO-UIS 2006, pp. 58 and 73).

18. Around 2006, salaries of civil servant teachers were about twice that of government-paid contract teachers (median for 15 SSA countries). Contract teachers hired by communities earned about one-sixth of civil servant teachers. Contract teachers hired by communities comprised about one-third of primary school teachers in Benin, Cameroon, Mali and Togo and as much half in CAR, Congo, and Madagascar (UNESCO-UIS 2011, p. 51).

Introducing these types of reforms is complex, in part because of the often poor cooperation between governments and teacher unions. But the need is pressing. For example, surveys conducted in 2010 in Tanzania and Senegal (AERC and World Bank 2011) found that the average number of hours per day primary school pupils are taught was 2 hours and 4 minutes in Tanzania compared with the official schedule of 5 hours and 12 minutes (i.e., 40 percent), and 3 hours and 15 minutes in Senegal compared with the official schedule of 4 hours and 36 minutes (71 percent). A study for Madagascar (for 2007) concluded that many aspects of the pedagogical process are poorly managed and many tasks essential for student learning were neglected. About 20 percent of teachers did not prepare daily lesson plans, school directors rarely followed up with their teaching staff on student performance, communication from teachers to parents on student learning was often perfunctory, pupils' absence was rarely recorded and communicated to parents, and in only 15 percent of the sample schools did all the teachers and school directors consistently perform the tasks considered essential by Malagasy educators (Lassibille 2012).

After qualified and committed teachers, the next most important input for the quality of learning are *high-quality teaching and learning materials*, especially textbooks. This is especially true in the SSA context where many teachers have little training, class size is large, duration of the actual school year is short, a high percentage of parents are illiterate, and homes lack alternative reading materials. Countries known for their rapid progress in education, such as Korea, Singapore, and (more recently) Vietnam, gave high priority at an early stage to ensuring universal access to quality textbooks (Fredriksen and Tan 2008).

While comparative data are scarce, a number of country studies show that textbook availability in SSA is low, and textbook costs are high. Supplementary teaching and learning materials, such as school libraries, is even scarcer. For example, a recent study of primary school textbook availability found that, in 23 SSA countries surveyed around 2010, there were on average slightly fewer than two pupils per book in reading and math. Books in other subjects are much scarcer, and there are large differences between urban and rural areas. And books are even scarcer in secondary education (UNESCO-UIS 2011).

The increase in quality and decline in prices of electronic teaching and learning materials, and the widespread availability of mobile phones, will radically change the options available over the next decade. It is unclear how this will affect financial requirements. It is clear, however, that electronic teaching and learning materials will not be a panacea for dealing with the current massive shortage and that, to harness the opportunities electronic materials offer, countries will need to put even more effort into building effective systems to deal with teaching and learning material issues.

Addressing the type of education challenges discussed in this chapter will often require major changes in policies as well as programs and budget trade-offs that are complex, knowledge- and capacity-intensive, and politically sensitive. Few African countries have the institutional capacity required to handle this transformation effectively. In particular, *"countries need much stronger capacity to deal with the political economy of reforms and with technical constraints on implementation"* (UNESCO 2007).

Capacity-building in the education sector has been given much attention over the last decades, including by donors, but progress has been elusive. The single most important constraint in most countries is currently less a shortage of technical expertise in education planning and management (except in some fragile states) than low institutional capacity to mobilize, utilize, and retain existing expertise; to monitor performance; and to hold managers and teachers accountable for outcomes. As noted in World Bank (2011b): "In sum, to strengthen an education system means to align its governance, management, financing, and incentive mechanisms to produce learning for all. This means reforming accountability relationships among all participants in the system so that these relationships are clear, coordinated, and consistent with their assigned functions and that they support national education goals."

Success in developing better performing systems will require strong political leadership to manage the often difficult political economy of education reform, including handling inter-sectoral linkages. In addition, the budget trade-offs are becoming more difficult; the growing demand for post-primary education requires equitable trade-offs and keen knowledge of what is at stake to ensure that adequate funding to enhance quality and equity in basic education and to provide second-chance programs for out-of-school youth and young adults is maintained.

Improve relevance of technical and vocational skills development (TVSD)

Africa needs TVSD systems that can respond effectively both to the cutting-edge skill needs of a modern, knowledge-based economy and to those of the majority of the labor force engaged in the rural sector and informal economy. To develop such systems is a complex challenge. Existing systems suffer from a multitude of weaknesses: poor quality and relevance, weak links with employers, a lack of sustainable funding, and perception by parents and students of TVSD as second-rate education. Further, while clear success stories exist, there is no blueprint applicable to all countries. Established as well as newly industrialized countries have successfully followed quite different approaches. For all, however, good quality *basic education* is the essential foundation for further skills development in both the formal and informal sector (Adams, de Silva, and Razumara 2013).

Priority actions to address weaknesses in technical and vocational education and training include:

- *Improve the governance of TVSD* by strengthening the regulatory role of governments and the coordination of public-private training programs.
- *Raise the quality of TVSD* through a skills-based approach to training, upgrading the skills of master craftsmen, and modernizing traditional apprenticeship systems.
- *Establish national certification frameworks* for validating the skills acquired.
- *Develop national skills inventory and labor market information systems* that analyze the supply and demand of labor and track the growth sectors of the economy.
- *Foster the development of partnerships* between schools, training providers, and employers to increase the relevance of training and lifelong learning.
- *Address the special constraints of providing training for workers in the informal sector.*

Revitalize tertiary education

This chapter has focused on the importance, especially for SSA, to catch-up in the development of *basic human capital*. However, Africa cannot hope to build the full human capital it needs for the future without also *urgently revitalizing tertiary education*, which is the engine of a knowledge economy and an incubator of skilled labor. As economies expand and become more complex, they require workers with the technical and cognitive skills to assimilate ideas, adapt new technologies, open new frontiers in science and innovation, generate new knowledge, and manage complex institutions and systems. Tertiary education provides the capacity skills that SSA badly needs for technological absorption and adaptation, competitiveness, and innovation. It also enables countries to start new industries that can create more productive jobs, better linkages, and a wider range of exports.

Priority actions in tertiary education, described in more detail below, need to be undertaken simultaneously in order to maximize the return on investment. These actions include:

- *Expand access.*
- *Improve quality.*
- *Improve relevance.*

African countries have devoted a relatively large proportion of their GDP and government budgets to tertiary education, which is allocated on average 20 percent of the education budget. Despite this effort, SSA's higher education coverage (7 percent enrollment in 2010) is by far the lowest of any region; it is at the level of Latin America in the early 1970s and East and South Asia in the early 1990s. This partly reflects the legacy of nearly non-existent post-secondary education at the time of independence: the Gross Enrollment Ratio (GER) was only of 0.1 percent in 1960. Thus, while student numbers have increased rapidly since then, they have done so from a very low base; SSA's GER for tertiary education increased by only 3 percentage points between 1990 and 2010 while the GERs of South Asia, Latin America and East Asia increased by 11, 23, and 24 points, respectively. The average coverage, moreover, masks large differences by country.

But to simultaneously expand access and improve quality and relevance is a formidable challenge. As countries all over the world are experiencing, simply expanding tertiary education is no panacea: if quality remains low and there are major mismatches between the training provided and labor market demands, unfilled jobs will continue to co-exist with growing levels of graduate unemployment. Thus, the needed educational expansion must be balanced with policies to improve quality and relevance. It will be a major political challenge to achieve this balance and to pay for both the expansion and improved quality. Most tertiary education systems in SSA lack the institutional, financial, and academic resources to absorb growing demand resulting from broader access to secondary education. As a result, an explosion of undergraduate student enrollment is now threatening to erode any remaining capacities of national systems for research and postgraduate education.

With few exceptions, universities across Africa face quite similar challenges (Butler-Adam 2012). On the whole, they are elite systems. There has been rapid growth in enrollments, but country systems remain small and competition for places is intense. Demand for Birhigher education has outstripped capacity, leading to overcrowding and concerns about the quality of offerings. Humanities and the social sciences enroll most students, while enrollment in science, engineering, technology, and medicine are low. This distribution of enrollment reflects the higher costs of delivering such courses and weak foundation in the sciences at the secondary level. Many universities have set a target of 60 percent enrollment in the sciences, but few are able to meet the target. Enrollment in graduate level courses is very low; doctoral enrollment comprises only one percent of total enrollment. As a result, the scope for training future professors for the fast-growing student population and scientific and technical leaders for the economies is limited. There is a growing shortage of university teachers. The current cohort of academic staff is aging, and few young people are choosing an academic career. Also, brain drain is high. Finally, pressure on resources to improve access to higher education is squeezing funding for R&D.

Given Africa's low coverage of higher education and the severe financial, academic, and infrastructure constraints on rapid expansion, the pressure on innovation and new thinking is perhaps even more important here than in other regions. In particular, governments must proactively assess how they can use the rapidly evolving web-based learning methods and other technological developments to revolutionize the delivery of tertiary education, often through public-private partnerships. It may be that the government's role as a provider of tertiary education will diminish. Instead, government will take a sharply increasing role in facilitating quality assurance and developing well-organized certification services for students who have gone through web-based learning programs, whether these services and programs are provided by the private sector or by government-sponsored institutions.

Build human capital for knowledge and innovation-driven economies

The role of knowledge and innovation as drivers of economic growth has risen sharply in recent decades. This development has particular importance for education, given the sector's role in creating, adapting, and transmitting knowledge. The importance is not limited to the knowledge economy; knowledge and innovation are key drivers of productivity throughout the economy — ranging from agricultural yields to the effectiveness of public service delivery. Therefore, education and training programs must both respond to the skills demanded by the present economic structure and anticipate emerging skill needs to support the growth sectors. And the role of education is not limited to higher education and research but includes basic human capital formation starting with literacy and numeracy.

Priority actions beyond building basic skills include:
- *Broaden access to quality upper secondary education* to strengthen the critical link between basic and higher education and the bridge between the school system and the labor market.

- *Strengthen the articulation between education and jobs* by addressing mismatches between skill supplies and labor market demands and misalignment arising from evolving skill requirements; revising program content to better respond to labor market demands; and fostering partnerships between schools, training providers, and industry.
- *Broaden the system of delivering initial training and, in particular, skills upgrading* to include different pathways of lifelong learning through online and on-the-job training.
- *Channel tertiary education toward the creation of innovative capacity and scientific and technical knowledge* and proactively link academic institutions to business and industry.
- *Invest at least 2 percent of GDP in R&D* and provide incentives for tertiary institutions and industry to collaborate in applied research in strategic areas.

Reinforce training and skill development through regional cooperation

Globalization is greatly intensifying the need for regional cooperation in education. Beyond the growing internationalization of higher education and research, regional cooperation offers benefits in many areas including lifelong learning, curriculum development, quality assurance, open education resources, and the use of ICT. Increasingly, national decisions in these areas have implications beyond national borders. Moreover, the cross-border *movements of education and health workers* and the *trade of education and health services* are likely to grow sharply. This exchange will deepen the capacity of higher education in small states, leverage economies of scale, and reduce the time it takes for countries to develop the skilled workforce needed in select priority areas.

Priority actions to harness such benefits include:

- *Develop an ambitious regional vision for transformational change of education systems in Africa.* Such a vision will help raise the level of ambition at the country level, facilitate collective actions on common issues, strengthen the hand of in-country reformers, and promote cross-country knowledge sharing and benchmarking.
- *Increase the support for regional networks and centers of excellence* to strengthen joint research, deepen national capacity, and leverage economies of scale.
- *Establish common educational standards and certification systems* to increase the flexibility and mobility of labor across the continent.
- *Strengthen inter-country and inter-university exchanges* of staff, students, research, and partnerships with the private sector.

Leadership for implementation

Realizing the *transformative change* in education and health systems needed to reach the Africa 2050 vision will, for most countries, require sustained long-term actions at a scale beyond that achieved over the past 40 years. Sustained action is needed both to deal with the legacy of slow human capital formation in the past and to respond to, and help shape, increasingly complex, rapid, and unpredictable national, regional, and global developments. The challenges in implementing the suggested action agenda will be daunting and, given the long-term nature of human capital formation, the choices made over the next decade will be particularly critical to attaining the 2050 vision. However, given the right conditions, rapid catch-up growth is possible. The most important of such enabling conditions is *strong, broad-based national political leadership* that makes accelerating human capital formation a strategic national development priority. Thus, implementation of the actions needed is not limited to the ministries of health and education. Stiglitz (1996) underscores just how critical such leadership was to the economic success of East Asian countries. He concluded that the "real miracle of East Asia may be political more than economic" and that what seemed to lie at the root of sustained success was not the individual set of policies but rather their nexus, the policy choices that governments made, the manner in which they were implemented, and the flexibility and responsiveness that was built into institutions.

ክለብርሃን አምባዬ ኮንስትራክሽን
MITSUBISHI
THE BRAND YOU CAN TRUST
GREY GOOSE

PART II
SECTION B:
DIVERSE, COMPETITIVE ECONOMIES – PRIVATE INVESTMENTS TO CREATE JOBS

Maintaining Macroeconomic Stability and Increasing Resilience

Chapter 9

Jose Fajgenbaum and Anupam Basu

In the 1960s, many African countries gained independence. Driven by the desire to raise living standards across the continent, many of their leaders adopted a development strategy that relied on an extensive system of government interventions and controls for economic management. The main instruments of economic management were price controls, import licensing, foreign exchange restrictions, controls on bank credit and interest rates, taxation of the agricultural sector, and establishment of public enterprises in strategic sectors.

In Sub-Saharan Africa (SSA), following a modest increase in per capita income and strong export growth in the 1960s, there was a marked deterioration of economic performance during the 1970s. The growth rates of real GDP and per capita income decelerated, and aggregate export volume trended downward. An upswing in the terms of trade in the 1960s was followed by a downturn in the 1970s in the wake of a surge in oil prices. In contrast, in North Africa, where the average growth rate in the 1960s had been lower than in SSA, growth performance improved in the 1970s.

After the adverse effects of the oil price shock of 1973, most countries began to experience the paralyzing influence of ill-conceived government interventions and controls. Savings and investment rates were inadequate to foster growth and meet the needs of human resource and infrastructure development, unprofitable public enterprises became an unsustainable burden on the budget, and the private investments needed for agricultural and industrial development were not forthcoming. The state-administered system of controls on domestic prices, crop marketing, credit allocation and bank interest rates, and the allocation of import licenses and foreign exchange made it extremely difficult for the private sector to function.

A rethinking of development strategies in SSA led an increasing number of countries to implement reforms to achieve macroeconomic stability and eliminate the government interventions that impeded economic activity, especially in the private sector. Economic performance was disappointing throughout the 1980s with a decline in per capita income, and inflation rates accelerated in the first half of the 1990s. Throughout this period, investment-savings gaps and fiscal imbalances remained large, financed by substantial inflows of foreign aid and external debt relief. Growth performance also weakened in North Africa during the 1980s and early 1990s. The first signs of economic recovery emerged only in the mid-1990s.

Overall economic performance of African countries during the period 1980 to 1995 was disappointing. However, there was some evidence that countries that had improved their macroeconomic policies and implemented sustained reforms performed better than those that were less successful in implementing structural adjustment reforms. Growth performance in the franc zone countries of West and Central Africa had been chronically weak because of a highly overvalued exchange rate. These countries launched new adjustment programs based on a substantial devaluation of the currency in January 1994 and, with a short lag, their economic performance improved.

The next section traces the economic performance of Africa since 1960, distinguishing between two sub-periods: 1960 to the mid-1990s and the strengthened performance from the mid-1990s to date. The third section focuses on investment and savings, beginning with a review of recent trends in investment and saving rates, followed by policy recommendations to raise these rates to the levels that are required in the coming decades to sustain high growth rates. The concluding section outlines the macroeconomic policy framework for the sustained, inclusive high growth needed to achieve the Africa 2050 vision.

Broad Trends in Africa's Economic Performance (1960 – 2011)[1]

From 1957 to 1968, 33 African countries joined the international community as independent nations. Eight more countries gained independence between 1974 and 1980. Only a few countries had gained independence prior to the 1950s: Liberia in 1847, Egypt in 1922, and Morocco in 1927. Only Ethiopia was never under colonial rule.

Weak economic performance between the 1960s and the mid-1990s

In the 1960s, many of Africa's new leaders adopted economic development plans to promote rapid industrialization and broad-based economic development. Governments relied on the taxation of agriculture, and often export these to finance. Some countries mobilized financial support from foreign development partners, including both bilateral and multilateral institutions, to supplement domestic resource mobilization. Early assessments of broad economic trends in the post-independence years faced the challenges of the transition to new governments and the limited economic database of the time. We report briefly here on the few that exist.

Worsening economic growth performance following an initial encouraging period

Africa's overall growth performance in the 1960s was encouraging and reflected several positive trends (Figure 9.1). In both SSA and North Africa real GDP growth was on average faster than population growth, although slower than the average for other developing countries (World Bank 1989). Economic growth weakened substantially during the 1970s, especially in the non-oil and non-mineral producing countries of SSA. In North Africa the average growth rate continued to improve in the 1970s.

---

1. The data for this chapter are drawn mainly from various past issues of the World Bank's African Development Indicators, the IMF's World Economic Outlook and the UNCTAD database.

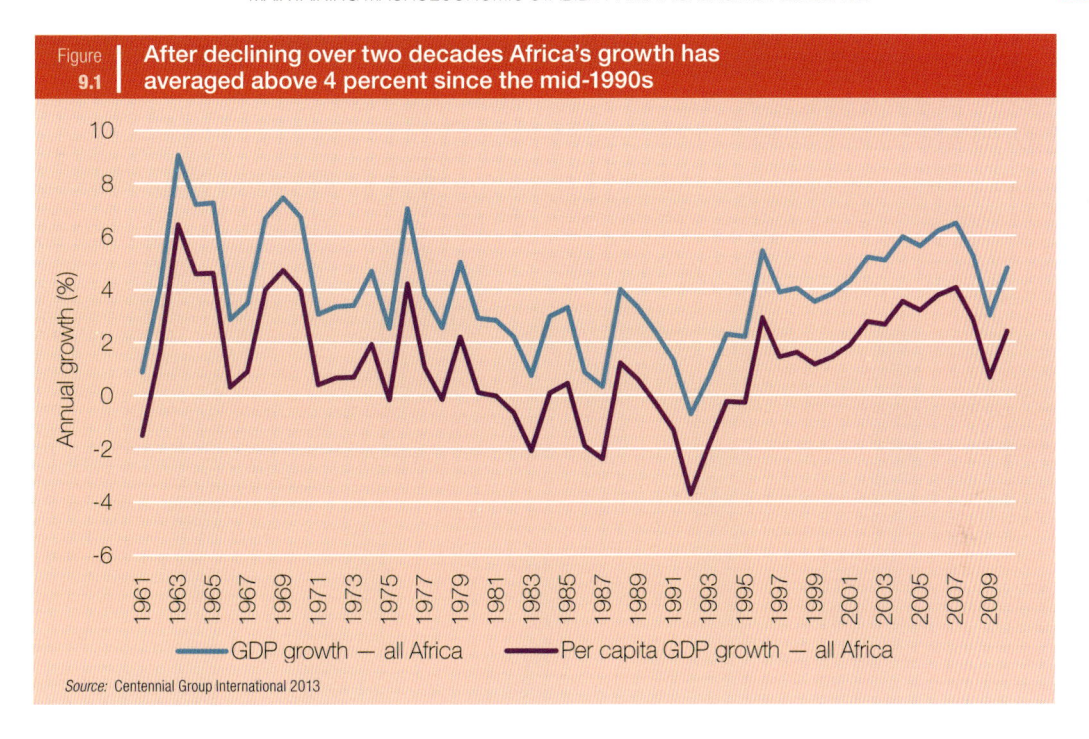

Figure 9.1 After declining over two decades Africa's growth has averaged above 4 percent since the mid-1990s

Source: Centennial Group International 2013

In the 1960s per capita GDP increased in both regions at an average annual rate of more than 2 percent. Growth in agricultural production (2.7 percent) was roughly the same as population growth in SSA countries, and agricultural exports increased at about 2 percent a year (World Bank 1989). Moreover, the volume of total exports from SSA grew on average at 6 percent a year, led mainly by oil exports. A surge in commodity prices in 1967 boosted exports and strengthened growth performance. In North Africa annual growth rates (in real terms) from 1965 to 1969 averaged 8 percent in industry (inclusive of oil and mining) and 4 percent in agriculture, which was noticeably faster than population growth (Global Coalition for Africa 2004).

Economic growth rates declined in SSA in the 1970s reflecting a deceleration of growth rates in the non-oil and non-mineral producing countries following a substantial worsening of their terms of trade. In these countries per capita GDP growth barely kept pace with the population growth rate. Aggregate export volume trended downward following the 1973 oil shock for all SSA countries (including oil exporters). Africa's share of total exports in world exports declined, and its share of world exports of primary commodities fell even more sharply. Agricultural exports from Africa's non-oil primary commodity exporters were also declining. Non-oil primary commodity exports remained narrowly concentrated on a few agricultural commodities, and exporters had yet to tap into the growing markets in other developing countries (especially Asia). Notable exceptions are Mauritius and Kenya, where efforts were made to diversify exports away from primary commodities.

In the 1960s and 1970s the growth performance of both regions was characterized by high volatility of annual growth rates (Figure 9.2).[2] The relatively undiversified structure of Africa's production and exports made it difficult to mitigate the negative impacts of both external and internal shocks.

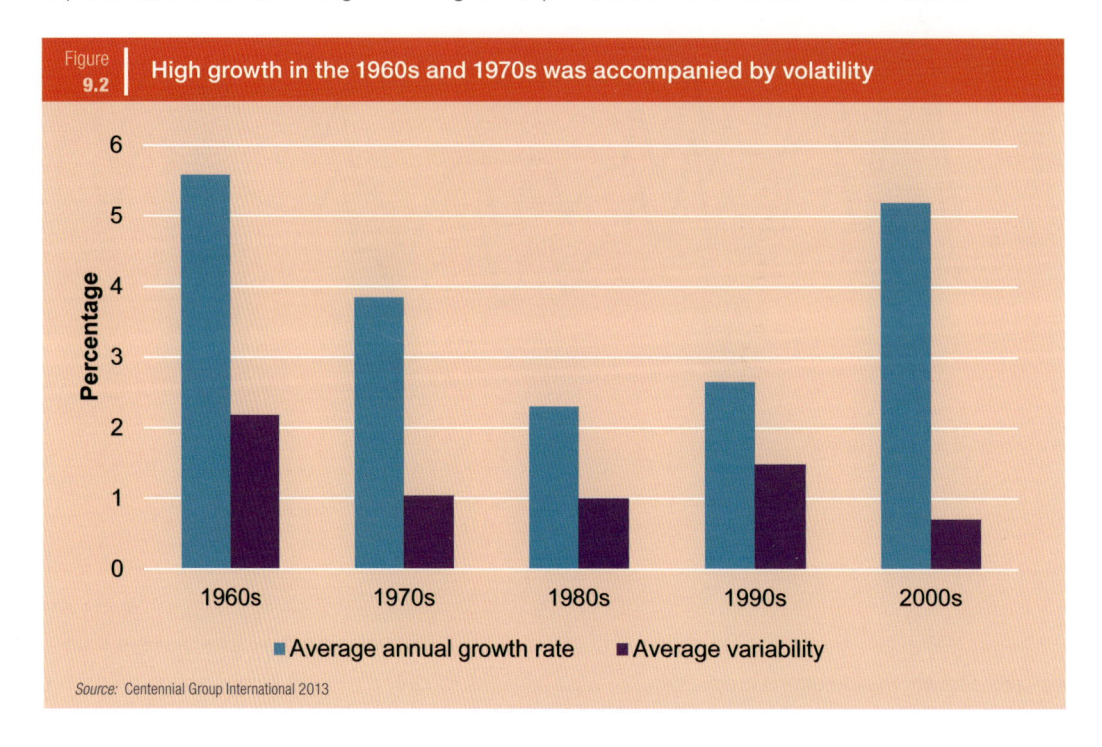

Figure 9.2 High growth in the 1960s and 1970s was accompanied by volatility

Source: Centennial Group International 2013

The oil shock of 1973 and the terms-of-trade losses of subsequent years (especially the early 1980s) were only part of the reason for the protracted slowdown in growth performance in the SSA countries. Serious structural weaknesses were also present (see Chapter 10). Even among Africa's oil-exporting countries where substantial resources were derived from the higher oil prices, there was little success in diversifying production and exports (World Bank 2000).

The urgent need for economic recovery triggered a rethinking of the interventionist economic development strategy. From the mid-1970s through the 1980s, an increasing number of countries began to implement economic reforms to achieve macroeconomic stability and remove structural distortions by phasing out these policies. Reforms also sought to restructure and privatize public enterprises in banking as well as in other sectors to improve economic efficiency, reduce the fiscal burden of unprofitable enterprises, and, most importantly, to support private sector development. The number of SSA countries pursuing such reforms increased sharply by the early 1990s.

---

2. Variability is measured by the average deviation from the mean.

The pace and intensity of reforms varied widely across SSA, and the reform efforts took time to bear fruit. Average annual growth rates continued to decline through the 1980s and the mid-1990s, and per capita GDP growth was negative as recovery began only in the second half of the 1990s. During this period, economic performance was particularly disappointing in the CFA franc zone countries where the problems associated with unsustainable fiscal and external deficits were compounded by a highly overvalued exchange rate. These countries, which had a fixed peg to the French franc, devalued their exchange rate in January 1994 and adopted structural adjustment programs that laid the foundation for economic recovery in the late 1990s. In North Africa, growth rates declined during the 1980s, and the annual improvements in per capita GDP (less than 1.5 percent) were on average much less than the previous two decades.

Throughout the economic reform process Africa faced serious macroeconomic challenges: tackling large fiscal and external current account imbalances, reducing inflationary pressures, increasing domestic savings and investment, and addressing external debt management problems. Once there was adequate progress in establishing macroeconomic stability, economic performance improved over an increasing number of countries.

Weak savings and investment efforts

Africa's savings rate remained low for almost four decades in both SSA and North Africa. A modest improvement in 1970s was followed by a downwards trend in the 1980s and no visible improvement through the mid-1990s. The investment rate rose in SSA in the 1960s and 1970s, while in North Africa it increased sharply in in the second half of the 1970s. But both regions saw an investment rate decline in the 1980s and virtually no improvement through the early 1990s. The investment rate has been higher than the savings rate for most of the period (Figure 9.3), and the resultant financing gaps were covered by aid inflows and foreign borrowing. Aid flows mainly benefited the SSA countries. Fiscal deficits remained large and were financed by foreign aid and debt relief operations.

Growing inflationary pressures, monetary expansion, and exchange rate policies

Annual inflation rates in the 1960s, as measured by the GDP deflator, were relatively low in both SSA (about 6 percent) and North Africa (about 2 percent) (World Bank 2000). However, inflation rates were markedly higher in the 1970s in both regions (13 percent and about 9 percent, respectively). The inflation rate accelerated further in the 1980s in SSA where it ranged from 20 to 30 percent. In North Africa inflation remained around 10 percent. For Africa as a whole the inflation rate was in the range of 10 to 20 percent during the 1980s.

Africa's inflation rate surged in the first half of the 1990s followed by a steep reduction between 1995 and 1997 (Figure 9.4). In the latter half of the 1990s inflation declined in SSA, with significant progress in an increasing number of countries (IMF 2004). In North Africa, inflation fell below 10 percent in Algeria, Egypt, and Libya while Morocco and Tunisia maintained their low-inflation environment (IMF 2009).

Figure 9.3 | Investment has generally outpaced savings in Africa

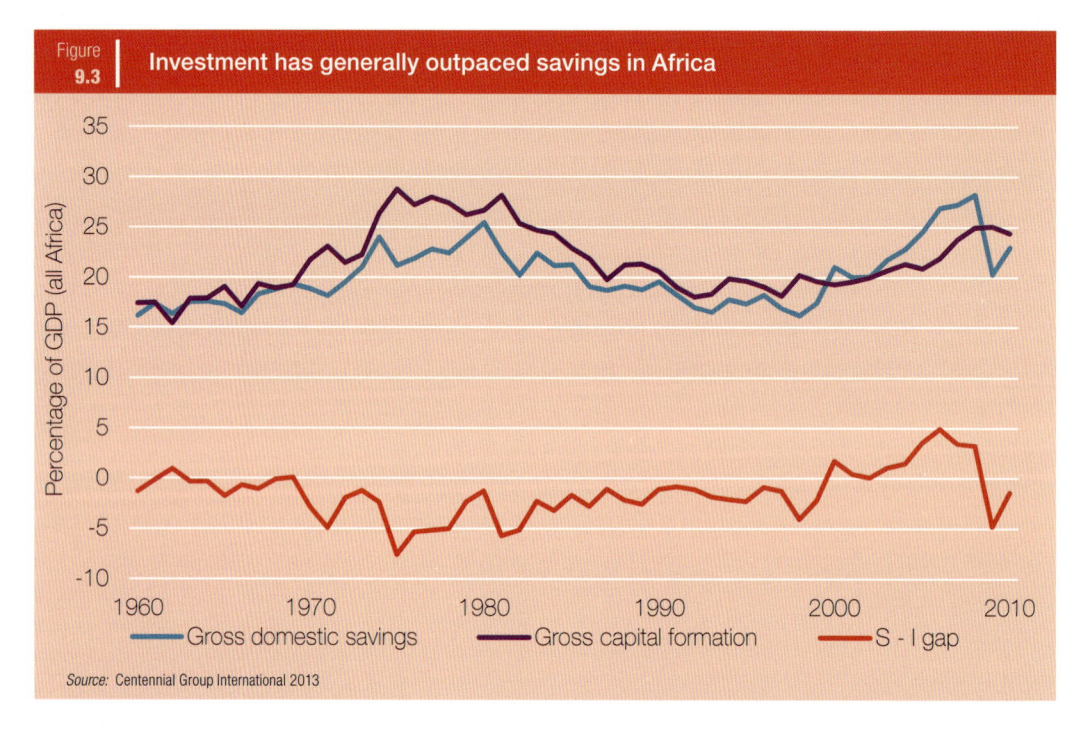

— Gross domestic savings — Gross capital formation — S - I gap

Source: Centennial Group International 2013

Figure 9.4 | After a surge in the 1990s, inflation has largely been brought down to more manageable levels

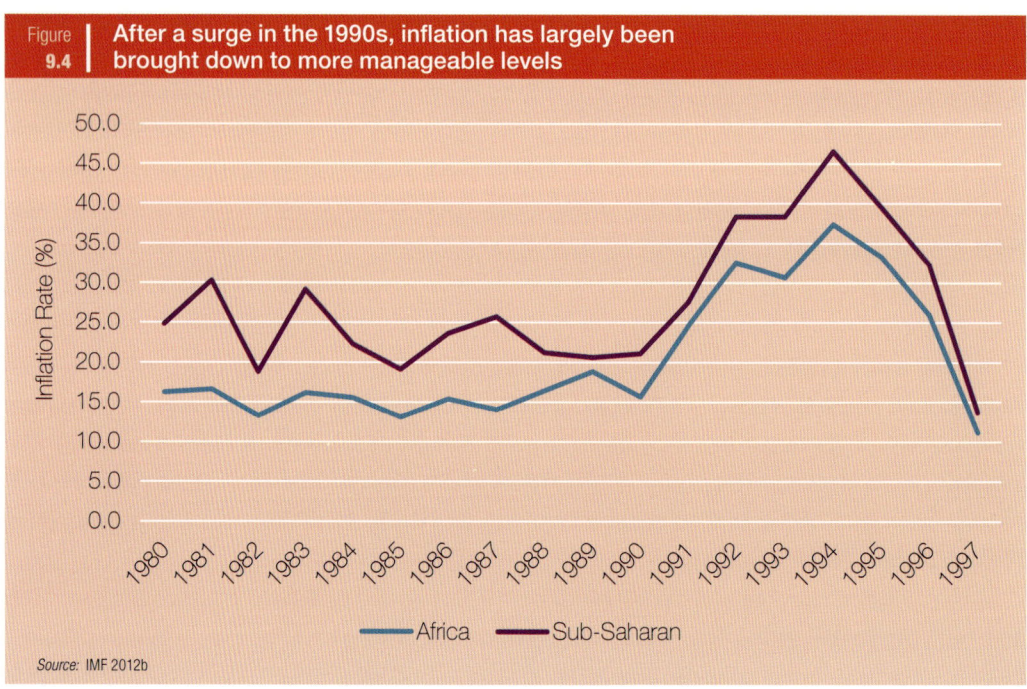

— Africa — Sub-Saharan

Source: IMF 2012b

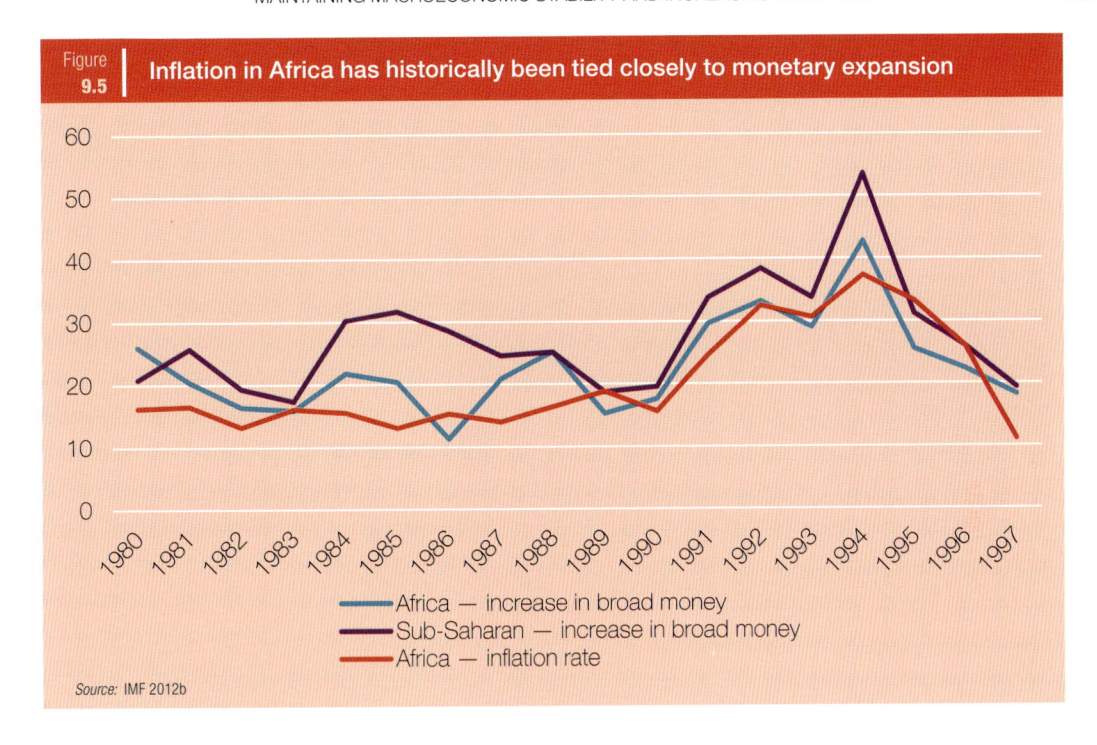

Figure 9.5 | Inflation in Africa has historically been tied closely to monetary expansion

- Africa — increase in broad money
- Sub-Saharan — increase in broad money
- Africa — inflation rate

Source: IMF 2012b

The movements in the inflation rate reflected closely the rates of monetary expansion in Africa (Figure 9.5). Both indicators moved sharply up in the early 1990s and then declined during 1995-97.

The inflation experiences of African countries with fixed exchange rates differed from those with more flexible regimes. For example, inflation rates in the CFA franc zone countries averaged well below 10 percent between 1975 and 1989 in contrast to double-digit inflation in many of the countries with flexible exchange rates (such as in Ghana, Sierra Leone, Uganda, and Zambia). Low inflation in the CFA franc countries reflected their special monetary and financial arrangements, which included a fixed exchange rate, a high degree of openness of the external capital account, and an independent common central bank. The effect of domestic credit expansion, large fiscal deficits, and investment-savings imbalances was channeled through a build-up of foreign debt and/or reduction of foreign reserves with little or no spillover into monetary expansion and inflation. In countries with flexible regimes the main cause of inflation was fiscal deficits entailing substantial monetary financing. In these cases, exchange rate devaluation can aggravate inflationary pressures by raising the cost of imports (especially of imported inputs), more so if domestic supply elasticity is low.

The inflationary impact of the 1994 CFA franc devaluation (50 percent in foreign currency terms) was large for a short period following the devaluation. The 14 franc zone countries all implemented the devaluation simultaneously and quickly launched macroeconomic programs to maximize the gains from the devaluation. The result was a temporary upturn in Africa's inflation in 1994, followed by a drop during 1995 to 1997.

Exchange rate devaluation per se has not always led to inflationary pressures. In countries with large differentials between the official exchange rate and the rate in the parallel market, devaluations tended to close this gap without significant inflationary effects when appropriately tight macroeconomic financial policies were in place. In this situation, domestic prices already reflected the parallel market exchange rate prior to the devaluation. The experiences of countries that moved from fixed to flexible exchange rate regimes indicate that high inflation and thriving parallel markets prevailed before the exchange rate reforms. Devaluation in these cases tended to align the official rate with the parallel rate and thus contributed little to inflationary pressures. In some cases it even alleviated fiscal pressures by increasing government revenues.

Many African countries implemented structural reforms of the financial sector during this period. Central banks were granted more autonomy in conducting monetary policy, interest rates were liberalized, credit allocation systems were phased out, and strict limits were introduced on government borrowing. The solvency of banks was thus improved and bank supervision and auditing practices were strengthened. Steps were also taken to shift from direct to indirect monetary policy implementation.

In the aftermath of the 1994 devaluation, the CFA franc countries implemented several financial sector reforms. Crop credit was included under an overall credit ceiling, credit controls were eliminated, and a new rating system for assessing creditworthiness was introduced to guide the central bank's refinancing policy. A system of indirect monetary management was launched within the framework of a regional interbank and money market. Money market auctions and a central bank discount window were introduced. A form of repurchase agreement was created to provide liquidity for banks, and interest rates were liberalized. Bank supervision capabilities and regulatory and prudential standards were substantially improved and enforcement strengthened.

Persistence of large fiscal deficits

From the beginning of the 1970s to the early 1990s, Sub-Saharan Africa's fiscal deficits fluctuated between 5 and 9 percent of GDP without a clear trend toward a narrowing of the deficit. A sharp reduction of the deficit was achieved during 1994-1997. A similar time profile applies to the whole of Africa (Figure 9.6).

Reform efforts in the 1980s and 1990s included a variety of fiscal measures; public investment programming was integrated within a coherent budgetary framework and supported by improvements in project selection and public expenditure management systems. More attention was given to government expenditures for human resource development (through emphasis on health and education) and poverty

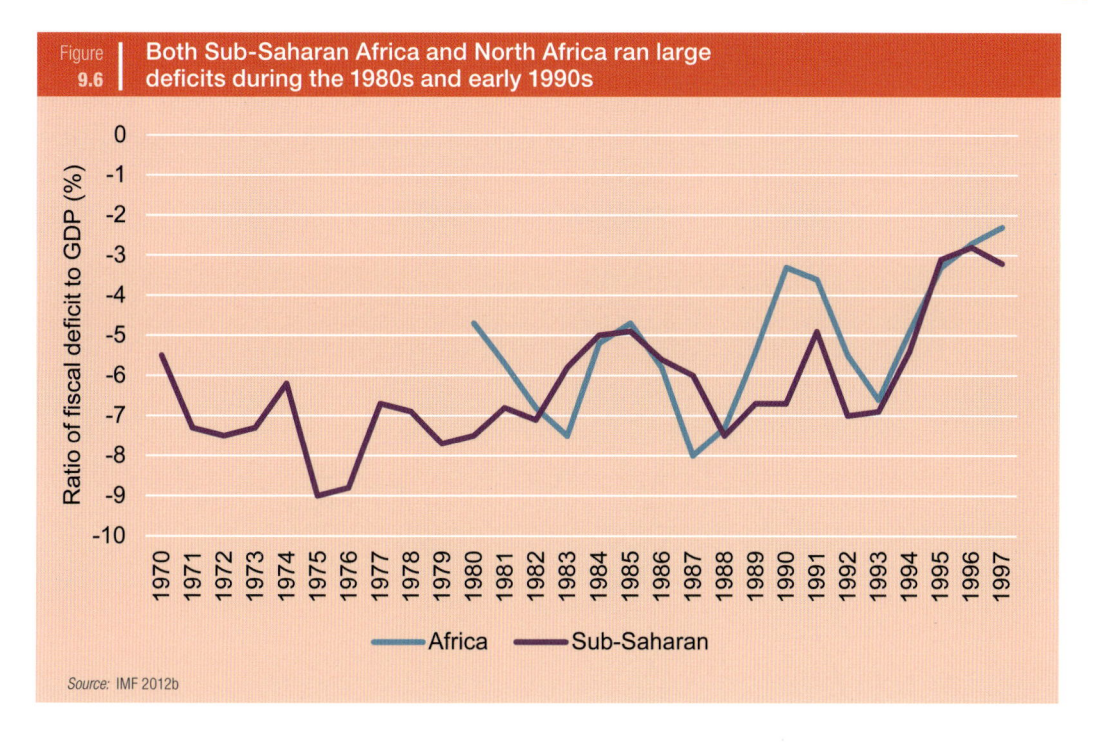

Figure 9.6 Both Sub-Saharan Africa and North Africa ran large deficits during the 1980s and early 1990s

Source: IMF 2012b

reduction. Measures were implemented to restructure the public enterprise sector, privatize some of these enterprises, and reduce the sector's reliance on budgetary subsidies and domestic bank credit. A number of countries (the Gambia, Ghana, Lesotho, and Mali) took steps to reduce the civil service wage bill as a percentage of GDP and improve the wage structure.

On the revenue side, steps were taken to improve tax administration, broaden the tax base, and rationalize tax structures. Efforts were made to reduce reliance on taxation of foreign trade and shift toward taxes on domestic transactions and sources of domestic income. Reform of import tariffs in the Gambia, Kenya, Madagascar, Niger, Senegal, Tanzania, and Togo included reduction in the number and highest level of tariffs, reduction of exemptions, and conversion of specific to ad valorem taxes. In some cases, broad-based sales taxes replaced a multiplicity of sales tax rates, and Kenya, Malawi, Mali, Niger, and Senegal took steps to introduce value-added taxes. Kenya, Madagascar, Malawi, and Tanzania simplified personal income taxation by lowering the highest marginal rates, reducing the number of rates, reducing exemptions and deductions, and shifting to improved definitions of income.

Prolonged deficits in the external current account of the balance of payments

Mainly as a result of the fiscal imbalances, SSA's external current account deficits were substantial as a proportion of exports throughout the 1970s and the 1980s (averaging about 23 percent). These deficits began declining around the mid-1990s (Figure 9.7). For Africa as a whole, external deficits were smaller as a share of exports because of the lower share in North Africa.

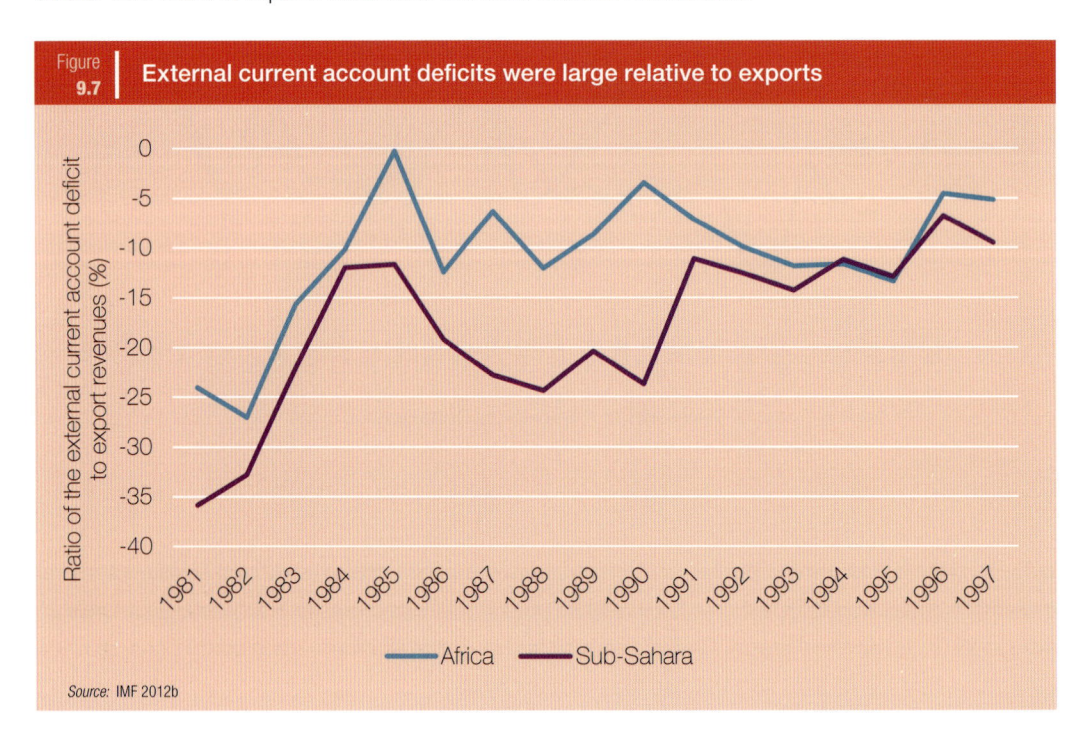

Figure 9.7 External current account deficits were large relative to exports

Source: IMF 2012b

A growing debt problem and repeated recourse to debt relief

The large deficits in the fiscal and external current accounts were financed by substantial foreign borrowing in SSA. Consequently, SSA's external debt to GDP ratio increased from 25 percent in 1973 to about 70 percent of GDP by the mid-1990s (Figure 9.8). The external debt service ratio to exports for SSA rose from 8 percent in 1974 to about 20 percent by the mid-1990s. These ratios followed similar trends for Africa as a whole.

Bilateral official creditors sought to alleviate Africa's debt burden through repeated rescheduling operations on increasingly concessional terms, mainly (but not exclusively) for the low-income countries. Various initiatives were undertaken by the Paris Club, the IMF, and the World Bank to provide broader debt relief to heavily indebted poor countries with severe debt burdens and to strengthen the links between debt relief, poverty reduction, and social policies. Debt relief, combined with substantial foreign

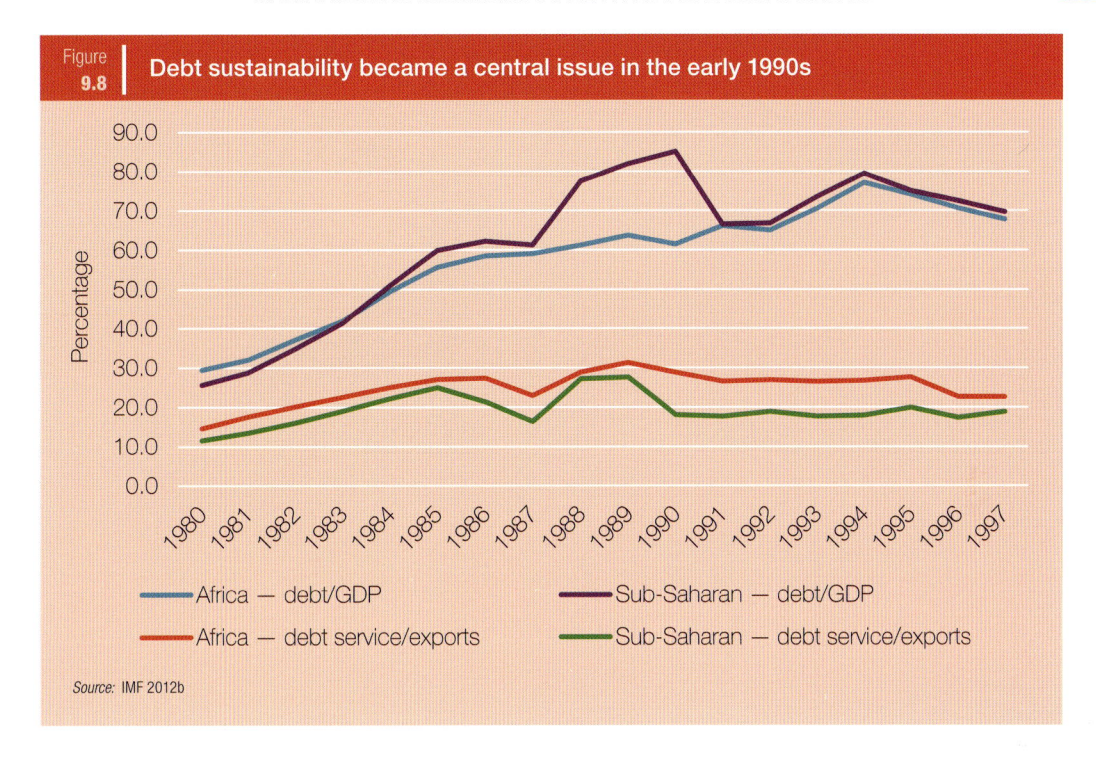

Figure 9.8 Debt sustainability became a central issue in the early 1990s

— Africa — debt/GDP
— Sub-Saharan — debt/GDP
— Africa — debt service/exports
— Sub-Saharan — debt service/exports

Source: IMF 2012b

aid inflows, allowed African countries not only to finance their fiscal and external imbalances but also to gradually build up a much-needed (albeit modest) cushion of foreign reserves. In SSA reserves increased from less than one month of imports in 1980 to slightly more than 3 months of imports (Figure 9.9).

The contribution of reform efforts to economic recovery

Success in implementing reforms differed widely across countries as well as across the various areas of policy reform. A World Bank study examined the experience of 29 countries and reported that those with the maximum improvement in macroeconomic policies between 1981-86 and 1987-91 achieved the strongest improvements in economic performance, per capita GDP, and industrial and export growth rates (World Bank 1993). Agricultural growth rates also accelerated in countries that reduced the tax burden on farmers. The report concluded that the countries studied had in general been more successful in improving their macroeconomic, trade, and agricultural policies than in reforming their public and financial sectors. A later IMF staff study reviewed the adjustment experiences of two groups of countries during 1986-93, comparing countries that had implemented broadly appropriate policies for at least three years (the sustained adjusters) with those that were less successful in sustaining the implementation of their programs (weak adjusters). The sustained adjusters improved their external competitiveness, implemented structural reforms to cushion the impact of terms-of-trade losses, and performed better than the weak adjusters. In addition, the strong adjusters achieved positive and higher rates of per capita real

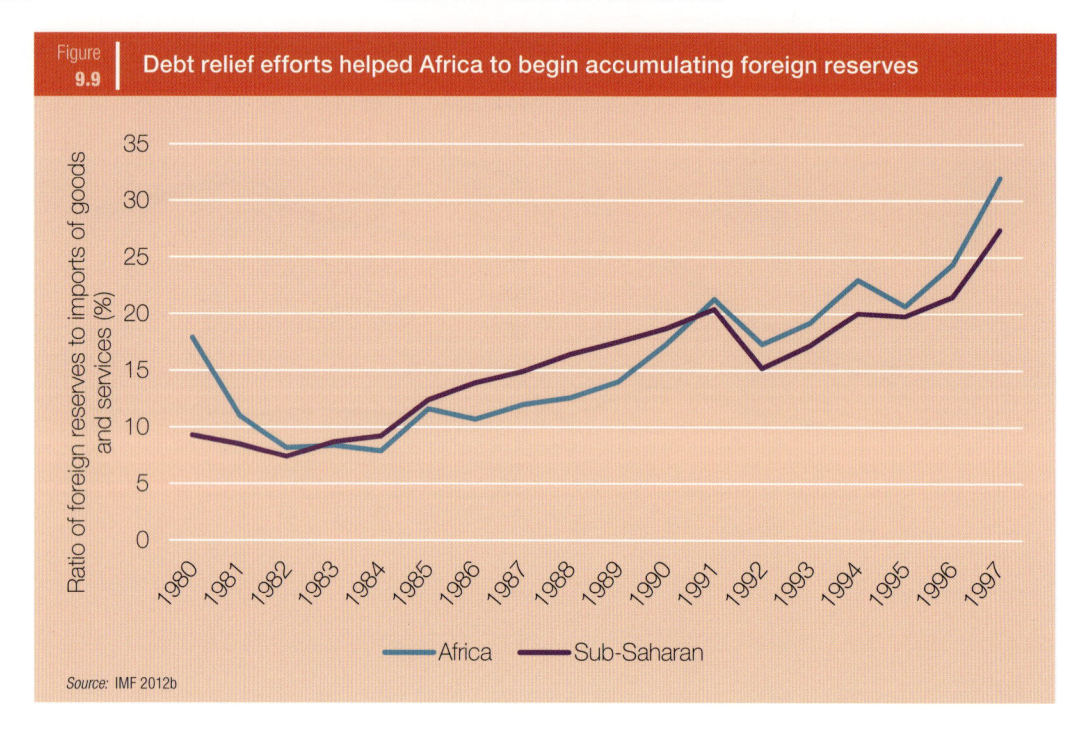

Figure 9.9 Debt relief efforts helped Africa to begin accumulating foreign reserves

Source: IMF 2012b

GDP growth and higher rates of government savings and investment growth than the weak adjusters, which experienced negative per capita income growth and declines in domestic savings and investment in both the public and private sectors (Hadjimichael et al. 1995).

A growing number of countries implemented reform programs, often over extended periods, and evidence of improved economic performance gradually emerged. An IMF staff study found that the economic performance of SSA countries had improved markedly between the periods 1981-84 and 1995-97 (Calamatsis, Basu, and Ghura 1999). It noted that after recording negative growth rates of per capita GDP through most of the 1980s and the five-year period 1990-94, the growth rate of per capita real GDP rose to 1.2 percent during 1995-97. More than twice as many countries experienced positive growth rates during 1995-97 than the 16 that had achieved increases in per capita GDP during 1990-94. Growth performance was significantly weaker in countries affected by past or continuing political turmoil. The growth rates in conflict-affected countries (including Burundi, Comoros, the Democratic Republic of the Congo, Rwanda, Sierra Leone, Swaziland, and Zambia) remained negative or declined.

Strengthening of macroeconomic performance since the mid-1990s

Growth, resilience, and inflation

Africa's macroeconomic performance improved markedly over the last decade and a half, with not only higher growth rates but also important gains in reducing inflation and thus in macroeconomic stability. Africa's GDP growth increased considerably from the early to mid-1990s and has averaged around 4.6 percent a year since then (Figure 9.10). Moreover, despite the weak global economic environment that followed the onset of the global financial crisis of 2008-09, annual growth averaged a remarkable 4.8 percent during 2007-11. Most countries shared in this solid expansion.

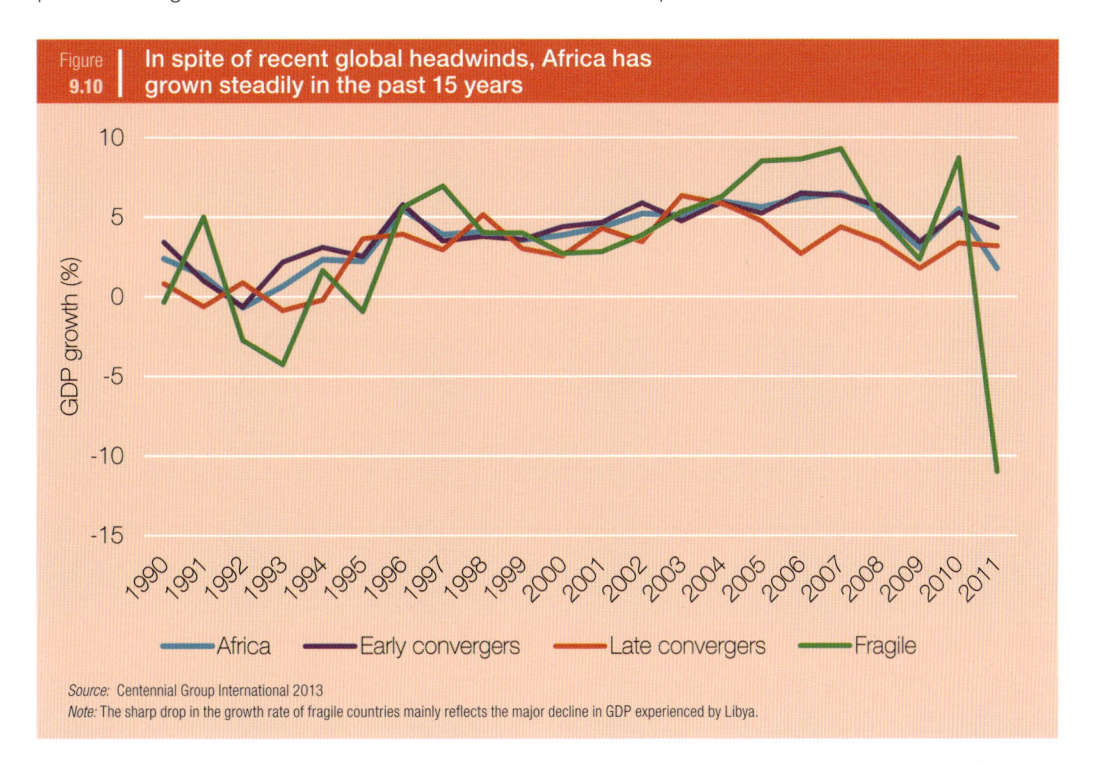

Figure 9.10 In spite of recent global headwinds, Africa has grown steadily in the past 15 years

Source: Centennial Group International 2013
Note: The sharp drop in the growth rate of fragile countries mainly reflects the major decline in GDP experienced by Libya.

As noted above, the improvement in economic performance is to a considerable extent the result of important policy efforts, including the wide-ranging reforms implemented by many countries prior to and in the context of the various debt-relief initiatives of the 1990s, and also by a number of countries that had not been eligible for relief. Africa's growth performance also benefited from a considerable improvement in its terms of trade in recent years and the associated increase in production of natural resources in several countries.

The reforms were instrumental in introducing dynamism to the economies, as evidenced by higher economic growth and a remarkable strengthening in resilience (see Figure 9.11) (Boorman et al 2013).[3]

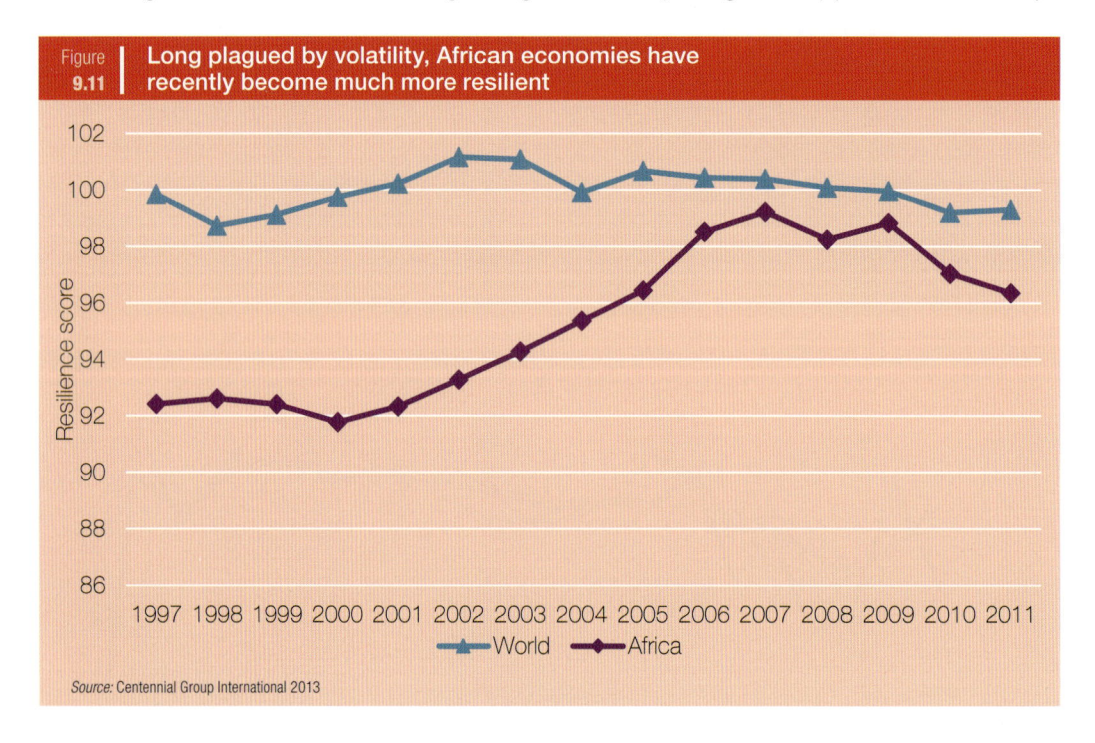

Figure 9.11 Long plagued by volatility, African economies have recently become much more resilient

Source: Centennial Group International 2013

A review of the resilience sub-indexes tellingly reveals that, overall, African countries performed well in "external robustness" and "private debt" (see Table 9.1). Resilience was relatively weak, however, in the areas of "government effectiveness," "governance," "monetary policy," "export diversity," and "export independence."

Africa's inflation rate has dropped markedly during the last decade and a half, although it remains higher than that of the advanced countries and other regions (Figure 9.12). The decline in inflation from the mid-1990s in a number of countries reflects the tapering off of the impact of the significant devaluation of the CFA franc in 1994. The relative increase in inflation since 2007 most likely reflects rising food prices, given food's prominent place in Africa's consumption basket. What is remarkable is the major improvement among the fragile countries;[4] their inflation rate approached the average for the region by the late 1990s. Also noteworthy is the decline in inflation among the late convergers (see Chapter 1), from about 25 percent in the mid-1990s to low single digits currently.

---

3. In the aftermath of the global financial crisis, Sub-Saharan Africa's GDP growth fell to 1.6 percent in 2009, but it rebounded to 4.6 percent in 2011, reflecting the strengthening in resiliency. The focus here on Sub-Saharan Africa is an attempt to isolate the improvement in the region's resilience from the adverse economic impact on some Northern African countries associated with the Arab Spring.
4. See Chapter 1 for the definition of early converger, late converger, and fragile.

Table 9.1 Resilience Index (world average=100)

	Resilience	Fiscal policy	Government effectiveness	Governance	Monetary policy	Banking soundness	Export diversity	Export independence	External robustness	Private debt	Reserves
Algeria	116	114	86	81	97	108	86	91	136	114	137
Botswana	106	109	93		94	110	77	94	121	111	119
Namibia	103	109	89	91	95	109	98	92		110	104
South Africa	102	104	93	97	101	97	104	98	110	104	100
Uganda	100	106	83	79	87	115	102	103	113	112	100
Ghana	97	103	92	83	98	109	93	93	109	112	100
Mauritius	97	102	97	93	96	107	94	98	104	92	108
Togo	97	121	73	76	96	102	103	95	117	109	99
Cameroon	97	112	79	77	98	106	95	101	112	113	98
Morocco	97	102	89	88	98	102	98	99	110	104	100
Egypt	97	97	83	88	94	99	109	104	107	110	99
Kenya	97	104	83	83	88	113	105	102	109	108	95
Benin	96	108	82	81	97	102	91	98	115	113	101
Swaziland	95	112	84	81	95	110	91	86	108	112	106
Malawi	95	106	87	79	94	120	95	99	102	111	90
Tanzania	94	103	81	79	87	104	104	101	112	112	99
Mozambique	93	110	81	80	94	116	85	96	115	106	94
Madagascar	93	103	78	76	95	103	96	102	116	113	94
Burkina Faso	92	107	78	80	96	101	89	101	109	112	100
Senegal	91	102	80	78	97	97	98	102	112	110	99
Seychelles	91	137	94	82	95	103	85	88	95	92	101
Niger	90	111	81	79	98	101	80	100	107	114	99
Ethiopia	90	109	82	75	78	107	97	106	108	115	93
Tunisia	89	106	88	89	98	99	94	91	112	105	84
Nigeria	89	110	80	80	94	109	75	86	117	113	103
Mali	89	106	76	83	96	100	82	98	111	113	101
Zambia	84	109	81	83	96	97	76	88	112	113	96
Côte d'Ivoire	84	93	73	75	97	103	97	88	111	111	100
Gabon	84	111	81	78	98	105	71	76	114	115	100
Angola	83	109	81	78	93	105	65	80	115	111	109
Sudan		100	72	72	90	106	63	103	92	115	88

Source: Centennial Group International 2013
Note: Dark green > 110 (more than one standard deviation above world average); Light green 100-10 (less than one standard deviation above world average; Light red 90-100 (less than one standard deviation below world average); Dark red <90 (more than one standard deviation below world average

Figure 9.12 | Even Africa's fragile countries have had recent success managing inflation

Source: Centennial Group International 2013
Note: Inflation for Fragile countries from 1994 to 1996 was over 60%

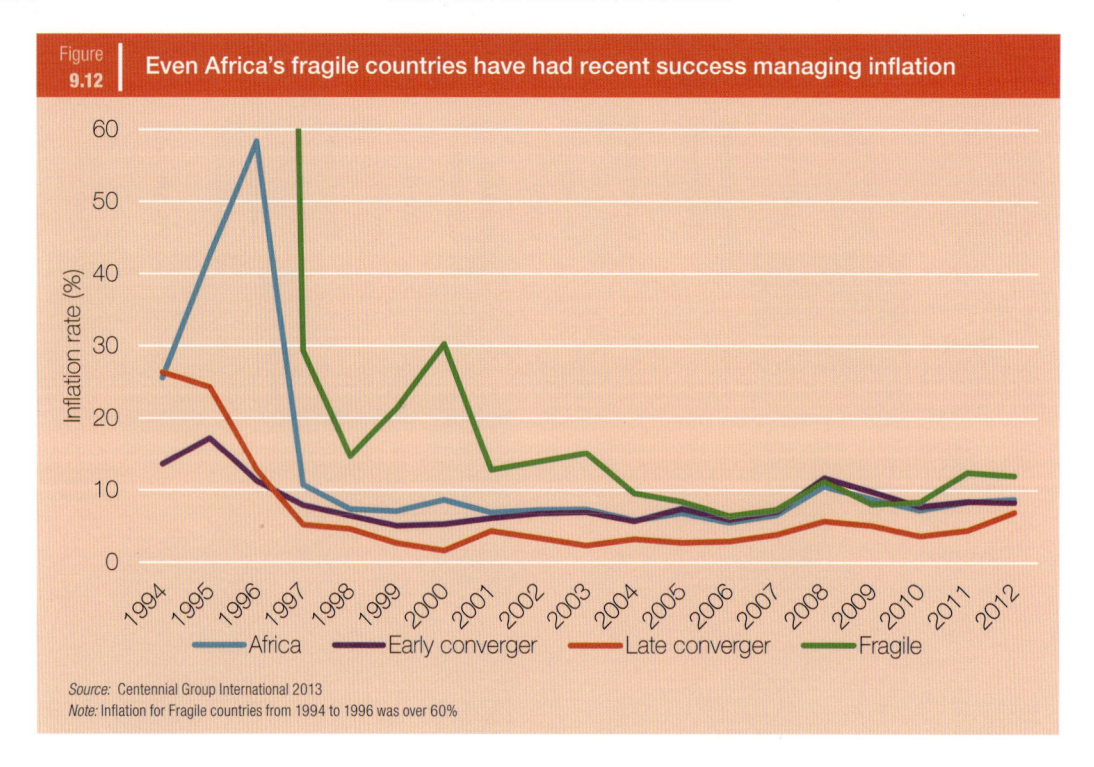

Inflation rates vary across countries reflecting individual policies and circumstances. In 2011, the Sub-Saharan countries with conventional exchange rate pegs recorded an inflation rate of 3.6 percent, whereas those without such a peg recorded an inflation rate of 10.4 percent (IMF 2012a). Inflation in the Sub-Saharan oil importing countries (excluding South Africa) was 13.2 percent, reflecting the jump in world oil prices.

Many African countries have improved considerably their monetary policy management over the last decade and a half. Most of the countries without a conventional exchange rate peg have introduced indirect instruments to control monetary aggregates, and some of these countries have adopted inflation targeting frameworks. Those with exchange rate pegs have kept a prudent credit policy. Many countries have increased the autonomy of their central banks, enhancing the banks' capacity to control inflation. Nevertheless, despite important efforts, progress in containing inflation rates has been limited in recent years. As mentioned above, inflation has been relatively high in some countries, suggesting that monetary policies may need to be strengthened, even if part of the recent inflationary developments reflect the impact of higher food and fuel prices.

Public finances

Fiscal policy in Africa, as measured by the government overall balance, has been prudent during the last decade, showing significant surpluses in the period 2004 to 2008 (largely accounted for by the fragile and late-converging countries) that turned into small deficits in the aftermath of the global financial crisis of 2008-09. These deficits have been largely similar to those prevailing in other regions but, as Figure 9.13 shows, Africa's public finances were more severely affected by the crisis than other regions. In particular, government revenue fell considerably while government spending remained relatively stable (Figures 9.14 and 9.15).

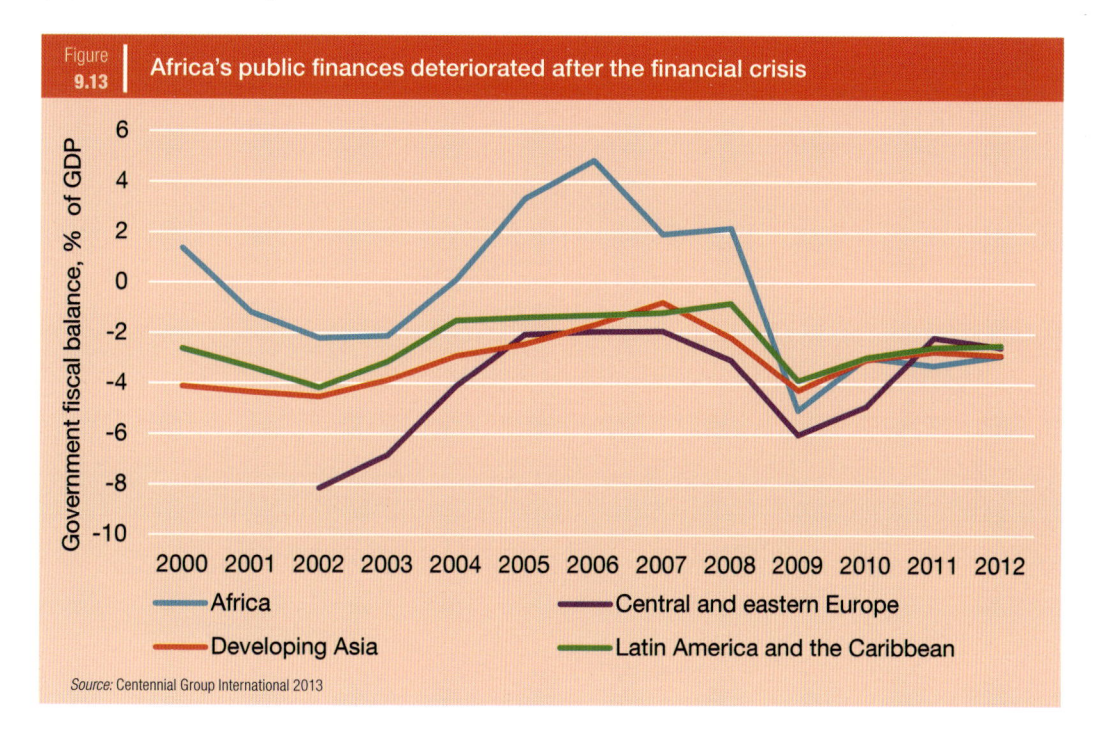

Figure 9.13 | Africa's public finances deteriorated after the financial crisis

Source: Centennial Group International 2013

Not surprisingly, the aggregates mask large differences among the various groups of countries. Both the fragile and late convergers showed large overall surpluses during 2004 to 2008 (Figure 9.16). The surpluses of the late convergers turned into a small deficit in the aftermath of the global crisis; the overall balances of the fragile countries fluctuated significantly but remained in surplus. The overall balances of the group of early convergers showed a similar pattern but with deficits throughout almost all of the period.

Figure 9.14 Government revenues dropped, more than in other regions, during the crisis

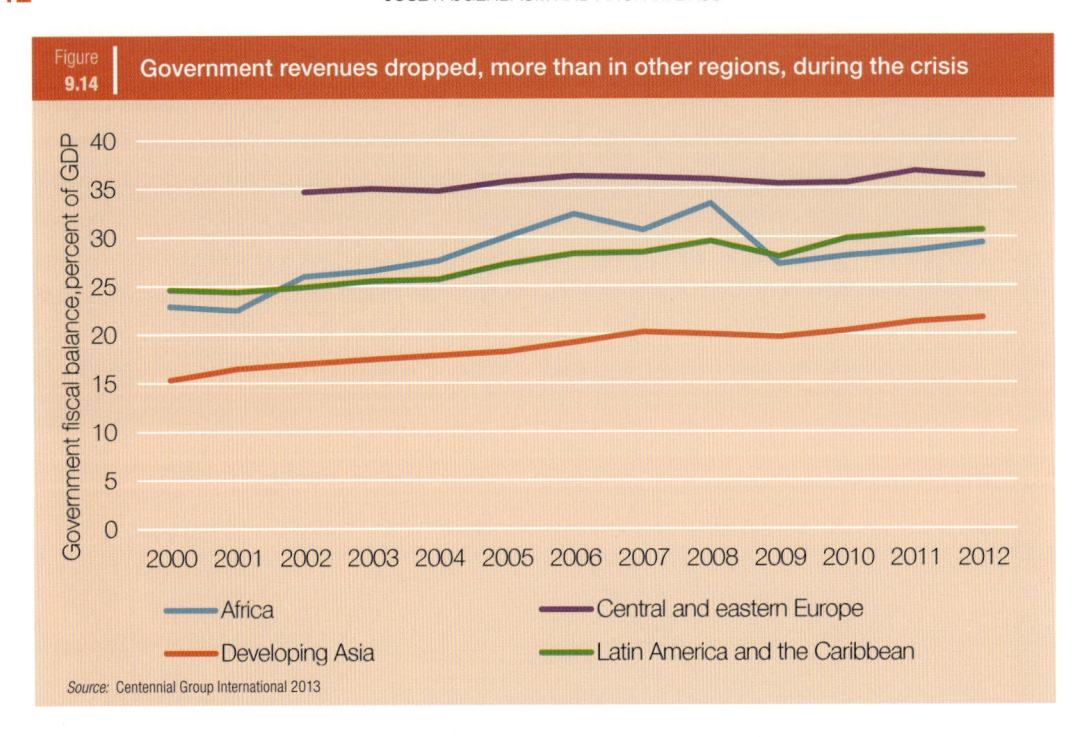

Government fiscal balance, percent of GDP — Africa, Central and eastern Europe, Developing Asia, Latin America and the Caribbean

Source: Centennial Group International 2013

Figure 9.15 Government expenditures in Africa have remained relatively stable since 2007

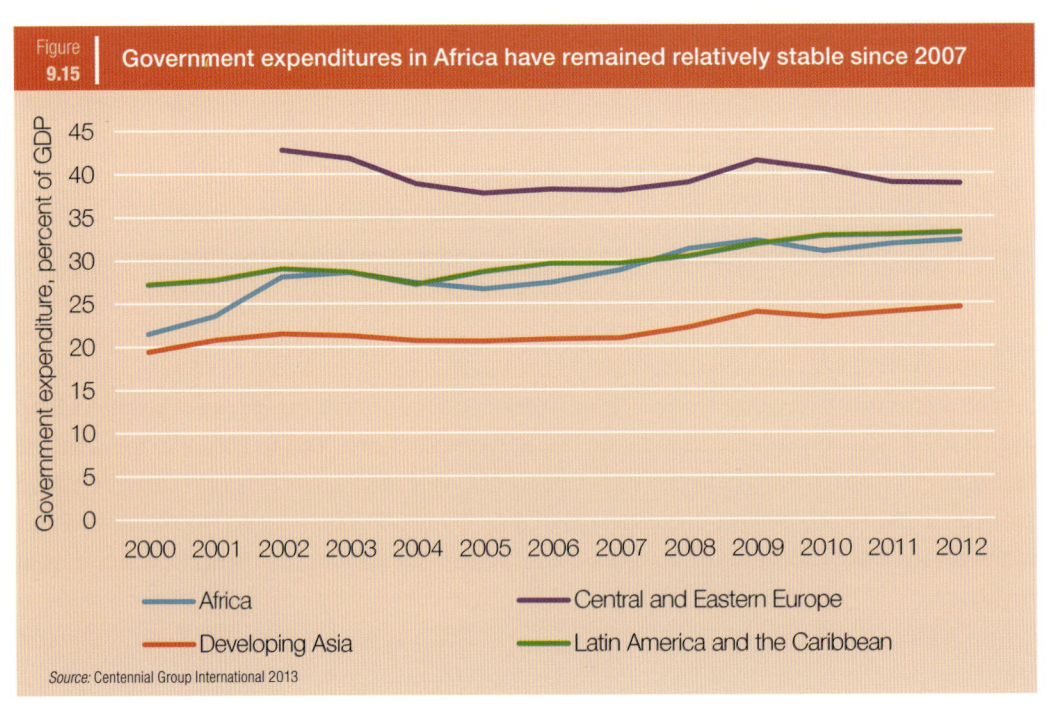

Government expenditure, percent of GDP — Africa, Central and Eastern Europe, Developing Asia, Latin America and the Caribbean

Source: Centennial Group International 2013

Figure 9.16 Public finances have varied greatly across the continent

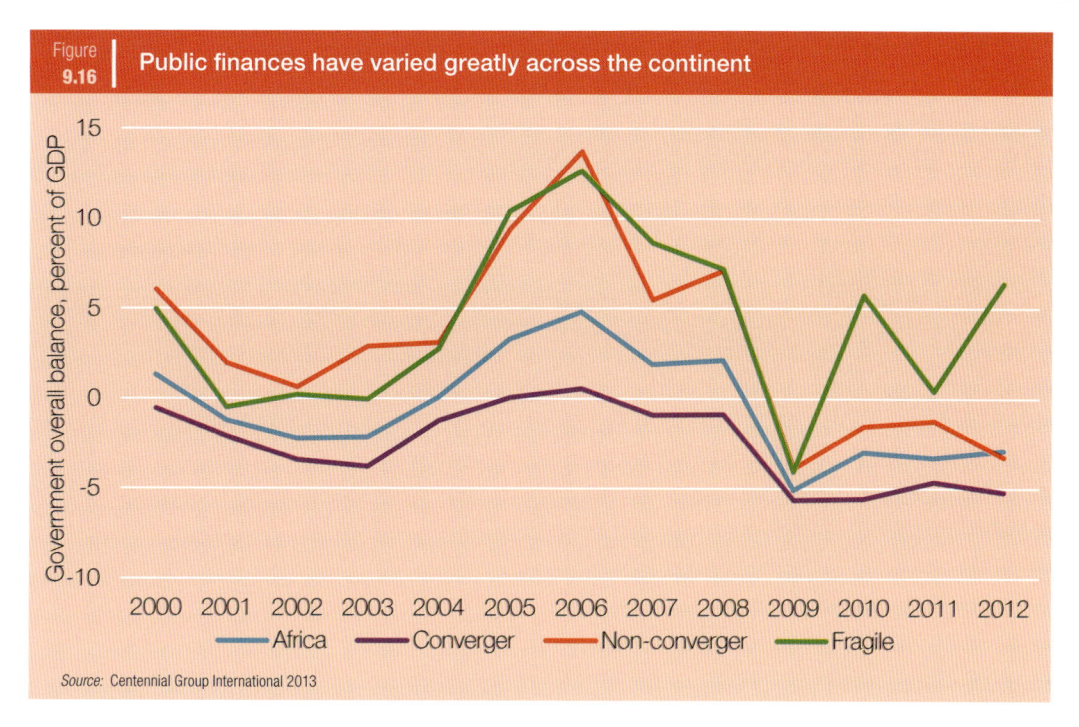

Source: Centennial Group International 2013

This performance reflects a considerable increase in government revenue since the early 2000s (Figure 9.17), mainly attributable to the fragile and late convergers, as revenue of the early convergers remained relatively flat. This increase is likely related to the large proportion of resource exporters among these countries.

Government spending also rose markedly in the early 2000s in all the subgroups (Figure 9.19). All groups continued to increase government spending, but the increases among the fragile and late converger countries have been significantly larger, indicating a strong correlation between increases in government revenue and expenditure. Such a pro-cyclical behavior raises concern about the sustainability of macroeconomic stability, given the large proportion of resource-rich countries in these groups, especially in the event of a weakening in the terms of trade (Loser 2013).

As shown in Figure 9.18, Africa's government expenditure is quite similar to that of Latin America but considerably higher than that of fast-growing Asia. Indeed, Africa's government revenue ratio to GDP, while similar to that of Latin America, is considerably higher than that of fast-growing Asia.

Despite the overall positive performance, many African countries show enormous infrastructure gaps, weak human development indicators, and poor income distribution. Fiscal policies should play a key role in improving these conditions. To this end, there is a need to address structural weaknesses on the revenue and expenditure sides and thereby prevent them from constraining growth potential.

Figure 9.17 Government revenues are larger in fragile states and early convergers

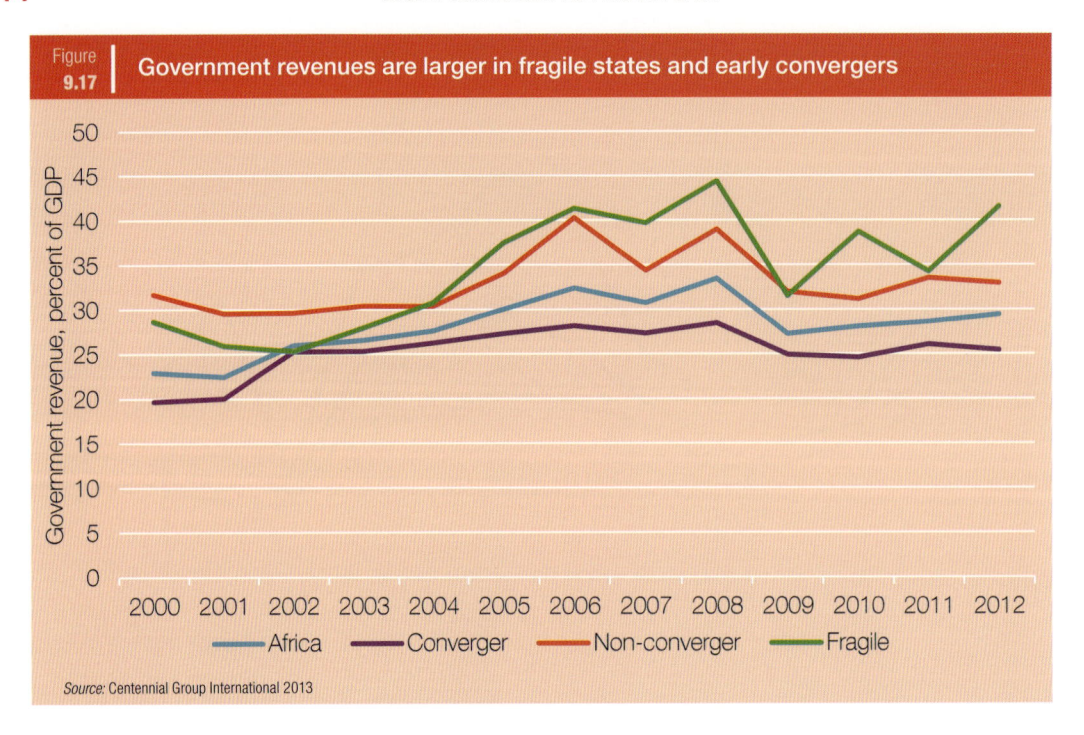

Source: Centennial Group International 2013.

Figure 9.18 Increases in government spending have mirrored increases in government revenues

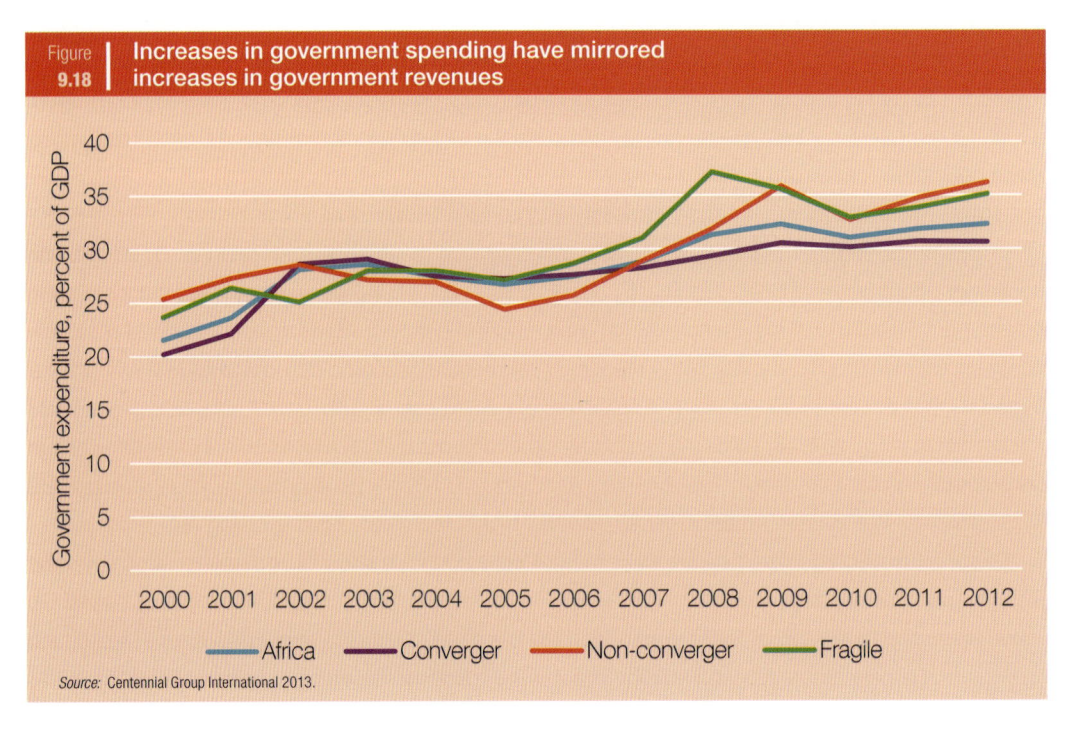

Source: Centennial Group International 2013.

Public debt

Africa's public debt declined considerably as a ratio to GDP in the context of the 1990s debt relief initiatives, (see Figure 9.19), thereby making the debt burden sustainable. While the public debt ratio bottomed out in 2008, it has increased significantly since then due to the fiscal stimulus packages adopted following the global financial crisis. This increase is largely attributable to the group of early converger countries (Figure 9.20). All other regions also show an increase in 2009 or 2010, for similar reasons, but their debt ratios stabilized immediately thereafter and in developing Asia even returned to the previous lower level by 2012.

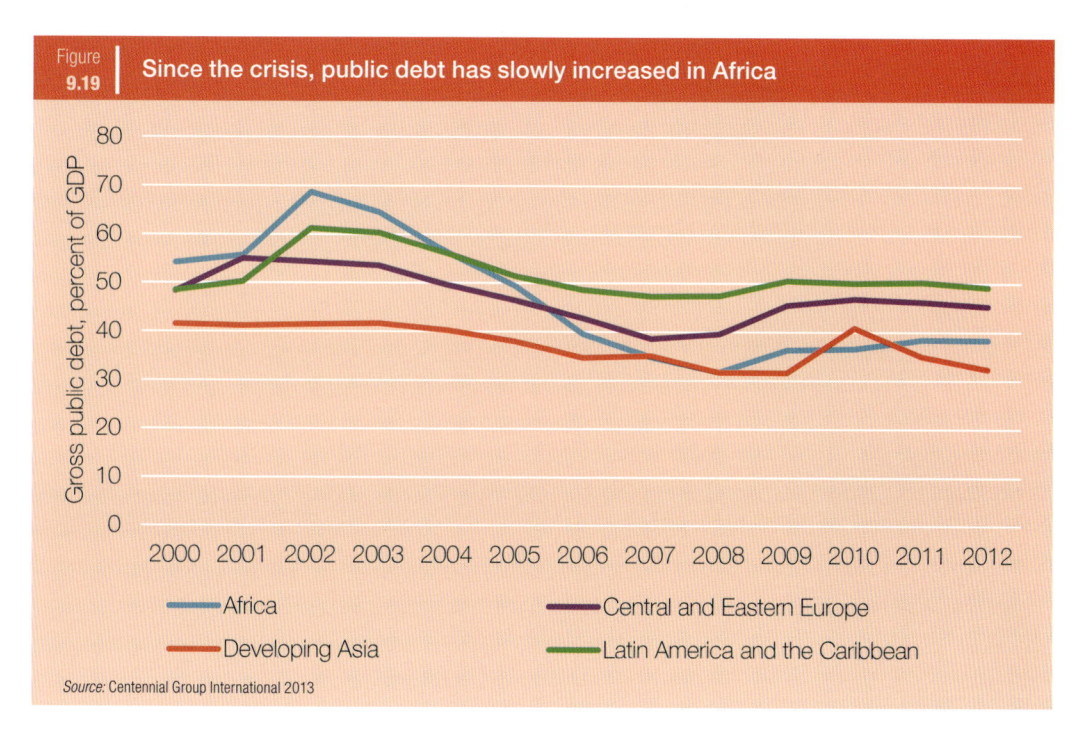

Figure 9.19 | Since the crisis, public debt has slowly increased in Africa

Source: Centennial Group International 2013

Given the depressed economic situation of Europe–a continent that accounts for a large share of Africa's exports–it is understandable that the fiscal stimulus measures have been difficult to unwind without affecting economic activity.

Balance of payments

Mirroring the strengthened macroeconomic policies of the last decade and a half, as well as the contribution of the improved terms of trade, Africa's external current account showed large surpluses from 2004 until 2008, that is, until the onset of the global financial crisis. The current account balances turned into small, sustainable deficits, but they have been more than financed by FDI and portfolio inflows.

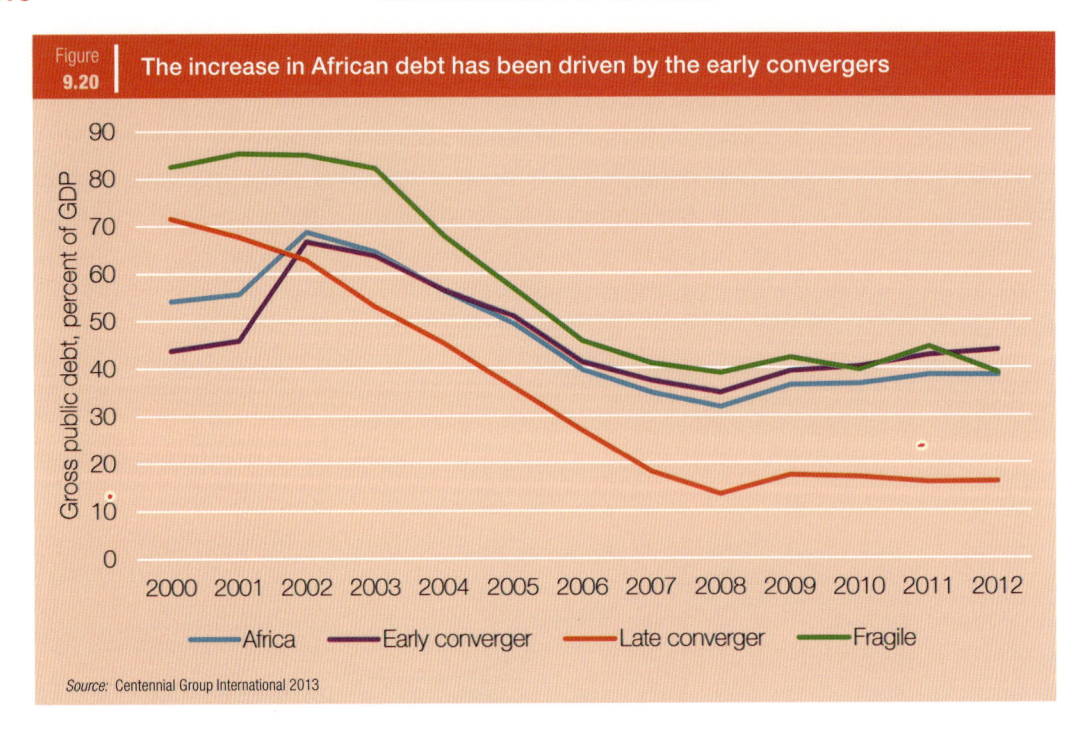

Figure 9.20: The increase in African debt has been driven by the early convergers

Gross public debt, percent of GDP, 2000–2012, for Africa, Early converger, Late converger, and Fragile.

Source: Centennial Group International 2013

Developing Asia and Latin America show similar trends. In contrast, Central and Eastern Europe show a contrasting trend as easy access to external borrowing led to a boom in consumption that was reversed in the aftermath of the global crisis (Figure 9.21).

The trends for the groups of late converger and fragile countries are considerably more pronounced (most likely reflecting a higher incidence of the gains in terms of trade). The group of early convergers also shows a strengthening of the current account balance until 2006 and steady decline thereafter; although their deficit does not raise major concern, further declines may be worrisome (Figure 9.22).

Investment and Savings Needs for Sustained High Growth

Growth, investment, and savings: Recent performance

Growth

The growth path for the group of early convergers has been similar to that of the continent as a whole, although with less volatility in recent years (see Figure 9.10). Volatility is greatly influenced by the high instability of the fragile countries. Growth performance of the group of late convergers is significantly

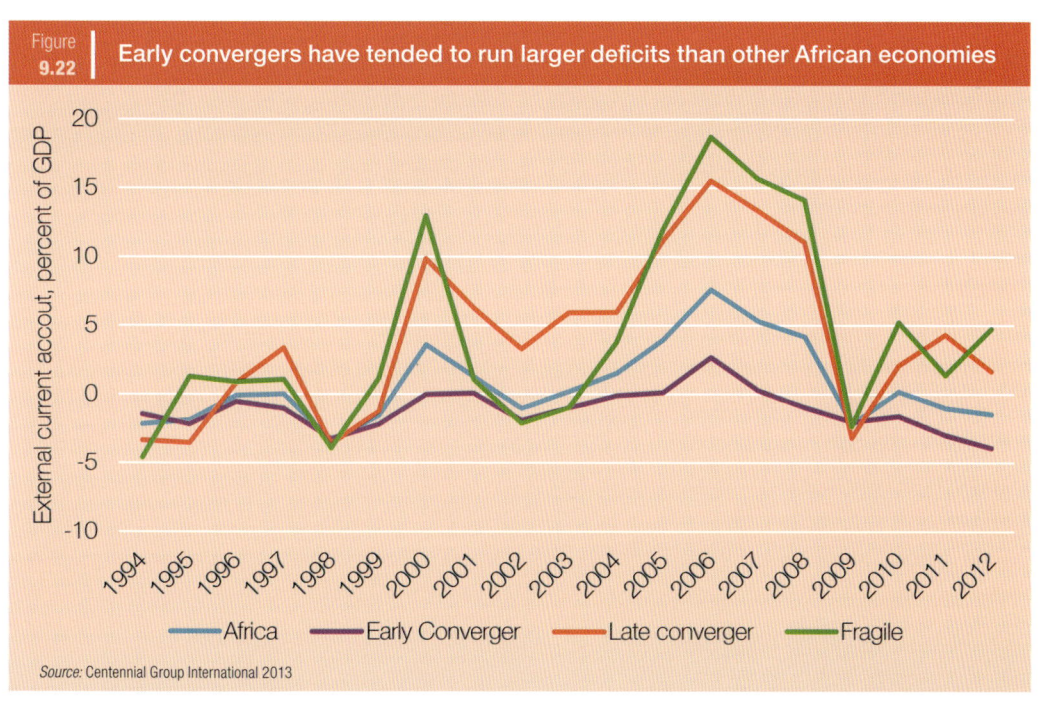

MAINTAINING MACROECONOMIC STABILITY AND INCREASING RESILIENCE

Figure 9.21 | In spite of the crisis, Africa has managed its current account balance well

Source: Centennial Group International 2013

Figure 9.22 | Early convergers have tended to run larger deficits than other African economies

Source: Centennial Group International 2013

weaker than the other groups, with somewhat lower volatility than the fragile group. More importantly and of greater concern is that the group of late convergers shows a declining trend in GDP growth since the early 2000s.

Africa is expected to maintain a moderate rate of growth over the next few years, with some growth attributable to new natural resource production in several countries. But the weaker performance of recent years also suggests that the important reform efforts described above need to be reinforced for GDP growth to accelerate. It will be especially important to create the conditions for Africa's low investment and savings rates to rise markedly.

Investment ratio

Africa's investment as a share of GDP is too low to support high rates of real GDP growth for long. The investment rate fluctuated around 20 percent over the past three decades but has risen to about 23 percent of GDP since 2007. These rates are quite similar to those of Latin America, but they are significantly lower than the average for emerging market and developing countries, and markedly lower than those of the fast-growing countries in developing Asia (see Figure 9.23).

The investment ratios of the group of early convergers have been quite similar to those of the continent, but the decline in their rates over the last few years is disturbing and contrasts with the increases observed in the other two groups (Figure 9.24). The decline may reflect a drop in FDI associated with the eurozone crisis. The investment ratios for the group of fragile countries have been volatile and lower than the average during the period under review. The considerable increase since the early 2000s, however, is remarkable. By contrast, the investment ratios for the late convergers, while also volatile, have been significantly higher than the average and show a major uptick since 2000, reflecting the high proportion of resource-exporting countries in this group and the capital-intensive nature of natural-resource production.[5]

Savings rates

As in the case of investment, Africa's savings represent too low a share of GDP. The savings rate compares poorly with those of other regions (except for Latin America and the Caribbean) and particularly of the fast-growing countries, as shown in Figure 9.25. It averaged well below 20 percent of GDP during 1980-2011; although it rose steadily from 2001 to about 23 percent in 2006-07, it has declined to about 20 percent in recent years. This decline is striking given the income gains arising from the significant improvements in terms of trade.

The regional averages mask very large disparities among African countries. For instance, about half of the Sub-Saharan countries have a savings rate of less than 15 percent of GDP (IMF 2012a). Moreover, as shown in Figure 9.26, the group of early convergers has had higher savings rates than the average

---

5. The investment ratios in the North African countries are markedly higher than those in the Sub-Saharan countries, but real GDP growth rates are considerably lower. This finding suggests a higher capital-output ratio (i.e., lower productivity of capital) in the North African countries than in the Sub-Saharan countries.

Figure 9.23 African investment trails behind many emerging economies

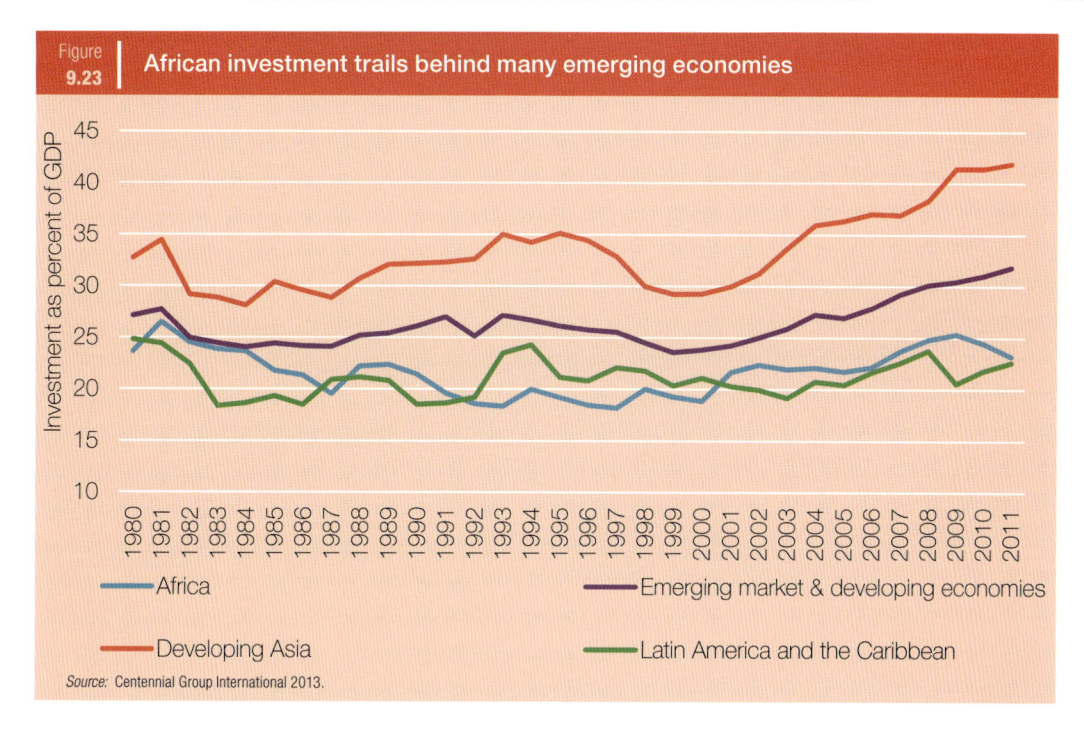

Source: Centennial Group International 2013.

Figure 9.24 Although late convergers have seen a recent rise in investment, the meager performance of Africa's early convergers is worrisome

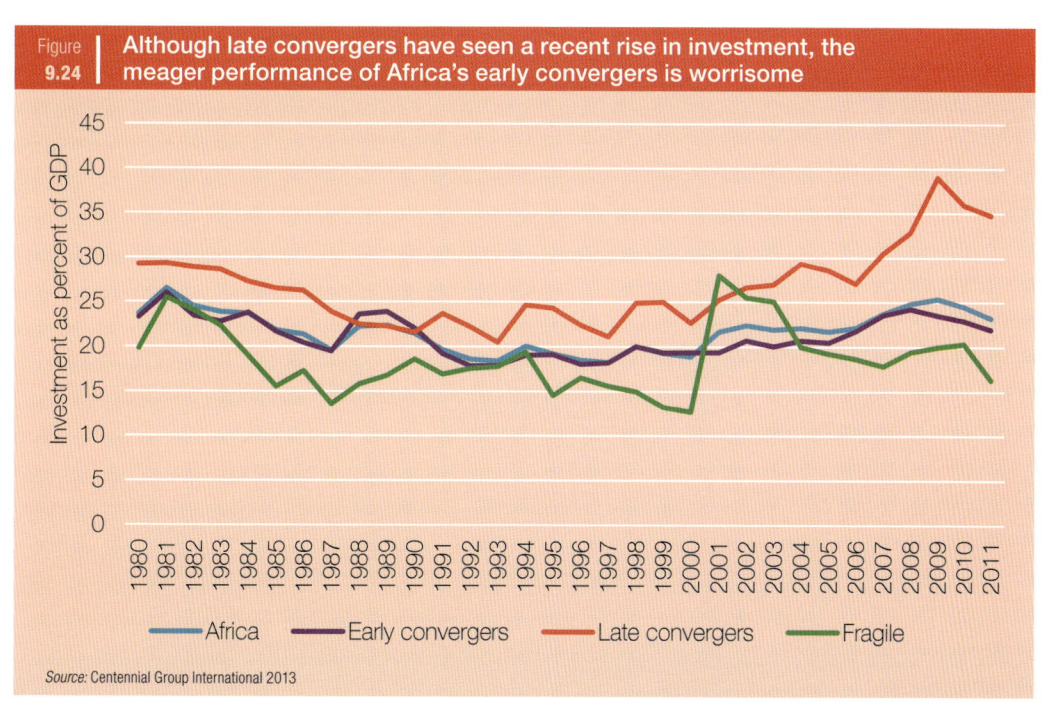

Source: Centennial Group International 2013

Figure 9.25 African savings rates trails those in Developing Asia

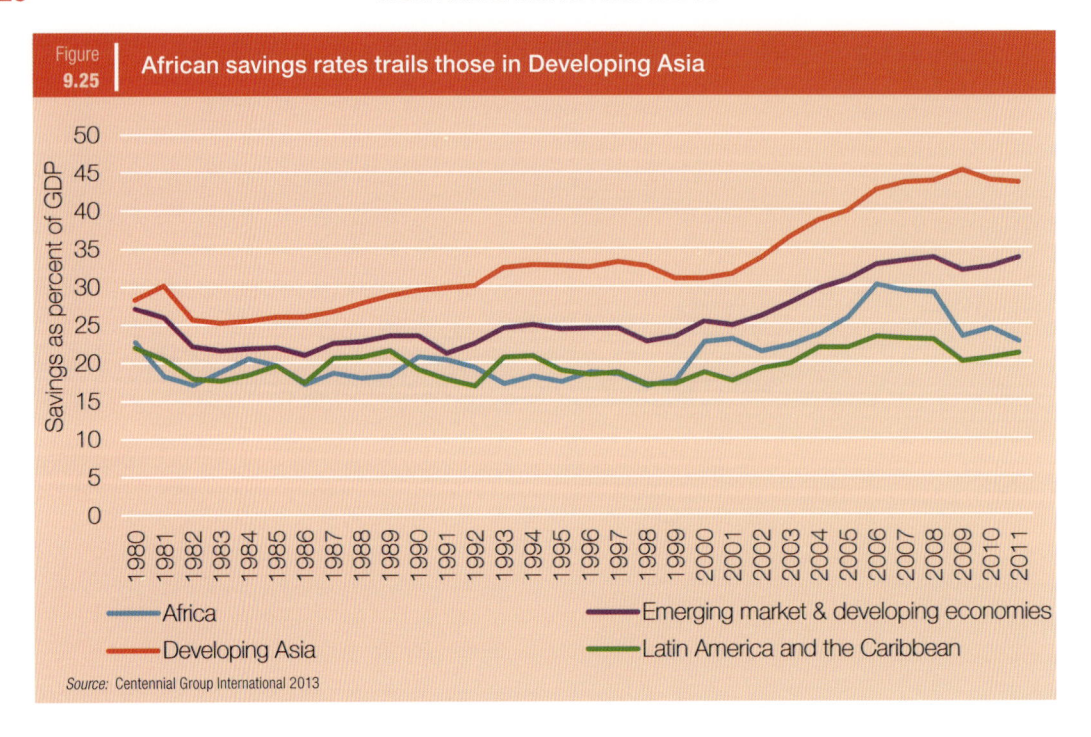

Source: Centennial Group International 2013

Figure 9.26 Late convergers have had higher rates of savings than early convergers

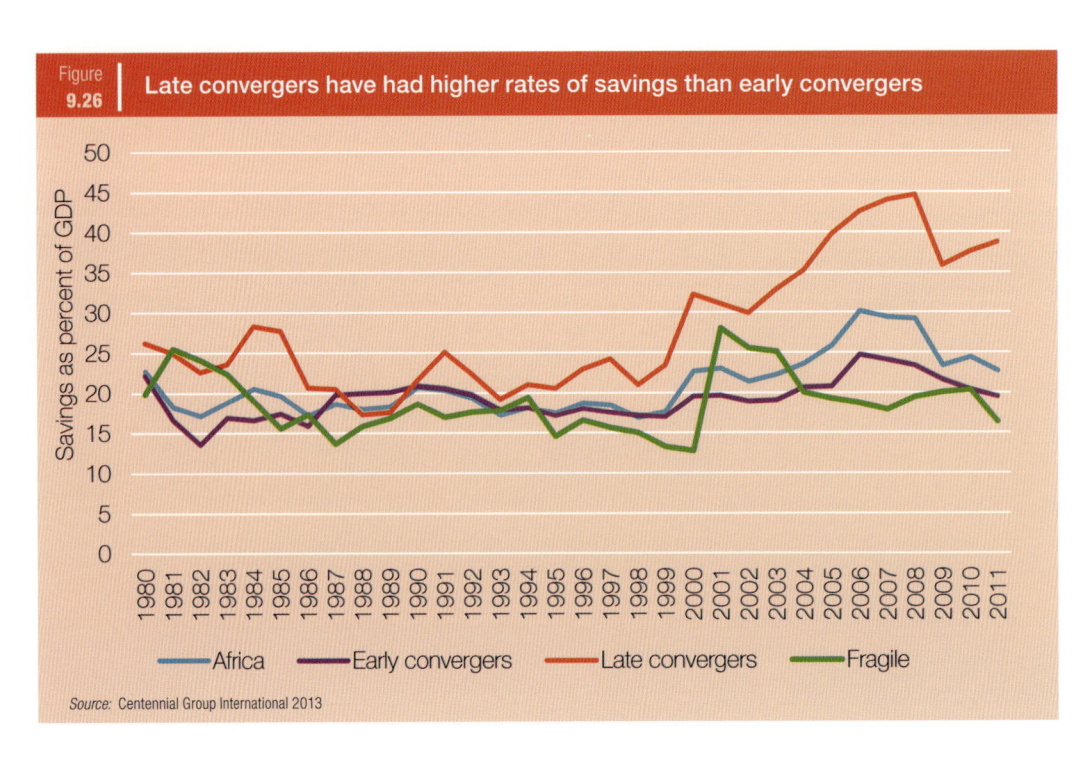

Source: Centennial Group International 2013

for the continent as a whole for most of the period under review. However, since 2005, these countries have experienced a sharp deterioration, surprisingly falling below the continent average in recent years. The savings rates of the group of late convergers have shown wide fluctuations, but their levels are considerably higher than the average for the continent, reflecting the high proportion of resource-exporting countries in this group and the size and volatility of the rents obtained from such exports. As in the case of the investment rates, the group of fragile countries has lower savings rates than the other groups. The recent increase to just below the average for the continent is noteworthy and may reflect increased rents from exports of natural resources.

Policy recommendations to achieve higher investment and savings ratios

The low investment and savings rates raise concerns about the sustainability of Africa's growth prospects. The following sub-sections propose a list of steps and policies that are the minimum necessary to create the conditions for Africa's low investment and savings rates to rise markedly.

To realize the Africa 2050 vision, particularly sustaining the GDP growth rate of 6.5 percent a year in the convergence scenario (see Chapter 1), Africa will need to raise its investment to an average of about 30 percent of GDP.[6] To reach this continent-wide average, those countries that already have high investment-to-GDP ratios – especially the capital-intensive natural resource producing countries – will need to raise their investment ratios well above this figure; correspondingly, the other countries will need to increase somewhat less. The increase in investment will help close the wide existing infrastructure gap and build an infrastructure that supports the targeted rate of GDP growth. The investment rate of those countries that also need to invest to close very large gaps in housing and the associated infrastructure (water, sanitation) will also need to increase above the 30 percent rate.

It is expected that the new, higher investment will be more productive as it will bring in new technology. Higher, more productive investment, together with the policies proposed in other chapters of this book – especially regarding education and health – will raise TFP growth and generate considerable employment opportunities.

Correspondingly, savings will need to rise to some 26 percent of GDP a year to avoid balance of payments problems while allowing for the imports associated with higher investment.[7] As in the case of investment, African countries that already have high savings to GDP ratios – especially those with high rents from natural resource extraction – will need to raise their savings rates well above this level. The increase in savings needs to be supported by higher FDI, especially in non-resource extractive activities.

---

6. Such a ratio will still be lower than the average for the emerging market and developing countries (see Figure 9.24). The ratio is based on the average incremental capital output ratio of 4.8 recorded during 2007-11 and a TFP growth of 1.6 percent a year. The average investment ratio envisaged in the growth model used for the Africa 2050 study is 30.4 percent of GDP.
7. The implied external current account deficit of 4 percent of GDP is expected to be more than financed by FDI and sustainable external financing, thus allowing for some accumulation of international reserves.

As growth rises, domestic savings will increase accordingly and become a more important source of financing for investment, leading to a virtuous cycle of higher investment, savings, and growth, as well as a sustainable balance of payments position.

An investment rate of 30 percent and a savings rate of 26 percent are achievable, but important efforts are needed to make them a reality. These efforts, outlined below, are mutually reinforcing and create a virtuous cycle; they aim at establishing the basis for sustainable, high economic growth. They include:

- *Implementing a sound macroeconomic policy framework* that allows both the government and the private sector to plan ahead and thus create an environment for increased investment. Moreover, the framework should generate mutual trust and confidence in economic policies, enabling the private sector (domestic and foreign) to play a key role as an engine of growth. An important aspect of the policy framework is a stable and efficient tax regime (see below). Such a framework is also critical to help curb capital flight and encourage the repatriation of the considerable resources Africans are holding abroad. Deposits held by Africans at BIS-reporting banks alone amount to $345 billion.[8]

- *Improving infrastructure.* Poor infrastructure (especially in power, water, communication, transportation, and logistics) is one of the greatest constraints on economic growth, especially because it leads to high costs and loss of productivity (Fujita, Tsuruga, and Takeda 2013). Thus, policy-makers need to re-balance government expenditure toward much higher public investment, which will help crowd-in private sector investment (as a consequence of the complementarity between public and private investment) and lead to more dynamic and growing economies. Moreover, given the limited resources available to governments, the re-balancing effort needs to be supplemented by the adoption of a (or strengthening of the existing) legal framework to encourage domestic and foreign private sector participation in enhancing infrastructure through public-private partnerships (PPPs) and other such arrangements.

- *Developing constructive and collaborative relations between the state and the private sector.* Policies are needed that reduce the cost of doing business by establishing a business environment in which economic agents are not constrained by red tape and unnecessary regulations. Regulatory certainty and institutional reforms that enhance governance and the rule of law are critical to promote a dynamic private sector.[9] They also should improve the state's efficiency, effectiveness, and responsiveness by professionalizing and upgrading the competence of the civil service and strengthening accountability.

---

[8]. This is only a portion of the assets Africans own abroad, as some financial assets are most likely held in, or channeled through, non-BIS-reporting financial institutions; assuming that Africans also hold deposits in offshore financial centers in about the same share as those in BIS-reporting banks, some $55 billion would need to be added to that amount. Ideally, the value of real estate properties and other assets Africans own abroad should be included, but these are difficult to quantify.

[9]. In the case of resource-rich countries, policy makers also need to remove, inter alia, uncertainties over ownership, tax treatment, and allocation of mineral rights.

- *Building up of a well-qualified labor force* that is able to adopt and adapt, and eventually develop, new technologies associated with new investments. Improving the labor force calls for investment in the quality of and access to education, as well as training (see Chapter 8). Policies that encourage immigration of professionals may be needed as well.
- *Developing a seamless Africa and open markets* that allow the exploitation of economies of scale (see Chapter 14) and promote greater competition in domestic and regional markets.
- *Increasing foreign direct investment* by, in addition to the points listed above, giving such investment equal treatment to domestically generated investment. FDI is generally associated with bringing new technologies, as has been the case of foreign involvement in the exploitation of natural resources, and therefore plays a key role in raising TFP and growth.
- *Establishing an advanced and efficient financial system* is essential to the development of capital markets that finance investment activities. The rapid spread of pan-African banking systems, as well as the introduction of a framework that facilitates taking advantage of portfolio capital inflows (frontier markets) should help in this regard. An efficient, competitive, and well-regulated financial system will help encourage financial savings, which are relatively low in Africa.[10] Higher financial savings will help deepen financial intermediation and, eventually, develop a dynamic domestic capital market.[11] These steps could be supplemented by a comprehensive social security system that includes affordable compulsory membership for all employees.
- *Increasing public sector savings* is also important. Governments could do so by ensuring fiscal sustainability and re-balancing government spending to make room for higher public investment. The public enterprises should also add to public savings by becoming more efficient and thus improving their profitability. More generally, public savings can be increased considerably by enhancing the public sector's effectiveness and governance. In the case of resource-rich countries, stabilization and wealth funds, as discussed in Chapter 12, need to play an important role in this regard.

Action Agenda

The policy reforms and associated hard-won improvements in macroeconomic performance that African countries have attained need to be preserved, but further efforts are needed to ensure the sustainability of these improvements and thus achieve high growth. The following sections address the macroeconomic areas where such further efforts may need to be considered.

It is difficult to propose a single macroeconomic policy framework for all African countries given the diversity of income levels, circumstances, institutions, and endowments. Nevertheless, it is generally recognized that for economic activity to expand rapidly and equitably on a sustainable basis,

---

10. For example, in 2011 the average ratio of bank assets to GDP was 48 percent in Sub-Saharan Africa, compared with 60 percent in Latin America and the Caribbean and in the Middle East, and 163 percent in Asia.
11. In the case of the smaller economies, consideration could be given to the development of regional capital markets in order to take advantage of economies of scale.

macroeconomic policies need to ensure stability and predictability. These aspects are critical to create an environment that enables economic agents to plan ahead, fostering high private sector investment and savings, and thus promoting high economic growth.

Broadly, stability and predictability require a clear commitment from policy makers to implement *sound fiscal policies* along with *sound monetary policies,* consistent with debt and balance of payments sustainability. Ideally, these policies would be supported by a *flexible exchange rate regime,* which would allow for an independent monetary policy and would provide countries with a critical policy instrument to help absorb external shocks. (Many African countries have had a fixed exchange rate regime or have belonged to a currency union for years, and such arrangements, properly managed, may also help support macroeconomic stability.) Attention to policies that *improve resilience* is also warranted. These policies form the core of the action agenda summarized here and described in more detail below:

- **Establish sound fiscal policies** that ensure the sustainability of public debt and so provide macroeconomic stability, mobilize revenues efficiently and allocate resources equitably, create an environment of certainty to foster investment, and address revenue volatility, sustainability, and intergenerational equity, where needed. Specifically, fiscal policy priorities should be on increasing employment, and improving social equity. Tools include improved public spending allocation and management and tax policy to increase government revenue.
- **Establish sound monetary policies** and **flexible exchange rate regimes** that enhance the ability to control inflation. Tools will differ across the different country situations but include adopting inflation-targeting frameworks, targeting the monetary aggregates, assessing existing exchange arrangements, establishing stabilization or liquidity funds, strengthening the financial system, and moving toward an advanced capital market.
- **Establish policies that strengthen resilience** with a particular focus on improving performance in government effectiveness and governance and, as appropriate, improving monetary policy, export diversity, and export independence.

Fiscal policy

From a macroeconomic point of view, sound fiscal policies call for the maintenance of overall fiscal deficits that ensure public debt sustainability and thus preserve macroeconomic stability. From a microeconomic point of view, sound fiscal policies call for an effective and equitable revenue mobilization system, as well as an efficient resource allocation process geared toward improving human and physical capital and reducing inequality. In both realms, governments should provide the certainty that future fiscal policies will remain sound. Certainty should help lower the cost of capital and so foster higher private investment and savings, which will promote faster economic growth and contribute to the development of an inclusive society. Good governance requires that fiscal policies be conducted in a framework of transparency and accountability. In the case of mineral-exporting countries, sound fiscal policies also address revenue volatility, sustainability, and intergenerational equity.

The current provision of public goods and services does not meet the population's needs in many countries, neither in quality nor in quantity, given the very severe gaps in education, health, and infrastructure. These gaps are frequently a consequence of pressures caused by the growth of other current expenditures (including very large generalized subsidies in a number of countries). If not addressed, these gaps are likely to widen as current spending continues to rise with the size of bureaucracies, inefficient outlays, and eventually population aging.

The current priorities and goals of fiscal policy need to focus on establishing an environment for sustainable, high, and inclusive economic growth, and thereby achieve three critical objectives: 1) increase employment, 2) reduce inequality, and 3) improve equity:

Increase employment by investing in infrastructure. By closing the enormous gap in infrastructure (see Chapter 13), e.g., transport, logistics, energy, water resource development, schools, hospitals, and sanitation, public investment (including through PPPs) will help create employment directly in the formulation and construction of projects, the production of inputs for projects, and the operation and maintenance of new facilities (Foster and Briceno-Garmendia 2009). Public investment also crowds-in private investment and so would create employment indirectly by improving the efficiency of the economy and laying the basis for faster growth. This is the multiplier effect. Moreover, given Africa's rich human factor endowment, labor-intensive construction methods, where appropriate, should be given preference over capital-intensive ones.

Reduce inequality by investing in human capital. Government spending to enhance human capital needs to increase (see Chapter 8). The current quality of education denies many the skills needed to access employment and thereby reduces the dynamism of the economy. Moreover, poor health care denies many future. Spending that improves the quality of health and education services at all levels will endow the population with the necessary tools to take advantage of opportunities and thus reduce inequality. It is therefore imperative that budgets provide adequate resources to build the human resources for the future, including improving school infrastructure, educational materials and equipment, clinics, and hospitals.

Improve equity by meeting basic needs. Policies that raise growth can significantly advance social equity goals. But explicit policies to advance equity, such as enhancing social protection, food security, and nutrition, are also needed. In some countries (like South Africa), government may play a role in the development of low income housing, within its budget constraint. African policy makers may want to consider establishing conditional transfers programs like those in Latin America (e.g., Bolsa Familia and Oportunidades) that have had some success not only in reducing poverty but also in increasing economic activity and creating important centers of development.

Addressing the infrastructure and human capital gaps and reducing misallocation and waste requires governments to improve public expenditure allocation and management, including the public procurement process, and to implement a targeted system of subsidies where they are essential. However, these steps may be insufficient to cover the needed increase in public expenditures. Accordingly, to avoid widening the overall fiscal deficit, government revenue will need to rise considerably, even after assuming that gains in efficiency spending and subsidy reduction could be significant.[12] Revenue will also need to rise over time in order to eliminate Africa's aid dependency.[13] Africa can potentially benefit from its youth bulge in the coming decades (see Chapter 5), but eventually its population will begin to age and countries will see increases in spending associated with aging, as is already the case in North Africa. A strong safety net should become affordable as countries become richer). One approach would be to build a social security system that covers all working people, with special protection for the poor using conditional transfers.

The tax structure in African countries needs to serve the dual objectives of raising revenue while promoting economic growth. It is difficult to propose an ideal tax structure to a continent with such a diversity of countries and with such different endowments, but it is possible to outline some key features that could be considered:

- Flat corporate income taxes, at a rate that makes countries competitive and attractive to FDI;
- Relatively progressive personal income taxes with a limited number of brackets and a low threshold;
- Value-added taxes that applies uniformly to all consumer goods and services;
- A set of selected excise taxes, especially on fuel consumption; low import duties; and an up-to-date system of real estate taxes (administered by local governments); and
- A contributory social security system.

In addition, natural resource exploitation will need to be subject to a clear tax structure, including a system of royalties linked to the value of the resource (see Chapter 12).

The tax system should have almost no exemptions or preferential arrangements in order to reduce tax avoidance and evasion. The pros and cons of any exemptions or preferential arrangements need to be evaluated carefully against their opportunity costs, including a potential proliferation of such exemptions or preferential arrangements that would undermine the integrity and efficiency of the tax system. The tax system needs to be supported by an effective and efficient tax administration, using best practices and latest technologies and avoiding discrimination among taxpayers.[14]

Monetary and exchange rate policies

The long-term nature of the Vision laid out in this book would suggest that there is no need to address monetary policy, which has a relative short-term focus. However, experience has made abundantly clear that price and financial stability are essential to establish and sustain strong economic growth.

---

12. In addition, the elimination or important reduction of implicit subsidies, especially those on fuel consumption, should yield considerable revenue gains. Measures will be needed to ameliorate the effect of the subsidy elimination or reduction on the most vulnerable segments of the population. Over time, as the population becomes richer, even such measures should be eliminated to make room for other priority spending, including that related to population aging.

13. In 2011, budgetary grants amounted 2.4 percent of GDP for SSA (excluding Nigeria and South Africa) and 0.75 percent for the continent as a whole.

14. Many countries have followed the advice of international financial institutions and centered their efforts on large taxpayer units. These efforts may have encouraged firms to remain small and thereby forgo the benefits of scale and possible access to credit and new technologies, thus hampering growth potential.

As noted above, many African countries have improved considerably their monetary policy management over the last decade and a half, especially as a result of increasing the autonomy of their central banks and the resulting enhancement of their capacity to control inflation. Those countries with flexible exchange rate regimes have introduced indirect instruments to control monetary aggregates and have implemented them successfully; some have adopted inflation-targeting frameworks, which have been successful as well. Those with conventional exchange rate pegs (especially under currency unions) have kept prudent credit policies. Nevertheless, Africa's inflation rates are higher than those in other regions suggesting that monetary policies need to be strengthened especially because the poor are hurt the most by the inflation tax.

Monetary policy needs and the appropriate tools depend very much on the exchange rate regime and the degree of development of the financial system:[15]

- *Countries with a flexible exchange rate regime and a more developed financial system* are best served by the adoption of inflation-targeting frameworks, which have proven to be quite successful in reducing inflation and keeping it low. Adoption of such a framework requires a high degree of autonomy of the Central Bank in conducting monetary policy and government deficits that do not condition the growth of money supply (i.e., no fiscal dominance). South Africa has been a leader in this area among emerging markets.
- *Countries with a flexible exchange rate regime but with an underdeveloped financial system* need their Central Bank to directly target the monetary aggregates. As the financial system develops and an interbank market becomes operational, the Central Bank may start to control such aggregates through indirect instruments such as open market operations. With further development of the financial system, monetary authorities should move toward creating the basis for an inflation-targeting framework.
- *Countries that have a fixed exchange rate regime or are part of a currency union,* most notably those in the West African Economic and Monetary Union (WAEMU) and the Central African Economic and Monetary Union (CEMAC), will need to assess how well these exchange arrangements are serving them, especially in view of the large diversity of country endowments and economic development.[16] If these regimes continue, it is important that credit policy remains cautious and consistent with preserving price stability and external competitiveness.

The establishment of a stabilization/liquidity fund that removes the pro-cyclicality of fiscal spending associated with fluctuations in export earnings will facilitate considerably the conduct of monetary policy in resource-rich exporters, under any exchange rate regime (see Chapter 12). Similarly, the establishment of a sovereign wealth fund would help reduce the excessive pressure on domestic resources that a natural resource boom typically causes. Moreover, the combination of these two types of funds

---

15. We take the view that a flexible exchange rate regime is preferable to a fixed one because it provides the authorities with an important macroeconomic policy instrument and because it allows the exchange rate to act as a shock absorber.
16. CEMAC is the official, French-language acronym for the organization - Communauté Économique et Monétaire de l'Afrique Centrale.

will lead to a more stable macroeconomic environment and therefore lower exchange rate tensions than otherwise. This combination provides a strong foundation for monetary policy based on an inflation-targeting framework.

The conduct of monetary policy will also be strengthened by a sound and developed financial system as a precursor to an advanced capital market. To this end, it would be critical to adopt a regulatory and supervisory framework that is in line with international best practices. Such a financial system will facilitate the external liberalization of capital markets.

As financial integration spreads worldwide, African countries have to prepare for eventual integration with that framework. Liberalizing capital markets without adequate preparation in structural reform and financial soundness, however, would be premature and costly. The costs and benefits as well as the timing of external liberalization should be carefully weighed. Specifically, the potential benefits of integration and the associated modern financial technologies ought to be weighed against the likely costs of substantial volatility of capital flows. Countries will have to be prepared with an appropriate strategy for managing capital flows.

Policies to strengthen resilience

Strengthening economic resilience is urgent in many African countries because much recent growth has been driven by terms-of-trade improvements (see Appendix 9.1). The steady rise of commodity prices over most of the last decade is likely to be an anomaly and a return to greater price volatility is likely. Countries must improve their resilience in order to protect overall growth from volatility. The elements of resilience in which African countries are weakest (the red columns of Table 1 above) and hence those in which the biggest improvements are necessary are strongly linked to the reform agendas set out in this book, in particular monetary policy (above), governance and government effectiveness (Chapter 4), export diversity (Chapter 10), and management of natural resource revenues (Chapter 12).

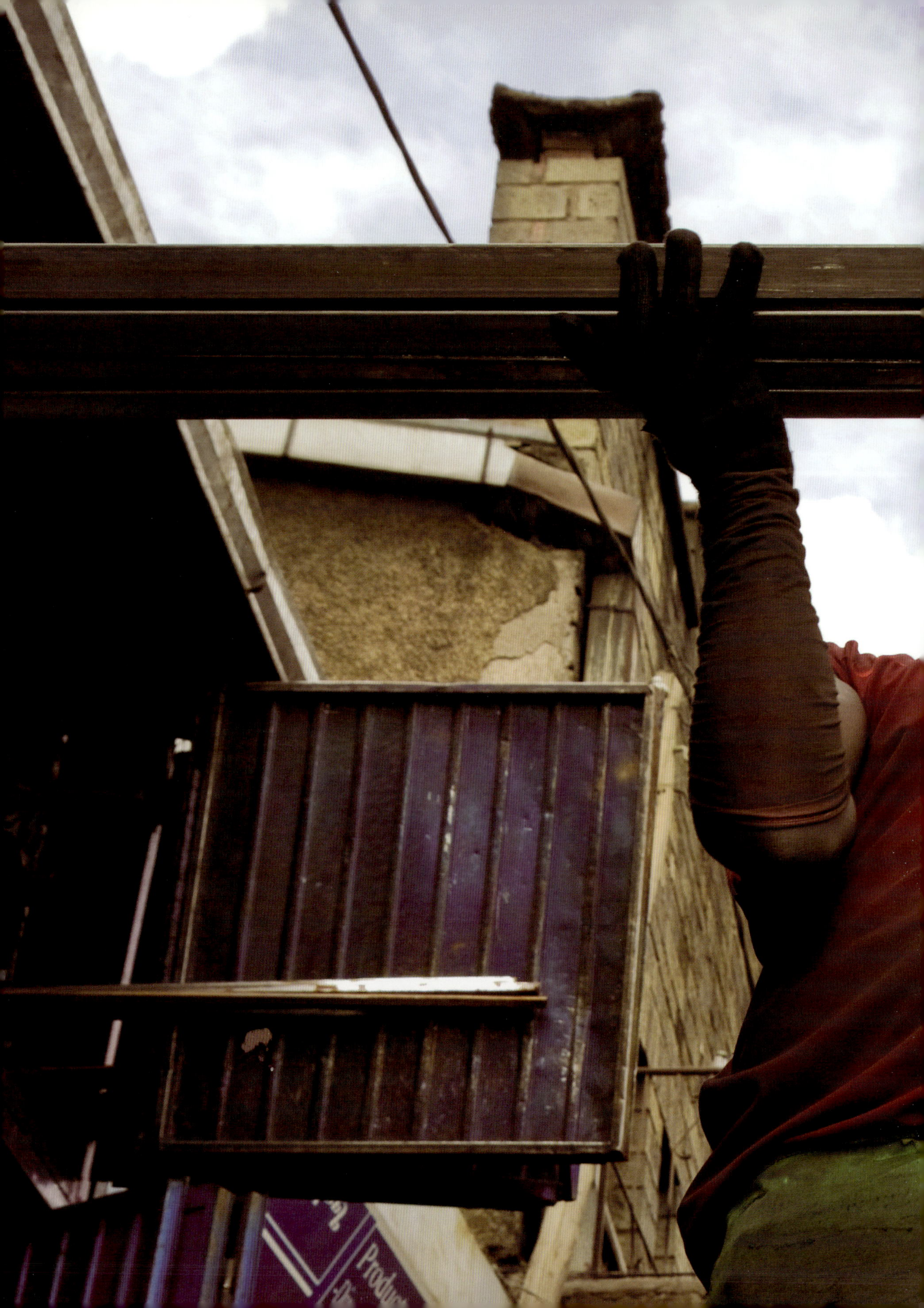

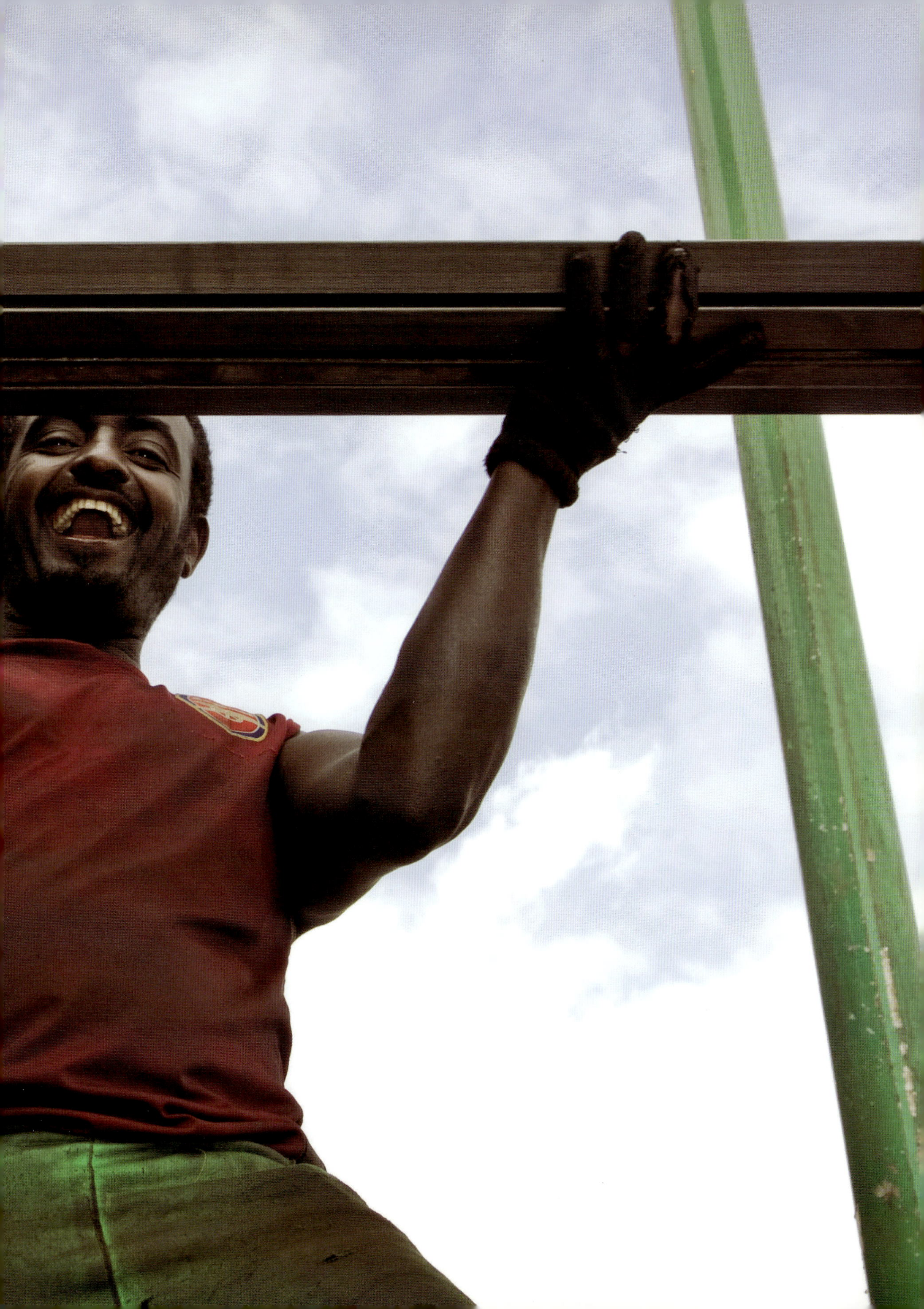

Enhancing Growth, Competitiveness, and Job Creation

Chapter 10

Anil Sood and Anupam Basu

African economies have enjoyed higher growth rates since 1995 and have also been relatively resilient to the 2008 crisis. Growth rates pre- and post-1995 illustrate the acceleration (Figure 10.1). The acceleration in growth results from high global demand for the continent's natural resources and rising commodity prices, from efforts on the macroeconomic front, and from fundamental reforms; foreign aid inflows and concessional debt relief (including debt forgiveness) played an important role in supporting the reform efforts. African economies' resilience to the latest global crisis, while positive, also reflects limited integration with the global economy, particularly in the financial sector. Though the performance with respect to GDP per capita has been less positive due to the relatively high rates of population growth, GDP per capita grew at over 2 percent, double the rate of the previous 15 years.

Growth remains vulnerable. By some estimates, one quarter of the growth in GDP in Africa is attributable to changes in commodity prices/terms of trade. The concentration of Africa's exports in commodities makes its growth vulnerable to downtrends in demand and prices; a decline in terms of trade of 10 percent would entail a decline in GDP of 2 percent.

Africa faces a daunting challenge on the jobs front. If African countries are to turn their population growth into a demographic dividend and maintain social cohesion, they must prepare to create a very large number of jobs. Between 2010 and 2050 Africa's working age population (20 to 64 years) is expected to increase from 465.50 million to 1.18 billion (under the low variant scenario of the UN's population projections); the corresponding 2050 forecasts of the working age group for the medium and high variant population projections are 1.25 billion and 1.33 billion, respectively. These projections suggest that by 2050 the number of new job seekers per year will have increased to between almost 16 million under the low variant to almost 20 million under the high variant projections (compared to 14 million today). As in other parts of the world, nine out of every ten jobs in Africa are in the private sector. Accordingly, job creation requires, inter alia, a vibrant private sector growing at sustained high rates.

Note: The authors gratefully acknowledge contributions by Jose Fajgenbaum, Herve Ferhani, and Kendra White.

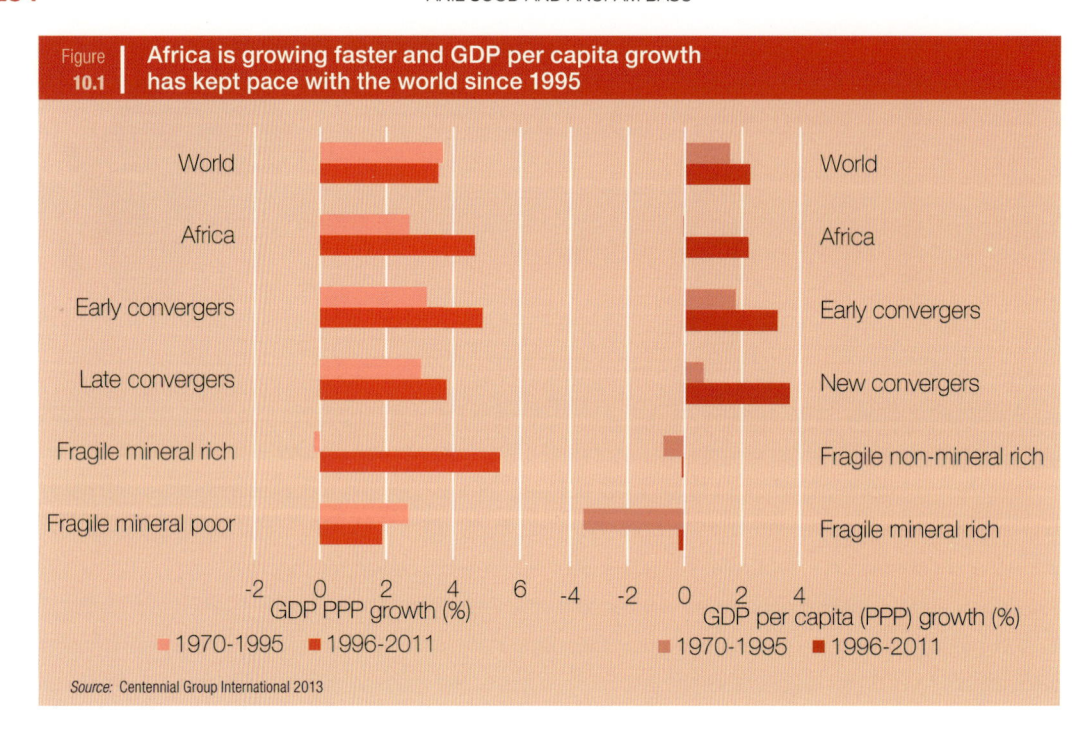

Figure 10.1 Africa is growing faster and GDP per capita growth has kept pace with the world since 1995

Categories (left panel, GDP PPP growth %): World, Africa, Early convergers, Late convergers, Fragile mineral rich, Fragile mineral poor

Categories (right panel, GDP per capita (PPP) growth %): World, Africa, Early convergers, New convergers, Fragile non-mineral rich, Fragile mineral rich

Legend: 1970–1995, 1996–2011

Source: Centennial Group International 2013

The jobs challenge combined with vulnerability in economic growth makes it vital for African countries to pursue job-intensive diversification of their economies based on improved global competitiveness. Efforts to transform and diversify African economies well beyond commodities into high-productivity, job-intensive activities such as agro-processing, manufacturing and a wide range of services must continue. Sustained high growth would require increased exports based on improvements in global competitiveness and productivity.

Current Status: Economic Structure, Employment, Competitiveness, and Productivity

Past reforms in African countries have focused on removing barriers to market competition and private sector development; however, much more needs to be done to engage the private sector as the primary engine of growth. Although the private sector accounts for a dominant share of GDP, aggregate domestic demand, and employment, it remains underdeveloped in many respects. Micro-, small-, and medium-size enterprises (MSMEs) account for most of the private sector enterprises and employment, with most workers in low productivity non-wage jobs and informal employment. The transition from agriculture to other sectors, especially job-intensive manufacturing, and in general from low-productivity to higher productivity firms and value-added activities is far from complete. Africa ranks very low on most global competitiveness indicators, and despite recent improvements total factor productivity (TFP) is low relative to other regions. As a result, Africa's export structure is concentrated in a few primary products, and its share of global exports has remained low (more so if fuel exports are excluded).

Economic structure

Many African countries have undertaken reforms to remove barriers to market competition and private sector development. Reforms have included restructuring and privatizing public enterprises, removal of price controls, elimination of exchange controls, reduction of import tariffs and non-tariff barriers, and removal of selective controls on bank credit and interest rates. In addition, many countries have worked to improve the business environment and investment climate, all with the basic objective of enhancing the role of private sector participation in the economy.

The private sector in Africa today is relatively large (IZA 2011). It accounts for about two-thirds of total investment and four-fifths of total consumption, and its share of aggregate domestic demand is substantial in both North Africa (58 percent) and Sub-Saharan Africa (SSA) (69 percent). However, in both regions the ratio of private sector demand to GDP has been declining as government expenditures have been increasing. The private sector also accounts for three-quarters of total domestic bank credit and 90 percent of total employment.

MSMEs account for a dominant share of private sector firms, up to 90 percent of all businesses in Sub-Saharan Africa (IFC 2013). The vast majority of MSMEs (90 percent) are micro-enterprises (MEs, employing 1 to 9 employees) operating mainly in the informal sector (Fjose, Grunfeld, and Green 2010). Hence, small and medium-sized enterprises (SMEs, employing 10 to 250 employees) account for a relatively small share of all MSMEs in most countries, although this share is relatively large in Ghana and Tunisia (Fjose, Grunfeld, and Green 2010). Unlike the micro-enterprises, the SMEs generally operate in the formal sector.

In most African countries the transition from agriculture to other sectors is far from complete. The share of agricultural value-added, after dropping in the 1970s and 1980s, has held steady since 1995 at around 16 percent of GDP (in constant 2005 prices). Since 1995, mining and utilities' share of GDP has increased sharply, reflecting to a large extent increases in world fuel prices. The share of value-added by the manufacturing sector (potentially more labor-intensive than mining or utilities) has dropped to 10 percent and is well below the share in Latin America and, particularly, developing Asia (Table 10.1); manufacturing has contributed little to job creation. The share of the services sector has increased noticeably compared to 1980 and is approaching that in developing Asia. The services sector has been the main source of both new employment and gains in labor productivity.

Table 10.1 Africa is still undergoing its sectoral transformation

Sectoral value-added contributions to nominal GDP (%)	Africa 1970	Africa 1980	Africa 1995	Africa 2000	Africa 2010	Latin America 2010	Developing Asia 2010
Agriculture, hunting, forestry, fishing	25.1	19.1	16.5	15.2	16	5.7	10.1
Industry	30.7	42.2	32.7	35.5	38.4	32.6	41.3
Mining, manufacturing, utilities	25.8	36.5	28.3	31.3	33.3	26.2	35.2
Manufacturing	13.8	12.5	14.7	12.8	10	16.1	24.6
Mining & Utilities	12	24	13.7	18.6	23.2	10.1	10.6
Construction	4.9	5.7	4.3	4.2	5.1	6.4	6.1
Services	44.2	38.7	50.8	49.2	45.6	61.7	48.6

Source: UNCTAD 2013b

Employment and the jobs challenge

Labor force participation rates have been stagnant in both North Africa and SSA, with a small increase in the female participation rate balancing a modest decline in the male participation rate. Table 10.2 shows trends in labor participation and unemployment within North Africa and SSA, as compared with East Asia and Latin America. Overall the male participation rate (76 percent) is substantially higher than the female participation rate (55 percent), which reflects the striking gap in North Africa (74 vs. 24 percent).

The unemployment rate has declined noticeably in North Africa (from 13.8 percent in 1995 to 9.6 percent in 2010). The much higher unemployment rate persists among women as compared with men in North Africa (16.4 vs. 7.4 percent in 2010).

Youth unemployment rates in North Africa (23.1 percent) and SSA (11.4 percent) are significantly higher than the overall unemployment rates in the two regions. In a number of countries the youth unemployment is two to three times as high as overall unemployment; unemployment rates are higher for women than for men in both regions. The gender disparities are more substantial in North Africa – 34.4 percent for women vs. 18.5 percent for men – and may reflect in part the higher per capita incomes and safety nets than in SSA.

The combined share of wage and salaried workers and employers in total employment has been rising. Stable, wage-paying jobs account for a predominant share of employment in North Africa (62 percent). In contrast, in SSA the share of vulnerable employment (comprising own-account workers and family workers) remains very high (77 percent) (Table 10.3). A large part of the vulnerable employment is informal employment, which exists in both the informal and formal sectors.

Table 10.2 — Participation rates are low and unemployment high for females in North Africa

	North Africa 1995	North Africa 2010	Sub-Saharan Africa 1995	Sub-Saharan Africa 2010	East Asia 2010	Latin America & Caribbean 2010
Labor Force Participation (%)						
Overall	48.5	48.8	69.6	70.2	72.5	66.2
Male	75.3	74.1	78.2	76.1	79.2	79.8
Female	21.9	24	61.2	64.4	65.6	53.2
Unemployment						
Total	13.8	9.6	7.9	7.6	4.2	7.2
Male	11.4	7.4	7.3	7.1	4.8	5.9
Female	22	16.4	8.7	8	3.5	9.1
Youth	29.4	23.1	12.4	11.4	8.9	14.5
Male	25.6	18.5	11.4	10.8	10.5	11.9
Female	39.2	34.4	13.5	12.2	7.2	18.5

Source: World Bank 2012a

SMEs account for a substantial share of total employment in African countries, although the share varies widely across countries. The average share of SMEs in total employment is above 50 percent, with much higher shares in some countries, e.g., Egypt, Ghana, and Kenya. The average share among the early convergers is about 34 percent compared with 19 percent for the countries classified as late convergers and fragile.[1] South Africa is an outlier at 82 percent. Workers in SMEs represent a significant share of the total formal labor force in manufacturing.

Table 10.3 — Three-quarters of employment in SSA is vulnerable employment

Status in Employment	North Africa 1995	North Africa 2010	Sub-Saharan Africa 1995	Sub-Saharan Africa 2010	East Asia 2010	Latin America & Caribbean 2010
Wage & salaried workers (employees) (%)	47.2	52.1	17.5	21.7	35.4	63.5
Employers (%)	10.3	10.1	1.1	1.4	2.3	4.6
Share of vulnerable employment in total employment (%)	42.6	37.7	81.4	77	62.2	31.9

Source: World Bank 2012a

---

1. As discussed in Chapter 1, the convergence scenario modeled in the Africa 2050 study classifies 19 African countries as "early convergers" based on their GDP and TFP growth, 15 as "late convergers," and 20 as "fragile."

In SSA, informal non-farm enterprises (NFEs), which include household enterprises (HEs) and MEs, account for a significant share of the total labor force (28 percent) (Fox and Sohnesen 2012). The share of informal employment in total non-agricultural employment is quite large (58 percent on average) but it varies widely, between 33 percent in South Africa and almost 82 percent in Mali within the sample of eleven countries for which data are available (ILO 2013).

Overall the share of the primary sector in total employment has been declining gradually, while the employment shares of the secondary and tertiary sectors have been rising. Agriculture accounts for the largest share of employment in SSA (62 percent) but less in North Africa (28 percent). The secondary sector accounts for the lowest employment share in both North Africa (22 percent) and SSA (8.5 percent). The tertiary sector's employment share has risen in both regions in the past 15 years but more markedly in SSA. In North Africa, this share has remained nearly constant, accounting for about half the total employment (Table 10.4).

Table 10.4 The share of industry and services in employment remains very low in SSA

Sectoral shares in Total Employment	North Africa 1995	North Africa 2010	Sub-Saharan Africa 1995	Sub-Saharan Africa 2010	East Asia 2010	Latin America & Caribbean 2010
Agriculture	33.1	28.4	67.2	61.9	35.0	16.2
Industry	19.2	21.7	8.0	8.5	28.7	22.2
Services	47.7	49.9	24.7	29.6	36.4	61.6

Source: World Bank 2012a

In the past decade, overall labor productivity has increased over the past decade in both SSA and North Africa, with the agriculture and services sectors both contributing to the increase (Dihel et al. 2010). In both regions the improvement in agricultural productivity has been sustained for a longer period compared with other sectors. In contrast, labor productivity in industry has fallen in both regions.

The key challenges then are to translate the labor force expansion to jobs growth, to achieve a structural shift of the labor force away from agriculture to the non-agricultural sectors and to diversify the production base. Growth rates of non-agricultural employment and of the employment of wage earners and employers have been sluggish and account for the high share of vulnerable employment, particularly in Sub-Saharan Africa. Diversification of the economy will increase the likelihood that stable, wage-paying jobs will account for an increasing share of total employment. Since the 1970s the share of agriculture in real GDP has declined in most sub-regions of the developing Asian countries, while the shares of manufacturing, industry as a whole, and services have risen. Diversification of the production base has contributed to a significant diversification of the sectoral pattern of employment, especially in the two sub-regions of East Asia and Southeast Asia. Similar diversification in SSA would help move toward more stable wage-paying jobs that will help address poverty and inequality.

Global competitiveness

With the exception of a very few countries, Africa ranks very low on global competitiveness compared with all other regions. In the often-cited Global Competitiveness Index (2012), no African country ranks in the top 50 countries; South Africa (52), Mauritius (54), Rwanda (63), and Morocco (70), rank in the upper 50th percentile. The vast majority of African countries rank at the very bottom of the many indexes related to competitiveness (Figure 10.2).

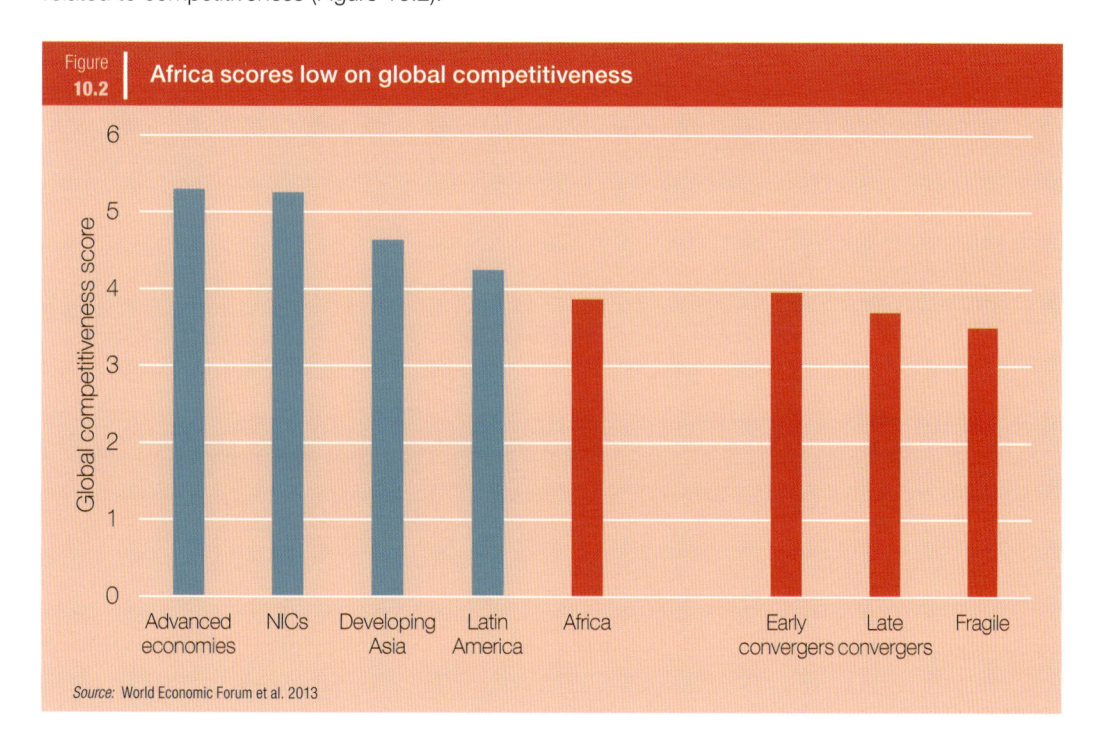

Figure 10.2 | Africa scores low on global competitiveness

Source: World Economic Forum et al. 2013

The lagging competitiveness of African economies is reflected in Africa's trade performance. Africa's exports are concentrated in oil, minerals, and, to a lesser extent, agricultural commodities. Its overall share of global exports has risen somewhat in the last decade but remains very low at around 1 percent, if fuel, minerals, and other primary commodities are excluded (Figure 10.3).

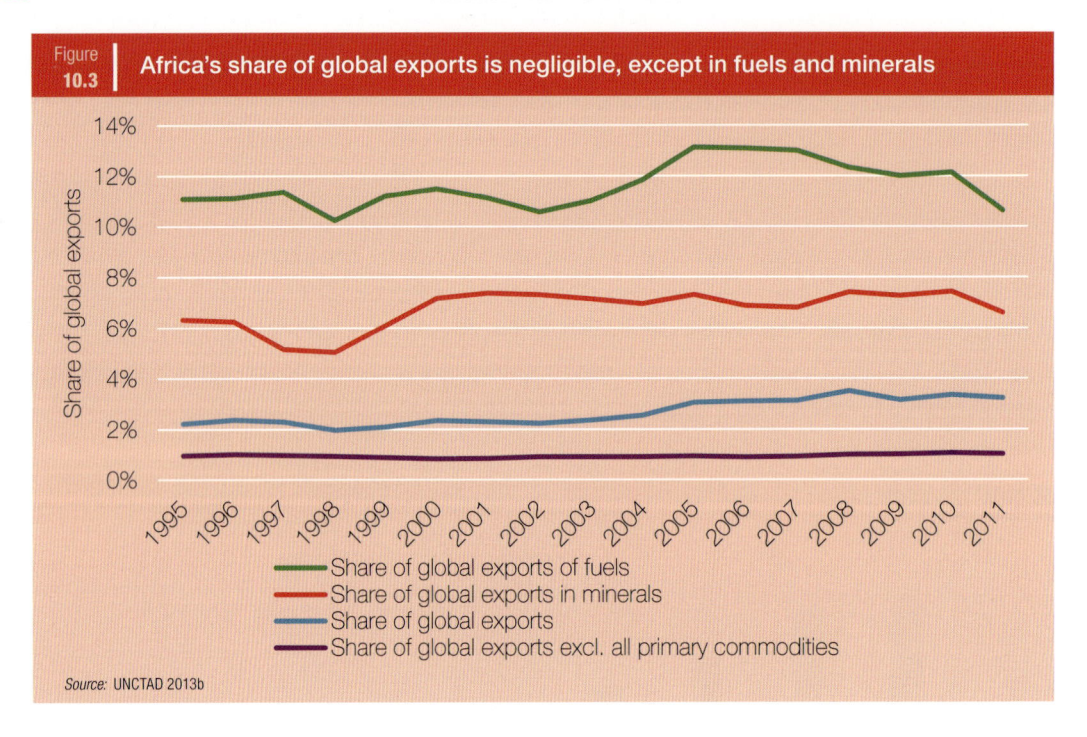

Figure 10.3 | Africa's share of global exports is negligible, except in fuels and minerals

— Share of global exports of fuels
— Share of global exports in minerals
— Share of global exports
— Share of global exports excl. all primary commodities

Source: UNCTAD 2013b

Total factor productivity

Africa's performance with respect to TFP – a key determinant of competitiveness – has improved in recent years, but there is a long way to go. The performance of African economies in TFP level and growth rates shows marked progress since 1995 as reflected in the movement of most African countries between Figures 10.4 and 10.5. Though improving, the level of TFP in African economies is very low — again with the exception of a handful of countries.

TFP performance detracted from GDP growth in the 1980-1995 period but now contributes significantly to growth in most countries in Africa. It has accounted for more than one-third of the growth since 1995. TFP contribution differs by country category (Figure 10.6). At the positive end, TFP contributed close to 40 percent of the growth performance of early convergers post-1995. At the other end, TFP contribution remains negative in the fragile states without mineral resources.

Factors Underlying Africa's Competitiveness, Productivity, and Growth

The major factors that underpin competitiveness, productivity, and resulting growth fall under two broad categories: the climate for investment and the needed skills/human capital. The determinants of the investment climate include the macroeconomic environment, prevalence of competition, needed

ENHANCING GROWTH, COMPETITIVENESS, AND JOB CREATION

Figure 10.4 — Starting from a very low base....

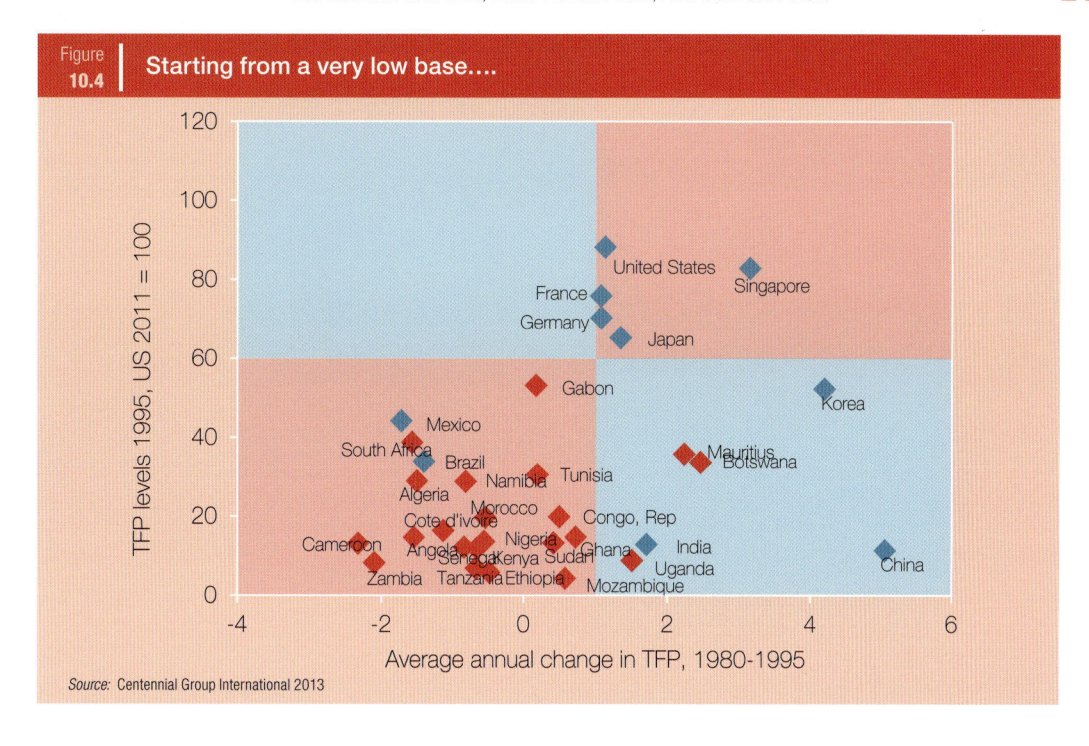

Y-axis: TFP levels 1995, US 2011 = 100
X-axis: Average annual change in TFP, 1980-1995

Source: Centennial Group International 2013

Figure 10.5 — ...African economies have been catching up

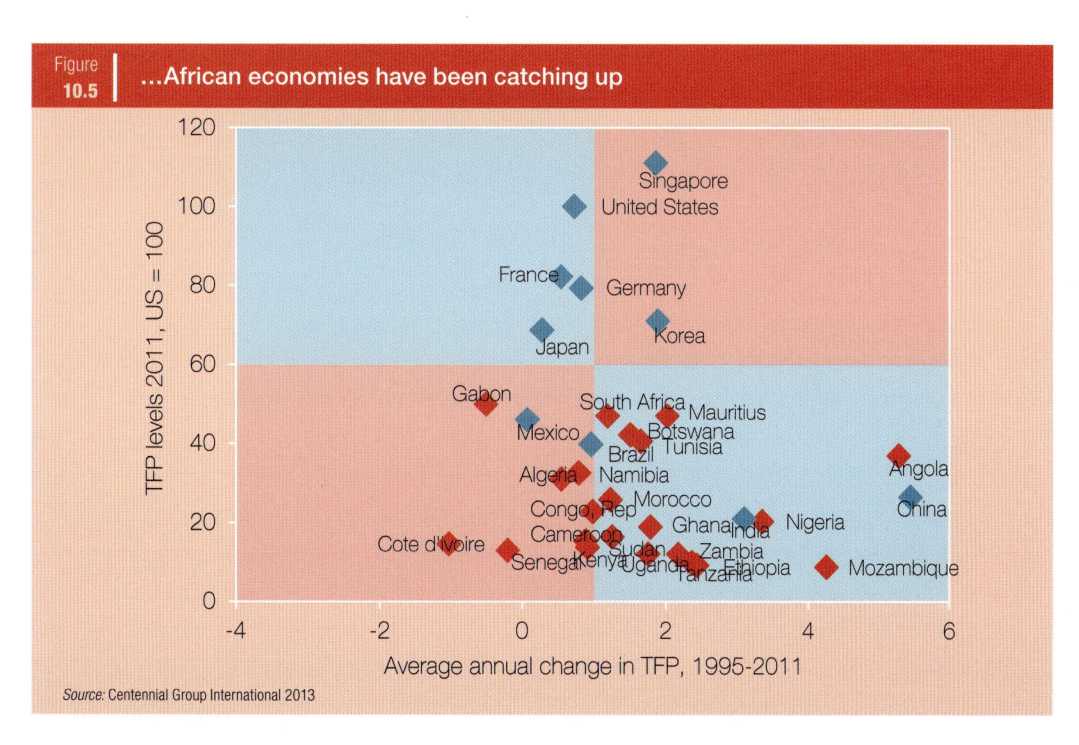

Y-axis: TFP levels 2011, US = 100
X-axis: Average annual change in TFP, 1995-2011

Source: Centennial Group International 2013

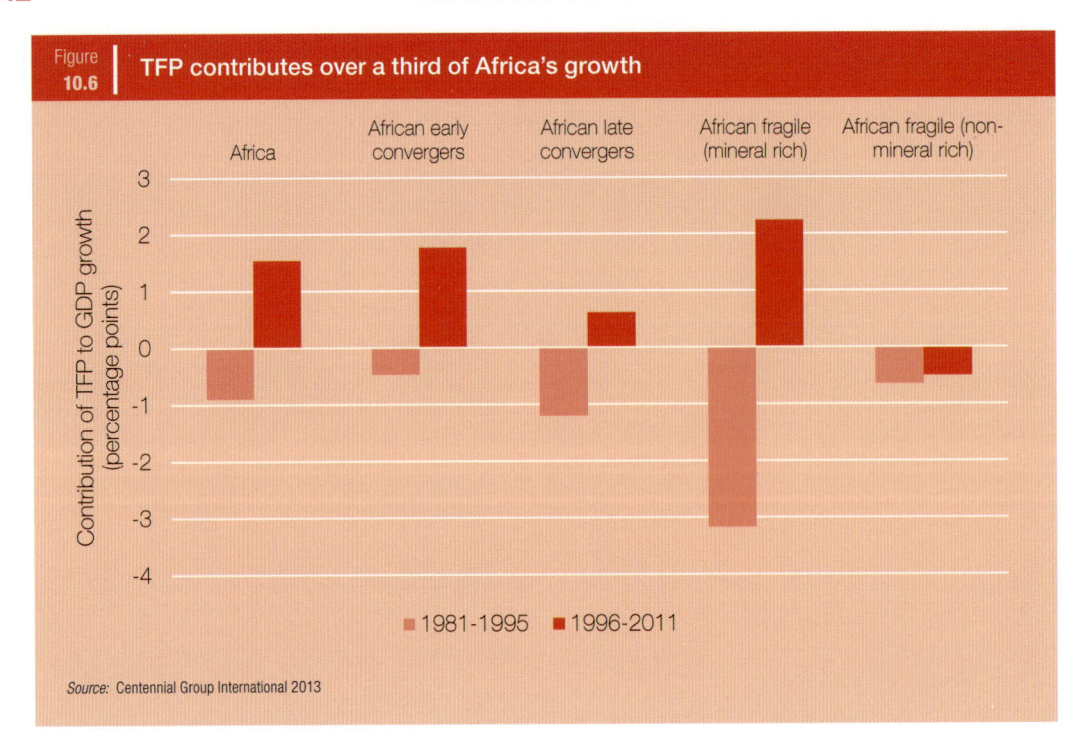

Figure 10.6: TFP contributes over a third of Africa's growth

Bars show contribution of TFP to GDP growth (percentage points) for Africa, African early convergers, African late convergers, African fragile (mineral rich), and African fragile (non-mineral rich), comparing 1981–1995 and 1996–2011.

Source: Centennial Group International 2013

infrastructure, access to finance, business environment, and, importantly, governance, including rule of law. Skills and human capital matched to the requirements of the economy are fundamental, including for growth in productive jobs.

These topics are briefly discussed below; some are treated in greater depth in other chapters (e.g., governance in Chapter 4 and human capital in Chapter 8).

Macroeconomic environment

Improved policies and reforms, such as more sustainable fiscal policies, controlled inflation, and better-managed debt, have contributed to macrostability in many African economies. Savings and investment rates have improved over the past 10 years, though even higher savings rates are required for long term growth. The investment rate fluctuated around 20 percent of GDP during 1980 to 2011, and it has risen to about 23 percent since 2007 (Figure 10.7). These ratios are similar to those seen in Latin America, but they are significantly below the average in emerging markets and far lower than the average in fast-growing developing Asia. Savings rates have generally fallen short of investment, fluctuating around 20 percent in recent years. Again, these rates are below the emerging markets' average and should be increased to help ensure sustained long-term growth. The investment-savings gaps, particularly the underlying fiscal deficits, were financed by substantial foreign aid inflows and debt relief (including debt reduction under the Heavily Indebted Poor Countries Initiative [HIPC] and debt forgiveness under the Multilateral Debt Relief Initiative [MDRI]).

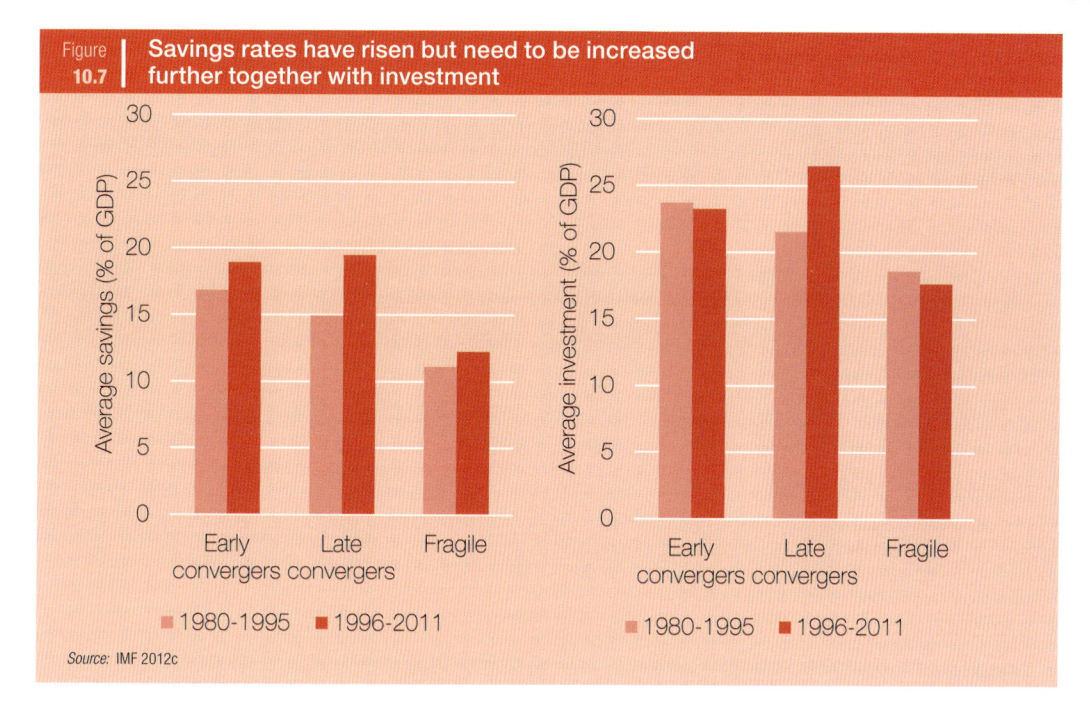

Figure 10.7 | Savings rates have risen but need to be increased further together with investment

Source: IMF 2012c

Competition and trade

African enterprises face little competition. Lack of competition is evident in the gap between Africa and the advanced economies across a number of indicators of market competition — intensity of local competition, extent of market dominance, and effectiveness of anti-monopoly policies. Africa's scores on all three indicators have been consistently lower (Table 10.5). Facing very little competition, African enterprises lack the impetus for raising productivity and competitiveness.

With the exception of a handful of countries, Africa's economies, and thus its national markets, are small (see Chapter 14). The cost of trading across borders SSA is higher than in any other region across most of the indicators shown below (Table 10.6). The high costs reflect both gaps in infrastructure and the inadequate state of trade facilitation services. High costs of trading between countries result in very limited, and declining, intra-Africa trade; it has fallen from a peak of over 20 percent and now stands at 11.3 percent. The current level is a little over half of the level in Latin America (20.4 percent) and less than a quarter of that in developing Asia (52.6 percent) (Figure 10.8).

Domestic entry and other regulations also undermine competition. The professional services sector in East Africa offers an example of a number of regulations, restrictions, and constraints imposed by the countries in the region (Dihel et al. 2010). Professional services are associated with higher labor productivity, lower transaction costs, and improved production processes. There is a large gap between the potential contribution these services could make and the small contribution they do make today in Africa. National markets for professionals and professional services in East Africa remain underdeveloped, and regional markets are fragmented by restrictive policies and regulatory heterogeneity. Kenya, Tanzania, and Uganda all impose severe entry restrictions on engineering and legal services. Licensing and qualification requirements inhibit competition. Operational regulations (such as fees and advertising) also undermine the growth of a strong professional services sector.

Table 10.5 Lack of competition is a serious concern for African economies

	2006-2007	2007-2008	2008-2009	2009-2010	2010-2011	2011-2012	2012-2013
Intensity of local competition							
Advanced economies	5.5	5.6	5.6	5.5	5.5	5.5	5.5
Africa	4.1	4.3	4.5	4.5	4.5	4.4	4.3
Extent of market dominance							
Advanced economies	5.0	5.1	5.1	4.9	4.7	4.7	4.7
Africa	3.3	3.3	3.4	3.5	3.5	3.5	3.5
Effectiveness of anti-monopoly policies							
Advanced economies	5.3	5.3	5.2	5.1	5.0	4.9	4.8
Africa	4.0	4.0	4.0	4.1	4.1	4.1	4.1

Source: World Economic Forum et al. 2013

Table 10.6 Cost of trading across borders is high

	Documents to export (number)	Time to export (days)	Cost to export (US$ per container)	Documents to import (number)	Time to import (days)	Cost to import (US$ per container)
East Asia & Pacific	6	21	923	7	22	958
Eastern Europe & Central Asia	7	26	2134	8	29	2349
Latin America & Caribbean	6	17	1268	7	19	1612
Middle East & North Africa	6	19	1083	8	22	1275
OECD high income	4	10	1028	5	10	1080
South Asia	8	32	1603	9	33	1736
Sub-Saharan Africa	8	31	1990	9	37	2567
North Africa	7	13	809	8	18	973

Sources: World Bank and IFC 2012

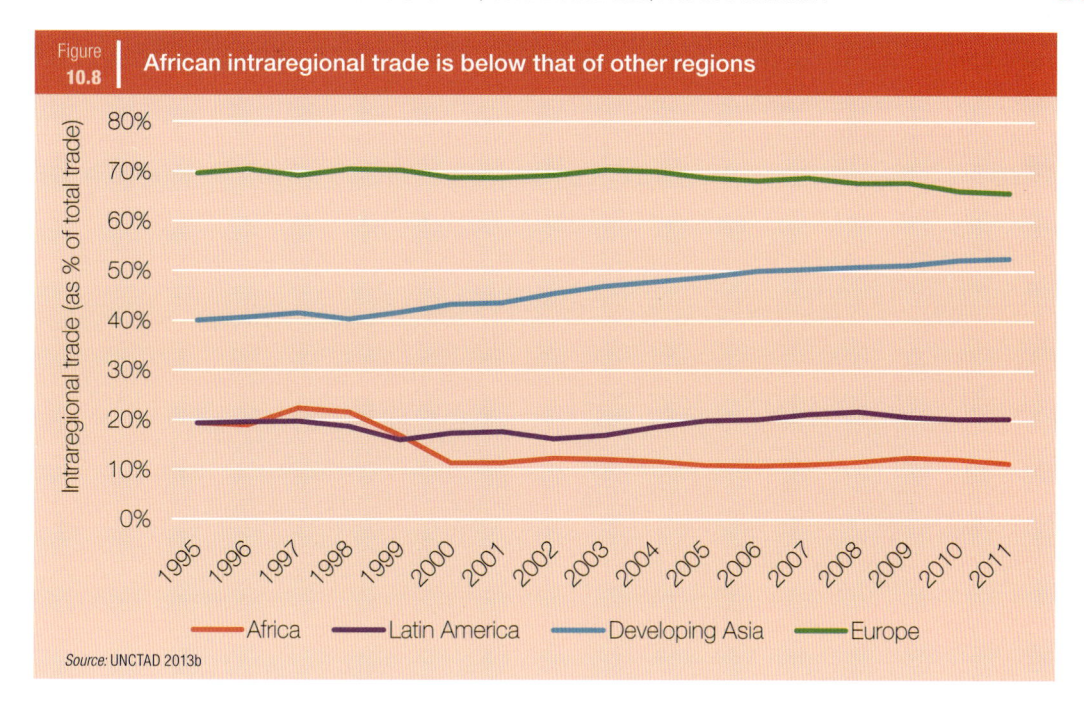

Figure 10.8 African intraregional trade is below that of other regions

Source: UNCTAD 2013b

The pattern of trade means that African enterprises face competition in export markets mostly with respect to commodities. Africa's exports have been concentrated in commodities, while its imports show a concentration in manufactures (Figure 10.9). The share of exports of fuels and minerals in total exports has risen sharply since 1995. The pattern of exports is also reflected in Africa's export concentration index, which is higher than any other region, particularly for the oil-rich economies (Table 10.7).[2] As discussed earlier, an export structure concentrated in a few commodities means that African economies are highly vulnerable to external shocks originating from global commodity markets.

Business environment

Indicators of the business environment, such as the Doing Business indicator, show that Africa lags behind developing Asia and Latin America, with very few countries in the top 50. There are significant differences across countries, particularly between early convergers and other economies (Figure 10.10), as well as some notable examples of countries, e.g., Rwanda, that have registered marked improvement in recent years. In one area, the ease of starting a business, however, Africa ranks above Latin America and developing Asia, with early convergers ranking particularly high (Figure 10.11).

African countries fare poorly in the areas of control of corruption, regulation quality, and rule of law. The design and implementation of regulatory and investment climate policies is subject to state capture by firms or individuals and manipulation to serve vested interests. Moreover, a combination of complex

---
2. The Herfindahl-Hirschmann index has been used to measure export concentration; its value varies between 0 and 1 (maximum concentration).

political and institutional factors can often impede the process of reducing industrial concentration and promoting competition in major economic sectors (as in South Africa). Recent data on the Control of Corruption index in the World Bank Governance Indicators (WGI) show that in 2011 only one country (Botswana) in Africa was ranked in the top quartile with most countries in the third and fourth quartiles. Only one country, Mauritius, is ranked in the first quartile for regulatory quality. No African country makes the first quartile for the government effectiveness indicator. Finally, only Mauritius makes it into the first

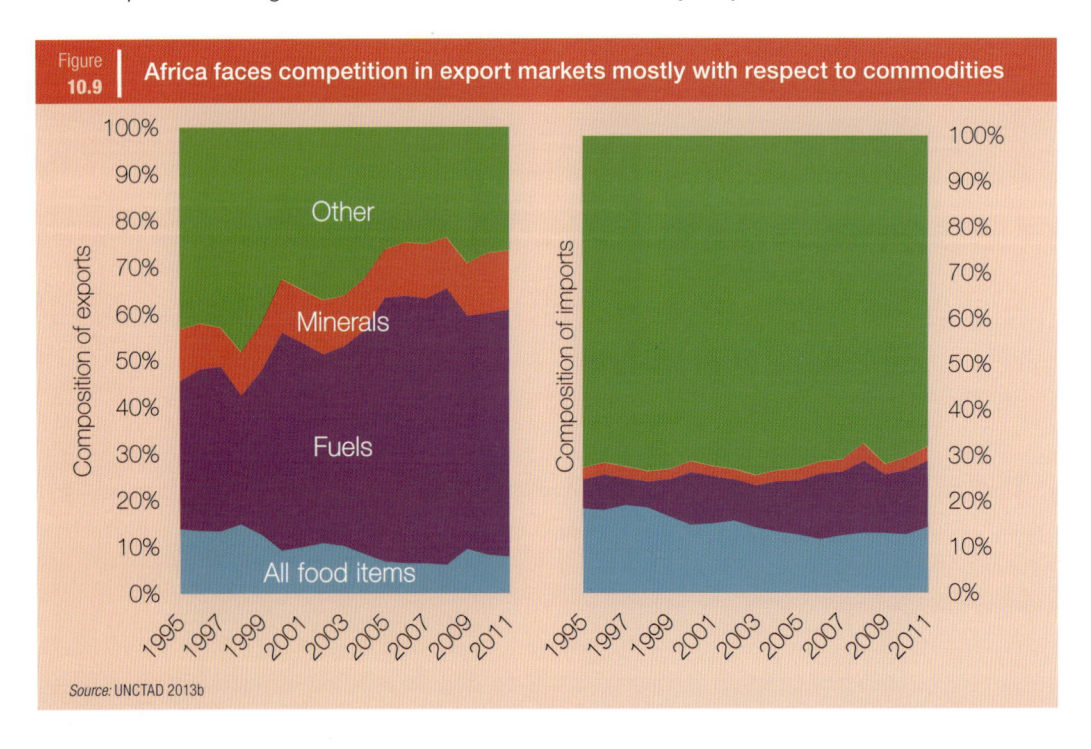

Figure 10.9 Africa faces competition in export markets mostly with respect to commodities

Source: UNCTAD 2013b

Table 10.7 Africa's exports are concentrated in a small number of products and a small number of trading partners

Export Concentration Index	1995	2000	2005	2010	2011
World	0.05	0.07	0.08	0.08	0.08
Developed economies	0.06	0.07	0.07	0.06	0.06
Transition economies	0.18	0.22	0.29	0.32	0.34
Developing economies	0.09	0.13	0.14	0.13	0.13
Africa	0.24	0.33	0.44	0.39	0.41
Latin America	0.09	0.11	0.12	0.13	0.14
Developing Asia	0.09	0.13	0.13	0.12	0.12

Source: UNCTAD 2013b

ENHANCING GROWTH, COMPETITIVENESS, AND JOB CREATION   247

quartile for the rule of law. Most African countries fare poorly (Figure 10.12), mainly due to weak implementation. Contract enforcement is a challenge in many countries and, in some, individuals' physical security is at risk.

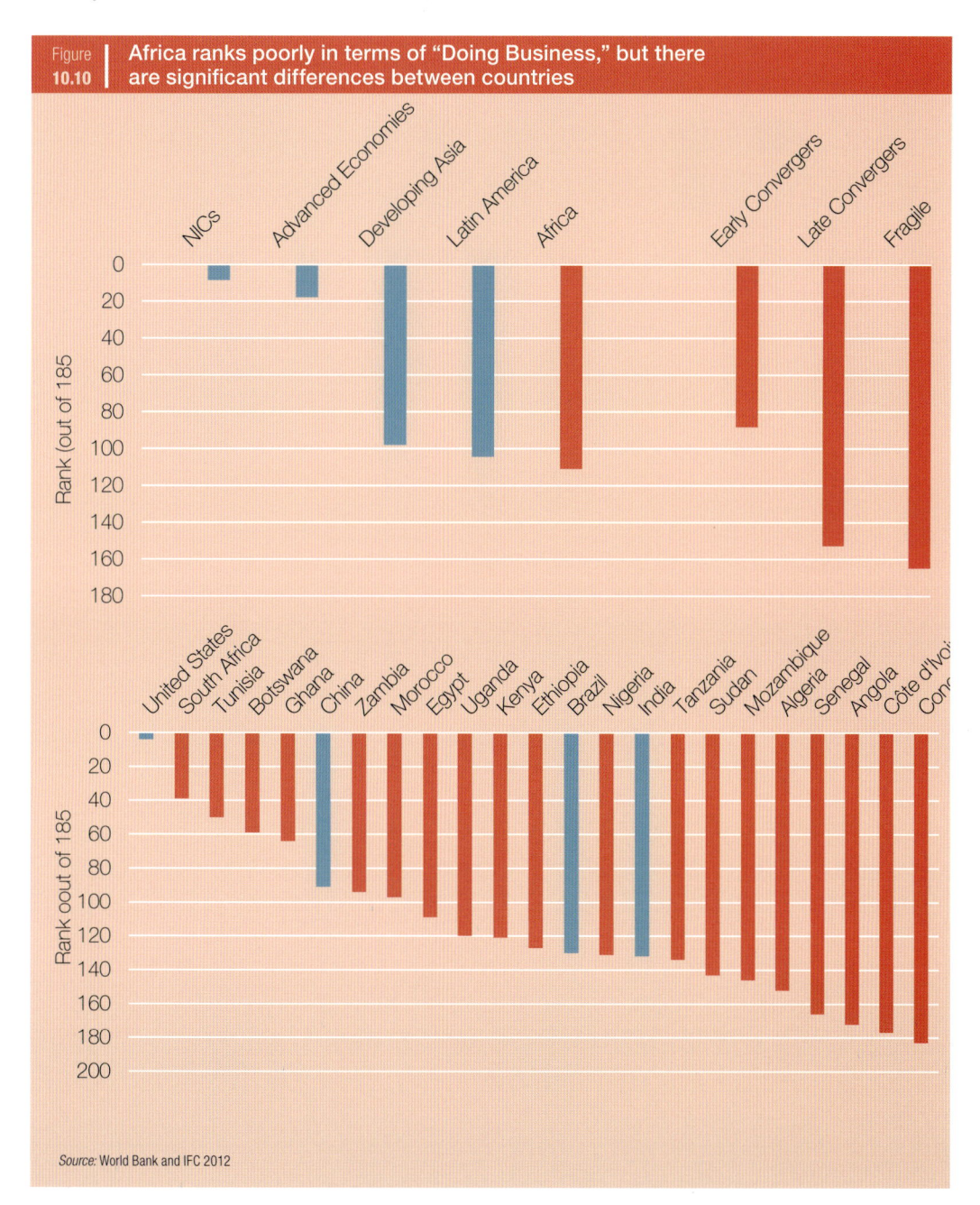

Figure 10.10 Africa ranks poorly in terms of "Doing Business," but there are significant differences between countries

Source: World Bank and IFC 2012

Figure 10.11 Africa is average in terms of starting a business, with early convergers ranking relatively high

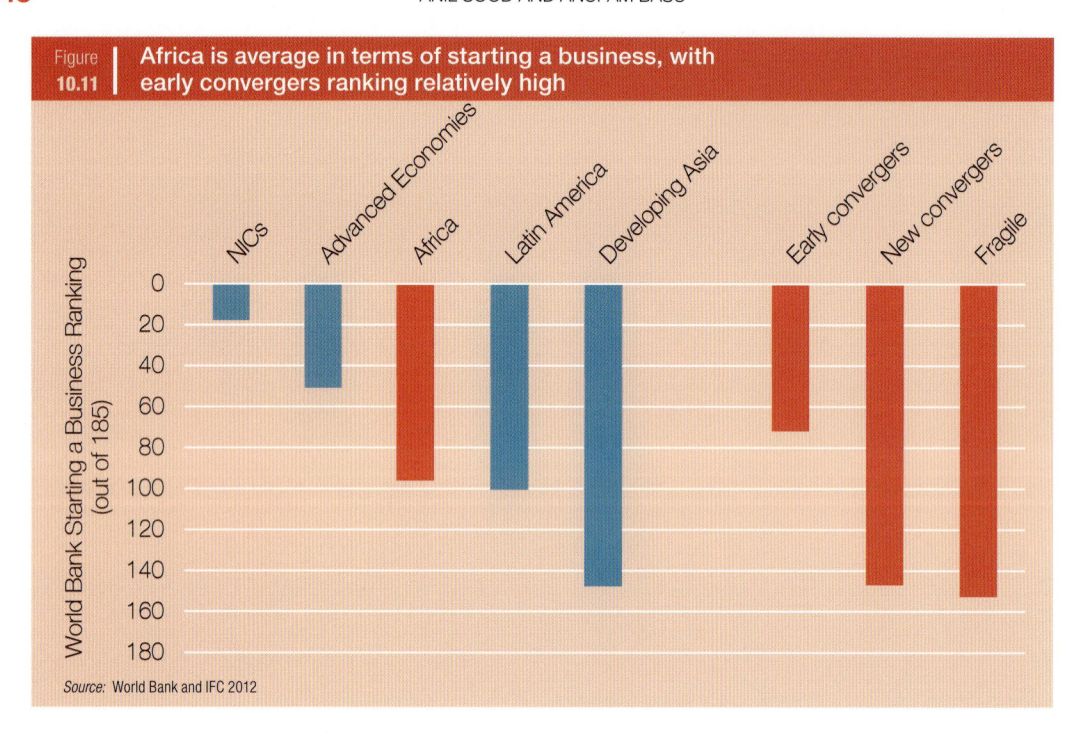

World Bank Starting a Business Ranking (out of 185) — NICs, Advanced Economies, Africa, Latin America, Developing Asia, Early convergers, New convergers, Fragile

Source: World Bank and IFC 2012

Figure 10.12 Most African countries rate poorly on rule of law

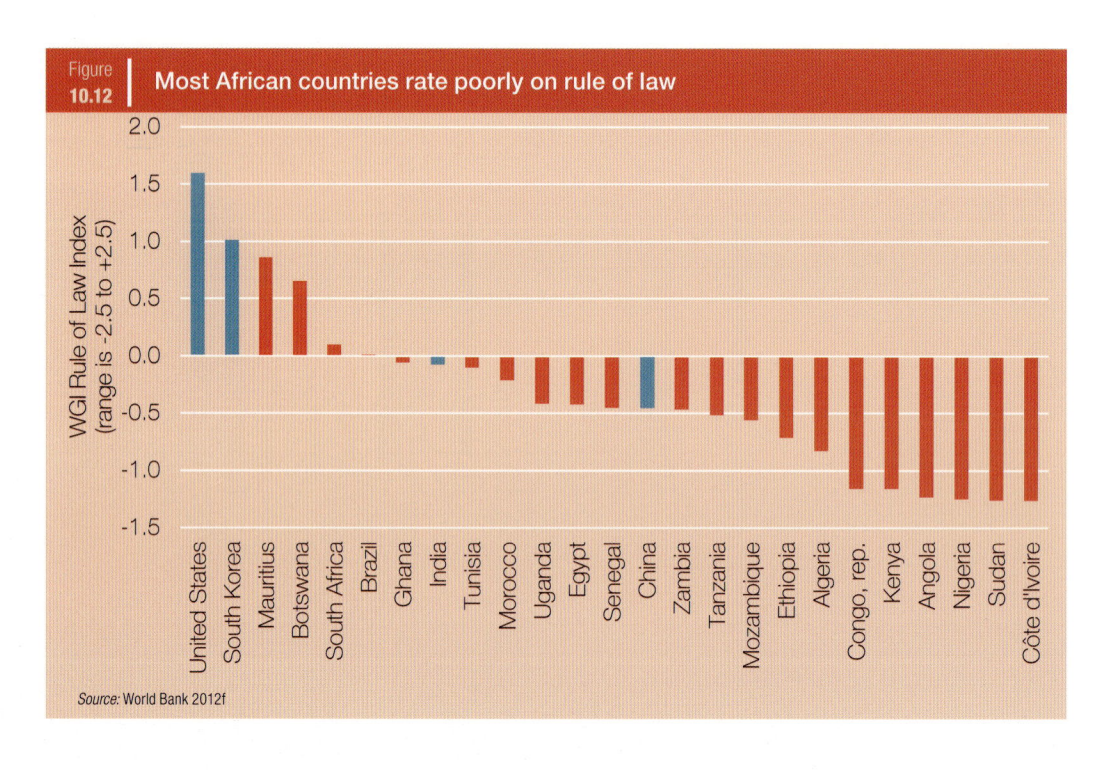

WGI Rule of Law Index (range is -2.5 to +2.5) — United States, South Korea, Mauritius, Botswana, South Africa, Brazil, Ghana, India, Tunisia, Morocco, Uganda, Egypt, Senegal, China, Zambia, Tanzania, Mozambique, Ethiopia, Algeria, Congo, rep., Kenya, Angola, Nigeria, Sudan, Côte d'Ivoire

Source: World Bank 2012f

Labor markets in Africa are more rigid than in other regions of the world. Strict laws regulate employer-employee relations, including those related to hiring, maximum hours of work and overtime, minimum wage, protection against dismissal without cause, and severance pay (Fox and Gaal 2008). High mandatory benefits, social insurance, and labor taxes also contribute to raising labor costs. Despite the rigid labor laws, investment climate surveys suggest that firms consider labor regulations in most countries to be less of an obstacle to investment and expansion than constraints in infrastructure, access to credit, and worker skills. Again, these conditions vary across countries. South Africa lies at the extreme. Of the 144 countries rated by World Economic Forum, it ranks 144th on cooperation in labor-employer relations, 140th on flexibility of wage determination, 143rd on hiring and firing practices, and 134th on pay and productivity.

The dominant, binding constraints to competitiveness lie in the area of infrastructure — power, transportation, logistics, and information and communications technology (ICT) – both within and between countries. These constraints lead to high costs and losses in productivity and can significantly undermine competitiveness. The poor quality and high costs are due in part to inadequate infrastructure investment but even more so due to poor policies and management of infrastructure assets. Africa's infrastructure is rated very poorly (Figure 10.13). Most significant, 24/7 access to power is rare, and power outages constrain productivity. Roads and rail transport are a major constraint and deficits in transportation infrastructure raise costs. With the exception of telephony, prices of infrastructure services are very high, partly due to cost factors but also to high profits enabled by lack of competition (Table 10.8).

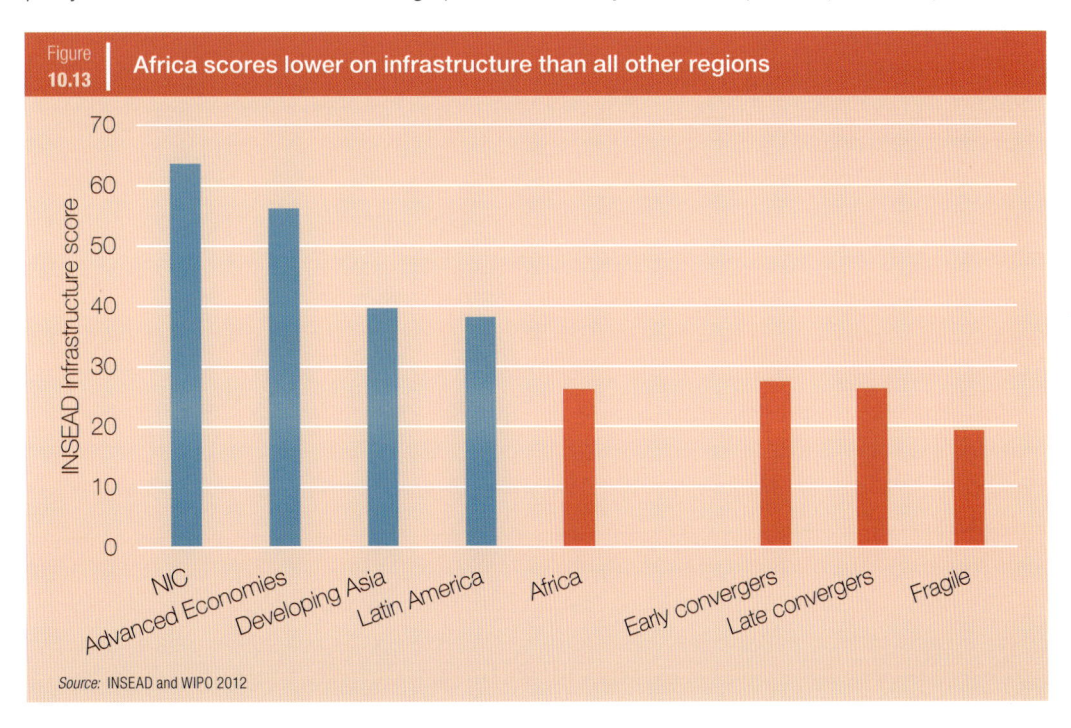

Figure 10.13 Africa scores lower on infrastructure than all other regions

Source: INSEAD and WIPO 2012

Table 10.8 — Africa's infrastructure costs are also higher

Infrastructure	Sub-Saharan Africa	Other developing regions
Power Tariffs ($ per kilowatt-hour)	0.02-0.46	0.05-0.10
Water Tariffs ($ per cubic meter)	0.86-6.56	0.03-0.60
Road Freight Tariffs ($ per ton-kilometer)	0.04-0.14	0.01-0.04
Mobile Telephony ($ per basket per month)	2.60-21.00	9.90
International Telephony ($ per 3-minute call to the U.S.)	0.44-12.50	2.00
Internet Dial-Up Service ($ per month)	6.70-148	11.00

Sources: Authors' estimates based on Africon 2008; Banerjee et al. 2008; Eberhard et al. 2008; Minges et al. 2008; Teravaninthorn and Raballand 2008; Wodon 2008a and 2008b
Note: Ranges reflect prices in different countries and various consumption levels. Prices for telephony and internet service represent all developing regions, including Africa.

There has been tremendous progress in ICT, particularly in mobile telephony, which is reflected in the lower costs shown above. ICTs directly contribute 7 percent of Africa's GDP. ICT is beginning to address some of the challenges facing agriculture and food security (information systems/platforms for stakeholders), climate change (satellite and GPS), education (access to information and resources), financial services (mobile banking), health (communication and data collection), modernizing government (social media to reinforce democratic processes and foster innovation), and regional trade and integration (improving efficiency and coordination of trade and transport, port, customs and border management and data sharing). Good practice examples of innovative ICT initiatives can be seen in the areas of crop insurance, village mapping, money transfers and telemedicine, in Kenya, Malawi, Senegal, and Mali, respectively (Yonaza et al. 2012).

Availability of and access to finance is limited and is a major obstacle to growth. Several factors make African finance both small and shallow. Africa is a large and sparsely populated continent, making outreach to scattered users costly. Prevalent informality hampers access to information on borrowers and curtails household enterprises' and MSMEs' access to finance. Enforcement of creditors' rights is weak due to unreliable courts as governance issues plague the judiciary and many other institutions. As a result, a large part of the population is un-banked. Sub-Saharan Africa has 2.7 bank branches per 100,000 residents compared to 7.4 in developing East Asia. Mobile phone technology is surmounting this challenge in some countries as evidenced by the success of the M-Pesa network covering Kenya and neighboring countries, which gained 14 million users within 4 years of its launch in 2007. Finally, African banks typically invest mostly in government securities rather than lending to the private sector. As a result, long-term finance is elusive; it especially affects funding for infrastructure, housing, and enterprises.

The pattern of urbanization, particularly in SSA, is undermining the growth potential typically afforded by the transition from a predominantly rural economy. Urbanization has been driven less by an urban demand for labor linked to fast industrialization (as in 19th century Europe or now in Asia) than by the relative lack of opportunity in most rural areas. Sprawling development of exceptionally large metropolises has created huge unmanageable zones that lack the needed infrastructure and basic services of urban roads, transport, drainage, safe drinking water, and electricity. Beyond the modern administrative and commercial centers of many large African cities is the widespread prevalence of slums or what are usually called "unstructured districts" ("Quartiers sous intégrés" in French) lacking the most basic facilities. Some of these unstructured districts/slums have already become lawless areas controlled by rival gangs involved in various illicit activities.

Skills, innovation, and entrepreneurship

The education level and skills endowment of the labor force lag behind other regions, and the mismatch with the required skills may be growing. The percentage of labor force with primary and secondary education–40 percent have completed lower secondary — remains low, though it is improving. The percentage with tertiary education shows a similar trend. Within tertiary education, there is very limited emphasis on engineering and other professional education (management, accounting, law). The quality of education is a major issue (see Chapter 8).

Africa's status with respect to innovation is the lowest among all regions, with North Africa faring better than SSA (Figures 10.14 and 10.15). African economies also rank poorly on indexes of technological development, technology level of output and exports, and progress toward becoming knowledge economies.

Africa lacks world-class universities, which are widely recognized as catalysts for development through their role in producing the knowledge, skills, and innovations required for economic growth. Only one African university (University of Cape Town, South Africa) ranks among the top 200 universities in the world, as compared with four to six from the Republic of Korea alone. Both the level of tertiary education and the share of students in technical fields are low. Africa's share of engineers is the lowest of all regions (Asia has the highest); only 4 percent of SSA graduates study engineering compared to 20 percent in Asia. Only 2 percent of Sub-Saharan students study agriculture, which, though comparable to other regions, is low relative to the importance of the sector in the region and the challenge of transforming the sector. Public and private expenditure on R&D is also the lowest of all regions at 0.4 percent of GDP. Furthermore, university-industry partnerships and linkages are weak, and there is very limited progress toward urban "clusters" that typically drive innovation and technology development as well as the creation and growth of enterprises.

Entrepreneurship is vital for Africa's growth and for much-needed job creation. It also contributes to Schumpeter's "creative destruction," innovation, and technological progress. There is a positive correlation between entrepreneurship and improvements in TFP (Figure 10.16). Few African economies rank in the top half of the 118 economies that are rated in the index of entrepreneurship (Figure 10.17). As discussed earlier, African enterprises are predominantly small and in the informal sector. Entrepreneurship

Figure 10.14 — African economies rank poorly in innovation...

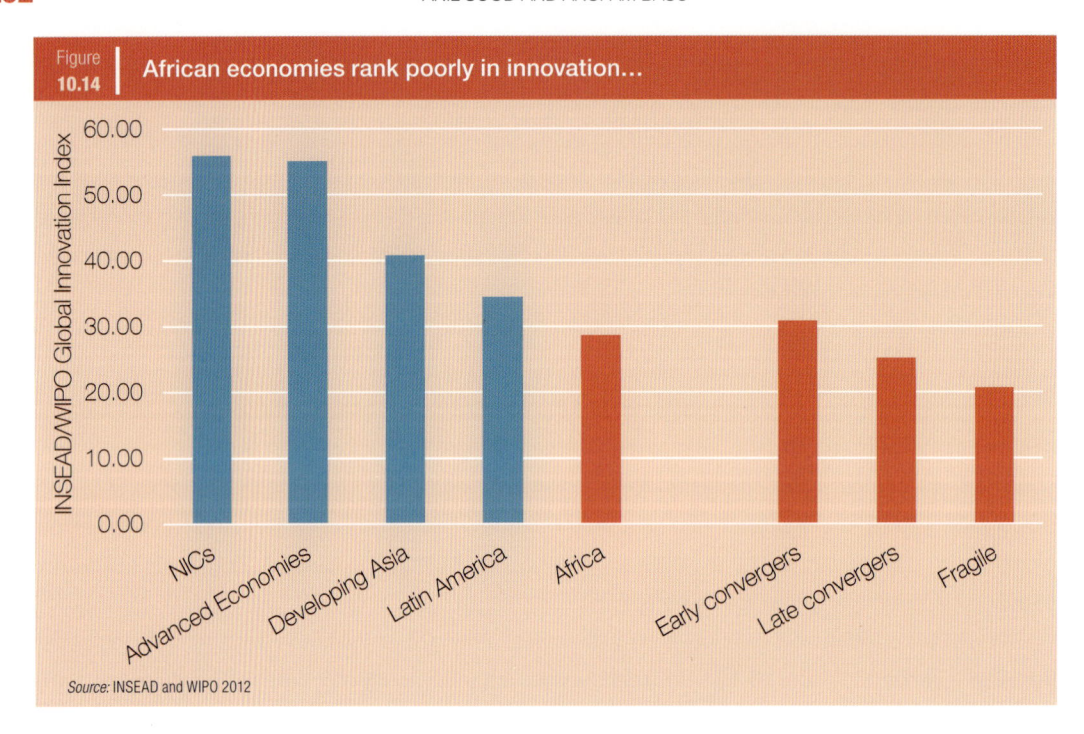

INSEAD/WIPO Global Innovation Index values by group: NICs ~56, Advanced Economies ~55, Developing Asia ~41, Latin America ~34.5, Africa ~29, Early convergers ~31, Late convergers ~25, Fragile ~21.

Source: INSEAD and WIPO 2012

Figure 10.15 — ...but some African economies rate higher for innovation than others

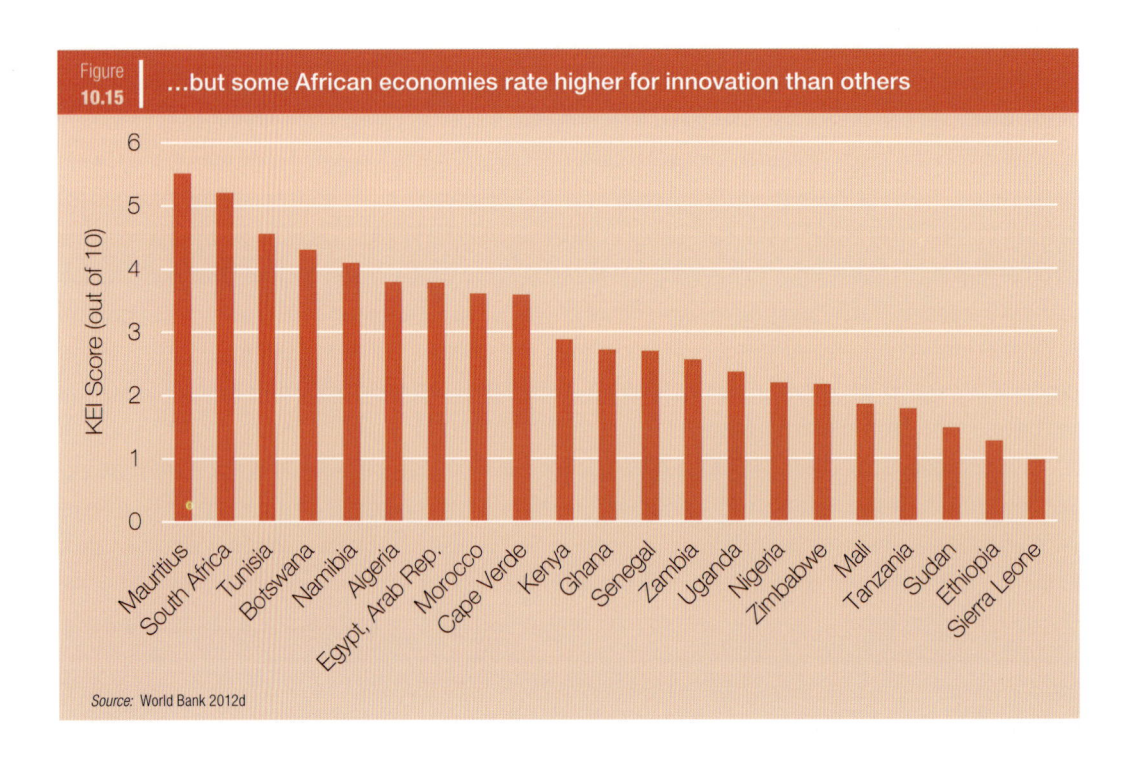

KEI Score (out of 10) by country: Mauritius ~5.5, South Africa ~5.2, Tunisia ~4.6, Botswana ~4.3, Namibia ~4.1, Algeria ~3.8, Egypt, Arab Rep. ~3.8, Morocco ~3.6, Cape Verde ~3.6, Kenya ~2.9, Ghana ~2.7, Senegal ~2.7, Zambia ~2.55, Uganda ~2.4, Nigeria ~2.2, Zimbabwe ~2.2, Mali ~1.9, Tanzania ~1.8, Sudan ~1.5, Ethiopia ~1.3, Sierra Leone ~1.0.

Source: World Bank 2012d

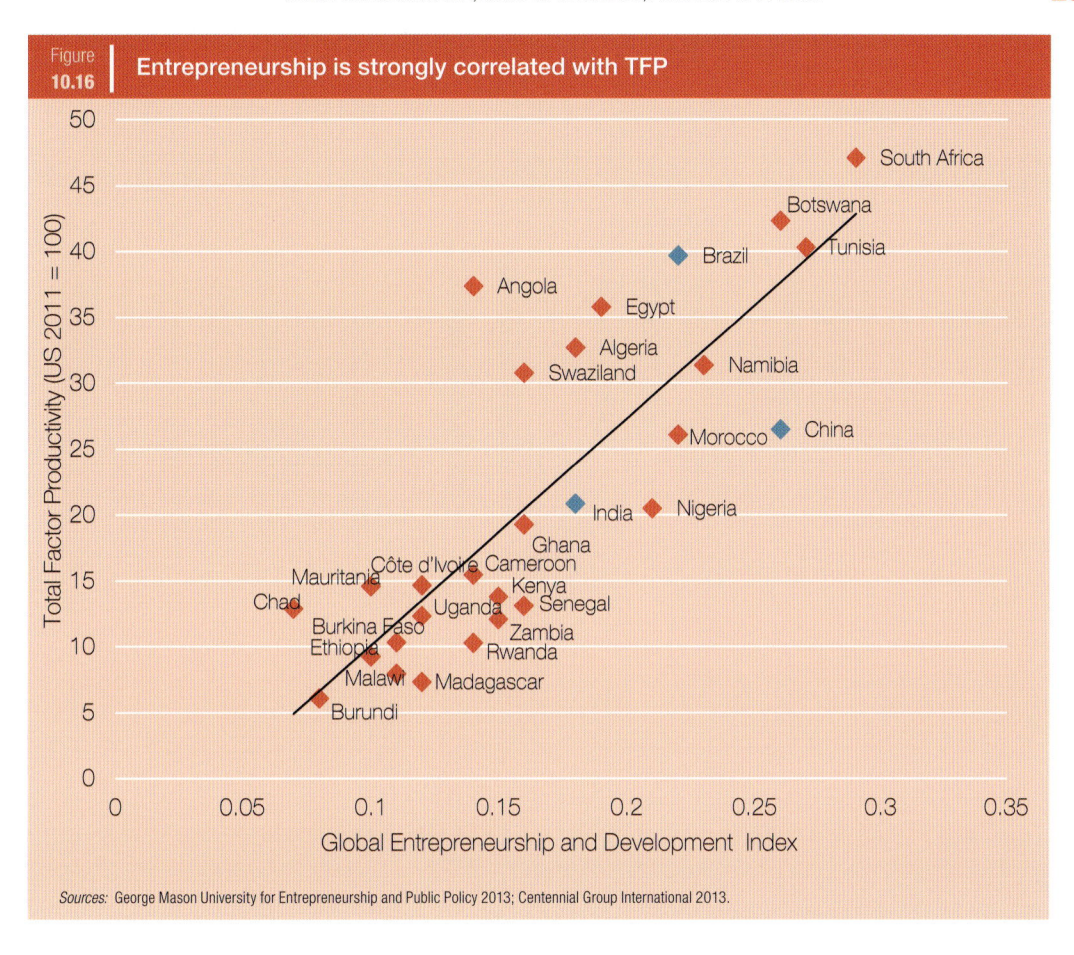

Figure 10.16 | Entrepreneurship is strongly correlated with TFP

Sources: George Mason University for Entrepreneurship and Public Policy 2013; Centennial Group International 2013.

is visible mostly in MSMEs, notably in women-owned household enterprises. At the other end of the spectrum, there are very few large, global companies in Africa that could be the pulling force and, for example, drive "factory Africa"; African companies are missing from the Fortune Global 500.

Innovation and entrepreneurship in Africa are largely of the catch-up variety, based on replicating existing products. There are very few examples of frontier or pioneering innovation and entrepreneurship, which require breakthroughs in science and technology. Again, there are differences across countries. South Africa, Botswana, Tunisia, and Mauritius consistently outperform the rest of the region when it comes to issues such as total factor productivity, entrepreneurship, and innovation. These countries also outperform major emerging market economies such as Brazil, India, and China. Africa lacks a skilled labor force, especially in important sectors such as research and technology, in which innovation and entrepreneurship are cultivated. For example, Africa only has about 55 percent of the researchers per 1000 workers that China has and only 1 percent of the technicians per 1000 workers that Brazil has.

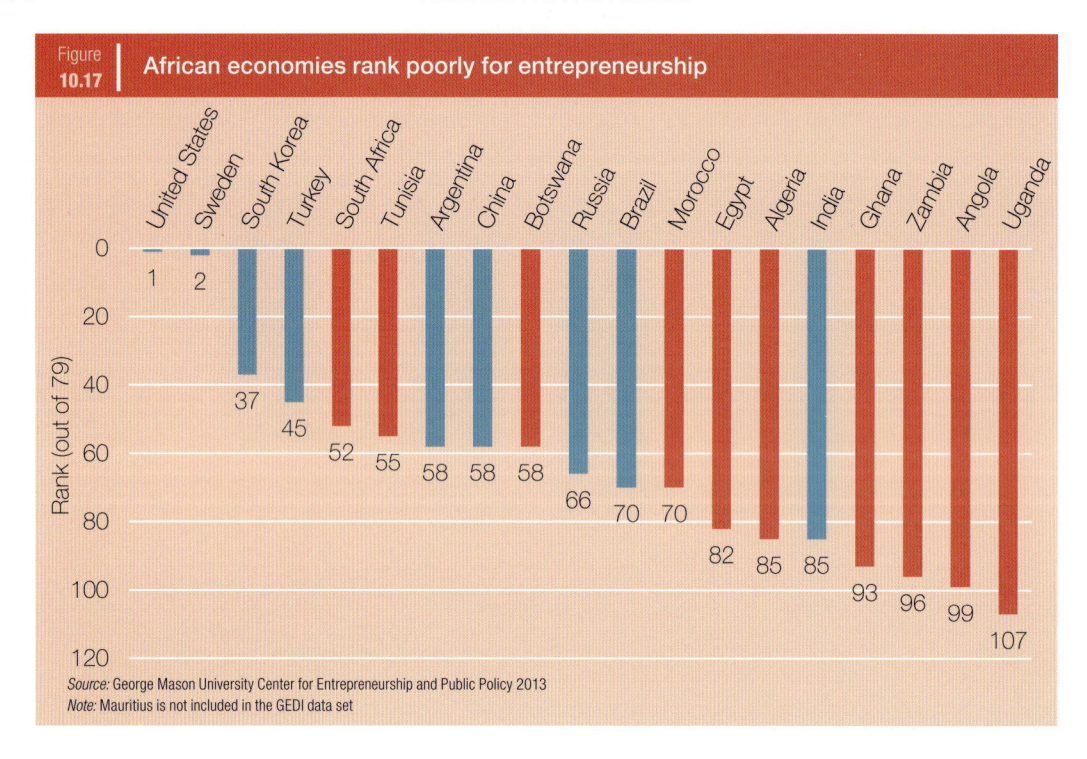

Figure 10.17: African economies rank poorly for entrepreneurship

Rank (out of 79):
- United States: 1
- Sweden: 2
- South Korea: 37
- Turkey: 45
- South Africa: 52
- Tunisia: 55
- Argentina: 58
- China: 58
- Botswana: 58
- Russia: 66
- Brazil: 70
- Morocco: 70
- Egypt: 82
- Algeria: 85
- India: 85
- Ghana: 93
- Zambia: 96
- Angola: 99
- Uganda: 107

Source: George Mason University Center for Entrepreneurship and Public Policy 2013
Note: Mauritius is not included in the GEDI data set

Foreign direct investment

FDI is important for Africa for a number of reasons. It is widely acknowledged for its positive effect on growth and productivity, and it is potentially a source of technology, a wide range of skills and know-how, and spillovers into domestic enterprises through integration into supply chains. It has played an important role in improving competitiveness in African firms.

FDI to Africa has grown significantly in recent years (Figure 10.18). Africa was an attractive destination for FDI in the early 1970s when it accounted for some 5 percent of global FDI inflows and close to 30 percent of the inflows into developing economies. Thereafter, Africa's share trended downwards; by the 1990s FDI flows to Asia expanded dramatically, bringing Africa's share of global inflows to less than 1 percent in 2000 and of inflows to developing countries to under 5 percent. This trend was reversed over the past decade, and absolute levels of FDI into Africa rose sharply, from $9.7 billion in 2000 and to $43 billion in 2011 (Figure 10.19). North Africa and West Africa have been the two sub-regions attracting most of these inflows, followed by East Africa. Egypt, Morocco, Nigeria, and Tunisia have been the major destinations. Inflows have declined in the last three years due to political uncertainty but remain important at 2.6 percent of GDP. Sources of FDI now include new entrants, dominated by China, and there has also been some increase in intra-Africa investment.

ENHANCING GROWTH, COMPETITIVENESS, AND JOB CREATION

Figure 10.18 Africa was an attractive destination for FDI in the early 1970s

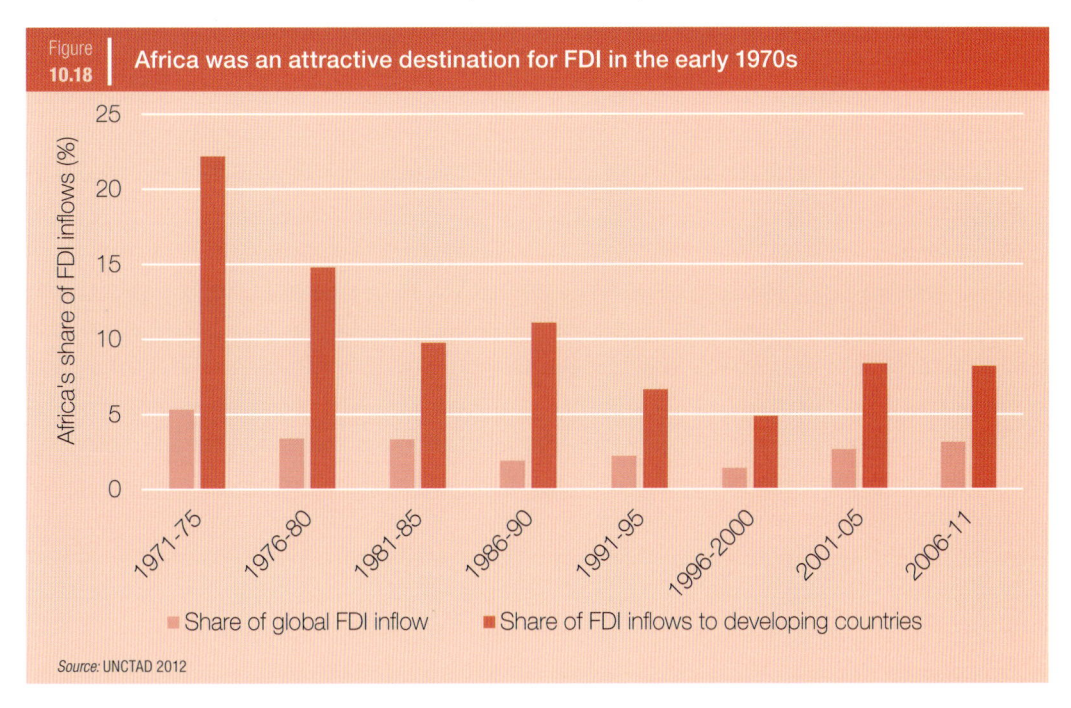

Source: UNCTAD 2012

Figure 10.19 Absolute levels of FDI into Africa rose sharply between 2000 and 2011

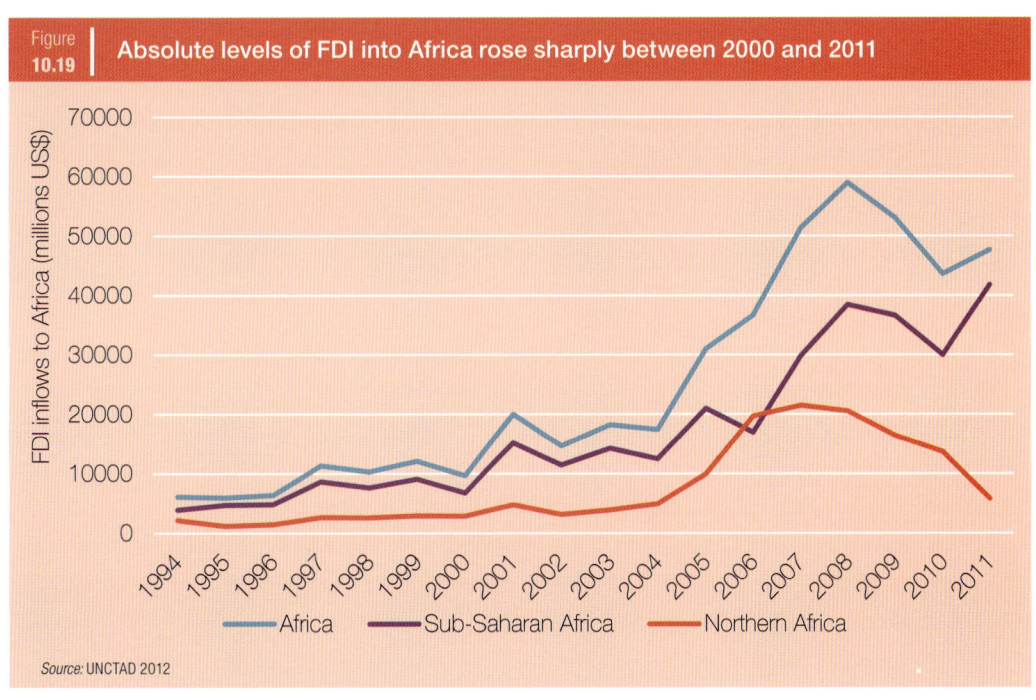

Source: UNCTAD 2012

Foreign investors in emerging markets are now more positive about Africa than those in developed economies. Their perceptions point to some barriers that are specific to increasing FDI into Africa. They rank an unstable political environment, corruption, and weak security as the leading barriers to investment, followed by infrastructure. In contrast, domestic enterprises rank infrastructure and access to finance at the top of the list.

In summary, with a handful of exceptions, African economies fare poorly on the determinants of global competitiveness. Higher savings and investment rates will be needed to sustain higher growth rates over the long-term. A number of elements of the investment climate merit urgent attention. A lack of competition contributes to a lack of impetus among African firms to improve productivity and competitiveness. The high costs of trading across borders, resulting from inadequate infrastructure and trade facilitation services, have impeded the expansion of both regional and global trade and, hence, the exposure to foreign competition.

Africa lags behind other regions across many Doing Business indicators; most African countries are in the bottom two quartiles for the World Bank's indicators of control of corruption, regulatory quality, government effectiveness, and rule of law. Binding constraints in power, transport systems, trade logistics, and ICT contribute to high costs and productivity losses for African firms, undermining their competitiveness. The lack of much-needed infrastructure and basic services (such as roads, transport systems, drainage, drinking water, and power) in urban areas has contributed to the growth of sprawling slums instead of urban clusters of productive, job-creating enterprises.

The education level and skills endowment of the labor force lag behind other regions, and the mismatch with the required skills may be growing. Africa's status with respect to innovation and entrepreneurship is the lowest among all regions. FDI to Africa, which can contribute to enhanced productivity and competitiveness, has grown significantly in recent years but there has been variation across countries and over time.

Vision Africa 2050

The preceding two sections have discussed the current status of African economies with a special emphasis on the determinants of competitiveness. With that backdrop, this section makes the leap to what Africa could be in 2050. The section focuses on the marked improvements in competitiveness, productivity, and a wide range of underlying factors that could underpin Africa 2050. The section that follows then lays out the bold action agenda for Africa to realize this Vision.

African economies, with very few exceptions, would be characterized by macrostability and high rates of savings and investment that would enable the much-needed increase in investment, particularly but not only, in human capital and infrastructure.

The economies would be more diversified and much less concentrated in commodities. The share of oil and minerals would have fallen significantly in favor of light manufacturing, trade, and social and other services, including tourism. Agricultural output would have moved to higher value-added products, and productivity would have increased considerably, allowing labor to move out of agriculture. Exports would be similarly diversified in their composition with Africa taking over some areas now dominated by developing Asia.

Firms across Africa would serve larger, more integrated regional and global markets. At the same time, they would be open to competition — domestically and through trade. The continent would be seen as an attractive destination of FDI diversified across sectors and from both (today's) developed economies and emerging markets, with its share in global FDI exceeding 10 percent.

Most economies would boast a thriving enterprise sector. The sector would comprise a mix of companies of different sizes including some 20 to 30 African companies that count among the top 500 global companies (e.g., in extractive industries and ancillary services, agro-industry, trading, and renewable energy) investing across Africa and the globe. Most enterprises would be in the formal sector, specialized, and taking advantage of the economies of scale afforded by larger markets. The majority of those that remain in the informal, household enterprise sector would be closely linked to the formal sector, including as part of production or service networks and supply chains.

TFP levels would have continued to catch up with best practice. Many economies would reach the level of Chile today. Productivity gains would be supported by the upgraded education and skills of the workforce, including management skills of entrepreneurs and professional (accounting, legal, consulting) services. Businesses of all sizes, including entrepreneurs and traders in the informal household enterprise sector, would have access to needed finance from a deeper financial sector, including non-bank financial institutions. Financial services to household enterprises would be supported by mobile banking.

Upgraded national and regional infrastructure and the resulting high quality of services at low costs would support enhanced competitiveness. With very few exceptions, the continent would enjoy 24/7 power, clean water, access to roads (with the vast majority of the population within two kilometers), and an air network with hubs in major capitals, efficient ports, and extensive ICT with full internet access. Hydropower would enable a plentiful supply of electricity to high-density centers. Smaller hydro (e.g., pico hydro) and solar stations would ensure clean electrification of remote areas, facilitating access for all to ICT and the internet.

A well-functioning, regionally and globally networked science-technology-innovation (STI) system built around world-class universities (with some 10 to 15 ranked among the world's top 200) would serve the continent. Universities and businesses would be concentrated in efficient urban "clusters" that would support continuous innovation adapted to Africa's needs. Urban centers would account for close to 90 percent of GDP.

The overall result would be reflected in much higher scores for most countries on the Global Competitiveness Index and, vitally, in much-needed growth in employment and good jobs.

Action Agenda

The continent faces a challenging multi-pronged agenda for action to bridge the very large gap between the Vision for 2050 outlined above and the current status discussed earlier. Labor-intensive diversification based on enhancement of competitiveness and productivity will be needed to sustain growth and create much-needed jobs. Successful implementation of this agenda would enable African economies to take advantage of growth and diversification opportunities in agriculture and agro-processing to meet the changing food consumption patterns of a more affluent Africa and for export; construction of much-needed national and regional infrastructure; value-added and ancillary industries and services related to the extractive natural resource sector; social services (health and education); tourism; retail and trade, including global trading in minerals and agricultural commodities; and light manufacturing.

The agenda with respect to the required macroeconomic environment, improvements in governance and the rule of law, infrastructure, urbanization, and the development of requisite skills and human capital is set out in the related chapters. This section focuses on four areas that are central to growth and private sector development – competition; markets and trade; technology development, innovation, and entrepreneurship; and the business environment –all in the support of the objective of creating jobs. It also covers measures specific to job creation within the new business environment. Priority actions, described in more detail below, include:

- **Foster competition and competitiveness** through policies that reduce barriers to entry; improve access to business services for SMSEs in both rural and urban areas; improve transport, energy, and finance infrastructure; and reduce regulatory burdens;
- **Integrate markets with respect to goods, services, and the movement of people** by lowering tariff and non-tariff barriers, improving connectivity, facilitating cross-border trade, and harmonizing trade and investment regimes across countries in order to increase the size of the markets in which businesses participate;
- **Promote technology development, innovation, and entrepreneurship** through investment in the capacity and quality of education (see Chapter 8), increased expenditure on research and development, implementing reforms needed to increase FDI, and increased regional collaboration;
- **Improve the business environment for private sector firms** through promulgation of business regulations that are sound, streamlined, consistently applied, and transparent with the goal of minimizing corruption and state capture; and
- **Address the challenges associated with job creation** including rural-urban migration, worker productivity, informal employment, women's entry into market activities, and youth unemployment.

Realizing the bold Vision for 2050 will require Africa to promote inclusion in order to mitigate the risks of increased inequality due to rapid urbanization and widening productivity gap between agriculture and other sectors (see Chapter 7). All components of the action agenda must include attention to the needs of the informal sector. It is important to ensure that services and innovations are available to and benefit all

Africans, including the poor and vulnerable and those living in remote areas. China, India, and South Africa offer good examples of inclusive innovation — lowering the costs of goods and services to make them more affordable and readily accessible to poor people and to enhance income-earning opportunities.

Foster competition

Fostering competition, including through entry and growth of enterprises, requires both putting in place pro-competition policies and curbing anti-competitive behavior demonstrated by state or private monopolies, strong vested interests, and instances of state capture. The regulatory barriers to the entry and exit of firms, which limit competition in input and output markets, should be removed to bring them in line with best international practice.

Regulatory policies should aim to level the playing field between small and large firms. Compared with large firms, the costs of unreliable power supply are more burdensome, and the burden of fixed costs (license and permit fees) are greater for smaller firms. The burden of regulatory requirements (the number of procedures, the time required to comply with them and the costs of compliance) needs to be progressively reduced to allow domestic firms to become competitive in a global setting.

The proposed action agenda has significant potential for promoting synergy between the various parts of the private sector, by reinforcing supply and demand side linkages between the informal and formal sectors, large and small firms, and the farming and manufacturing sectors. For example, improvements in basic infrastructure and financial services would facilitate the participation of domestic firms in the value chain of production and raise firm productivity. The provision of services (especially transport and finance) to the rural sector is essential for connecting rural and urban markets and forging production linkages between agriculture and industry. These services (especially banking) would also facilitate linkages between firms in the formal and informal sectors. Improvements in infrastructure and financial services are also essential for domestic firms to connect with both regional and global markets. Reductions in regional transport costs would be immensely beneficial for landlocked countries.

Integrate to expand markets and facilitate trade

Africa must continue to aggressively pursue movement toward more integrated markets in goods, services, and the movement of people. Lessons can be learned from the more successful regional economic communities (RECs) (e.g., the East African Community [EAC] in some areas, the Economic Community of West African States [ECOWAS] in others) and from other regions of the world (see Chapter 14). Actions need to go beyond lowering tariff barriers to genuinely opening up, reducing non-tariff and behind-the-border barriers, improving connectivity, facilitating cross-border intra-Africa trade in food, other goods and services, and harmonization of trade and investment regimes. Greater openness to global markets is essential for domestic African firms to benefit from economies of scale and for learning-by-exporting.

To reap the benefits of competition, African firms need to expand their markets beyond their national boundaries to participate in regional and global markets. The existing private sector dominated by numerous small firms and a large informal sector catering mainly to domestic markets has to be transformed into a dynamic modern private sector with firms growing in both numbers and size and conducting their business in the formal sector. This transformation can be achieved through promotion of export-oriented and labor-intensive light manufacturing industries as well as other labor-intensive sectors such as tourism. Without such transformation, economies will be unable to accommodate the projected substantial growth in the workforce and to productively employ the large numbers of laborers expected to move out from agriculture as farm productivity improves.

Trade logistics in each country need to be substantially improved through trade facilitation measures to sharply reduce the cost, complexity, and time spent in completing customs clearance, obtaining bank credit, and paying customs duties. Improving logistics is essential to encourage firms to access (both regional and non-regional) foreign markets for exports and to procure inputs at competitive world prices. National and regional infrastructure for power, transport, port facilities, and broadband and telecommunication services should be expanded and upgraded to lower costs. Regional infrastructure should be integrated to improve connectivity both regionally and globally.

Pro-competition policies combined with larger markets would provide the impetus for investment —domestic and foreign — to take advantage of expanded opportunities. At the same time, Africa would be able to diversify its export markets beyond its traditional partners to include the more rapidly growing emerging market economies and, most importantly, to link into global supply chains.

Promote technology development, innovation, and entrepreneurship

African economies can realize large gains from tapping into expanding global knowledge, which is increasingly possible through trade, FDI, access to members of the African diaspora, and information in print and on the Internet. It requires African countries to build a foundation to diffuse and encourage the adoption of new technologies. To this end, Africa needs a massive increase in the capacity and quality of education and in investments in technology and innovation, particularly early stage technological development and grassroots innovation. Many sectors will require workers with specialized knowledge — a prerequisite for an STI system that can serve as a major source of growth. But all workers will need the soft skills — creativity, innovation, communication, managerial, and entrepreneurial skills — necessary for success in business.

Most economies in Africa could pursue innovation and entrepreneurship of the catch-up variety. The underlying requirements are clearly getting the fundamentals (such as economic and business basics, access to finance, availability of needed infrastructure services) right. A few economies that are technologically more advanced and have already achieved high levels of TFP (e.g., South Africa, Mauritius, Botswana, and Tunisia) can start to lay the foundation for pioneering or frontier innovation and entrepreneurship, which requires a more demanding environment — strong tertiary education particularly in science and engineering, appropriate intellectual property rights, availability of venture capital, a tax regime that promotes research and innovation, and science and technology parks or export processing zones.

More effort must be put into promoting research and development, including raising research and development expenditures, mostly in the private sector, from the very low current level of 0.4 percent of GDP to some 2 to 3 percent. Africa must also invest in building world-class universities with links between universities and research centers and industry, so that skills and degrees are relevant and useful in the job market. Such linkages can also underpin the development of urban clusters that can enable agglomeration economies, support the emergence and growth of businesses, and help meet Africa's jobs challenge.

FDI can bring in much needed technology, know-how, and managerial capability across sectors. Implementing fundamental reforms to address political instability, corruption, concerns about safety and bureaucratic obstacles will help make the business environment more predictable and appealing. Enhancing competition to promote the development of professional services can help to build and support entrepreneurial capacity.

Regional collaboration in STI can bring substantial gains. Collaboration to leverage STI systems in countries where they are relatively developed will help achieve faster results in other African countries at lower cost. Regional collaboration should help to develop centers of excellence in selected areas of particular relevance to the continent such as extractive industries and ancillary services, agriculture, small solar power and hydropower units, and ICT. These are best established and operated as public-private partnerships (PPPs), including with global organizations.

Improve the business environment with a focus on private sector development

The key challenge in this area is to foster an environment that enables and promotes entry (and allows exit) of enterprises and their continued growth, unconstrained by regulatory and other barriers. Such an environment is vital to support the transformation and growth of informal household ventures to SMEs in the formal sector and from there to larger enterprises.

African governments need to formulate sound, streamlined, and unambiguous regulations and to publish the related implementation rules, as well as all decisions based on them. The regulations that govern government-firm relations need to be transparent in design and implementation to facilitate public scrutiny and merit public confidence. Effective implementation of regulatory policies depends also on the quality of public services and the civil service, the degree of the administration's independence from political pressures, and the credibility of the government's commitment to the policies.

To prevent corruption and state capture, decisive actions are needed to eliminate discretionary authority, inadequate accountability, and monopoly power. To prevent the undue influence of particular groups on government policymaking at the cost of broader social interests, governments need to include in their policy dialogue a broad range of interest groups, such as business associations that represent smaller firms, and civil society groups and consumer organizations that would be affected by the policies under consideration. Proper accountability for the exercise of public authority should be sought through vigilant and competitive legislatures and a free and independent media to provide strong legislative oversight, enhance the transparency of government-firm transactions, and make the public aware of the costs of corruption.

Public confidence in the regulatory system requires that governments not only enforces but also abides by the rule of law. There should be clear conflict-of-interest laws and standards of public conduct. Cases of corruption or other improper financial transactions would be dealt with through a proper judicial process. Some countries have relied on independent, autonomous bodies to investigate and prosecute suspects, prevent corruption, and educate the public. For example, Botswana established a Directorate of Corruption and Economic Crime for this purpose in 1994 and conducted an active publicity campaign to inform and educate the public (World Bank 2005b).

An advanced and efficient financial system is essential to help encourage higher financial savings, deepen financial intermediation, and eventually develop dynamic domestic (or, where needed, regional) capital markets that finance investment activities. In light of the low population density and small national markets, cross-border approaches will be needed. The rapid spread of pan-African banking systems, as well as the introduction of a framework that facilitates taking advantage of portfolio capital inflows (frontier markets) should also help in this regard. Technology, like M-Pesa, can be employed, and alternative channels such as stores and post offices can minimize fixed costs.

Governments and the public sector have an important role to play with respect to the above agenda, but the results will ultimately be driven by investment by the private sector — foreign and, increasingly, domestic.

Address specific barriers to job creation

The primary environment for promoting job creation is that the fundamentals for growth and private sector development are in place, and that the broad agenda of promoting labor-intensive diversification of African economies is successfully implemented as laid out in the set of policies and reforms discussed above. The second element of the jobs agenda is that of addressing the most visible problems of job creation that arise in a variety of country situations in the African context. These include the challenges related to rural-urban migration, informal employment, women's entry into market activities, and youth unemployment.

To facilitate rural-urban migration, early efforts are required to extend adequate health and education services in both rural and urban areas to better prepare rural migrants for entry into the urban job market. In the rural sector opportunities for absorbing labor in productive off-farm activities should be pursued. On the demand side of the urban labor market, public policies need to focus on the development of functional cities (with good infrastructure and a network of competing firms and suppliers) that could provide the basis for developing a dynamic urban private sector, and for taking advantage of the productivity spillovers from jobs in industrial clusters, dynamic cities, and global value chains.

Informal employment in agriculture and in household enterprises will remain a key feature of African economies for some time to come. Therefore, a critical challenge is to improve worker productivity and prospects of better paying jobs in the informal sectors. More broad-based access to higher levels of education beyond the primary level would provide the informal sector with better human capital. Efforts to improve the informal sector's access to inputs, finance, and markets would facilitate the employment of the better-educated new entrants to the sector. Improvements in the business environment that reduce the costs of complying with government regulations will help to reduce the incentives for firms to operate in the informal sector. In addition, opportunities for linking informal sector firms with formal sector firms should be seized.

Governments should make greater efforts to facilitate women's entry into high-productivity market activities by removing obstacles to their access to productive assets such as education, capital, and land to support entrepreneurship. Regulations that prevent women from having equal employment opportunities need to be eliminated.

The challenge of youth unemployment merits special attention. The education system — including vocational training — should provide youth with education and skills that respond better to the needs of the private sector. On-the-job training and apprenticeships can help the youth adapt better to the work environment of the private sector.

Finally, government plays a key role in hiring new graduates and setting public sector wages. Public sector hiring and wage policies should take into account the realities of the macroeconomic situation and avoid maintaining wages and non-wage benefits more generous than in the private sector.

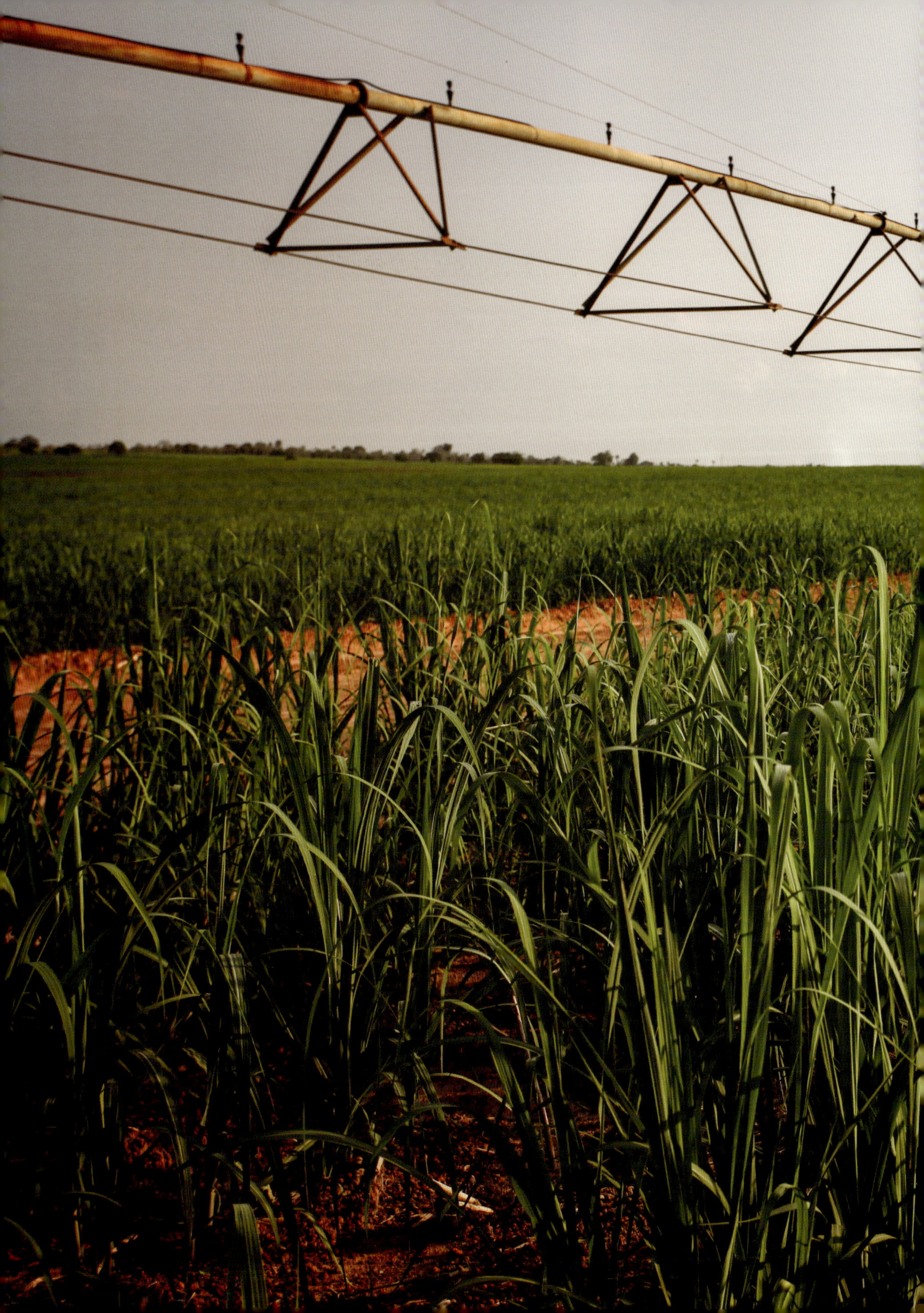

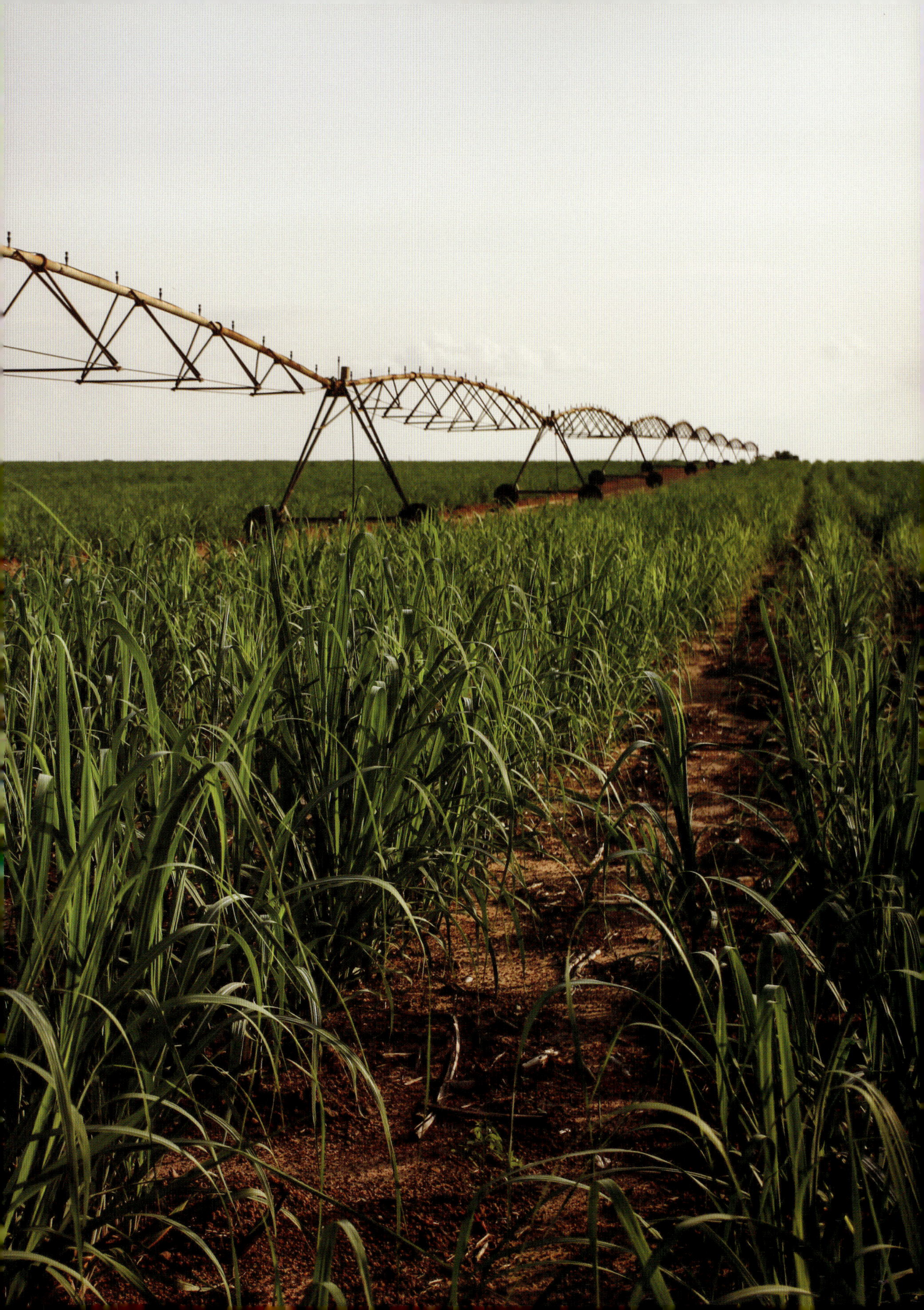

Transforming African Agriculture

Chapter 11

John Murray McIntire

Africa has long and unsuccessfully confronted the linked problems of agricultural growth and food security. Beginning in the 1970s both agricultural and food production per capita fell for 20 years across Africa. There has been a gradual revival of agriculture since the early 1990s, in parallel to the recovery of political stability and economic growth. But agriculture faces expanded challenges in this century that must be met if the problems of food security, agricultural growth, and employment are to be solved. Africa can meet those challenges, but only if it invests adequately in infrastructure, incentives, research, social protection, and the global public goods of biodiversity and carbon sequestration.

The Challenges

The challenges to African agriculture are: (i) raising agricultural productivity to accelerate the delayed shift of labor and national product into industry and services; (ii) slowing high population growth, which leads to greater land pressure and progressively blocks the traditional avenue of rural growth via land expansion; (iii) seizing the opportunity provided by economic growth in the service, industrial, and natural resource sectors, which will expand demand and induce technical and land use changes, including both farm consolidation and farm fragmentation; (iv) addressing the chronic problems of food insecurity and malnutrition and their relation to the fiscal and management capacities of African states; (v) mitigating climate change, whose effects are projected to be especially adverse for Africa's agricultural potential; and (vi) developing public policies — investments and incentives — that reverse the historic discrimination against agriculture and stimulate it to reach its potential.

This chapter first reviews the productive potential of African agriculture in 2010 and then sketches a vision of African agriculture, organized around feasible agricultural development paths through 2050. It focuses on crop agriculture, about which the most reliable and comprehensive projections have been

Note: The author acknowledges the advice of Gerald C. Nelson and Mark Rosegrant of the International Food Policy Research Institute (IFPRI), and of Mario Herrero and Dolapo Enahoro of the International Livestock Research (ILRI), in obtaining, using, and interpreting the results of the IFPRI IMPACT model of global agriculture.

made. It then defines obstacles to development along those paths before concluding with recommendations about removing or avoiding those obstacles. The chapter makes general recommendations across the paths on public investment and incentive policies and on policies affecting the returns to private interests. It does not make country-level recommendations or specific projections of outcomes.

Economic Growth and Agriculture

Africa's growth saga is well known. Growth of gross national income (GNI) per capita was negative across much of Sub-Saharan Africa, and at times in North Africa, until the new century. It has since expanded at an average of slightly more than 2 percent per year, with many countries growing rapidly toward middle-income status stimulated by economic reforms, an end to many conflicts, infrastructure investments, a rapid increase in the numbers of educated people, and, in some countries, development of natural resources.

It is very likely that African countries can continue to grow and even increase their rate of growth as their secondary, tertiary, and natural resource sectors expand. Even if agriculture's growth rate is slower than that of services and industry, development of secondary and tertiary sectors will benefit agriculture by providing demand for food and other rural goods, by lowering input and intermediation costs (notably transport and logistics), by developing broader financial markets, and by generating urban income to remit to rural residents.

This chapter develops two scenarios of agricultural growth in Africa linked to the Africa 2050 macroeconomic model used to develop the aggregate scenarios described in Chapter 1 and the IFPRI IMPACT model (IFPRI 2012). The Africa 2050 model estimates GDP as a function of labor force, capital stock, and total factor productivity (TFP) for 186 countries and is described in Annex 2. The IFPRI work takes exogenous rates of population growth and per capita income growth (IFPRI 2012) and projects them forward in a model designed chiefly to evaluate the effect of climate change on poverty and food security. We refer mainly to the Africa 2050 model in discussing economic growth at the country level and mainly to the IFPRI IMPACT model in discussing constraints to moving along defined agricultural development paths.

The Africa 2050 scenario presented in Chapter 1 classifies countries as "early convergers" (countries whose total factor productivity (TFP) is converging with that of advanced economies), "late convergers" (countries whose TFP begins to converge with that of advanced economies over the next decade), and fragile countries (whose TFP grows more slowly than that of the advanced economies). TFP growth is driven by technological change, sectoral shifts of labor (notably from agriculture to industry and services), better education, and more productive infrastructure. The three scenarios (convergence, business-as-usual, and downside) discussed in Chapter 1 reveal dramatic differences in economic outcomes, including per capita income, by 2050 based primarily on differences in productivity growth (see Table 11.1)

Table 11.1 — Incomes in 2050 depend crucially on productivity growth assumptions

	Annual Per Capita Income Growth Rate, 2012-2050 (%)		
	2050 Scenarios		
	Convergence	Business-as-usual	Downside
Africa	4.7	1.9	0.9
— early convergers	4.9	2.0	1.1
— late convergers	3.5	1.4	0.3
Asia	4.2	4.2	4.2

	Per Capita GDP as share of Global Average (%)			
	2011	2050 Scenarios		
		Convergence	Business-as-usual	Downside
Africa	27	52	20	14
— early convergers	30	64	23	17
— late convergers	32	41	20	13
Asia	64	106	115	117

Source: Centennial Group International 2013

Several regularities of economic growth affect agriculture and are common to the vision defined here: (i) agriculture's shares of GDP, population, and the labor force fall as GDP per capita grows; (ii) agriculture's value added grows under the impetus of technical change and market access, and (iii) as a result of the first two, agriculture's labor productivity rises.[1] While Africa has lagged in the transition to higher rural productivity (Binswanger-Mkhize, McCalla, and Patel 2010), and in the associated demographic shifts, there is no reason to expect that it will do so forever. Indeed, countries that have grown more rapidly in the past decade have begun to show a decline in the labor and GDP shares of agriculture as other sectors have advanced.

The growth of population and population density will vary.[2] Growing population will lead to higher population density in good agricultural areas; density will increase more slowly in marginal and protected areas. Total population (rural population) grew at a rate of 2.7 percent (1.9 percent) from independence until 2010. As discussed in Chapter 5, Africa's late demographic transition means that its population growth will continue at only a modestly diminished rate for many years, with the result that even the UN's medium variant population projections foresee 2.4 billion in Africa by 2050 (132 percent more than in 2010) (UN 2013).

---

1. Discussed for instance in Collier and Dercon (2009) and in Binswanger-Mkhize, McCalla, and Patel (2009).
2. The models referred to for this paragraph vary, which creates some inherent error in the resulting calculations. The population projections are the UN medium scenario (UN 2013). The projected areas in the major crops are from the IFPRI IMPACT Model (IFPRI 2012).

Some of the basic transformations will happen by 2050 (Table 11.2). The demographic transition will have occurred as population growth will have fallen to slightly more than 1.5 percent across all convergence groups.

Table 11.2 | **African incomes can grow faster than population in the convergence scenario**

	2010	2030	2050
Total population, millions			
Early convergers	647.0	958.1	1295.2
Late convergers	127.6	197.4	273.2
Fragile	253.4	396.7	548.7
Population growth, annual %			
Early convergers	2.4%	2.0%	1.5%
Late convergers	2.5%	2.2%	1.6%
Fragile	2.7%	2.3%	1.6%
GDP per capita, 2010 PPP$			
Early convergers	3299	7692	21741
Late convergers	3591	5278	13937
Fragile	1862	3403	8513

Source: Centennial Group International 2013

Farming population density — the ratio of rural population to the projected area in the major crops — will rise by nearly 20 percent from 2010 to 2050 among early convergers. Stress on farming land resources will therefore be relatively high because of the incomplete transition of labor from rural to urban areas. This stress will be acute in the fragile states, which would have endured 40 years of slow growth and be confronted, in 2050, with a much higher level of farming population density, much greater internal income inequality, and a much smaller share of regional income.

African Agriculture in 2010

The broad performance of African agriculture has been summarized in Binswanger-Mkhize, McCalla, and Patel (2009), by the InterAcademy Council (2004), and the McIntyre et al. (2009) and is highlighted in Box 11.1. The salient features of African agriculture are its low land and labor productivity, small export shares, lower food security, and greater weather risks compared to other regions.

Three broad factors — rapid population growth, slower growth of cultivated land than of population, and slower growth in irrigated area — led to falling productivity after independence in the 1960s. Almost without exception, the continent saw falling per capita agricultural and cereals production until about 1990. There has been some recovery over the past two decades, but output is now barely 10 percent higher than it was in 1990.

Box 11.1 | African agriculture performance (by Koji Makino)

Agriculture is the principal source of employment and of poverty reduction in Africa. It accounts for 64 percent of the continent's employment, 34 percent of its GDP, and one third of its economic growth (World Bank 2008).

The real growth rate for the agricultural sector averaged a low 2.2 percent between 2002 and 2006 but doubled to an average of 4.4 percent between 2007 and 2011. Grain production in Africa tripled from 1961-1963 to 2008-2010 (UNDP 2012) mainly because of an expansion in the harvested areas (see Figure 11.i). Agricultural productivity itself (cereal yield per hectare) virtually stagnated. In contrast, Asia achieved its green revolution and substantially increased its production mainly on the basis of steady improvements in its agricultural productivity. Yields in Africa are around one-third the levels in Asia and Latin America.

Figure 11.i: Increases in African agricultural output have largely come from increased harvested areas, not higher yields

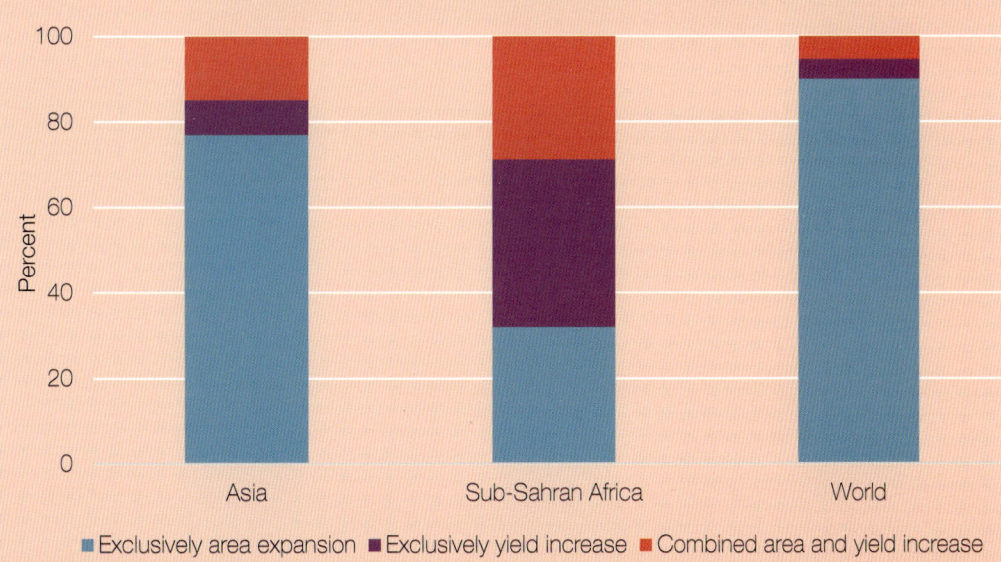

■ Exclusively area expansion ■ Exclusively yield increase ■ Combined area and yield increase

Source: UNDP 2012

Although Africa increased its production through expansion of cultivated land in the past, population pressure has meant a decrease in per capita cultivated land. Combined with stagnant productivity, this has resulted in a 13 percent reduction in per capita cereal production between 1961-1963 and 2008-2010.

> **Box 11.1** | **African agriculture performance (by Koji Makino) (continued)**
>
> Strong population pressure combined with economic growth has led to a rapid increase in food consumption and demand. The imbalance between domestic supply and demand was addressed by boosting the volume of cereal imports (see Figure 11.ii), resulting in much higher import dependence — 74 percent for wheat and 41 percent for rice.
>
> **Figure 11.ii: The trade deficit in cereals has widened for Sub-Saharan Africa over the past 40 years**
>
> *Source:* UNDP 2012
>
> Food expenses account for 50 to 70 percent of each household's budget, much higher than in other regions. As a result, households are particularly vulnerable to external conditions, such as poor weather and price hikes. Africa is the only region where the number of hungry grew over the past two decades from 175 million to 235 million. The prevalence of hunger stands at about 23 percent — with nearly one in four hungry (FAO, IFAD, and WFP 2012).
>
> Transforming agriculture in Africa to boost production dramatically is one of Africa's major challenges.

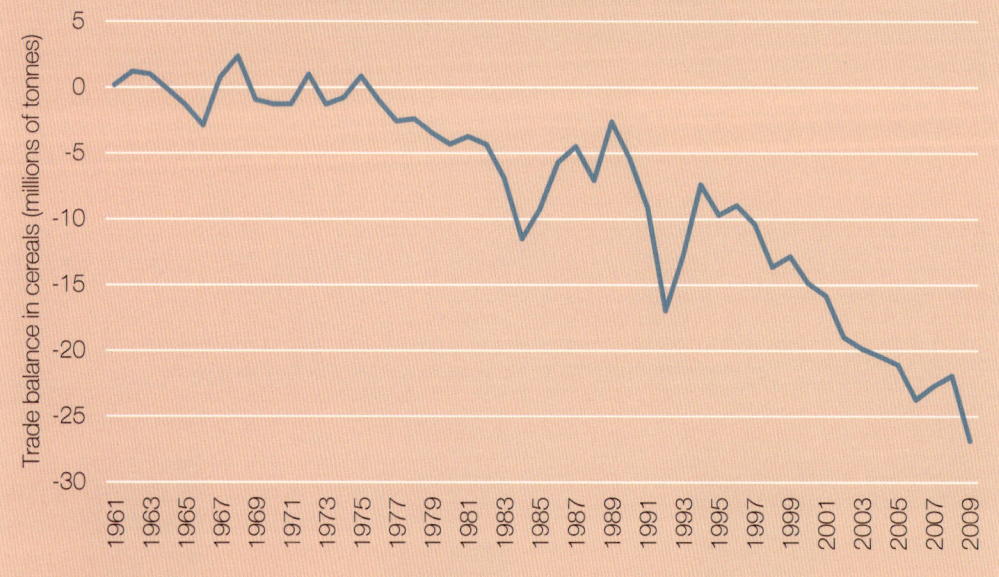

The productivity of rural Africa is low compared to urban. The value of agricultural GDP is now roughly $250 billion, half of which is accounted for by North Africa alone. The ratio of urban-to-rural GDP per capita in 2010 was 2.0 in North Africa and an astonishing 5.5 in Sub-Saharan Africa.

The corresponding ratios are 4.0 in China, 2.7 in Vietnam, 2.1 in Mexico, and 2.7 in India (IFPRI 2012). Realizing Africa's agricultural productivity potential would not only improve trade competitiveness and food security, it would almost reduce urban-rural inequalities.

African remains the least food-secure region. Estimates of annual per capita food production growth across Sub-Saharan Africa were on average only 0.2 percent in the 1990s. The number of Africans classified as "food insecure" was estimated at more than 30 percent in the 1990s. The food-insecurity situation barely improved after 2000 and deteriorated during the world grain price increases of 2007-2008 and 2010.

Another measure of food insecurity is malnutrition, where Africa is also at great risk. Estimates of the shares of malnourished persons in total populations across Sub-Saharan Africa were on average more than 25 percent in the 1990s. Corresponding values in Algeria, Egypt, and Tunisia were only 4 to 6 percent in 2000 but were dramatically higher in Morocco at nearly 20 percent of the population. The least food-secure nations are those with rapid population growth (e.g., Kenya), those in marginal agricultural environments with low and variable rainfall (e.g., Niger, Chad, Mali), or those where HIV/AIDS has been most severe (e.g., southern Africa).

Agriculture Paths to 2050

Most African agriculture will evolve along one of five broad paths for Sub-Saharan Africa and two for North Africa. The paths are to a large extent determined by the characteristics of land and the availability of water. In the transformation scenario, there can be some movement of land between paths, mostly from Path 4 to Path 1. But much of the change in output will come from a more productive use within the path. The paths are:

- Sub-Saharan Africa
    - Path 1 — Extensive, mechanized farming
    - Path 2 — Intensive export farming
    - Path 3 — Intensive peri-urban farming
    - Path 4 — Subsistence farming
    - Path 5 — Reserves, game ranching, and tourism
- North Africa
    - Path 6 — Irrigated farming
    - Path 7 — Rainfed farming

In moving along these paths, much of African agriculture in 2050 could overcome a century of foreign domination and bad policy to achieve global success in a continent that is very different from the present.

The baseline scenario discussed below is based on the IFPRI IMPACT model, which begins with country classifications by population variables (size, growth, rural/urban shares), productivity growth (crop yields), cropped areas, consumer demand by commodity, and climate change scenarios. The model generates crop yields as functions of the climate change scenarios. It projects rates of growth in cropped area and multiplies crop yields times cropped areas to give crop production. Those outputs enter a multi-market model of international trade to generate prices, consumption, and international trade values.

Under a transformation scenario Africa would have many more high- and middle-income consumers and trade partners. Agriculture would produce a much lower share of national incomes and employment. Median economies would be middle income, and several would be high income. Most countries would be heavily urbanized, creating a great diversity in population density within and across countries. Nearly all would have much lower trading costs, internally and with the rest of the world. And rapid technical changes in world agriculture would have been developed and applied in Africa, making its rural workers more competitive and export-oriented.

Table 11.3 shows the evolution of area and value of production along each of the seven paths for a baseline scenario and a transformation scenario. The transformation scenario involves changing present agricultural systems into ones that are: (i) a much smaller share of GDP; (ii) a much smaller share of the labor force; (iii) more productive in returns of land, labor, and investment; (iv) more market oriented, with Path One and Path Two having become major exporters; and (v) much more input-intensive, especially for modern planting materials, fertilizers, and irrigation water.

The transformation scenario involves a shift of land and labor between paths, faster development of irrigation, and accelerated yield increases to approach those of other emerging market countries. In the transformation scenario the paths would, with one exception, be commercial and oriented to international trade, be competitive with the least-cost global exporters, generate profits and wages that provide middle to high incomes for rural people, and create significant environmental risks that require regional and international cooperation to mitigate.

The discussion of the paths to 2050 takes first the perspective of what the major production systems can be expected to look like in 2050, and second the perspective of what must be done to remove obstacles along those paths so as to create those systems in 2050. Despite the common aspects by 2050, the paths of African agriculture will diverge greatly with respect to their enterprise composition, shares of GDP, share of the labor force, labor productivity, and trade orientation. These divergent paths have common policy measures needed to move along them, and those measures are discussed with respect to the chief obstacles. With respect to TFP in agriculture, we discuss below the potential for and barriers to technical change and more productive infrastructure.

The paths sketched below show what African agriculture can look like in 2050 — a mix of much more high-technology commercial farming, much less subsistence agriculture, and much less low-yield pastoralism. The transformation of African agriculture toward competitive commercial farming along the seven paths will require broad policy measures: (i) much better infrastructure and research services to shift rainfed lands from less to more productive paths, which will allow farmers to achieve yields more like that of the better lands in Sub-Saharan Africa and elsewhere in the world; (ii) much faster irrigation development and better water management in both Sub-Saharan Africa and North Africa; and (iii) a

Table 11.3 — Agricultural production would grow dramatically in the transformation scenario

	Area, ha million			Value of Production, $bn		
	2010	2050(a)	2050(b)	2010	2050(a)	2050(b)
Path 1: Extensive mechanized rainfed farming	43	58	115	30	64	529
of which, irrigated	4	7	31	3	12	205
of which, rainfed	39	51	84	27	52	324
Path 2: Intensive export farming	51	73	99	73	168	725
of which, irrigated	0	1	0	2	10	78
of which, rainfed	51	72	99	70	158	648
Path 3: Intensive peri urban farming	49	70	81	67	160	563
of which, irrigated	1	2	5	4	16	125
of which, rainfed	48	68	77	63	144	438
Path 4: Subsistence farming	54	76	60	47	113	254
of which, irrigated	1	1	2	2	10	81
of which, rainfed	53	75	58	45	104	172
Path 5: Reserves, game ranching, tourism	34	49	43	38	93	226
of which, irrigated	2	4	10	3	14	116
of which, rainfed	32	44	32	35	79	110
Path 6: North African irrigated farming	8	9	14	32	63	278
Path 7: North African rainfed farming	19	20	23	26	47	116
Total	257	354	435	313	710	2690

Source: IFPRI 2012
Note: 2050(a) IFPRI baseline scenario; 2050(b) Agricultural transformation scenario

general convergence of crop yields toward world levels on both irrigated and rainfed lands throughout the continent, including the faster irrigation development under the second set of policy measures. Path One and Path Two are particularly important as they offer the greatest potential for income and export growth.

Five of the paths lead to prosperity in 2050, but prosperity is only possible with much higher productivity than is expected in the baseline scenario. We first describe the principal characteristics of the paths and then discuss the transformational measures required to push these paths to faster convergence with rural incomes and productivity in competitor countries.

Appendix 1 provides projections of the baseline scenario cropped areas by path for the principal grains (maize, wheat, sorghum, millet, and rice), oilseeds and legumes (soybean, groundnut, edible beans) and others (cassava, yams, sugarcane, fibers, fruits, and vegetables). Appendix 2 provides projections of the baseline scenario yields for the same goods. Appendixes 1 and 2 are derived from the IFPRI IMPACT Model and do not reflect the changes in productivity needed to reach the convergence scenario.

Agricultural Paths in Sub-Saharan Africa

Path 1 — Extensive mechanized farming

Path 1 offers major opportunities for increased production and exports. This system will cover most of the semi-arid and sub-humid areas with good market access, including parts of West Africa from Guinea to Cameroon and East/Southern Africa from Angola, through Zambia and the DRC, to Tanzania. In terms of farming systems, Path 1 will be "maize-dominant" and "cereal-root crop mixed" systems (Dixon, Gulliver, and Gibbon 2001).

In the baseline scenario of Path 1, there would only be modest growth rates of area (irrigated or rainfed) and of value of production per hectare. The value of production would have grown at an annualized rate of 1.9 percent from 2010 through 2050. Among the rainfed crops, wheat, cotton, cassava, and sorghum would have gained ground with respect to maize, while rice and vegetables would have grown the most rapidly among the irrigated crops.

The transformation scenario of Path 1 would produce quite dramatic changes in area, production, and the value of production by 2050. The area under irrigated farming would have expanded at an annual rate of 5.1 percent (compared to 1.4 percent in the baseline). The value of production (irrigated and rainfed) would be more than four times as much as in the baseline; the value of production per hectare would have grown at an annualized rate of 4.7 percent compared to 1.1 percent in the baseline.

The transformation of Path 1 — the most export-oriented and high-income form of African agriculture in 2050 — is in essence a move out from Paths 3, 4, and 5. In other words, land formerly used less productively moves into Path 1, where yields rise more rapidly owing to better land conditions, cheaper transport, more input use, and the planting of more productive crops. The transformation scenario's effects on area, output, and value of output would, in turn, induce major secondary changes in land use, technology, and production relations.

Land use. The countries contributing the most to Path 1 are Tanzania, Angola, Zambia, Zimbabwe, DRC, and, in West Africa, Guinea, Cote d'Ivoire, Ghana, Nigeria, and Cameroon. In those countries, Path 1 will evolve on two tracks of land use. The first is what has happened elsewhere in the land abundant world — the United States, Canada, Brazil, Thailand — by expansion of new or existing farms onto unused land. The second track involves consolidation of small and medium-sized farms into larger ones. In the transformation scenario, these tracks would have joined by 2050 and the path would look like its counterparts in what are now the upper- and middle-income countries, with much larger median farm size and many fewer small subsistence farms. This path was blocked until market access improved — road, rail, and rarely inland water transport costs fell sharply as investments in infrastructure paid off and as competition developed in the transport industries, forcing costs to fall and making farmers more able to export or to compete with imports in regional markets.

Resources, scale, and technology. Fertile soils and abundant land will allow crop and livestock production at export parity costs. The principal commodities would be maize, rice, cassava, soybeans, groundnuts, and cotton. Average farm sizes will be more than 50 hectares and, at the extreme, would cover thousands of hectares. Farm size will grow under two forces. Large enterprises will be started in less populated areas (see, for example, World Bank 2009a for an extended discussion of the middle rainfall zone known as the Guinea Savannah) where commercial opportunities are good; this is most likely in Zambia, Angola, Mozambique, and parts of Tanzania. Second, large farms will emerge from the consolidation of small farms and underused land as laborers leave rural areas for urban jobs and, in so doing, sell or rent their lands; this is most likely in West and Central Africa.

Such farms would spread across the intermittent rainfall zones (600-1500 mm/year) and irrigation would not generally be used in production except for paddy. There would be mechanization for land clearing and preparation, cultivation, weeding, application of chemicals, harvesting, transport, and processing. The farms along this Path would use modern plant cultivars and be involved in continuous global research to develop new cultivars adapted to hotter, more variable climates. Their crop productivity per unit of land and per unit of labor would be competitive with the best global regions. Finally the large increase in production would both meet domestic demand and permit a major increase in exports to world markets.

Production relations. Farming would be exclusively commercial, incomes would be high, and poverty would have largely disappeared, except among landless workers with few skills. Farmers would use markets for land, products, inputs, finance, and risk management. The larger enterprises that will become characteristic of Path 1 farms would be managed by a class of influential farmers who would be important in domestic politics and in world trade discussions, given the importance of global markets for their businesses and given the financial weight of their enterprises. The power of these businesses and their political influence in the countryside would tilt labor relations toward large producers and against laborers and competing small producers. Foreign direct investment will not be a necessary condition for large farms, but there will be substantial FDI as a source of technology and market access.

Specific barriers to Path 1. The principal obstacles to the expansion along Path 1 are national land administration systems that discourage commercial investment in agriculture; poor logistics at ports and on domestic roads and rails; financial constraints in normal years and periodic crises caused by domestic inflation or over-borrowing on land values; water conflicts domestically and with neighboring countries; and intellectual property issues related to cultivars and farm chemicals. Regulatory demands involving foreign and domestic trade, intellectual property, logistics, and water markets will require new capacities in national administrations.

Land conflicts. Path 1 farming will pose special problems for the more land-abundant African countries. These countries — Angola, Tanzania, the DRC, Zambia, parts of Nigeria, South Sudan, and parts of West Africa — have underused land, so they are under constant pressure, foreign and domestic, to give land to potential large farmers who argue that they can use it more productively than small farmers. Given the weakness of many national land administrations, the land-abundant countries run the risk of depriving local communities of their land rights, leading to the same kinds of land conflicts that have occurred in Brazil or in parts of Asia.

Path 2 — Intensive export farming

Path 2 would extend and intensify the historical systems of beverage crops, spices, and other tree crops in humid areas with good market access.

In the baseline scenario of Path 2, there would be very slow growth of area (irrigated or rainfed) and of value of production per hectare. The value of production would have grown at an annualized rate of 2.1 percent from 2010 through 2050. Among the rainfed crops, cocoa and coffee would have grown slightly more rapidly than the others, while the food crops, notably maize and cassava, would barely have changed in area or in production. Irrigated farming would contribute very little to Path 2 in 2010 or in 2050 under the baseline scenario.

The transformation scenario of Path 2 would produce significant changes in area, production and the value of production by 2050. The transformation of Path 2 crop farming is more difficult than that of Path 1 because Path 2 depends significantly on tree crops (coffee, cocoa, oil palm, coconut, rubber, and cashew), which might be more sensitive to climate change and on roots and tubers (yams and cassava), whose rates of yield growth might be harder to sustain than those of the major cereals and oilseeds because of lower global research investment.

The main effect in Path 2 is for the value of production per hectare to grow much more rapidly — at an annual rate of 4.1 percent compared to 1.2 percent under the baseline. Because of rising yields in food crops compared to export crops, which are constrained by pests and diseases, the value of production of rice, maize, and cassava would have grown more rapidly than that of coffee and cocoa by 2050.

The transformation of Path 2 — a mix of export and food crops — is an intensification of existing sub-humid and humid cropping systems. There is not so much a shift of land among uses, as is seen in Path 1, as an extension of current trends in areas suited for Path 2 crops. The transformation scenario in Path 2's effects on area, output, and value of output would, in turn, induce fewer secondary changes in land use, technology, and production relations than Path 1. But new logistical problems, especially traceability, will develop in the export sectors.

Scale and technology. The commodities characterizing this system — coffee, cocoa, oil palm, rubber, sugarcane, pineapple, flowers, tea, timber — will be grown on a mix of large estates associated with processing, storage, and trade facilities, and smallholdings, which will be largely specialized and sell to the estates and other processors. Incomes per hectare will be high for owners and operators, though landless laborers, with few modern skills, will continue to be poor. This path will be completely novel in some respects — plant cultivars will be largely genetically modified organisms (GMOs), with traits both for production and consumption purposes. Agrochemical use will be rare because of organic food preferences in both export and African markets and because GMOs will make agrochemicals unnecessary in many situations.

Skilled labor use in processing will have replaced unskilled labor, and field techniques will be carefully managed to avoid the environmental costs of erosion and water pollution. In other respects, this path will look much like its predecessors. Techniques will be highly labor-intensive, field mechanization will be less common than in Path 1 (because of the practical impediments with mechanized cultivation and harvesting and related product quality problems), and the locus of production will remain in humid or highland areas. Exporting to OECD markets and to the middle-classes of China, India, and Latin America with organic preferences will impose strict product traceability standards, which will in turn require new skills in the public and private regulatory sectors.

Production relations. The share of sales in output will be 100 percent. Demand from middle- and high-income African markets will have grown substantially and will induce growth of specialty products for regional consumption as well as for export. African countries, after a long struggle to move beyond primary production and first-transformation, will have industrialized to the extent that they capture practically all of the value added from transforming Path 2 goods into consumer products (chocolate, processed coffee and tea, packaged fruits and vegetables, furniture). Product quality and traceability will have emerged as major advantages of African origins, especially for "organic" or "fair-trade" labels.

Political relations. Processing and trade will be undertaken by many fewer operators than will be production, because of nucleus estates and contract farming. Political influence will emerge from alliances between (the many) growers and (the fewer, richer) processors and exporters. Union movements will find it difficult to develop because of the costs of organizing many small- and medium-scale producers. But even in the absence of farmer's unions, labor relations will be contentious as producers' organizations will contest the market power of processing and trading firms, particularly if the latter continue to be dominated by foreign investors.

Path 3 — Intensive peri-urban farming

Path 3 will dominate domestic markets by producing a very wide variety of food crops, with a mix of power, fertilization, and irrigation techniques. Dairy cattle, poultry, and swine would constitute the bulk of livestock production.

Little would change *in the baseline scenario*. There would be modest growth of irrigation from a low base; rainfed areas (which are projected to be 97 percent of cropped area in 2050) would grow at an annualized rate of less than 1 percent, so that per capita rainfed areas would be less in 2050 than in 2010. Crop yields would barely grow at all in the rainfed areas. The value of production in rainfed areas would barely exceed the rate of population growth.

The transformation scenario to 2050 is modest. Irrigated area would grow slowly to be less than 10 percent of Africa's irrigated area in 2050. Rainfed areas would dominate (more than 15 times the area under irrigation in 2050), though the expansion of rainfed land in Path 3 would be limited by competition with urban land use. The value of output would grow much more rapidly in irrigated conditions; such growth in peri-urban areas is likely to create significant environmental costs and public health issues with agrochemicals that national regulators would have to manage carefully.

Scale and technology. The swelling of urban populations will have radically changed domestic food production. Farm size will vary greatly as small producers complete with large ones in many instances as the transport and communication scale penalties will have largely disappeared. Subsistence production will have been largely abandoned. Commercial growers for urban markets will use new and sophisticated techniques for producing fruits, vegetables, and condiment crops for urban markets (for example, the conurbations of Abidjan, Addis Ababa, Dakar, Dar es Salaam, Johannesburg, Khartoum, Kinshasa, Lagos, Maputo, and Nairobi). The production cycle will be nearly constant throughout the year and even throughout the day as abundant demand and cheaper energy allow processing, transport, and trade to occur 24 hours a day. GMO plant cultivars will have been developed for local demands and will be produced with irrigation and a wide mix of soil fertility and management techniques according to local soil, water, and climate circumstances. As with Path 2, extremely fast and reliable communications will allow even small growers to produce custom goods for markets at all distances.

Political relations. Political influence will emerge from groups of integrated growers, processors, and supermarket operators. Downstream labor relations will be contentious as union movements will develop against large, vertically integrated processing and trading firms. Land conflicts will occur constantly during the development of this type of farming because of competition between agriculture and urban land uses. Though many farmers will have become affluent, landlessness will be widespread and laborers without modern skills will always be on the margin of poverty as they can only find manual work that is difficult to mechanize.

Environmental costs. The constant pressure of insects and plant and animal diseases in the humid tropics will always harm the productivity of farming and stock-raising. Farmers and research systems must develop agrochemicals to block that pressure, generate better biological control, or develop plants and animals that resist diseases and parasites. The environmental costs of intensive peri-urban agriculture will be very high where pesticides are the principal control measure, especially the costs imposed by agrochemicals on workers' health and on water quality. The proximity of intensive agriculture to cities will cause large soil, water, and air pollution costs; reducing those costs so as to avoid large human and animal health costs will be the major job of national regulators. It is therefore most critical in Path 3 that new non-chemical controls be found, including through the use of biotechnology and integrated pest management.

Path 4 — Subsistence farming

The baseline scenario in Path 4 is a long and somber decline. Irrigated areas would have nearly vanished, and rainfed cropping would decline in per capita terms. Crop production would barely keep pace with population growth; much of new crop production would be in low value starches, notably pearl millet, sorghum, and cassava. Because of the shift of the better Path 3 lands into Path 1, there may even be yield declines in the baseline scenario of Path 4.

The transformation scenario of Path 4 would provide higher incomes than the baseline scenario but only under very optimistic assumptions about irrigation expansion and the value of production from each irrigated hectare. Because of the more rapid shift of the better Path 3 lands into Path 1 in the transformation scenarios, there are yield declines in the baseline scenario of Path 4 especially among food crops that receive little global research investment. All productivity indicators for Path 4 crops would remain well behind those achieved in other regions and far behind those in the more productive areas of other paths.

Path 4 will subsist in areas of sparse rainfall and poor market access, such as the northern Sahel, the upper highlands of East Africa, and the few areas that remain thinly settled in East and Southern Africa. Emigration from those areas will, through its effect on the labor force, cause the dependency ratio to rise. The share of poor people in this system will be the highest among the seven paths and, for that reason, demands for income support and other forms of social protection will be strongest on this path.

Scale and technology. Path 4 will most resemble the situation today in the semi-arid tropics of Africa and in the coldest, least accessible highlands. The main goods will be coarse grains (millet, sorghum, and maize), cassava, and ruminant livestock. Lack of technical change, persistently bad terms of trade related to high transport costs, and underinvestment in public infrastructure will have prevented incomes from growing. Because many workers will have left, owing to the scarcity of remunerative work, operated holding size may even have declined except on large ranches in the drier areas. Small farmers, using hand techniques and applying little or no mineral fertilizer, will continue to produce for subsistence needs, selling only sporadically in markets.

Political demands for support. These areas will remain poor and depend on government transfers for disaster relief, ordinary income support, infrastructure, and social capital. They will have little political influence except through populism based on "family farm" or "sons of the land" appeals. This class of farm will remain poor and will therefore demand financial support in exchange for political loyalty. Governments will be forced, as is now the case with isolated farming areas in middle-income and high-income countries, to choose between providing social protection for such areas or making major investments in infrastructure and social services that are disproportionate to those in more productive parts of the same country.

Path 5 — Reserves, game ranching, and tourism

Path 5 will be characterized by sparsely populated and lightly cultivated areas used for tourism, hunting, very extensive game ranching, and limited commercial forestry or set aside as preserves of biodiversity or carbon sequestration. This path, concentrated in East and Southern Africa, the hardwood forests of humid central Africa, parts of the Sudan, and parts of the Sahel, is the one with the greatest uncertainty related to climate change and global policies. The set-aside nature of these lands requires international political and financial assistance to create and defend them against agricultural and industrial encroachment.

Resources, scale, and technology. The few operational holdings — such as game ranches, tourism parks, and commercial forests — will be very large. If global assistance is forthcoming, then such areas will have: (i) low population density and employment; (ii) extensive activities — tourism, game ranching, hunting, conservation forestry, biodiversity, and carbon sequestration; and (iii) majority government ownership and management of resources. If such assistance is not forthcoming then the drier parts of these areas will be converted to commercial farming and ranching, while the wetter ones will be exploited for commercial forestry. If such reserves are private, their owners/managers will be politically influential because they will control rents. Labor conflicts will not be important because labor use in this system will be marginal. Land conflicts will be common and potentially violent as farmers in adjacent areas make claims on the reserves.

Developing Path 5 will require substantial external resources if significant areas of it are held to produce international public goods, such as biodiversity or carbon sequestration. The African countries will, justifiably, argue that if they incur opportunity costs in forestry, livestock, and agriculture, then they should be paid for doing so. Regional and continental cooperation will be needed to develop common positions to preserve these areas — the humid hardwood forests of the Congo Basin, the Serengeti, grazing areas of East Africa, and the West African Sahel — to prevent resource grabs by foreign investors or local governments.

Agricultural Paths in North Africa

Path 6 — Irrigated farming

The baseline scenario in Path 6 is for a long period of negative growth in per capita output caused by the limits on new irrigated areas and by the failure of crop yields to grow. The transformation scenario implies that the rate of growth of production value per hectare triples from 1.4 percent per year in the baseline scenario to 4.0 percent per year in the transformation scenario over the period 2010 to 2050.

Path 6 requires better water use efficiency to ensure the passage to global agriculture. The irrigated farming systems north of the Sahara are largely concentrated in Egypt, where rice and wheat are the major crops. The chief issue is water management so as to reduce production costs, unlike in Paths 1 and 3 (especially) where the main water issue is development of new irrigation. While North Africa — Libya,

Algeria, Egypt, extending southward into Sudan and Chad — is thought to have the largest volumes of groundwater storage and of renewable freshwater (MacDonald et al. 2012), it will be expensive to extract those volumes using boreholes for irrigation and/or urban uses. Realistic projections of irrigable area in Path 6 are that it cannot grow faster than 1 percent annually so the only expansion possibilities are diversifying the cropping pattern into higher-value crops and raising yields across the cropping pattern.

Path 7 — Rainfed farming

In Path 7, better land policies are needed to allow the consolidation of smaller into larger farms that is needed to accommodate the shift of workers from rural to urban jobs while meeting the demand for more production and more exports.

Path 7 will converge slowly in the physical sense that yields of its products — rainfed cereals and oilseeds, and orchard crops — will take many years to reach levels found in the temperate countries of Europe. The main form of convergence in Path 7 will be through the pressure of relative wages, which will induce mechanization and other technical changes that will cause Path 7 farming to become like that of its European and Latin competitors. Path 7 countries will become more competitive not because of reaching yields like those in Europe and Latin America, but because of reaching equivalent unit costs through having lower wages that compensate for inferior yields per unit of land.

Obstacles to Agricultural Transformation

Expansion of crop land, greater irrigation investment, better water management, and technical change to raise yields would improve rural incomes throughout Africa, with positive effects on malnutrition and income inequality between urban and rural areas. Realizing those effects across the principal agricultural paths in this vision of African agriculture to 2050 confronts obstacles in the forms of: (a) land availability arising from high population growth, (ii) water resources, (iii) climate change, (iv) technology generation and transfer, and (v) farm size and type.

Land availability and population growth

Population growth is a potential obstacle to agricultural development because higher population density increases land scarcity and reduces income per family in the absence of intensification.

Harvested area in Sub-Saharan Africa grew by about two-thirds from 1961 to 1999; it grew less rapidly in North Africa because of both moisture and land constraints. Overall cropland per capita has become scarcer; annual and permanent cropland fell by some 1.7 percent over the period 1961-2010, notably in Southern Africa. At the same time, irrigated area per capita failed to expand, falling by some 0.8 percent across Africa, especially in Central and South Africa, though it did expand modestly in Eastern Africa.

The FAO projects that harvested area (FAO 2010) will grow by another 39 percent from 1998 to 2030. The IFPRI IMPACT model projects that the rainfed and irrigated areas under the main cereal, oilseed, fiber, fruit, and vegetable crops will grow by 0.6 percent from 2010 to 2050 in the converging countries (about 1 percent in the late converging and fragile states). For the most populous countries (Nigeria, Ethiopia, and DRC, which account for 37 percent of Africa's harvested land in 2010), significant new land expansion per capita is only possible in parts of central Nigeria and in lower, hotter areas of western Ethiopia (leaving aside the special case of DRC where environmental and security reasons make it difficult to expand cropped area). Major new cultivation is only possible in a few of the Path 1 countries, notably Angola, Tanzania, Mozambique, and Zambia. *It is therefore likely that Africa will have reached a nearly constant total cultivated area by 2050 and that the most populous countries will have long since exhausted new land for crops and livestock.*

Water resources

The productivity gap between African and Asian agriculture and the rural growth gap over the past 40 years are due in part to the greater prevalence of irrigation in Asia. The area equipped for irrigation (Alexandratos and Bruinsma 2012) in Africa was only 6 million hectares between 2005 and 2007, which was some 3 percent of arable land, compared to 90 million hectares in South Asia (42 percent of arable land). The effect of irrigation is limited by the fact that three countries — Sudan, Madagascar, and South Africa — account for most of Sub-Saharan Africa's irrigated land.

The rates of growth of irrigation throughout Africa are low and have not risen. Growth of irrigated area was 1.9 percent from 1961-1997 but fell to 0.7 percent from 1997-2007 and is projected in the baseline scenario to fall to only 0.5 percent annually from 2007 to 2050. The growth of irrigated area in North Africa was only 0.12 percent from 2000 to 2010 and is projected (in the base line scenario) to be essentially zero from 2010 to 2050.

Irrigation has great potential in Africa but has to date contributed relatively little to agricultural growth. First, much of West and Central Africa is wet enough that sustainable agriculture is possible without irrigation; rainfall is heavy and sufficiently reliable that here is little demand for irrigation. Second, the major rivers in Africa cover many countries and cooperation among riparians on river basin management for irrigation and other purposes has been slow and expensive. Third, costs of irrigation development with full water control, on large and small farms alike, have been high.

A fourth issue is the accessibility of the large groundwater volumes south of the Sahara. A recent review finds that those volumes are quite large relative to those from annual rainfall and from surface water but warns that "Strategies for increasing the use of groundwater throughout Africa for irrigation and urban water supplies should not be predicated upon the widespread expectation of high yielding boreholes" because most of the groundwater in Africa south of the Sahara is of low yield (MacDonald 2012).

Technology generation and transfer

It is generally accepted that African soil resources are more fragile and have fewer nutrients than those of other continents. Agricultural expansion will therefore need more nutrients from fertilizers to accelerate the growth required to converge with other regions and to replace nutrients lost to depletion.

There is less agreement about how much of that expansion requires mineral fertilizer use. The FAO projects that agricultural production in Sub-Saharan Africa can grow at a rate of 2.5 percent (2.4 percent for crops) from 2010 to 2030 and at a rate of 2.1 percent (1.9 percent for crops) from 2030 to 2050 (Alexandratos and Bruinsma 2012). Of that growth, 20 percent would be attributable to cultivation of new land, 6 percent to higher cropping intensity, and 74 percent to higher yields per unit of land. The FAO projections create an annual average growth rate, therefore, of 1.3 percent across all crops and countries. The IFPRI IMPACT model, which takes climate change into account, implies that it will be difficult to generate such yield increases in many situations. For example, average maize yields in Nigeria, Tanzania, Sudan, Zimbabwe, and Ethiopia actually decline over the long term in the IMPACT model, as do those of irrigated rice in Cote d'Ivoire, Mali, Senegal, Tanzania, and Mozambique.

The dominant share of yield per unit of land in higher output focuses attention on the gaps between African crop yields and those in competing countries, especially in Path 1 crops (chiefly maize, rice, wheat, soybeans, groundnuts, and cotton) and irrigated rice (Paths 1 and 6). The FAO projects that African countries could close the yield gaps, even accounting for less favorable production conditions of water, soil, and temperature. Some of the gaps can be closed by using fertilizers more intensively.[3] The FAO projects that African fertilizer consumption would grow at an annual rate of 3.7 percent from 2005/07 to 2030 and at a rate of 3.1 percent from 2030 to 2050; the corresponding rates per hectare would be 3.1 percent and 2.6 percent, respectively. Those growth rates are projected to be more than nine times as high as those in developed countries and more than 2.5 times those in developing countries. The great majority of this additional fertilizer consumption would be on cereals and oilseeds in Path 1 and Path 3, with much less growth in root and tree crop systems (Path 2 and some of Path 3), as has been recent experience (InterAcademy Council 2004).

What are the barriers to more fertilizer use? The barriers to more fertilizer use are first information and second economic. Average fertilizer use per hectare or per farm has been low in many African countries because farmers lacked access to fertilizer or because they did not know how to use it well. This information barrier will become lower over time as information and transport services become cheaper, and it should not be a long-term issue, given the experience of rapid growth in fertilizer use in other developing countries with tight land constraints.

The principal constraint is economic. African farmers faced bad production incentives for many years, as shown in the Krueger, Schiff, and Valdes studies (1991-1992). Poor incentives, especially from suppression of producer prices and overvalued exchange rates, lowered output and input demand at the

---

3. Alexandratos and Bruinsma (2010) cite the work of Smil (2002), which found that nitrogen fertilizer contributed some 40 percent of the increase in per capita food production between 1950 and 2000, and that the share was even larger in Indian grain sector in the 1970s and 1980s.

same time, with a clearly adverse effect on fertilizer use and on soil fertility. While those incentives have greatly improved, the recent updating by Anderson and Masters shows that many African countries still repress farmers' incomes and their input use by continuing the bad policies of the past (2009). Weak incentives will always be a constraint to the use of fertilizers and nutrient-responsive cultivars. Realizing the long-term vision of African farming requires making incentives more competitive.

Barriers to intraregional trade in inputs constitute an additional economic constraint related to incentive distortions. Fertilizer trade within Africa is not important in 2010 (IFA 2010) but must become much larger as Africa develops its natural gas — needed to produce urea as a source of nitrogenous fertilizers on cereals — and as it develops its phosphate resources — needed to produce more oilseeds, grain legumes, cereals, and pasture crops.

What are constraints to more efficient fertilizer use? More efficient fertilizer use implies achieving more output for a given application of nutrients. The FAO projections note substantial historical gains in fertilizer efficiency, owing to precision agriculture and to biotechnology, although these gains have leveled off in advanced countries. There is potential for greater nutrient efficiency in poor countries, from the same factors that have stimulated efficiency in rich countries. Other factors that will advance efficient fertilizer use in Africa, in all paths, are increased formal education and the learning-by-doing that will come from greater familiarity with fertilizer use.

Can organic or low-input farming complement mineral fertilizers? One possibility for increasing the efficiency of mineral fertilizer use is to complement it with organic fertilizers from biomass, notably animal manures, crop residues, and nitrogen-fixing plants. Extensive evidence, going back to experiments done in the 1930s in many farming systems, has shown that organic soil fertility management can improve crop productivity. At the same time, organic practices can make mineral fertilizers more efficient and can produce environmental benefits by limiting fertilizer runoff into bodies of water and improving the sustainability of soils.

While the benefits of organic soil fertility amendments are undeniable, it is not clear that such practices can raise productivity from a low base without modern plant cultivars and mineral fertilizers. After all, much of African farming is today organic and has been so for centuries, with the result that much of it remains unproductive. In addition, the expansion path of traditional low-input farming by land expansion has had adverse environmental effects because it has shortened fallows, induced deforestation, and extended into marginal lands where livestock would ordinarily be a better form of resource use.

Low-input farming offers limited sustained growth prospects because it is a form of recycling. Farmers can reap the benefits of such practices as applying manures, plowing under crop residues, intercropping with annual legumes, or fallowing with nitrogenous trees, but each cycle of application is less productive than the previous one to the point that organic systems reach a steady state unless there are incremental inputs in land or nutrients.

A second growth limitation to low-input practices is that they have opportunity costs in land use unless external resources can provide the organic inputs. Producing animal manures requires pasture or browse land; intercropping with legumes reduces the area in the main crop; fallowing removes land from the crop production cycle. The limitations imposed on low-input farming by cycle losses and by land scarcity do not mean that organic farming should be discouraged; they do mean that efforts to promote low-input farming must be complemented by crop innovations that respond to low input levels and that fetch higher prices in organic markets.

A third issue with low-input practices is that they are highly labor-intensive. While labor intensity can substitute for fertilizers and other chemical inputs to some extent in maintaining yields per unit of labor, labor-intensive farming as an economy-wide strategy is limited because it does not allow labor to move to other sectors.

Farm size and type

The core policy question of farm size — should policy promote large or small farms — is often misunderstood as having a single answer that is applicable to most situations.[4] This question can only be answered with respect to the level of rural wages compared to the scarcity of land and to the costs of mechanization, all of which vary across farming systems and evolve over time. Answers about farm size in African agriculture are more complex than on other continents because of its extreme heterogeneity, and it is impossible to say that one type or scale of farm enterprise should be the model across many situations. It is, in fact, dangerous to attempt to do so because it leads to land grabs in the name of higher productivity.

Beyond the false question of optimal farm size, the scenarios shown here cannot shed light on the evolution of farm size because existing models either do not treat population shifts appropriately (Nelson et al. 2010) or because they do not analyze changes in sectoral GDP in enough detail (Kohli, Syzf, and Arnold 2012). Despite these gaps in the path analysis, we can summarize here much of what is known on the subject.

When wagers are relatively low, small farms do not inherently produce at higher unit costs than large ones, provided that they have market and input access that is comparable to large farms. In some instances, small farmers may even produce at lower costs on small farms because they employ family labor for which they incur lower supervision costs and hence achieve better net productivity; larger farms must use hired labor, with higher supervision costs, or mechanization and hence have difficulty achieving significantly higher productivity than small farms. As relative wages rise or as land becomes scarcer, both selective mechanization and hiring occur. These developments slowly begin to favor larger farms because they can bear the higher fixed costs of draft animals or machines and because they can manage hired labor more effectively through skilled employees or contracts that provide better incentives to workers. But even where mechanization and hiring have become common, there is a range of

---

4. Paul Collier asks: "Is an exclusive commitment to smallholders warranted?" (Collier and Dercon 2009).

farm sizes and types — for example, in cotton-growing areas of West Africa, in maize-growing regions of East and Southern Africa, or among coffee producers of East Africa — that can compete in the same markets. In such conditions there is no strong profitability reason to favor large farms, especially farms that are 50 to 1000 times the size of small and medium ones, and there are strong equity reasons not to favor very large farms. The only reason to favor large farms with policy incentives is where good land is abundant, where that land has no local claimants, and where profitable output markets exist.[5] In such cases, standard investment incentives can be given to large operators under the relevant national investment codes, subject to environmental and social safeguards because of the risks of land grabs and/or the risks of environmental damage associated with large scale production of some goods (especially livestock, sugar cane, and cotton).

Smallholders are currently important with regard to shares of output, input demand, and employment. Their productivity is comparable enough — sometimes greater, sometimes lesser — to large farms that there is no reason to discriminate against small farms. Moreover, small farms are the victims of discrimination in many instances, notably in access to water and finance, so that their relative productivity would be even better were such discrimination to be eliminated.

The competitiveness of small holders will change over time. As African economies shift into manufacturing and services, labor will move out of rural jobs and into urban ones (Ferroni 2012). One result of this move will be farm consolidation, especially in the grain-oilseeds-fibers system (Path 1) because it is more generally mechanized in response to rising wages than the other systems. The inevitable reduction in the number of small farms in much of Africa does not mean that small farms should be ignored with respect to access to markets and inputs. It does mean their weight in policy discussions will fall over time and will become more concentrated in farming systems (especially the second and third paths) where crop type, lesser need for large scale irrigation, and market proximity will favor labor intensive small farms over large mechanized farms.

African farms achieve lower yields and are uncompetitive in world markets for the most heavily traded crops — maize, wheat, rice, and soybeans. One reason is low use of fertilizers and modern plant cultivars, despite recent progress in maize, wheat, and rice. Clearly Path 1 will require higher input use because it cannot achieve yields competitive with those of North American, Latin American, or European producers of grains, oilseeds, and fibers without using more modern variable inputs. Because these inputs are divisible, the requirement for more variable inputs per unit of land does not strengthen the case for interventions in favor of large farms.

---

5. "No local claimants" is extremely unlikely, so it is more realistic to say "where local claimants can be fairly compensated for their lands" including the value of lost access to water, grazing, hunting and other common properties.

Dependence on higher quantities of variable inputs in Path 1 (especially) implies that farmers using more variable inputs depend more on lower logistic costs (e.g., port charges for fertilizers), more on financial intermediation because their cash needs are deeper, and more on research outputs because the cultivars they plant require constant updating from research in order to maintain competitiveness, respond to new plant diseases, and adapt to changing factor prices.

China's experiences provide valuable insights on the questions of farm size and input use. After the policy reforms of the late 1970s, China raised its agricultural output and productivity growth substantially despite most of its producers being small farmers (Fan, Nestorova, and Olofinbiyi 2010). At the same time its small farmers increased input use, notably water and fertilizers. The Chinese experience shows that small farm size can support higher productivity and lower poverty, while absorbing the higher quantities of inputs needed to raise productivity. We do not minimize the difficulty of replicating this experience in Africa, but China's experience shows that small farms are not an insurmountable obstacle to Africa's agricultural transformation provided that policy does not discriminate against them.

Transport costs are a particular burden on small farmers. A cross-country study (Dorosh et al. 2012) found "a statistically significant association between travel time and agricultural production in [Sub-Saharan Africa]"; and that "improvements in road [infrastructure] could facilitate a substantial increase in agricultural production [in a case study of Mozambique]."

Many studies have shown that isolation is associated with lower rural productivity, more poverty, and greater risk of catastrophic losses of assets.[6] Unit transport costs are high because (i) roads are absent or bad, (ii) fuel prices are high, and (iii) the strength of competition weakens as a function of remoteness to markets and size of markets, causing prices to rise. A recent survey by World Bank staff (Teravaninthorn and Raballand, 2008) found that *transport prices paid* by African users are elevated. It did not find that transport *costs* are especially high compared to other continents. It found that *prices paid by users* exceed the sum of fixed and variable costs because lack of competition, often caused by weak policy, allows operators to take rents (i.e., prices to users are higher than the total costs of providers).

Climate change

Climate change will constitute a general obstacle to Africa's agricultural transformation (see Chapter 15). High rates of yield growth are needed in the major crops if African farming is to catch up to that in its chief developing country competitors. The many recent studies on climate change have shown that tropical countries may not achieve such high rates of yield growth because of the risks from higher and more variable temperatures, more variable rainfall, and more violent storms, all of which might cause lower potential productivity.[7] A summary from the IPCC found that "… climate change is likely to reduce potential agricultural output in the long term" and that "… adverse effects are especially marked in Africa"

---

6. Thurlow and Wobst (2004) found rural poverty in Zambia to be higher in remote areas; Stifel and Minten (2003) showed rural poverty to be higher, and rice productivity to be lower, in more remote places of Madagascar. Binswanger, Khandker, and Rosenzweig (1993) make this conclusion very broadly across Indian agriculture; as does Fafchamps (2003) for livestock production in Niger.
7. For more information, view Nelson et al. (2010), IFPRI (2012), Willenbockel (2012), and Cline (2007).

(Parry and Rosenzweig n.d). For example, estimates of cassava yield losses owing to climate change might be around 10 percent in low-income countries, the losses in rice and sorghum could be about 8 percent and, while there might be a small gain in maize yields, losses of wheat yield would be higher" (Nelson et al. 2010).[8]

A review of climate change in Africa, using both biophysical and economic models (Nelson et al. 2010) predicts that a baseline climate change scenario affecting temperature, water availability, and crop productivity would:

- Reduce yields of the major rainfed cereals in low-income (middle-income) developing countries by an average of 1.8 percent (2.2 percent) in maize and 1.5 percent (11.8 percent) in wheat over the entire period 2000 to 2050;
- Have minor effects on cassava and sorghum yields in both low-income and middle-income developing countries;
- Have a mixed effect on rice yields, increasing them slightly in low-income countries and reducing them by about 1 percent in middle income countries;
- Cause maize prices to rise by 68 percent in a baseline climate change scenario compared to one with perfect mitigation of climate change effects, with effects of 35 percent for rice and 31 percent for wheat;
- Have large effects on cropped area in some low-income countries, notably Nigeria, Niger, Sudan, Ethiopia, and Tanzania depending on the degree of climate change; and
- Increase numbers of malnourished children by about 10 percent in low- and middle-income developing countries alike, while having a small effect on calorie availability in both, all relative to the perfect mitigation scenario.

Parts of East and Southern Africa are likely to be among the most severely affected by climate change. A study of Malawi, Mozambique, South Africa, Tanzania, Uganda, and Zambia (Hertel, Burke, and Lobell, 2010) concluded that:

- The cereal price changes associated with a medium global warning scenario are modest, but those associated with warmer (cooler) scenarios could be much higher (lower);
- World price changes would affect global trade patterns, offering increased opportunities to African countries via higher prices for some exports;
- Under some pessimistic scenarios, climate change could cause staples prices to rise by some 10 to 60 percent by 2030 with the secondary effect that poverty rates could rise steeply in parts of Africa (Hertel, Burke, and Lobell 2012);
- Total poverty numbers would rise substantially in the six countries studied under the most severe warming (high-price) scenario; and
- Source of income affects the impact of global warming on incomes, with rural non-farm labor and urban labor being most adversely affected.

---

8. This refers to all low-income developing countries, not only those in Africa.

African countries need to at least plan for dealing with pessimistic case effects on the order of:
- Yield declines of up to 40 percent in South African maize;
- Smaller harvested areas in Nigeria, Ethiopia, and DRC, three of the four most populous countries;
- Declines in calorie availability in low- and middle-income countries alike; and
- Increases in numbers of malnourished children in low- and middle-income countries.

Action Agenda

Priority actions, described in more detail below, for promoting the transformation of agriculture to its most productive uses include:
- **Reducing population growth** to allow higher rural income per capita;
- **Promoting irrigation** as appropriate to the water availability and cropping patterns of each agricultural path;
- **Adapting the roles of the state** to support more productive agriculture by, as appropriate, changing existing roles (e.g., development and maintenance of infrastructure); developing new roles (e.g., supervision, regulation, and mediation); improving access to land; creating targeted social safety nets; promoting regional cooperation; and assuring access to world markets;
- **Promoting the acceleration of technical change** through investing in agricultural research and technology transfer, improving the sustainability of small farms, making use of biotechnology, and addressing human diseases that reduce agricultural labor productivity; and
- **Preparing for climate change.**

Reducing population growth

Long-term rapid population growth impedes the growth of rural incomes and explains in part the failure of much of rural Africa to converge with competitors. Population growth does not have a strong relation with the agricultural paths but is related to the two main sub-regions of the continent. The expected average rate of rural population growth in Sub-Saharan countries of 1.9 percent is nearly four times that of the 0.46 percent projected for China, India, Mexico, Turkey, and Vietnam and about 3.3 times as high as the rest of the globe. This is not true of the early convergers (Egypt, Morocco, and Tunisia) in North Africa, whose population growth rate is expected to decrease to 0.70 percent through 2050. *A declining rate of rural population growth that would allow higher rural incomes per capita is vital for Sub-Saharan Africa. Achieving such a decline requires better access to family planning services and assuring that women have equal access to health, education, and labor market opportunities* (see Chapter 5).

Promoting irrigation

Irrigation development will vary by scale and agricultural path because of water availability and the cropping patterns of each path. Both large-scale and small-scale irrigation will grow in Paths 1 and 3. Full water control is likely to remain unnecessary in path Two, which has better rainfall and crops that do not need irrigation. Irrigation may remain unprofitable for cost reasons in Paths 4 and 5. In Path 6, which is almost entirely irrigated, growth of cultivated land is projected to be very low through 2050 and hence growth can only come from higher yields through better water management.

Promoting irrigation along the various paths depends on national and international policies. Three measures will be particularly important at the national level. The first is to reduce the costs of irrigation development across all paths. Many countries continue to tax irrigation equipment, for example, which contributes to the high cost of water control on small operations. The second is to extend modern energy supplies, especially off-grid energy and renewables, so that the variable costs of lifting water become cheaper. The third is to promote competition in irrigation investment, just as in the transport industry, so that builders are less able to extract rents on water control investments.

Cross-border measures to promote irrigation are the most difficult and have to date taken generations.[9] Solving water management problems in the principal river basins and lakes to realize their irrigation potential will require years and strong political goodwill among riparian states. Such efforts are particularly important on large projects where multi-purpose uses of water (irrigation, power, flood control) across many countries are needed to ensure their economic and financial viability.

Changing the role of the state

The productive role of the state will be quite different in 2050. State commercial companies — in farming, ranching, processing, trading, and selling — will have disappeared. The state, in its productive role, will concentrate on building and maintaining public infrastructure, which will remain important in roads, water and energy distribution, and delegate responsibility for, water and telecommunications to the private sector.

African states will face new challenges in their supervisory roles. They must first regulate private infrastructure (which will dominate in telecommunications, energy generation, water production, and ports) to avoid monopolies that are costly to their export sectors. Second, states must mediate land, labor, and other resource conflicts among private agents of different political stature in order to avoid resource grabs that are politically destabilizing. *The main regulatory role of the state in agriculture will be to limit costly externalities arising from intensive farming. Such externalities can occur in food safety, prevention and treatment of zoonoses, and management of the environmental impacts of intensive*

---

9. The history of the "Office de Mise en Valeur du Fleuve Senegal" and its predecessors extends over 50 years; it took 40 years for the Water Charter to manage the Senegal River to be signed, and Guinea, the source of most of the Senegal River water, has participated only intermittently in the OMVS institutions. There have also been extended political and technical conflicts over management of waters of the Nile, the Niger, Lake Victoria, the Zambezi, and Lake Malawi most of which continue today.

farming — preserving water quality, preventing adverse human and animal health effects of farm chemicals, managing the widespread use of GMOs throughout the food chains, and preserving biological reserves against encroachment by farms and cities.

African states must improve secure and equitable access to land. The main step to improving access to land is to begin in earnest the process of land titling in areas of high export potential. Because those farms bear the highest risks for investment and recurrent finance, whether operated by Africans or foreigners, they have the greatest needs for protection against expropriation and unexpected claimants.

Improving access to land for some users may damage the claims of others. The outstanding example of such collateral damage will be smallholders who, because of policy bias against them, may lose land or water rights to large operators who have been granted preferential access in the (mistaken) belief that they are inherently more productive. *In seeking to improve land security, African land policy must continuously evaluate land claims against an objective standard of productivity rather than one that assumes that large operations are always superior.*

African states will face new challenges in their internal income distribution roles, particularly in resolving the income gaps that will grow between subsistence production and the commercial paths and between the urban sectors and agriculture in general. Such income inequalities can be partially offset through funding for social safety nets, public service pricing, and tax and trade policies affecting output prices. *The fiscal and targeting capacities of governments will increase with sustained economic growth, especially in the early converging countries, but governments at all levels must still strengthen their capacities to create social safety nets, target tax expenditure, and manage the environmental costs of growth.*

Greater regional cooperation. Transformation along the shifting agricultural paths to 2050 will require greater regional cooperation. Such cooperation includes water use for hydropower, flood control, and irrigation; collaboration on management of trans-boundary biodiversity, which is urgently needed to protect wildlife; joint work on the international effects of climate change, especially for disease control, water management, and flood control; and regulation of integrated African financial markets as the latter become a much larger share of operational funding for all scales and types of farms.

Ensuring better access to world markets. Five of the seven 2050 agricultural paths (all but subsistence farming and reserves) require cost reductions for regional trade within Africa and for global trade with African partners in order to thrive. Lower trade costs will derive from higher investment in infrastructure, including rehabilitation of the old rail network and construction of new ones, and in private trading services. Associated with this new investment must be faster logistics — a higher turnover from each infrastructure site at a given level of investment — which will generally occur under pressure from domestic producers who benefit from cheaper trade. *Beyond investments in infrastructure and better incentive policies, African states must do more to improve their access to markets through trade agreements, starting with regional trade in Africa.*

Accelerating technical change

The transformation of African agriculture will only be realized if African scientific institutions, public and private, contribute scientifically to global technology generation, and if African states, organized by sub-regions, invest in the necessary science to accelerate technical change. Accelerating technical change in African farming faces four broad issues — adapting external innovations; generating innovations and promoting change on small and dispersed farms; making good use of biotechnology; and responding to emerging problems in health and in minor crops.

Continuing global technology generation is inevitable and can benefit Africa enormously if global research is adapted to regional conditions. The progress of global research means that a lack of biological technologies is not likely to be a constraint in Paths 1 and 3 for some time. Those paths will specialize in crops where international research can be transferred, especially in cereals, oilseeds, and fibers, and where productivity in those crops is projected to grow for many years. IFPRI (2012, referring to the work of Evenson and Rosegrant (1995)) shows a continued trend of growth in the yields of major crops for many years. The yield gap between Africa and other regions in transferrable crops, and even in crops that are only partly transferrable such as cassava, can be closed without any further increase in the technological yield maximum.

Improving the productivity and sustainability of small farms is feasible.[10] It is imperative to address the productivity problems of small farms, given that they will remain the principal type of rural organization in Africa for decades. The main step to increasing the productivity of small farms is to reduce their costs of market participation and to provide them with better technologies.

The high costs of market participation — communication, transport, storage — is a significant tax on African agriculture. These high costs have three parts: (i) costs imputable to low transport and communications infrastructure density, also allowing for the decrepit condition of many of Africa's rails; (ii) high fuel and vehicle taxes because of the low share of income taxes in public incomes; and (iii) lack of competition in trucking on existing roads. Such costs will erode as infrastructure density and population density increase but will always remain higher on small farms because the connection costs of market access are higher on small units. Realizing the transformation scenario requires that aggressive action be taken to reduce such costs.

Higher communication costs lower productivity and do so even more at low infrastructure densities because of the absence of network effects. Communication costs are being cut rapidly through mobile telephones, which also provide access to data, finance, and information about jobs and investments. Mobile phones have had positive effects on price discovery and productivity in rural India (farming and fishing), East Africa (crops), and Niger (grain trading).[11] In the presence of good regulation for competition,

---

10. Peter Hazell (2011) asks five questions about small farmers that are relevant to this discussion.
11. Antoine Kantiza (2012) cites relevant examples from Uganda, Burundi, and Kenya, where isolation of farmers is extreme. Other research supporting this argument is Sife, Kiondo, and Lyimo-Macha (2010) for central Tanzania; Mittal, Gandhi, and Tripathi (2010) in four states of India; and Aker (2010) for grain trading in Niger, a country which suffers particularly from high transport costs and associated high domestic price variability.

there are no major impediments to wider telecommunications penetration continuing to reduce rural transactions costs. The important complementary measures to be taken by governments are: (i) to allocate licenses competitively; (ii) to regulate providers to prevent collusion; and (iii) where needed, to subsidize fixed costs of "last mile" connections in sparsely populated areas through provision of telecommunications services or through subsidized public provisions of rural roads and water supplies.

Making good use of biotechnology is essential. The trend of global farm technology will be to use more biotechnology products to raise crop yields, develop new products, and adapt to biotic and abiotic stresses, notably those caused by global warming. African farmers have benefited from biotechnology products, as summarized in a recent book on agricultural innovation in the continent (Juma, 2011), while simultaneously suffering from national policies and from measures in OECD nations that impede use of GMOs. Valuable research is deferred or ignored altogether because it uses GMOs. This policy bias — against research in African conditions and against the use of existing GMO cultivars in cotton, maize, sorghum, fruits, and vegetables — is damaging to African farmers because it makes them less competitive compared to foreign growers who do use GMO products.

To close the biotechnology gap in African agriculture it is important for the African Union to lead a continuous continent-wide review of biosafety and public information issues related to GMO products, and to the use of biotechnology in general.[12] This review would: (i) identify specific biosafety risks and propose measures to manage those risks in a way that develops public confidence in biotechnology; (ii) review capacity needs in biotechnology in terms of labs and African scientists; (iii) advise member governments on regulations, tools, and capacities so that they may make more well-informed national biosafety policies; (iv) support African scientists in using biotechnology; and (v) inform the African public about the benefits and risks of biotechnologies of all types, including GMOs.

The development and regulatory capacities of African states in biotechnology, especially for GMOs, must be strengthened so that products derived from biotechnology can be used safely and with public confidence. Regulatory capacity building is all the more urgent in the smaller countries which will require assistance in bio-regulation from their larger neighbors and from regional organizations.

There are at least two other emerging priorities for agricultural research throughout Africa. One involves the interactions among animal health, human health, and labor productivity. Human disease reduces labor supply and lowers returns to labor because of seasonality; hence disease control, especially for malaria, is especially important in farming because of seasonal shifts in labor productivity (e.g., it matters less if you are sick during the dry season than if you are sick at planting or weeding time).

A second emerging problem in Africa and in other tropical regions is lack of technologies for minor crops. Specifically, a lack of new technologies will continue to hamper productivity gains in Paths 2 and 4. The dry areas that constitute Path 4 are resource poor. In the absence of irrigation, it has been very difficult to raise productivity in traditional livestock or in millet and sorghum. The productivity barrier in

---

12. As done by Cooke and Downie (2010) for Zambia, Kenya, and South Africa and more generally by Juma in his recent book (Juma 2011).

Path 2 will be, in some instances, crops and livestock that are specific to local tastes and hence are "orphaned" from the point of view of international research that can be used in Africa. Path 5 will require new technologies for protecting livestock. In addition, the impact of climate change has not been as well studied in such commodities because their international value is smaller.

African countries have traditionally underinvested in agricultural R&D and technology transfer. As a result their rates of domestic innovation and productivity growth are lower and their capacities to absorb external innovations are weaker. Increasing the impact of agricultural research in Africa requires action on the following four issues:

- Spending for agricultural research and for development of African scientific capacities must be a renewed priority at all levels to support African farmers in becoming more competitive in global markets;
- Increased effort in agricultural research and technology transfer must have an explicit focus on small farmers and must be related to the cost conditions — transport, communications, water supply — in which they operate;
- Barriers to imported innovations, especially in irrigation equipment, fertilizers, and planting materials, must be reduced; and
- African food consumption depends to an unusual degree on root and tuber crops, where global research is weaker than for cereals and oilseeds; this demands a special and extensive effort, involving dedicated biotechnology, to raise yields of such crops.

African food production will increasingly depend on two crops — maize and cassava — that can benefit from generations of crop improvements. This crop improvement, while undeniably positive for incomes and nutrition, bears the risk of narrowing the genetic base in maize and cassava if a few commercial cultivars become dominant, which would increase the chance of catastrophic harvest failures resulting from a few pathogens. This risk of narrowing of the genetic base of major food crops must be addressed through a coordinated pan-African effort in plant breeding and pathology to identify sources of broad-based resistance.

Adapting to climate change

Climate change is expected to adversely affect output of many African farm commodities via its effect on yields and on areas suitable for production. Water will become scarcer in some areas and there will be more floods in others. The risks of higher human and animal disease related to greater vector spread are also likely to increase. All of these factors — potentially lower yields, larger and more frequent storms, graver health risks, higher price variability — call for policy adaptations for which many African countries are unprepared.

The main adaptation to such projected impacts will be to invest in insurance. A particular problem of climate adaptation in Africa is the prevalence of small farms whose poverty and market isolation prevent them from self-insuring, either through physical investments or through financial instruments. Support to small farmers through research will be negligible in the short term because of the small feasible rates of genetic gain in the yields of the principal crops that are important sources of income and food security to small farmers. Appropriate forms of public insurance for smallholders are:

- Strengthening legal and management agreements for regional water bodies, which are at particular risk (electricity production sharing, irrigation management, and biodiversity are all notable risks from high and low water levels);
- Holding greater financial reserves, or contracting forward, against exceptional import bills for food and fuel if world prices become more variable with higher temperatures and more severe storms;
- Defining programs to create jobs for those who have lost income or work, notably in rural areas affected by extreme climate events; and
- Investing in regional research on plant materials and farming practices that will resist higher temperatures and deeper flooding.

Appendix 1: Cropped Areas by Path in IFPRI IMPACT Baseline (thousand hectares)

All countries	2000	2010	2020	2030	2040	2050	Annual Growth Rates
Path One							
All irrigated crops	3,183	3,674	4,261	4,963	5,808	6,827	1.5%
sugarcane	277	306	338	374	414	459	1.0%
rice	1,311	1,595	1,944	2,372	2,898	3,545	2.0%
vegetables	246	287	336	393	461	540	1.6%
wheat	324	356	394	436	486	543	1.0%
maize	303	338	378	423	474	531	1.1%
All rainfed crops	37,022	39,191	41,640	44,403	47,521	51,041	0.6%
cotton	3,932	4,345	4,816	5,353	5,965	6,663	1.1%
wheat	1,901	1,997	2,112	2,250	2,416	2,613	0.6%
maize	12,049	12,142	12,256	12,389	12,541	12,709	0.1%
groundnut	887	957	1,036	1,127	1,232	1,351	0.8%
cassava	6,442	6,864	7,316	7,799	8,317	8,871	0.6%
sorghum	8,571	9,251	10,005	10,841	11,769	12,803	0.8%
Path Two							
All irrigated crops	444	493	547	608	677	755	1.1%
other	198	219	242	268	297	329	1.0%
vegetables	1	1	1	1	2	2	2.0%
All rainfed crops	47,208	50,844	55,072	59,965	65,614	72,123	0.8%
maize	3,973	4,004	4,042	4,086	4,136	4,192	0.1%
rice	394	404	416	429	443	458	0.3%
cassava	2,091	2,228	2,374	2,532	2,700	2,880	0.6%
cocoa	3,994	4,635	5,379	6,243	7,245	8,408	1.5%
coffee	2,045	2,259	2,496	2,757	3,045	3,364	1.0%
Path Three							
All irrigated crops	996	1,139	1,307	1,503	1,732	2,003	1.4%
sorghum	125	138	152	167	184	203	1.0%
rice	183	223	272	333	407	498	2.0%
vegetables	266	311	363	425	498	584	1.6%

All rainfed crops	45,721	48,988	52,744	57,048	61,973	67,605	0.8%
maize	3,952	3,983	4,020	4,064	4,113	4,168	0.1%
rice	3,446	3,533	3,631	3,740	3,860	3,993	0.3%
vegetables	1,229	1,311	1,399	1,495	1,599	1,711	0.7%
groundnut	1,849	1,993	2,158	2,347	2,564	2,813	0.8%
other crops	14,877	16,626	18,614	20,880	23,463	26,413	1.1%
Path Four							
All irrigated crops	518	576	642	716	799	894	1.1%
subtropical fruits	81	92	105	120	138	157	1.3%
sorghum	83	92	101	111	123	135	1.0%
other crops	198	219	242	268	297	329	1.0%
All rainfed crops	48,949	52,973	57,533	62,693	68,530	75,130	0.9%
pearl millet	16,245	17,757	19,426	21,268	23,301	25,547	0.9%
maize	1,985	2,000	2,019	2,041	2,065	2,093	0.1%
vegetables	136	145	155	166	177	190	0.7%
cassava	1,085	1,154	1,229	1,308	1,394	1,485	0.6%
total oilseeds	2,451	2,453	2,460	2,474	2,493	2,518	0.1%
Path Five							
All irrigated crops	1,984	2,277	2,625	3,040	3,534	4,126	1.5%
sugarcane	142	157	173	191	212	235	1.0%
rice	680	827	1,008	1,229	1,501	1,836	2.0%
vegetables	180	211	246	288	337	394	1.6%
All rainfed crops	30,039	32,202	34,682	37,516	40,749	44,432	0.8%
pearl millet	3,852	4,215	4,615	5,058	5,547	6,087	0.9%
sorghum	2,445	2,632	2,840	3,071	3,327	3,612	0.8%
vegetables	601	641	684	731	782	837	0.7%
maize	2,202	2,219	2,239	2,264	2,291	2,322	0.1%
groundnut	1,634	1,761	1,907	2,074	2,265	2,485	0.8%
Path Six							
All irrigated crops	7,385	7,617	7,868	8,141	8,437	8,760	0.3%

wheat	1,674	1,696	1,720	1,746	1,773	1,803	0.1%
vegetables	865	900	937	976	1,016	1,058	0.4%
other crops	1,268	1,274	1,279	1,285	1,290	1,296	0.0%
			Path Seven				
All rainfed crops	18,517	18,772	19,062	19,388	19,749	20,149	0.2%
wheat	4,359	4,269	4,182	4,101	4,024	3,950	-0.2%
other crops	5,027	5,167	5,314	5,467	5,627	5,795	0.3%
other grains	3,073	3,028	2,983	2,938	2,895	2,852	-0.1%
vegetables	2,408	2,498	2,591	2,687	2,787	2,891	0.4%
total oilseeds	2,357	2,479	2,607	2,742	2,884	3,034	0.5%

Source: IFPRI 2012

Appendix 2: Crop Yields by Path in IFPRI IMPACT Baseline (mt/ha)

All countries	2000	2010	2020	2030	2040	2050	Annual Growth Rates
Path One							
All irrigated crops							
sugarcane	83.6	85.0	93.4	101.0	106.8	109.4	0.5%
rice	1.7	1.9	2.3	2.8	3.2	3.6	1.5%
vegetables	8.2	8.9	10.7	12.4	14.1	15.2	1.2%
wheat	3.1	2.8	3.3	3.8	4.3	4.7	0.8%
maize	2.1	2.7	3.2	3.7	4.2	4.6	1.6%
All rainfed crops							
cotton	0.3	0.3	0.4	0.4	0.5	0.5	0.9%
wheat	1.5	1.8	2.1	2.3	2.6	2.9	1.3%
maize	1.5	1.6	2.0	2.2	2.3	2.5	1.1%
groundnut	0.6	0.5	0.6	0.6	0.7	0.7	0.2%
cassava	8.4	9.4	10.7	11.6	12.6	13.3	0.9%
sorghum	0.8	0.9	1.1	1.2	1.3	1.5	1.2%
Path Two							
All irrigated crops							
other	7.0	8.7	12.1	16.6	22.4	28.9	2.9%
vegetables	4.4	4.6	5.7	6.9	8.3	9.7	1.6%
All rainfed crops							
maize	1.5	1.6	1.9	2.1	2.3	2.5	1.1%
rice	0.8	0.9	1.0	1.1	1.2	1.3	0.9%
cassava	8.4	9.4	10.7	11.7	12.6	13.4	0.9%
cocoa	0.4	0.5	0.5	0.5	0.5	0.6	0.5%
coffee	0.4	0.4	0.4	0.4	0.5	0.5	0.5%
Path Three							
All irrigated crops							
sorghum	1.7	2.2	2.9	3.6	4.3	4.9	2.1%
rice	1.7	1.9	2.3	2.7	3.1	3.5	1.5%
vegetables	8.2	9.0	10.7	12.5	14.1	15.3	1.2%
All rainfed crops							
maize	1.5	1.6	2.0	2.2	2.3	2.5	1.1%
rice	0.9	0.9	1.0	1.1	1.2	1.3	0.9%
vegetables	4.9	5.6	6.5	7.4	8.1	8.4	1.1%
groundnut	0.6	0.5	0.6	0.6	0.7	0.7	0.2%
other crops	1.7	1.8	2.0	2.1	2.2	2.2	0.5%

Path Four							
All irrigated crops							
subtropical fruits	12.2	13.4	16.2	19.1	22.0	24.5	1.4%
sorghum	1.7	2.2	2.9	3.6	4.3	4.9	2.1%
other crops	7.0	8.7	12.1	16.6	22.4	28.9	2.9%
All rainfed crops							
pearl millet	0.7	0.8	0.9	1.0	1.2	1.3	1.4%
maize	1.5	1.6	1.9	2.1	2.3	2.5	1.1%
vegetables	4.9	5.6	6.6	7.5	8.2	8.5	1.1%
cassava	8.3	9.3	10.5	11.5	12.5	13.2	0.9%
total oilseeds	0.7	0.6	0.7	0.8	0.8	0.9	0.6%
Path Five							
All irrigated crops							
sugarcane	84.5	85.9	94.4	102.2	108.1	110.7	0.5%
rice	1.7	1.9	2.3	2.8	3.2	3.6	1.5%
vegetables	8.3	9.0	10.8	12.6	14.3	15.4	1.2%
All rainfed crops							
pearl millet	0.6	0.7	0.9	1.0	1.1	1.3	1.4%
sorghum	0.8	0.9	1.0	1.2	1.3	1.4	1.1%
vegetables	4.9	5.6	6.6	7.5	8.2	8.5	1.1%
maize	1.5	1.6	1.9	2.1	2.3	2.5	1.1%
groundnut	0.6	0.5	0.6	0.6	0.7	0.7	0.2%
Path Six							
All irrigated crops							
wheat	4.7	5.0	5.4	5.6	5.7	5.6	0.4%
vegetables	14.0	13.0	16.3	19.6	22.2	23.3	1.0%
other crops	15.1	15.7	17.1	18.3	18.7	18.2	0.4%
Path Seven							
All rainfed crops							
wheat	0.8	1.0	1.2	1.3	1.4	1.4	1.2%
other crops	4.1	4.3	4.7	5.2	5.5	5.8	0.7%
other grains	0.6	0.9	1.1	1.2	1.2	1.2	1.5%
vegetables	3.8	4.1	4.7	5.3	5.8	6.1	1.0%
total oilseeds	0.8	0.7	0.8	0.9	1.0	1.1	0.7%

Source: IFPRI 2012

Appendix 3: Value by Path in Transformation Scenario ($bn at 2010 world prices)

All countries	2000	2010	2020	2030	2040	2050	Annual Growth Rates
Path One							
All irrigated crops							
Total value	2.4	5.5	13.6	33.4	81.0	205.0	8.9%
sugarcane	0.3	0.4	0.8	1.3	2.1	3.3	5.0%
rice	0.5	1.4	4.0	11.9	33.2	100.0	10.8%
vegetables	1.2	2.7	6.5	15.2	34.8	76.7	8.4%
wheat	0.1	0.2	0.5	1.2	2.8	6.7	8.1%
maize	0.1	0.1	0.4	1.0	2.2	5.9	9.3%
All countries rainfed							
Total value	17.2	29.1	52.7	96.5	172.4	323.6	5.9%
cotton	1.5	2.4	5.2	11.1	22.9	45.1	6.8%
wheat	0.3	0.7	1.6	3.3	6.6	14.3	7.5%
maize	1.6	3.1	6.4	13.0	24.3	51.2	7.0%
groundnut	0.3	0.5	0.9	1.7	2.9	5.1	5.6%
cassava	3.5	6.8	13.8	27.4	50.6	98.8	6.7%
sorghum	0.6	1.6	3.6	8.0	16.6	35.7	8.1%
Path Two							
All countries irrigated							
Total value	1.5	3.2	7.3	16.5	36.1	77.7	7.9%
other	0.8	1.8	4.4	10.8	24.7	55.2	8.4%
vegetables	0.0	0.0	0.0	0.0	0.1	0.1	8.0%
All countries rainfed							
Total value	56.0	91.3	150.5	248.7	397.2	647.5	4.9%
maize	0.5	0.9	1.8	3.4	5.9	11.6	6.2%
rice	0.1	0.1	0.2	0.4	0.8	1.5	6.1%
cassava	1.1	2.0	3.9	7.1	12.2	22.2	6.0%
cocoa	3.0	4.1	5.7	7.8	10.8	14.9	3.2%
coffee	2.1	2.7	3.6	4.7	6.2	8.2	2.7%
Path Three							
All countries irrigated							
Total value	2.8	5.9	13.0	28.3	60.1	125.3	7.6%
sorghum	0.0	0.1	0.1	0.3	0.5	1.0	7.9%
rice	0.1	0.2	0.4	1.0	2.5	6.6	9.3%
vegetables	1.3	2.5	5.3	10.6	21.1	40.1	6.9%
All countries rainfed							

Total value	49.6	77.1	120.6	188.8	284.2	437.6	4.4%
maize	0.5	0.9	1.6	2.7	4.4	8.0	5.5%
rice	0.6	1.0	1.8	3.0	5.0	8.7	5.3%
vegetables	3.5	5.6	8.8	13.4	19.9	27.9	4.2%
groundnut	0.6	0.9	1.4	2.3	3.4	5.1	4.1%
other	15.1	23.9	37.4	58.1	85.0	122.5	4.2%
Path Four							
All countries irrigated							
Total value	1.5	3.3	7.5	17.1	37.7	81.4	8.0%
subtropical fruits	0.5	0.9	2.1	4.4	9.2	18.6	7.4%
sorghum	0.0	0.0	0.1	0.2	0.3	0.7	7.9%
other	0.8	1.8	4.4	10.8	24.7	55.2	8.4%
All countries rainfed							
Total value	34.6	48.4	67.8	94.8	127.1	172.2	3.2%
pearl millet	2.9	5.6	9.5	15.6	24.6	37.9	5.1%
maize	0.3	0.4	0.6	0.9	1.2	1.9	4.0%
vegetables	0.4	0.5	0.7	1.0	1.2	1.5	2.7%
cassava	0.6	0.8	1.3	1.8	2.5	3.7	3.7%
total oilseeds	0.5	0.8	1.1	1.5	1.9	2.4	3.1%
Path Five							
All countries irrigated							
Total value	2.5	5.1	11.3	25.0	53.6	116.2	7.7%
sugarcane	0.1	0.2	0.4	0.7	1.1	1.7	5.0%
rice	0.2	0.6	1.6	4.0	9.7	25.2	9.3%
vegetables	0.9	1.7	3.6	7.3	14.4	27.4	6.9%
All countries rainfed							
Total value	27.2	36.4	48.9	65.5	84.1	110.0	2.8%
pearl millet	0.7	1.2	2.0	3.3	5.1	7.6	4.9%
sorghum	0.2	0.3	0.5	0.8	1.3	2.0	4.8%
vegetables	1.7	2.3	3.1	3.9	4.8	5.7	2.4%
maize	0.3	0.4	0.6	0.9	1.2	1.8	3.7%
groundnut	0.6	0.7	0.9	1.2	1.5	1.9	2.4%
Path Six							
All countries irrigated							
Total value	27.7	42.4	70.4	115.3	180.3	277.9	4.6%
wheat	0.9	1.4	2.0	2.9	3.9	5.5	3.6%
vegetables	7.0	9.2	15.6	25.1	38.2	54.5	4.1%
other	11.6	15.9	22.8	32.2	41.8	52.9	3.0%

	Path Seven						
All countries rainfed							
Total value	22.1	31.3	44.6	63.0	85.8	115.8	3.3%
wheat	0.4	0.7	1.0	1.3	1.7	2.3	3.5%
other	12.4	16.5	22.5	30.7	39.7	50.9	2.8%
other grains	0.1	0.2	0.4	0.5	0.6	0.7	3.4%
vegetables	5.3	7.6	11.0	15.5	21.5	28.9	3.4%
total oilseeds	0.6	1.0	1.8	2.9	4.4	7.0	5.0%

Source: IFPRI 2012

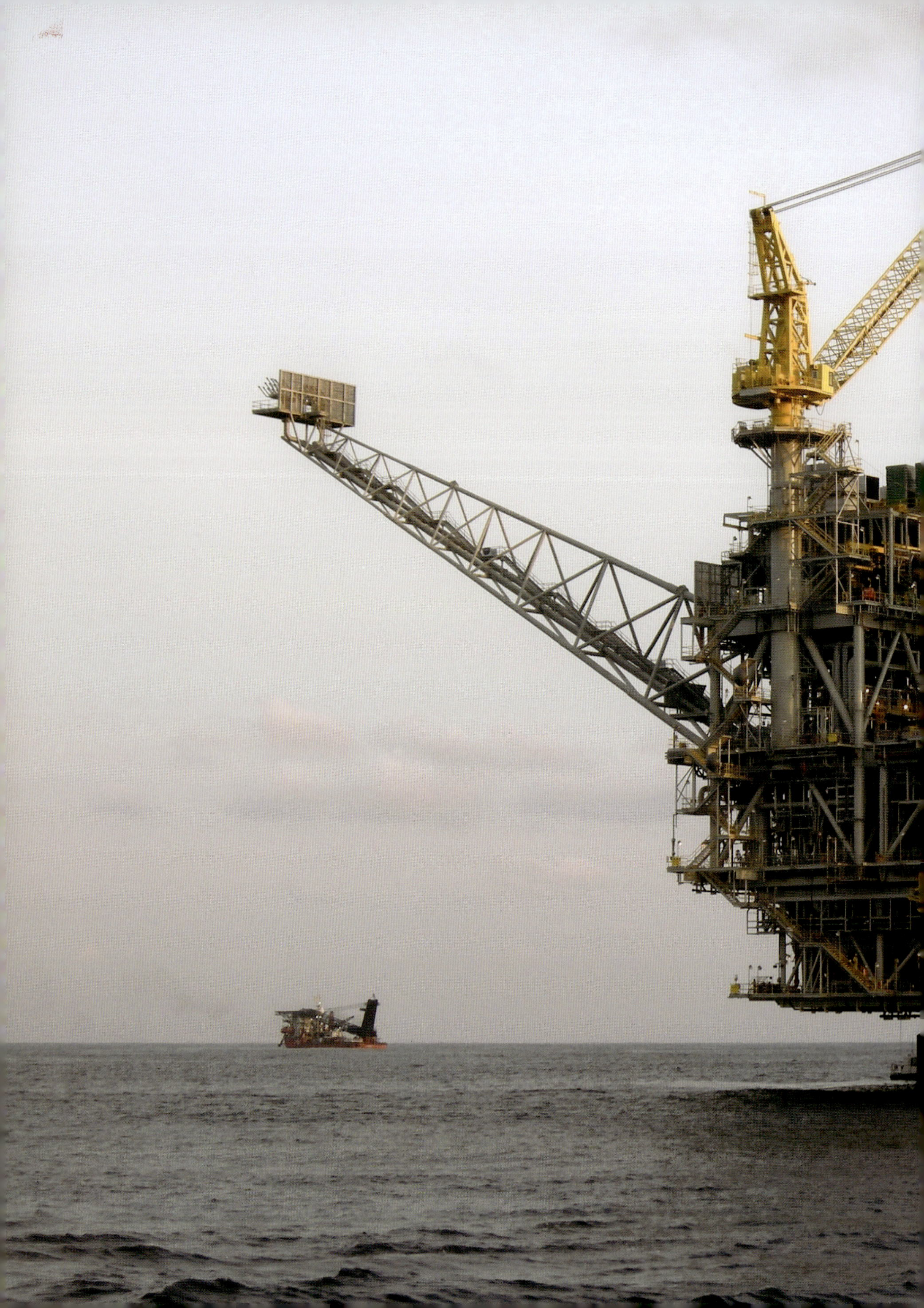

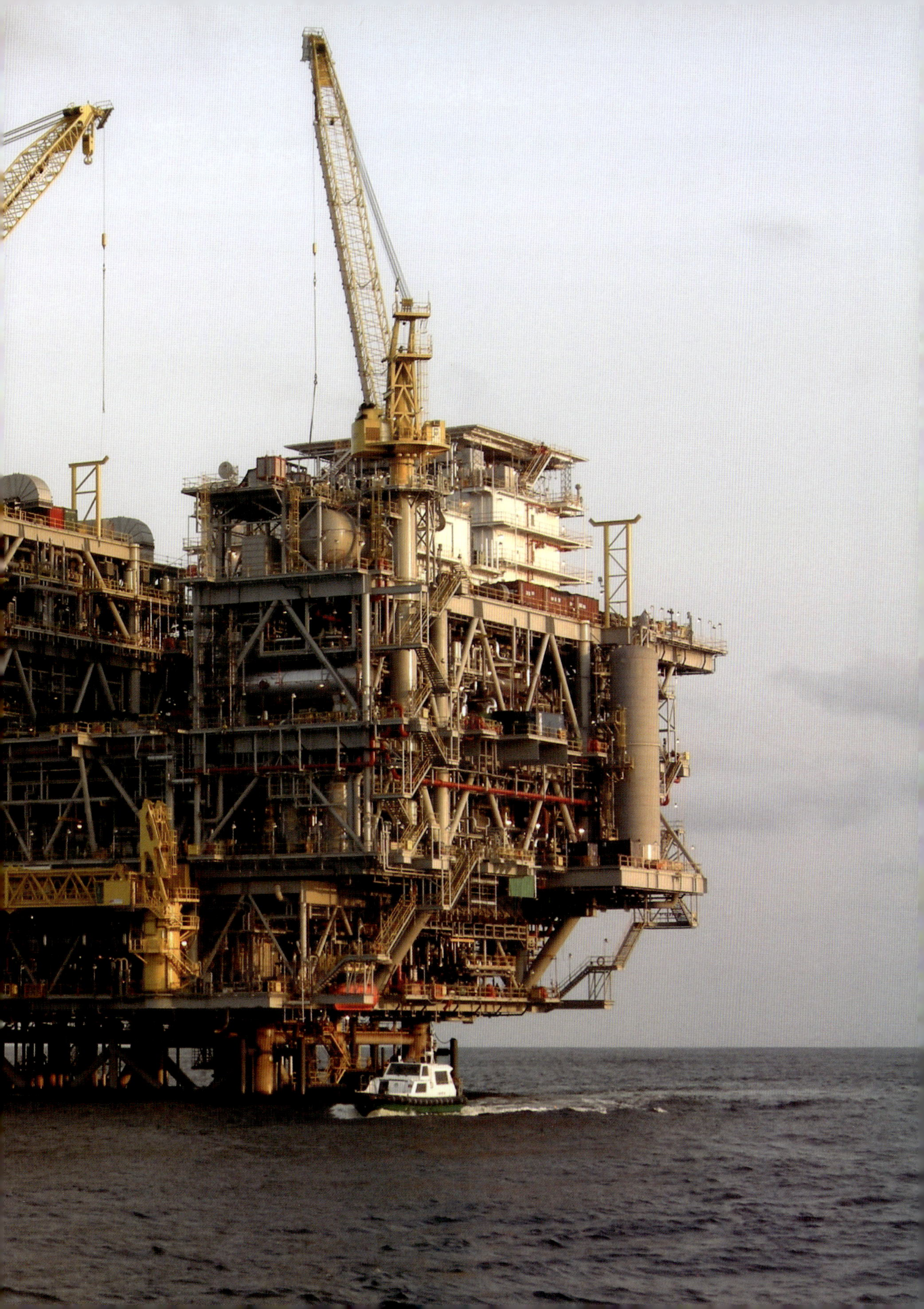

Chapter 12

Harnessing Natural Resources for Diversification

James Bond and Jose Fajgenbaum

The natural resource sectors (oil, gas, and mining – the extractive industries) are important parts of the economy of many African countries. If harnessed right, these natural resources can constitute a huge opportunity for development. By exploiting its natural resource base, Africa could in essence convert its underground minerals and agricultural potential into human and physical capital to create inclusive growth. By 2050, Africa could become factory and granary to the world, just as Britain and the United States were the factories and the United States and Argentina the granaries in the second half of the 19th century, followed by China and Australia in the 20th century.

This is a vision of economic convergence for Africa's resource-rich economies in which these countries catch up with other high- and middle-income countries to narrow the gap in per capita income and development outcomes. Over the next 40 years the African continent could build on its natural resource and agricultural production base to become an important supplier of intermediate and finished goods and agricultural products, relying on a diversified private sector and a high degree of economic and geographic integration. Africa's factories and agribusiness processing centers, linked by world class regional infrastructure (rail, road, electricity, and ICT) to its raw material production centers and farms, could transform these inputs into intermediate and finished products for export to clients on the continent and across the world. By 2050 Africa could also possess a significant service sector, particularly in natural resource extraction-related activities such as mining finance, technical design, and environmental and social analysis. The continent could be home to major multinational corporations operating in the extractive industries across the globe.

The key challenge faced by Africa's resource-rich countries is to transform the resources in the ground into assets that lead to strong sustainable growth, economic diversification, reduction of inequality and poverty, and equity between generations. This chapter reviews the natural resource sector and outlines the key policy actions that Africa's governments will need to put in place to achieve the vision of convergence.

Africa and extractive industries remain inextricably linked. In many African countries, the natural resources sector constitutes a significant proportion of the formal economy. Africa is also an important player on the world stage for many mineral resources. It has this role, in part, because of its historical legacy as the continent where many of today's extraction techniques were first developed (copper and cobalt in Zambia; gold, platinum, and diamonds in South Africa; bauxite[1] in Guinea; liquefied natural gas in Algeria; and phosphates in Morocco). The continent still boasts very rich deposits of ores that are much higher grade than elsewhere on the planet (bauxite in Guinea, copper in the Democratic Republic of the Congo, gold in Ghana, iron ore in Liberia and Guinea, and phosphates in Morocco).

Extractive industries have shaped the economies of many post-colonial African countries. The oil and gas industry has defined Nigeria's past four decades of economic development and has left significant governance and social development problems in its wake. The DRC's copper, cobalt, diamonds, and coltan[2] have fueled armed conflict and political instability in the east of the country and elsewhere. Guinea's fabulous bauxite reserves have enabled it to survive epic macroeconomic mismanagement since independence in 1956.[3] On the other hand, Botswana's extraordinary success in moving from a very poor colony to a well-performing middle income country in less than half a century has largely been ascribed to the responsible management of its diamond resources (see Box 12.2). South Africa has a strong, dynamic world-class private sector and modern infrastructure largely built upon and financed by developments in the mining industry for over a century, even as some of its traditional resources reach exhaustion. Mozambique's exploitation of its gas and coal reserves has fueled inclusive growth, which has largely erased the scars of its post-independence upheavals. More recently, responsible management of gold and gemstone production in Tanzania and gold and oil and gas in Ghana has created economic growth that is transforming these countries' economies and creating strong private sectors.

For good or for ill, the extractive industries have a very significant impact on the economies of Africa's resource rich countries. The challenge for Africa's policymakers is to apply the right combination of policies to ensure that this impact is positive and leads to the kind of inclusive growth necessary for economic convergence.

The next section of this chapter starts with a discussion of Africa's natural resource endowment and the opportunities and challenges it presents. It then discusses the track record of African economies in extraction, transformation, and processing and outlines the conditions for downstream processing to proceed. The final section briefly presents the vision for Africa's extractive industries in 2050. The chapter concludes with recommendations for policy measures for the continent's resource-rich countries to converge with other emerging market economies. The recommendations cover measures related to natural resource rents[4] and their management as well as broader economic management to enable inclusive development and private sector-led diversification of the economies.

---

1. Bauxite is the raw material for aluminum.
2. Coltan is an ore combining columbite and tantalite, from which the elements niobium and tantalum are extracted. Tantalum is used to manufacture capacitors for electronic products such as integrated circuit chips, and is therefore present in minute quantities in almost all electronic devices. Coltan mining has been cited as helping to finance armed conflict in the Eastern Congo and is termed a conflict mineral.
3. The author of this chapter remembers visiting Guinea's tropical capital Conakry in the mid-1980s and seeing row upon row of snow plows sent by the Soviet Union in exchange for Guinean bauxite under the barter trade agreement between the two countries.
4. Resource rent is defined as the difference between the value at market prices of the resource in the ground and the cost of its discovery and extraction.

Historical Context

Mining and oil and gas have been important sectors in the continent's economic development for over a century. But today, with a few exceptions, Africa's mineral resource endowments in terms of proven reserves turn out to be rather modest at a global level (see Tables 12.1 and 12.2), ranging from 1 percent of world total reserves for iron ore to 26 percent for bauxite. Africa's production, too, of most key bulk minerals such as oil and gas, coal, and iron ore mirrors its fairly modest global reserve position and does not stand out as exceptional. There are some exceptions: Africa is still by far the most important reserve base and producer of gemstones, titanium, and bauxite.

Table 12.1 | Africa contains modest portions of many of the world's most valuable resources

	Unit		Reserves end 2011 World	Africa	%	Production 2011 World	Africa	%	Reserves/Production (years) World	Africa
Oil	M Tons	1	234300	17600	8%	3995.6	417.4	10%	59	41
Gas	Bn Cubic Metres	1	208400	14500	7%	3276.2	202.7	6%	64	72
Coal	M Tons	1	860938	32895	4%	5933	219.9	4%	145	150
Iron Ore	M Tons	2	170000	2500	1%	2800	70	3%	61	36
Bauxite	M Tons	2	29000	7600	26%	220	20	9%	132	380
Titanium Ore	M Tons TiO2	3	692	140	20%	6.7	2.0	30%	103	69
Copper Ore	M Tons Cu	2	690	50	7%	16.1	1.3	8%	552	40
Gold	000 Tons Au	2	51	9	18%	2.7	0.3	12%	159	28
Gemstones	$ billion value	2	No data available			80	50	62%	No data available	

Sources: British Petroleum 2012; US Department of the Interior and US Geological Survey 2012

That Africa possesses only modest shares of global proven reserves today may be an indication of lower investment in mining exploration in recent years on the African continent. Investments in exploration, the key step before reserves can be certified, are lower in African countries than elsewhere because of the greater risk faced by mining companies on the continent and the more arduous investment environment that Africa represents. In addition, technological advances and higher commodity prices have made extraction of lower-grade ores located in other parts of the world economically viable. These are now included in global reserve figures where previously they were not, which lowers Africa's share of the total. However, because Africa's resources are for the most part of higher grades than in other parts of the world, if commodity prices decline, Africa's resources would be among the last to be shelved, and its share of the total reserve base would increase.

Table 12.2 | Several African nations have vast stocks of hydrocarbons

Oil	Billion barrels 1991	2001	2011	Billion tons 2011	Share of Total	Reserves/Production (years)
Algeria	9.2	11.3	12.2	1.5	0.7%	19.3
Angola	1.4	6.5	13.5	1.8	0.8%	21.2
Chad	-	0.9	1.5	0.2	0.1%	36.1
Congo-Brazzaville	0.7	1.6	1.9	0.3	0.1%	18.0
Egypt	3.5	3.7	4.3	0.6	0.3%	16.0
Equatorial Guinea	0.3	1.1	1.7	0.2	0.1%	18.5
Gabon	0.9	2.4	3.7	0.5	0.2%	41.2
Libya	22.8	36	47.1	6.1	2.9%	*
Nigeria	20	31.5	37.2	5	2.3%	41.5
Sudan	0.3	0.7	6.7	0.9	0.4%	40.5
Tunisia	0.4	0.5	0.4	0.1		15.0
Other Africa	0.8	0.6	2.2	0.3	0.1%	27.0
Total Africa	60.4	96.8	132.4	17.6	8.0%	41.2
Total World	1032.7	1267.4	1652.6	234.3		54.2

Gas	Trillion cubic metres 1991	2001	2011	Trillion cubic feet 2011	Share of total	Reserves/Production (years)
Algeria	3.6	4.5	4.5	159.1	2.2%	57.7
Egypt	0.4	1.6	2.2	77.3	1.1%	35.7
Libya	1.3	1.3	1.5	52.8	0.7%	*
Nigeria	3.4	4.6	5.1	180.5	2.5%	*
Other Africa	0.8	1.1	1.2	43.5	0.6%	63.4
Total Africa	9.5	13.1	14.5	513.2	7.0%	71.7
Total World	131.2	168.5	208.4	7360.9		63.6

Source: British Petroleum 2012

Natural resource endowments: Opportunities and challenges

It is part of the conventional wisdom that natural resources have been a curse for Africa. But the effects of mineral resource endowments on the economy and social structures are complex and by no means predetermined.

It has often been stated that Africa's mineral wealth has not contributed as much as it should have to the development of the continent. It seems that in many cases Africans have stood by as foreign firms extracted their resources. The firms have paid taxes and royalties to national governments that either have not had the capacity or have lacked the governance mechanisms to ensure their use for broad-based growth. In the worst cases, resource rents have led to Dutch disease (discussed below) and loss of competitiveness or to widespread corruption, which has hollowed out local traditions and institutions and created a culture of rent-seeking and extraction. At worst, it has led sometimes to armed conflict and war.

It is true that, looking at the past, some countries with very strong endowments seem to have had greater difficulty putting in place the strong institutions needed for inclusive growth. However, in actual fact, there does not seem to be any clear-cut statistical correlation between resource endowments (measured as the share of resource rents in GDP) and growth over a long period (Figure 12.1). Moreover, recent economic research suggests there is little causal link between oil wealth and conflict, based on cross-country analysis and correcting for other explanatory variables (Cotet and Tsui 2013). While this research is narrower than the subject of this chapter both in terms of the commodity reviewed (oil) and the specific outcome (conflict, as opposed to other negative impacts), the rigor of the analysis underpins the broader conclusions of this chapter.

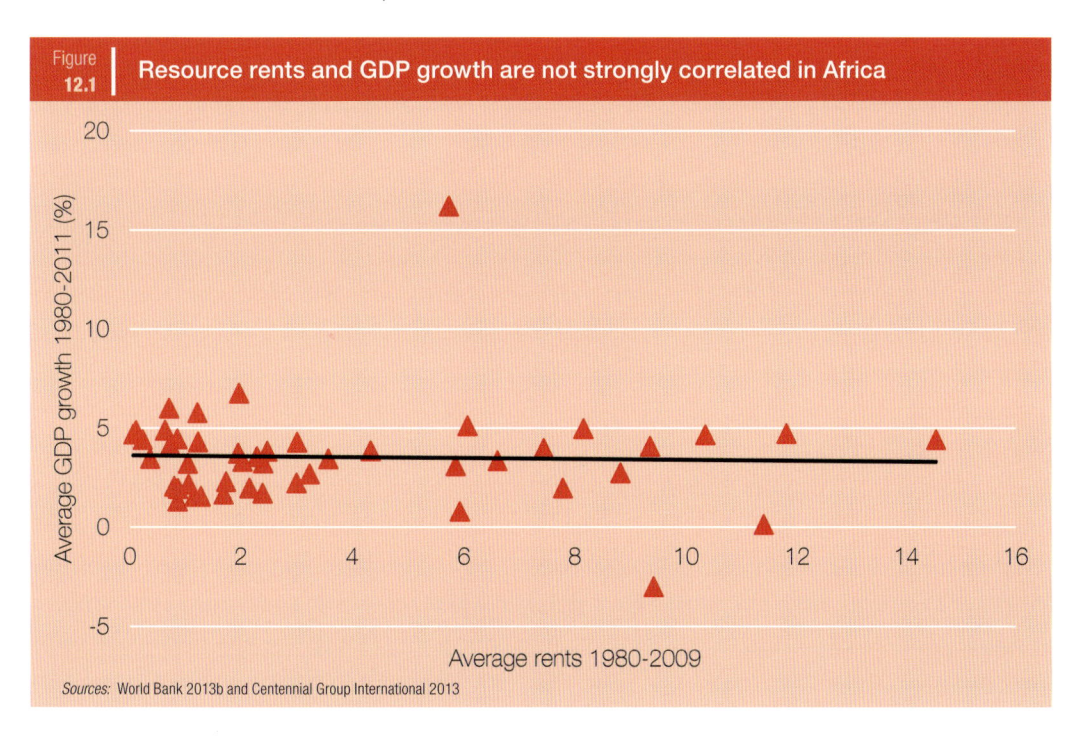

Figure 12.1 Resource rents and GDP growth are not strongly correlated in Africa

Sources: World Bank 2013b and Centennial Group International 2013

Mining and oil and gas make little direct contribution to the local economy, except for the rents they generate. Extractive industries are highly capital-intensive and neither create many jobs nor contribute significantly to the development of skills and human capital, whether in Africa or in other parts of the world. Mining and oil and gas operations have few forward or backward linkages to the rest of the economy and have often been managed as virtual enclaves without much impact on the economies of host countries other than payment of taxes and royalties. They do however have a very significant impact on the physical environment because of the operations involved in extracting the ore and disposing of tailings (mining waste). Mining and oil and gas can also have very significant effects on local communities, which, in some cases, can be beneficial. However, for the most part they have tended to be deleterious, particularly during the construction phase when imported labor can introduce prostitution, sexually transmitted diseases such as HIV/AIDS, and petty crime. During the production phase tensions can arise between local communities, the central government, and production companies (e.g., in the Niger and Escravos Deltas in Nigeria), when local communities deem the sharing of the proceeds of resource extraction as unfair.

As the body of experience with extractive industries deepens, we are beginning to see greater positive interaction between extractive industries and the rest of the economy, particularly in countries where resources have been developed more recently (oil and gas in Ghana, ilmenite[5] in Madagascar, coal in Mozambique). The improvements are due in part to clearer requirements imposed on investors by host countries, who now require firms to better integrate their operations with the local economy, and in part to a greater appreciation by mining and oil and gas companies themselves of the long-term costs to their shareholders of negative environmental and social impacts.

Specific macroeconomic challenges

Resource-rich countries face a set of macroeconomic challenges that other developing countries do not. In the context of the process of transforming the natural resources into inclusive growth, resource-rich countries need to avoid the boom-and-bust cycles associated with resource earnings (Figure 12.2). In addition, they need to address the distortions caused by spending in excess of the economy's absorption capacity and the attendant increases in inflation and real appreciation of the currency, a phenomenon frequently linked to resource booms.[6] Policies need to be designed with a view to minimizing the adverse effects of an eventual permanent decline in resource earnings as the resources become exhausted. These effects can be severe.

Many resource-rich African countries have experienced boom-and-bust cycles linked to volatility in resource earnings and a pro-cyclical fiscal policy, in which considerable and frequently inefficient spending increases associated with positive earnings shocks and abrupt reversals following adverse earnings shocks. Expenditures frequently follow fluctuations in resource earnings; resource-rich countries

---

5. Ilmenite is mined for use in the production of titanium dioxide, a powder widely used as a base pigment in paint, paper, and plastics.
6. These distortions include overheating of the economy and the real appreciation of the currency, which through relative price changes leads to declining tradable sectors, a phenomenon known as "Dutch disease." It can also lead to the breakdown in governance, increased corruption, and the tendency toward wasteful public spending ("white elephants").

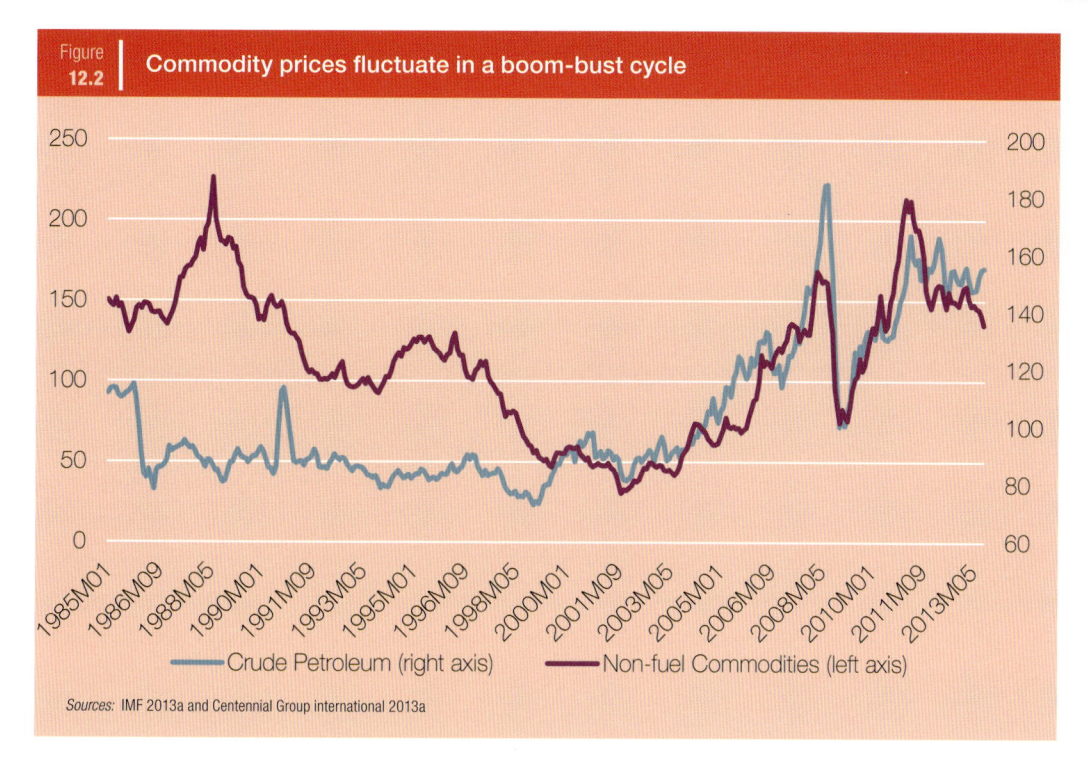

Figure 12.2 Commodity prices fluctuate in a boom-bust cycle

Sources: IMF 2013a and Centennial Group international 2013a

overspend when times are good, i.e., when resource prices and associated revenues are high, and then cut back spending when resource prices and revenues decline. The commodity price cycle that followed the global financial crisis was recent evidence of this phenomenon.

A pro-cyclical fiscal policy involves a complex and costly expenditure-decision process with potential negative effects on the quality and efficiency of public spending. Furthermore, it leads to macroeconomic volatility, which effects the private sector's consumption and investment planning and decisions and thus hampers growth potential.

In Africa, limited public oversight and parliamentary checks and balances often exacerbate the problem. In good times fiscal resources may be directed to "white elephant" investments of marginal development value or to financing recurrent expenditure such as civil servant salaries. An excessively large and relatively well-paid public sector attracts the best talent, impoverishing other sectors, and drives up the cost of non-tradables within the economy. So-called "Dutch disease" results from the appreciating currency which renders tradable sectors less competitive. In bad times, budgets may be cut indiscriminately across the board, undermining the sustainability of investments in the social sectors and infrastructure. Schools are hit with unpaid salaries and lack of textbooks, and infrastructure maintenance is neglected.

Extracting and transforming Africa's resources

Extracting resources more equitably

In economic terms, production of natural resources generates a resource rent. Resource rents increase when commodity prices increase; the richer the ore body, the greater its value in the ground and so the higher the resource rent. On balance, African countries do not receive as large a share of the resource rents as other regions of the world.

Taxing natural resource production well above a country's income tax rates is justified by the sovereign ownership of the underground resource and the rent that this resource generates. Resource-specific taxes are justified to ensure equitable sharing between the investor company and the sovereign owner of the resource. Governments argue–with some justification–that a significant portion of this resource rent should accrue to the host country, hence the need for a specific resource tax over and above economy-wide taxes (income and value-added or sales taxes). The key challenge for all resource-endowed countries is how to set up a fiscal framework to tax resource rents at levels that maximize fiscal flows to the country but do not dissuade investor companies from exploring and producing the resource. The problem is compounded because commodity prices vary in unpredictable ways and, with them, the value of the resource rent itself, which can introduce wild swings in tax revenue and company profit. A combination of a country's corporate income tax and a royalty tax that is linked progressively to the value of the natural resource is one option to address these challenges.

For the purposes of this chapter we have categorized African countries into three groups: resource dominant, in which resource rents represent 10 percent or more of GDP in 2009; resource available, with resource rents between 2 and 10 percent of GDP; and resource poor, with resource rents less than 2 percent of GDP (Table 12.3). Naturally, this classification of countries will change as new reserves of minerals and oil and gas are discovered in coming years.

This definition of resource dominant, resource available and resource poor is based not on the absolute value of the resource rent but on its impact on the economy as a whole. Economies with fairly significant mining sectors such as Namibia (diamonds, uranium) or Madagascar (ilmenite) figure as resource poor either because a fairly diversified economy reduces the impact of the mining sector (Namibia) or because of the very low resource rent of the mined commodity (the market price of ilmenite is only marginally above its cost of extraction in Madagascar) and therefore the rent represents only a marginal part of GDP. A country that is only obtaining a marginal share of the resource rent due to overly generous tax terms may also be categorized as resource poor.

Table 12.3 Some African nations are heavily reliant on resource rents, while others lack them entirely

Resource Dominant	2009	Av. 2000-2009	Resource Available	2009	Avg. 2000-2009
Congo, Rep.	53.7	63.3	Mali	9.8	5.0
Equatorial Guinea	46.2	69.4	South Africa	7.5	5.1
Libya	46.1	53.4	Cameroon	6.6	8.9
Gabon	41.1	46.6	Ghana	6.6	2.6
Angola	38.4	56.0	Cote d'Ivoire	5.8	5.1
Mauritania	37.7	23.6	Tunisia	5.5	5.4
Chad	33.6	30.6	Zimbabwe	4.7	4.6
Algeria	25.1	33.5	Mozambique	4.7	4.3
Nigeria	24.5	35.2	Tanzania	4.3	2
Zambia	17.6	10.5	Burkina Faso	3.5	0.6
Sudan/South Sudan	16.2	17.1	Botswana	3.0	3.2
DRC	14.9	10.2	Morocco	2.2	1.5
Guinea	14.8	9.4	Togo	2	1.2
Egypt	10.5	15.0			

Resource Poor	2009	Av. 2000-2009		2009	Av. 2000-2009
Liberia	1.4	0.3	Swaziland	0	0
Senegal	1.3	0.4	Benin	0	0
Burundi	1.1	0.5	Cape Verde	0	0
Namibia	0.9	0.9	Comoros	0	0
Sierra Leone	0.8	0.4	The Gambia	0	0
Niger	0.8	0.4	Guinea-Bissau	0	0
Ethiopia	0.2	0.1	Lesotho	0	0
Eritrea	0	0	Malawi	0	0
Kenya	0	0	Mauritius	0	0
Madagascar	0	0	Sao Tome and Principe	0	0
CAR	0	0	Seychelles	0	0
Rwanda	0	0	Somalia	0	0
Uganda	0	0	Djibouti	0	0

Source: World Bank 2013b

Resource extraction cycle

Extraction of oil and gas and minerals follows a fairly well-defined cycle for all countries (Table 12.4), and in each country it is governed by a legal and contractual framework that depends on the country's specific oil and gas, mineral, and investment legal codes. The degree to which a mining or oil and gas extraction operation is governed by law or by contract varies from country to country.

The extraction cycle commences with exploration, for which the investor must generally obtain an exploration permit. Once economically viable oil, gas, or mineral resources have been discovered, the investor generally has then to obtain a production contract before developing the resource and investing in production facilities. During the life of the oil or gas field or the mine, production parameters (such as minimum investment amounts) and tax and royalty payments are defined by this production contract, which generally also defines social and environmental responsibilities and any required end-of-life remediation steps. In some cases these parameters are contained in a country's legal framework instead. Processing oil, gas, or minerals into usable intermediate or end products (petroleum products, metals) may or may not be carried out in the country of production. If it is, the legal framework and tax regime are for the most part those of other industrial sectors.

Table 12.4 The same framework applies to most resource deposits, although it depends on a country's legal complexities

	Legal Framework		Resource Taxation	
	Oil and Gas	**Minerals**	**Oil and Gas**	**Minerals**
Exploration	Exploration permits auctioned off under a competitive process	Exploration permits granted on a first-come first-served process	Exploration bonus paid for right to explore	No bonus paid (but minimum investment commitment)
Production	Production sharing contract	Concession contract	Royalty; Oil production tax; Equity stake for government	Royalty; Mineral production tax; (Often a tax holiday is granted for the initial years)
Processing	Refining and processing are generally undertaken as part of the legal framework covering industry		Refining and processing are taxed at normal income tax rates. Petroleum products have specific excise taxes in addition to any economy-wide value-added or sales tax	

Source: Centennial Group International 2013

Attribution of exploration and production permits

Oil and gas exploration permits are generally auctioned off in blocks (a block is a defined acreage for exploration), and potential investors' bids include an initial cash payment (called a signature bonus) to the government, as well as investment or exploration commitments. The government selects the highest bidder based on a combination of the signature bonus and investment commitment. Mining exploration permits, in contrast, are traditionally granted on a "first come, first served" basis and seldom include cash payments. This practice reflects the generally lower resource rent of the mineral compared to oil and gas and the lower degree of competition for mining exploration acreage.

At the production stage, oil production permits are generally production sharing agreements that specify a significant equity share for the government in the investment itself.[7] The government is thus both a sovereign regulator and a shareholder. Once the oil field is under production the government receives, because of its equity in the field, either a cash payment equal to the value of its oil (on top of royalties and taxes due to it as sovereign), or it takes physical delivery of a percentage of total oil production, which it will often then market directly or refine through its national petroleum company.

Many mining production contracts, on the other hand, have been straightforward concession agreements that define royalties and taxes as well as the investor's obligations but do not include an equity share of the investment for the government. There are, however, important exceptions to this practice and increasingly, as commodity prices have risen in the past decade, governments have sought a stake in the equity of the mining operation as well.

Africa's record with resource extraction contracts

On balance, African countries negotiate a worse deal on resource rent sharing than other countries. Although it is difficult to obtain hard data concerning the resource rent-sharing terms of natural resource production contracts in Africa, abundant anecdotal evidence suggests that African countries receive on average a lower share of resource rents than countries in other regions of the world.

The lower share of resource rents that African countries obtain represents, in part, the higher risk and cost of investing in the African continent. Governments in Africa have the reputation of being less predictable; the risk of expropriation is higher, at least based on the historical record; there is a greater risk of armed conflict; and Africa's infrastructure endowment is poorer. All of these factors represent risks or, in the case of infrastructure, costs that investors will need to offset through a higher return on their investment, and therefore a larger share of the resource rent. Risk and return are strongly correlated, and African countries must grant investors more of the resource rent because of the perception that Africa is a risky place to do business.

But higher risks and increased infrastructure costs are not the only reasons for the less favorable contractual terms. A lower share of the resource rent also reflects the weaker negotiating stance that African governments generally have in their negotiations with private investors compared to other parts of the world. African governments often have lower capacity and less extensive information, and especially do not make enough use of external expert advice to assist them in their negotiations.

Corruption lowers government take as well. Side payments to officials and persons of influence do not only come out of investors' profits (which is the private sector's share of the resource rent) but to a very large extent out of the government's share. Thus, these payments reduce the governments' formal

---

7. The government's equity share is often carried, i.e., financed by the private investor and reimbursed out of future cash flow.

share of the resource rent. African countries are probably no more corrupt than those in other parts of the world, but there are fewer external checks in Africa in the form of the transparency that civil society oversight would bring. Therefore, corruption may have a greater impact on reducing the government's share of resource rent.

In recent decades African countries have started to base their mining codes and oil and gas legislation, including their fiscal frameworks, on standardized best practice following policy advice provided notably by the World Bank. This initiative has been praised by industry because it provides them with a more rational framework for comparison between countries and reduces the dimensions in negotiations between the two parties. It should also have significant advantages for civil society because it has the potential of providing them with a standardized comparison. But despite being based on a common framework, the precise fiscal terms are almost never known beyond the relevant ministries (mining or energy, and in some cases the ministry of finance). Confidentiality is often explained on the grounds that these sectors are strategic. Whatever the merits of this argument, the resulting lack of transparency prevents public scrutiny, favors side payments and corruption, and leads to poor development outcomes.

Transforming and processing Africa's resources – Who gets the benefits?

Spin-offs from processing raw materials locally

Africa's resources are mostly exported for processing elsewhere. To a large extent Africa exports its raw materials for processing and inclusion into finished products in other parts of the globe. For example, although Africa possesses 26 percent of world bauxite reserves and produces 9 percent of world bauxite, in 2011 it only produced 4 percent of primary aluminum (US Department of the Interior and US Geological Survey 2012; International Aluminum Institute 2013). There are, however, important exceptions to this rule, notably for precious metals and copper/cobalt where high transport costs and the high value of the finished metal make it more economical to process them locally.

Mining and oil and gas production are capital-intensive activities that do not create much direct employment. Without local processing, the potential opportunities for job creation, development of skills and human capacity, and linkages to the rest of the economy are lost. For decades the continent's leaders have lamented the export of Africa's raw materials elsewhere for processing and have tried to encourage or coerce investors into integrating their activities downstream by investing in processing capacity in the region. From an economic point of view this position may have been misguided.

Oil, gas, and mineral processing are not very profitable businesses. Transformation processes such as oil refining, gas treatment, and mineral processing can at best hope to cover their long-run marginal costs over long periods, with significant overshooting and undershooting around the trend line. On average they do not generate significant profits or value added, and their contribution to GDP is small. A processing plant will need to have a geographic advantage of some sort to be able to buck the overall trend of low profitability and generate a profit over long period.

> **Box 12.1** | **Mining ownership in Zimbabwe and South Africa**
>
> The mining sectors in Zimbabwe and South Africa have been important drivers of economic activity for these countries for over a century, producing gold, platinum, diamonds, and other minerals. In both countries mines were developed – at least initially – by foreign investors, creating well-known companies such as Anglo-American, Goldfields, de Beers, and others.
>
> Following majority rule, there was significant dissatisfaction with the lack of equity in the sharing of the resource rent. In both countries, there has been a concern to transfer ownership of the sector to formerly disadvantaged nationals.
>
> South Africa attempted to change the ownership structure of its mining industry in 2004. The Mineral and Petroleum Resources Development Act sought, among other things, to expand opportunities for historically disadvantaged South Africans to enter the mineral industry and obtain benefits from the exploitation of mineral resources; and to promote employment, social and economic welfare, as well as ecologically sustainable development. Companies were required to lodge a social and labor plan on how they intended to expand opportunities for historically disadvantaged persons. The Mineral and Petroleum Resources Development Act (incorporating the Mining Charter) also required a mining company to have ownership by historically disadvantaged South Africans at a level of 15 percent by April 30, 2009, and 26 percent by April 30, 2014, transferred at fair market value. A review of this legislation undertaken by the government in 2010 concluded that it had not been fully successful in transferring significant assets to new investors (9 percent had been transferred by 2009) and opened questions about whether the priorities should focus on improved fiscal terms for the government rather than transfer of capital ownership to political elites. However, the 2014 target has been maintained and guidance has been provided about other aspects of the charter (e.g., dividend payments, job creation, and training). The government retains wide-ranging discretionary powers in the sector.
>
> In 2010 Zimbabwe passed an indigenization law under which foreign companies must transfer a controlling stake (51 percent) to indigenous nationals over a five year period. An "indigenous Zimbabwean" is defined as "any person who before the 18 April 1980" - the official founding date of Zimbabwe - "was disadvantaged by unfair discrimination on the grounds of his or her race." This ruling has created opportunities for politically well-connected individuals to benefit from the rent transfer (the UK press has referred to it as "racketeering by regulation") and has had a chilling effect on investment in the Zimbabwean mining sector. It will not, however, increase the share of rent that goes to government to pay for investments in human and physical capital.
>
> In terms of investment outcomes in the mining sector following the introduction of the new legislation, South Africa has fared better than Zimbabwe. South African mines continue to attract capital, both domestic and foreign, although at a much lower level than in the past. Whether this is a reflection of the more modest targets imposed in the law or a greater sense of legal due process open to investors in South Africa, is not clear.

In the case of oil refining, the geographic advantage is being located close to key market hubs such as Rotterdam in Europe (at the mouth of the Rhine and barge transport into Germany), Singapore in Asia, and the Gulf Coast in the United States. Locating refineries close to these key market hubs minimizes overall transport costs because the cost of transporting crude oil to refineries is significantly lower than the cost of transporting refined products to a market hub.[8] Most African refineries are located far from the market hubs and, therefore, lose money in economic terms and need to be subsidized to remain in service (either directly from the treasury or through administered prices for locally refined petroleum products which keep them above the cost of imports). This transport cost structure explains why only 1 percent of world refinery throughput takes place on the African continent, even though Africa represents 3.9 percent of world petroleum product consumption and produces 10.4 percent of the world's oil (British Petroleum 2012).[9]

In the case of aluminum smelting, the geographic advantage is due not so much to proximity to major market hubs as access to cheap energy because of the extremely high energy cost of transforming alumina (an intermediate product between bauxite ore and metal aluminum) into aluminum. The only way an aluminum smelter can generate a positive margin over a long period is to be able to buy electrical energy at a price far below its average world cost, generally because the smelter has access to extremely cheap hydroelectricity (e.g., smelters in Ghana, Cameroon, Canada) or has a contract to buy energy at a very low marginal cost (Mozal smelter in Mozambique, which has a contract with South Africa's ESKOM at fractions of a cent per kWh). If a smelter does not have access to cheap electricity it cannot hope even to break even. Iron ore is to some extent in a similar situation.

There are exceptions to this geographic disadvantage, notably in the case of precious metals such as gold, silver, the platinum group metals, and copper. In Africa, ores of these metals are generally processed at or close to the mine. The high monetary value of the metal compared to the onerous transport costs of the ore justify refining into metal at the point of extraction. But even so, their processing does not create much employment nor do they have significant linkages to the rest of the economy.

Record on downstream processing in Africa's industries

With a few notable exceptions such as diamond processing in Botswana (see Box 12.2), the record of downstream processing in Africa, when it has occurred, has not been good. As indicated above, most African processing plants already have a major handicap compared to optimally located plants. In addition, unit investment costs in Africa have almost always been much higher than those in other parts of the world, in part because of the poor infrastructure endowment, which increases construction costs, and in part because of poor procurement practices. For example, a Memorandum of Understanding signed in mid-2012 between the government of Nigeria and a private US-Nigerian joint venture for the construction of refining capacity of 180,000 barrels/day (9 million tons/year) sets the investment at $4.5 billion, three times the estimated world average for the investment cost for a moderately complex refinery of a similar capacity (Bala-Gbogbo 2012, Favennec 2001). Nigeria is an expensive place to do business and Nigerian refineries will find it difficult to compete.

---

8. Petroleum products are transported in smaller, more technically sophisticated vessels than crude oil, which costs more per ton-mile.
9. 3.6 percent of world refinery capacity is located in Africa, but has a very low utilization rate due to its poor profitability.

> **Box 12.2 | Botswana – Diamond Sorting Initiative**
>
> The discovery of the Orapa diamond pipeline in 1967 by De Beers introduced diamond mining to Botswana, which has transformed the country from one of the poorest economies in the world to one of the fastest growing middle income countries in the world. Diamond production was undertaken through the Debswana joint venture, a 50/50 partnership between the Government of Botswana and De Beers.
>
> In May 2006, the government and De Beers established DTC Botswana, a subsidiary of Debswana, to sort and value Debswana's production and to make aggregated diamond mixes available for sale in Botswana for local manufacturing. A building was constructed with a total capacity to process 45 million carats and to accommodate up to 600 employees. It incorporates state-of-the-art sorting equipment.
>
> Today, DTC Botswana is the largest and most sophisticated rough diamond sorting and valuing operation in the world. DTC Botswana sells and markets rough diamonds to 21 cutting and polishing companies licensed by the Government of Botswana to carry out cutting and polishing activities locally. DTC Botswana aims to facilitate, drive, and support the creation of a sustainable and profitable downstream diamond industry in Botswana that will deliver additional value for Botswana's diamonds. With further development of the downstream diamond industry, there is likely to be continued job creation in the coming years. The downstream activities add value to the local diamond industry through cutting and polishing of diamonds and ultimately manufacturing of jewelry.
>
> The establishment of DTC Botswana also acts as a potential catalyst for the development of new business clusters such as banking, security, information technology, and tourism, and for other international businesses to invest in Botswana.
>
> *Source:* Centennial Group International 2013

Moreover, where processing plants have been set up in Africa, with the exception of Botswana, not only have their geographic disadvantages made them largely uneconomic, but they have also not been good at developing world-class skills either because of poor profitability or often poor management, even though they may represent an important source of local employment. For example, before its privatization in 2002 the Zambian state-owned enterprise ZCCM, which smelted copper ore into copper and cobalt metals, was the most important source of employment in the Zambian Copper Belt, employing thousands of workers. But its operating techniques were decades old because of the lack of investment in its plants, and the skills it imparted were not very useful outside its own operations. Similarly, the Nigerian state-owned petroleum company NNPC has had great difficulty in keeping its oil refineries operating due to low profitability and poor maintenance and has not been able to provide significant skills to the workers in the Nigerian refining industry.

Conditions for downstream processing to succeed

The disappointing outcome from downstream processing in the past does not mean that it should be forgone in all cases going forward. There are some important success stories for downstream processing such as the one just described in Botswana and others in countries like South Africa and Morocco, and there is still a case to be made for it if the conditions are right. In order to work and make a positive contribution to the economy, downstream processing must respect three criteria:

- A significant geographic advantage other than reserves of the natural resource itself;
- Investment and ownership by the private sector, to ensure effective management; and
- A competitive environment without reliance on operating or price subsidies.

A Vision for Africa's Extractive Industries in 2050

In 2050 Africa could be the factory and granary to the world, just as Britain and the United States were the factories and the United States and Argentina the granaries in the second half of the 19th century, succeeded in the 20th century by China and Australia.

This vision will need Africa's workers, who are young and energetic, to become highly skilled, productive, and cost-effective. If it is realized, this vision would confer on African countries highly diversified economies where the extractive industries are only a small part of total output but that produce the inputs for its highly competitive manufacturing and service industries. In this vision Africa will have avoided the resource curse and turned it into a blessing.

Resource-rich African countries can converge with the advanced and emerging market economies if they use their resources now to build a diverse economy alongside their extractive industries. If they do, natural resource rents will over time represent a much smaller share of GDP, in part because of the inevitable decline of extractive industries on the continent between now and 2050 but mostly because of growth in other sectors of the economy. Africa's resource importance is declining compared to other parts of the world, and the fiscal revenue available to African countries from the extractive industries could well decline over the next 40 years.

Policymakers of resource-rich African countries need to take action on specific policy measures now or they are likely to miss an important opportunity for economic convergence.

Action Agenda

All African countries with natural resource exports will need to implement the following measures to get onto the convergence path. Two relate specifically to natural resources; the other two relate to broader economic policy. All are described in more detail below.

Actions relating to the natural resource sector:

- *Obtain a greater share of resource rents,* through better informed negotiations with mining and oil and gas companies, and greater transparency and public accountability to reduce opportunities for corruption.

- *Manage their resource rents effectively,* by establishing rigorous macroeconomic management based on fiscal rules to offset boom-and-bust cycles and to address intergenerational tradeoffs. Stabilization and wealth funds should be created where needed.

Actions relating to broader economic management:

- *Invest fiscal revenues to create inclusive development,* notably in public infrastructure and human capital.
- *Foster a diversified private sector alongside extractive industries* to provide the basis for strong, inclusive growth. Doing so will require, in particular, a better business environment and greater integration of Africa's economies (see Chapters 10 and 14).

Natural resource-related policy measures:

To *obtain a greater share of resource rents* policy makers must:

Ensure *greater transparency* in their extractive industries through public disclosure of the fiscal and other terms of resource extraction contracts.[10]

- *Call on world class expertise when negotiating new contracts.* Financial assistance can be obtained through the facilities managed by the African Development Bank and the World Bank.

Greater transparency in contracting would lead to more equitable sharing of resource rents. The first step would be transparency across the region about the precise ratio of rent sharing, i.e., what tax and royalty rates and other parafiscal levies private investors have to pay. Currently, the terms of contracts governing the extraction of natural resources in Africa are difficult to obtain, even for government officials not in the relevant sector ministry.

Nationalization is not a solution. In past decades some countries (not only those in Africa), frustrated by the unfair sharing of resource rents and the raw deal they believed they were getting, resorted to nationalization (replacing private investors by state-owned companies) or indigenization (transferring a portion of ownership of existing assets to nationals) as a means to increase the national share of the resource rent. These strategies have not proved to be good options for Africa any more than they have in other parts of the world: where oil, gas, and mineral extraction is undertaken by a state-owned enterprise, the outcome frequently combines both inefficiency and corruption. By almost any measure most natural resource-based state owned companies, such as Sonatrach in Algeria (oil and gas) and Gécamines in the DRC have significantly underperformed compared to their private peers. Transferring a portion of the capital to nationals creates very significant opportunities for rent-seeking and corruption without addressing the central issue of inequitable sharing of the resource rent between the investor and the government. Part of the solution is for national and foreign companies to be treated equally in the tendering process.

---

10. Such transparency, involving disclosure of actual fiscal terms, goes beyond Extractive Industries Transparency Initiative which publishes financial flows paid by the private investor to the government, and as such does not provide an estimate of the resource rent sharing.

To get a better deal for their countries, African governments will need to take into account that they are operating in a competitive environment, and private investors have the choice to go elsewhere. Three types of actions are needed—most notably, those that reduce investors' costs and perceptions of political risk, but also those that enhance governments' negotiating capacity and those that eliminate corruption. By reducing their handicaps and having negotiators who are world-class, honest, and very well-informed, the terms of the deal will become much better balanced.

Greater transparency is the best way to reduce or eliminate corruption. Given the widespread lack of transparency in the extractive industries, several global initiatives have been launched to improve outcomes for resource-rich countries (Box 12.3).

To *manage their resource rents effectively* policy makers must:
- *Apply fiscal management rules to address cyclicality* of resource and non-resource revenues, e.g., non-resource primary fiscal balance target or structural primary fiscal target.
- *Implement a monetary policy framework based on inflation targeting, unless a monetary union is in place.*
- *Consider the creation of stabilization and wealth funds,* managed independently and domiciled in an external bank of international standing.
- *Nurture the development of resource clusters.*

Resource-rich countries need to implement policies that deal with volatility and intergenerational trade-offs. Potentially important tools in the management of fiscal flows are stabilization/liquidity funds, designed to help avoid boom and bust cycles, as well as wealth funds to help manage the economic distortions associated with resource booms and to address intergenerational issues. The following sections elaborate on fiscal rules for the management of resource flows and on the use of resource funds.

Fiscal rules to promote macroeconomic stability

To delink public spending from the dynamics of resource earnings for macroeconomic stability purposes, policymakers can adopt fiscal rules that define a sustainable public spending pattern that is protected from the volatility of resource earnings. Such rules would smooth public spending over time by allowing for larger (or smaller) government deficits when resource earnings are lower (or higher) than their long-term potential level.[11]

This section focuses on two alternative rules or approaches, both of which establish short- to medium-term fiscal targets that take into account fiscal sustainability in the longer-term. They consist of the adoption of (1) a non-resource primary fiscal balance or (2) a structural primary fiscal balance.[12] Both

---

[11]. These rules call for a well-defined formula and expert judgment to estimate long-term potential resource earnings and the benchmark/reference price of the natural resource. As the resource horizons and price developments are uncertain, this potential needs to be updated with some frequency.

[12]. Targeting the non-resource or structural primary fiscal balance is more appropriate than targeting the corresponding overall balances because it allows for the formulation and assessment of fiscal policy independent of changes in interest payments.

Box 12.3 Global transparency initiatives for resource-rich countries

The Extractive Industries Transparency Initiative (EITI), the most important global initiative on natural resource governance, aims to improve transparency of payments by oil, gas, and mining companies to governments or government agencies such as state-owned enterprises, as well as transparency in the use of revenues by host country governments. EITI has been implemented in 37 resource-rich countries, of which 18 are fully compliant with EITI principles and 19 are candidate countries. One country has been suspended.

EITI has issued a set of reporting guidelines, a Statement of Principles, and six criteria that represent the global minimum standard for EITI implementation:

- Regular publication of all oil, gas, and mining payments by companies to governments; all revenues received by governments from companies; data made available to a wide audience in a publicly accessible manner.
- Payments and revenues are the subject of a credible, independent audit, applying international auditing standards.
- Payments and revenues are reconciled by a credible, independent administrator.
- This approach is extended to all companies including state-owned enterprises.
- Civil society is actively engaged as a participant in the design, monitoring, and evaluation of this process and contributes toward public debate.
- A public, financially sustainable work plan for all the above is to be developed by the host government, including measurable targets, a timetable for implementation, and an assessment of potential capacity constraints.

African countries are important players in EITI, representing over half of all the countries involved in the initiative. Currently, 10 of the EITI-compliant countries (Central African Republic, Ghana, Liberia, Mali, Mauritania, Mozambique, Niger, Nigeria, Tanzania, and Zambia) are from the African continent, as are 11 of the candidate countries (Burkina Faso, Cameroon, Democratic Republic of the Congo, Gabon, Guinea, Republic of Congo, São Tomé and Principe, Sierra Leone, and Togo). The one suspended country – Madagascar – is from Africa as well. EITI has had a significant and positive impact on transparency in financial flows in the oil, gas, and mining sectors of its member countries, reducing opportunities for corruption and improving outcomes.

The Kimberley Process Certification Scheme (Kimberley Process) is an international governmental certification initiative set up by governments, industry, and civil society to prevent the trade in diamonds that fund conflict. Launched in January 2003, the scheme requires governments to certify that shipments of rough diamonds are conflict-free. Currently, 75 governments participate in the Kimberley Process. Its technical provisions are implemented by governments, but its tripartite structure means that non-governmental organizations and the diamond industry hold official status as observers and take part, along with member states, in all working groups and decision-making processes.

> **Box 12.3** **Global transparency initiatives for resource-rich countries (continued)**
>
> Natural Resource Charter is a global initiative designed to help governments and civil society effectively harness the opportunities created by natural resources. The Natural Resource Charter provides twelve precepts to inform and improve natural resource management. It was drafted by an independent group of experts in economically sustainable resource extraction and has no political sponsorship. It is a common framework for addressing the challenges of natural resource management. The Charter can be viewed here: http://natural-resourcecharter.org/precepts.
>
> Publish What You Pay (PWYP) is a global network of civil society organizations that undertakes public campaigns and policy advocacy to encourage disclosure of information about extractive industry revenues and contracts. The network is diverse, with over 650 member organizations across the world including human rights, development, environmental, and faith-based organizations. In about 30 countries, network members have joined forces to create civil society coalitions for collective action to enhance transparency of natural resource revenues. More information can be found at http://www.publishwhatyoupay.org/.
>
> In addition to these global initiatives, several global advocacy NGOs focus on the issue of revenue transparency and corruption, either as part of a broader mandate (Oxfam: http://www.oxfam.org/en/about/issues/natural-resources) or as their key objective (Revenue Watch [http://www.revenuewatch.org/] and Global Witness [http://www.revenuewatch.org/]).
>
> The success of these various initiatives has been mixed. There is a consensus that EITI has had a very significant effect both on transparency of funds flows and on norms of behavior, particularly in the oil and gas sector. On the other hand, the Kimberley Process has been a mitigated success at best. Overall however, these initiatives have together raised global awareness of the issues surrounding corruption and lack of transparency in resource-rich countries, including in particular within the civil societies of African countries, and are having a beneficial impact on the way these industries are managed.
>
> *Source:* Extractive Industries Transparency Initiative 2013

approaches involve the establishment of a stabilization/liquidity fund, which accumulates revenues in good times that can be used to cover public spending in bad times, relative to long-term potential resource revenues. By smoothing public spending over the cycle, they effectively help achieve a more stable macroeconomic environment. Under either approach, a more stable macroeconomic environment will help improve the spending quality and efficiency of both the public and private sectors by allowing for better expenditure planning.

The non-resource primary balance is the overall primary balance excluding all tax and royalty collection from natural resource activities. It measures the effect of government operations on domestic demand, given that resource earnings are originated externally. Using the non-resource primary balance as a target helps delink fiscal policy from the volatility of resource earnings. The structural primary balance is the overall primary balance excluding the cyclical component of resource and non-resource revenue.

The implementation of this approach requires an independent institutional framework to ensure credibility of the estimates of the cyclical component. Moreover, estimating this component of revenue (and the associated output gap) may be quite a complex task, a key reason for its limited worldwide use.

Stabilization/liquidity fund to address volatility in resource earnings

The size of a stabilization/liquidity fund should be determined mainly by the expected volatility in earnings (due to variations in the resource price), especially the extent of the swings, with just a minimum or no accumulation of funds over the commodity price cycle. Such a fund requires adequate transparency and public oversight to prevent corruption and mismanagement. The fund also needs to be supported by the capacity to develop medium-term forecasts of resource revenues. These funds are in essence a type of self-insurance and may be expensive when weighed against a country's pressing development needs. Countries could instead opt for market-based instruments to deal with earnings volatility (e.g., futures contracts) or for a minimum liquidity buffer based on, for example, value-at-risk models. But these approaches are technically complex, costly, and difficult to explain to stakeholders, as well as politically risky. Therefore, it would seem advisable for resource-rich African countries to adopt a stabilization/liquidity fund now while international prices are still relatively high by historical standards. Some countries have already gone this route as shown in Box 12.4.

Wealth fund for intergenerational equity

Efficient use of resource rents also has an important time dimension. Resource-rich countries need to make the trade-off between extracting the resource now and leaving it in the ground for future generations. Moreover, for a variety of reasons (including uncertain future price developments) they may consider it advisable to extract now, setting aside some of the proceeds for future use in the form of financial assets. The exhaustible nature of natural resources calls for intertemporal decisions about how much resource earnings to consume and invest, and how much to save.[13] This decision may involve a complex sociopolitical process. While saving a portion of the resource earnings makes sense, a balance has to be found between the welfare of future generations and the immediate needs to reduce poverty and invest in physical and human capital, which are critical for building an inclusive society and may well have a high social rate of return. This tradeoff is especially acute for African countries where such expenditure is crucially needed. Similarly, spending resources beyond the economy's absorptive capacity is not desirable either because it will lead to the distortions typically associated with Dutch disease.[14] Thus, for a lasting impact on development, part of the resource earnings needs to be saved. Moreover, the portion that is to be saved into a wealth fund is closely related to the value society attaches to intergenerational equity and has important implications for short- and long-term macroeconomic policies.[15]

---

13. Despite their large resource earnings, many resource-rich African countries have had very low savings to GDP ratios.
14. For instance, most oil-exporting African countries record very high levels of government spending in relation to non-resource GDP (around 50 percent of GDP), thereby generating intense price pressures on domestic resources.
15. A priori, the shorter the reserve horizon, the more important are the intergenerational (and fiscal sustainability) considerations, and therefore the larger portion or resource earnings to be saved.

> **Box 12.4 | African countries with stabilization or wealth funds**
>
> Stabilization funds offset commodity price swings to smooth fiscal resource availability and government spending over the commodity cycle. Wealth funds invest financial assets from resource extraction for use by future generations. Wealth funds and stabilization funds established by African resource-rich countries include:
>
> - Botswana adopted in 1994 a Sustainable Budget Index Principle that ensures that resource revenue is invested or saved. Since then, a large stock of savings has been accumulated in its Pula Fund, which is managed by the Bank of Botswana. The fund also acts as stabilization mechanism when resources fall sharply (as occurred in 2009).
> - Nigeria adopted in 2004 a budgetary rule whereby oil revenue is linked to a historical average of oil prices (adjusted in budget negotiations). Excess oil revenue was deposited in the Excess Crude Account (ECA). Resources from this account can be drawn when revenues are short of the target. Withdrawals took place in 2009, when oil prices dropped sharply, but also in 2010 and 2011, despite the strong oil price recovery and contrary to Excess Crude Account's stabilization function. Because the Excess Crude Account did not have legal backing, Parliament replaced it in 2011 by establishing a sovereign wealth fund with three components: a stabilization fund, a fund to finance domestic priority infrastructure investments, and a fund for longer-term purposes. The sovereign wealth fund became operational in 2012, with an initial allocation of US$1 billion.
> - Ghana has recently put in place a legal framework governing oil revenue; oil revenue is calculated on the basis of a five year moving average. 70 percent of such revenue will be allocated to the budget and the rest split between a stabilization fund and a heritage fund.
> - Other resource-rich countries (e.g., Angola, Chad, Guinea, Equatorial Guinea) have accumulated significant assets offshore, without formally establishing a stabilization or wealth fund.
>
> Source: IMF 2012a

Quality of public investment

Another key issue is the quality of the investment financed by the earnings from the resource boom, as this has implications for growth and economic diversification as well as for building an equitable society with a well-designed social protection system. Many resource-rich African countries need to build up their project formulation and implementation capacity, as well as strengthen their capacity to enhance the quality and effectiveness of education and health services. They also need to increase their absorptive capacity. These efforts are critically important and require considerable time to bear fruit. Therefore, countries should avoid rushing into wasteful spending that will hinder achievement of these goals.[16] Moreover, rushing may lead to an unwarranted real appreciation of the currency caused by

---

16. It may also lead to significant governance, rent-seeking, and corruption problems, which underscores the need to build and maintain sound institutions.

jumps in non-tradable good prices and thus an otherwise avoidable loss of competitiveness. Once both the absorptive capacity of the economy and the ability of government officials to design and implement investment projects have been built, a cautious use of revenue from natural resources should play an important role in transforming the country.

Because the exploitation of mineral resources does not generally lead to significant increases in employment given its capital-intensive nature, policymakers need to plan government spending and investment carefully with a view to fostering economic sustainability, including through diversification of the economy. Enhancing infrastructure and human capital, removing bottlenecks and distortions, and encouraging ancillary activities, non-resource exports, and other employment-intensive activities (especially agriculture, agroindustry and services) would help contain the real appreciation of the currency.[17] Moreover, diversification into these activities is critical for job creation and long-term development as employment in mineral resources is likely to decline over time in relative (and, in some countries, in absolute) terms.

The fiscal rules or approaches described above (the non-resource primary balance and the structural primary balance) are key for fiscal policy to be consistent with the objective of building a wealth fund. The deficits in those balances represent the amount of resource earnings that is being consumed and/or invested by the government. It would seem appropriate for policy makers to target deficits that are somewhat larger in the early years of the resource boom in order to help address the pressing needs that prevail in most resource-rich African countries by scaling up high-priority investment in human and physical capital and in poverty reduction.[18] These deficits will need to be smaller in subsequent years, consistent with fiscal and external sustainability. The size of these deficits would also need to take account of the resource reserve horizon of the particular country. The shorter the time horizon, the smaller the deficit necessary to avoid an abrupt spending adjustment when resource revenue or the intergenerational fund are exhausted; such an adjustment would otherwise disrupt economic activity and the provision of services.

Having determined the portion of natural resource earnings to save in a wealth fund, countries need to decide how such a fund is to be managed. Chile's Economic and Social Stabilization Fund (ESSF, formerly the Copper Stabilization Fund; see Box 12.5) and Norway's Oil Fund offer good examples. Countries will also need to decide whether—and to what extent—it would be advisable for the wealth fund to lend to the private sector given that the domestic capital market is underdeveloped and bearing in mind that such lending should reflect due diligence and would add pressures on domestic resources.[19] Along

---

17. However, as the country becomes richer with the resource boom, some real appreciation of the currency will be unavoidable.
18. How much larger these deficits could be depends on the absorption capacity of the economy and the project formulation and implementation capacity, which should increase over time, and—linked to these issues—the need to avoid pushing up the price of non-tradable goods.
19. Transparency and accountability should help direct such lending to socially profitable projects and thus avoid the temptation of lending to entities or individuals just because they are closely associated with government officials.

Box 12.5 Chile's structural overall balance rule and wealth funds

Chile has been recognized for the rigor and boldness of its macroeconomic management and its ability to weather the boom and bust cycle of its main export, copper. It has applied the kinds of rules outlined in this chapter to deal with the cyclical nature of commodity prices and created two successful wealth funds.

The Structural Overall Balance Rule. Chile started implementing a structural fiscal balance rule in 2001 with the objective of determining the level of fiscal spending consistent with the government's structural revenue. This rule detaches such spending from fluctuations in the copper price, as well as in economic activity and other factors. This allows the government to save in boom times and thus avoid drastic adjustments to fiscal spending during unfavorable economic periods. Initially, implementation of the rule did not have legal backing, but it was formalized under the Fiscal Responsibility Law in 2006. In 2011, the Ministry of Finance created the Fiscal Council; its main role is to guarantee independence in the estimation of the structural variables and to verify the structural balance estimates.

The methodology to calculate the structural balance has been improved over time, mainly to better estimate structural revenue. For example, following the recommendations of an Advisory Committee, the 2011 budget excluded from structural revenue proceeds from temporary tax measures with a legal deadline and cyclical adjustments to other revenue and to interest income on financial assets held by the Treasury.

The structural overall balance target has also changed over time. The target was set initially at a surplus of 1 percent of GDP, in order to cover the losses of the Central Bank of Chile. The surplus was reduced to ½ percent of GDP in 2008, as the government considered that the Economic and Social Stabilization Fund had accumulated substantial resources. In 2009, faced with the global crisis, the government reduced the target to zero. (The methodological change of 2011 implied that the 2009 target actually was a deficit of 3 percent of GDP.) The target has been adjusted since then and is expected to converge to a structural deficit of 1 percent in 2014.

The Economic and Social Stabilization Fund (ESSF). The ESSF replaced the Copper Stabilization Fund (which was created in 1985) in 2007 and has the same macroeconomic stabilization objectives, as established by the FRL. The ESSF aims at accumulating excess copper revenues when the price of copper is high in order to transfer resources back to the budget when the price of copper is low, thereby smoothing out government expenditure. The ESSF receives all fiscal surpluses that exceed 1 percent of GDP, the structural fiscal target until 2009 when the government implemented a fiscal stimulus package to counteract the adverse effects of the global crisis. In October 2011, the government adopted a series of measures recommended by a panel of experts to improve the transparency of fiscal policy and to minimize the discretion in its application.

The Central Bank of Chile appoints the members of the Financial Committee; they must have vast experience in the economic and financial areas. The Committee reports to the Ministry of Finance and is responsible for advising the Minister of Finance on long-term investment policy and all other matters related to investment, on selecting fund managers, and on the contents and structure of the reports of the ESSF. Although the ESSF does not report to Congress, good governance is assured by the fact that Congress decides on the government's budget. The General Treasury produces the Fund's financial statements in accordance with International Financial Reporting Standards.

> **Box 12.5** | **Chile's structural overall balance rule and wealth funds (continued)**
>
> Management of the ESSF follows the Generally Accepted Principles and Practices, known internationally as the "Santiago Principles," agreed by the International Working Group of Sovereign Wealth Fund in Santiago, Chile in September 2008. In 2012 the government published a self-assessment of Chile's compliance with these voluntary principles with a view to improve the publicly available information about the ESSF and to show that it is managed in accordance with best international practices.
>
> As of end-2011, the market value of the assets of the ESSF amounted to $13.2 billion. As a stabilization fund, it must remain relatively liquid and therefore has to take a short-term view regarding its investments; its return was 5.1 percent in 2011. External managers play a key role in managing the Fund's resources, although the Financial Committee defines the strategic allocations (66.5 percent in sovereign bonds, 30 percent in money market instruments, and 3.5 percent in inflation-indexed sovereign bonds; the currency exposure is 50 percent to the US dollar, 40 percent to the euro and 10 percent to the yen). The Central Bank of Chile prepares daily, monthly, quarterly, and annual reports on the state of the Fund and performance of its investments, which are submitted to the Ministry of Finance and the General Treasury.
>
> The Pension Reserve Fund. It was also created in 2007, and its purpose is to address an expected future fiscal shortfall in the area of pensions and social welfare. Specifically, the fund backs the state guarantee for old-age and disability solidarity pension benefits, as well as the solidarity pension contribution, as established by the pension reform. Given its nature, the fund takes a longer-term view for its investments than the ESSF, and therefore it invests in a broader range of asset classes. As of end-2011, the fund had accumulated $4.4 billion. The fund must receive a minimum annual contribution of 0.2 percent of GDP. If the fiscal surplus exceeds this amount, the contribution can be increased by the amount of the surplus up to 0.5 percent of the previous year's GDP. The Fund is managed in a similar fashion as the ESSF.
>
> *Source:* Chilean Ministry of Finance 2012

the same lines, once a wealth fund is established, countries need to decide how much to consume and invest from the wealth fund or from its return, balanced against the need to preserve wealth for future generations.[20]

Discussing the tax regime appropriate for resource-rich countries is beyond the scope of this chapter, but taxation on the non-resource sectors of the economy is closely related to the discussion on wealth funds. Many resource-rich countries worldwide reduced the tax burden on these sectors, given the high revenues from resource activities. This reduction (or subsidy) could help diminish the distortions of the tax system, but it would—obviously—lower the portion of resource earnings that could be saved into a wealth fund and, indirectly, add to pressures on domestic resources. Moreover, many countries (e.g., Angola, Mexico, Nigeria, Trinidad and Tobago, and Venezuela) with low tax revenue from the

---

[20]. An approach based on the permanent income hypothesis would be advisable to guide such a decision, allowing for an initial period of higher spending to address pressing needs, as indicated above.

non-resource sectors experienced major adjustment needs and costs when they experienced a severe drop in resource earnings due to a major decline in commodity prices. Again, society will need to balance these considerations when deciding on the portion of resource earnings to be saved in a wealth fund.

Monetary and exchange rate framework

A stability/liquidity fund and a wealth fund, to the extent they can be set up and made to work, would help considerably in the conduct of monetary policy, as the first removes the pro-cyclicality of fiscal spending and the second prevents the excessive pressure on domestic resources that a natural resource boom would cause. Similarly, in a more stable macroeconomic environment, exchange rate tensions will be significantly less than otherwise.

The combination of the two funds provide a strong foundation for monetary policy to be based on an Inflation Targeting (IT) Framework, especially given the absence of fiscal dominance (i.e., that government deficits do not condition the growth of money supply). Some African countries are already using such a framework with success. Others will require time to develop the conditions necessary for its introduction. The IT framework will allow the implementation of a flexible exchange rate policy, which will, in turn, help reduce the impact of external shocks.[21]

Some resource-rich African countries have a fixed exchange rate or are part of a currency union, most notably those in WAEMU and CEMAC. If these regimes continue, it would be important that credit policy remain cautious and consistent with preserving external competitiveness. The combination of a stability/liquidity fund and a wealth fund provides a similar strong foundation for such a policy.

Broad economic policy measures

Nurturing the development of resource clusters

Although downstream processing may not have been a very significant success in Africa because of the continent's geographic and other disadvantages (low infrastructure endowment, low labor productivity), the extractive industries have over the years created positive spinoffs in other ways. Most notably, ecosystems of firms providing support functions to oil, gas, and mining operations have emerged organically around the extractive sector. For example, West African oil producers like Cameroon and Nigeria have seen the creation of internationally competitive support firms in oil logistics, maintenance and other associated services, some of which started as subsidiaries of international firms and others as local start-ups. South Africa has a record in the mining industry of hosting the best providers of mining services, from geologists and mining engineers to specialized banks, which now operate internationally. These clusters

---

21. The argument that a flexible exchange rate regime will lead to an unwarranted appreciation of the currency and that a fixed exchange rate regime will not is misleading. If the conditions for a real appreciation are present, it will happen irrespective of the exchange rate regime: through a nominal and thus real appreciation under the flexible regime or through a rise in the price of non-tradable goods. To avoid such conditions, the key is for policies to create the basis for sustained improvements in competitiveness of the non-resource tradable sectors including through investment in human and physical capital and the removal of bottlenecks and distortions, as discussed above.

provide employment, create world-class capacity, and possess strong links into the rest of the economy, and are a model for African resource-based sectors going forward. They are not significantly capital intensive and have been good at creating specialized human capacity, often of a world-class nature.

In addition to sound macroeconomic policies and effective management of public finances through fiscal rules and funds, governments can proactively seek to nurture these related-industry clusters to increase the positive spillovers of their natural resource sectors. This will require creating a business-friendly regulatory environment and economy and providing specialized targeted infrastructure. For example, a country with offshore oil production might target the development of its port, an efficient low-cost ICT infrastructure, and a modern commercial legal framework that favor the installation of service firms for the delivery of services such as offshore platform maintenance, cleaning and hospitality, oil-field geology, and crude oil trading. High-quality and low-cost communications services will allow local firms to bid for projects outsourced from the headquarters of producing companies. Ease of setting up firms and simplified tax procedures will lower the barriers to entry for local entrepreneurs. Availability of visas and work permits for foreign workers will allow them to work locally, facilitating the transmission of skills.

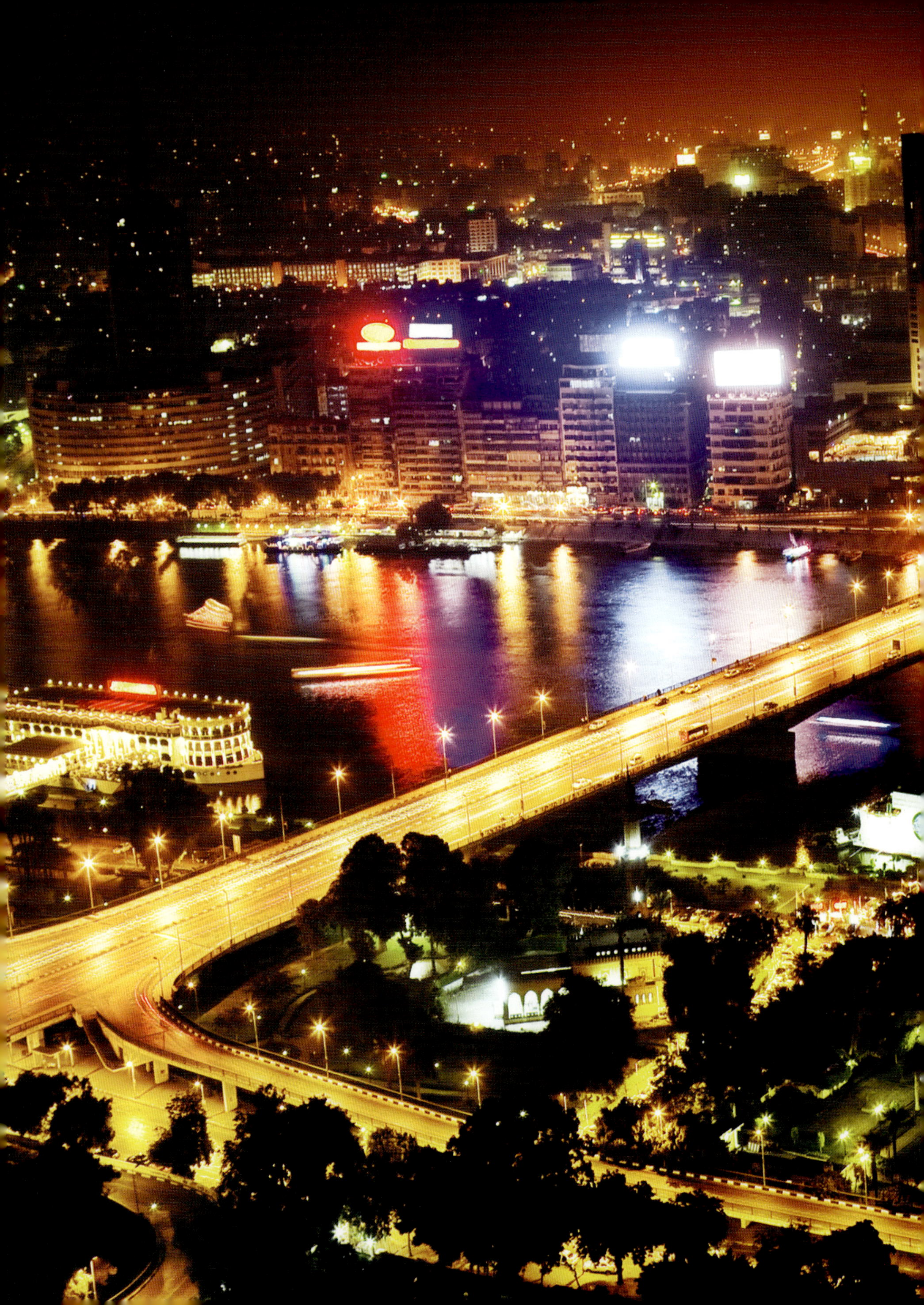

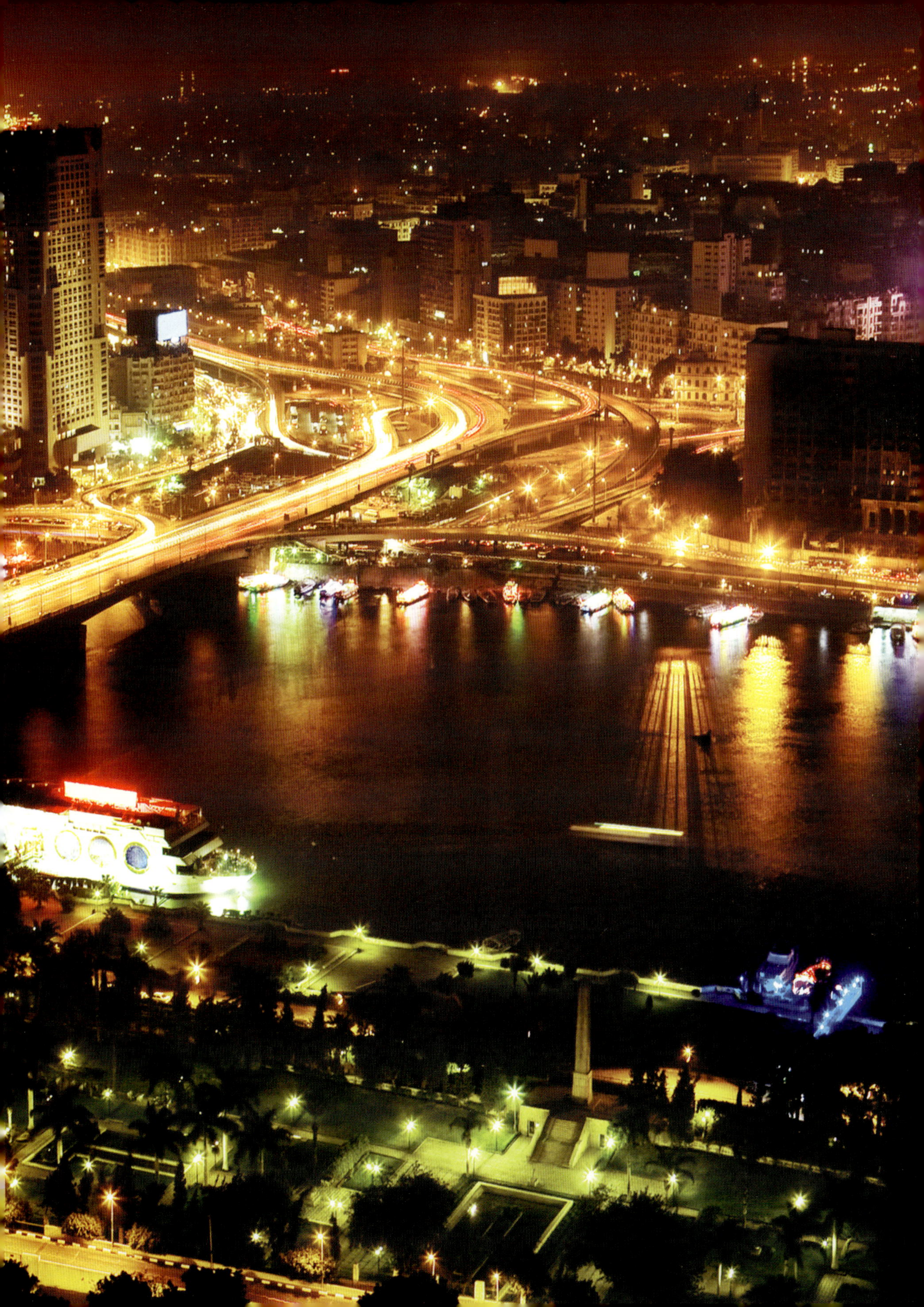

Managing Urbanization for Growth

Chapter 13

Jeffrey Racki, Praful Patel, and David DeGroot

The fast-evolving process of urbanization will transform Africa's future. Urbanization can be harnessed to build an effective urban platform for the continent's social and economic development but only by putting in place the right policies to capture the benefits of urban growth. The scope and scale of urban growth requires a fundamental change to current practices of making sporadic, large scale infrastructure investments. Cities must be enabled to facilitate and finance ongoing investment programs in partnership with local businesses and communities.

Over the next 40 years, Africa will have the fastest growing cities in the world. The vision of urbanization for 2050 depicts 1.5 billion African city-dwellers living in well-managed urban centers with adequate access to basic services, land, and shelter. How African leaders manage this increase in urbanization will determine the extent to which countries in the region become effective partners (and competitors) in the global economy. Public policy will play a major role in allowing African countries to capture the benefits of the urban transition while mitigating its risks. But policy will have little influence on the underlying urban transition itself. To realize the 2050 vision, African governments must radically transform their approaches to their cities. Instead of focusing almost exclusively on externally-financed support for discrete infrastructure investments, they must envision a broader approach that develops the systems necessary to underpin sustainable investments in urban infrastructure and services.

This chapter puts forward an agenda for achieving the 2050 vision focused on unlocking a more systematic approach to urban development and management. A key component of the agenda is the development of new partnerships for urban development and management between tiers of government, with the private sector, and with citizens. The new partnerships will focus on using local resources to leverage the financing needed to support urban growth. National governments will play a leading role in repositioning and strengthening local city managers to meet the challenges of urban growth. And all partners must develop strengthened capacity for city planning and management to meet projected demand for land and services.

The first section describes the massive urban transition that lies ahead for Africa. It highlights the potential of urban centers, appropriately managed, to contribute significantly to productivity increases, growth, and achievement of Vision 2050. The second lays out the challenges of urban policy that African economies must overcome to realize this potential. The next outlines the vision for African cities in 2050 and for their management. The chapter concludes with an Action Agenda for realizing the vision.

Urban Transition

Over the next 40 years, Africa will have the fastest growing cities in the world. Figure 13.1 show the dramatic growth projected for 2010 to 2025. About 800 million Africans will either migrate to, or be born in, urban areas in the next four decades. By 2050 Africa's cities and towns will house nearly 1.5 billion people, 60 percent of the region's projected population (UN-Habitat and UNEP 2010) (Figure 13.2). African cities are already the fastest growing in the world, and by 2050, the continent could be home to up to 15 mega-cities of more than 10 million inhabitants. Even already highly urbanized Egypt will see its urban population double by 2050.

The new urban population will be relatively young (see Chapter 5). With projected population growth rates in excess of 2 percent, the median age will continue to drop from the current 19.7 years. The number of youth (aged 15-24) will increase from 205 million today to between 330 and 450 million, the majority of whom will live in urban areas. These demographic shifts can lead to higher productivity and per capita incomes or to unmanageable social tensions, violence, and conflict. The Arab Spring demonstrates how youth disillusionment can rapidly gain momentum, particularly in urban areas where access to services and opportunities has lagged.

The urbanization dynamics will create growing demand for urban land and services. Declining fertility rates in urban areas will be offset by declining household sizes and mortality rates, as well as rising economic activity, per capita incomes and education levels. Africa's demographic dividend will be reaped or lost in its cities.

Importantly, around 70 percent of Africa's urban growth will take place in secondary cities. Large infrastructure investments and often-idiosyncratic institutional arrangements will continue to be required in the largest metropolises, but the needs of secondary cities will also have to be systematically addressed. Rapidly growing secondary cities will be home to more than half a billion new residents who will be seeking services, opportunities, and shelter in market towns that typically have had very little infrastructure but that are not bound by scarcity of land.

African leaders must manage this massive urban transition to ensure their place in the global economy. The seismic demographic shifts will generate growing pressure for urban land, services, and economic opportunities. Africa's cities will be the loci of much job creation. The size of urban markets, rising income of urban residents, and concentration of economic activity could make cities dynamic centers for higher productivity jobs — offering the prospects of a better life to more than one billion people. If policy-makers respond appropriately, urbanization offers a pathway to sustained and inclusive growth. But if people

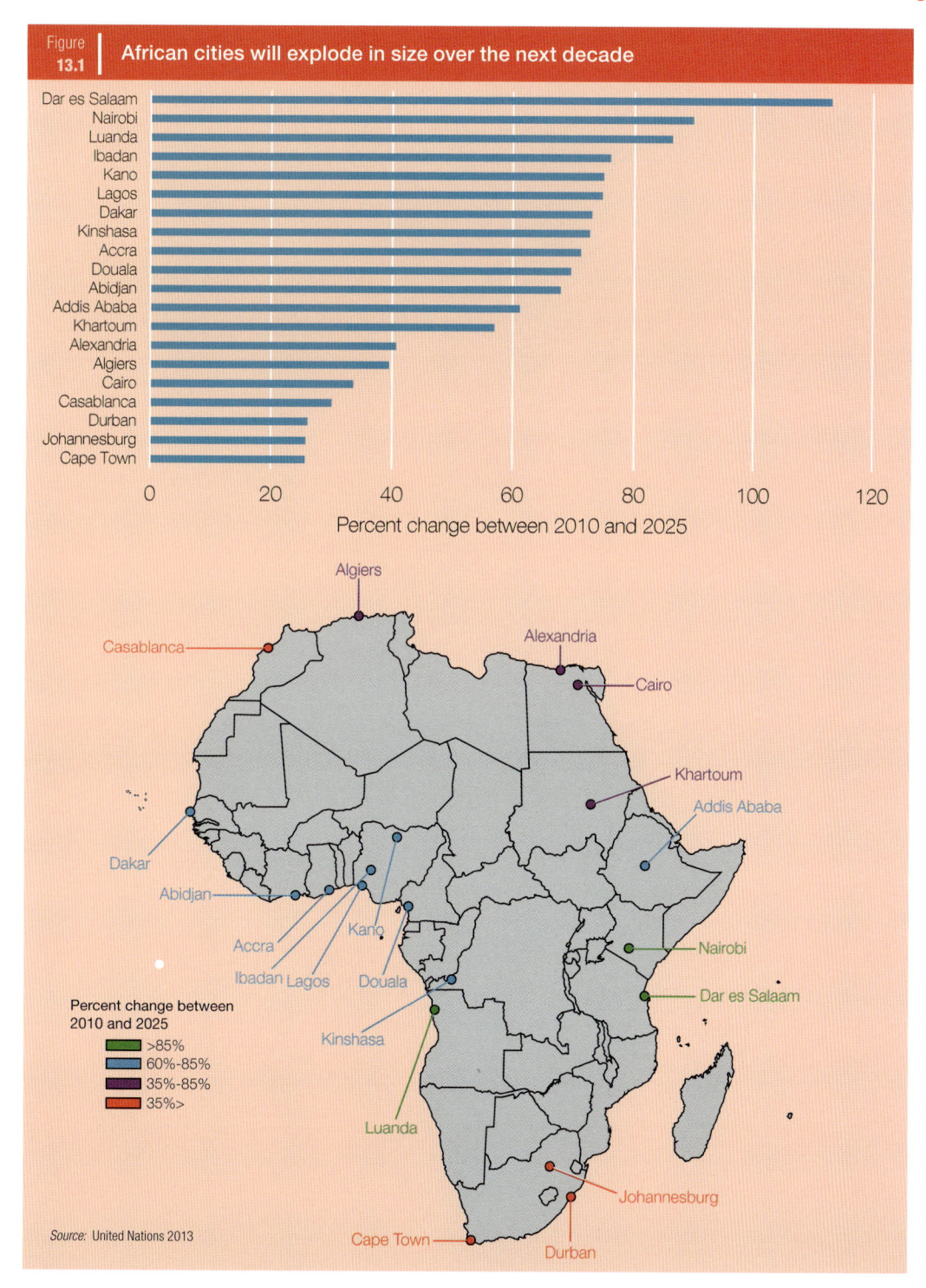

MANAGING URBANIZATION FOR GROWTH 341

Figure 13.1 African cities will explode in size over the next decade

City	
Dar es Salaam	~115
Nairobi	~90
Luanda	~87
Ibadan	~77
Kano	~75
Lagos	~75
Dakar	~74
Kinshasa	~73
Accra	~70
Douala	~70
Abidjan	~68
Addis Ababa	~62
Khartoum	~57
Alexandria	~41
Algiers	~40
Cairo	~34
Casablanca	~30
Durban	~26
Johannesburg	~26
Cape Town	~25

Percent change between 2010 and 2025

Percent change between 2010 and 2025
- >85%
- 60%–85%
- 35%–85%
- 35%>

Source: United Nations 2013

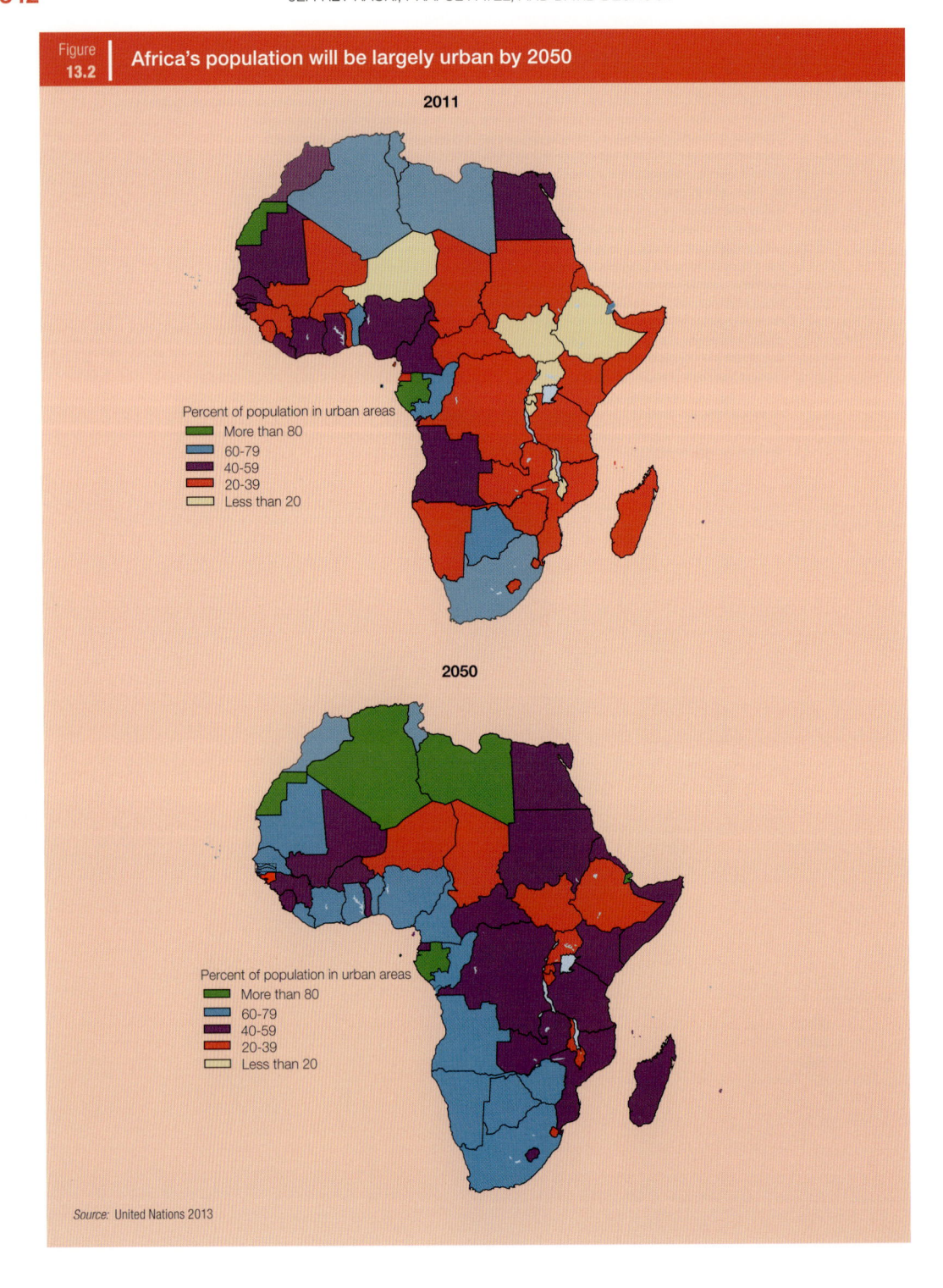

Figure 13.2 | Africa's population will be largely urban by 2050

2011

Percent of population in urban areas
- More than 80
- 60-79
- 40-59
- 20-39
- Less than 20

2050

Percent of population in urban areas
- More than 80
- 60-79
- 40-59
- 20-39
- Less than 20

Source: United Nations 2013

are illiterate and unskilled, cities dysfunctional, and economies trapped in extractive activities and crony capitalism, urban areas will be poor and violent — offering only the desperation of hopelessness to residents facing only the prospect of growing inequality and instability. Well-managed urban areas will be a critical prerequisite to a future of dignity and equitable opportunity.

The ability of urban areas to become the engines of economic growth directly determines the rate and sustainability of national economic performance, and hence the development outcomes and political stability of the country. In rapidly urbanizing countries virtually all GDP growth is concentrated in the cities as the rural share of GDP growth steadily declines. The countries that are addressing the urbanization challenge effectively are achieving near double-digit growth rates (China, Ethiopia, Ghana, and Uganda); those that are not continue to reap uneven economic performance and instability.

Globally, urbanization has proved an unstoppable process. International trends show that urbanization generates significant opportunities for growth, poverty reduction, and environmental sustainability. Specifically, urban centers:

- *Make a disproportionate contribution to productivity growth and job creation.* They have the potential to function as sources of economic dynamism by virtue of the spatial concentration of productive activity, entrepreneurs, workers, and consumers. Dense constellations of firms and workers bring markets and suppliers in close proximity and thus facilitate the sharing of infrastructure, services, and information; the matching of the distinctive requirements of firms for different types of premises; and innovation in products and processes.
- *Provide economies of scale for the financing and development of major facilities*, particularly through leveraging local and national tax bases for public infrastructure investment (such as for integrated public transport systems or ports).
- *Are dynamic sites of social, political, and cultural interaction and fusion.* Rising personal mobility makes urban centers places where people from many different languages, traditions, and belief systems come together. Long recognized as the centers of creativity and innovation, cities are also the most likely places for political unrest to emerge.
- *Are vital in efforts to curb the use of non-renewable resources, reduce pollution and other forms of environmental degradation, and promote climate mitigation and adaptation.* Higher density, more compact cities with mixed land uses can reduce the amount of energy needed for transportation and community services.

However, urban growth can also be associated with growing levels of inequality and environmental damage. These trends are pronounced in many African cities, where inequality is conspicuous, levels of social exclusion are high, and the environmental sustainability of urban settlements is low.

Public policy will play a major role in determining the ability of African countries to assure that the benefits of the urban transition outweigh its risks. But policy will have little influence on the underlying urban transition itself. Africa's urban moment is now — its cities are already swelling with the population influx, but they are not yet choked or overwhelmed by it. Most countries have the physical space, the physical networks, and the embryonic institutions to meet the challenge — but only if they start acting now.

Core factors that will determine the extent to which the cities fulfill their prospective role as drivers of economic growth include: the level, quality, and competitiveness of their services; the efficiency and sustainability with which these services are delivered; the predictability of their governance and accountability functions; the reliability of their regulatory implementation and business environment; the effectiveness of the operation of their land, housing, and transport markets; their ability to strategically plan and implement initiatives that address environmental challenges; and their enhanced livability derived from high-standard infrastructure linkages to attractive hinterlands. These are the attributes necessary to make African cities globally competitive, attracting international investment, opening up local capital markets and local investment, encouraging businesses to locate there, and fostering dynamic new business initiatives and a thriving start-up/innovation culture as well as a nurturing environment for micro and small enterprise development.

Urban growth will require the transformation of millions of hectares of land for businesses, housing, public spaces, and circulation. The table below presents projections (over the period leading to 2050) of land transformation in Africa's ten largest countries[1] by urban land cover in 2000. It gives a sense of the scale of transformation implied in the urbanization process for Africa. Even the most conservative projection (0 in the table) shows several-fold increases in urban land cover for Sub-Saharan countries over the next 30 years. Urban land cover has expanded significantly in North Africa as well: Casablanca's periphery grew about 15 percent per year from 1995 to 2004, and Algiers grew at 4 percent per year from 1987 to 2008. With the possible exception of South Africa, no country in the region has any comparable experience with developing land for urban uses on this scale

Physical expansion will require increased capacities of the associated water and sewerage systems, sanitation and solid waste management, roads and drainage, parks and recreation, electricity supply, and urban transport — all of which are to be provided on a massive scale by cities that, for the most part, have failed to meet much less pressing service demands to date. Recent studies have shown that despite the economic gains made by Africa over the past decade, and to a much greater extent than in Asia, there has been a significant increase in urban slums and a worsening of urban poverty levels. Innovation will be key to providing services in these conditions.

The massive change in land use is a huge institutional and financial challenge. But the urban transformation also offers an enormous opportunity for the region. Just as China's urbanization has lifted half a billion people out of poverty, assembling, servicing, and mobilizing investment on millions of hectares of new urban land could create enormous numbers of jobs, assets, and opportunities for inclusive growth

---

1. Similar data on all of the continent's countries can be found in Angel et al. 2012.

Table 13.1 Cities will require much more land in the coming decades

Country	Urban Land Cover (Hectares) 2000	Annual Density Decline (%)	2010	2020	2030	2040	2050
South Africa	506,638.0	0	596,440	669,589	744,816	810,855	867,722
		1	659,169	817,838	1,005,396	1,209,653	1,430,632
		2	728,494	998,910	1,357,143	1,804,591	2,358,713
Nigeria	464,192.0	0	689,925	960,546	1,262,215	1,584,014	1,905,194
		1	762,485	1,173,214	1,703,812	2,363,071	3,141,135
		2	842,677	1,432,967	2,299,905	3,525,288	5,178,855
Algeria	341,628.0	0	441,035	546,608	638,411	713,574	775,619
		1	487,419	667,628	861,765	1,064,527	1,278,779
		2	538,681	815,443	1,163,260	1,588,088	2,108,350
Sudan	274,226.0	0	424,902	606,435	808,233	1,022,544	1,231,588
		1	469,590	740,701	1,091,000	1,525,456	2,030,545
		2	518,977	904,694	1,472,696	2,275,714	3,347,803
Ghana	263,057.0	0	380,554	514,953	657,802	803,391	940,988
		1	420,577	628,965	887,939	1,198,518	1,551,427
		2	464,809	768,220	1,198,593	1,787,979	2,557,871
Egypt	260,941.0	0	313,174	383,490	477,936	589,404	695,724
		1	346,111	468,396	645,146	879,287	1,147,055
		2	382,512	572,100	870,856	1,311,743	1,891,174
Morocco	136,949.0	0	163,665	196,566	230,548	260,808	285,860
		1	180,878	240,086	311,208	389,080	471,303
		2	199,901	293,241	420,086	580,439	777,047
Ethiopia	120,328.0	0	182,980	283,614	436,250	642,808	898,806
		1	202,224	346,406	588,876	958,957	1,481,881
		2	223,492	423,102	794,899	1,430,596	2,443,209
DRC	120,291.0	0	193,283	312,105	479,821	693,986	939,523
		1	213,610	381,205	647,690	1,035,305	1,549,012
		2	236,076	465,605	874,290	1,544,493	2,553,888
Cote d'Ivoire	85,926.0	0	118,266	159,400	204,093	250,415	295,922
		1	130,704	194,691	275,497	373,576	487,893
		2	144,450	237,796	371,882	557,309	804,400

Source: Angel et al. 2012

Note: The table shows projected urban land requirements to 2050 for the ten African countries with largest urban land cover in 2000. The total urban land cover in 2010 for the ten countries was about 2.6 million hectares representing about 70 percent of the continental total of about 3.6 million hectares.

across the whole region. Exploiting this opportunity will require a radical reconception by governments of their role and functions in a broadly based and accelerating urban development process. Embracing the inevitability of massive demand for serviced urban land, and acting in a timely fashion to meet that demand, are fundamental to ensuring that the region's urban growth is productive, environmentally sustainable, and equitable.

Urban Policy Challenges

To realize their potential as effective engines of growth, African cities must meet six challenges, common throughout the region.

1. The development of *political and institutional platforms* that enable cities to support equitable growth. City-level authorities require sufficient real authority, resources, and accountability over core urban management functions to be able to guide and coordinate development in responding to the demands of urban growth. Real authority requires:
- The assignment of adequate authority over key urban development functions, particularly those of spatial planning and control, land and housing development, basic infrastructure services (such as water, solid waste, sanitation, and energy), and public transportation services.
- Clear accountability of staff to city-level leadership, particularly in the case of senior administrators and technical specialists, including authority to hire, fire, and compensate staff appropriately, as well as protection from the all-to-frequent rotation of officials between local authorities.
- A transparent and predictable fiscal and financial framework for urban infrastructure investment and management, including the provision of adequate local revenue sources with sufficient discretion over rate-setting, and a predictable and fair basis for the transfer of national revenues to local governments.

Basic policy frameworks exist in most African countries, but implementation is uneven. Entrenched interests impede functional, personnel, and fiscal decentralization in many countries, skewing resource allocation in favor of central agencies that are not directly accountable to citizens. Excessive regulatory control of devolved powers, such as interference in tariff-setting, or highly unpredictable resource transfers, prevent effective medium-term planning and delivery. Even in countries that are increasing capital resource transfers to cities, central agencies often earmark highly projectized investments that do not always address local priorities, are usually one-off, and so not linked to more comprehensive integrated planning requirements, and do not involve adequate local consultation resulting in little local ownership of the assets.

2. Effective *partnerships between locally elected officials and their constituencies.* A significant number of African countries now have cities and/or local governments run by officials who have been selected through some form of a popular election process. Elections establish the framework for systems of

transparency, accountability, and inclusion in the management of the cities, including consultation in the formulation of development plans and the annual capital budget, public scrutiny in the management of public funds and the assignment of contracts, and public oversight in the operation and management of public assets. However, continued regulatory over-reach by central government and dependence on unpredictable central transfers prevent local officials and citizens from establishing performance-based delivery contracts and accountability mechanisms that address citizens' real needs and priorities.

3. Adequate *technical skills and organizational capacity* to manage complex urban systems. Most African cities are operating with very low bases of technical and management capacity across all the essential competency areas.

- First, staffing complements are often unaffordably large but still lack the skill profiles necessary to undertake functions effectively. Continued control over senior and specialist positions by central agencies exacerbates the capacity shortfalls, as ill-timed rotations and inappropriate deployments weaken the capacity of city leadership to hold officials to account and to establish effective capacity to provide and operate services. The reluctance of qualified staff to move to fast-growing secondary cities and towns is exacerbated by poorly developed (or non-existent) schemes of service for local governments. The result is a self-fulfilling prophecy, where the view that cities are too weak to be entrusted with the responsibilities denies them the one fundamental ingredient essential to building their capacity — learning by doing.
- Second, the tools for effective planning and management are undeveloped, and the regulatory authority for enforcing the application of these tools is often subject to centralized authorization (or even direct management). Hence, key elements in the development of well-functioning cities, such as (i) market regulation (land use, setting and collection of fees, directing the location of infrastructure investments to influence/manage housing development, coordinating public transport) and (ii) forward planning (funds are severely limited and/or unpredictable, limiting the value of producing realistic plans that enjoy effective consultation with communities) that has the requisite tools for implementation and enforcement, is generally not functionally effective.

4. Getting the *basics to support growth* right. Many cities in Africa are already demonstrating robustness in taking advantage of the benefits of agglomeration, serving as the locus for job creation, the emergence of dynamic micro- and small business activities and innovation focused on local market opportunities, and providing the context in which nearly all GDP growth is taking place across the continent. In Tunisia, for example, 9 out of 10 industrial establishments are located within one hour of a large city. However, much of the accelerating economic activity in cities is taking place because of the natural ability of dense agglomerations to act as incubators despite the costs of inefficient functioning. Faster growth requires key reforms in:

- Service delivery, where levels of access and deficiencies in the quality and reliability (24/7) of the services represent significant additional costs to economic activities and discourage potential investors. The lack of technical and management expertise in the service delivery agencies, the limitations on their ability to ring-fence their finances, the lack of proper regulation and tariff setting, and the absence of incentive and accountability systems to foster sound performance are common to urban service delivery entities in most African cities.
- Undeveloped land and housing markets that confine economic growth to the informal sector and weaken the ability of cities to finance land and infrastructure development from rising urban land values. Weak property rights systems, in particular, constrain the efficient functioning of urban land and housing markets. The constraints arise from uncertain ownership rights, poor title recording systems, and complex legal processes to assert property rights for purposes of investment and development. In Egypt, for example, up to 90 percent of property transactions are unregistered, and 71 registration procedures are required for a transaction. One consequence of the poor functioning of the land, housing, and housing finance markets is the rapid growth of unserviced squatter settlements (disproportionately large in Africa as compared to other rapidly urbanizing regions).
- Costly spatial planning, where the absence of effective planning tools and land use management and building regulatory regimes, as well as the inability to plan realistically in the absence of predictable capital development funding, result in: (i) uncontrolled settlement straining already low-capacity service delivery agencies; and (ii) the expansion of the cities along the same settlement patterns as introduced under colonial regimes — - i.e., very low densities that add substantially to the costs of infrastructure and transportation and undercut the potential agglomeration benefits of urbanization. In Morocco, for example, new cities (*villes nouvelles*) are being constructed miles away from economic centers.

5. *Managing cities for the impacts of climate change.* Outside of the metropolises, most African cities are relatively new with modest-sized populations. Future settlement patterns, which will house the majority of the urban settlers, will therefore be new, allowing for provisions to be made for the cities to contribute to global initiatives to reduce carbon emissions and to take measures to cope with the effects of climate change. But the economic dependence of a significant number of landlocked countries on a relatively limited number of coastal cities makes it imperative to improve the capacity of African ports to address the prospects of rising sea levels. Similarly, many of the major economic centers in the interiors are located in areas highly vulnerable to flooding and/or highly dependent on stressed water resources. These vulnerabilities are accentuated because central agencies have yet to take the lead in developing policies, strategies, and funding to deal with climate change that include enabling arrangements for cities to define and pursue a critical role in tackling climate change. Moreover, the specific actions and related instruments necessary to deal with climate change is effects — more efficient, denser, and well-planned

spatial development patterns; more efficient and integrated public transport and traffic management systems; and bulk infrastructure and drainage networks, as well as land use and building standards designed to cope with shifts in weather patterns — are lacking.

6. *Roles of major metropolitan areas, regional clustering of cities with complementary economic functions, and regional links to key coastal port cities.* Some countries are making substantial progress both within their own boundaries and across national borders, e.g., the Gauteng triple metropolis is increasingly well integrated and is directly connected to Maputo, and Cairo is well connected to coastal cities to the north and east. However, similar corridors and clusters in the rest of the continent are largely at the discussion stage.

Vision for 2050

The above challenges notwithstanding, Africa is in the early stages of urbanization. An ambitious vision for 2050 is plausible and is outlined below. In 2050, 1.5 billion Africans would live in well-managed urban centers with adequate access to basic services, land, and shelter. These cities would play a critical role in the continent's social and economic wellbeing, with vibrant urban economies providing a growing source of employment, driving economic growth, and playing a leading role in the continent's political and cultural life. Ongoing investment in and maintenance of urban infrastructure services will be financed from this growth, particularly through expanding and efficient land markets, providing an effective platform for African enterprises to compete globally.

By 2050, Africa's urban centers, ranging from regional metropolises to primary economic centers, secondary commercial centers, and tertiary market towns, would:

- Serve as effective platforms for driving economic growth and job development. Prospective local and global investors would be able to take for granted infrastructure network standards and health and education systems that are world-class. The supporting service and market-oriented environments would effectively incubate small- and medium-size businesses. The service efficiency and proximity attributes of cities and towns would be fully exploited, encouraging technology, service, and product innovation. Expanded economic activity would have generated robust fiscal bases encouraging the participation of the capital markets in the funding of the cities. Economies of scale promoting regional integration would be realized in the development of urban clusters – mega-cities linked by mega-corridors (for example, Mombasa-Nairobi-Kampala in East Africa and Lagos-Accra-Dakar in Western Africa) and efficient coastal cities that form the market entry points for the rest of the continent (for example, the Johannesburg/Maputo corridor).
- Operate within sound national institutional and regulatory frameworks enabling cities to function as systems in which public sector regulation and public sector goods investment are private sector-friendly, thus promoting the emergence of a flourishing private sector, including in the land and housing markets and in urban transportation services.

- Operate within sound political and fiscal enabling frameworks based on firmly grounded legislation and regulation, clearly identified functional assignments for service delivery, and reliable fiscal systems ensuring adequate, predictable resource flows to meet functional responsibilities within effective upward and downward oversight structures.
- Operate with well-functioning social contracts, whereby budgeting, investment decisions, and operational performance follow transparent and accountable procedures, routinely meet satisfactory audit standards, and deliver services to standards that address citizen expectations.
- Generate steadily improving standards of living. Efficient spatial planning would enable cities to capture economies of scale (reversing the colonial inheritance of diseconomies of scale in city form). Routine and effective collaboration with central agencies would maximize the scale benefits and related efficiency gains in both the systemic management of the urban economy and the integrated planning and operation of service delivery. Strategic collaboration with the center would provide the critical mass necessary for the major investments required to establish essential city infrastructure platforms. Partnership arrangements with the private sector would be undertaken as a matter of course by cities when service delivery efficiency gains could be made. More efficient connectivity of the cities to their own hinterlands would enhance quality of life opportunities and strengthen rural economic opportunities.
- Significantly reduce urban poverty by increasing access to infrastructure, health, and education services through the sustained, accelerated delivery of infrastructure works in slums and squatter settlements, complemented by portable tools (e.g., conditional cash transfers or vouchers) made available to qualified households.
- Address climate change imperatives through sound national policies that institutionally and fiscally equip cities to: develop and implement programs for mitigating generation of greenhouse gases through efficiency gains in transportation systems, management of solid waste, and well-planned settlement patterns and land use systems; promote adoption of eco-friendly technologies and practices including energy-efficient site planning and building systems; and introduce programs for system-wide adaptation to the impacts of climate change.

Action Agenda

To realize the 2050 vision, African governments must radically transform their approaches to their cities. Instead of focusing almost exclusively on sporadic, externally-financed support for discrete infrastructure investments, they must take a broader approach that develops the systems necessary to support sustainable investments in urban infrastructure and services. Infrastructure investment remains a priority, as one part of an iterative strategy in which countries establish systems that enable the effective management of urban growth – City Enabling Systems (CESs) — that:

- clearly assign functional responsibilities to urban governments
- establish the legal and regulatory frameworks for the functional and fiscal operations of urban local governments
- determine predictable sources of local revenues, including a transparent architecture for central-local fiscal transfers
- introduce guidelines and practices that support good governance and strengthen accountability
- support the development of enhanced institutional capacity and performance of urban local government.

Broadly, African countries fall into three categories in respect of developing CESs:
- countries that are seriously and thoroughly attempting to create effective enabling environments for cities (e.g., South Africa, Ethiopia, Ghana, Uganda, Tanzania, Morocco, and Tunisia)
- countries that are trying, with still limited success, to create effective city enabling environments (e.g. Egypt, Zambia, Senegal, Mali, Mauritania, Benin, and Swaziland)
- countries that have no serious initiatives to introduce CESs.

Clearly, the development of CESs must go hand in hand with massive investments in urban infrastructure and services. A symbiotic relationship between the development of CESs and these investments is required not only to ensure that current investment in infrastructure results in sustainable service delivery but also to progressively increase the resources necessary to finance future investment.

Linking current investment financing to increased local capacity will require strengthening the performance of city governments. National governments can utilize their inter-governmental fiscal transfer system to encourage and reward city government performance. Fiscal transfers can reward progress made by each city in implementing its responsibilities, as determined by independently conducted performance assessments. Resource allocations would be scaled up proportionate to the demonstrated capacity of the city to undertake the investments. Enhanced performance by the cities would, in turn, influence the extent to which sustainable domestic municipal finance markets would evolve, and against which funding for city development would be expanded.

A three-step approach

A wide array of initiatives will eventually be required to meet the 2050 vision. But for the next decade the critical focus of governments' urban policies and strategies must be on establishing effective and well-functioning CESs, including a much more systematic approach to analyzing and subsequently addressing CES constraints.

The *first key step* in establishing a systematic approach is *analyzing the current policy and regulatory frameworks within which urban local governments function.* A clear analysis of gaps and weaknesses in CESs will allow tailored support to be provided relative to the needs of each country. The three key areas for CES assessment are:

- **Strategic enabling environment.** For cities to manage and drive economic growth they must operate in a clear and predictable policy and legislative environment. Cities should be supported to prepare realistic population growth projections over the medium term. These projections should correspond to core infrastructure investment and land acquisition plans, including forward-looking adjustments of urban boundaries and medium-term capital investment plans to support productive urbanization. Analysis of the strategic environment for urban management requires a review of:
    - *Enabling legislation.* Delivery responsibilities and revenue assignments must be both clear and balanced allowing local governments and investors to proceed with confidence. Most countries in the region do not currently meet this requirement, with legal frameworks little changed from colonial times. These Local Government Acts commonly distinguish between urban and rural/traditional local authorities (as in, e.g., Zimbabwe, Swaziland, Ghana, and Sudan), give cities little relevant authority in urban management, and retain strong powers for central governments. Weak national Ministries of Local Government are ineffective in supporting larger cities. In a number of countries, decentralization initiatives have muddied the local government legislative environment. In Zambia, for instance, almost 20 years of political wrangling over decentralization policy has blocked effective local government reforms and performance; in Ghana, local government reforms have yet to be meaningfully implemented. Many countries, particularly in North Africa (Tunisia, Egypt), are reviewing governance arrangements and reconsidering the role and functions of local governments. This review presents an important opportunity, although the specific type of enabling legislation will vary depending on each country's specific circumstances. The gold standard for enabling legislation in the region is South Africa's 1994 constitution that clearly sets out the structure and responsibilities of local governments, supported by very specific legislation delineating municipal finance regulations, PPP practices, and other key areas. Ethiopia's federal nature required that regional states enact urban local authority legislation, with the Ministry for Urban Development providing effective central support.
    - *Urban policy and city strategies.* Many countries in the region have nominal urban strategies but most rest quietly on bookshelves. Effective national urban strategies will focus on removing impediments to growth rather than commanding specific outcomes. South Africa's excellent national spatial development strategy, for instance, can be summarized as a) assuring all citizens have access to adequate basic services and b) investing heavily in areas — almost entirely urban — where growth potential is greatest. The chapter on the urban sector in Ethiopia's current five year "Growth and Transformation Plan" focused on removing impediments to growth. Useful national urban strategies can only be executed through realistic city level strategies. Johannesburg's "iGoli 2002" and "iGoli 2010" set

the regional standard for near-term transformation and medium term growth strategies; the 19 largest cities in Ethiopia are already implementing this two-step approach, as are a number of other cities in the region. But many cities are still mired in the neo-colonial master plan cul-de-sac, vainly attempting to force growth into static zoning plans thereby stifling the initiative of citizens, denying opportunities to the working poor, and compiling expensive infrastructure backlogs as informal settlements continue to grow.

- *Fiscal and financial frameworks.* Transparent, reliable fiscal and financial systems are critical for good urban governance and sustainable service provision. Political will is required to install and maintain effective systems, and experience shows that ministries of finance are the crucial levers in achieving sound intergovernmental frameworks that promote growth while limiting contingent liabilities. Analysis of the financial environment for urban management requires a review of the adequacy and flexibility of local assigned revenue instruments, the arrangements for the sharing of national revenues to finance urban development and management, and the rules and procedures for city governments to access domestic capital markets. In Egypt, for example, own-source revenues account for only 6 percent of total city revenues, 90 percent of which is spent on staff salaries.

- **Accountability, transparency, and performance.** For cities to effectively drive growth, local officials must be empowered and encouraged to respond to local needs and priorities. With very few exceptions, elected city officials throughout the region are not primarily accountable to their constituents. Dominant political parties deploy local government candidates with little or no regard for management capacity, and central ministries responsible for local government frequently interfere with local officials. The effectiveness of local governments in meeting citizen's priorities can only be judged when objective evidence is available. Cities in Namibia, South Africa, Swaziland, and Ethiopia commission and publicize annual reports and are independently audited, but this practice is not common in the rest of the region. Ethiopia has very successfully instituted independent annual performance assessments for its 19 largest cities and is now planning to extend its performance-based grant system to 25 additional cities. South Africa's National Treasury and Fiscal and Finance Commission both regularly assess local government performance. But, again, these good practices are not common in the rest of the region.

- **City and local government capacity.** City and local government management requires a multi-disciplinary skill set quite distinct from generic public administration, but few countries in the region have addressed this core requirement. Zambia's Local Government Training Institute has been functioning at a basic level since the mid-1990s, and South Africa has a wide-ranging array of local government training programs provided through both private and public entities. Ethiopia's Civil Service College (ECSC) has, since 2006, offered an Urban Management Master's Degree based on the highly regarded degree program of the Institute for Housing and Urban

Development Studies,[2] and its more than 2,000 graduates have thoroughly overhauled city management across the country. Donor-driven training programs come and go irregularly in many other countries. To achieve the Africa 2050 Vision, the region needs a steady supply of effective urban managers, and the most cost-effective delivery method is to follow the ECSC model of adapting suitable existing curricula. In addition, national local government associations should be revitalized following the example of the South African Cities Network (SACN), and local government career paths should be strengthened and brought into consonance with skilled labor market conditions.

Thorough assessment of the key elements of national CESs across the region should not be an expensive or time-consuming exercise. Based on the CES assessment, each country can define the reform and capacity-building work program required to support productive urbanization. Experience in the region shows that key reforms can be designed and adapted to local realities in a short period of time. With the Ministry of Finance in the lead, Zambia completely revamped the design of its intergovernmental fiscal architecture in less than a year. Ethiopia installed its performance-based grant system in about 18 months. The key to successful reforms is, as always, effective champions within key agencies. In the absence of these champions, there is no track record of effective urban reforms in the region.

The *second key step* is for cities to *project the urban growth they must accommodate to 2050, translate these projections into requirements for expanding the supply of serviced land, and begin the incremental processes of planning, assembling, and servicing that land.* CES reform and capacity-building are necessary but in no way sufficient. Very few countries in the region have track records in systematic urban land assembly and delivery despite the fact that developable land is readily available around most of the region's cities. With a few notable exceptions, urban investments in the region over the last 40 years have been disjointed, projectized, and wholly inadequate to meet the demands of increasingly rapid urbanization. In much of the region traditional (central) authorities are reluctant to cede control of portions of their domains for urban expansion. In other countries public land management agencies are similarly reluctant. Systematic programs to acquire and service land for urban expansion must be tailored to the realities of each country, and internal strictures that make financing land acquisition nearly impossible must be reexamined.

Countries that are serious about achieving a productive and sustainable 2050 urban vision — as evidenced by clear progress in implementing CES reforms and effective capacity building — should be supported in developing and implementing medium-term urban land expansion programs. The region's cities must focus on keeping ahead of demand instead of ignoring growth. Adequate supply of serviced, affordable urban land will be the key to productive private investment by both firms and households, especially in secondary cities and towns. Again, defining urban land expansion requirements is a manageable

---

2. The Institute is an international centre of excellence of the School of Economics (ESE) and the Faculty of Social Sciences (FSS) of the Erasmus University Rotterdam, The Netherlands, offering post graduate education, training, advisory services and applied research.

exercise. South Africa's Reconstruction and Development Program was initially defined based on work undertaken over about 18 months. Existing methodology provides an excellent entry vehicle for preparing systematic urban land expansion needs assessments throughout the region.

The *third key step* to achieving the 2050 urban vision for Africa is to *address financing issues.* Acquiring and servicing land will be possible only if cities have access to adequate finance. The three required elements for implementation of coherent, predictable intergovernmental fiscal and financial systems work together in a unified approach:

- **Local own-revenue bases.** Own-revenue assignments should be matched to delivery assignments. As African cities grow in both population and economic importance, parliamentarians and national officials must transition to supportive — rather than command — roles, allowing cities sufficient autonomy to charge and collect rates, tariffs, and fees adequate to sustain the services and infrastructure required for growth. Africa's rising middle class must play a key role in financing the infrastructure to support urban growth. Central government interference in setting local government tariffs is common in the region. City governments in Ethiopia, South Africa, Namibia, and Swaziland are empowered to raise own-revenues largely consonant with delivery responsibilities and are increasingly able to use these local sources of finance to invest in infrastructure to support growth – which in turn provides them with further revenues. In most other countries, authorized own-revenue bases are inadequate to meet service delivery assignments. In most instances property taxes and rates are a critically important own-revenue source, with strong potential to finance infrastructure investment. In North Africa, prior to the Arab Spring, urban land values doubled every three years. Assistance may be required in updating registries and valuations.

- **Intergovernmental fiscal arrangements.** Ministries of finance must be assisted to make choices on intergovernmental transfer systems including sources and formula. Both South Africa and Ethiopia share portions of general revenues. Other countries may wish to identify specific sources, such as revenues from extraction of primary resources that are national public goods or shares of nationally collected taxes. Allocation formulae should be transparent, as should conditions for disbursement of funds. The provision of funding should reward good performance by local governments. Accumulated arrearages and debts should be cleared allowing cities to begin with a clean slate. South Africa's intergovernmental fiscal framework features a constitutionally mandated division of revenues and predictable intergovernmental grants operating through a medium-term budget. Ethiopia's federal system features revenue sharing to the regional states, and the federal government has overlaid a transparent, performance-based grant that promotes good urban governance with co-financing from the regions. Many other countries in the region — including Zambia, Zimbabwe, Kenya, and Ghana — have historical experience with relatively well-functioning intergovernmental fiscal systems that have not been maintained for a variety of reasons. And many countries have *ad hoc* intergovernmental systems or, as in several of the West African countries, deconcentrated systems that enforce local government dependence on the center.

- **Domestic municipal finance markets.** For cities to drive growth, create jobs, and enable private investment, responsive domestic sources of finance for investment by creditworthy city governments must be available widely across the region. Ministries of finance must play a role in fostering sound markets that do not impose contingent liabilities on the central fiscus. Obviously, development of sustainable municipal finance throughout the region will take time and must, in any event, be based on the emergence of creditworthy, capable city-borrowers. Until recently, very few domestic financial markets in the region have had the resources and capacity to provide municipal finance, and creditworthy municipal borrowers have been in very short supply. This picture is rapidly changing as external and sovereign investment accelerates into the region. Banks and pension funds will require support to understand how municipal financial markets work. Cities will require support to become creditworthy, both as an indicator of overall good governance and as a prerequisite to sustainable local borrowing without recourse to sovereign guarantees. In Morocco, for example, cities have buoyant revenues and recurring budget surpluses, indicating a lack of capacity to invest.

Domestic municipal finance markets can be mobilized in a variety of ways. Medium-term plans should be developed to support key domestic financiers in learning and adopting good municipal lending practices. As creditworthy cities begin to emerge, lending and bonds in manageable amounts should be facilitated between cities and lenders, without sovereign guarantees. In countries with relatively sound financial sectors and significant resource inflows a combination of lending regulatory reform and capacity-building with lenders may be adequate. Municipal finance intermediaries are common in West Africa and may, with adequate reforms, provide a basis for sustainable lending. Development of specialized municipal lenders may also be feasible. South Africa's Infrastructure Finance Corporation (INCA), for example, played a key role in priming its municipal finance market. Partners should adopt a programmatic approach, fostering domestic market development instead of crowding out through direct lending to cities.

Finally, getting to the 2050 vision for African cities will require at least ten-year commitments from governments, cities, and partners, requiring both patience and perseverance. To be successful, these commitments must encompass the three key areas of work: reforming enabling environments, getting ahead of demand for land and services, and fostering sound fiscal and financial frameworks to finance large scale programs of urban infrastructure investment.

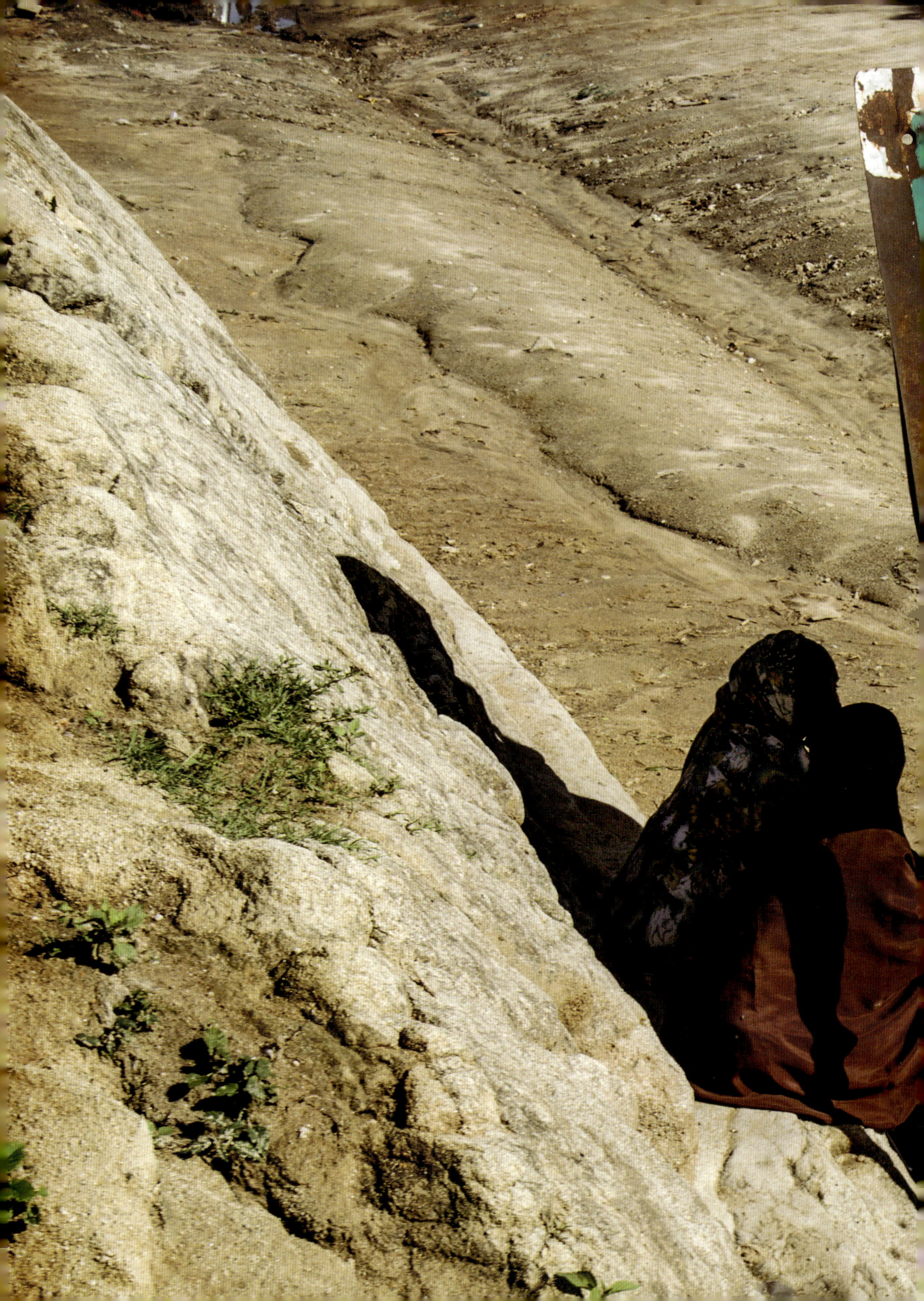

PART II
SECTION C: INTEGRATED CONTINENT – BIGGER MARKETS TO FOSTER INVESTMENT AND HIGHER PRODUCTIVITY JOBS

Enhancing Regional Cooperation and Integration on the Continent

Chapter 14

Harinder S. Kohli

Why Africa Should Strive for Regional Cooperation and Integration

Five basic imperatives of regional cooperation and integration will allow the continent to realize its full economic potential:

- First, permit individual economies to specialize over the medium term, an essential precondition for escaping the "middle-income trap" that has engulfed many countries in Latin America and some in Asia;
- Second, overcome the reality that the size of the domestic markets in most African economies — with the exception of South Africa, Nigeria, Egypt, and one or two other countries — are small by global standards and thus not large enough to permit the economies of scale needed by firms to be globally competitive;
- Third, accelerate the economic growth of landlocked and other slow-growing economies by linking them more closely with neighboring fast-growing and coastal growth hubs;
- Fourth, allow skillful and joint management of regional commons thus mitigating risks related to terrorism and the drug trade; addressing the economic and security concerns of fragile states, resolving disputes within and between countries, fighting the spread of diseases such as HIV/AIDS, and adapting to climate change; and,
- Fifth, provide a bridge between actions of individual African countries and the rest of the world. To have voice and regional influence on the global agenda and governance, Africa will need to formulate a unified position on a range of global issues, which can only be achieved through regional dialogue and cooperation.

This chapter is focused on the first four imperatives. Chapter 16 is devoted to Africa's role in the world, including closer economic relations with the fast-growing emerging economies in Asia, the Middle East, and Latin America.

Economic Imperatives for Regional Cooperation

Specialization and economies of scale

Half of the countries in Africa are middle-income. The region as a whole has a per capita income of $1875 (2012 market exchange rates), a third higher than that of South Asia. A key challenge facing the continent is how to build on its recent success and transition to the ranks of upper middle-income and high-income economies.

The Growth Commission led by Nobel laureate Michael Spence found that a major characteristic of the economies that have successfully avoided the middle-income trap and made an effective transition to becoming high-income economies was their ability to specialize (Kharas and Kohli 2011). Successful economies developed a competitive advantage in the global marketplace by proactively building unique skill sets and creating economies of scale. Specialization and economies of scale in turn allowed the economies to enhance productivity and competitiveness.

Specialization involves investing in activities with greater value added and higher TFP and shifting resources — labor and capital — from labor-intensive activities whose viability depends on low wages (and hence lower per capita income) into economic activities that have higher innovation and technology content, allowing greater returns to both capital and labor. The resulting higher wage levels in turn raise people's living standards and boost the country's per capita income.

A closer look at high-income countries (both developed and newly industrialized countries) as well as high-growth East Asian economies reveals that, with the exception of a few large economies, most high-wage economies have achieved some degree of specialization in the global market place. Some of the many possible examples are: Korea in electronics, shipbuilding, and automobiles; Japan in highly specialized machine tools, automobiles, and innovation in and design of consumer and industrial electronics; the United States in financial services, information technology, innovation in and design of electronics, commercial airplanes, biotechnology, higher education, and military equipment; France in nuclear power plants, fashion, and international tourism; the UK in financial and other services; Singapore in financial services, tourism, shipping and airlines, and biotechnology. China has also become the manufacturing hub for the globe and India has become a world leader in IT services and seeks to do the same in pharmaceuticals.

Countries' success in moving toward specialization on a global scale allowed them to raise their productivity. This in turn has allowed local firms to achieve higher profitability while investing in activities that made it possible for them to pay higher wages to their employees with requisite skills. However, to successfully achieve specialization, firms need ready access to markets that are large enough to yield economies of scale at the national or regional level before they can compete in the global market place. Unfortunately, most African countries would currently find this very difficult to achieve in domestic markets alone.

In 2012, 1.1 billion people lived on the African continent. Thus, one in every seven human beings calls Africa home. The region's population exceeds the population of four continents: North America, Latin America, Europe, and Australia. But, African economies are small. Table 14.1 shows the total size and the share of the global economy of the 15 largest economies in the world in 2012 in purchasing power parity (PPP). None of the 54 African economies rank among the largest economies in the world (Table 14.2).

Table 14.1 | No African nation reaches the top rankings of the world's largest economies

Rank	Country	PPP 2012 $ billions (Current)	% World in 2012
1	United States	15,685	18.9%
2	China	12,406	14.9%
3	India	4,684	5.6%
4	Japan	4,628	5.6%
5	Germany	3,197	3.9%
6	Russia	2,513	3.0%
7	Brazil	2,356	2.8%
8	United Kingdom	2,336	2.8%
9	France	2,254	2.7%
10	Italy	1,833	2.2%
11	Mexico	1,759	2.1%
12	Korea	1,614	1.9%
13	Canada	1,488	1.8%
14	Spain	1,411	1.7%
15	Indonesia	1,217	1.5%
	World	83,140	

Source: IMF 2013b

Two basic conclusions stand out. First, even though in terms of the size of their population at least four African countries — Nigeria, Ethiopia, Egypt, and South Africa — are large, the size of their economies is relatively small from a global perspective because of their modest per capita income. And, second, because most individual African economies are small by global standards, local firms operating exclusively in their home country markets would find it extremely difficult to achieve economies of scale with the possible exception of exports of mineral and energy resources.

Only through closer regional cooperation that facilitates much greater regional trade and investment and expands their home markets can African countries aspire to create global firms, become upper-middle-income countries, and realize the vision of Africa in 2050 articulated in this book.

Table 14.2 | Most African economies are relatively small

	Country	Market Ex. Rates	PPP
1	South Africa	384	582.4
2	Nigeria	269	448.1
3	Egypt	257	540.0
4	Algeria	208	272.9
5	Angola	119	128.3
6	Morocco	98	171.2
7	Libya	82	77.4
8	Sudan	60	85.3
9	Tunisia	46	105.3
10	Ethiopia	42	103.3

Source: IMF 2013b

Faster growth in landlocked countries

The continent has 16 landlocked countries; they are home to 274 million people or a quarter of its population. The average per capita income in landlocked countries is $668 (market exchange rates, 2012), compared to $1,875 for the continent as a whole. Much of the difference can be attributed to countries' own resource endowments and stages of development. But at the same time there is no question that being landlocked has put these countries at a significant disadvantage and makes their efforts to climb out of poverty much more difficult.

There is wide agreement among economists that one precondition for accelerating the growth of the landlocked economies in Africa — and of similar economies elsewhere — is better connectivity, not only to their neighbors in the region but also to economies in other continents. Physical connectivity — including robust transport and communications links — are essential for moving goods, services, and people. For landlocked countries, improved infrastructure would significantly lower the cost of all imported products and make export of local products both feasible and more competitive. In addition, easy connectivity permits people-to-people exchanges and allows faster spread of new information and innovation.

Indeed, to the extent that physical connectivity is the bedrock of all efforts aimed at promoting regional cooperation and integration, the biggest beneficiaries of regional cooperation in Africa would include the landlocked countries. The resultant higher growth would help narrow the disparities of incomes within Africa and create new markets for local businesses.

Joint management of regional commons

A number of common challenges and threats — some natural and others man-made — that can seriously affect long term growth and Africans' well-being can best be tackled through cooperation at the regional level. Large parts of Africa's agricultural lands are threatened by droughts, and continued climate change poses an increased risk of flooding in low-lying river basins and coastal areas. Collaboration on water resource management and adaptation to climate change should be a priority. Additionally, many countries still suffer from very high prevalence of HIV/AIDS, tuberculosis, malaria, and other tropical diseases (see Chapter 8). Recently, many national authorities, international agencies, and private groups have started to intervene aggressively at the national level. But, these issues require regional approaches to detection, information sharing, control, and response.

The challenge in Africa is to facilitate and accelerate further regional integration within the continent's political and institutional environment while maintaining openness to the rest of the world. East Asia has done so effectively; Africa may take into account its experience.

Past Efforts on Regional Cooperation and Integration[1]

Africa's leaders have long cherished the idea of an integrated or seamless continent that overcomes the limitations excessive fragmentation imposes on the continent's development. As enunciated by one of the foremost leaders of Africa's struggle to end colonial rule, the dream has been to overcome *"The greatest wrong which the departing colonialists had ever inflicted on us, and which we now continue to inflict on ourselves in our present state of disunity, was to leave us divided into economically unviable states which bear no possibility for development"* (Nkrumah 1973). The belief that close cooperation among nations will facilitate economic progress is widely shared.

Early regional groupings in Africa had a mixture of economic, political, and security-oriented objectives. The countries attached importance to all three objectives because they needed to feel secure in each of these areas. The quest for security was logical for newly independent countries, some of which had had to fight vicious liberation wars. With time, the concerns about political survival and defense have softened, allowing the economic rationale for integration to receive greater emphasis. This evolution justifies the label of Regional Economic Communities (RECs), which came to be attached to these regional groupings.

The drive for regional cooperation in Africa also includes a strong element of foreign policy and diplomacy. Indeed, the long-term goal of all of the RECs is to develop into unions of federated states. This paper focuses on regional economic integration, but the broader judgments on progress on the economic component of integration must take into account the reality that the main actors still pursue multiple objectives.

Several regional organizations were set up over time, starting in 1917 with the precursor of today's East African Community (EAC). The process intensified, and the numbers multiplied after more and more countries gained independence in the 1960s. After much internal churning, the number of RECs has now dropped to 14, ranging in size from a low of 3 member countries, in the case of the Community of the

---

1. This section is based on a background paper prepared by Emmanuel Akpa for Centennial Group International.

Great Lakes States, to a high of 28 members, in the case of the Community of Sahel-Saharan States. Each of today's 54 sovereign countries belongs to 2 or more RECs. Thus there is considerable overlap in membership that creates the "spaghetti-bowl" phenomenon.

The RECs expected particular development outcomes from the larger economic space to be achieved by integrating the member country markets. They expected the removal of barriers to trade to lead to expanded regional trade and investment. They looked to the larger market to help induce higher enterprise profitability, and thereby strengthen the global competitiveness of the region, thus helping to increase domestic and foreign investment. And they counted on intra-group cooperation on the use of regional public goods to help crowd-in externalities and improve their management.

The protocols to bring about these outcomes typically called for policy reforms to liberalize intra-regional trade; free up cross-border movement of labor and capital; harmonize business laws, investment policies, and regulations; and enhance cooperation in infrastructure development and the management of infrastructure services. It was assumed that these outcomes would help strengthen economic growth in the member countries.

Considerable effort has gone into creating the RECs and establishing their operational programs but true integration lags. Agreements have been reached on direction, and institutions to manage the processes of integration have been created. But the process of reaching agreement on the protocols and implementing them has been taxing, particularly with 54 sovereign states whose national institutions are patterned after five different European traditions and who use as many official languages.

The more active RECs made some progress on integration in the 1990s when general macroeconomic and trade reforms provided a context for advancing the regional integration agenda. Those general trade reforms included the elimination of quantitative restrictions (quotas and non-automatic licensing), the simplification of tariff schedules, and the elimination of rate cascading. The key element that the regional integration agenda added to this broader agenda was the common external tariff, which was adopted and implemented at varying speeds in the West African Economic and Monetary Union (WAEMU), the Economic Community of West African States (ECOWAS), the Common Market for Eastern and Southern Africa (COMESA), the Southern Africa Customs Union (SACU), the Central African Economic and Monetary Community (CEMAC), the Arab Maghreb Union (AMU), and the EAC. By 2010, the general trade reforms had achieved significant openness in the reforming countries, and the addition of the regional dimension measures made the RECs move in the direction of full customs unions.

The common external tariffs typically have four bands, with the rates of zero for social goods and food, 5 percent for capital goods and raw materials, 10 percent for final consumer goods, and 20 percent for luxury goods. Thus, the simple average MFN tariff now stands at 12 percent in the case of the EAC and COMESA; at 11 percent in the case of ECOWAS and WAEMU; and at 9 percent in the case of SACU. The reduction has been more modest in the cases of CEMAC, where it dropped to 17 percent, and AMU, where it dropped to 15 percent (World Bank 2013b).

Some unfinished business remains regarding tariffs, particularly deciding what level of interim protection to provide for infant industry. Discussions are ongoing in ECOWAS, EAC, and COMESA about the level at which to set a possible fifth rate as well as the list of products to which that rate would apply. The decision is taking time, and the delay means that the common external tariffs are not fully in place. After this issue is settled, the spaghetti-bowl phenomenon may further delay completion. Additional time will be required to work out the treatment accorded to beneficiary products depending on the trading pairs of RECs affected.

The general trade reforms discussed above extended to non-tariff barriers (NTBs) as well, thereby enabling the RECs, as with tariff reform, to pursue the integration agenda by adding the regional dimension of trade reforms to measures of greater general outward orientation. The abolition of quantitative restrictions is a major step forward, as it promotes resource allocation efficiency and also reduces scope for trade-inhibiting discretion at customs. The introduction of systems of automated processing of trade transactions (SYDONIA/ASYCUDA) was packaged as part-and-parcel of the introduction of common external tariffs. In this guise, the RECs underwrote an important reform that helps reduce time taken in processing trade documents and eliminates discretion and red tape.

The RECs have thus far established a good record on the provision of transport links in trade corridors, beginning with the sharing of port facilities and the creation of bonded warehouses for, and the provision of physical transport of merchandise to, landlocked partners. The adoption of regionally acceptable insurance documents facilitates trade further. Finally, the more active RECs have implemented free movement of people across borders, together with visa-free short-term (90-day) residence for citizens of one country in partner countries (e.g., ECOWAS, EAC), and a few have taken steps to allow free movement of capital (e.g., EAC).

Many of the necessary institutions and agreements have been put in place that would support further integration and development of regional markets. However, progress on implementation has been very uneven. Impediments to achieving the goals rather than simply creating the structures and formulas of the integration agenda include:

- the multiplicity of RECs, which spreads limited attention and capacity thinly and so encourages formalism — accession to a union but with limited capacity to follow through on the substance
- overlapping REC memberships, some of which produce conflicting arrangements and, occasionally, complete blockage in areas such as developing sensible rules of origin;
- persistent strong vertical links with former colonial metropoles, where privileged trade and development assistance arrangements remain vital and have stood in the way of attempts to strengthen horizontal links with neighbors; and
- delays in domestic policy reform, which cause corresponding delays in the acceptance and implementation of cross-border trade reforms.

Status of Regional Trade and Investment Flows

Despite the long-standing efforts and the political and institutional initiatives, intra-regional trade between African economies is among the lowest of the major geographic regions of the world (see Table 14.3).

Table 14.3 African intraregional trade is low by global standards

Region	(Percent of total trade)
North America	48
Latin America	27
Europe	71
CIS	20
Africa	13
Middle East	9
Asia	53

Source: WTO 2012

In 2011 African intra-regional trade (13 percent) was about half that of Latin America (27 percent), one-fourth of East Asia (53 percent), and only one fifth of the European Union (71 percent). While consistent and reliable data are not readily available on intra-regional investment flows in Africa, their magnitude is believed to be equally modest.

Three fundamental reasons account for the current overall very low two-way trade in Africa. First, the economies have relatively low overall trade-to-GDP ratios when compared to East Asia and Europe. Second, African exports are dominated by commodities, whose main markets are large economies in OECD countries, China, and India. Few African companies (except for some South Africa-based firms) produce goods and services needed by neighboring countries. Finally, Africa's largest economies — South Africa, Nigeria, and Egypt — have limited direct trade with each other.

Yet, from a business perspective there appears to be a significant unexploited potential for greater trade and investment flows within the region, provided the current barriers are removed. The economies are linked by a contiguous landmass, and the people share a common heritage and history. It should be natural for the consumers within the region to prefer similar (though not necessarily the same) products, and local companies should have a competitive advantage in forging business relations with their local counterparts and in marketing to the consumers in other parts of Africa.

Lessons from Other Regions[2]

Africa's efforts for greater regional cooperation and integration can benefit from the key lessons on integration in Europe, the Americas, and East Asia over the last half-century. The key conclusions from this experience are discussed further below.

The EU is commonly regarded as the most successful and effective example of regional cooperation and integration. Indeed, people involved in such efforts elsewhere in the world often use the EU as the basic reference point, if not the model to emulate. This is mainly due to Europe's steady move during the past fifty years toward ever-deeper and broader political and economic integration. NAFTA is another common reference point in discussions on regional trade, but unlike the EU, NAFTA is essentially a trade agreement. Countries in South America have discussed regional integration since their independence from Spain but actual progress toward regional cooperation was negligible until the so-called "new regionalism" efforts started with the advent of a new political and economic environment during the past two decades.

Political commitment and leadership. Perhaps the most important lesson of the past experience in regional cooperation in Europe and the Americas is that strong political commitment and leadership in support of the basic objectives and direction of the regional cooperation and integration efforts is absolutely essential for a far-reaching initiative like the "Europe Project." Indeed, the leadership must come personally from the top political leaders (e.g., head of states), in at least the catalyst countries. Such leadership and ownership is vital at the initial stages to agree on the basic vision and to generate necessary broad public support, and it remains critical during the subsequent implementation stages to resolve issues and disagreements that inevitably arise among technocrats and specialized institutions.

Willingness to cede sovereignty. A second central lesson is the critical importance of the recognition by the countries that to create a larger and more efficient (competitive) single market in turn requires also a willingness on their part to cede sovereignty on some economic matters. The national leaders have to accept that, for the greater common good of the region as a whole, individual countries have to accept some loss of national sovereignty in favor of institutions that include all members of the community.

Creation of supranational institutions. The third lesson follows directly from the first two. Effective regional integration requires creation of supranational institutions to carry out effectively many of the functions for which nations agree to cede sovereignty.

Willingness to adjust economies, cost of integration, and financial transfers. In most discussions on economic cooperation and integration, the focus is either on the economic and political benefits or on the technical issues concerning the design of specific initiatives and programs. Two important social and financial (and ultimately political) issues, while often implicitly or explicitly acknowledged, do not receive as much attention as they deserve given their vital importance to the political economy of such efforts. First, creation of larger markets and reaping the benefits from them by definition means that individual

---

2. This section is partly based on the conclusions of the paper "Regional Economic Cooperation and Integration: Lessons of Experience from Europe and the Americas" prepared by the Centennial Group for the Asian Development Bank.

national economies, sectors, and firms must adjust and restructure. Political leaders supporting regional cooperation must understand this need for restructuring and be willing to take steps necessary to facilitate these economic adjustments despite their short-term costs. Second, while most of the benefits of liberalization become visible only over time and are spread over the population at large, the burden of adjustment often falls on a smaller set of groups who are both more vulnerable and often more vocal (less developed countries and regions, inefficient companies, and communities reliant economically on uncompetitive units and activities). The financial and human costs of adjustment to them can be felt and seen more immediately. Unless the short-term negative impact of such adjustments is cushioned, the public's focus on the short-term social costs of liberalization can cloud recognition of the longer-term benefits, dissipating the political support so vital to the longer-term regional cooperation efforts.

Multi-pronged approach and sequencing. There is a strong consensus among economists with interest in issues of regional economic integration that economic and societal gains from regional cooperation can be maximized by meeting three main conditions: i) creating the largest regional markets possible, with one or more developed markets acting as the anchor; ii) conceiving regional cooperation policies within a framework of openness to global markets (e.g., MFN approach); and iii) creating a single (common) market for all goods, services, and factors of production (capital and labor). The European efforts seem to meet all three conditions. This has not been true in the Americas or Asia.

Variable geometry (multi-speed integration). At some crucial junctures in Europe, when it was not possible to reach full and unanimous agreement between all parties to proceed with a major new initiative, the community decided to adopt the so-called "variable geometry" approach under which a core group of countries agreed to proceed with the new initiative while leaving the door open for other countries to join later when they were ready. Adoption of a single currency, such as the euro, is one recent example.

Gradual broadening and deepening. With all the political commitment and leadership it enjoyed, European integration started modestly with a coal and steel community and only six member states. Over the subsequent fifty-plus years, it has been vastly deepened and broadened into a strong political and economic union with 28 member countries (with many more under consideration and others eager to join) and with an economy and population larger than that of the United States. The original vision of a federated Europe is clearly closer to being realized. Such a federated region is not on the horizon either in the Americas or Asia.

The European efforts have accordingly moved much further and have been much more successful in getting close to the original vision of the founders than has been the case elsewhere. As a result, Europe today has the highest proportion of intra-regional trade in the world. Although history, culture, income level, and specific local circumstances account partly for the different outcomes, there are a number of general lessons that are not region-specific and that contribute to the different outcomes. The discussion below is focused on these general lessons, with implications for Africa.

The launching of the federated "Europe Project" arose from a unique and fortuitous coming together of history, shared culture, widespread desire for change, and strong and committed political leaders. These in turn allowed visionaries like Jean Monnet to put forth a very powerful and persuasive vision of a new, more peaceful, and cooperative federated Europe. Monnet's vision was accepted and actively promoted by the then leaders of the two largest and richest nations on the continent: France and Germany. The fact that these two countries were willing to put aside centuries of animosity and jointly promote the vision of a new Europe, and were also willing to cede national sovereignty in some sensitive areas, brought tremendous credibility to the project and persuaded other countries to join. Importantly, while the countries signed off on a bold vision for the longer term, they also adopted a pragmatic step-by-step approach to implementing this vision, leading to progressively broader and deeper integration. Use of "variable geometry" was an integral part of this pragmatic strategy. Creation of powerful supranational institutions was also essential as was the agreement to set aside substantial financial resources to offset the cost of the reforms.

In the Americas, in sharp contrast to Europe, most of the above preconditions for far-reaching regional cooperation were not present, and the region adopted a considerably less structured and much more fragmented approach. Due to lingering suspicion between the major actors and in the absence of a shared vision and goals, there was no political will to embark on a journey that would encounter strong domestic resistance. As a result, Europe and the Americas adopted very different approaches that have yielded very different outcomes.

East Asia today has the highest intra-regional trade after Europe (53 percent versus 71 percent). By some estimates intra-regional investment accounts for almost half of all cross-border investment. But this impressive flow of regional trade and investment resulted from a very different approach than that in Europe.

East Asia's regional integration is the result of a market-driven, bottom-up approach under which businesses have provided the impetus for intra-regional trade and investments by setting up regional production networks. Unlike Europe, East Asian businesses were not driven by any top-down directives from the political leadership or creation of supranational institutions. Indeed, in Asia, regional institutions followed the moves by the business community. And the recent political decisions to create regional free trade (ASEAN) or economic communities (Asia Economic Area) were taken after large-scale regional trade and investments had already become a reality. Asia still does not have any supranational institutions with the kind of authority that the European Commission has. ASEAN does have a secretariat, but with a small staff and only limited authority. So far, the member countries have not ceded sovereignty on any major issues.

The cultural, historic, economic, and social backgrounds of Asia and Africa contrast with those of Europe and the Americas. Asia and Africa are huge, heterogeneous regions of 42 countries and 54 countries, respectively. The historic, cultural, political, and economic imperatives in Asia during the 1960s and 1970s and in Africa today are fundamentally different than those prevailing in Europe when it embarked on its journey toward a federated Europe in the immediate aftermath of World War II.

Africa's path to regional cooperation and integration will have to be different from Europe for the following reasons:

- Unlike Europe, there appears to be no overwhelming desire among the public at large or among political leaders to embark on a project that will blur the boundaries of nation-states.
- Realistically and politically, Africa's integration cannot be based on a vision that has insufficient mass support and no concrete demonstration of clear benefits. Regional cooperation efforts must be justified and judged first and foremost on their economic costs and benefits.
- The region is in reality an amalgamation of at least five distinct sub-regions (North Africa, West Africa, Central Africa, East Africa, and Southern Africa). Establishing sub-regional cooperation is the way to move forward, rather than attempting a single all-encompassing vision and road map for all 54 countries.
- As recently independent nations, most African countries jealously guard their national identities, and many still have lingering political differences and problems with each other (for example in the Maghreb). As a result, the level of mutual trust (or lack of it) is more like that in Latin America and Asia than in Europe.
- The economic and social disparities in Africa (and also Asia) are a multiple of those in Europe. And there is still a lack of strong political commitment and leadership for regional integration. Given these political and economic realities, a top-down approach to conceiving and implementing comprehensive regional initiatives is unlikely to succeed. Instead, it would be much more prudent to attempt a step-by-step bottom-up approach.

As Asia has done since the start of its journey toward regional cooperation and integration, Africa will need to find its own approach to regional cooperation that reflects its historic, cultural, political and economic realities as well as the world economy today, while applying relevant lessons from Europe, the Americas, and Asia.

Action Agenda

Given the potential economic benefits of regional cooperation, the region must pursue all avenues to enhance cooperation and create more efficient regional markets. Overall, regional economic cooperation requires a much more flexible, pragmatic, and agile approach than was the case in Europe. In many respects, Africa's approach may build on Asia's adoption of a flexible and step-by-step approach. A pragmatic strategy would allow Africa to continue with ongoing initiatives and pursue additional regional programs and projects voluntarily agreed among the countries concerned. This strategy does have its limitations and can advance regional cooperation only up to a certain point.

Initiatives for broader and more comprehensive regional cooperation — in trade (e.g., creation of a single market), financial integration (creation of truly regional financial markets), and indeed even significant physical connectivity projects — would remain conditional on a much more conducive environment in four inter-related areas: stronger political support in the key countries, willingness to share or cede some sovereignty in economic matters, consensus to give real authority and resources to autonomous regional institutions (many regional and sub-regional institutions already exist but their authority is limited), and availability of financial and human resources necessary to support economic integration.

The framework for Africa's regional cooperation strategy could consist of the following main elements:

- Rely on a *pragmatic step-by-step bottom-up approach* rather than on conceiving and implementing a comprehensive pan-African vision or grand plan as was done in Europe.
- Follow the *open regionalism* approach that will keep the region open to the rest of the world. Asia has benefited greatly by adopting this approach. So would Africa.
- Adopt the *variable geometry or multi-speed* cooperation approach, under which a few like-minded countries can start working together while allowing other countries to join at a later time of their choosing. Successful outcomes of initial efforts would open the way for subsequent gradual deepening and widening the scope of cooperation over time. Indeed, Africa's current strategy with RECs at its core fits with this concept. Recent progress in the EAC (see Box 14.1) could serve as a good example for the other RECs.
- Continue to focus on *sub-regional cooperation through the RECs.* Different sub-regions would inevitably have different scope and speed of regional cooperation, with some working on only a limited number of areas while others pursue a more comprehensive and ambitious agenda. Over the longer term, these RECs could be succeeded by a seamless Pan-African economic space.
- In the meantime, it would be helpful to reduce the number of RECs to five as some African policy makers have already suggested, allowing the *five major sub-regions* — North Africa, West Africa, Central Africa, East Africa, and Southern Africa — to be treated distinctly. In each, the focus must be on the issues and concerns of immediate common interest to the countries and on which it is feasible to reach a consensus in a reasonable time. At the same time, any opportunities for countries to collaborate across sub-regional boundaries should be encouraged and actively promoted.
- Make *physical connectivity* the foundation of pan-African regional cooperation initiatives. Physical connectivity is the bedrock for promoting and building true regional markets for goods and services and, therefore, is an essential building block for opening trade and for tackling regional commons problems. Such physical connectivity is also of paramount importance to the land-locked countries.
- Tackle *regional commons* issues at the sub-regional level in order to find solutions expeditiously and efficiently. While there are some truly *global commons* (HIV/AIDS, avian flu, climate change), most commons issues have regional or even sub-regional roots and solutions.

> **Box 14.1 | East African Community — Ahead of the rest**
>
> The EAC was founded in 1967, collapsed in 1977, and was revived in July 2000. It now has five members: Burundi, Kenya, Rwanda, Tanzania, and Uganda, with a total population of about 135 million and GDP per capita of about $490. The EAC has been a common market since 2010, and there are plans to move to an economic union with a common currency by 2015. There are also plans for a political union, the East African Federation, in the not-too-distant future.
>
> The trade corridor of the EAC supports active overland trade, and the infrastructure links are better developed than those in western or southern Africa. The countries also see more scope than elsewhere to complement one another in the valuable tourism business, which creates an incentive for cooperation in two areas that are important for regional integration: facilitation of cross-border movement of goods and people and management of the natural environment.
>
> Overall, the EAC is ahead of the rest of Africa in progress on reforms toward integration. Though it only re-emerged in 2000, its policy reforms in the areas of trade facilitation and business environment improvements place it ahead of any other REC in Africa. The superior performance of EAC is illustrated in the World Bank's Doing Business Results of April 2012, which reported that over the seven years preceding the review (2005 to 2012), all five EAC countries implemented a large number of business regulatory and trade facilitation reforms of importance to local entrepreneurs. Table 14.i below compares the rankings of RECs. The EAC does better than all the rest, with the exception of SACU.
>
> **Table 14.i: The EAC has done relatively well moving toward integrated reform**
>
> | REC | Ease of Doing Business — Rank 2006-09 Latest |
> |---|---|
> | SACU | 78 |
> | EAC | 116 |
> | AMU | 125 |
> | COMESA | 125 |
> | ECOWAS | 153 |
> | WAEMU | 165 |
> | CEMAC | 173 |
>
> *Source:* World Bank 2012c

In summary, regional cooperation and integration is essential for Africa's longer-term growth, much more so than perhaps any other region of the world. Given the relatively small size of individual economies, the only way to allow African businesses to develop economies of scale and become globally competitive is to create larger "domestic" markets. This in turn is critical for the region to diversify away from its current heavy reliance on commodities and develop competiveness in agro industry, manufacturing and services. The vision for 2050 should be to create a seamless Africa that allows uninterrupted trade and investment flows. To realize this vision, the region needs to focus on policies and strategies that will lead to practical results in terms of much higher regional trade and investment. To accelerate the pace of regional cooperation and build momentum for subsequent bolder steps, countries should look for low-hanging fruit with immediate and visible effects to demonstrate leaders' determination to accelerate the pace of regional cooperation. For example, to facilitate greater trade and investment flows within the region, the countries should consider adopting open sky policies and granting pan-African business visas to facilitate travel of business leaders within the continent. Instead of waiting for a continental consensus, individual countries should consider taking such actions unilaterally.

Appendix 1: Active Regional Economic Communities

- **Arab Maghreb Union (AMU):** 5 members: Algeria, Libya, Mauritania, Morocco, Tunisia
- **West African Economic Community (CEAO):** 7 members: Benin, Burkina Faso, Ivory Coast, Mali, Mauritania, Niger, Senegal
- **Central African Economic and Monetary Community (CEMAC):** 6 members: Cameroon, Central African Republic, Chad, Congo Equatorial Guinea, Gabon
- **Community of Sahel-Saharan States (CEN-SAD):** 28 members: Benin, Burkina Faso, Chad, Comoros, Guinea, Kenya, Ivory Coast, Liberia, Libya, Mali, Mauritania, Niger, Sao Tome and Principe, Sudan, Central African Republic, Eritrea, Djibouti, The Gambia, Senegal, Egypt, Morocco, Nigeria, Somalia, Tunisia
- **Common Market of Easter and Southern Africa (COMESA):** 18 members: Burundi, Comoros, Djibouti, Egypt, Eritrea, Ethiopia, Kenya, Libya, Seychelles, Swaziland, Madagascar, Mauritius, Rwanda, Sudan, Uganda, Zambia, Zimbabwe
- **East African Community (EAC):** 5 members: Burundi, Kenya, Rwanda, Tanzania, Uganda
- **Economic Community of Central African States (ECCAS):** 10 members: Burundi, Cameroon, Central African Republic, Chad, Congo, Equatorial Guinea, Gabon, Rwanda, Sao Tome and Principe, Democratic Republic of the Congo
- **Economic Community of West African States (ECOWAS):** 16 members: Benin, Burkina Faso, Cape Verde, Ivory Coast, The Gambia, Ghana, Guinea, Guinea-Bissau, Liberia, Mali, Mauritania, Niger, Nigeria, Senegal, Sierra Leone, Togo
- **Economic Comunity of the Great Lakes Countries (EGGLC):** 3 members: Burundi, Rwanda, Democratic Republic of the Congo
- **Indian Ocean Commission (IOC):** 5 members: Comoros, Madagascar, Mauritius, Reunion, Seychelles
- **Intergovernmental Authority on Development (IGAD):** 7 members: Djibouti, Eritrea, Kenya, Somalia, South Sudan, Sudan, Uganda
- **Mano River Union (MRU):** 4 members: Ivory Coast, Guinea, Liberia, Sierra Leone
- **Southern African Development Community (SADC):** 14 members: Angola, Botswana, Democratic Republic of the Congo, Lesotho, Malawi, Madagascar, Mauritius, Mozambique, Namibia, Seychelles, South Africa, Swaziland, Tanzania, Zambia
- **West African Economic and Monetary Union (WAEMU):** 8 members: Benin, Burkina Faso, Ivory Coast, Guinea-Bissau, Mali, Niger, Senegal, Togo

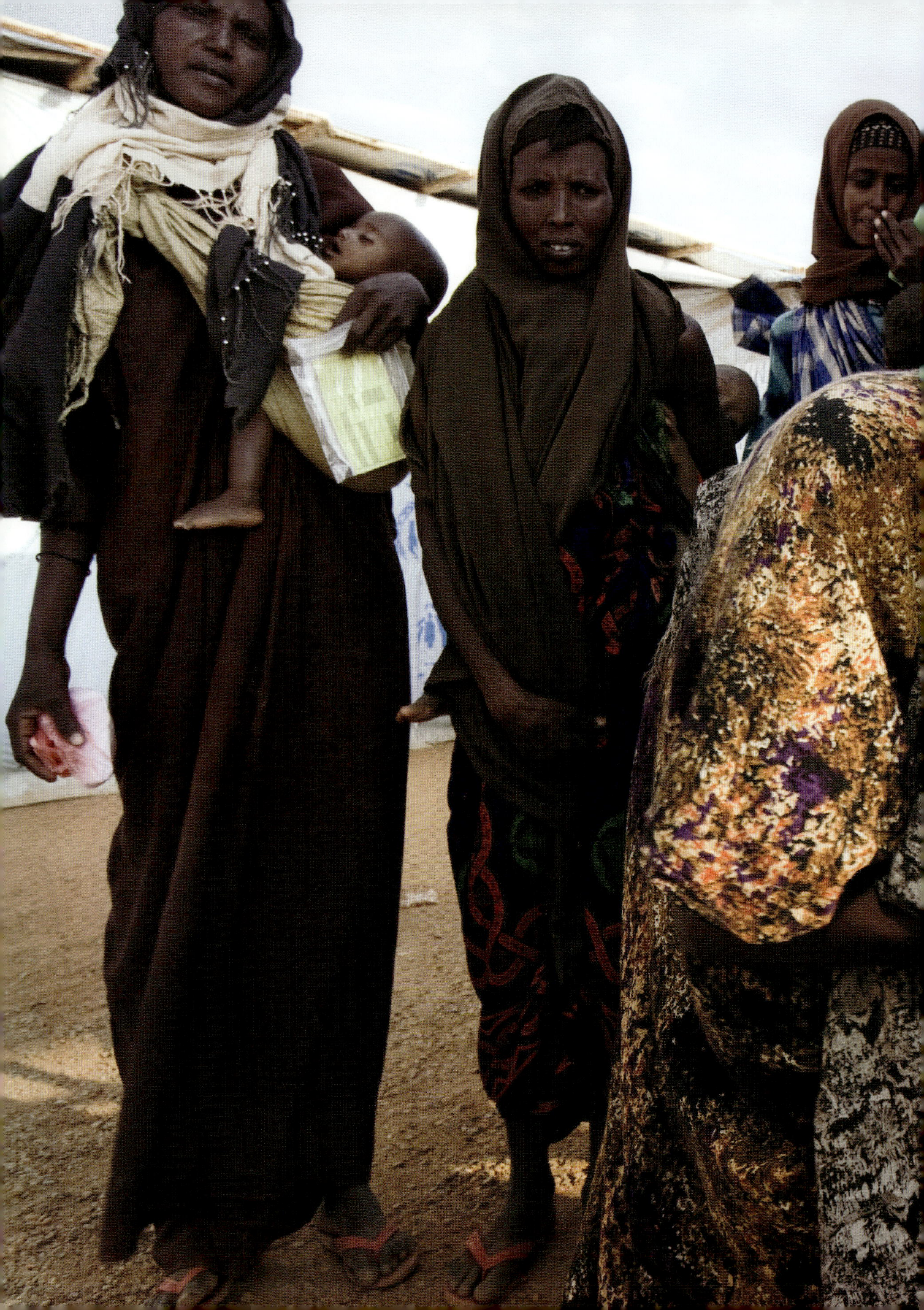

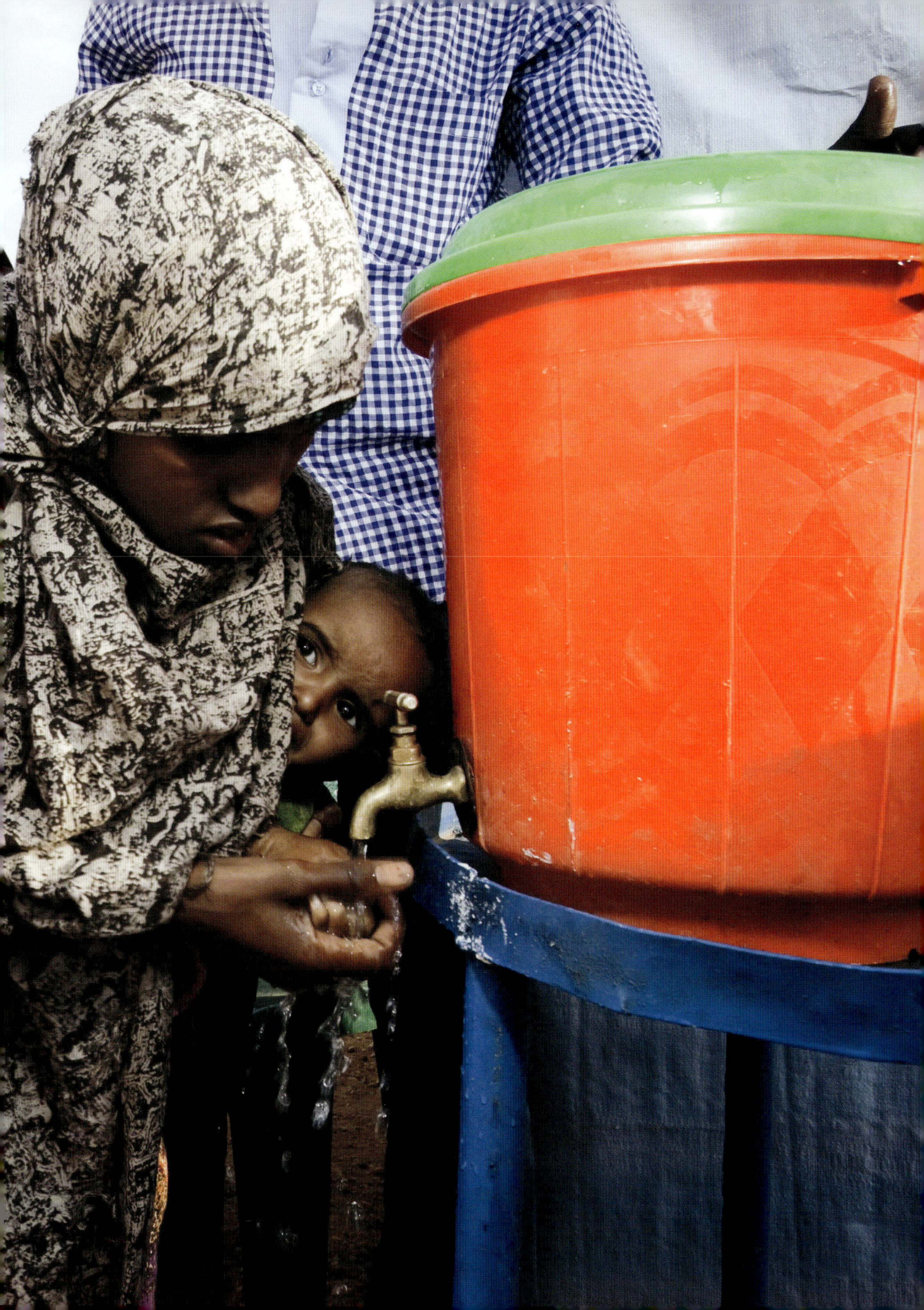

Mitigating and Adapting to Climate Change

Chapter 15

Tomonori Sudo

Climate change is already a reality. Various phenomena such as rises in global average temperature; floods and drought due to changes in precipitation; an increasing number of large-scale typhoons, hurricanes, and cyclones; and other extreme weather events have been observed. And, in the long run, rises in sea level caused by the melting of glaciers and ice sheets in the Antarctic and many other serious phenomena could be realized. The Intergovernmental Panel on Climate Change (Field et al. 2012) predicts that greenhouse gases (GHGs) will continue to increase, leading to serious climate change unless appropriate actions are taken promptly. The effects of climate change could threaten human lives and damage the social capital and fruits of development that both advanced and developing countries have accumulated over decades and centuries.

Developing countries are particularly vulnerable to climate change. In addition to being adversely affected by the consequences of climate change — torrential downpours, drought, the submerging of low-altitude areas due to a rise in sea level — their ability to adapt to climate change is limited. African countries are of particular concern for their vulnerability to climate change, as many of their inhabitants depend on the natural environment for their livelihoods and are vulnerable even under the current climate conditions. Thus, climate change will introduce new risks to the continent adding to current environmental and socioeconomic stressors.

A number of studies on the effect of climate change, mitigation and adaptation, and other climate-related activities have been implemented in developing countries. Many developing countries have analyzed the risks caused by climate change and have formulated mitigation and adaptation policies that have been submitted as National Communications to the Secretariat of the United Nations Framework Convention on Climate Change (UNFCCC) (UNFCCC 2010).

Climate change issues are also a critical development agenda, and development partners have worked to incorporate climate change issues into their development cooperation policies and strategies. The OECD has developed policy guidance to integrate climate change adaptation into development cooperation (OECD 2009b). The World Bank featured climate change issues in its 2010 World Development Report (World Bank 2010b), noting that although climate change is one of many issues that developing countries face, "left unmanaged, climate change will reverse development progress and compromise the well-being of current and future generations." Japan has been an active player in the international community in its effort to combat climate change. In 1997, the Japanese government announced the "Kyoto Initiatives," advocating proactive assistance to developing countries for countermeasures against climate change. Of particular note for Africa, the Yokohama Action Plan, compiled at the Fourth Tokyo International Conference on African Development in 2008, discusses "Addressing Environmental Issues and Climate Change," along with the need to promote measures for mitigating or adapting to climate change, water resources conservation, hygiene, and education for sustainable development.

Against this backdrop, this chapter discusses the challenges and ways to address climate change in Africa. The second section gives an overview of the general discussion on the importance of such countermeasures; the third summarizes the effects of climate change in Africa and the situation regarding GHG emissions; the fourth, fifth, and sixth discuss challenges and opportunities regarding climate change, respectively focusing on mitigation measures, adaptation measures, and on funding, technologies and market mechanisms related to countermeasures against climate change. Finally, the chapter concludes with recommendations for addressing climate change in Africa.

Dealing with Climate Change

Effects of climate change

Developing countries are highly vulnerable to natural disasters. Over 95 percent of the people killed in natural disasters between 1970 and 2008 lived in developing countries (Field et al. 2012). The suffering can be measured not only in human causalities but also in economic losses. Between 2001 and 2006, economic losses from natural disasters were smaller in developing countries than losses in developed countries in absolute terms but higher as a percentage of GDP (about 0.3 percent vs. less than 0.1 percent) (Field et al. 2012). Countermeasures against climate change need to include adaptation alongside mitigation. Mitigation refers to efforts to reduce the rate of climate change or the magnitude of its effects; adaptation refers to strengthening countries' capacity (adaptive capacity) to reduce the vulnerability of people and natural systems to risks related to climate change.

Mitigation and adaptation

Mitigation includes introducing renewable energy, promoting energy conservation, reducing the methane gas generated from livestock waste, and increasing CO_2 sequestration by, for example, afforestation, reforestation, and forest conservation. However, these measures must be promoted in such a way that they do not impair the benefits of development. Therefore, governments need to formulate plans and strategies to balance development policies and mitigation policies at the national and sectoral level. In addition, governments need to establish socioeconomic systems where resources are utilized efficiently and effectively, and to promote development and deployment of low-carbon technologies that allow these plans and strategies to be realized.

Measures to deal with the effects of climate change — adaptation — include strengthening adaptive capacity against the increasing number of meteorological disasters and infrastructure development to deal with the medium- to long-term effect of climate change. These effects are influenced by very diverse factors and cannot be fully foreseen. Thus, adaptation measures need to be assessed locally, taking into consideration the features of the regions, sectors, and communities concerned, as well as alongside nationwide measures. In order to assure steady pursuit of adaptive measures in developing countries, governments need to formulate National Adaptation Plans (NAPs) and other appropriate strategies and plans at the national and sector level. These plans should take into consideration the results of scientific analyses, such as impact assessments, backed up by scientific data. However, due to the uncertainty of the effects of climate change, formulating policies based on a precautionary approach and a "no-regrets policy" will be required, in a way that meets the countries' development.

Furthermore, when developing plans and designing projects, governments need to be aware of the risk of maladaptation that exacerbates rather than reduces the vulnerability to climate change, for example, landfill in low-lying areas that inadvertently increases flooding by impairing drainage. Adaptive measures need to be examined with sufficient caution during implementation in order to prevent maladaptation, after discerning the vulnerability of the targeted strata and how they are affected by climate change.

Africa and Climate Change

Greenhouse gas emissions in Africa

As a region, Africa has among the world's lowest GHG emissions and contributes the least to ongoing global warming, while the economic growth of advanced countries, as well as, more recently, China, India, and other emerging countries, was associated with large amounts of GHG emissions that accompany industrialization. The percentage of global GHG emissions in Africa is lower than that of any other region. In 2005, the total GHG emissions from the African region were only 6 percent of the global total (Figure 15.1). Moreover, GHG emissions per capita in the African region are 2.56 tons, which is less than half the global average of 5.85 tons per capita (World Resources Institute 2012).

Some individual countries, however, have large emissions. For example, per capita emissions from Equatorial Guinea, the Central African Republic, Libya, Gabon, South Africa, Seychelles, Angola, and Botswana exceed the global average (Figure 15.2).

This situation could change. Some 30 African countries suffer from a chronic shortage of electricity, and 585 million people (about three-quarters of the population in Sub-Saharan Africa) cannot access modern energy. Of these people, about 85 percent live in rural areas and use firewood and other biomass fuels for cooking. Energy demands are expected to rise rapidly due to economic growth and population increases in recent years. If African countries choose to depend on fossil fuels to meet these growing energy demands, GHG emissions from Africa will increase significantly. In addition, GHG emissions due

Figure 15.1 | African emits less GHG than any region

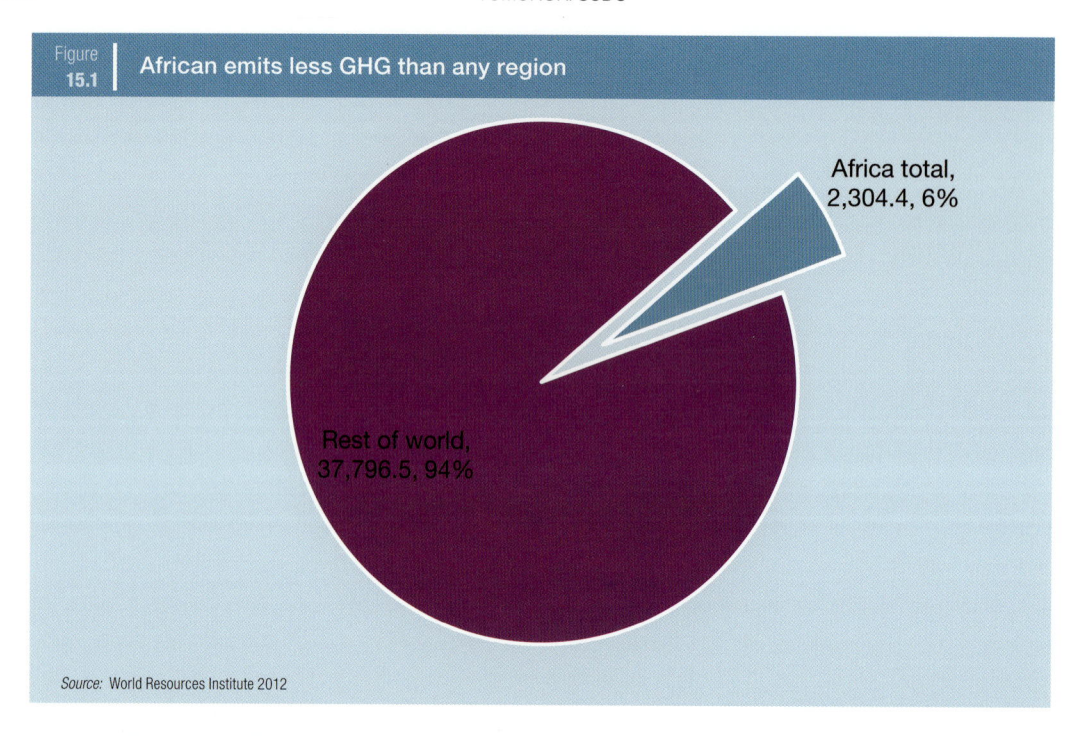

Africa total, 2,304.4, 6%
Rest of world, 37,796.5, 94%

Source: World Resources Institute 2012

Figure 15.2 | Some African states exceed the global average for GHG emission

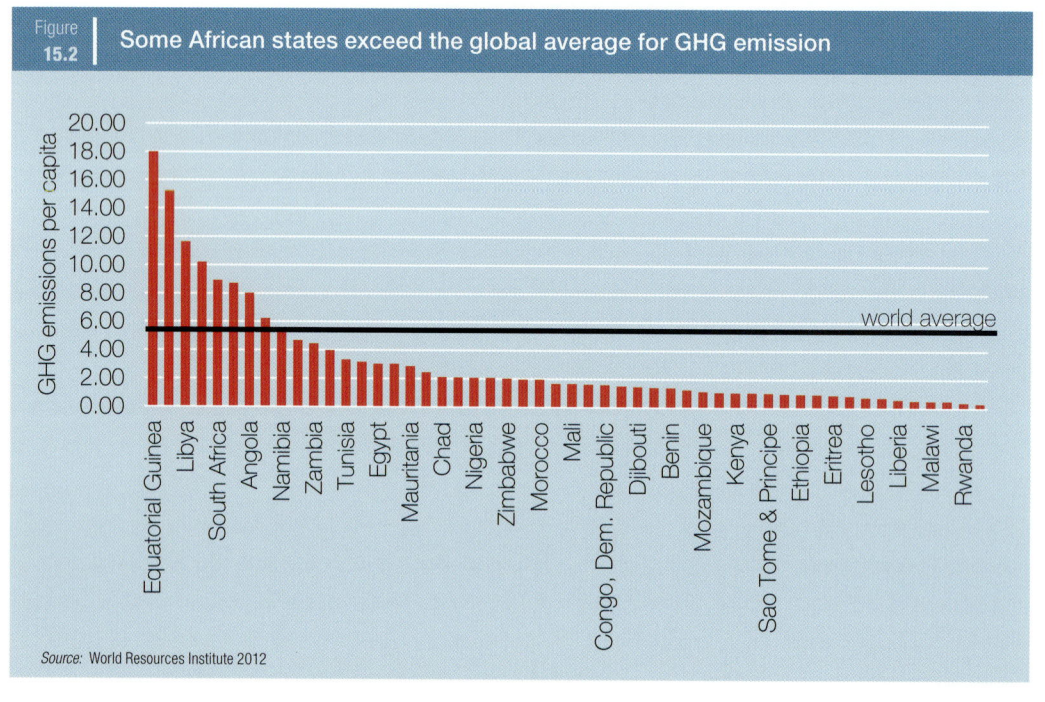

GHG emissions per capita

world average

Equatorial Guinea, Libya, South Africa, Angola, Namibia, Zambia, Tunisia, Egypt, Mauritania, Chad, Nigeria, Zimbabwe, Morocco, Mali, Congo, Dem. Republic, Djibouti, Benin, Mozambique, Kenya, Sao Tome & Principe, Ethiopia, Eritrea, Lesotho, Liberia, Malawi, Rwanda

Source: World Resources Institute 2012

to land-use and/or land use change are comparatively high in some African countries and are at risk of increasing further due to change in land use from forest to farms and urban areas in response to address increasing food demand and growing urbanization.

Impact of climate change in Africa

Africa is one of the regions most affected by climate change. Table 15.1 summarizes climate change trends in Africa and their future impact. The temperature has risen by 0.5°C In the past 100 years, and the effects of El Niño and La Niña phenomena have been exacerbated by global warming. The effect of climate change on incomes is estimated to reach 1.9 to 2.7 percent of GDP. In addition, about 75 to 250 million people will be threatened due to increased water stress, and an additional 80 million people will be at risk of malaria.

Table 15.1 The changing climate is a serious risk factor for much of Africa

Trends	Impacts
• Africa is warming: Africa is 0.5°C warmer than it was 100 years ago. Tendency toward greater extremes; global warming will exacerbate El Niño and La Niña effects • Vulnerability is rising: the income effects of climate change are approximately 1.9–2.7% of GDP in Africa • Uncertainty remains: the precise effects of climate change on Africa are not well understood at the country level since very few countries have their own climate change scenarios and risk assessments	• Increased water stress: 75-250 million more Africans will be at risk of water stress by 2025; arid and semi-arid lands are likely to increase by up to 8%; 25–40% of animal species in national parks in Sub-Saharan Africa are likely to be become endangered • Food insecurity: parts of the Sahara are expected to suffer agricultural losses of up to 7% of GDP • Threats to health: an additional 80 million people will be at risk of malaria • Sea level rises: coastal zones, especially in East Africa, will face increased flooding with the adaptation bill reaching 10% of GDP

Source: World Economic Forum 2008

Climate change has already begun to take its toll in Africa. In the past several decades, the average rainfall in Sub-Saharan Africa has shown a decreasing trend. Average monthly rainfall in the 2000s has decreased by as much as 7 millimeters compared to the 1951-1980 period. The reduction ratio is 2.5 times that of Asia and more than 10 times that of Latin American and the Caribbean countries. The instability and decrease in rainfall poses a food security threat to Africa, where an overwhelming proportion of agriculture depends on rainfall.

In addition, abnormal temperatures, droughts, wildfires, and other climatic disasters take place more often in Africa than anywhere else in the world except after East Asia and the Pacific. Even though other natural disasters, such as floods and violent storms, occur less frequently in Africa than in other areas, their number has increased at the second highest rate in the world and the size of the affected population has tripled in the past decade (UNDP 2012). Climate change is believed to aggravate the frequency and intensity of extreme weather phenomena. There are concerns that this in turn could have serious effects not only on agriculture and water resources but also on ecological systems and gene resources, as exemplified by the expansion of disease vector habitats and the extinction of plant and animal species (Field et al. 2011).

Mitigation Measures

As noted above, Africa contributes the least to ongoing global warming while the economic growth of advanced countries and emerging countries was characterized by large volumes of GHG emissions that accompanied industrialization. In many African countries, economic development and poverty reduction are the most urgent issues, and expectations are high that these will be realized by following the same path toward industrialization as in the advanced and emerging countries. Moreover, there is an urgent need for improved access to energy in view of the fact that three-quarters of the population in the region have not had access to energy and have endured chronic electricity shortages and because energy demands are expected to increase as the economies and populations grow.

The current lack of economic infrastructure development is an important challenge for Africa, but this situation also presents an opportunity for Africa to move toward greener and more sustainable development, in a manner unlike that adopted by the advanced and emerging countries. Africa has a potential to develop renewable clean energy. For example, Africa holds 15 percent of the global hydroelectric power generation potential, of which only about 10 percent has been developed (World Bank 2012f). There is also high potential for photovoltaic power, solar thermal power, wind power, geothermal power, and biomass energy. In addition, there is a potential for Africa to improve efficiency of energy and resource use by leapfrogging to more efficient technologies and infrastructure.

Africa also has great potential for carbon sequestration and storage. The tropical forests in Africa's Congo Basin constitute the second largest forested area in the world. However, these forests have been shrinking and deteriorating due to farmland conversion, excessive logging, forest fires, and other factors. According to the FAO, the global forest area shrank by about 13 million hectares a year on average between 2000 and 2010. Of this, Africa accounts for 3.4 million hectares (FAO 2010). The need to conserve forests, where natural resources and carbon are stocked, has increased. The Congo Basin is an effective carbon sequestration and storage resource and is also high in biodiversity. It could benefit from introducing Payment for Ecosystem Services (PES), such as Reducing Emissions from Deforestation and Forest Degradation plus conservation (REDD+), the sustainable management of forests and enhancement of forest carbon stocks. PES could add new economic value to natural resources that have not yet been appropriately valued.

The sub-sections that follow present a sector-by-sector discussion of the challenges and opportunities related to mitigation measures.

Energy sector

Improving access to energy is important for making progress in industrialization and an accompanying poverty reduction, as well as for expanding access to education and health services. To address the increase in energy demand, African governments need to consider stable energy while preventing pollution and conserving the natural environment.

Africa has abundant potential for renewable energy across the continent. Photovoltaic power and solar thermal power could be obtained from the ample sunlight in the Sahara Desert and surrounding areas, geothermal energy is found mainly in the Great Rift Valley, copious hydroelectric capacity is found mainly along large international rivers, and wind power capacity is found mainly in the coastal areas. Those resources could help the continent establish a low carbon society, if governments promote the use of renewable energy and the cleaner use of limited fossil fuel resources appropriate to the economic and technology level of each country.

Developing efficient power transmission networks and regional power interchange systems based on power pooling would allow a more efficient and stable power supply and would reduce GHG emissions. In remote regions, access to energy could be improved by utilizing small-scale power generation by hydroelectric power, solar power, wind power, and biomass power, as well as independent small-scale grids. The use of low-carbon energy requires efforts on the user side such as energy conservation in addition to those on the supplier side. Energy users in rural areas need to transition from the traditional types of fuel and methods to more thermally efficient, modern methods.

Transportation and urban sectors

Developing transportation infrastructure is also important to promote economic growth. But economic growth could lead to increasing fuel demands and GHG emissions as road transportation demands increase. If the development of high-traffic arterial roads is insufficient, the increased travel time caused by traffic congestion could hinder economic growth and lead to excess fuel consumption. Furthermore, if the transportation infrastructure is vulnerable to the increase in natural disasters due to climate change, the transport of necessary goods could be impaired in times of disaster, and economic activities could be impeded until recovery is achieved. Therefore, low-carbon, resilient transportation systems need to be included in transportation system development.

Urbanization has progressed rapidly in Africa (Chapter 13). Urban plans should be revised to allocate urban functions more efficiently, according to the development stage of the city. In the medium to long term, the goal should be disaster-resilient, low-carbon urban development to the extent possible. The introduction of railroads and Bus Rapid Transit systems may be possible, mainly in large- and medium-scale cities.

Forest management

Africa has an abundance of diverse forest resources. Forest conservation is important for increasing the water-retention capacity of the soil and mitigating the scale and frequency of natural disasters, as well as for retaining a resource for absorbing GHGs. In other words, forest conservation is expected to have both mitigating and adaptive effects. Currently, Africa has one of the highest rates of forest reduction in the world. The percentage of forest coverage in the Sub-Saharan region fell from 31.2 percent in 1990 to 28.1 percent by 2010. This reduction is attributable to the excessive exploitation of forest resources caused by population growth, the accompanying fulfillment of basic needs, and economic development, as well as the conversion of forests to other uses. Mitigation measures aimed at reducing GHGs by curbing forest reduction in developing countries, were on the agenda for the first time at the 11th meeting of member countries (Conference of Parties) to the UNFCCC. Subsequently, Reduced Emissions from Deforestation and Forest Degradation (REDD) was officially adopted as one of the topics for consideration under the Bali Action Plan at the 13th meeting, and it was decided in the Copenhagen accord at the 15th meeting to pursue the development of a REDD+ framework. The introduction of PES under REDD+ is expected to provide an incentive for forest conservation in the Congo basin and other places where forest destruction is underway.[1]

In forest conservation, it is important for the policy makers and project developers to consider residents who depend on forest resources for their livelihoods. It is also important for the government to promote the sustainable use of forest resources in a way that contributes to sustainable forest management, poverty reduction, and regional development. Communities that depend on forests for their subsistence have sometimes used appropriate forest conservation techniques as part of their regional traditions. These indigenous technologies could be incorporated into national forest conservation planning. Sustainable forest management also needs to be promoted for reviving deteriorated forests through trading sustainably produced lumber along with planting and replanting trees in Africa and other areas.

Adaptation Plans

There is growing concern about extreme weather, such as the historic drought in the Horn of Africa in 2011, and its effects on food security. Even if a significant reduction in CO_2 is realized globally, it will still take a long time for GHG concentrations in the atmosphere and the climate system to stabilize, and the adverse effects from future climate change could expand. Especially in Africa, where many of the poor live in rural areas and depend on natural resources for their livelihoods, including rain-fed farming, climate change is a huge threat to achieving inclusive development since poor people will be the most affected by the impact of climate change. Water resources are not used only for drinking water and cultivating food but also for power generation and in industrial processes. In addition, due to rapid urbanization and population increases, improvements in urban infrastructure such as water supply, sewerage, and drainage systems have been delayed, and measures to combat floods are also urgently required. It is

---

1. JICA has assisted in forest conservation programs in the Congo Basin, Gabon, Ghana, Malawi, and other countries.

necessary for governments to consider appropriate water resource management including management of forests as a source of water, improvements in agricultural productivity, improvements in water supply and sewerage systems, and reuse of water as appropriate.

Another threat that climate change poses to development is through the increase in natural disasters. The higher frequency of natural disasters and their increased intensity may lead to a loss in human, social, and natural capital and could wipe out efforts to reduce poverty that have been made to date. Efforts to prevent disasters and reduce their impacts will be essential to securing the benefits of development.

Furthermore, future climate conditions must be taken in to account, not just with regard to existing infrastructure but also in the planning of new infrastructure. For example, an irrigation facility would require the installation of water-saving equipment so as to withstand the changes in precipitation brought by climate change. To create a society and economy capable of withstanding the effects of medium- to long-term climate change, developing economies in Africa (and elsewhere) will need to focus on building climate change-proof infrastructure.

In many cases, water resource management and disaster prevention will require a cross-border response. Especially in Africa, with its many international rivers, cooperation among watershed nations is important. In this area, benefits are maximized through cooperation as opposed to through settlement of disputes. A policy dialogue among countries and the formation of cooperative groups involving various stakeholders — private enterprises, citizen organizations, and communities — could maximize benefits as well as accelerate regional integration, which in turn could lead to expanding markets and new business opportunities (AfDB 2012b).

To tackle those challenges and take advantage of opportunities, African countries need to improve climate information for informed decision making, tailored solutions including development of early warning systems, seasonal forecasts, and regional-level climate change projections. The sub-sections that follow discuss, by sector, the challenges and opportunities concerning response measures.

Agricultural sector

Africa has traditionally been very vulnerable to shocks such as droughts and floods because it is dependent on rainwater and lacks adequate distribution systems. For example, between 2010 and 2011, the Horn of Africa region suffered a severe drought, and more than 10 million people faced a serious food crisis. While the region has periodically suffered severe damage in the past, the rainwater cycle has become more irregular in recent years, and the amount of actual precipitation has been declining.

Agriculture is a vital source of wealth and a means to poverty reduction in Africa (Chapter 11). Indeed, agriculture's share of employment is 65 percent and of GDP, 32 percent. In the past, Africa increased production by expanding its cultivated acreage; however, cultivated acreage per capita has been declining due to demographic pressure, and, coupled with stagnant land productivity, this has resulted in a drop in grain production per capita.

Economic growth and strong demographic pressure have caused food consumption to expand rapidly, worsening the domestic supply and demand balance and increasing the continent's dependency on food imports. In other words, Africa is highly vulnerable to external conditions such as a sharp increase in international food prices and bad weather due to climate changes.

Improvements in agricultural productivity are urgently required in Africa, but improving productivity alone will not necessarily make the region less vulnerable or more resilient. Further measures should be considered for the government and farmers, for example: agricultural infrastructure development such as irrigation facilities to help farmers adapt to climate change, development of crop and cultivation methods, and the introduction of agricultural techniques adaptive to climate change.

The private sector can play an important role in assisting local farmers to improve their productivity and in enhancing the commercial value of products through investment and technology transfer, making agricultural products competitive in the market. Particularly, FDI in agriculture is needed for strengthening the agricultural production and agro-processing capacity of African countries, and it is important for governments to continue to promote it. However, if plans are poorly structured and implemented, international agricultural investment could have unintended negative effects on the political stability of the recipient nation, as well as on its social cohesion, human security, sustainable food production, food safety on a household level, and environmental protection. It may also result in local residents losing access to resources they depend on.

Land transactions are a very sensitive issue. In Africa, where laws and regulations concerning land use are not well established and where communal land use is a traditional norm, international land transactions can trigger a serious, emotionally charged backlash. At the L'Aquila Summit in 2009, the G8 nations highlighted the Promotion of Responsible Agricultural Investment, a comprehensive approach to promoting global agricultural development through increased investment while mitigating the negative effects of international agricultural investment. In September 2009, the seven "Principles of Responsible Agricultural Investment that Respects Rights, Livelihoods, and Resources" were announced (FAO et al. 2010; World Bank et al. 2013). The expectation is that through agricultural investments conducted in line with these principles, agricultural infrastructure will be developed and technology to improve agricultural productivity by sustainable methods will be introduced.

The agricultural sector is the most vulnerable to climate change. Therefore, it could be useful to consider establishing a structure to cover losses from climate aberrations, such as through a climate index insurance policy.

Disaster prevention and reduction

In recent years, many African countries have been hit by large-scale natural disasters, such as floods, droughts, coastal erosion, and mudslides. The increasing frequency of natural disasters has brought additional risks and attendant influences on social and economic development. The effects are varied, and a case-by-case response is required. At the UN World Conference on Disaster Prevention in 2005, the Hyogo Framework for Action was adopted as an international framework for disaster prevention. In accordance with this framework, it is important for governments to establish disaster prevention plans in line with the priority that each country places on them.

In order to respond to large-scale disasters accompanying future climate change, meteorological and climate observation capabilities must be improved and an early warning and evacuation system structure constructed on the bases of an accurate meteorological and climate change forecasting system. In addition, governments need to improve their climate change risk management capabilities in infrastructure development at a sector level (such as agricultural development, water resources management, and traffic) to incorporate disaster prevention and rapid recovery from disasters into planning in all sectors. Hosono (2012) points out that there are three kinds of gaps between the capabilities required for disaster prevention and the actual levels of such capabilities: (1) the level required for addressing expected impact of disaster (a disaster scenario), (2) the level required for a level exceeding a disaster scenario, and (3) the level required to respond to long-term changes. In some cases, the traditional techniques handed down in the community or the technologies used in other developing countries are more favorable than the latest technology to close these gaps. In such cases, south-south or triangular cooperation may be effective.

To respond to a temporary shortage of funds in case a massive disaster occurs, systems such as standby-type loans and insurance could be utilized as safety nets.

Water resources management

Water resources are an important component of almost all development sectors. Water demand is expected to increase due to the expansion of agricultural and industrial production and the energy sector, in addition to the increasing demand for safe water supply for human lives. At the same time, the changes in precipitation accompanying climate change and the decreased water retention capability due to the reduction of forest resources are all likely to cause unstable water supplies. Africa has not been able to fully develop the potential of its rich renewable water resources (UNECA, AU, and AfDB 2011). Therefore, developing these resources and appropriately managing them are important issues for Africa.

Africa has a number of international rivers including the Nile and the Congo, and approximately three-quarters of its surface water resources, estimated at 4.6 trillion cubic meters annually, are concentrated in eight major international rivers (World Bank 2009b). Therefore, it is essential to conduct cross-border water resource management and to establish master plans and enhance governance for optimal Integrated Water Resource Management (IWRM) within each watershed. This would include the appropriate development of surface and ground water and the purification and recycling of industrial and living discharge water. Africa has established an Africa Water Vision for 2025. This vision aims to provide an environment in which all people will have equal access to water resources and be able to use these resources for power generation and agriculture. It also creates an enabling environment for IWRM and designates integrated regions based on watersheds (UNECA, AU, and AfDB 2011).

Reservoirs can be an effective response to an unstable water supply (World Bank 2009b). However, a safe water supply will have a different meaning for urban and rural areas. In urban areas, improvements in the water supply system will be required to deal with the increase in population caused by migration to cities. On the other hand, since many people lack access to safe water in rural areas, one urgent issue for the governments is to establish a system and infrastructure for a stable supply of safe water in rural communities.

Funding, Technology, and Market Mechanisms Associated with Climate Change Measures

The funds required to implement these measures is huge. Africa faces vast needs for infrastructure improvement. According to an estimate by the AfDB, the funding needs accompanying climate change measures will be around $9 to 12 billion annually, if Africa is to take the low-carbon development route. Importantly, if appropriate measures are not taken now, the incremental cost rises to an estimated $13 to 19 billion (AfDB 2011b).

At the 16th meeting of the Conference Parties to the UNFCCC, the Cancun Agreement was established (UNFCCC 2012), which clearly stated that between 2010 and 2012, developed countries would provide funding aid of almost $30 billion to developing countries in the area of climate change (fast-start financing). It also established a Green Climate Fund that would make $100 billion in funds available annually by 2020 (long-term funding).

As indicated in Figure 15.3, the flow of funds is on the increase. The funds include not only ODA but also a large amount of FDI from the private sector. Governments need to work to mobilize private funds, not just public funds, to finance climate change measures. For further mobilization of funds for climate change measures, African countries need to strengthen the absorptive capacity for climate funding and improve the enabling environment for private investment.

Specifically, governments need to engage diverse actors comprehensively in the following: (i) planning and establishing climate change policies, such as Nationally Appropriate Mitigation Actions (NAMAs) and National Adaptation Plans (NAPs), as part of their development policies; (ii) information sharing and dissemination with related parties in transparent manner; and (iii) implementation of measures based on an appropriate budget. The climate change program loans now being implemented in Indonesia and Vietnam provide examples of donor support schemes for these activities. In these schemes, the donor and the government engage in dialogue on the provision of financial support, through which they monitor and evaluate the implementation status of a climate change policy scheme matrix. These schemes provide an efficient way for governments to implement climate change policies, such as NAMAs and NAPs, as part of their development policies, work toward transparently sharing and disseminating information with related parties, and implement measures based on an appropriate budget (Sudo et al. 2009, Fujikura and Toyota 2012). Furukawa et al. (2013) have surveyed the effects of general budget support in the health sector and concluded that although there have been certain improvements in budget allocations

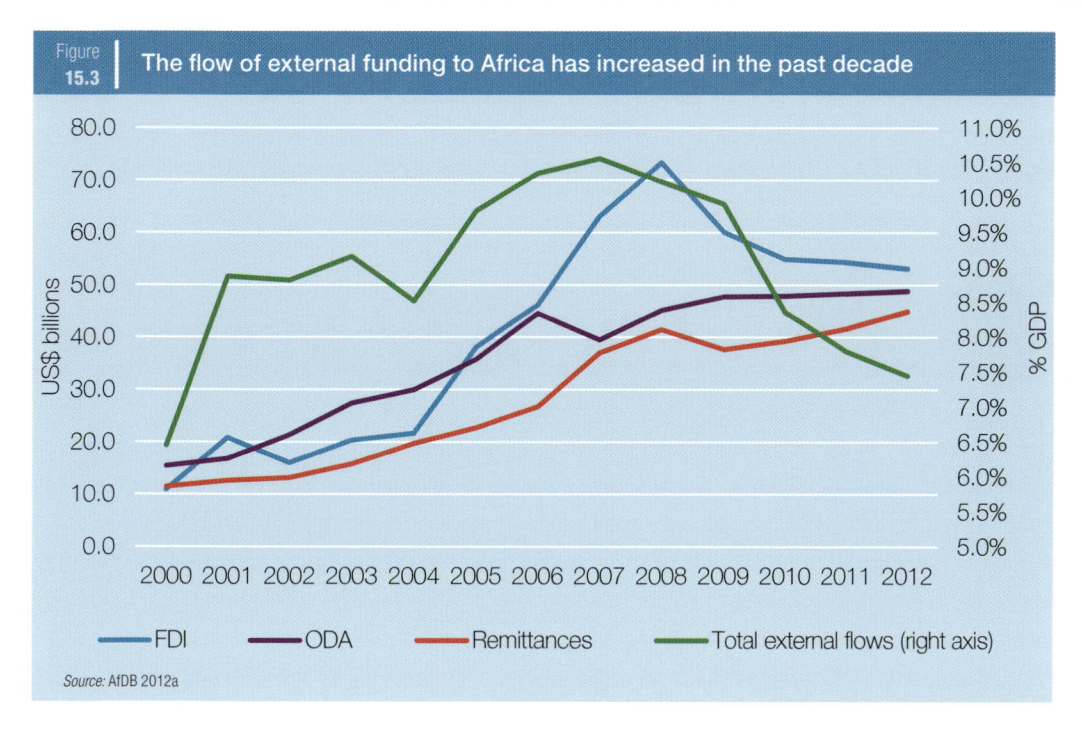

Figure 15.3 The flow of external funding to Africa has increased in the past decade

Source: AfDB 2012a

in this sector, these have had a limited effect on improving health indicators. They comment that general funding support and the complementary effects of the projects and programs require attention. The complementary effects between policy, budget, and project, as pointed out before, should be considered carefully when deciding on climate change investments.

There is also a strong need in Africa for appropriate low-carbon technologies for enhancing development that is resistant to the effects of climate change. The Cancun Agreements also included an agreement to establish a Climate Technology Center and Networks to expand and promote the development and transfer of technology for mitigation and adaptation, and to understand and support technical needs in developing countries. In addition to training, various activities will be required, to promote the use of appropriate technology, improve data-gathering capabilities, and establish systems to share knowledge.

These technical and investment needs could create an attractive market for private companies. Establishing an attractive market environment for private companies to introduce technology and investments could help promote climate change measures in the private sector. The Clean Development Mechanism, one of the market mechanisms introduced under the Kyoto Protocol, was expected to promote the active participation of the private sector in the mitigation business, and over 5,500 projects have been registered to date. However, as of the end of December 2012, only 104 projects, a mere 1.9 percent, were in Africa. It has been pointed out that the current Clean Development Mechanisms have not been able to fulfill the functions intended at the Kyoto Protocol due to the complexity of the applications and fundraising for low-profit projects (Fujikura and Toyota 2012). The use of market mechanisms, such as a simplified Clean Development Mechanism or a bilateral offset credit system mechanism, could act as an incentive for private companies to provide investments and technical transfers, and efforts to improve the system and develop the ability to effectively utilize these mechanisms are important.

Action Agenda

Climate change is a cross-cutting issue and a problem that has a global dimension and impact. It requires a comprehensive approach spanning various strata from the individual and community level to the governmental and regional/global level. And there is a need to resolve the apparent disconnect generated between a policy-based top-down approach and a community-based bottom-up approach (Fujikura and Tawanishi 2011). In addition, the activities of each actor must be considered from the perspective of externalities that influence the actions of others. For example, an adaptive policy taken by one community might trigger a maladaptation that could exacerbate the disaster damage in another. Therefore, to effectively implement climate change measures, information sharing among a wide range of actors is important, from the international level to the community level.

Although Africa has the world's lowest amount of GHG emissions, it is affected the most by climate change. For Africa to maximize its natural resource potential in a sustainable, low-carbon way and be resilient to external shocks such as climate change, it must engage in sustainable development in which everyone can receive the benefits of growth. In other words, Africa is in a position to target sustainable development through inclusive and resilient green growth. Africa's climate change measures are themselves the start of a new development process.

Based on the discussions above, we offer the following priority actions for the effective promotion of future climate change measures in Africa.

Establish climate change policies in accordance with the conditions of each country as part of its development policies, share and disseminate this information with stakeholders in a transparent manner, and implement the policies with appropriate budget allocation.

The climate change policies established by governments, such as Nationally Appropriate Mitigation Actions (NAMAs) and National Adaptation Plans (NAPs), are prepared as part of each country's development policy, and it is desirable for these climate change policies to generate co-benefits that will contribute to sustainable development (Fujikura and Toyota 2012). Many countries in Africa have already created NAMAs and NAPs. These clear, foreseeable, and stable policies lend credibility to the activities of actors, including in private investment. In establishing these policies, the opinions of actors in the private sector and civil society organizations, as well as those of women and the poor, should be actively incorporated along with those of the government. Furthermore, although the use of data based on scientific analysis is recommended wherever possible, it is also necessary for the policy makers to respond to the needs of their own countries based on precautionary principles and the concept of a "no-regrets" policy, taking into consideration the capabilities of the subject sector, region, and community.

Schemes such as climate change loans can be effective to support these activities, in addition to supporting projects or programs. Great care should be taken, however, with regard to the complementary nature of policy, budget, and project policy, as well as the leverage effects of general funding support.

Support access to information as well as innovation through R&D as important means to identify opportunities for low-carbon and climate-resilient growth and promote effective green growth in Africa.

Access to information is the most important factor in today's society, not only for disseminating climate change policies but also for providing disaster information or information concerning low-carbon technologies and funding access. It is also important for a country in determining how it can apply climate change measures implemented by other nations or communities or what effect they could have. Making greater use of information and communication technology is one way to improve access to this information. Sharing information and knowledge through policy dialogue is another effective method. In addition, the NAMAs established by each country require monitoring, reporting, and verification, and securing the transparency and accountability of information through monitoring, reporting, and verification will enable the implementation of appropriate climate change policies in a plan-do-check-act cycle. Furthermore, access to technical information will promote a country's introduction of technology that is internationally available and could lead to the development of technology-enabled leapfrogging. Appropriate technical information includes not only cutting-edge technologies but also information on traditional technologies, which can be very useful. Technology transfers are expected to include not only transfers from developed countries but also transfers between developing countries through south-south and triangular cooperation (Hosono 2012).

Using environmental education to enhance people's awareness of climate change is important for inclusive growth, particular for the poor, who are vulnerable to the effects of climate change, and also for women and future generations.

Establish an enabling environment where everyone, including the private sector, can participate in various climate change measures.

It is important for the public sector to establish a path toward the creation of a low-carbon economic society resilient to climate change through policies and system improvements. However, the public sector itself neither manufactures nor conducts business transactions on its own. Everyone, not just private companies and civil society organizations, but also poor and socially vulnerable people, is involved in economic and social activities. In view of the public and external nature of global-scale climate change, the participation of all is required for a low-carbon, socioeconomic model that is resilient to climate change.

Particularly high expectations are placed on the private sector's participation in climate change measures, because of its capacity to provide funds, technology, and employment. In addition to support from the policy side, actions will be required to promote the participation of the private sector including establishing a conducive investment climate (with macroeconomic stability), establishing fair and transparent legal systems, promoting business models such as public-private partnerships, and providing support and seed money for establishing projects.

Use market mechanisms effectively along with use of public funds and promotion of capability development.

The implementation of specific climate change measures requires funds and implementation capabilities. The Cancun Adaptation Framework requires $100 billion in funds to be made available annually by 2020 together with systematic technology transfer; this includes sizable needs in African countries. The effective use of funds is required, as well as the development of ways to maximize the effects of development and climate change measures while minimizing additional costs. Funding for climate change was discussed at the 2011 High Level Forum on Aid Effectiveness, and the partnership document it adopted calls for the promotion of consistency, transparency, and predictability in effective climate change finance and a broad approach toward development aid (OECD 2011a).

Public funds are also expected to provide leverage in obtaining private funds. Establishing a structure and environment to promote private investment can contribute to an overall increase in private investment, beyond climate change measures. Moreover, by monitoring and evaluating the efforts of the donors involved, even more effective cooperation could be possible. Lamhauge, Lanzi, and Agrawala (2012) have conducted studies on monitoring and evaluation methods with regard to several donors' support for adaptation measures. Such monitoring and evaluation methods focusing on the role of donors should be examined in the future.

Market mechanisms like Climate Development Mechanisms and bilateral offset credit mechanisms, or innovative mechanisms like PES, including REDD+, can be easy for African countries to work with. In order for these mechanisms to be used effectively to benefit African countries, it is necessary to develop the capabilities of the African countries themselves and to introduce these mechanisms into international society so they can become even easier to use.

The challenge of climate change in Africa, as elsewhere, is best addressed through collaboration and partnerships among a wide range of stakeholders.

An approach to climate change must be taken with the participation of all people. There is a need to cooperate in implementing the optimal climate change measures, with different countries and development institutions providing all the cooperation knowledge they have amassed to date for everyone to use. Further knowledge is being amassed in the academic and private sectors. All of this knowledge needs to be utilized in an complementary manner to establish a low-carbon economic society with the ability to withstand climate change so that all people, including the poor, will be able to receive the benefits of development. Optimal solutions will involve establishing networks with various actors while keeping in mind international negotiations, technology, and funding trends in the climate change field. To do this, we recommend establishing a broad collaboration among international organizations, other aid organizations, CSOs, universities, autonomous bodies, private companies, and others, as well as providing bridges for exchanges among various actors and mediating policy dialogues between communities and governments.

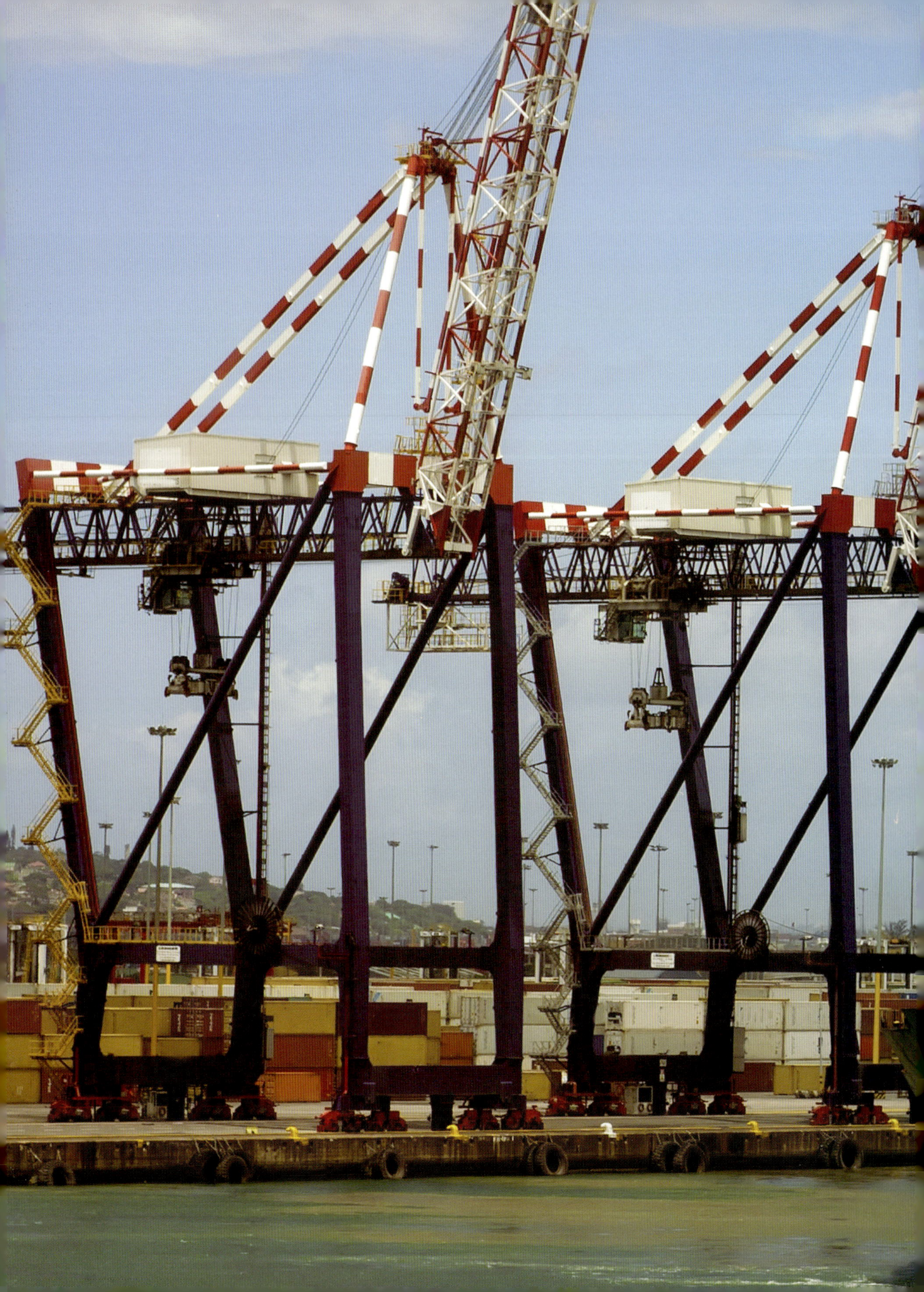

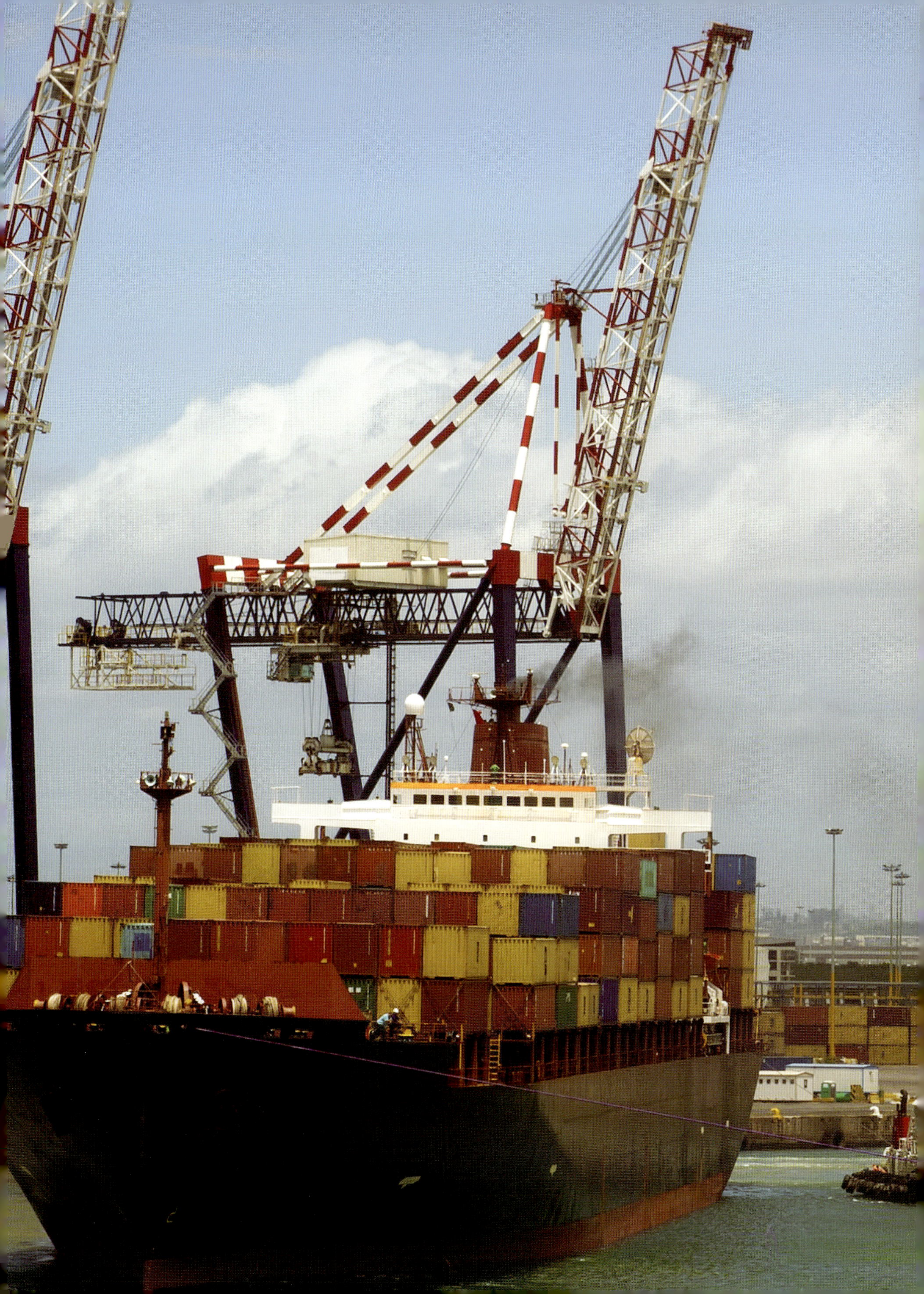

Repositioning Africa in the World

Chapter 16

Graham Stegmann and Fantu Cheru

Africa has long had contacts with China and India. But over the past 50 years, Africa's external relationships have been dominated by ties with the OECD countries. For the most part, relations have been asymmetrical, reflecting past colonial links and Western economic dominance, cemented by migration and the use of English, French, and Portuguese as official languages. Over this period, the overwhelming majority of development, humanitarian, and emergency assistance; investment; and preferential trade arrangements (PTAs) came from the OECD countries, with terms largely set the wealthy powers. The international financial institutions were dominated by majority shareholders from OECD countries. UN development agencies too had to respond to the policy positions of their major contributors. African voices were raised, but core decisions were made elsewhere.

The rise of China, India, and other emerging economies, and their increasing engagement with the continent of Africa, have brought changes. High levels of growth in emerging economies have fuelled an almost insatiable demand for oil, gas, and other raw materials from Africa, bringing higher returns from commodity exports and greater availability of affordable consumer goods. The increased income has enabled some African countries to improve their infrastructure and productive capacity, leading to impressive economic growth. Sustained growth in many African countries has changed perceptions of the continent, both as a prospective customer and as a reliable partner in which to invest. A new generation of African leaders has begun to emerge, and regional and continental institutions are being strengthened.

The rebalancing of relations continues, and the center of gravity continues to shift. Economic relations between Africa and its old partners remain substantial, but Africa's relationship with the emerging economies is now almost as important economically (Chaturvedi et al. 2012; Woods 2008). Significantly, there are signs that African countries are beginning to approach their relations more pragmatically, taking them less for granted and making their own interests explicit. They increasingly recognize that partners are engaged with Africa in pursuit of their own interests and that Africa must do likewise.

New opportunities will open up for Africa in a multipolar world where more than half of global GDP comes from developing and emerging economies. Africa will have the policy space to drive the development process on its own terms. Trade and investment will predominate in relations with the rest of the world. Development aid will become less important and be replaced by cooperation, knowledge exchange, and technical know-how, some of it in furtherance of global initiatives.

By 2050 Africa could become a growth pole with an important place on the global stage. Under the convergence scenario developed in Chapter 1, it would no longer be just a supplier of raw materials, but also a source of manufactured and capital goods. It would be economically integrated, energy- and food-secure, with sound infrastructure. Its sizeable middle class and young population would provide a burgeoning consumer market. Brain drain would be a thing of the past; talent would still be highly mobile but increasingly attracted to Africa. Africa would have taken responsibility for its own security, the promotion of peace, and for the management and prevention of conflicts.

None of this can be taken for granted. Africa would still be a relatively minor economic partner for both the OECD and emerging market economies. There would be few free rides, and global competition would be intense, with both old and new partners. Africa will continue to be buffeted by events outside the continent, including global business and financial cycles. The current economic crisis and introspection in much of the developed world and the slowdown in China and India underline the uncertainties that lie ahead and the risks that have to be managed. Africa cannot assume that it will receive preferential treatment. But it can move from being essentially a passive onlooker, reacting to events elsewhere, to being an active participant in global councils. It would be able to articulate an African view and to have it taken into account; it could help set the agenda.

To achieve this vision, Africa countries will have to be proactive, take initiative, and show leadership. Countries will have to work together and manage multiple relationships. Notwithstanding the rhetoric of respect for African-led priorities, of non-interference, and of mutual benefit, it is evident that much of the motivation of Africa's partners, old and new, has come from the pursuit of their own national interests (Kragelund 2008; Chaturvedi et al. 2012). Economic and political differences will remain, but African countries would be able to form partnerships on a more equal footing based on mutual economic interests. Bilateral relationships would be secondary to multilateral engagement. Most economic exchange would be market- rather than state-determined.

This chapter provides first a brief introduction to Africa's external economic relationships over the past 50 years, seen through the prisms of aid, trade, and investment. It then considers the likely evolution of these relations and the implications for Africa. The concluding section offers recommendations on action that should be taken if Africa is to realize its potential.

Evolution of Old and New Partnerships

Development aid: a donor-led agenda

Much of the motivation of Africa's partners, old and new, has been the pursuit of their national interests. The preferred mode of engagement for most of the partners has been bilateral, almost exclusively so in the case of China, which has largely adopted a turnkey approach to aid. Major donors have established fora for dialogue with Africa on the continental level, holding regular meetings at head of state or ministerial level, but these have all been donor-initiated and funded (Cheru & Obi, 2010; Li et al. 2012; FOCAC 2006). Over the past 50 years, donor governments have largely set the policy agenda.

For some OECD countries, trade, investment, and aid policies have at times been separate, each with its own objectives, the product of shifting and at times competing policy priorities. But the political dimension, previously evident in rivalries between Western countries and the former Soviet Union, has re-emerged in the past decade in response to conflicts in Iraq, Afghanistan, and Syria, and as the economic crisis puts donor budgets under greater scrutiny. For the emerging market countries, aid has always been subsidiary to foreign policy considerations, and assistance has bundled trade, investment, and aid.

In the 1960s, more than 30 countries in Africa and another handful in Southeast Asia gained independence. The challenges facing these new countries, especially those in Africa, were great. Many were landlocked, infrastructure was minimal and designed to serve colonial interests, education and health services were sparse, and resources were poorly used and institutions nascent. The OECD countries, in particular, felt a moral and political commitment to assist.

From 1960 to 1990, flows of official development assistance (ODA) from OECD Development Assistance Committee (DAC) countries to developing countries rose steadily in nominal terms. The allocation of aid reflected Cold War rivalries, and the former colonial powers naturally gave priority to their ex-colonies (OECD 2011b). However, as a percentage of DAC countries' combined GNI, aid fell between 1960 and 1970 (see Figure 16.1). Early optimism about the impact of aid faded in the 1970s, both as progress stalled in Africa and as oil price shocks put pressure on donor budgets. The overall aid level then oscillated between 0.27 percent and 0.36 percent of GNI for a little more than 20 years.

Following the stagnation in African growth in the late 1970s and early 1980s, development assistance increased in real terms throughout the 1980s, and the focus shifted toward policy reform, specifically reducing the role of the state and expanding the space for market forces to tackle both social and economic issues. The main barriers for development were now seen to be unsustainable macroeconomic policies in developing countries and regulations and policies that prohibited markets from evolving: in summary, too much government and not enough market. The new approach did not work well (Riddell 2008). African governments reluctantly acceded to conditions imposed but failed to implement reforms on which there was no domestic political consensus and which often hurt vested interests. When it became evident that market-oriented policy reforms were not reducing poverty as expected, more development assistance was targeted to the poor. It was also recognized that the state had to play a new role, especially for investments in human capital via health and education and in agriculture.

The collapse of the Soviet bloc at the end of the 1980s had a marked impact on development. The loss of desire to keep developing countries on one or other side of the East-West divide came at the same time as fiscal retrenchment in many donor countries. As a result, real net ODA fell by nearly a third

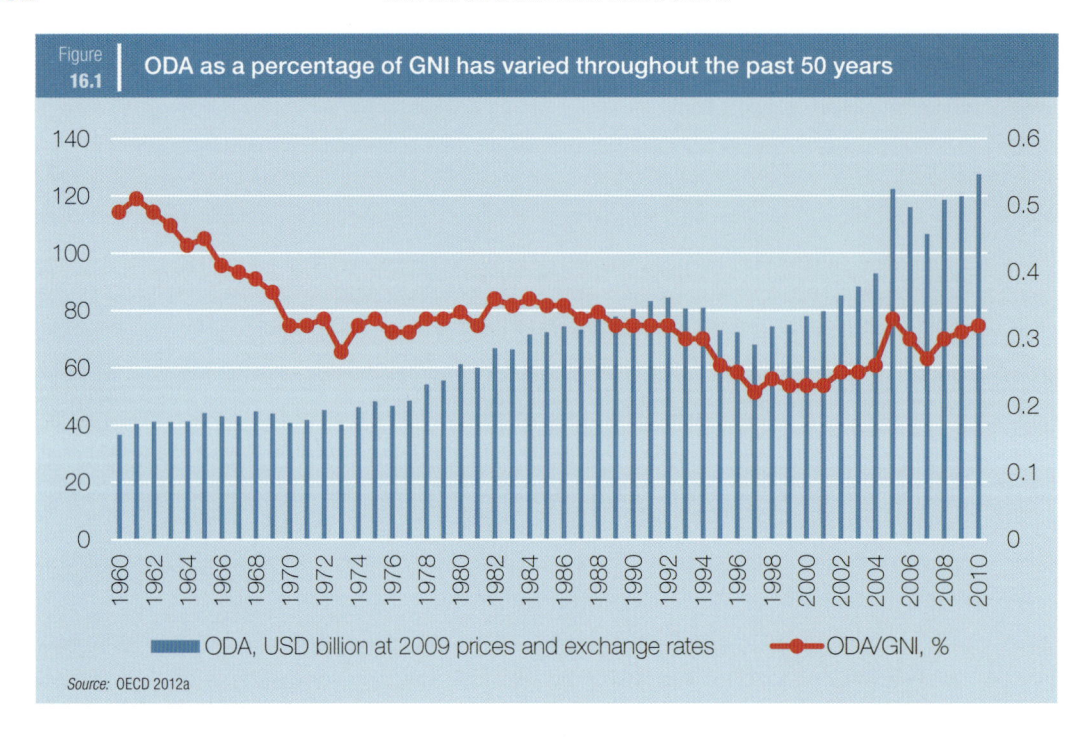

Figure 16.1 ODA as a percentage of GNI has varied throughout the past 50 years

ODA, USD billion at 2009 prices and exchange rates — ODA/GNI, %

Source: OECD 2012a

across the decade. In Latin America and Asia, much of the loss was more than countered by a rise in private flows, but not in Africa. In addition, competition for aid dollars rose globally, and significant assistance was diverted to countries in Central and Eastern Europe.

Aid started to rise in 1998, but it was still at its historic low as a share of GNI (0.22 percent) in 2001. Since then, a series of high-profile international conferences have helped to boost ODA flows. In 2002, the International Conference on Financing for Development held in Monterrey, Mexico, set firm targets for each donor and marked the upturn of ODA after a decade of decline. An increasing amount of aid began to be directed to the social sectors and to responses to humanitarian and emergency needs, with many bilateral donors reducing their allocations to agriculture and infrastructure.

Aid levels to Africa showed a dramatic increase from 2001 onwards. Africa has been on the agenda of each G8 summit since 2002. The inclusion of quantifiable targets in summit documents, particularly in Gleneagles in 2005, has maintained some momentum and brought a degree of accountability. Results are published; commitments are monitored by a Progress Panel headed by Kofi Annan as well as a number of international NGOs. In 2005 — following a request from African heads of state — United Nations Economic Commission for Africa (UNECA) and the DAC developed a Mutual Review of Development Effectiveness. Through this biennial consultation, African leaders and policy makers engage with OECD counterparts to assess commitments, monitor performance, and identify good practice on the continent.

The 2010 G20 Summit in Seoul marked an important paradigm shift. Previously it was felt that "the constituency for aid is suspicious of growth, and the constituency for growth is suspicious of aid" (Collier 2007). Following Seoul, growth was highlighted as the policy objective, with priority given to supporting the drivers of growth. There was recognition that progress depends on a wide range of factors and must be underpinned by wider coherence of trade, investment, aid, migration, and domestic policy (Council of European Union 2012).

New partnerships

Over the past decade new partnerships have begun with emerging market countries. Engagement has expanded rapidly and substantially over the past decade. The change has been driven by a perception of Africa as a continent with unrealized potential, but much more by the need to secure energy and other mineral resources to support the high rates of growth in emerging market economies. Initially, engagement, investment, and trade were concentrated in a limited number of resource-rich and, in particular, oil-exporting countries, but non-resource-rich countries are now benefitting as well (UNCTAD and UNDP 2007; UNCTAD 2013a; Mawdsley 2012).

From the start, there have been obvious differences in the conceptualization and execution of development assistance between the OECD countries and the emerging market partners. The latter do not consider themselves providers of traditional aid. They prefer to use the language of solidarity, mutually beneficial development, and South-South cooperation.

The differences are four-fold. First, for the new partners, assistance is very clearly part of an integrated external policy, driven primarily by domestic interests rather than by development results or Millennium Development Goal (MDG) targets. Interventions are directed and managed almost exclusively on a government-to-government level, although private companies may be charged with implementation. Emerging market countries feel no compulsion to observe DAC best practice guidelines or to participate in donor coordination or harmonization. They have not imposed policy conditions when providing aid, although non-policy conditions are a regular feature of trade and investment agreements (Mawdsley 2012; Woods 2008).

Second, the major part of new assistance is in the form of concessional loans, not grants, much of which is channeled through Export-Import (EXIM) Banks, alongside export credits, and executed by state-owned or state-selected enterprises. Much of the assistance is directed to infrastructure and the productive sectors, and very little has gone to the social sectors where OECD donors have concentrated since the 1990s.

Third, almost all of the new aid is for discrete projects. There is little or no budget or sector support. Fourth, there is explicitly no macroeconomic policy or other conditionality attached to loans. This distinction is blurred, however, by the close association of development assistance and investments in, or access to, natural resources.

OECD partners have questioned the approach adopted by emerging market countries. They argue that it risks increasing debt levels by financing unproductive projects or by extending loans to countries unable to pay, and that China and India are in effect free riders on the initiative for Highly Indebted Poor Countries (HIPC). The evidence has not supported these concerns (Reisen and Ndoye 2008; Berthelemy 2009). Western donors have also been concerned that DAC norms and standards relating to democracy, human rights, and good governance are not being observed. However, recent assessments found no convincing evidence that the availability of aid from the emerging economies encourages poor governance in Africa (Woods 2008; Brautigam 2008).

Composition and flow of resources

The volume of assistance from emerging market economies that qualifies as ODA is difficult to estimate. Figures are not reported in the common format used by DAC, and headlines focus on commitments rather than disbursements. In addition, even when figures become available, it is difficult to distinguish between export credits, concessional aid, and technical assistance. The aid estimates presented here, therefore, relate predominantly to OECD donors.

External financial flows to Africa have trebled over the past decade as shown in Table 16.1. In 2011, external finances recovered to pre-crisis levels with FDI, ODA, and remittances estimated at $152 billion. External flows doubled as a share of Africa's gross domestic product from 6.8 percent in 2000 to 12.3 percent in 2006 but were still only an estimated 8.2 percent in 2011. In 2010, OECD countries still accounted for about 40 percent of total FDI to Africa. For Sub-Saharan Africa, FDI and ODA remain the key sources of finance (AfDB 2012a).

Table 16.1 ODA, FDI, and remittances are all key sources of external financing for Africa

	2001	2002	2003	2004	2005	2006	2007	2008	2009	2010	2011	2012
ODA	16.8	21.4	27.4	30.0	35.8	44.6	39.6	45.2	47.8	47.9	48.4	48.9
Portfolio investment	-3.3	-0.1	-0.4	6.8	5.8	22.2	12.8	-27.0	-2.1	12.2	7.7	16.2
FDI	20.9	16.1	20.4	21.7	38.2	46.3	63.1	73.4	60.2	55.0	54.4	53.1
Remittances	12.6	13.2	15.8	19.8	22.7	26.8	37.0	41.5	37.7	39.3	41.6	45.0
Total External flows	47.1	50.6	3.3	78.3	102.5	140.7	152.5	133.1	143.6	154.4	152.1	163.2

Source: AfDB 2012a

Multilateral assistance

Total aid to Africa in 2011 amounted to $51.7 billion, of which the multilaterals accounted for $18.5 billion. The European Union institutions and the World Bank each accounted for just over $6 billion and the AfDB $2.4 billion. The World Bank has been a leading force intellectually; much of the aid policy debates described above have been centered on the World Bank and IMF Boards, both dominated by the most advanced economies. Only in the smaller AfDB did regional member countries form a majority and have a decisive say in the election of the president. Despite the UN's ostensible position as a global body, its institutions have had much less influence, with the exception of emergency and humanitarian assistance and peacekeeping.

Meanwhile there has been a proliferation of channels as new institutions have been established, often with a narrow remit, to focus on new priorities. International NGOs (mainly Western) have gained an increasingly prominent role, not only as proponents of more aid but also as critics. By 2006, according to the Development Cooperation Report 2009, there were about 225 bilateral donor agencies, 242 multilateral agencies (of which 24 were development banks), and about 40 UN agencies, working in development cooperation (OECD 2009a). The global aid architecture has become increasingly complex, making it ever harder for African countries to successfully manage relationships with donors, including in-country. Across all the different types of donors, the common rhetoric of "country ownership" was little reflected in practice.

European Union

The EU (member states together with the European institutions) is the biggest player in global development, providing aid worth $69.7 billion in 2010, of which 48 percent was disbursed in Africa in 2010. The European Commission (EC) itself manages a large part of the aid ($12.7 billion grants, $8.3 billion loans and equity). EU aid delivered by the European Commission and other European institutions has for some time been rather more contractual than most bilateral assistance, subject to reasonably transparent rules and procedures and providing for a known level of medium-term financing. The EU policy framework reflects the fact that expenditure comes from a number of separate budgets each with its own objectives. As a result, aid through the EC is less focused on low-income countries than most bilateral aid.

For most of Africa, the main EU source is the 2000 Cotonou Partnership Agreement between the African, Caribbean, and Pacific (ACP) and the EU and its member states, which provides a 20-year framework covering trade and investment as well as aid. Assistance is financed from the European Development Fund as negotiated and agreed with member states. North African countries benefit from bilateral agreements under the European Neighborhood Policy, which builds on earlier association agreements and is structured around a privileged relationship, offering political association, economic integration, and increased mobility. North Africa also benefits from the Union of the Mediterranean, (which aims at economic integration and democratic reform in North Africa and the Middle East supported by regional and sub-regional projects.[1]

Summits are held with Africa every three years, alternately in Africa and the EU. The EU has looked to the AU Commission as a partner on continent-wide issues. The EU/Africa Strategy 2007 signed with the AU Commission is intended to promote a stronger political dialogue around four key objectives: (i)

---

1. Formerly known as the Barcelona Process, relaunched in Paris in July 2008.

consultation on issues of common concern; (ii) promoting peace, security, democratic governance and human rights, gender equality, and sustainable economic development; (iii) jointly promoting a system of effective multilateralism; and (iv) promoting a broad-based and wide-ranging people-centered partnership. The EU has also provided financial and technical support to capacity building of the AU Commission and, in particular, to support the peace and security operations (ECPDM 2009; Council of Europe 2007).

United States

The United States provides about a quarter of global development assistance and is by far the largest donor in financial terms, although it ranks 19th of the 23 DAC donors in terms of aid in relation to the size of the economy. Over the last decade the United States has increased the aid budget, reaching a high of $30 billion in 2010, increasing from 0.1 percent GNI in 2001 to 0.21 percent in 2010. 39 percent of aid from the United States goes to Africa. American assistance is driven by a national security strategy to advance American values and interests, bringing together diplomatic, defense and development efforts. 27 entities are involved in American development cooperation; USAID and the State Department are the two key drivers. Assistance from USAID is heavily earmarked by Congress.

The Obama administration set out its new strategic orientations on development in 2010. It outlined an approach based on three elements: a policy targeted at sustainable development; an operational model focused on effectiveness and results, underscoring the importance of country ownership and promoting effective division of labor among donors; and a whole-of-government approach that harnesses development capabilities across government. Balancing strategic national interests and development objectives remains a challenge when deciding aid allocations.

Japan

Japan's aid program started as economic reparations after World War II and remains primarily focused on Asia. Eschewing a military or security role, Japan concentrates on economic relations and is explicit that development cooperation is in its own interest in the long term.[2] The Ministry of Foreign Affairs (MFA) plays a key coordinating and policy role and the Japan International Cooperation Agency (JICA) manages most aid implementation.

There has been stability in Japan's approach, but questions have been raised periodically about whether it was playing a role consistent with the size of its economy. The 2003 revisions to its ODA Charter include a poverty dimension within the overall growth and self-help policy orientation, making it more consistent with the 2001 DAC guidelines on poverty reduction and facilitating cooperation with other donors.

---

2. The stated aim in its revised ODA Charter of 2003 is "to contribute to the peace and development of the international community, and thereby help to ensure Japan's own security and prosperity."

Until 2000 Japan was the largest bilateral donor in financial terms, but it has since slipped to fifth as the Japanese economy has stagnated. According to the DAC, total Japanese aid in constant 2010 dollars declined from $12.08 billion in 2002 to $11.02 billion in 2010, the only major donor to show a decline over this period (OECD 2012b). In 2010, Japan's ODA represented 0.2 percent of its GDP, which places it at the low end of donors measured against the UN target of 0.7 percent (OECD 2012b).

Since the early 1990s, Japan has reassessed its relations with Africa and adopted a more proactive approach to African affairs, as shown by the Tokyo International Conference on African Development (TICAD) first convened in 1993 and held every five years since then. Japan's assistance to Africa focuses on boosting growth, accelerating infrastructure and capacity development, empowering farmers, promoting sustainable growth, creating inclusive societies, and consolidating peace, stability, and good governance. The proportion of Japanese aid allocated to Africa has increased over the decade, and Japan has met the targets it set itself under TICAD. In 2011, DRC was Japan's third largest aid recipient and eleven of Japan's top 30 aid recipients were African. Given the importance of Japanese programs in Asia, however, less than a quarter of disbursements were to Africa (OECD 2012c).[3] In May 2013 at the TICAD V meeting Japan announced combined private and public support to Africa of $32 billion, including ODA of approximately $14 billion over the next five years (Japanese Ministry of Foreign Affairs 2013).

Japan has a strong preference for bilateral aid (over 80 percent) and has pursued an independent rather than coordinated path. Almost half of its aid has been in the form of loans, reflecting its concerns about the visibility of Japanese aid and its role in foreign affairs. The rise of, and relations with, China remain sensitive. Japan provides mainly project financing and has always emphasized state-to-state relations, channeling less than other OECD donors through NGOs or other in-country partners. It has been more technocratic and less engaged than Western donors with policy dialogue and policy conditionality. Japan has given a stronger push to global issues, including climate change, conflict, and terrorism.

China

China has had long historical, political and economic relations with Africa. China's current aid, trade, and investment strategies are closely intertwined and promote national interests, in particular access to raw materials, while also benefiting Africa. While the renewed interest in Africa was very much influenced by China's desire to enhance its global status as a rising power and to promote its "going out policy," Africa's abundant natural resources, such as oil and gas, needed by China to fuel its growing economy make it an attractive partner. In January 2006, the Chinese government issued an Africa Policy Paper, declaring its commitment to a new strategic partnership with Africa based on five principles: "peaceful coexistence, respect for African countries' independent choice of development path, mutual benefit and reciprocity, interaction based on equality, and consultation and cooperation in global affairs" (People's Republic of China 2006, Brautigam 2008).

---

3. Only one African country (DRC) was among the top ten recipients of Japanese bilateral aid. The top four were India, Indonesia, Vietnam, and China.

Chinese aid is almost exclusively bilateral and is given almost entirely without conditions relating to recipients' domestic policy or governance. Financial assistance is tied to the purchase of Chinese goods and services and is designed to benefit Chinese companies. China has favored what it calls a "full-form technical and managerial cooperation" including managing projects on behalf of beneficiaries, lease management, and joint ventures — in effect "turnkey" projects for delivery of roads, power plants, hospitals, schools and government offices as complete packages (PRC 2011; UNCTAD 2010). These projects often involve resource-for-infrastructure deals, and Chinese construction companies have been the main beneficiaries. Some aid is also provided as interest-free loans, mainly for infrastructure projects, which are usually written off as debt relief, or as export buyer's credit for Chinese equipment and construction services.

China provides aid almost exclusively on a bilateral basis. But it has also sought to engage on a continental level, establishing in 2000 the Forum on China-Africa Cooperation as a platform for dialogue on a "just and equitable" international order and cooperation between China and Africa. This approach, including high-level political attention and a more positive portrayal of the continent, is very attractive to African countries disenchanted with the Western approach, often considered to be paternalistic. China's own experience and spectacular growth also appears to offer an alternative model of development. More recently, however, some Africans have started to query the value of Chinese assistance, noting the similarities it has with Western engagements in Africa and that China is as much a competitor as a partner.[4]

India

India has been at the heart of the Non-Aligned Movement and of South-South cooperation. Traditionally, Indian development assistance has been a marginal component in the overall foreign policy framework. In the last decade, aid has had a higher priority in Indian foreign policy (Beri 2008; Sharma 2009), and a new body for governing India's development assistance, the Development Partnership Administration (DPA), was set up in 2012 under the Ministry of External Affairs (MEA).

As in the case of China, aid, trade, and investment are closely coordinated, and the government provides significant support to investment and trade from Indian companies. India is also similarly motivated to secure energy, raw materials, and markets to fuel its growing economy, particularly since the economic liberalization of the 1990s.

An important driver in India's Africa policy is energy security. It is projected that by 2030 India will become the world's third largest consumer of energy. India possesses few proven oil reserves, and it is seeking to diversify sources of energy supply away from the volatile Middle East to develop stronger economic ties with the African continent. Currently around 24 percent of India's crude oil imports are sourced from Africa (Madan 2006; Sharma and Mahajan 2007; Cheru and Obi 2010; Vines et al. 2009).

---

4. See for instance Sanusi 2013.

Figures on India's aid are difficult to obtain. However the share of India's official development assistance going to Africa is relatively small; total aid to Africa was $23 million in 2009/10. Most aid to Africa has been in the form of technical cooperation, providing training in India, capacity building, and project-related consultancy services. EXIMBANK has played a critical role in facilitating the entry of Indian private sector companies into Africa, including the financing of major capital projects in Africa. As of mid-2012, close to 54 percent (or $4.2 billion) of total Exim lines of credit went to 24 African countries. There is also close coordination in the promotion of consultancies and other professional services firms from India.

India has consolidated its presence in Africa through the India-Africa Forum Summit, first held In April 2008 in New Delhi; a second Forum was held in May 2011. Though modest by comparison with the Forum on China-Africa Cooperation the Summit demonstrated India's longer-term interest. Commitments were made to increase existing lines of credit from $2 billion to $4 billion, provide duty free access for poorer countries, double trade from $25 billion to $50 billion by 2011, expand aid for capacity building and training, and provide a $200 million line of credit to AU/NEPAD to support regional integration.

Brazil

Brazil's economic and political relationship with Africa was transformed under the presidency of Luis Ignacio Lula da Silva. Though less active than China and India, Brazil has openly courted African countries to secure access to Africa's large market and to resources vital for Brazil's fast-growing economy (ABC 2010b).

Brazil is a resource-rich country, and its policy is less driven by resource-seeking. Oil constitutes a large part of Brazil's imports from Africa (mostly from Angola and Nigeria) at present, but following the discovery of oil in Brazil in 2007, it has become clear that Brazil will no longer be dependent on imported oil.

Consequently, aid, trade, and investment are less integrated than in China and India. Brazilian policymakers see Africa's biggest potential as providing a consumer market for their country's manufactured goods. In addition, aid and technical assistance are channeled to African countries to some extent to gain their support for Brazil's quest to secure a permanent seat on the UN Security Council. Some recipients of Brazilian aid are resource-poor but possess ample unused land for agricultural production, including biofuels (CEIRI 2011; ABC 2010a). Brazil's engagement in Africa is moving beyond commercial interests to embrace social development programs and knowledge transfer, particularly to the agricultural/biofuel sector, including sharing of tropical agriculture technologies and of policy expertise

While initial engagement focused on the lusophone countries for historical reasons, Brazil's African engagement now extends to a wide range of countries throughout Africa. The number of technical cooperation projects has risen rapidly over the past decade, putting Brazil among the key players in South-South knowledge transfer. Africa received about half of Brazil's development budget of $90 million between 2003 and 2008 (World Bank and IPEA 2011; Pariota and Pierri 2013).

The Trade Dimension

Although trade with the emerging economies has increased rapidly over the past decade, OECD countries remain Africa's major market. Africa has three dominant trading partners: the EU, China, and the United States. Each is a multiple of the next largest market in volume. Intra-Africa trade remains under 10 percent of Africa's total trade. The main transport lines for imports and exports run to the coast, built to promote external rather than regional trade. Africa has benefited from PTAs, particularly with OECD countries, but their value is being eroded as tariffs are reduced globally and non-tariff constraints remain constant. This section provides a brief overview of the main patterns of trade to date.

Declining share of trade with traditional partners

In the 1980s and 1990s about two-thirds of Africa's exports went to the advanced countries, and a similar share of total imports came from them. Since then, growth in African exports has doubled, characterized by very rapid growth in exports to emerging economies and some growth to advanced economies. The OECD countries remain the largest market and in 2011 accounted for some 59 percent of exports, as shown in Figure 16.2.

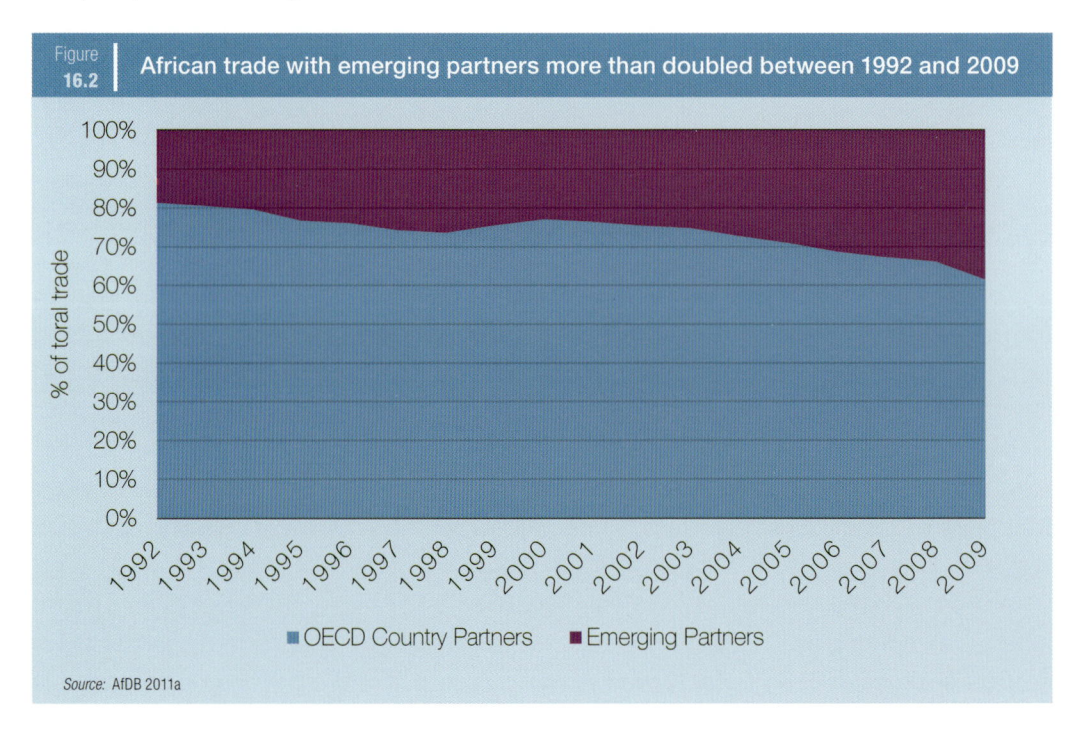

Figure 16.2 African trade with emerging partners more than doubled between 1992 and 2009

Source: AfDB 2011a

The headline numbers obscure the fact that a handful of African countries account for the bulk of trade with both OECD countries and the emerging market economies and that exports are heavily dominated by hydrocarbons and minerals. The top five hydrocarbon exporters — Algeria, Angola, Egypt, Libya, and Nigeria — experienced an 89 percent increase in exports between 2001 and 2010. Europe and the United States account for about a third of all oil exports from Africa, but this share has been gradually decreasing in recent years as China and India increase their imports. Demand for non-oil commodities from Africa, such as gold, platinum, diamonds, iron, and copper, is also shifting from Europe and the United States, mainly to China. By the end of 2010, 12.9 percent of Africa's non-oil exports went to China, almost five times more than a decade earlier. Dependence on exports of natural resources makes Africa vulnerable to volatility in global commodity prices. Emerging market countries' share of total trade grew from 23 percent in 2000 to 37 percent in 2009 (see Table 16.2). The United States' share of Africa's trade was more than three times China's in 2000, but China surpassed the United States in 2009 and is now Africa's largest trading partner (Freemantle, 2010). From the perspective of Africa's trading partners, Africa is still a small market. Africa as a whole provides less than 9 percent of EU imports and exports, half of which is with North Africa. All ACP countries, for example, provide only 4.8 percent of EU imports and exports. For the United States, Africa is a minor trading partner, providing just 2 percent of exports and 4 percent of imports; over three-quarters of US imports are crude oil, which conditions US strategic interests accordingly. China is the largest partner among the emerging market economies. Africa's importance to China is as a strategic supplier of raw materials; but in total volume of Chinese trade, Africa is a minor partner. If Africa were a single country its total trade would still be less than China's trade with the United States, Japan, South Korea, Taiwan, Hong Kong, or Germany.

Table 16.2 China has become more and more important for Africa in the past decade

	2009 Trade	2009 Exports	2009 Imports	2000 Trade	2000 Exports	2000 Imports
Share traditional partners (%)	63.5	67.6	59.0	77.0	78.3	75.4
EU25	44.3	43.0	45.6	53.5	51.3	56.4
Other trading partners	6.1	6.1	6.1	7.5	6.6	8.8
United States	13.1	18.4	7.3	16.1	20.4	10.1
Share emerging partners (%)	36.5	32.4	41.0	23.0	21.7	24.6
Brazil	2.5	2.4	2.7	1.7	2.0	1.3
China	13.9	13.1	14.7	4.7	4.6	4.9
India	5.1	6.0	4.0	2.3	2.4	2.1
Total Value	673.4	350.8	322.5	246.4	142.4	104.0

Source: AfDB 2011a

Trade agreements

Debates on the comparative value of aid and trade and on the use of mixed credits linger but are no longer center stage. Evidence shows that there are positive links between openness to trade and economic growth. Unfortunately, successive rounds of multilateral trade negotiations have highlighted the difficulties that many low-income countries face in capturing benefits from new market access and trading opportunities. More recently African countries have been urged to liberalize their imports, a sensitive issue for countries with weak fiscal positions reliant on trade taxes.

The stalemate on the WTO Doha Round has left PTAs as the main market-opening mechanism. PTAs continue to evolve and are not confined to North–South trade. In a narrow sense, preferential arrangements are not in conformity with WTO rules, which under the most-favored-nation (MFN) clause extend to all WTO signatories the trade concessions given to any one member. Since the 1970s Africa has had PTAs with both East and West. There are many similarities across the agreements, including lower tariffs, higher quotas, or quota-free access.[5]

The importance of PTAs has eroded as MFN rates have been lowered. PTAs have, however, generated benefits for Africa, although the size of such benefits is contested.[6] Benefits are not evenly distributed and depend on the composition of each country's exports; for instance, exports of sugar and bananas accounted for 73 percent of preferences under the Cotonou Agreement.

The debate has shifted toward issues of how countries manage investment, government procurement, competition, and trade facilitation. The ongoing discussion among the EU, the EC, and the ACP countries is a likely indicator of future trends.[7] The case is not clear cut; the political leverage of individual countries and regions varies, and the prospect of development assistance makes it harder to resist agreement.

---

5. EU-EBA (everything-but-arms): Duty-free entry without quotas for all products although transitional arrangements were put in place for three sensitive products, bananas, sugar, and rice. Cotonou Agreements: Forty-eight Sub-Saharan countries have preferential access to EU markets. United States-AGOA: Preferences enabled countries like Kenya, Lesotho, and Swaziland to develop their clothing industries. OECD-GSP (Generalized System of Preferences): Provides the same level of preferences available under the EBA for those countries committed to implementing core international conventions on human rights, labor rights, environmental protection, and good governance; however, to date, only Cape Verde is covered. China-FOCAC (Forum on China-Africa Cooperation): More than 4,700 items covering 95 percent of commodities from Africa are tariff-free. India: Duty-free tariff preference scheme for 34 least-developed African countries covering 94 percent of total tariff lines, including products such as cotton, cocoa, aluminum ores, copper ores, cashew nuts, cane sugar, clothing, and non-industrial diamonds.

6. The OECD concluded that preferential access to Quad (United States, EU, Japan, and Canada) agricultural markets generated on average an additional $1.4 billion of exports for the countries concerned (2007). The value of EU preferences is estimated to be some 4 percent of beneficiary country exports—rather higher than the benefits generated by United States or Japanese preferences. The difference arises from higher preference margins, greater commodity coverage, and less stringent rules of origin.

7. Despite opposition from developing countries, the EU tried in the Doha discussions to establish WTO rules on how countries manage investment, government procurement, competition, and trade facilitation (the Singapore issues). With the stalemate in the Doha round, the EU has switched its efforts to promote this agenda to the Economic Partnership Agreement (EPAs) providing for reciprocal liberalization of merchandise trade intended to replace the Cotonou trade preferences. The EC argues that the Cotonou Agreement already contains provisions relating to investment and a mandate to negotiate further and that full EPAs could help accelerate regional trade integration by providing a dynamic stimulus and a coordinating mechanism to undertake reforms. This would liberalize intra-Africa trade on an MFN basis, improve the business climate and competitiveness, and enhance the credibility of regional integration by locking in reforms in an international treaty. ACP countries argue that Cotonou does not stipulate that an investment agreement should be part of an EPA, nor is there any WTO obligation to include investment provisions in a regional trade agreement. They argue that such rules would constrain their choices in crucial policy areas for managing their domestic economies and have continuously resisted proposals for reciprocity in agreements. The ECA and some independent studies have argued that the proposed EPA approach would produce serious adverse consequences, such as job losses, closure of industries or deindustrialization, loss of revenue, and disruption of the economic integration process underway in the ACP regions.

Investment in Africa: Growing Rapidly but Concentrated

Reliable data on the volume and sectoral distribution of FDI in Africa from emerging market economies are hard to come by. Nevertheless, based on available data from UNCTAD, important trends are discernible. According to UNCTAD, developing countries accounted for 45 percent of global FDI inflows in 2011, of which the share of East and Southeast Asia was 22 percent. Africa's share was 2 percent (UNCTAD 2012).

Between 2005 and 2011, Africa attracted on average $40 billion annually in FDI. In real terms, FDI to Africa in 2011 was $43 billion, much lower than the $53 billion reported in 2009 (UNCTAD 2012). The decline in FDI inflows to the continent in 2011 was caused largely by the fall in investment in North Africa, which has traditionally been the recipient of about a third of inward FDI to the continent. In particular, inflows to Egypt and Libya, which had been major recipients of FDI, came to a halt owing to their protracted political instability.

In contrast, inflows to Sub-Saharan Africa recovered from $29 billion in 2010 to $37 billion in 2011, a level comparable with the peak in 2008. A rebound of FDI to South Africa accentuated the recovery. The continuing rise in commodity prices and a relatively positive economic outlook for Sub-Saharan Africa contributed to the turnaround. In addition to traditional patterns of FDI to the extractive industries, the emergence of a middle class is fostering the growth of FDI in services such as banking, retail, and telecommunications, as witnessed by an increase in the share of services FDI in 2011 (UNCTAD 2012).

UNCTAD's medium-term baseline scenario projects that FDI to Africa will grow annually between $75 and $100 billion in 2013 and 2014 (UNCTAD 2012).The most recent estimates of total FDI flows and stock to Africa countries (UNCTAD 2013a) are shown in Table 16.3 below.

Table 16.3 Traditional partners remain the key source of FDI, but emerging markets are becoming increasingly important

	Flows		Stock	
Total world	$39,540	100%	$308,739	100%
Developed countries	$26,730	68%	$237,841	77%
European Union	$16,218	41%	$155 972	51%
North America	$9,281	23%	$53,412	17%
Developing economies	$12,635	32%	$68,890	22%
BRICS	$10,007	25%	$42,583	14%

Source: UNCTAD 2012

The largest stock of FDI is held by investors from France, the United States (each over $55 billion), and the United Kingdom ($46 billion), followed by Malaysia (which has only one-third as much), South Africa, China and India. The flow figures, however, show an increasing trend of investment from emerging market economies (UNCTAD 2012).

Mining has attracted the most FDI, but significantly only a quarter of the value of the so-called BRIC countries (Brazil, Russia, China, and India) investment in Africa was in the primary sector, the majority from state-owned enterprises in China and India. While labor costs in Africa are not yet very different from those in the BRICs, the duty-free, quota-free access provided by the EU and the United States have generated some manufacturing investments. The destination of FDI within Africa is shown in Table 16.4

Table 16.4 | FDI flows vary greatly throughout the continent

\> $3 bn	$2-3 bn	$1-2 bn	$500-999 mn	$100-499 mn	< $100 mn
Nigeria	Congo	Sudan	Madagascar	Zimbabwe	Swaziland
South Africa	Algeria	Chad	Namibia	Cameroon	Cape Verde
Ghana	Morocco,	DRC	Uganda	Cote d'Ivoire	Djibouti
(3)	Mozambique	Guinea	Equatorial Guinea	Kenya	Malawi
	Zambia	Tunisia	Gabon	Senegal,	Togo
	(5)	Tanzania	Botswana	Mauritius	Lesotho
		Niger	Liberia	Ethiopia	Sierra Leone
		(7)	(7)	Mali	Mauritania
				Seychelles	Gambia
				Benin	Guinea-Bissau
				CAR	Eritrea
				Rwanda	Sao Tome and Principe
				Somalia	Burkina Faso
				(13)	Cameroon
					Burundi
					Egypt
					Angola
					(17)

Source: UNCTAD 2012

Conflict and Climate Change Have Risen on the Agenda

The trajectory of Africa's economic and political relations with both traditional and new partners will very much depend on how the continent manages two important risks: conflict and climate change.

Conflict and security

The fragility of many African states, with weak central authority and competition for resources between rival ethnic or other groups, has provided fertile ground for conflict (see Chapter 6). Conflict within and between states has also provided opportunities for extremist and criminal networks to establish themselves and for security and police officials to operate with virtual impunity. Terrorist and criminal networks have come to be seen as real threats to the stability of African countries and to the conduct of beneficial international economic relations. For most OECD countries issues of peace and security, terrorism, drug trafficking, and money laundering are now clear priorities. Recent events in the Sahel have demonstrated just how quickly new threats can emerge, topple governments, and necessitate foreign military intervention. Responding to emergencies absorbs nearly 9 percent of total aid to Africa.

Security of transport routes has become a concern for trading nations across the globe. Almost 90 percent of Africa's imports and exports are carried by sea. Yet Africa is the only region that does not have a maritime strategy and has sparse naval or other security assets to deploy. It loses revenue as pirate operations drive up the cost of trade and as goods are diverted to other ports. Africa also loses substantially from illegal and unregulated fishing; a recent report puts the loss in West Africa as high as 37 percent of the region's catch. Lack of maritime policing also facilitates trade in illegal logging. The AU has begun to move toward a maritime strategy for the continent's waters. Establishing the necessary legal and regulatory framework will require unprecedented levels of cooperation as well as coordination between police, customs, and armed services (Institute of Security Studies 2012).

The major powers have long recognized the area's strategic importance but more recently have stepped up operations in response to maritime attacks, mainly from pirates (Institute of Security Studies 2012). Both China and India now participate in operations. India in particular has decided to project its military power in the Horn of Africa and the Indian Ocean region, which it considers part of its sphere of influence and through which the oil tankers that carry nearly all of India's oil imports must travel.

Climate change

Climate change is predicted to have a major impact on Africa even though Africa's greenhouse gas emissions are marginal (see Chapter 15). OECD country donor strategies now often include assistance with adaptation, better management of natural resources, and cooperation on energy and environmental matters. Nonetheless, at a global level donor policies are dictated by domestic and regional concerns, and international dialogue will continue to be dominated by exchanges between the old and new emitters.

Climate financing continues to be a difficult issue. The amounts required, the source of funding, burden sharing, the allocation of resources, and competing demands for mitigation and adaption all remain disputed. Reaching agreement and unlocking funds will take years, and there is no guarantee that poor countries will be the main beneficiaries. As current discussions on climate financing vividly illustrate, there is considerable scope for arguments about additionality, the basis for any new taxes, their incidence and impact, national or international collection, and how the resulting resources will be managed. There will be competing demands from potential beneficiaries and debates on the extent to which private sector activity can be leveraged in support. Africa urgently needs to develop national and regional strategies not only to adapt to climate change but also to participate in global discussions and find opportunities to use climate financing.

Global governance

Until recently, the structure of global governance reflected agreements made in the aftermath of World War II. But change has begun, stimulated, in particular, by the recent global financial crisis. The G7/G8 remains a key forum for coordination on political and security issues, but its role as pacesetter in international finance and economics has waned while that of the G20 has increased. Given its greater legitimacy, the G20 looks set to remain the central forum, but debates continue about the its composition, the extent to which weight should be given to representativeness rather than just economic size, how to balance inclusion with efficiency in discussions and decisions, and whether it is a forum for exchange rather than decision-making. Africa's only member, South Africa ranks only 28th in economic size globally.

What is Likely to Happen Next

Africa is unlikely to be the central concern of the major economies. All of them have major challenges domestically and, internationally, are focused on relations among themselves, on security and areas of actual and potential conflict, and on financial crises and systemic stability. The new leadership in China has signaled a stronger focus on its domestic agenda, maintaining and improving the quality of growth and tackling corruption. India and Japan will remain focused on regional issues and on growth. Competition in trade will grow; countries and private sector institutions with funds to invest will continue to seek the highest return consistent with risk, as seen vividly in the comparison of flows to Africa to total global flows.

Ensuring global stability will remain a goal in an economically and financially integrated world and will require narrowing the gap between rich and poor and implementing public policies to stimulate and regulate trade and markets and to manage common goods. The gap between the rich and poor will be as much within as between countries (see Chapter 7). Inequality will receive more attention, and development policy and practice will continue to evolve.

Trade and investment come center stage

Trade and investment, not aid, will predominate in economic relations among countries. FDI from all partners, trade, remittances, and philanthropic giving will all offer greater opportunities to support economic development. Some will still come with strings attached, but in a healthy global economy, Africa will be able to make its own choices, not simply take what is on offer.

Patterns of production and trade will continue to evolve. China's days of being the low cost supplier to the world appear numbered, as witnessed by the rise of textile production in Bangladesh and Vietnam. Africa could take the place of China as a key link in the supply chain of goods by taking advantage of geographical proximity to many OECD countries. But to do so it will have to improve its infrastructure, develop rapid transport links, and remove other barriers to production and trade (see Chapter 10).

Investment is not guaranteed. The current slowdown in the global economy will affect the demand for raw materials from Africa, at least in the short run. The economic crisis has also reduced investment flows to African countries. Going forward there will always be finance for higher return projects, and Africa can be expected to benefit, provided that risks can be managed. Once growth returns, however, so will competition for investment funds.

Demand for energy will continue. Africa's share of global reserves is strategically important. New hydrocarbon discoveries and untapped potential make it an attractive region for countries with rapidly growing energy needs, particularly the emerging economies. There will be opportunities for value addition in the energy sector and for using revenues to support development of a vibrant industrial sector that can be sustained after natural resources are exhausted (see Chapter 6).

Securing a seat at the table will take time. Despite the broadening of dialogue from the G8 to the G20, the pace and volume of international negotiations will continue to give primacy to large economies and to effective regional organizations at the expense of smaller countries. Governance of existing international economic and financial institutions will adjust only slowly because many members have a vested interest in the status quo. New institutions, such as the proposed BRICS Development Bank (Brazil, Russia, India, China, South Africa), are also likely to be dominated by the policy interests of major shareholders. In order to have a voice, Africa will increasingly need to develop continental positions; in order for that voice to be heard, it will need to make the most of its representation in multilateral institutions and the presence of its large economies in narrower fora such as the G20.

Preferential access will disappear. The Doha Round may not be resumed. The EU and United States have ambitions to complete within two years a Transatlantic Trade and Investment Partnership (TTIP) to liberalize trade between them, in part as a response to increased competition from China and India, and to protect jobs. The proposed Trans-Pacific Partnership (TPP) would similarly free trade between key American and Asian countries. Trade deals are increasingly likely to be completed by regional blocs. By 2050 it is likely that Africa will no longer get significant preferential treatment. International attention will focus on non-tariff barriers, labor standards, environmental and health regulations, intellectual property rights, services, and public procurement.

More regional trade will be needed in addition to diversification of products and international markets. By 2050, around 50 percent of global GDP will be generated in Asia, and Africa must adjust trade relations accordingly.[8] But Africa cannot rely on any single market or assume a wholesale switch to emerging markets. As long as the pace of growth continues, China will predominate, but the rich countries will continue to provide high-value markets and to represent a considerable proportion of global trade and investment. The continent must be flexible and diversify to meet the changing demands.

Expansion of intra-Africa trade will help bind countries together, create larger markets, and assist the process of integration. Much of the success of the Association of Southeast Asian Nations (ASEAN) was founded on regional trade liberalization and cooperation. It brought together countries with very

---

8. This is under the African convergence scenario. In other scenarios, Asia's share of global GDP would be slightly greater.

disparate backgrounds, some of which had recently been in conflict. Intraregional trade represents 50 percent of total trade in Asia and 65 percent in the EU. Their experience shows that economic liberalization and increasing openness to trade increase the share of trade in GDP, both within the region and with the wider world.

Global issues will loom larger. International dialogue and resources are likely to increasingly focus on collective concerns, such as climate change, resource scarcity, security, disease, and the health of the global financial system. For Africa, resource transfers in support of global initiatives will not readily replace traditional development assistance (North et al. 2008). OECD countries in particular will hang back on climate financing until they see the emerging markets make what they regard as commensurate efforts, including reducing emissions and making financial contributions. New financing mechanisms, international taxes, or levies, are therefore unlikely to be agreed upon quickly or to be directed predominantly to poorer countries.

National interests will dictate partners' policy. For all partners, relations with developing countries will be increasingly defined with more explicit regard to national interests, contained within a broader foreign and security policy, and designed to secure domestic and parliamentary support. This focus will bring the traditional partners more into line with the stance already adopted by the emerging market countries.

Aid is losing importance and its volume will decline. Aid is only one element in a mix of financial flows to Africa, and it is not the most important. Today it still makes a significant contribution to the development budgets of a number of African countries, but as African economies grow it will be increasingly replaced by trade and investment. There is now a greater skepticism about aid in the OECD countries and politicians are faced with stronger demands to address domestic concerns first. The sense of post-colonial moral obligation has dimmed and been replaced by concerns about macroeconomic and policy stability, the rule of law, property rights, and tackling corruption. Given budget constraints, donors are already cutting back aid and looking to reduce the budget burden by widening the definitions of oda (for instance, to include more conflict-related expenditure) and by leveraging more from the private sector. At best, aid levels are likely to stagnate. The 0.7 percent benchmark, achieved by only a handful of donors, will become irrelevant.

By 2050 traditional Western development aid will have long since been eclipsed. Emerging market economies will have cemented an integrated approach based primarily on national needs. Any aid on concessional terms to Africa from traditional or emerging partners will be financially insignificant; the residual will be focused on responses to emergencies, humanitarian needs, technical know-how, and knowledge transfer, or as part of support of broader global initiatives. For African governments, domestic revenue mobilization and access to international capital markets will offer a more predictable and stable source of development finance.

In the process, partners will differentiate more between African countries. The EU is already promoting differentiation, moving away from the concept of "developing countries." The Agenda for Change approved in May 2012 concentrates EU activities on two broad priorities: (i) human rights, democracy, and good governance; and (ii) inclusive and sustainable economic growth, with a strong focus on leveraging private sector money. The Commission proposes allocating funding according to country needs assessed using several indicators, including fragility and vulnerability, ability to generate domestic resources, access to other sources of finance, investment in education, health and social protection, progress on democracy and good governance, and the potential impact of EU funding, especially on political reform and private sector investment.

Aid will be concentrated on fewer countries. Bilateral development assistance driven by poverty objectives is likely to be concentrated on a smaller number of poor countries, on post-conflict states, and in response to humanitarian crises. More assistance at the grassroots level will come through philanthropic funds and international NGOs, most operating directly rather than through the national budget. The countries most affected will be solidly-performing but small African countries without extractive resources that are outside zones of conflict and therefore of little strategic interest to the West. The paradox remains that development and humanitarian aid will continue to be most urgently needed in countries where the prospects of its working effectively and productively are poorest.

Results will matter. The focus on aid quality rather than quantity will increase: "with limited ODA growth on the horizon, aid effectiveness and the use of aid-effectiveness principles will play a more prominent role in realizing greater development impact in the near term" (US Department of State 2008).

The post-2015 MDGs could be helpful but will not be critical. The High-Level Panel on the post-2015 MDGs recognized the need to promote a single and coherent post-2015 development agenda that integrates economic growth, environmental sustainability, and social inclusion. They highlighted four key objectives: reshaped and revitalized global governance and partnerships; protection of the global environment; sustainable production and consumption; and strengthened means of implementation, including financing for development.

The diversity of development actors will continue. There will still be a variety of channels providing concessional resources. Foreign investment (direct or through investment funds), trade, remittances, and philanthropic giving will all offer greater opportunities to support development. International NGOs and national counterparts will become more influential and be conduits for higher levels of resources than most bilateral agencies. They will have the capacity to bypass governments by assisting communities directly and transferring money to individuals (e.g., via mobile banking). They will be more concerned with delivery, efficiency, and meeting targets (which the donor will largely define) than with more systemic questions.

The influence of multilateral development institutions will decline. Limited aid budgets will be directed on the basis of results, not necessarily to those most in need, and priority given to nationally directed action. This development will further erode the comparative advantage of the multilateral institutions. The UN in particular will continue to have a political role as a forum for global discourse, but most of its agencies will be increasingly irrelevant. The World Bank is likely to find a niche in global public goods, but as a number of large borrowers graduate from the World Bank's International Development Association (IDA), its concessional funds will be concentrated in Africa. IDA and AfDB cannot both claim precedence as channels for resources for Africa and will be forced to reduce overlaps and build a stronger partnership based on division of labor.

African countries will have a choice. In the future, multilateral and bilateral aid agencies will have reduced influence; therefore, countries will be able to choose globally from a wide variety of ways to design, finance, and deliver projects.

Action Agenda

Going forward, Africa's major partners will continue to juggle multiple objectives, and policy will evolve in response to events. The future is uncertain. There will be risks but also opportunities. For Africa the message is clear: the continent cannot wait for its partners to decide; it must take control of its own future. This section proposes an action agenda for Africa and outlines recommended roles for its partners, both old and new. The agenda will have to be implemented at multiple levels — national, sub-regional, and continental — and the formulation must engage the domestic private sector, civil society organizations, and other non-state actors. Partners will be called on to mesh their aid, trade, and investment priorities with the expressed country priorities, recognizing that solutions may include regional initiatives as well. Priority actions for countries and their old and new partners, described in more detail below, include:

- **Development strategy:**
  - *Countries* articulate a development strategy based on growth, jobs, and inclusion, and accept only assistance that is aligned with this strategy.
  - *Partners* align aid, trade, and investment with the country strategy; focus on growth, jobs, and inclusion; and emphasize quality and impact of initiatives over costs and volume, identifying new modalities and instruments of aid as needed.
- **Investment environment:**
  - *Countries* provide an enabling and conducive environment for investment. Major priorities include promoting macroeconomic stability, strengthening accountability, reducing corruption, and maintaining internal peace and security.
  - *Partners* provide aid and investment flows that are predictable, transparent, and disbursed in support of domestic policy improvements; make mutual dialogue and transparency the foundation for an equal partnership with countries; avoid introducing policies, such as credits to national suppliers, that undermine country strategies; and support African-led conflict management.

- **Regional cooperation:**
  - *Countries* participate fully in key regional and international institutions and work to identify regional solutions to common problems.
  - *Partners* add support for regional integration to their bilateral approaches.
- **Infrastructure development:**
  - *Countries* invest in national and regional infrastructure, such as transport and power; prioritize human capital development, particularly in science and technology; and support trade facilitation efforts.
  - *Partners* work to enhance productive capacity through support for infrastructure development and education in science and technology, with a focus on building capacity in Africa.
- **Sector development:**
  - *Countries* use natural resources to promote diversification and work to enhance the productivity of agriculture.
  - *Partners* broaden the scope of engagement to sectors other than extractive industries and take a long-term perspective on natural resource development; demand transparency from multinationals; and promote agriculture by reducing non-tariff barriers and distortive production subsidies to own agriculture.

Africa takes the lead

Africa must have a compelling long-term vision rooted in what Africa itself will do and allowing it to become more self-confident and willing to set the agenda with its partners. Knowledge, sharing of lessons, and experience will be more important. More key economic and trade decisions will be made on a multilateral basis, between blocs, and between private sector players. Bilateral, government-to-government relationships will be less important; therefore Africa will have to make sustained efforts to develop regional and continental positions on the most significant policy questions.

Articulate an African development agenda and accept only that assistance which is aligned with these priorities. At the domestic level, African governments should insist that their homegrown development strategies and the priorities already identified by individual African countries, the AU, and NEPAD be the basis for negotiations with partners. They must remain steadfast that the emerging partners reorient their trade, investment, and aid policies to complement and support such priorities. Moreover, the emerging market partners should be sensitive in their engagement with individual African countries to the regional dimension of their investments and take appropriate measures to ensure that national-level projects contribute to African strategies to strengthen intra-regional trade.

Inspire confidence through macro-economic stability, sound, and predictable policies to provide an enabling and conducive environment for domestic and external investment and to create the conditions for inclusive development.

Use natural resources to promote African industrialization. Africa's abundant natural resources, if properly managed, could serve as a foundation for the continent's industrialization and could create more backward and forward linkages with the other sectors of the economy (see Chapter 12). Resource-seeking has often been the primary motivation of investors, and they have paid scant attention to the continent's priorities of industrialization and job creation. Investments in the natural resource sector should be guided by the African Mining Vision adopted by the AU in the 2009, the African Productive Capacity Initiative adopted by the AU and NEPAD in 2004, and the Plan of Action for the Accelerated Industrial Development of Africa adopted during the 2008 AU Summit. Greater transparency in extractive industries must be assured through public disclosure of the fiscal and other terms of resource extraction contracts; at the same time, the playing field for contract negotiations must be leveled through the use of world-class legal expertise (see Chapter 12).

Enhance the productivity of African agriculture. Africa's recent impressive growth has been driven by commodity exports, but agriculture remains the main source of employment and livelihood for the majority of the population. Africa must take a more strategic approach to the sector so that the necessary rural infrastructure, research, and skills can be upgraded to unleash the productivity of the sector (see Chapter 11). The Comprehensive African Agricultural Development Plan provides a reference point. Land-lease agreements should require prior consultation of the affected communities, spell out the obligations of commercial farms to downstream peasant farmers and pastoralist communities, and establish from the outset a regular system of monitoring and evaluating compliance that involves all stakeholders. Countries should insist that all potential investors and stakeholders adhere to articulated strategies for development of agriculture and support of agricultural communities.

Invest heavily in national and regional infrastructure and encourage partners to do likewise. Africa's huge infrastructure gap is well-documented, and high transport costs are identified by private firms as the major impediment to doing business in Africa (see Chapter 10). High costs have a negative impact on productivity and on intra-African trade. Priority regional infrastructure projects have been identified in the Program for Infrastructure Development in Africa (PIDA), a continental framework for the development of infrastructure. Partners must consult with the sub-regional economic communities since the sequencing of PIDA priorities may vary from region to region, particularly in corridor development. Countries should promote co-financing arrangements with existing infrastructure finance mechanisms such as the Africa Infrastructure Facility of the AfDB, the World Bank, and the Development Bank of Southern Africa (DBSA).

Prioritize human capital development in science and technology. Africa's strategy for industrialization and economic diversification cannot succeed without development of technological capacity through increased investment in science and technology (see Chapter 8). Partners continue to provide training and scholarship programs for large numbers of African students, but the current focus is too general and uncoordinated, making it difficult to deploy graduates in critical sectors of the economy once they completed their studies. Countries should insist that partners review and reorient their capacity development programs to fit African priorities in close consultation with African governments and their respective institutions of higher education.

Support African efforts for trade facilitation. Trade facilitation has been hampered and costs increased by lack of access to suppliers or buyers credit, guarantees, and other services. It is in the interest of emerging market partners to support strong promotion services, including one-stop facilitation of administrative approvals; provision of specialized physical, customs-related, and technical infrastructure; matchmaking between investors and local suppliers; and provision of accurate information on individual countries' laws and regulations to private economic agents. Support for the removal of blockages to sub-regional trade would increase competitiveness and productivity and, by breaking down barriers within the continent, create larger markets attractive to investors and to suppliers. In parallel, countries need to develop better trade policy capacity so that negotiations take place on a more equal footing. Regional economic cooperation institutions must prioritize areas where they seek key results; aim for high-quality, high-impact commitments to lower trade transaction costs and the cost of key inputs (notably services); and improve the regulatory environment for businesses and consumers.

Strengthen accountability and reduce corruption. Coordinated action is required by Africa and its partners to increase both political and economic transparency and accountability (see Chapter 4). Without such accountability the Africa 2050 vision outlined in Chapter 1 cannot be realized. In addition, Africa and its partners must reduce the incidence of and scope for corruption and bribery, take action against offenders (both those who offer and those who take payment), and require return of stolen assets.

Participate fully in key international institutions including the G20 and allied bodies dealing with banking and finance. African institutions and networks must be systematically developed to provide the knowledge base needed for effective participation. With the explosion of IT-accessible knowledge, assimilation will be as important as generation. Not all African countries can engage in all institutions; there has to be some conscious sharing of roles and mutual representation.

Maintain peace and security, including economic security of trade routes and territorial waters. The old partners will no longer put boots on the ground and will be reluctant to pay the very high costs of external peacekeepers. Partners can provide information and technical support, but leadership must be taken in Africa at regional and continental levels. This new responsibility will require unprecedented levels of cooperation and coordination, as well as smart investment in the security sectors.

Emerging countries come onboard

The relationship between Africa and the emerging partners will continue to grow, and great care should be taken to ensure that the relationship does not end up replicating the unequal relationship that has characterized Africa's relationship with traditional partners. To build the foundation for a sustained relationship with win-win outcomes, emerging partners need to identify the areas where their trade, investment, and aid policies align with Africa's own priorities.

Broaden the scope of engagement to include sectors other than extractive industries. Trade and investment by emerging market partners have to date been concentrated in the extractive sector, replicating the pattern of economic relations between Africa and its traditional partners, which was characterized by commodity exports and the importation of manufactured goods. The new partners should use their resource flows to enhance technology transfer and technological learning in support of Africa's process of industrialization and diversification.

Take a long-term perspective on natural resources development. The new partners must adopt a strategic approach to building local technical capacity in the extractive sector that takes into account equitable distribution of resource rents with producer countries in ways that will benefit both partners. Complementary investments in infrastructure designed to facilitate access to Africa's resources should also address the needs of the non-resource sectors of the economies. Emerging market partners should align their strategies with the African strategies outlined in the African Mining Vision and the AU Principles on Land Development.

Focus on building Africa's productive capacity through infrastructure development. Africa has established its own priorities in PIDA. Partners should align their engagement accordingly and respect these priorities.

Prioritize science and technology education in Africa. Technological advance has been a key driving force in the emerging market countries, accounting for the major part of productivity growth. The emerging market countries can contribute immensely to resolving Africa's shortage of skilled labor by helping the continent embark on a progressive upgrade of technological capacity through expanded programs of capacity building and educational exchanges. Programs should respond to African priorities and be developed in consultation with African stakeholders. The aim should be to help Africa exploit its potential by leapfrogging in knowledge acquisition, enterprise creation, and global economic linkages.

Strengthen support for regional integration in Africa. Emerging market partners have, to date, preferred to conduct their relationships with Africa at a bilateral level, with little or no link to regional development priorities. However, small countries achieve economies of scale through regional integration. Emerging market partners can assist by providing more support for regional projects as an important step toward developing regional markets and enhancing intraregional trade and investment opportunities. Support for the development of regional infrastructure is key as it would help reduce transaction costs, improve export competitiveness, and boost inter-regional trade and investment.

Use mutual dialogue and transparency as the foundation for equal partnership. Mutual confidence will be supported by openness. There must be public disclosure of official aid and investment flows as a foundation for monitoring mutual accountability; disclosure of royalties collected and the terms and conditions of sharing the revenues with partner governments; transparency in procurement of goods and services linked to major construction and extraction projects; and strengthened mutual review mechanisms.

OECD partners

The traditional partners currently provide 90 percent of development assistance and frequently dominate discussions of trade and investment. Greater self-confidence in an Africa buoyed by sustained growth, and the advent and weight of the emerging market economies is leading to an evolution in the historical patterns. The web of relations with Africa is complex, but change is in the interests of both parties. If OECD countries want to continue to support Africa they should:

Learn the lessons of experience. Assistance will be most effective when flows are predictable, transparent, and disbursed alongside and in support of domestic policy improvements. Where required, conditionality will probably fail; programs need to be owned by the governments implementing them.

Promote growth, jobs, and inclusion, moving beyond aid to a coherent set of policy measures covering aid, trade, and investment. The need for aid will decrease significantly with macroeconomic stability, moderate inflation, high rate of investment, aggressive efforts at domestic resource mobilization, and structural changes to favor a growing manufacturing sector. Donors should tailor resource allocation and their development strategies accordingly.

Emphasize the quality and impact of development aid rather than costs and volume. This revised focus will require active harmonization in support of country-defined targets and indicators and a shift in prime accountability from donors to citizens. More attention should be paid to the agreed targets on harmonization and development effectiveness.

Help build science and technology capacity in Africa, including through centers of excellence, knowledge platforms, and exchange and linkages to African education institutions.

Develop new modalities and instruments to bring together the private and public sectors, new ways of raising and using resources to support national and regional initiatives in Africa, as well as global programs on, for example, adaptation to and mitigation of global warming.

Demand transparency from multinationals. Europe is moving toward legislation that would require oil, gas, mining, and timber companies to publish their payments, project by project, to foreign governments, thereby making it harder to disguise bribes to corrupt officials. This move follows recent rules adopted by the US Securities and Exchange Commission that delete tax exemptions for companies reporting in countries where criminal law prohibits disclosure. OECD partners must insist on an effective exchange of information between tax authorities and positive enforcement.

Promote African agriculture by reducing non-tariff barriers and eliminating distortive production subsidies to developed country farmers.

Continue to support African-led conflict management, including through finance, training, exchange of information, and technical training.

Avoid the reintroduction of competing export credits or other subsidies to national suppliers. The temptation to protect national interests may arise in response to competition from emerging markets or the push to create jobs at home. These new barriers would introduce economic distortions, raise costs, provide the recipient with lower value, and detract from efforts to introduce better procurement.

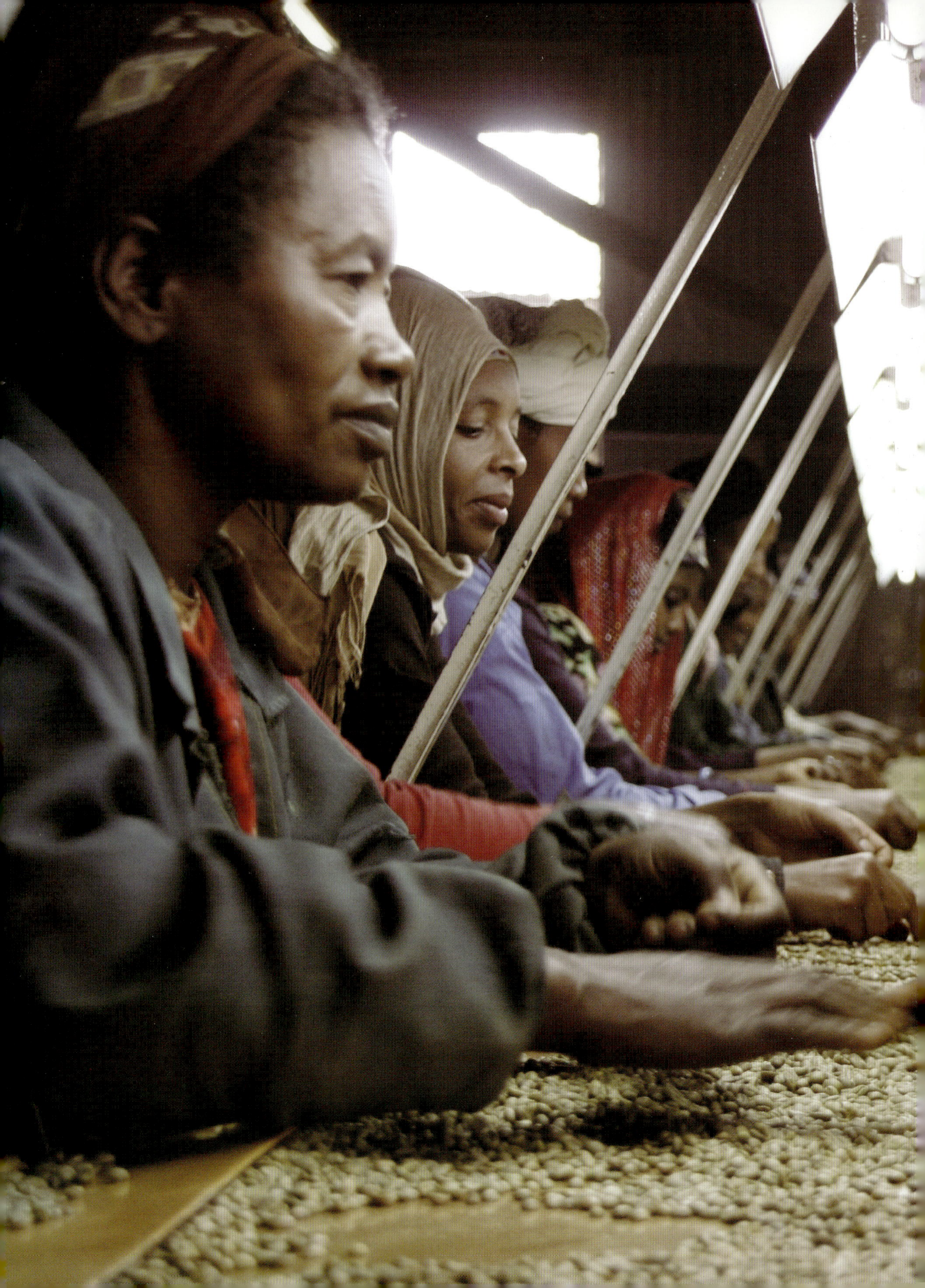

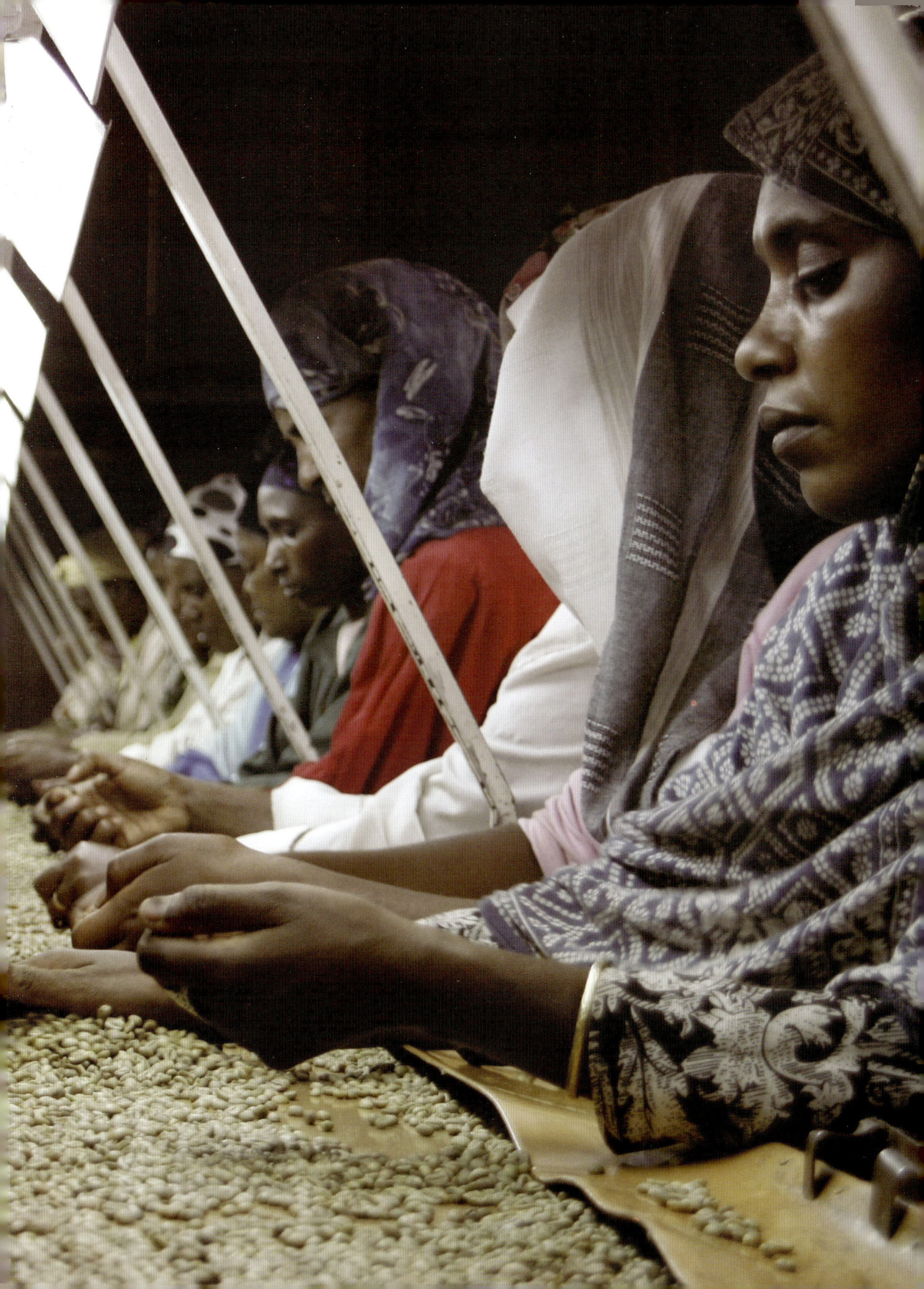

Commodity Terms of Trade in Africa: A Fragile Blessing

Annex 1

Claudio M. Loser

Africa, Latin America, and the oil-producing areas of the Middle East developed their commercial links with the rest of the world on the basis of commodity exports. Over time this has changed somewhat, particularly as some countries like Brazil, Mexico, and South Africa developed more advanced economies and moved up the technology scale, with more complex industrial exports. Nonetheless, commodities continue to be at the center of their exports, be it agriculture, minerals, or oil. As of 2011, commodities represented about 82 percent of African exports, a proportion that has risen from 71 percent in 1995, as prices and output have gone up sharply. The equivalent numbers for Latin America and the Caribbean were 51 percent and 60 percent respectively, and for the Middle East 75 percent and 80 percent. The increase in commodity prices, well in excess of these regions' import prices, has resulted in a marked improvement in terms of trade. They increased by more than 70 percent since 2000 for Africa, 50 percent for Latin America and about 45 percent for the Middle East. Clearly the impact of this enormous change in relative prices has resulted in a large transfer of resources, to an extent that had not been observed in the last 30 years. The rise of China and India, as well as the Newly Industrialized Countries (NICs) of Asia and other Asian countries, has secured a more stable demand for commodities, even as supplies have been growing worldwide. Accordingly, African prosperity has appeared to consolidate, as had previously been the case in the oil-exporting Middle East, and as is occurring in Latin America simultaneously.

The main question that needs to be faced by the commodity-exporting regions in the world is if this prosperity would remain for the long haul or if it would end. Furthermore, how will the economy react if conditions reverse? The answer, as described in this annex, is that it will not be easy. A reversal of prices will have a major impact on income and thus on growth through the expected multiplier effects of a decline in export income. Output has risen in the export sector and the general economy. A slowdown in the advanced and emerging world due to cyclical issues will cause a shock.

Maybe more importantly, as emerging markets like China, India, Brazil, and Mexico mature demographically and economically, the increase in demand observed in the last few decades will not be sustained and exporters will need to adapt to these new circumstances. Complacency among policymakers tends to reflect a benign view of the future. However, the past may repeat itself in terms of periods of growth and prosperity followed by times of crisis and reform. The last 150 or more years bear witness to this pattern, maybe not in Africa, but certainly in the western hemisphere, be it north or south of the Rio Grande or Asia or Eastern Europe. The warning lights cannot be dismissed and thus, the quantitative assessment of the consequences of a slowdown should become part of policymakers' tools.

General Discussion of Terms of Trade and Output Measurement[1]

The revolutionary process of globalization, increased trade opportunities, and reduced import restrictions of recent decades have resulted in a major increase in the importance of trade transactions in total GDP. Export and import prices have therefore taken on a growing importance in determining nations' real incomes, making the effects of changes in these prices an integral part of macroeconomic developments. In particular, the effect of changes in terms of trade (defined as the ratio of the price of exports to the price of imports) is central to the measurement of available resources to a specific economy.[2] Over longer periods of time terms of trade may revert, as has been the experience over the last 30 years, dampening the average annual effect on real gross domestic income (GDI). However, in more recent times, GDI has grown at a faster rate than GDP in many countries because of improved terms of trade. This has been the experience in Africa and Latin America in the last 10 years and in the Middle East over an even longer period of time. In these economies foreign trade plays a large role and makes export and import prices important determinants of prosperity.

The definition of real GDI is subject to debate. As discussed by the National Accounts Manual, GDI measures the purchasing power of the total income generated by domestic production. It is a concept that exists in real terms only. When the terms of trade change, there may be a significant divergence between the movements of GDP in output terms and real GDI. The difference between the change in GDP in output terms and real GDI is generally described as the "trading gain" (or loss). The differences between movements in GDP in output terms and real GDI are sometimes very large. As imports and exports have become increasingly large relative to GDP, and the commodity composition of imports and exports is very different, the scope for trading gains and losses is substantial (System of National Accounts 2008).

Domestic product is calculated in volume terms in order to measure the real change that occurs from one period to another. Aggregates of income also are not broken down into a quantity and a price component. They may, however, be calculated at constant purchasing power, which is described as being in real terms. When moving from domestic product in volume terms to national income in real terms, the effect of changes in the terms of trade between the total economy and the rest of the world must be taken into account. GDP is no longer identical to domestic final expenditure and deflation of

---

1. This discussion draws heavily on European Commission, IMF, OECD, UN, and World Bank 2008 and Reinsdorf 2009, as well as material from the Australian Statistical Office.
2. As described in European Commission, IMF, OECD, UN, and World Bank 2008: "If the prices of a country's exports rise faster (or fall more slowly) than the prices of its imports (that is, if its terms of trade improve) fewer exports are needed to pay for a given volume of imports... Thus, an improvement in the terms of trade makes it possible for an increased volume of goods and services to be purchased by residents out of the incomes generated by a given level of domestic production."

GDP must allow for the deflation of imports and exports as well as of domestic final expenditures. There is an impact on real income of changes in import and export prices. This is generally done by calculating what is known as the trading gains and losses from changes in the terms of trade.

Trading gains or losses are measured by Equation 1, described in greater detail in the Technical Appendix:

$$T = \frac{X - M}{P} - \left(\frac{X}{P_x} - \frac{M}{P_m}\right) \tag{1}$$

where X is exports at current values; M is imports at current values; P_x is the price index for exports; P_m is the price index for imports; and P is a price index based on some selected numeraire.

As noted by the National Accounts Manual, there is one important choice to be made in the measurement of trading gains or losses: the selection of the price index P with which to deflate the current trade balance. There is vast but inconclusive literature on this topic, but one point on which there is general agreement is that the choice of deflator P can sometimes make a substantial difference to the results. Thus, the measurement of real GDI can sometimes be sensitive to the choice of P and this has prevented a consensus from being reached on this issue. In any event, according to the National Accounts Manual, trading gains or losses should be treated as an integral part of the System of National Accounts. The choice of the appropriate deflator for the trade balance should depend on the particular circumstances of a country, and practical solutions are required, even with no consensus. No matter how it is defined, the formula to be used would be: *GDP in volume terms + the trading gain or loss resulting from changes in the terms of trade = real GDI*

In discussing this issue, Reinsdorf (2009), within the US Department of Commerce, describes the best adjustment as follows: the difference between real GDI and real GDP can be decomposed into two key terms: the change in the terms of trade weighted by the average share of trade in GDP, and the change in the relative price of tradables (to the rest of the economy) weighted by the average share of the trade balance in GDP.[3]

On that basis, the present discussion uses the following equation:

$$dy^*/y_0^* = (x_1/y_0)[(dpx/px) - (dpm/pm)] + (ca_1/y_0) \times (drer/rer) \tag{2}$$

where *dy/y* is the difference between GDI and GDP, on the basis of changes in the terms of trade, and *rer* is the real exchange rates denominated in local currency (appreciation entails a decline and vice versa), and *ca* is the current account balance. On a multiple-period basis the equation is:

---

3. Estimates based on US national accounts data for 1974 to 2007 show significant terms of trade effects in many years. Trading gains subtract at least 0.21 percentage points from real GDI a quarter of the time, and they add at least 0.18 percentage points a quarter of the time. Occasionally, however, the shocks are much larger. The petroleum price shocks that occurred at the end of 1973 and in 1980 subtracted more than a full percentage point from real GDI, and the one in the first half of 2008, in combination with rising prices of other imports, subtracted almost 2 percentage points from the annualized growth rate of real GDI (Reinsdorf, 2009).

$$dy_t^*/y_0^* = (\pi_{1tot} (1 + (dy_i^*/y_{i-1}^*))-1) \tag{3}$$

The measurement captures the effect of the terms of trade beyond a year. If a change occurs for one year only, the impact will be for that year alone. If the change extends for several years, the formula accounts for this effect over time.

The estimate is calculated on the assumption that the base GDP and GDP changes are not adjusted for terms of trade. In practical terms, most emerging economies do not have an explicit calculation of the trading gains and losses. Thus the proposed adjustment provides an effective tool to capture these movements. These adjustments to GDP only reflect the initial income effect of the change in terms of trade. It does not reflect the multiplier effect of higher income on output, either of tradable or other commodities on account of increased demand. This effect will be reflected in the GDP estimates of the following years.

Developments in Terms of Trade, Exports, and Imports

Over the long term, terms of trade for commodity-exporting regions and countries have shown a marked secular cyclicality. During the last century, terms of trade increased after World War I, collapsed during the Great Depression, and then tended to increase at the time of World War II. Subsequently, commodity prices tended to fluctuate with the world business cycle, although they showed a sharp declining tendency until the 1970s, when, at least for energy exporters, terms of trade rose sharply. Even this increase was reversed later, in response to the sharp slowdown associated with the anti-inflationary measures of the early 1980s. The events from the 1930s until the 1970s gave rise to the import substitution theories in developing countries, particularly promoted in Latin America, by Raul Prebisch, the head of the UN Economic Commission for Latin America and the Caribbean (ECLAC). ECLAC supported the development of domestic industries on the basis of an expectation of secular declines in the terms of trade for developing countries, and not only in Latin America.[4]

While the experience of Africa since independence through 2000 has been one of cyclical reversals in the terms of trade, more recently, it has been one of solid increase, helped by economic growth in a number of emerging economies, and particularly in the NICs, China, and India. This experience is shared by other developing regions, particularly Latin America and the Middle East (Figure A1.1), although the effect on advanced commodity producers like Australia and Canada is also remarkable.

In any event, the volatility in terms of trade for these regions has been much more marked than that of the advanced economies, as seen in Figure A1.2. The movements in terms of trade were also much more limited in developing Asia. Table A1.1 presents the average annual rate of change in terms of trade and the standard deviation for each region. While the Middle East shows the highest average annual change over the period, it also has the greatest volatility, as measured by the standard deviation. This

---

4. See Kohli, Loser and Sood 2011, Bulmer-Thomas 2003, and Franko 2003.

COMMODITY TERMS OF TRADE IN AFRICA: A FRAGILE BLESSING

Figure A1.1 Rising world demand for raw materials since 2000 has helped push commodity prices up

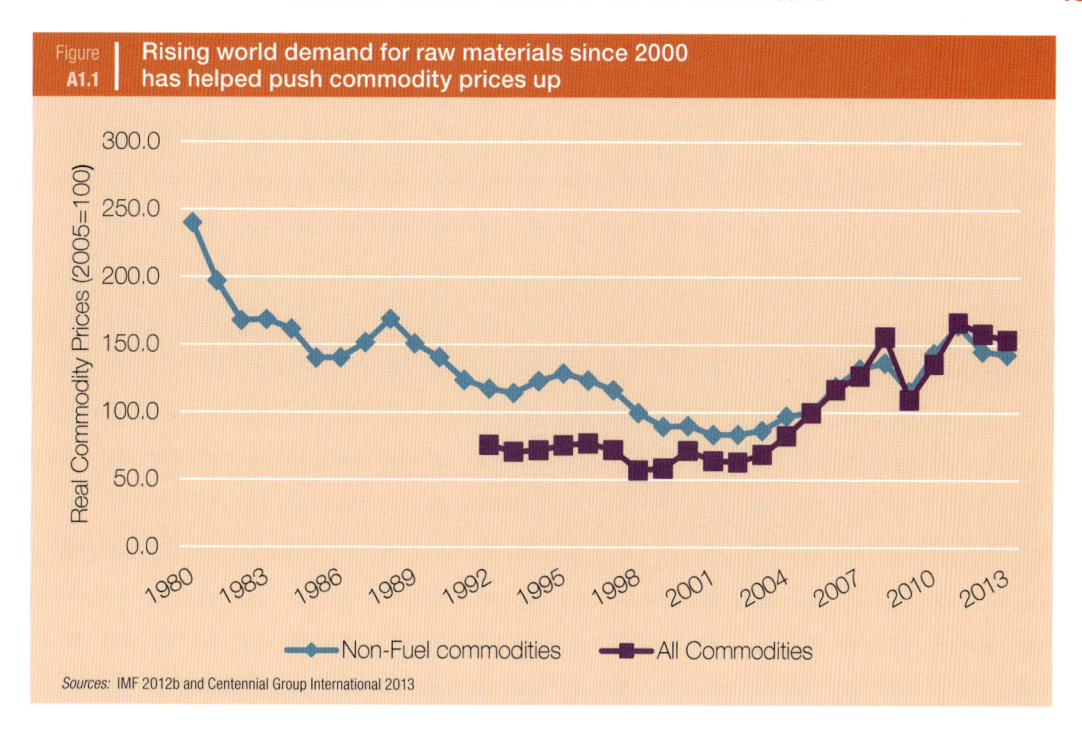

Sources: IMF 2012b and Centennial Group International 2013

Figure A1.2 The terms of trade of the developing world are highly volatile

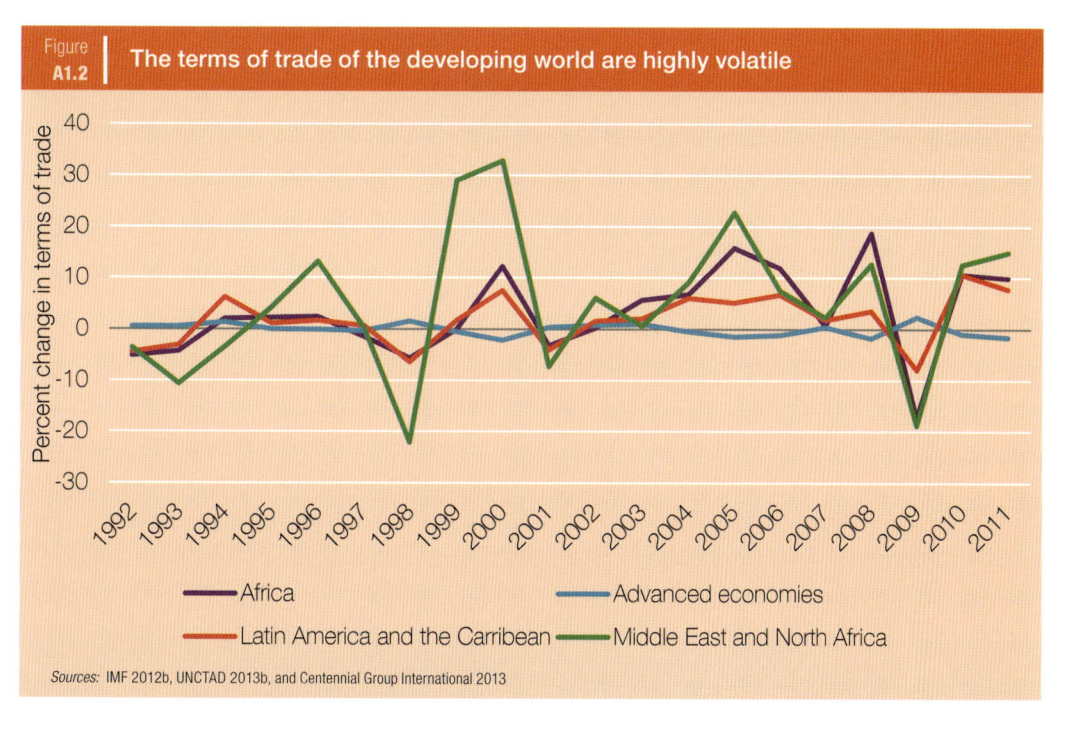

Sources: IMF 2012b, UNCTAD 2013b, and Centennial Group International 2013

Table A1.1 | Terms of trade changes (in percent, average, and standard deviation 2000–2011)

Region	Average	Standard Deviation
Advanced economies	–0.4	1.4
Emerging market and developing economies	1.9	3.1
Developing Asia	–0.7	2.5
Latin America and the Caribbean	3.4	5.2
Middle East and North Africa (5)	7.0	12.2
Africa	6.0	9.8
Export-Intensive (6)	9.6	16.1
Non-Export-Intensive	3.5	3.9

Note: There is an overlap of countries for the Middle East and North Africa, as defined in WEO, and Africa, which for the purposes of this paper, includes all African countries. Export-intensive refers to countries with a ratio of exports to GDP of 20 percent or higher, as described in Appendix 2.
Sources: IMF 2012b, UNCTAD 2013b, and Centennial Group International 2013

applies for goods and for goods and services. Africa follows, although with smaller average rates of increase, and the rate of change and volatility are much higher for export-intensive countries. Non-export intensive countries have tended to show volatility in line with what is observed in Latin America. By obvious contrast, developing Asia, the more dynamic destination of exports from these regions, shows a negative trend in terms of trade, while the advanced economies show very small negative or non-existent changes and relatively low volatility.

The changes in commodity prices and in terms of trade have been very similar, as seen in Figure A1.3.[5] For Africa and Latin America, terms of trade have tended to move less markedly than the comprehensive real commodity index, in part because its imports cover commodities. They have also tended to be below the non-fuel commodity index, as they have a fuel component in exports, even if with a smaller share than in the commodity index estimated by the IMF. The Middle East's terms of trade, in contrast, moved in line with the all-commodity index until 2005 but has moved in tandem with the others since then. In all cases, it is clear that terms of trade have had a strong secular cyclicality that suggests that the current high terms of trade may well reverse, as was the case in the past. The possible impact of a reversal should therefore be a major concern for policymakers.

The broad regional estimates do not make a distinction between commodity exporters and commodity importers. If that distinction were made, commodity exporters would show a larger gain during episodes of price increases. Importers would actually show a loss in terms of trade.[6] However, when Africa is divided between export intensive and more balanced "other" Africa, the terms of trade effects are considerably stronger in the first group, as can be seen in Figure A1.3b, which is constituted by 24

---

5. This is confirmed in section 4, on the basis of regressions of terms of trade as explained by commodity prices.
6. When Africa is divided between export intensive and more balanced "other" Africa, the terms of trade effects are considerably stronger in the first group, which is constituted by 24 countries. By contrast, for the group of 26 countries defined as less export-intensive has tended to have smaller changes in terms of trade, even though by 2011, all groups showed an equivalent increase in terms of trade as compared to 2005.

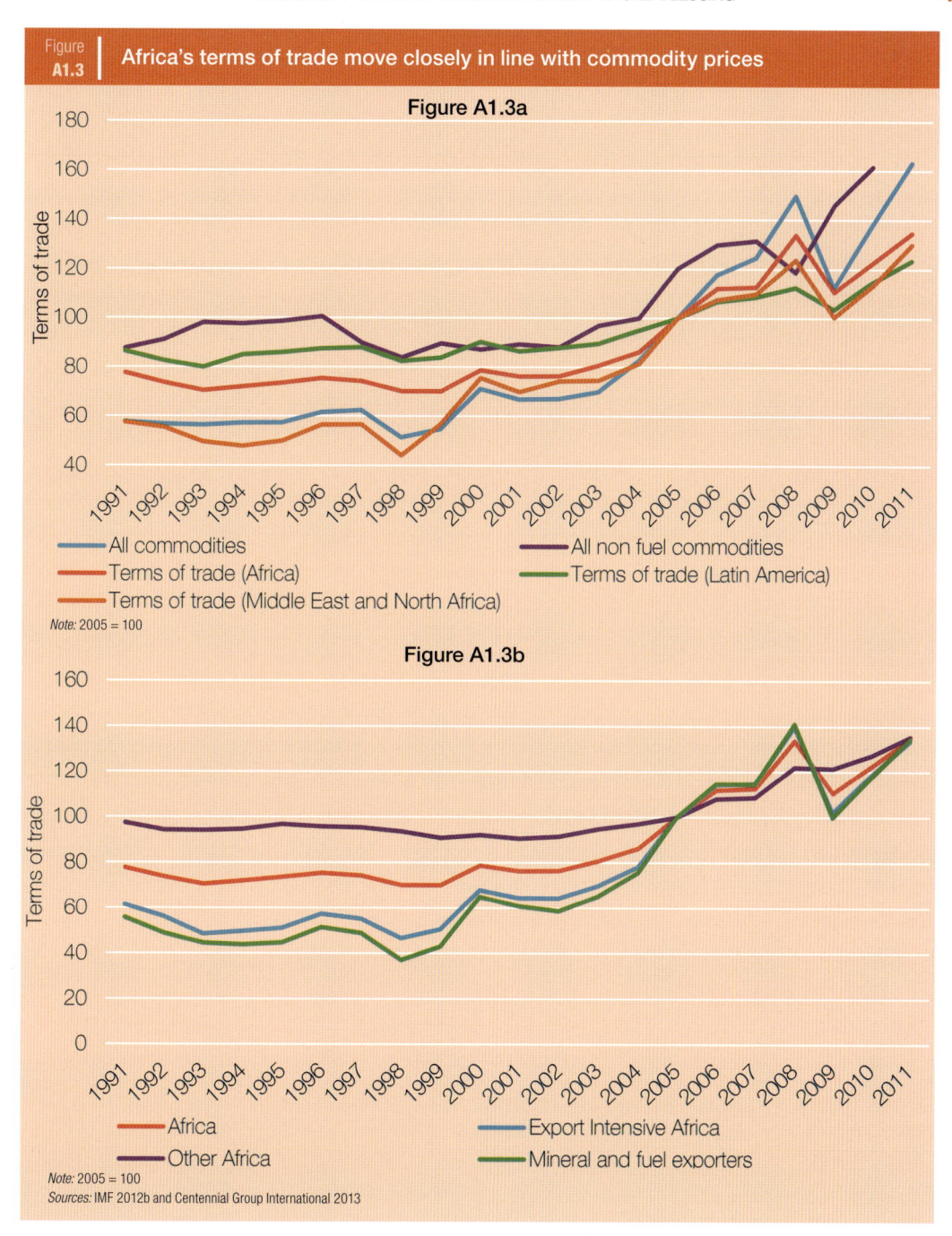

Figure A1.3 — Africa's terms of trade move closely in line with commodity prices

Figure A1.3a

Legend:
- All commodities
- All non fuel commodities
- Terms of trade (Africa)
- Terms of trade (Latin America)
- Terms of trade (Middle East and North Africa)

Note: 2005 = 100

Figure A1.3b

Legend:
- Africa
- Export Intensive Africa
- Other Africa
- Mineral and fuel exporters

Note: 2005 = 100
Sources: IMF 2012b and Centennial Group International 2013

countries. Moreover, the behavior of terms of trade for this group, which includes all commodity exports is not very different from a smaller group of 12 countries defined as mineral and fuel exporters. By contrast, the group of 26 countries defined as less export intensive has tended to have smaller changes in terms of trade, even though by 2011, all the groups showed an equivalent increase in terms of trade compared to 2005.

The impact of terms of trade has had a significant effect on imports and exports. In general, exports have increased in real terms, helped by the increase in commodity prices, although tempered by the effect of the real appreciation of national currencies at times of increases in terms of trade or export volumes and depreciations at times of declines.[7] In any event, export volumes have tended to be linked due to terms of trade effects. However, the pace of export growth in recent years has fallen below that of GDP, possibly reflecting the dampening effect of the real appreciation of the currencies. This has been evident in Africa, although not to the same extent as in Latin America. Nonetheless, the ratio of exports to GDP has tended to move at a considerably different pace than the volume of imports. If export volumes are adjusted by the impact of terms of trade, the picture changes drastically; actually, import volumes are more closely associated with the purchasing power of exports, including both prices and quantities. In Africa, the ratio of exports (in volume terms) to GDP has declined persistently since 2001, for a cumulative total of about 30 percent, after a sustained increase during the 1990s. The earlier change was most likely associated with a process of trade liberalization, although to a lesser extent than was the case in Latin America.

Figure A1.4 presents the different variables for Africa and Latin America, on the simplifying assumption that all terms of trade effects reflect changes in the prices of exports, while import prices are estimated to change at the same pace as the domestic GDP deflator adjusted by real exchange rates, and thus would not account for changes in relative prices.[8] In both cases, it is clear that exports in volume terms behave very differently than imports, as a proportion of GDP. However, when exports are corrected for their purchasing power, namely adjusted for terms of trade, imports tend to follow export behavior more closely. In other words, as the export receipts of the countries in Africa and Latin America have increased because of higher prices, there has been a concurrent change in the level of imports, particularly in the last 10 years. The increases in imports has been associated with increases in both consumption and investment, in response to the sharp rise in the purchasing power of exports.

---

7. Real exchange rate movements are explained by many factors other than terms of trade, including changes in the amounts and directions of capital flows, as well as domestic macroeconomic policies, sometimes associated with the changes in terms of trade. The real exchange rate is also influenced by the degree of protection granted to domestic import substituting industries. Thus, it is not always easy to identify the pure effect of commodities.

8. In theory the adjustment could be made on the basis of export prices and import prices separately, and not on terms of trade. The results may not deviate too much if that approach is taken. However, for simplicity, the estimates presented here follow the simpler approach. Furthermore, no adjustment is made to account for movements in real exchange rates, as all variables would change in the same proportion because they would be adjusted by the real exchange rate. Also, in practical terms, available information on regional African real exchange rates is only available in IMF statistics since 2000. The series is available for Latin America since the early 1990s from the same sources, although alternative series exist for earlier periods from ECLAC.

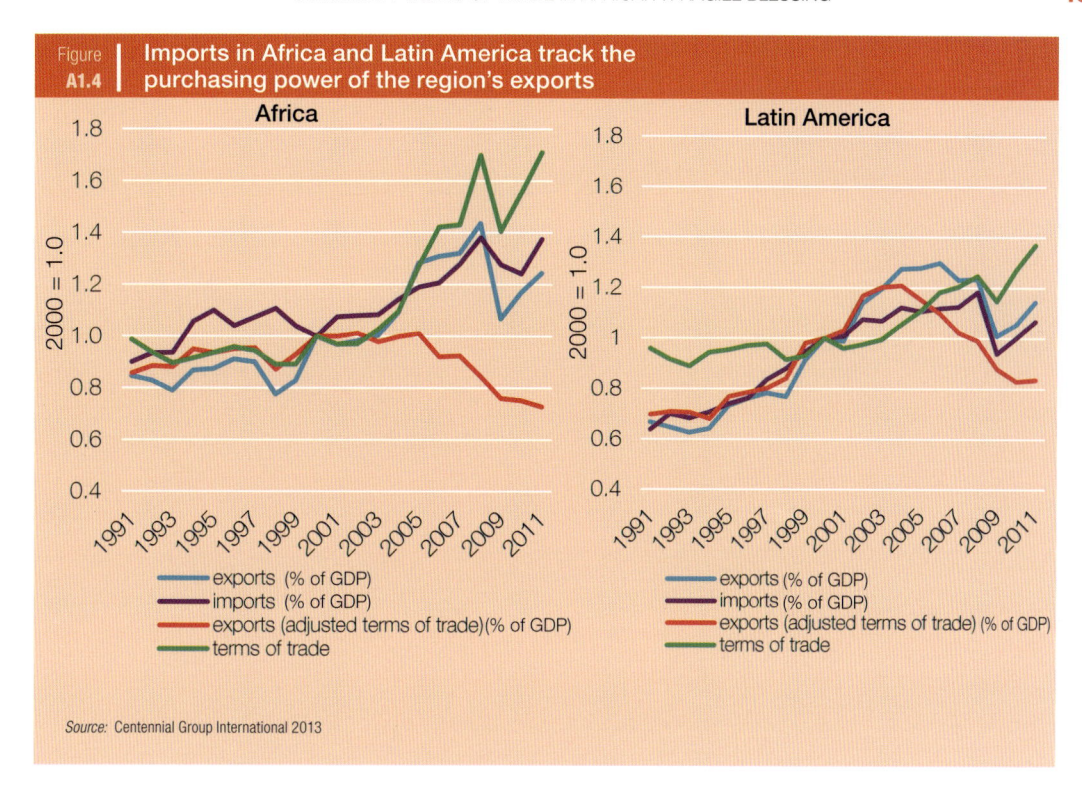

Figure A1.4: Imports in Africa and Latin America track the purchasing power of the region's exports

Africa and Latin America charts (2000 = 1.0), 1991–2011, showing: exports (% of GDP), imports (% of GDP), exports (adjusted terms of trade) (% of GDP), and terms of trade.

Source: Centennial Group International 2013

While the ratio of exports to GDP has declined in Africa and Latin America in recent years, this does not entail stagnation of exportable output and of exports. On the contrary, export volumes have increased significantly, but growth has been outpaced by other sectors of the economy, reflecting in part the large increase in purchasing power due to increased export prices. Investment, as well as both private and public consumption, has therefore risen rapidly to accommodate the growing prosperity, observed in recent years as terms of trade have skyrocketed. In any event, exports have moved with terms of trade, adjusted by real effective exchange rates as a proxy for domestic prices for exports. What is notable is the growth in export volumes in the 1990s and early 2000s, when terms of trade were generally stable. This should be mostly attributed to a general opening of emerging economies to trade. Subsequently, the increase in output has followed prices more clearly. Figure A1.5 shows the performance of exports (in volume terms) and terms of trade, including a series adjusted for real effective exchange rates.[9] The correlation is less obvious on the basis of simple econometric runs, most likely because of a complex investment process including lags and long gestation periods.

---

9. The adjustment for real effective exchange rates provides a better measurement of the relative price of exports with respect to the domestic economy. A real depreciation will increase the domestic relative price, while an appreciation will do the reverse. This effect is particularly important, as the real exchange rate reflected a steady appreciation of the currency both in Sub-Saharan Africa and Latin America starting in the early 2000s, when terms of trade started their most recent upward trend.

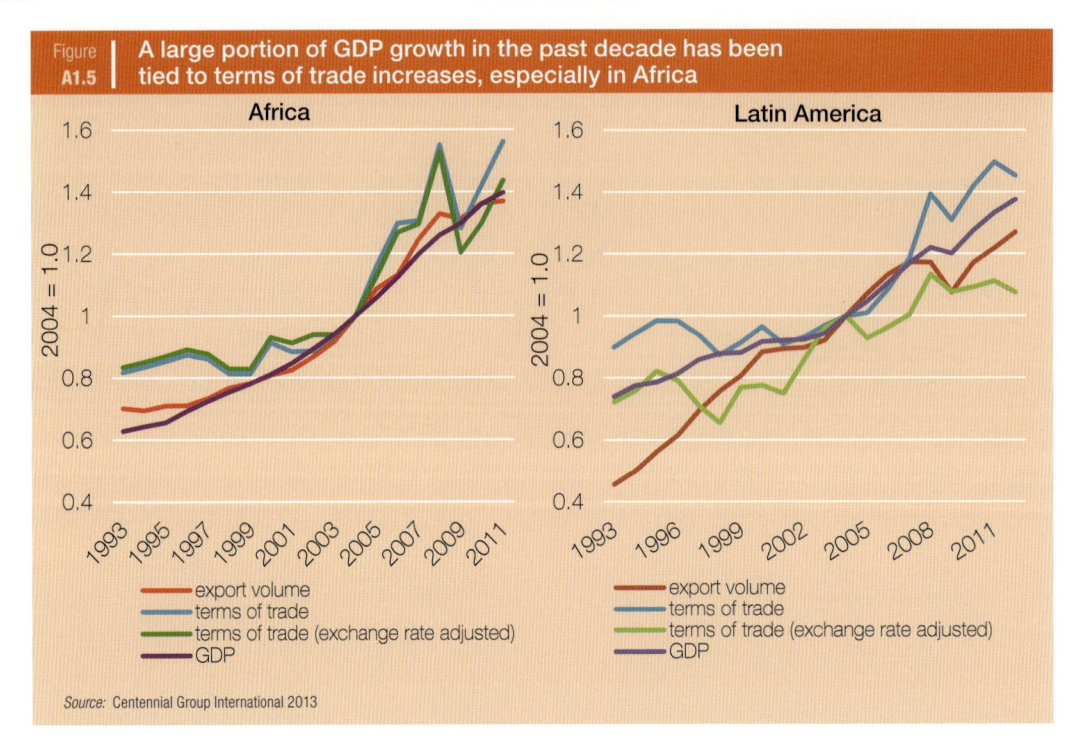

Figure A1.5 | A large portion of GDP growth in the past decade has been tied to terms of trade increases, especially in Africa

Africa / Latin America charts
- export volume
- terms of trade
- terms of trade (exchange rate adjusted)
- GDP

Source: Centennial Group International 2013

Finally, in Africa and Latin America, GDP appears to have been associated with the increase in terms of trade for the last 10 years or so, likely on account of increased exports and the impact of the commodity boom on the economy (Figure A1.5). In Latin America, GDP grew on a sustained basis, even with stable terms of trade in the 1990s, reflecting the significant structural changes that took place in that period, including the noted opening of the regional economies to greater competition and expanded trade opportunities.

Quantification of the Effects of International Price Shocks

As previously discussed, the impact of terms of trade on disposable income differs significantly from that on GDP. The key point is that terms of trade effects are not captured in the estimation of real GDP, i.e., GDP in real terms underestimates the income or purchasing power available to the country on account of the change in export prices.

On the basis of Equation 4 above, estimates of the cumulative change in prices on GDI were calculated for three regions and two sub-regions: Africa, Latin America, and the Middle East and North Africa as well as the group of export-intensive African countries and the remaining or "balanced" countries in Africa, as presented in Table A1.2. The direct effect of terms of trade changes over the last 11 years has been 1.2 percent of GDP a year in the case of Africa; 0.8 percent in the case of Latin America; and 1.7 percent in the case of the Middle East. The cumulative effect of these gains is very significant. According

Table A1.2 | The terms of trade effect has fueled growth but will not last forever

	Africa	Africa: Export-Intensive	Africa: Balanced	Latin America	Middle East & North Africa
GDI	6.8	7.7	5.7	4.5	6.9
GDP	5.6	6.3	4.9	3.7	5.2
Terms of trade effect	1.2	1.4	0.8	0.8	1.7
GDI change for 1% change in terms of trade (in %)	0.44	0.41	0.4	0.26	0.8
Per capita basis					
GDP	2.8	3.5	2.1	2.4	3
GDI	4	4.9	2.9	3.1	4.6
Terms of trade effect	1.2	1.4	0.8	0.7	1.6

Source: Centennial Group International 2013

to these estimates, and without accounting for changes in real GDP, African countries could lose the equivalent of 25 percent of GDP if prices were to decline to the levels existing in 2000;[10] Latin America would lose the equivalent of 12 percent, and the Middle East would lose the equivalent of 32 percent of GDP. Such losses are significant and should be seen as upper bounds in the short run. However, it is clear that terms of trade have declined sharply in the past, as witnessed in 2008–2009, and they have declined significantly and over long periods of time in earlier decades, like in the 1980s. On the basis of our estimates, a decline of 20 percent in terms of trade for Africa would result in a loss of available income of 8 percent in disposable income, with about 5 percent in Latin America and 16 percent in the Middle East. This impact would take place, even if output were to remain constant in real terms, which is extremely unlikely, as will be discussed in the next section.

The Impact of Commodity Prices on GDP and Export Volumes

The previous section discussed in detail the effect of prices on GDI. However, any estimate also requires the calculation of the impact of the external price shock on output, known in more simple terms as the multiplier effect of exports. Because of the nature of the problem, the assessment is better done using a simple econometric model. It should be borne in mind that the coefficients show correlation, not necessarily causality, and thus should be viewed with some caution in terms of interpretation.

The results for all regions are presented in Table A1.3. A first group of regressions shows the impact of different variables on GDP. The regressions include the terms of trade as independent variables, and either world GDP or a trend variable as additional variables. If world GDP is used as one of the explanatory variables, this variable and terms of trade are highly correlated and may distort the results. As an

---

10. The loss could be as high as 31 percent of GDP for export-intensive countries as a group. It amounts to 15 percent for the rest of Africa.

alternative, a trend variable is used as a proxy for the underlying growth in labor and capital and in TFP. It would have been preferable to use these factors specifically. However, for the sake of simplicity, and likely without loss of explanatory power, the trend variable is used showing a constant underlying rate of growth for the period of the regression.[11]

A second group of equations shows the high correlation between import volumes and exports adjusted for terms of trade. The result, illustrated in an earlier section, entails that a considerable portion of the increased purchasing power is spent abroad. In that sense, if and when a correction in prices occurs, the impact on domestic activity will be somewhat reduced, even though the impact on expenditure will move *pari passu* with the loss in terms of trade.

The analysis also indicates a reasonable correlation between terms of trade and export volumes, thereby indicating that domestic output of export goods reacts to price changes in international markets, although the degree of significance is not that high in the case of Africa. More research would be needed in this regard in order to distinguish the short-term and longer-term investment-related elasticities.

In summary, the econometric results show a high degree of significance for terms of trade, in addition to the trend variable. They confirm the experience in the main commodity exporting regions, regarding the multiplier effect of improvement in prices and also indicate significant elasticities of output to these changes in prices. This holds for all the regions under analysis.

Table A1.3 Terms of trade have a powerful impact on Africa's economic activity

	Terms of Trade	World GDP	Trend	Exports adjusted for Terms of Trade	Commodity prices	R-squared
Africa						
GDP	1.07**					0.87
GDP	0.13**	1.13**				1.00
GDP	0.18**		2.72**			1.00
Imports (% of GDP)				0.41**		0.78
Volume of exports	1.04**				0.51**	0.93
Terms of Trade						0.99
Terms of Trade		1.02**				0.85
Commodity prices		1.99**				0.84
Africa: Export-Intensive						
GDP	0.71**					0.92
GDP	0.16**	1.03**				0.98
GDP	0.21**		2.42**			0.98

---

11. The impact of different rates of growth in the trend variable does not change the result of the regression, nor the coefficients for terms of trade.

Table A1.3 — Terms of trade have a powerful impact on Africa's economic activity (continued)

	Terms of Trade	World GDP	Trend	Exports adjusted for Terms of Trade	Commodity prices	R-squared
Imports (% of GDP)				0.27**		0.5
Volume of exports	0.69**					0.87
Terms of trade					0.81**	0.95
Terms of trade		1.69**				0.9
Commodity prices		1.99**				0.84
Africa: Balanced						
GDP	1.62**					0.67
GDP	0.07	1.14**				1.00
GDP	0.061		2.91**			1.00
Imports (% of GDP)				0.69**		0.84
Volume of exports	1.95**					0.59
Terms of trade					0.26**	0.88
Terms of trade		0.48**				0.65
Commodity prices		1.99**				0.84
Latin America						
GDP	0.95					0.82
GDP	0.23**	0.68**				0.99
GDP	0.23*		1.73			0.99
Imports (% of GDP)				0.68*		0.9
Volume of exports	1.2					0.5
Terms of trade					0.36**	0.92
Terms of trade		0.7*				0.73
Commodity prices		1.99**				0.84
Middle East						
GDP	−0.07*					0.88
GDP	0.038**	1.18**				0.99
GDP	0.10*		2.81			0.99
Imports (% of GDP)				0.74		0.72
Volume of exports	0.87*					0.89
Terms of trade					0.48**	0.89
Terms of trade		1.03*				0.87
Commodity prices		1.99**				0.84

Sources: IMF 2012a and 2012b; Centennial Group 2013

Policy Implications of the Terms of Trade Effect

It is clear that fluctuations in prices have an immediate impact on available income, and thus on expenditure and output. Figure A1.6 provides an illustration of these magnitudes. It shows for Africa the levels of GDP, GDI (that is, GDP corrected by the effect of terms of trade), and GDP net of the effect of terms of trade on output, as previously described. Equivalent results are obtained for the other regions. It again shows the significant gap between output and income over time as a function of changes in terms of trade, and suggests the potential magnitude of the impact of lower prices. Over the 11-year period through 2011, according to the above estimates, GDP and GDI would have been lower by 11 percent and 24 percent respectively, had terms of trade remained at the same level as in 2000. Equivalent declines would have been observed with regard to per capita income.

On the basis of these estimates, it is possible to quantify the impact of a "terms of trade event" on the economy. The results provide broad orders of magnitude as they deal with regions and not specific countries; still, they quantify the possible impact of external shocks rather well. Table A1.4 presents a summary of the key findings. It shows the percentage increase in disposable income on the basis of the two main components: (a) the pure effect of terms of trade on income (which will be in excess of measured GDP and was developed in a previous section); and (b) the effect of the increased export receipts on real GDP (namely the multiplier effect on real output), as described in this article. The sum of the two effects will be the effect of the price change on disposable income. The table also includes the effect of terms of trade on the volume of exports.

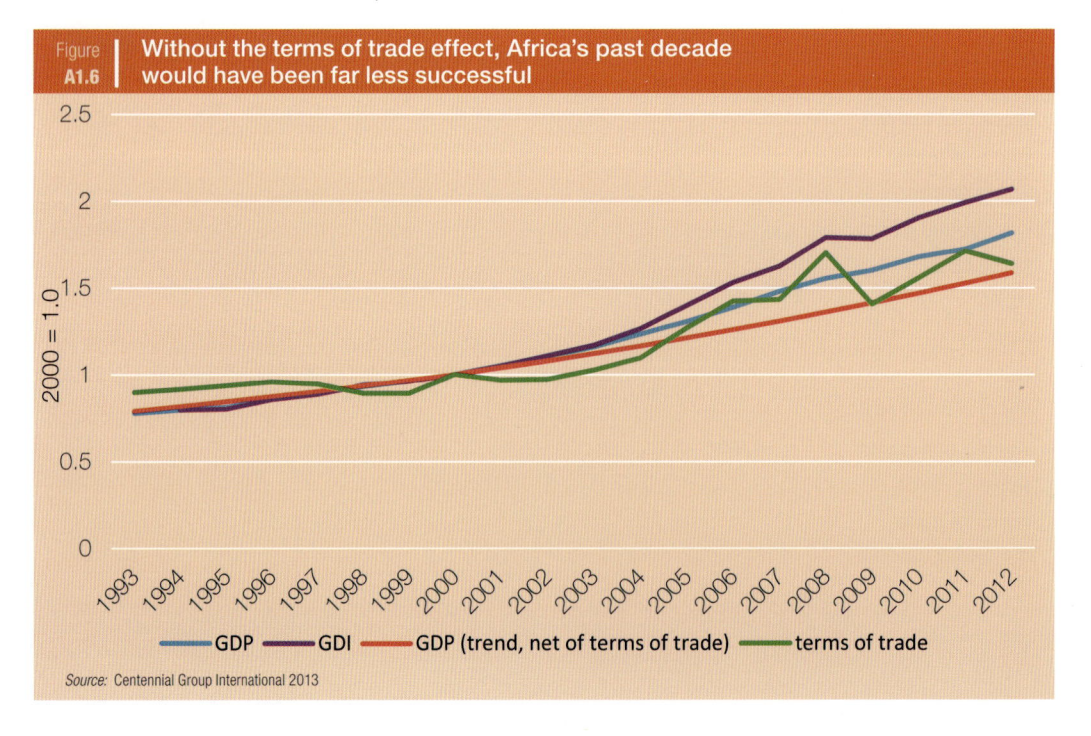

Figure A1.6 | Without the terms of trade effect, Africa's past decade would have been far less successful

Source: Centennial Group International 2013

On the basis of this information, a decline in world or regional activity or, as an alternative, an increase in world supply of commodities, will have a significant effect on the domestic economy. In the case of Africa, if terms of trade in the future were to stabilize at the current high levels, GDP growth rates would tend to fall to the trend growth rate of 3.4 percent, as the multiplier effect would disappear and the purchasing power of exports would stabilize. A decline in terms of trade of 10 percent for Africa would entail a decline in GDI of 6.5 percent; 5 percent in the case of Latin America and the Caribbean; and 9 percent for the Middle East. A decline of this nature, while steep, is not unusual. A 10 percent fall in commodity prices should be considered as plausible, as prices would still be about 50 percent higher than in 2003 and certainly still within the realm of the long-term cycle of commodity prices. Moreover, any argumentation that countries should not be concerned because GDP is growing beyond the terms of trade effect disregards the effect of export prices on domestic output.

Table A1.4 — A decline in the developing world's terms of trade would significantly impact their domestic economies

	Total impact on GDI	Multiplier effect on GDP	Pure terms of trade effect on GDI	Volume of exports
Africa	0.62	0.18	0.44	1.04
Africa: Export-Intensive	0.62	0.21	0.41	0.069
Africa: Balanced	0.46	0.06	0.4	1.95
Latin America	0.49	0.23	0.26	1.2
Middle East and North Africa	0.91	0.1	0.8	0.87

Source: Centennial Group International 2013

The impact of the terms of trade on GDP, GDI, and their respective growth rates is illustrated in Figures A1.7 and A1.8 for Africa. Equivalent figures can be presented for the other regions under consideration. Figure A1.7 shows the average growth rates for GDP and GDI for the period 1991–2012 and a scenario for the period 2013–2022. For the period through 2012, the graph presents the average rates of growth for 1991–1999, 2000–2008, and 2009–2012, against the actual level of terms of trade. For the future, the scenario assumes constant terms of trade for five years and a decline by 2 percent a year for the next five years. It is clear from the graph that GDP and GDI growth rates would fall substantially, even as terms of trade remain at current record levels. GDP growth rates would fall to the underlying business-as-usual levels unless reforms take place. Growth rates fall further during periods of terms of trade decline because of the reduced purchasing power of exports. Figure A1.8 shows the path of GDP and GDI, based on the levels for 2012. For GDP to continue on the historical growth path, terms of trade would have to continue to increase indefinitely. Under the more realistic assumption of plateauing terms of trade, followed by a moderate decline to levels well above the averages of 2000–2012, GDP would be 11 percent lower in 10 years than what would have been expected if the (unrealistic) historical rate of growth of the period 2000–2012 would have prevailed after 2012. Available income as measured by GDI will be lower by 15 percent.

At this point, a word of warning is needed. The numbers are estimates, and they fall within reasonable ranges on the basis of econometric tests. However, the true values will fall within a range around the projected values. Thus, the estimates should be approached cautiously. Nonetheless, even if the possible GDI/ GDP losses were to be one-third or one-half lower, they remain considerable and need to be taken into serious consideration in order to formulate a reasonable macropolicy for the medium term.

In any event, current levels of commodity prices are far from guaranteed to be stable over the long term. An assessment ignoring such a likely development would constitute a serious mistake by emerging and developed countries alike and needs to be corrected through appropriate economic policy. The consequences of inflated asset prices in advanced economies or the complacent and triumphalist dependence of governments on revenues from particular commodities (fuels, minerals, or agricultural goods) has had extremely negative effects throughout the history of Africa, Latin America, and the Middle East, and now the advanced world.

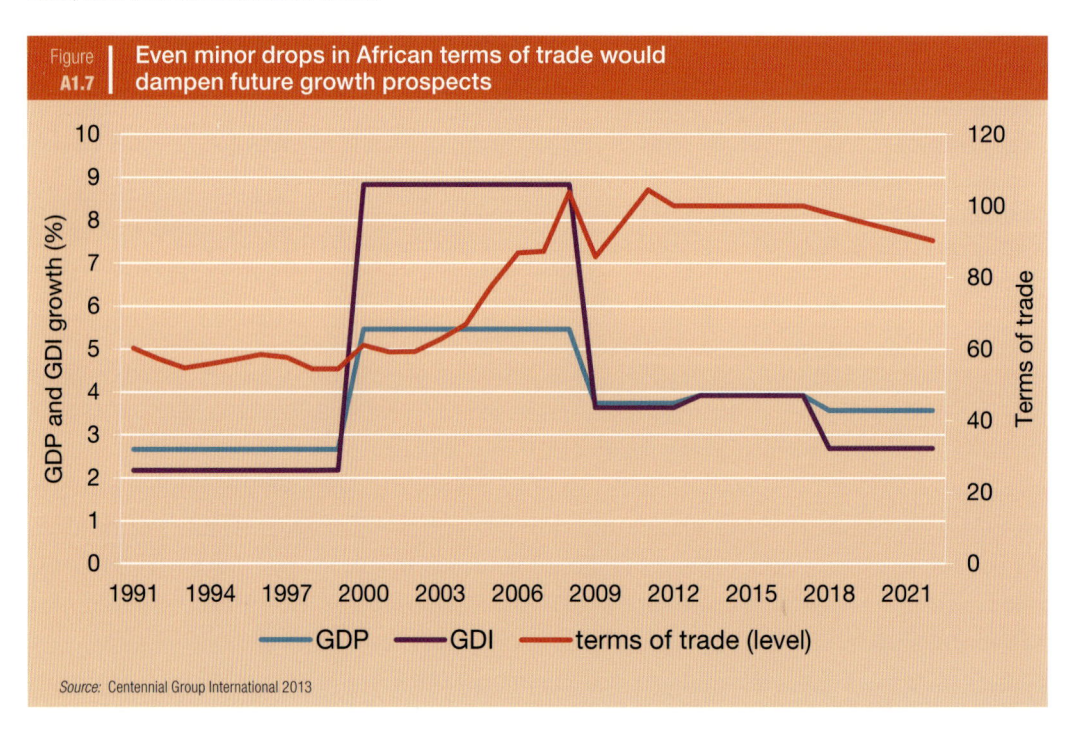

Figure A1.7 Even minor drops in African terms of trade would dampen future growth prospects

Source: Centennial Group International 2013

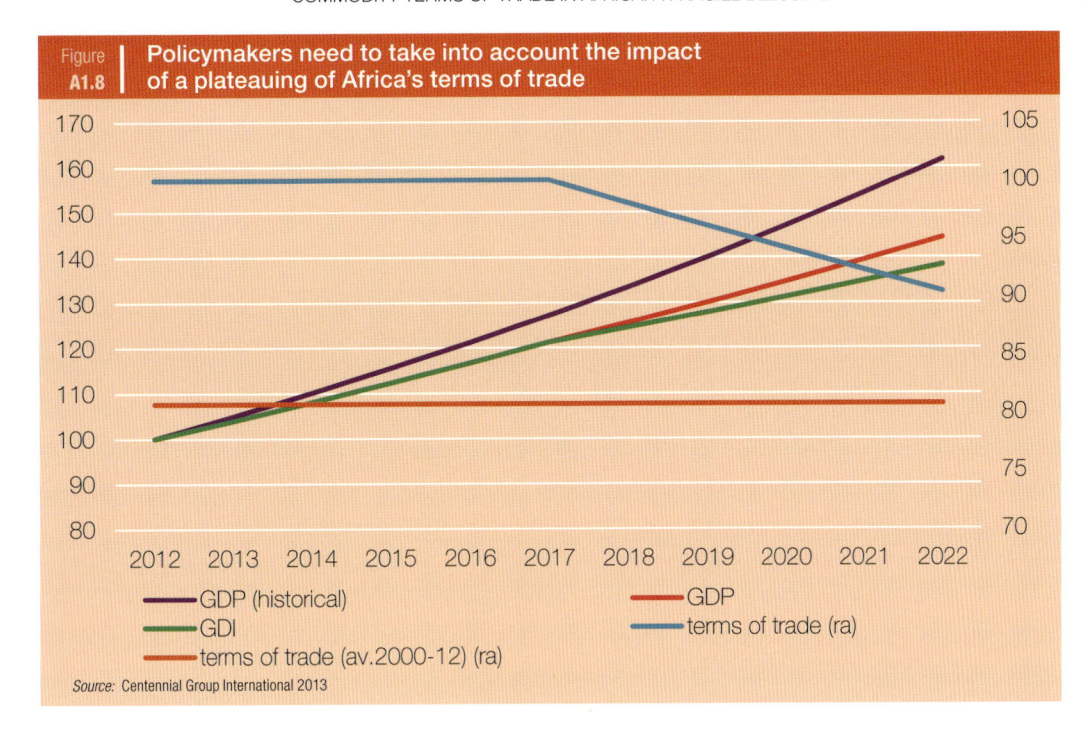

Figure A1.8 Policymakers need to take into account the impact of a plateauing of Africa's terms of trade

— GDP (historical)
— GDI
— terms of trade (av.2000-12) (ra)
— GDP
— terms of trade (ra)

Source: Centennial Group International 2013

Policies need to be formulated to incorporate the effect of possible changes in terms of trade.[12] A commodity stabilization fund equivalent to the Copper Stabilization Fund of Chile, together with structural fiscal targets—namely a budget that is based on long term trends and not only on current developments—would be optimal for these purposes. This requires a predictable path for exportable commodities and the readiness of authorities to offset the deviations from this trend through fiscal policy or a promotion of private stabilization schemes, when production and trade are in the private sector.

The adoption of structural fiscal targets, as they exist in Chile, would consolidate spending patterns by allowing better expenditure planning. A structural fiscal rule would smooth public spending patterns over time and reduce the pro-cyclicality of public expenditures observed at present, as governments adjust expenditure to correct for declines in revenue associated with export windfall reversals. A structural fiscal rule reduces the impact of cyclical revenue fluctuations on expenditures, as it allows for larger deficits and higher expenditures when the output gap is negative and vice versa. A structural fiscal rule applies automatically with no policy intervention and leads to savings when economic conditions improve, and vice versa, constantly smoothing public spending patterns. In particular, it helps to shield social spending and protect the more vulnerable in times of crisis.

---

12. The following discussion draws heavily on Fajgenbaum 2012.

A structural fiscal rule poses a number of complex implementation issues, such as calculating the output gap and projecting long-term commodity-related revenue. Accordingly, these issues need to be carefully addressed for the rule to work as desired. The details of these policy recommendations go beyond the scope of this annex, but abundant material is available (Fajgenbaum 2012).

Concluding Remarks

Gains in terms of trade in recent years have been a source of prosperity in Africa, as well as in Latin America and the Middle East. This article discusses in detail the behavior and the impact of terms of trade changes. The evidence shows clearly that GDI and GDP have been directly influenced by this performance. However, there is the clear likelihood that these trends will be reversed. The current situation has led to a degree of complacency among official and private economic agents that is not warranted. The impact of lower terms of trade can be staggering—a decline in GDI of about two-thirds of a percentage point for each percentage change in terms of trade. With a certainty that prices will fluctuate, and taking into account that they can show a secular downward trend, it is essential to prepare emerging economies for the lower price contingencies. Structural fiscal rules, preparation of the private sector, and a financial protection network are of the essence. Otherwise, volatility will take over and hinder growth and hurt the most vulnerable population groups in commodity exporters.

Appendix 1: Measurement of Trading Gains and Losses

As discussed by the National Accounts Manual, GDI measures the purchasing power of the total incomes generated by domestic production. The difference between the change in GDP in output terms and real GDI is generally described as the "trading gain" (or loss). As imports and exports have become increasingly large relative to GDP, and the commodity composition of imports and exports is very different, the scope for trading gains and losses is large.

The impact on real income of changes in import and export prices is generally done by calculating trading gains or losses, T, measured by the following expression:

$$T = \frac{X - M}{P} - \left(\frac{X}{P_x} - \frac{M}{P_m} \right) \quad (A.1)$$

where X is the exports at current values, M is imports at current values, P_x is the price index for exports, P_m is the price index for imports, and P is a price index based on some selected *numeraire*.

P_x, P_m, and P all equal 1 in the base year. The term in brackets measures the trade balance calculated at the export and import prices of the reference year, whereas the first term measures the actual current trade balance deflated by the *numeraire* price index. It is possible for one to have a different sign from the other.

As noted by the National Accounts Manual, trading gains or losses should be treated as an integral part of the System of National Accounts, on the basis of the following principle: (A.2)

GDP in volume terms + the trading gain or loss resulting from changes in the terms of trade = real GDI

In discussing this issue, Reinsdorf (2009), within the US Department of Commerce, describes the best adjustment as follows: the difference between real GDI and real GDP can be decomposed into two key terms: the change in the terms of trade weighted by the average share of trade in GDP, and the change in the relative price of tradables (to the rest of the economy) weighted by the average share of the trade balance in GDP.[13]

On that basis, the present discussion uses a simple formula:

$$dy^*/y^* = d(er^* (px^* - pm^*))/dy^* \qquad (A.3)$$

where dy/y is the difference between GDI and GDP, on the basis of changes in the terms of trade, and real exchange rates is er. It is important to note in this presentation that the volume changes of x (exports) and m (imports), respectively, are incorporated as part of GDP.

After manipulation, the operating formula for an annual change is:

$$dy^*/y_0^* = (x_1/y_0)[(dpx/px) - (dpm/pm)] + (ca_1/y_0) \times (drer/rer) \qquad (A.4)$$

where rer is the real exchange rate denominated in local currency (appreciation entails a decline, and vice versa), and ca is the current account balance. The relevant formula on a multi-year basis, i.e., based on the cumulative effect of terms of trade changes over time, for a three year period horizon would be: :

$$dy_3^*/y_0^* = (1 + (dy^*/y^*)_1) \times (1 + (dy^*/y^*)_2) \times (1 + (dy^*/y^*)_3) - 1 \qquad (A.5)$$

or in more general terms:

$$dy_t^*/y_0^* = (\pi_{1tot} (1 + (dy_i^*/y_{i-1}^*))-1) \qquad (A.6)$$

---

13. Estimates based on US national accounts data for 1974 to 2007 show significant terms of trade effects in many years. Trading gains subtract at least 0.21 percentage points from real GDI a quarter of the time, and that they add at least 0.18 percentage points a quarter of the time. Occasionally, however, the shocks are much larger. The petroleum price shocks that occurred at the end of 1973 and in 1980 subtracted more than a full percentage point from real GDI, and the one in the first half of 2008, in combination with rising prices of other imports, subtracted almost 2 percentage points from the annualized growth rate of real GDI (Reinsdorf 2009).

The result is the cumulative change of GDI relative to GDP, with regard to a base year. In this way, the measurement captures the effect of the terms of trade over a period of time extending beyond a year. If a change occurs for one year only, the impact will be for that year alone. If the change extends for several years, the formula accounts for this effect over time.

Appendix 2: Classification of African Countries

Country Export-Intensive Economies	Exports/GDP (%) Above 20%	Country Balanced Economies	Exports/GDP (%) Below 20%
Algeria	37%	Burkina Faso	16%
Angola	63%	Burundi	5%
Benin	22%	Cameroon	16%
Botswana	31%	Cape Verde	3%
Chad	43%	CAR	7%
Congo	69%	Comoros	2%
Côte d'Ivoire	42%	Egypt	8%
DRC	37%	Eritrea	15%
Equatorial Guinea	67%	Ethiopia	7%
Gabon	73%	Gambia	8%
Ghana	31%	Kenya	11%
Guinea	27%	Lesotho	13%
Guinea-Bissau	25%	Liberia	17%
Libya	44%	Madagascar	8%
Malawi	22%	Mauritius	8%
Mali	21%	Morocco	8%
Mauritania	71%	Niger	15%
Mozambique	24%	Rwanda	6%
Namibia	25%	Sao Tome and Principe	4%
Nigeria	43%	Senegal	11%
Seychelles	44%	Sierra Leone	9%
Swaziland	23%	South Africa	13%
Zambia	42%	Sudan	16%
Zimbabwe	29%	Tunisia	10%
		Uganda	10%
		Tanzania	16%

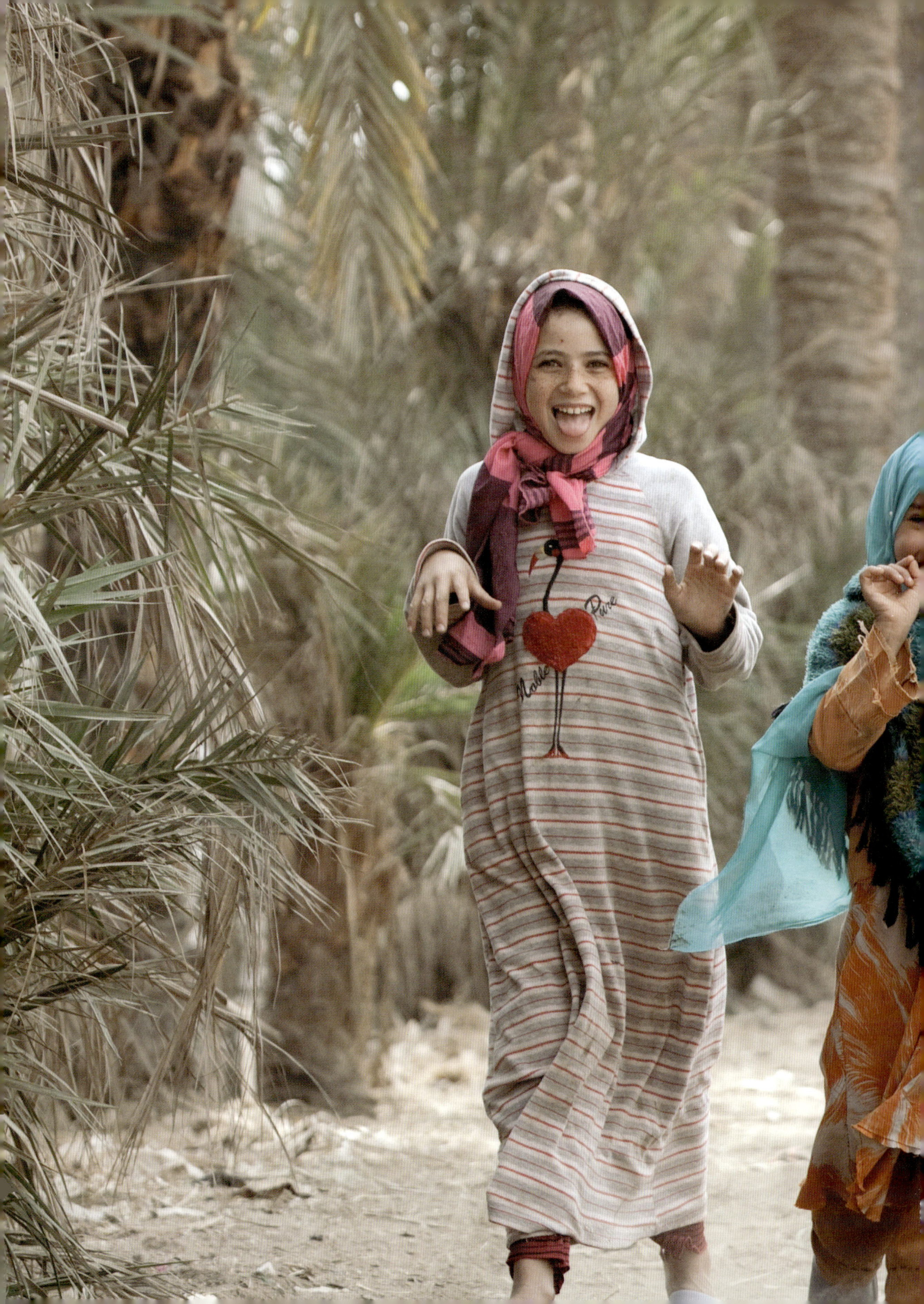
Pure
Noble

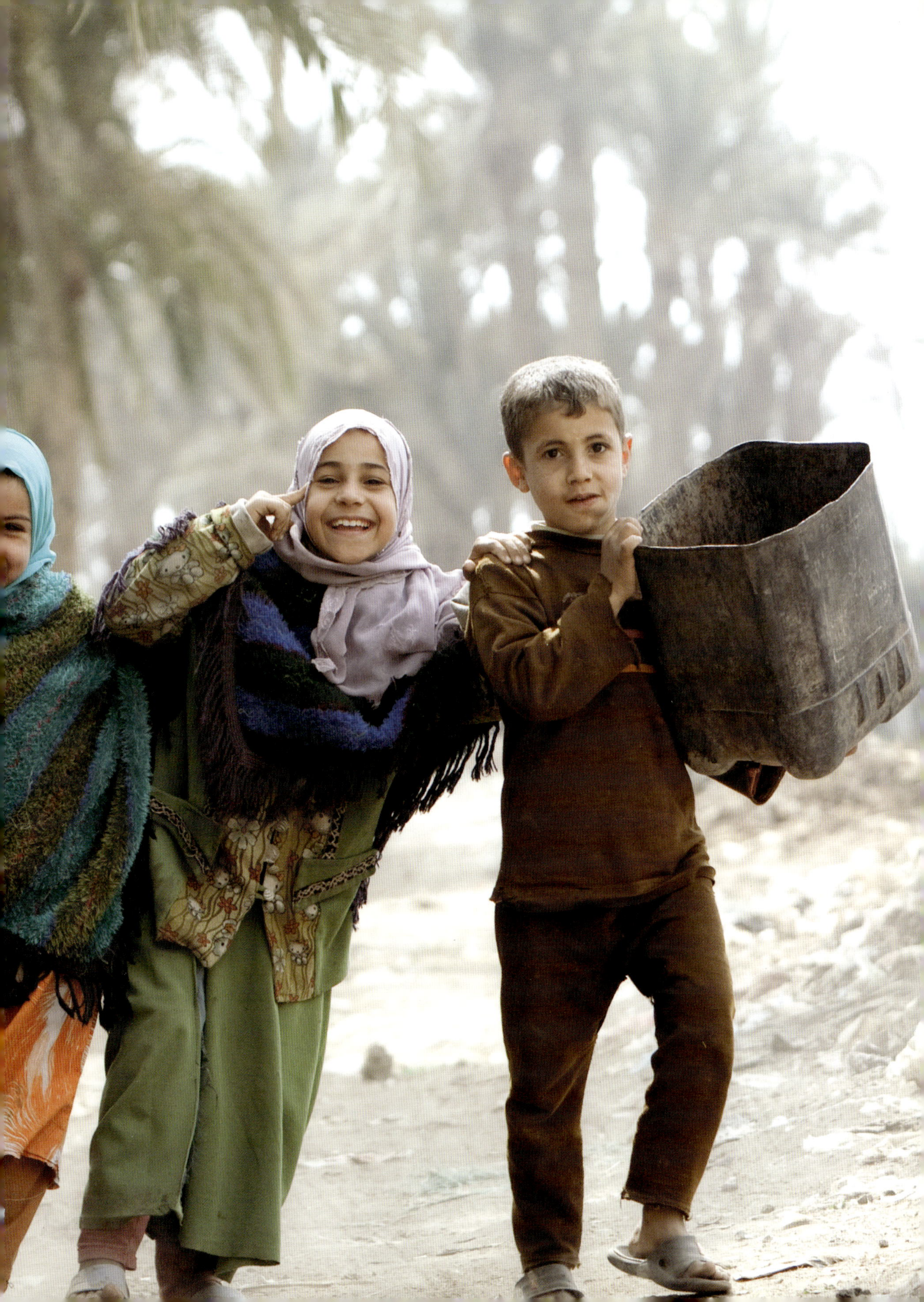

Model of Global Economy

Annex 2

Harpaul Alberto Kohli

The model used for the scenarios described in Chapter 1 estimates GDP as a function of labor force, capital stock, and total factor productivity for 187 economies between 2013 and 2050 under three different growth scenarios: the convergence scenario, the business-as-usual scenario, and the downside scenario. This section offers an abbreviated description of the model; a more detailed exposition, in Kohli, Szyf, and Arnold (2012), is available on request.[1]

As seen in Equation 1, a Cobb-Douglas function with constant returns to scale is assumed, with α equal to two-thirds:

$$GDP = TFP \times L^{\alpha} \times K^{1-\alpha} \qquad (1)$$

GDP figures are generated for three different measures: real GDP (constant 2010 prices), GDP PPP (constant 2010 PPP prices), and GDP at expected market exchange rates, which incorporates expected exchange rate movements and serves as the best proxy for nominal GDP.

The following is a summary of the process: The model first estimates annual real GDP growth for each country between 2014 and 2050. These estimates are applied to the previous values of real GDP, GDP PPP, and a measure equal to nominal GDP deflated by US inflation (on which GDP at market exchange rates is based) to derive the full series. Finally, to derive GDP at market exchange rates, real exchange rate changes are estimated and multiplied by nominal GDP deflated by US inflation to obtain GDP at market exchange rates.

Labor force growth stems from population growth and from changes in labor force participation rates. Population growth is based on the 2010 Revision of the UN's World Population Prospects, while labor force participation rates are projected separately, by gender, for seven age cohorts (15–19, 20–24, 25–29, 30–49, 50–59, 60–64, and 65+) to better capture cohort-specific trends. Male rates are projected directly; female rates are derived by projecting the difference between male and female rates for each age group. Labor force participation rates from 1980 through 2012 are taken from the ILO.

---

1. This annex is based on Kohli, Szyf, and Arnold 2012.

The cross-country, cohort-specific equations to forecast male rates are simple autoregressions of the following form:

$$\ln(M_{age,t}) = m_{age} \times \ln(M_{age,t-1}) \quad (2)$$

where M_{age} is the percent of males in age group *age* who are active in the labor force and m_{age} is a constant that varies for each age group.

The cross-country, cohort-specific equations to forecast the differentials between male and female participations rates are:

$$\ln(D_{age,t}) = d_{age} \times \ln(D_{age,t-1}) \quad (3)$$

where D_{age} equals the difference between the percentage of males in age group *age* in the labor force and the percentage of females in age group *age* in the labor force, and d_{age} is a constant that varies by age group. In both male and female models, for certain cohorts, rough upper or lower bounds are incorporated to address outliers. Observations that begin in 2012 beyond these bounds are not governed by the regressions but instead gradually converge over time toward the bounds.

Capital stock growth, based on an initial capital stock and yearly investment rates and depreciation, is defined as:

$$(1 + K\ Growth_t) = \frac{K_t}{K_{t-1}} = \left(\frac{I_{t-1}}{K_{t-1}}\right) - 0.06 \quad (4)$$

where K is the capital stock, 0.06 represents the yearly depreciation of 6%, and I_{t-1} is the capital investment from the previous year, which is defined as the previous year's GDP (measured in constant 2010 PPP dollars) multiplied by the investment rate as a share of GDP.

The initial capital stock is calculated using the Caselli method, with the following equation:

$$K_0 = \frac{I_0}{g + 0.06} \quad (5)$$

where K_0 is the initial capital stock, g is the average GDP growth over the subsequent ten years, 0.06 is the depreciation rate, and I_0 is the initial year's investment. For I_0, for each country, the earliest year for which there exists capital investment data (year *y*) is identified. The average of the investment rate values for year *y* and the two subsequent years is computed and treated as the initial investment rate. This smoothing out of fluctuations in the initial investment rate yields better estimates for certain countries with high volatility in the earliest investment rate values. This rate is then multiplied by the GDP in year *y* to determine I_0. The earliest year possible is chosen for this estimate because the longer the time frame before the projections commence, the more the yearly depreciations will reduce the effects on the model of any initial imprecision in capital estimates.

The model is calibrated by calculating TFP for an initial year (2013)[2] based on labor force, capital stock, and historical GDP, with GDP and capital stock measured in purchasing-power-parity dollars at constant 2010 PPP prices. For subsequent years, TFP is projected.

For the TFP projections, we differentiate four categories of countries: rich or developed, converging, non-converging, and fragile. All countries begin with a default TFP growth rate of 1 percent, which, with a high level of statistical significance, equals the average US rate over the past 40, 30, 25, and 20 years, and, which, also with a high level of statistical significance, equals the average rate of all non-converging countries over the same four periods. In our model, this is the fixed rate of productivity growth for non-converging, non-fragile countries.

Research shows that some growth differences between developing countries can be successfully modelled by separating them into two groups: converging and non-converging (Gill and Kharas 2007).

A country is deemed to be converging if its per capita income has rapidly converged over a 20-year period to that of best practice economies or if its 2001–2011 TFP growth is closer to what the model would predict for a converger (see below) than to what it would predict for a non-converger; the lower a country's productivity relative to the global best practice, the more quickly it converges. This convergence reflects technology transfers from richer innovating countries, technology leapfrogging, the diffusion of management and operational research from more developed countries, shifting underemployed agricultural workers to efficient export-led manufacturing, a steady increase in the average level of skills, building infrastructure to connect the unconnected to markets, and other ways that a country can shortcut productivity-improvement processes by learning from economies that are already at the productivity frontier.

Converging countries are modeled with a convergence "boost" that increases their TFP growth above the 1 percent US historical norm. The lower a converging country's productivity relative to that of the US, the larger the boost it receives and the quicker the catch-up.[3] The productivity growth of 14 of the 36 rich countries is treated the same as that of converging countries. Non-converging countries and 22 of the 36 rich countries maintain the default 1 percent yearly productivity growth and hence experience no convergence boost. The rich countries are divided into these categories based on their past TFP performance. The general equation for TFP growth is:

$$TFPGrowth = 1.0\% + CB - FP \tag{6}$$

---

2. IMF WEO GDP growth estimates are used for 2013.
3. TFP is used in the convergence term instead of the per capita income for three reasons. First, if the equation were to use GDP per capita, over time the TFP of a converging country would not converge to that of the US but instead to other values. Also, since the convergence equation represents convergence of TFP, we use TFP in order to make the equation consistent with its purpose. Third, using the convergence coefficient from past research in tandem with an income-based convergence term yields large discrepancies with the recent historical data for TFP growth for many countries; using TFP yields a better fit.

where *CB* is the convergence boost benefiting "converging" countries and *FP* is the productivity growth penalty suffered by fragile states.

The convergence boost is defined as follows:

$$CB = c \times 2.69\% \times \ln\left(\frac{TFP_{USA,t-1}}{TFP_{i,t-1}}\right) \qquad (7)$$

where *i* is the country, 2.69 percent is the convergence coefficient (derived from historical data), TFP is total factor productivity, and *c* takes a value between 0 and 1 and identifies whether a country is treated as a converger (*c* =1) or as a non-converger or fragile state (*c* =0) or as in an intermediate state of transition between being a converger and non-converger (0 < *c* < 1).

The fragile penalty *FP* is defined as

$$FP = f \times 1.5\% \qquad (8)$$

where *f* plays a role analogous to that of *c* in Equation 7 above. For each fragile country, *f* is set equal to 1, corresponding to a penalty in productivity growth of 1.5 percent, so that its productivity is assumed to fall by 0.5 percent a year. The coefficient of negative 1.5 percent is derived by identifying state failures and debilitating wars prior to the global financial crisis that lasted at least 2 consecutive years in 44 countries. The list of fragile states is the harmonized list prepared by the African Development Bank and the World Bank.

The projections of GDP growth are concluded by applying the labor growth, capital deepening, and productivity changes to each country over the period 2014–2050.

The measure of GDP at expected market exchange rates adjusts the GDP estimate by expected changes in the real exchange rate. First, an equation is derived to establish a theoretical relationship between a country's real exchange rate and its PPP income relative to that of the United States. Then, the country's modelled exchange rate converges toward the value that corresponds to its income in this theoretical equation. These relationships are not linear, and the countries for which increases in GDP PPP per capita lead to the largest appreciation of their real exchange rates are the countries whose incomes are between one-third and two-thirds that of the United States.

The model also projects the sizes of the low-, middle-, and high-income populations, again following Kharas, by measuring the number of people in each country with living standards -- in PPP terms — within a certain absolute range. An income distribution for each country is derived from the World Bank's Povcal and International Comparison Program.

The model calculates what share of the nation's income is available for consumption, and it distributes this consumption income over the population according to the income distribution. As the country's overall consumption income increases, the purchasing power of those at the bottom of the distribution increases, raising more to middle-income status.

For purposes of computing consumption income classes, the model projects changes in the share of the country's income available for consumption using the following equation:

$$\ln(C_{i,t}) = \alpha_1 \times \ln(C_{i,t-1}) + \alpha_2 \times \ln(GDPPCCap_{i,t}) + \alpha_0 \qquad (9)$$

where t is the year, i is the country, C is the ratio of consumption to GDP, $GDPPCCap$ is the minimum of each country's GDP PPP per capita and $50,000 PPP (in 2010 PPP international dollars), and α_0, α_1, and α_2 are constants.

The model can also account for changes in the terms of trade, which, in turn, affect GNI. The model multiplies the sum of imports and exports as a share of GDP by the percentage change in the terms of trade, yielding the percentage change in GNI. GNI increases lead to increases in both consumption and investment and hence GDP. The labor force increases result from increased demand for labor from the increased consumption and investment and productivity increases result from use of spare capacity or reduction of inefficiencies in response to the increased consumption and investment. Improvements in the terms of trade thus increase TFP, labor, and capital. The calibration of this effect is based on parameters derived from Loser (2013), which estimates for different regions how much increases in terms of trade increased GDP.

Separate projections are made for the convergence scenario, the business-as-usual scenario, and the downside scenario. The difference between the scenarios is how countries are classified, either as converging, non-converging, or fragile; how countries gradually transition between classifications; and, for the downside scenario, assumptions about the terms of trade.

For 145 countries the initial classification is based on the Kharas classification and for an additional 42 countries on a similar analysis of recent data. Under this classification, four African countries (Botswana, Cape Verde, Mauritius, and Mozambique) are classified as "convergers."

For the convergence scenario, a group of 15 additional African countries joins the "early convergers" and begins converging this decade. An additional group of 15 "late convergers" begins converging in the following decade. The remaining 20 countries currently considered "fragile" transition out of fragility over the next 30 years.

Under the business-as-usual scenario the four African countries that are currently converging are assumed to continue converging through 2050. All current non-convergers continue to not converge, and all fragile countries remain fragile.

In the downside scenario an additional five countries become fragile, non-convergers do not converge, and the four convergers gradually stop converging. This scenario also includes cyclical fluctuations in Africa's terms of trade. Specifically, starting in 2015 the terms of trade deteriorate by 15 percent over 5 years and then recover by 15 percent over the subsequent 10 years, after which this cycle repeats.

In all three scenarios, the transition of individual countries between converging and non-converging, or from fragile to non-converging, is gradual. That is, countries are made to adopt an intermediate state between fragile and not-fragile or between converging and non-converging, by varying the values of f and c in Equations 7 and 8.

References

Acemoglu, Daron, and James Robinson. 2012. *Why Nations Fail*. New York: Crown Business.

Adams, Arvil V., Sara Johansson de Silva, and Setareh Razamara. 2013. *Improving Skills Development in the Informal Sector: Strategies for Sub-Saharan Africa*. Washington, DC: World Bank.

ADEA. 2012. *Critical Knowledge, Skills, and Qualifications for Accelerated and Sustainable Development in Africa.* Synthesis Report for ADEA Triennale 2012, Association for Development of Education in Africa, Saint Paul, MN.

AERC, and World Bank. 2011. *Service Delivery Indicators: Pilot in Education and Health Care in Africa*. Washington, DC: AERC and World Bank.

Africa Progress Panel. 2012. *Africa Progress Report 2012: Jobs, Justice, and Equity; Seizing Opportunities in Times of Global Change*. Geneva: Africa Progress Panel.

———. 2010. *Africa Progress Report 2010*. Geneva: Africa Progress Panel.

African Development Bank. 2012a. *African Economic Outlook 2012: Special Theme; Promoting Youth Employment*. Tunis: African Development Bank.

———. 2012b. *Solutions for a Changing Climate: The African Development Bank's Response to Impacts in Africa*. Tunis: African Development Bank.

———. 2011a. *African Economic Outlook 2011: Africa and its Emerging Partners*. Tunis: African Development Bank.

———. 2011b. *The Cost of Adaptation to Climate Change in Africa*. Tunis: African Development Bank.

Africon. 2008. "Unit Costs of Infrastructure Projects in Sub-Saharan Africa." Background Paper 11, Africa Infrastructure Sector Diagnostic, World Bank, Washington, DC.

ABC. 2010a. A Cooperacao Tecnica do Brasil para a Africa. Brasilia: Agencia Brasileira de Cooperacao.

———. 2010b. *Dialogo Brasil-Africa em Seguranca Alimentar, Combate a Fome, e Desenvolvimento Rural*. Brasilia: Agencia Brasileira de Cooperacao.

Aitzhanova, Aktoty, Shigeo Katsu, Johannes F. Linn, and Vladislav Yezhov. Forthcoming. *Kazakhstan 2050: Towards a Modern Society for All*. New Delhi: Oxford University Press.

Aker, Jenny C. 2010. "Information from Markets Near and Far: Mobile Phones and Agricultural Markets in Niger." *American Economic Journal: Applied Economics* 2 (3): 46-59.

Alexandratos, Nikos, and Jelle Bruinsma. 2010. "World Agriculture toward 2030/2050: The 2012 Revision." ESA Working Paper No. 12-03, Global Perspective Studies Team, FAO Agricultural Development Economics Division, Food and Agriculture Organization of the United States, Rome.

Anderson, Kym, and William A. Masters, eds. 2009. *Distortions to Agricultural Incentives in Africa*. Washington, DC: World Bank.

Angel, Shlomo, Jason Parent, Daniel L. Civco, and Alejandro M. Blei. 2012. *The Atlas of Urban Expansion*. Cambridge, MA: Lincoln Institute of Land Policy.

Arnold, Drew, Jose Fajgenbaum, Vinod K. Goel, Tamara Ortega Goodspeed, Homi Kharas, Harinder S. Kohli, Claudio M. Loser, Nora Lustig, Jeffrey M. Puryear, Michael Shifter, Anil Sood, and Y. Aaron Szyf. 2013. *Latin America 2040: Breaking away from Complacency: An Agenda for Resurgence*. New Delhi: Sage.

Arvis, Jean-Francois, and Ben Shepherd. 2011. "The Air Connectivity Index: Measuring Integration in the Global Air Transport Network." Policy Research Paper No. 5722, World Bank, Washington, DC.

Bala-Gbogbo, Elisha. 2012. "Nigeria, Vulcan to Build New Refineries in $4.5 Billion Accord." *Bloomberg*. Published July 2. http://www.bloomberg.com/news/2012-07-02/nigeria-vulcan-to-build-new-refineries-in-4-5-billion-accord.html.

Banerjee, Sudeshna, Heather Skilling, Vivien Foster, Cecilia Briceno-Garmendia, Elvira Morella, and Tarik Chfadi. 2008. "Ebbing Water, Surging Deficits: Urban Water Supply in Sub-Saharan Africa." Background Paper 12, Africa Infrastructure Diagnostic, World Bank, Washington, DC.

Bannon, Ian, and Paul Collier. 2003. *Natural Resources and Violent Conflicts*. Washington, DC: World Bank.

Barro, Robert, and Jong-Wha Lee. 2010. *A New Data Set of Educational Attainment in the World 1950-2010*. NBER Working Paper 15902, National Bureau of Economic Research, Cambridge, MA.

Bayart, Jean Francois. 1985. *L'etat en Afrique: la politique du ventre*. Paris: Fayard.

Bayart, Jean Francois, Stephen Ellis, and Beatrice Hibou. 1999. *La criminalization de l'etat en Afrique*. Brussels: Complexe.

Belloncle, Guy. 1985. *Paysanneries Saheliennes en peril*. Paris: L'Harmattan.

Berif, Ruchita. 2008. "India Woos Africa." ISDA Strategic Comments, Institute for Defense Studies and Analysis, New Delhi, March 19.

Berthelemy, Jean-Claude. 2009. "Impact of China's Engagement on the Sectoral Allocation of Resources and Aid Effectiveness in Africa." Paper presented at the African Economic Conference, Addis Ababa, November 11-13.

Billaz, René. 2013. *Les défis alimentaires et environnementaux au Sahel sont gigantesques ; comment contribuer à les relever?* Lyon : Agronomes et vétérinaires sans frontières.

Binswanger, Hans P., Shahidur Khandker, and Mark Rosenzweig. 1993."How Infrastructure and Financial Institutions Affect Agricultural Output and Investment in India." *Journal of Development Economics* 41 (2): 337-366.

Binswanger-Mkhize, Hans P., Alex F. McCalla, and Praful Patel. 2010. "Structural Transformation and African Agriculture." *Global Journal of Emerging Market Economies* 2 (2): 113-152.

Bonfils, Michel. 1987. *Halte a la desertification au Sahel*. Paris: Karthala.

Bongaarts, John. 2010. *Poverty, Gender, and Youth: The Causes of Education Differences in Fertility in Sub-Saharan Africa*. Working Paper No. 20, The Population Council, New York.

Bongaarts, John, and John Casterline. 2012. "Fertility Transition: Is Sub-Saharan Africa Different?" *Population and Development Review* 38 (s1): 153-168.

Boorman, Jack, Jose Fajgenbaum, Herve Ferhani, Manu Bhaskaran, Drew Arnold, and Harpaul Alberto Kohli. 2013. "The Centennial Resilience Index: Measuring Countries' Resilience to Shock." *Global Journal of Emerging Market Economies* 5 (2): 57-98.

Brautigam, Deborah. 2008. *China's African Aid: Transatlantic Challenges*. Washington, DC: The German Marshall Fund of the United States.

British Petroleum. 2012. *BP Statistical Review of World Energy June 2012*. London: British Petroleum.

Bruns, Barbara, Deon Filmer, and Harry Patrinos. 2011. *Making Schools Work: New Evidence on Accountability Reforms*. Washington, DC: World Bank.

REFERENCES

Bulmer-Thomas, Victor. 2003. *The Economic History of Latin America since Independence*. Cambridge: Cambridge University Press.

Burnett, Nicholas, and Desmond Bermingham. 2010. "Innovative Financing for Education." ESP Working Papers Series 2010 No 5., Results for Development Institute and Open Society Institute, Washington DC.

Butler-Adam, John. 2012. *The Southern African Regional Universities Association: Seven Years of Regional High Education Advancement 2006-2012*. Johannesburg: SAURA.

Calamatsis, Evangelos A., Anupam Basu, and Dhaneshwar Ghura. 1999. "Adjustment and Growth in Sub-Saharan Africa." Work Paper No. 99/51, International Monetary Fund, Washington, DC.

CEIRI. 2011. "Cooperacao entre Brasil e Africa e Comemoradapela ONU." Published December 23.

Centennial Group International. 2013. Unpublished data. Washington, DC: Centennial Group International.

Chaturvedi, S., Thomas Fues, and E. Sidiropoulos, eds. 2012. *Development Cooperation and Emerging Powers: New Partners or Old Patterns?* London: Zed Books.

Cheru, Fantu, and Cyril Obi, eds. 2010. *The Rise of China and India in Africa*. London and Uppsala: Zed Books and NAI.

Chevenement, Jean Pierre, and Gérard Larcher. 2013. "Sahel : Pour une approche globale. " Rapport d' information no. 720, Commission des Affaires étrangères, de la Défense et des Forces armées, Sénat, Paris, France.

Chilean Ministry of Finance. 2012. *Chilean Self-Assessment of Compliance with Santiago Principles*. Santiago de Chile: Ministry of Finance.

Cline, William R. 2007. *Global Warming and Agriculture*. Washington, DC: Center for Global Development and Petersen Institute.

Collier, Paul. 2009. *War, Guns, and Votes: Democracy in Dangerous Places*. New York: Harper Collins.

———. 2007. *The Bottom Billion: Why the Poorest Countries Are Failing and What Can Be Done About It*. Oxford: Oxford University Press.

Collier, Paul, and Stefan Dercon. 2009. "African Agriculture in 50 years: Smallholders in a Rapidly Changing World." Paper prepared for the FAO/UNESDD Expert Meeting on How to Feed the World in 2050, Rome.

Collier, Paul, and Nicholas Sambanis. 2005. *Understanding Civil Wars.* Washington, DC: World Bank.

Commission on Growth and Development. 2008. *The Growth Report: Strategies for Sustained Growth and Inclusive Development*. Washington, DC: World Bank.

Cooke, Jennifer G., and Richard Downie. 2010. "African Perspectives on Genetically Modified Crops Assessing the Debate in Zambia, Kenya, and South Africa." A Report of the CSIS Global Food Security Project, Center for Strategic and International Studies, Washington, DC.

Cooper, Frederick. 2002. *Africa since 1940: The Past of the Present*. Cambridge: Cambridge University Press.

Council of Europe. 2007. "The Africa-EU Strategic Partnership." A Joint Africa-EU Strategy, Council of Europe, Strasbourg.

Council of the European Union. 2010. "Council Conclusions on the EU's Trade Policy." Written procedure, Council of the European Union, Brussels, December 21.

Cotet, Anca M., and Kevin K. Tsui. 2010. "Oil and Conflict: What Does the Cross-Country Analysis Really Show?" *American Economic Journal: Macroeconomics* 5 (1): 49-80.

Dayak, Mano. 1992. *Touareg, la tragedie*. Paris: CJ Lattes.

Demombynes, Gabriel, and Sofia Trommlerová. 2012. "What has Driven the Decline of Infant Mortality in Kenya?" Working Paper 6057, World Bank, Washington, DC.

di Gropello, Emanuela, ed. 2006. *Meeting the Challenges of Secondary Education in Latin America and East Asia: Improving Efficiency and Resource Mobilization.* Washington, DC: World Bank.

Di John, Jonathan. 2010. "The Concepts, Causes, and Consequences of Failed States: A Critical Review of the Literature and Agenda for Research with Specific Reference to Sub-Saharan Africa." *European Journal of Development* 22: 10-30.

Dihel, Nora, Ana Margarida Fernandes, Aaditya Mattoo, and Nicholas Strychacz. 2010. "Reform and Regional Integration of Professional Services in East Africa: Time for Action." Report No. 57672-AFR, Poverty Reduction and Economic Management Unit 2, Africa Region, World Bank, Washington, DC, October.

Dixon, John, Aidan Gulliver, and David Gibbon. 2001. *Farming Systems and Poverty: Improving Farmers Livelihoods in a Changing World*. Rome and Washington, DC: FAO and World Bank.

Dorosh, Paul, Hyoung Gun Wang, Liangzhi You, and Emily Schmidt. 2012. "Road Connectivity, Population, and Crop Production in Sub-Saharan Africa." *Agricultural Economics* 43 (1): 89-103.

Dubresson, Alain, Sophie Moreau, Jean-Pierre Raison, and Jean-Fabien Steck. 2003. *L'Afrique subsaharienne: Une géographie du changement*. Paris: Armand Colin.

Duggan, Victor, Sjamsu Rahardja, and Gonzalo Varela. 2013. "Service Sector Reform and Manufacturing Productivity: Evidence from Indonesia. Research Working Paper No. 6349, World Bank, Washington, DC.

Eberhard, Anton, Vivien Foster, Cecilia Briceno-Garmendia, Fatimata Ouedraogo, Daniel Camos, and Maria Shkaratan. 2008. "Underpowered: The State of the Power Sector in Sub-Saharan Africa." Background Paper 6, Africa Infrastructure Sector Diagnostic, World Bank, Washington, DC.

ECPDM. 2006. "Overview of the Regional EPA Negotiations: Pacific-EU Economic Partnership Agreement." ECDPM In Brief 14D, European Centre for Development and Policy Management, Maastricht.

Ellis, Stephen. 2009. "West Africa's International Drug Trade." *African Affairs* 108 (431): 171-196.

Engle, Patrice L., Lia C.H. Fernald, Harold Alderman, Jere Behrman, Chloe O'Gara, Aisha Yousafzai, Meena Cabral de Mello, Melissa Hidrobo, Nurper Ulkuer, Ilgi Ertem, and Selim Iltus. 2011. "Strategies for Reducing Inequalities and Improving Development Outcomes for Young Children in Low-Income and Middle-Income Countries." *The Lancet* 378, no. 9799: 1339-1353.

European Commission, IMF, OECD, UN, and World Bank. 2009. *System of National Accounts 2008*. New York: European Commission, IMF, OECD, UN, and World Bank.

Evenson, Robert R., and M. W. Rosegrant. 1995. *Productivity Projections for Commodity Market Modeling*. New Haven: Yale University Economic Growth Center.

Extractive Industries Transparency Initiative. 2013. "Extractive Industries Transparency Institute." http://eiti.org/

Fafchamps, Marcel. 2003. *Rural Poverty, Risk, and Development*. Cheltenham: Edward Elgar.

Fan, Shenggen, Bella Nestorova, and Tolulope Olofinbiyi. 2010. "China's Agricultural and Rural Development: Implications for Africa." Washington, DC: International Food Policy Research Institute.

FAO. 2010. *The Global Forest Resources Assessment 2010*. Rome: FAO.

FAO, IFAD, UNCTAD Secretariat, and World Bank. 2010. *Principles for Responsible Agricultural Investment That Respects Rights, Livelihoods, and Resources*. Rome: FAO.

Favennec, Jean-Pierre. 2001. "Refining: A Technical Summary Investments, Margins, Costs Probable Future Development." In *Petroleum Refining: Volume 5; Refinery Operations and Management* by Jean-Pierre Favennec, 117-172. Paris: Instit francais du petrole Publications.

Ferreira, Francisco H.G., and Martin Ravallion. 2008. "Global Poverty and Inequality: A Review of the Evidence." Policy Research Working Paper 4623, World Bank, Washington, DC.

REFERENCES

Ferroni, Marco, ed. 2012. *India 2040: Transforming Indian Agriculture*. New Delhi: Sage.

Ferry, Benoit, ed. 2007. *L'Afrique Face à ses Défis Démographiques*. Paris: AFD, CEPED, and Karthala.

Field, B. Christopher, Vicente Barros, Thomas F. Stocker, Qin Dahe, David Jon Dokken, Kristie L. Ebi, Michael D. Mastrandrea, Katharine J. Mach, Gian-Kasper Plattner, Simon K. Allen, Melinda Tignor, and Pauline M. Midgley. 2012. "Summary for Policymakers." In *Managing the Risks of Extreme Events and Disasters to Advance Climate Change Adaptation: A Special Report of Working Groups I and II of the Intergovernmental Panel on Climate Change*, edited by Christopher B. Field, Vicente Barros, Thomas F. Stocker, Qin Dahe, David Jon Dokken, Kristie L. Ebi, Michael D. Mastrandrea, Katharine J. Mach, Gian-Kasper Plattner, Simon K. Allen, Melinda Tignor, and Pauline M. Midgley, 1–19. Cambridge: Cambridge University Press.

Fjose, Sveinung, Leo A. Grunfeld, and Chris Green. 2010. "SMEs and Growth in Sub-Saharan Africa." MENON-publication no.14/2010, MENON Business Economics, Oslo, June.

FOCAC. 2006. "Declaration of the Beijing Summit and Beijing Action Plan 2007-2009." Ministry of Foreign Affairs, Beijing.

Fox, Louise M., and Melissa Sekkel Gaal. 2008. *Working out of Poverty: Job Creation and the Quality of Growth in Africa*. Washington, DC: World Bank.

Fox, Louise, and Thomas Pave Sohnesen. 2012. "Household Enterprises in Sub-Saharan Africa." Policy Research Working Paper No. 6184, World Bank, Washington, DC.

Francis, Paul A., S.P.I Agi, S. Ogoh Alubo, Hawa A. Biu, A.G. Daramola, Uchenna M. Nzewi, and D.J. Shehu. 1998. *Hard Lessons: Primary Schools, Community, and Social Capital in Nigeria*. Washington, DC: World Bank.

Franko, Patrice. 2003. *The Puzzle of Latin American Economic Development*. New York: Rowman and Littlefield.

Fredriksen, Birger. 2011. *Education Resource Mobilization and Use in Developing Countries: Scope for Efficiency Gains through More Strategic Use of Education Aid*. Washington, DC: Results for Development Institute.

Fredriksen, Birger, and Jee Peng Tan, eds. 2008. *An African Exploration of East Asian Education Experience*. Washington, DC: World Bank.

Fromkin, David. 1989. *A Peace to End All Peace*. New York: Henry Holt and Company.

Fujikura, Ryo, and Masato Kawanishi, eds. 2011. *Climate Change Adaptation and International Development: Making Development Cooperation More Effective*. London: Earthscan.

Fujikura, Ryo, and Tomoyo Toyota, eds. 2012. *Climate Change Mitigation and International Development Cooperation*. London: Routledge.

Fujita, Yasuo, Ippei Tsuruga, and Asami Takeda. 2013. "Policy Challenges for Infrastructure Development in Africa: The Way forward for Japan's Official Development Assistance (ODA)." In *For Inclusive and Dynamic Development in Sub-Saharan Africa*, 195-224. Tokyo: JICA Research Institute.

Furukawa, M., and J. Takahata. 2013. "Is GBS Still a Preferable Aid Modality?" Working Paper No. 50, JICA Research Institute, Tokyo.

Gakidou, Emmanuela, Krycia Cowling, Rafael Lozano, and Christopher J.L. Murray. 2010. "Increased Educational Attainment and Its Effect on Child Mortality in 175 Countries between 1970 and 2009: A Systematic Analysis." *The Lancet* 376 (9745): 959–974.

Garcia, Marito, Alan Pence, and Judith L. Evens, eds. 2008. *Africa's Future, Africa's Challenge: Early Childhood Care and Development in Sub-Saharan Africa*. Washington, DC: World Bank.

George Mason University Center for Entrepreneurship and Public Policy. 2013. *GEDI Index*. http://cepp.gmu.edu/research/geindex/.

Gill, Indermit, and Homi Kharas. *An East Asian Renaissance: Ideas for Economic Growth*. Washington, DC: World Bank.

Giri, Jacques. 1989. *Le Sahel au XXI eme siècle*. Paris: Karthala.

———. 1983. *Le Sahel demain: catastrophe ou renaissance*. Paris: Karthala.

Global Coalition for Africa. 2004. *African Social and Economic Trends: Annual Report 2003/2004*. Washington, DC: Global Coalition for Africa.

Gnessoto, Nicole, and Giovanni Grevi. 2006. "Sub-Saharan Africa." In *The New Global Puzzle: What World for the EU in 2025?*, edited by Nicole Gnessoto and Giovanni Grevi, 131-140. Paris: Institute for Security Studies.

Guengant, Jean-Pierre. 2012. *How Can We Capitalize on the Demographic Dividend? Demographics at the Heart of Development Pathways; Synthesis of Studies Conducted in WAEMU Countries and in Ghana, Guinea, Mauritania, and Nigeria*. Paris: French Development Agency and Institute for Research in Development.

———. 2007. "La démographie africaine entre convergences et divergences. " In *L'Afrique face à ses défis démographiques: un avenir incertain,* edited by Benoit Ferry, 27-121. Paris: AFD-CEPED-Karthala.

Guengant, Jean-Pierre, and John F. May. 201. "L'Afrique subsaharienne dans la démographie mondiale." ÉTVDES 4154: 305-316.

Guillaumont, Patrick, and Sylvianne Guillaumont Jeanneney. 2009. "State Fragility and Economic Vulnerability: What is Measured and Why?" Policy paper prepared for the *European Report on Development*, Barcelona.

Hadjimichael, Michael T., Dhaneshwar Ghura, Martin Muhleisen, Roger Nord, and E. Murat Ucer. 1995. "Sub-Saharan Africa: Growth, Savings, and Investment, 1986-93." Occasional Paper No. 118, International Monetary Fund, Washington, DC.

Hanushek, Eric, and Ludger Wößmann. 2007. *Education Quality and Economic Growth*. Washington, DC: World Bank.

Hazell, Peter. 2011. "Five Big Questions about Five Hundred Million Small Farms." IFAD Conference on New Directions for Smallholder Agriculture, Rome, January 24-25.

Heckman, James, and Flavio Cunha. 2006. *Investing in Our Young People*. Chicago: University of Chicago.

Herbst, Jeffrey. 2000. *States and Power in Africa*. Princeton, NJ: Princeton, NJ University Press.

Herderschee, Johannes, Daniel Mukoko Samba, and Moise Tschimenga Tschibangu, eds. 2012. *Résilience d'un Géant Africain Accélérer la croissance et promouvoir l'Emploi en RDC*. Kinshasa: Mediaspaul and World Bank.

Hertel, Thomas W., Marshall B. Burke, and David B. Lobell. 2010. "The Poverty Implications of Climate-Induced Crop Yield Changes by 2030." GTAP Working Paper Number 59, Global Trade Analysis Project, Purdue University, Indianapolis.

Hochschild, Adam. 1999. *King Leopold's Ghost*. Boston: Mariner Books.

Hoddinnot, John, Michele Adato, Tim Besley, and Lawrence Haddad. 2001. "Participation and Poverty Reduction: Issues, Theory, and New Evidence from South Africa." Discussion Paper 98, Food Consumption and Nutrition Division, International Food Policy Research Institute, Washington, DC.

Hoogeveen, Hans, and Dorica Andrews. 2012. *Are Our Children Learning? Literacy and Numeracy across East Africa*. Nairobi: Uwezo East Africa.

Hosono, Akio. 2012. "Climate Change, Disaster Risk Management." In *Scaling Up South-South and Triangular Cooperation*, edited by Hiroshi Kato, 15–41. Conference Volume Prepared for the Global South-South Development Expo 2012. Tokyo: JICA Research Institute.

ICF International. 2013. "STATcompiler." Updated November 20. http://www.statcompiler.com/.

ICIS. 2010. "Global Fertilizer Trade Map." *International Fertilizer Industry Association.* Updated December. http://www.africafertilizer.org/Markets/Library/Publications/Publication-Details-%281%29.aspx?publicationid=245&Keyword=.

IFAD, WFP, and FAO. 2012. *The State of Food Insecurity in the World*. Rome: FAO.

IFC. 2013. *SME Initiatives*. http://www.ifc.org/wps/wcm/connect/region__ext_content/regions/subsaharan+Africa/advisory+services/sustainablebusiness/sme_initiatives.

ILO. 2013. *Statistics and Databases*. http://www.ilo.org/global/statistics-and-databases/lang--en/index.htm.

REFERENCES

———. 2011. *Global Employment Trends*. Geneva: International Labor Organization.

IMF. 2013a. "IMF Primary Commodity Prices." Updated October 10. http://www.imf.org/external/np/res/commod/index.aspx.

———. 2013b. "World Economic Outlook Data: April 2013 Edition." Updated April. http://www.imf.org/external/pubs/ft/weo/2013/01/weodata/index.aspx.

———. 2012a. *Regional Economic Outlook: Sub-Saharan Africa; Maintaining Growth in an Uncertain World*. Washington, DC: International Monetary Fund.

———. 2012b. "World Economic Outlook Database." Updated October. http://www.imf.org/external/pubs/ft/weo/2012/02/weodata/index.aspx.

———. 2012c. *World Economic Outlook: Growth Resuming, Dangers Remain*. Washington, DC: International Monetary Fund.

———. 2009. *World Economic Outlook October 2009: Sustaining the Recovery*. Washington, DC: International Monetary Fund.

———. 2004. *Sub-Saharan Africa Regional Economic Outlook 2004*. Washington, DC: International Monetary Fund.

INSEAD, and WIPO. 2012. *The Global Innovation Index 2013: The Local Dynamics of Innovation*. Geneva and Fontainebleau: INSEAD and WIPO.

Institute of Security Studies. 2012. "Maritime Security in the Indian Ocean: Strategic Setting and Features." Paper No. 236, Institute for Security Studies, Pretoria.

International Aluminium Institute. 2013. *Primary Aluminium Production*. Updated October 21. http://www.world-aluminium.org/statistics/primary-aluminium-production/#data.

International Crisis Group. 2012. *The Gulf of Guinea: The New Danger Zone*. Dakar, Senegal: International Crisis Group.

International and Development Studies. 2009. *Small Arms Survey 2009: Shadows of War*. Geneva: Cambridge University Press.

IFPRI. 2012. "IMPACT Model." Updated July. http://www.ifpri.org/book-751/ourwork/program/impact-model

IZA. 2011. "How Large is the Private Sector in Africa? Evidence from National Accounts and Labor Markets." Discussion Paper No. 6267, Institute for the Study of Labor, Bonn.

Jacquemot, Pierre. 2013. *Economie politique de l'Afrique contemporaine*. Paris: Armand Colin.

Jacquemot, Pierre, and Serge Michailof. 2013. *Le développement du Sahel et en particulier du Mali : Leçons de l'expérience, enseignements de la recherche*. Paris : IRIS.

Japanese Ministry of Foreign Affairs. 2013. *Japan's Assistance Package for Africa at TICAD V*. Tokyo: Ministry of Foreign Affairs.

Jaramillo, Adriana, and Alain Mingat. 2008. "Can Early Childhood Programs Be Financially Sustainable in Africa?" In *Africa's Future, Africa's Challenge: Early Childhood Care and Development in Sub-Saharan Africa*, edited by Marito Garcia, Alan Pence, and Judith L. Evens. World Bank: Washington, DC.

Jayaram, Shubha. 2012. *Training Models for Employment in the Digital Economy*. Washington, DC: Results for Development Institute.

JICA. 2011. "JICA Climate-FT: Climate Finance Impact Tool for Mitigation and Adaptation, Version 1.0." Reference document, JICA, Tokyo.

JICA Research Institute. 2012. "Aiming for Promotion of Climate Change Mitigation Policies in Developing Countries." Policy Brief No.7, JICA Research Institute, Tokyo.

Juma, Calestous. 2011. *The New Harvest: Agricultural Innovation in Africa*. New York: Oxford University Press.

Kanbur, Ravi and Juzhong Zhuang. 2012. "Confronting Rising Inequality in Asia." In *Asian Development Outlook 2012*, published by the Asian Development Bank, 37-96. Manila: Asian Development Bank.

Kantiza, Antoine. 2012. "The Evaluation of Mobile Phone Application upon the Smallholder Farmer's Productivity." *e-agriculture*. Published December 5. http://www.e-agriculture.org/blog/evaluation-mobile-phone-application-upon-smallholder-farmers-productivity-east-africa.

Kharas, Homi, and Harinder S. Kohli. 2011. "What is the Middle Income Trap, Why Do Countries Fall into It, and How Can It Be Avoided" *Global Journal of Emerging Market Economies* 3 (3): 281-289.

Kohli, Harinder S., Richard Ackerman, Vinod K. Goel, R.A. Mashelkar, Homi Kharas, Hossein Razavi, Anil Sood, Inder Sud, Ashutosh Varshney, C.M Vasudev, Hariharan Ramachandran, Vivek K. Agnihotri, and Michael Walton. 2009. *India 2039: An Affluent Society in One Generation*. Manila: Asian Development Bank.

Kohli, Harinder S., Ashok Sharma, and Anil Sood. 2011. *Asia 2050: Realizing the Asian Century*. New Delhi: Sage.

Kohli, Harpaul Alberto, Y. Aaron Szyf, and Drew Arnold. 2012. "Construction and Analysis of a Global GDP Growth Model for 185 Countries through 2050." *Global Journal of Emerging Market Economies* 4 (2): 91-155.

Kragelund, Peter. 2008. "The Return of the Non-DAC Donors in Africa, Latin America, and Southeast Asia." United States Congressional Research Service Report for Congress, Washington, DC.

Krueger, Anne, Maurice Schiff, and Alberto Valdes. 1991-1992. *The Political Economy of Agricultural Pricing Policy*. Washington, DC: Johns Hopkins University Press.

Lamhauge, Nicolina, Elisa Lanzi, and Shardul Agrawala. 2012. "Monitoring and Evaluation for Adaptation: Lessons from Development Co-operation Agencies." OECD Environment Working Papers No. 38, OECD, Paris.

Lassibille, Gerard. 2012. "Teachers' Engagement at Work in a Developing Country." *Journal of African Economics* 22 (1): 52-72.

Lauglo, Jon. 2001. "Engaging with Adults: The Case for Increased Support to Adult Basic Education in Sub-Saharan Africa." Africa Region Human Development Working Papers Series, World Bank, Washington, DC.

Leonard, Kenneth, Gilbert Mliga, and Damien Haile Mariam. 2002. "Bypassing Health Centers in Tanzania." *Journal of African Economies* 11 (4): 441-471.

Levine, Ruth, Cynthia B. Lloyd, Margaret Green, and Caren Grown. 2009. *Girls Count: A Global Investment and Action Agenda*. Washington, DC: The Center for Global Development.

Levy, Brian. 2012. "Getting to 2050: A Long View of African Governance." Working Paper, Centennial Group International, Washington, DC.

Lewin, Keith, and Francoise Caillods. 2001. *Financing Secondary Education in Developing Countries: Strategies for Sustainable Growth*. Paris: UNESCO/IIEP.

Li, Anshan, Liu Haifang, Pan Huaqiong, Zeng Aiping, and He Wenping. 2012. "FOCAC Twelve Years Later: Achievements, Challenges, and the Way Forward." Discussion Paper No. 74, Nordic Africa Institute, Peking University, Uppsala.

Loser, Claudio. 2013. "Commodity Terms of Trade in Emerging Markets: A Fragile Blessing." *Global Journal of Emerging Market Economies* 5 (2): 99-115.

Loser, Claudio M., Jose Fajgenbaum, and Harinder S. Kohli, eds. 2012. *Mexico 2042: Achieving Prosperity for All*. New Delhi: Sage.

Lund, Frances, Michael Noble, Helen Barnes, and Gemma Wright. 2008. "Is There a Rationale for Conditional Cash Transfers for Children in South Africa?" Working Paper No. 53, Department of Social Policy and Social Work, University of Oxford, Oxford.

MacDonald, A. M., H. C. Bonsor, B. E. O, Dochartaigh, and R. G. Taylor. 2012. "Quantitative Maps of Groundwater Resources in Africa." *Environmental Research Letters* 7 (2).

Madan, Tanvi. 2006. "India." Energy Security Series, Brookings Foreign Policy Series, Brookings Institute, Washington, DC.

Maddison, Angus. 2007. *Contours of the World Economy 1-2030 AD: Essays in Macroeconomic History*. New York: Oxford University Press.

REFERENCES

Majgaard, Kirsten, and Alain Mingat. 2012. *Education in Sub-Saharan Africa: A Comparative Analysis*. Washington, DC: World Bank.

Makino, Koji. 2013. "Boosting Sustainable Agricultural Growth in Sub-Saharan Africa." In *For Inclusive and Dynamic Development in Sub-Saharan Africa*, 73-98. Tokyo, JICA Research Institute.

Mawdsley, Emma. 2012. *From Recipients to Donors: Emerging Powers and the Changing Development Landscape*. London: Zed Books.

May, John F. 2012. *World Population Policies: Their Origin, Evolution, and Impact*. New York: Springer.

McChrystal, Stanley. 2009. *Commander's Initial Assessment.* Published on August 30, 2009. http://media.washingtonpost.com/wpsrv/politics/documents/Assessment_Redacted_092109.pdf?sid=ST2009092003140.

McGann, James. 2011. *Global Go to Think Thank (Index).* University of Pennsylvania. Updated 2012. http://gotothinktank.com/rankings/.

McIntyre, Beverly D., Hans R. Herren, Judi Wakhungu, and Robert T. Watson, eds. 2009. *Agriculture at a Crossroads: Volume V; Sub-Saharan Africa Report*. Washington, DC: International Assessment of Agricultural Knowledge, Science, and Technology for Development.

McKinsey. 2012. *Africa at Work: Job Creation and Inclusive Growth.* New York: McKinsey and Company.

———. 2007. *How the World's Best-Performing Schools Come Out On Top.* New York: McKinsey and Company.

Meredith, Martin. 2011. *The Fate of Africa: A History of the Continent since Independence.* New York: Perseus.

Michailof, Serge. 2011a. "Are Conflict Prevention and Nation Building Feasible Goals?" *Monde-Cahiers du Quai d'Orsay*: 115-122.

———. 2011b. "Revolution verte et equilibres geostrategiques au Sahel." *La Revue Internationale et Strategique* 4 (8): 139-148.

———. 2010a. "The Challenges of Reconstructing 'Failed' States." *Field Action Science Reports*. http://factsreports.revues.org/696.

———. 2010b. *Notre maison brule au Sud*. Paris: Fayard/Comentaires.

———. 2005. "Cote d'Ivoire 2005: bienvenue sur le Titanic." *Comentaires* 110: 393-404.

Mine, Yoichi, and Mari Katayanagi. 2012. "Prevention of Violent Conflicts in Africa." JICA-RI Policy Brief No. 8, JICA Research Institute, Tokyo.

Mine, Yoichi, Frances Stewart, Sakiko Fukuda-Parr, and Thandika Mkandawire. eds. 2013. *Preventing Violent Conflict in Africa: Inequalities, Perceptions and Institutions*. New York: Palgrave Macmillan.

Mingat, Alain, Blandine Ledoux, and Ramahatra Rakotomalala. 2010. *Developing Post-Primary Education in Sub-Saharan Africa: Assessing the Financial Sustainability of Alternative Pathways*. Washington, DC: World Bank.

Minges, Michael, Cecilia Briceno-Garmendia, Mark Williams, Mavis Ampah, Daniel Camos, and Maria Shkratan. 2008. "Information and Communications Technology in Sub-Saharan Africa: A Sector Review." Background Paper 13, Africa Infrastructure Country Diagnostic, World Bank, Washington, DC.

Mittal, Surabhi, Sanjay Gandhi, and Guarav Tripathi. 2010. "Socio-Economic Impact of Mobile Phones on Indian Agriculture." Working Paper No. 246, Indian Council for Research on International Economic Relations, New Delhi, February.

Murotani, Ryutaro. 2013. "State-Building and Conflict Prevention in Africa." In *For Inclusive and Dynamic Development in Sub-Saharan Africa*, 329-347. Tokyo, JICA Research Institute.

National Intelligence Council. 2012. *Global Trends 2030: Alternative Worlds*. Washington, DC: Office of the Director of National Intelligence.

National Research Council. 1986. *Population Growth and Economic Development: Policy Questions* Washington, DC: National Academy Press.

Naudeau, Sophie, Naoko Kataoka, Alexandria Valerio, Michelle J. Neuman, and Leslie Kennedy. 2011. *Investing in Young Children: An Early Childhood Development Guide for Policy Dialogue and Project Preparation.* Washington, DC: World Bank.

Nelson, Gerald C., Mark W. Rosegrant, Amanda Palozzo, Ian Gray, Christina Ingersoll, Richard Robertson, Simla Tokgoz, Tingju Zhu, Timothy B. Sulser, Claudia Ringler, Siwa Msangi, and Liangzhi You. 2010. *Food Security, Farming, and Climate Change to 2050: Scenarios, Results, Policy Options*. Washington, DC: International Food Policy Research Institute.

Ngoupande, Jean Paul. 1997. *Chronique de la crise centre africaine*. Paris: L'Harmattan.

Nkrumah, Kwame. 1973. *Revolutionary Path*. New York: International Publishers.

North, Douglass C. 1990. *Institutions, Institutional Chance, and Economic Performance*. Cambridge: Cambridge University Press.

North, Douglass C., John Joseph Wallis, and Barry R. Weingast. 2009. *Violence and Social Orders*. Cambridge: Cambridge University Press.

OECD. 2012a. *Better Skills, Better Jobs, Better Lives: A Strategic Approach to Skills Policies*. Paris: OECD Publishing.

OECD. 2012b. *Development Co-operation Report 2012: Lessons in Linking Sustainability and Development*. Paris: OECD Publishing.

OECD. 2012c."OECDStat." Updated December 20. http://www.oecd.org/dac/stats/data.htm.

———. 2011a. "Busan Partnership for Effective Development Co-operation." Declaration, Fourth High Level Forum on Aid Effectiveness, Busan, Korea, November 29 to December 1.

———. 2011b. *DAC 50 Years: 50 Highlights*. Paris: OECD Publishing.

———. 2011c. *OECD Development Assistance Peer Reviews: Japan 2010*. Paris: OECD Publishing.

———. 2009a. *Development Co-operation Report 2009*. Paris: OECD Publishing.

———. 2009b. *Integrating Climate Change Adaptation into Development Co-operation: Policy Guidance*. Paris: OECD.

Oketch, Moses. 2007. "To Vocationalise or Not to Vocationalise? Perspectives on Current Trends and Issues in Technical and Vocational Education and Training (TVET) in Africa." *International Journal of Educational Development* 27: 220-234.

Oxenham, John. 2008. *Effective Literacy Programs: Options for Policy-Makers*. Paris: UNESCO International Institute for Educational Planning.

———. 2003. *Review of World Bank Supported Projects in Basic Education and Literacy 1977-2002: Comparison of Costs*. Washington, DC: World Bank.

Pariota, T.C., and F.M. Pierri. "Brazil's Strategy to Transform African Agriculture: Assessing the Technology, Knowledge, and Financing Platform." In *Agriculture and Food Security in Africa: The Impact of Chinese, Indian, and Brazilian Investment*, edited by Fantu Cheru and R. Modi. London: Zed Books and the Nordic Africa Institute.

Parry, Martin, and Cynthia Rosenzweig. n.d. "Climate Change and Agriculture." Intergovernmental Panel on Climate Change. http://cgiar.bio-mirror.cn/pdf/agm06/agm06_ParryRosenzweig_climatechange%26agr.pdf.

People's of Republic of China. 2011. *China's Foreign Aid.* Beijing: Information Office of the State Council.

———. 2006. *China's African Policy*. Beijing: The State Council.

Pina, Patriia, Tim Kotin, Vicky Hausman, and Edwin Macharia. 2012. *Skills for Employability: The Informal Economy.* Washington, DC: Results for Development Institute.

Prunier, Gerard. 2009. *Africa's World War: Congo, the Rwandan Genocide, and the Making of a Catastrophe.* Oxford: Oxford University Press.

REFERENCES

Reinhart, Carmen M., and Kenneth S. Rogoff. 2009. *This Time is Different: Eight Centuries of Financial Follies*. Princeton, NJ: Princeton, NJ University Press.

Reinsdorf, Marshall B. 2009. "Terms of Trade Effects: Theory and Measurement." Revised version of WP2009-01, Bureau of Economic Analysis, US Department of Commerce, October.

Reisen, Helmut, and Sokhna Ndoye. 2008. "Prudent Versus Imprudent Lending to Africa; From Debt Relief to Emerging Lenders." Working Paper 268, OECD Development Center, Organisation for Economic Co-operation and Development, Paris.

Riddell, R.C. 2008. *Does Foreign Aid Really Work?* New York: Oxford University Press.

Roemer, J. 1998. *Equality of Opportunity*. Cambridge, MA: Harvard University Press.

Romaniuk, A. 2011. "Persistence of High Fertility in Tropical Africa: The Case of the Democratic Republic of the Congo." *Population and Development Review* 37 (1): 1-28.

Rotberg, Robert I. 2003. "Failed States, Collapsed States." In *State Failure and State Weakness in a Time of Terror*, edited by Robert I. Rotberg. Washington, DC: Brookings.

Sanusi, Lamido. 2013. "Africa Must Get Real about Chinese Times." *Financial Times*. Published on March 11. http://www.ft.com/cms/s/0/562692b0-898c-11e2-ad3f-00144feabdc0.html#axzz2j9AldCp3.

Save the Children. 2012. *Born Equal: How Reducing Inequity Could Give Our Children a Better Future*. London: Save the Children.

Sharma, Devika, and Deepti Mahajan. 2007. "Energizing Ties: The Politics of Oil." *South African Journal of International Affairs* 14 (2): 37-52.

Shillington, Kevin. 1995. *History of Africa*. New York: St. Martin Press.

Sife, Alfred Said, Elizabeth Kiondo, and Joyce G. Lyimo-Macha. 2010. "Contribution of Mobile Phones to Rural Livelihoods and Poverty Reduction in Morogoro Region, Tanzania." *Electronic Journal of Information Systems in Developing Countries* 42 (3): 1-15.

Smil, Vaclav. 2002. "Nitrogen and Food Production: Proteins for Human Diets." *AMBIO: A Journal of the Human Environment* 31 (2): 126–131.

Stearns, Jason K. 2011. *Dancing in the Glory of Monsters: The Collapse of the Congo and the Great War in Africa*. New York: Public Affairs.

Stifel, David, and Bart Minten. 2003. "Transactions Costs and Agricultural Productivity: Implications of Isolation for Rural Poverty in Madagascar." Background paper for the Northeast Universities Development Consortium Conference, Yale University, New Haven, Connecticut, October 17-19.

Stiglitz, Joseph. 1996. "Some Lessons from the East Asia Miracle." *The World Bank Research Observer* 11 (2).

Sudo, Tomonori. 2013. "Countermeasures against Climate Change Africa." In *For Inclusive and Dynamic Development in Sub-Saharan Africa*, 301-328. Tokyo, JICA Research Institute.

Sudo, Tomonori, A. Sato, Y. Murakami, and M. Motohashi. 2009. "Promotion of Developing Country's Climate Policy Implementation: Applying Development Policy Loan." Paper presented at the Asia-Pacific Forum on Low Carbon Economy, Beijing, China, June.

Takeuchi, Shinichi, Ryutaro Murotani, and Keiichi Tsunekawa. 2011. "Capacity Traps and Legitimacy Traps: Development Assistance and State Building in Fragile Situations." In *Catalyzing Development: A New Vision for Aid*, edited by Homi Kharas, Koji Makino, and Woojin Jung, 127-154. Washington, DC: Brookings Institution Press.

Takizawa, Ikuo. 2013. "Toward Universal Health Coverage in Africa: Achieving MDGs with Equality and Beyond." In *For Inclusive and Dynamic Development in Sub-Saharan Africa*, 247-266. Tokyo, JICA Research Institute.

Teravaninthorn, Supee, and Gael Raballand. 2008. "Transport Prices and Costs in Africa: A Review of the Main International Corridors." Working Paper 14, Africa Infrastructure Country Diagnostic, World Bank, Washington, DC.

Thebaud, Brigitte. 1988. *Elevage et developpement au Sahel, quell avenir pour les eleveurs?* Geneva: BIT.

Thurlow, James, and Peter Wobst. 2004. "The Road to Pro-poor Growth in Zambia: Past Lessons and Future Challenges." Development Strategy and Governance Division Discussion Paper No. 16, Development Strategy and Governance Division, International Food Policy Research Institute, Washington, DC, December.

Tlemcani, Salima. 2010. "Sahel: vers l'Afghanisation de la region." *El Watan*. Published Sept. 20.

Toynbee, Arnold. 1972. *A Study of History*. Oxford: Oxford University Press.

UNAIDS. 2012. *UNAIDS Report on the Global AIDS Epidemic*. Geneva: UNAIDS.

———. 2011. *AIDS at 30: Nations at the Crossroads*. Geneva: UNAIDS.

UNCTAD. 2013a. "The Rise of BRIC FDI and Africa." *Global Investment Trends Monitor* Special Edition.

———. 2013b. "UNCTADSTAT." Updated April 29. http://unctadstat.unctad.org/ReportFolders/reportFolders.aspx.

———. 2012. *World Investment Report 2012*. Geneva and New York: United Nations.

———. 2010. *Economic Development in Africa Report 2010: South-South Cooperation; Africa and the New Forms of Development Partnership*. Geneva and New York: United Nations.

UNCTAD and UNDP. 2007. *Asian FDI in Africa: Towards a New Era of Cooperation Among Developing Countries*. New York: United Nations.

UNDP. 2013. "International Human Development Indicators." http://hdr.undp.org/en/statistics/.

UNDP. 2012. *Africa Human Development 2012: Towards a Food Secure Future*. New York: Regional Bureau for Africa, United Nations Development Programme.

———. 2011. *Human Development Report 2011: Sustainability and Equity; A Better Future for All*. New York: United Nations Development Programme.

UNECA, AU, and AfDB. 2011. *The Africa Water Vision for 2025: Equitable and Sustainable Use of Water for Socioeconomic Development*. Addis Ababa: United Nations Economic Council for Africa.

UNECA, AU, AfDB, and UNDP. 2011. *MDG Report 2011: Assessing Progress in Africa toward the Millennium Development Goals*. Addis Ababa: United Nations Economic Commission for Africa, African Union, African Development Bank, and United Nations Development Programme.

UNESCO. 2012a. *EFA Global Monitoring Report 2012*. Paris: UNESCO.

———. 2012b. *World Atlas of Gender Equality in Education*. Paris: UNESCO.

———. 2007. *EFA Global Monitoring Report 2008*. Paris: UNESCO.

———. 2005. *EFA Global Monitoring Report 2006*. Paris: UNESCO.

UNESCO-UIS. 2011. *Financing of Education in Sub-Saharan Africa: Meeting the Challenge of Expansion, Equity, and Quality*. Montreal: UNESCO-UIS.

———. 2006. *Teachers and Education Quality: Monitoring Global Needs for 2014*. Montreal: UNESCO-UIS.

UNFCCC. 2010. "Report of the Conference of the Parties on Its Sixteenth Session, Held in Cancun from 29 November to 10 December 2010." FCCC/ CP/2010/7/Add.1, United Nations Framework Convention on Climate Change, New York.

UN-Habitat and UNEP. 2010. *The State of African Cities 2010: Governance, Inequality, and Urban Land Markets*. Nairobi: United Nations.

UNICEF. 2013. "Multiple Indicator Cluster Surveys – Round 4." Updated October. http://www.childinfo.org/mics_available.html.

REFERENCES

———. 2012a. *Committing to Child Survival: A Promise Renewed*. New York: UNICEF.

———. 2012b. *Levels and Trends in Child Mortality*. New York: UN Inter-agency Group for Child Mortality Estimation.

United Nations. 2013. *World Population Prospects: The 2012 Revision*. New York: United Nations.

———. 2012a. "2012 Update for the MDG Database: Contraceptive Prevalence." http://www.un.org/esa/population/unpop.htm.

———. 2012b. *World Urbanization Prospects: The 2011 Revision*. New York: Population Division, United Nations Department of Economic and Social Affairs.

———. 2011a. *World Population Prospects: The 2010 Revision*. New York: Population Division, United Nations Department of Economic and Social Affairs.

———. 2011b. *World Urbanization Prospects: The 2010 Revision*. New York: Population Division, United Nations Department of Economic and Social Affairs.

UNU-IHDP, and UNEP. 2012. *Inclusive Wealth Report 2012: Measuring Progress toward Sustainability.* Cambridge: Cambridge University Press.

US Department of State. 2012. *Camp David Accountability Report: Actions, Approach and Results.* Washington, DC: US Department of State.

US Department of the Interior and US Geological Survey. 2012. *Mineral Commodity Summaries 2012*. Reston, VA: US Department of the Interior and US Geological Survey.

USAID. 2011. "Contraceptive Security Indicators." Updated 2012. http://deliver.jsi.com/dhome/whatwedo/commsecurity/csmeasuring/csindicators.

Van Creveld, Martin. 1991. *The Transformation of War*. New York: Macmillan.

Van Reybroucke, David. 2012. *Congo: Une histoire.* Paris: Actes Sud.

Varghese, N. Y. 2013. "Private Higher Education: The Global Surge and Indian Concerns." In *India Infrastructure Report 2012*: *Private Sector in Education*, published by the Infrastructure Development Finance Company, 145-156. London: Routledge.

Verspoor, Adriaan M. and the SEIA Team. (2008). *At the Crossroads: Choices for Secondary Education in Sub-Saharan Africa.* Washington, DC: World Bank.

Vines, Alex, Lillian Wong, Markus Weimer, and Indira Campos. 2009. *Thirst for African Oil: Asian Oil Companies in Nigeria and Angola*. London: Chatham House.

Wang, Haidong, Laura Dwyer-Lindgren, Katherine T. Lofgren, Julie Knoll Rajaratnam, Jacob R. Marcus, Alison Levin-Rector, Carly E. Levitz, Alan D. Lopez, Christopher J.L. Murray. 2012. "Age-Specific and Sex-Specific Mortality in 187 Countries, 1970-2010: A Systematic Analysis for the Global Burden of Disease Study 2010." *The Lancet* 380 (9859): 2071-2095.

WHO. 2012a. *Atlas of African Health Statistics 2012: Health Situation Analysis of the African Region.* Brazzaville: World Health Organization.

———. 2012b. *Global Tuberculosis Report 2012*. Geneva: World Health Organization.

———. 2010. *The World Health Report: Health Systems Financing; The Path to Universal Coverage*. Geneva: World Health Organization.

Willenbockel, Dirk. 2012. "Extreme Weather Events and Crop Price Spikes in a Changing Climate." Oxfam Research Report, Oxfam, Oxford, September.

Wodon, Q., ed. 2008a. "Electricity Tariffs and the Poor: Case Studies from Sub-Saharan Africa." Working Paper 11, Africa Infrastructure Country Diagnostic, World Bank, Washington, DC.

———. 2008b. "Water Tariffs and the Poor: Case Studies from Sub-Saharan Africa." Working Paper 12, Africa Infrastructure Country Diagnostic, World Bank, Washington, DC.

Woods, Ngaire. 2008. "Whose Aid? Whose Influence? China, Emerging Donors, and the Silent Revolution in Development Assistance." *International Affairs* 84 (6): 1205-1221.

World Bank. 2013a. *China 2030: Building a Modern, Harmonious, and Creative Society*. Washington, DC: World Bank and the Development Research Center of the State Council, People's Republic of China.

———. 2013b. "World DataBank." Updated August 1. http://databank.worldbank.org/data/home.aspx.

———. 2013c. "World Development Indicators." http://data.worldbank.org/data-catalog/world-development-indicators.

———. 2012a. *The 2013 World Development Report: Jobs*. Washington, DC: World Bank.

———. 2012b. "Corporate Scorecard: CO2 Emissions." Published August 24. http://corporatescorecard.worldbank.org/images/pdfs/tier1/122.pdf.

———. 2012c. *Doing Business 2012: Smarter Regulations for Small- and Medium-Size Enterprises*. Washington, DC: World Bank.

———. 2012d. *KEI and KI Indexes (KAM 2012)*. http://info.worldbank.org/etools/kam2/KAM_page5.asp.

———. 2012e. "Logistics Performance Index." http://www1.worldbank.org/PREM/LPI/tradesurvey/mode1a.asp.

———. 2012f. *World Development Indicators 2012*. Washington, DC: World Bank.

———. 2011a. *Global Development Horizons 2011: Multipolarity; The New Global Economy*. Washington, DC.

———. 2011b. *Learning for All: Investing in People's Knowledge and Skills to Promote Development; World Bank Group Education Strategy 2020*. Washington, DC: World Bank.

———. 2011c. *World Development Report 2011: Conflict, Security, and Development*. Washington, DC: World Bank.

———. 2010a. *African Development Indicators 2010*. Washington, DC: World Bank.

———. 2010b. *World Development Report 2010: Development and Climate Change*. Washington, DC: World Bank.

———. 2009a. "Awakening Africa's Sleeping Giant: Prospects for Commercial Agriculture in the Guinea Savannah Zone and Beyond." *Agriculture and Rural Development* 48.

———. 2009b. *Making Development Climate Resilient: A World Bank Strategy for Sub-Saharan Africa*. Washington, DC: World Bank.

———. 2008. *World Development Report 2008: Agriculture for Development*. Washington, DC: World Bank.

———. 2007. *Capturing the Demographic Bonus in Ethiopia: Gender, Development, and Demographic Actions*. Washington, DC: World Bank.

———. 2005a. *Expanding Opportunities and Building Competencies for Young People: A New Agenda for Secondary Education*. Washington, DC: World Bank.

———. 2005b. *World Development Report 2005*. Washington, DC: World Bank.

———. 2004. *World Development Report*. Washington, DC: World Bank.

———. 2000. *Can Africa Claim the 21st Century?* Washington, DC: World Bank.

———. 1993. *Adjustment in Africa: Reforms, Results, and the Road Ahead*. New York: Oxford University Press.

———. 1989. *Sub-Saharan Africa: From Crisis to Sustainable Growth*. Washington, DC: World Bank.

REFERENCES

World Bank, and IFC. 2012. *Doing Business 2013: Smarter Regulations for Small and Medium-Size Enterprises*. Washington, DC: World Bank.

World Bank, and IPEA. 2011. *Bridging the Atlantic: Brazil and Sub-Saharan Africa; South-South Partnering for Growth*. Brasilia: World Bank and IPEA.

World Bank, FAO, UNCTAD, and IFAD. 2013. "Knowledge Exchange Platform for Responsible Agro-Investment." https://www.responsibleagroinvestment.org/.

World Economic Forum. 2008. *Africa@Risk: A Global Risk Network Briefing*. Geneva: World Economic Forum.

World Economic Forum, World Bank, African Development Bank, and Ministry of Foreign Affairs of Denmark. 2013. *The Africa Competitiveness Report 2013*. Geneva: World Economic Forum.

The World Factbook. 2013. Washington, DC: Central Intelligence Agency. https://www.cia.gov/library/publications/the-world-factbook/.

World Resources Institute. 2013. "CAIT 2.0." http://cait2.wri.org/wri.

WTO. 2012. "International Trade Statistics 2012." https://www.wto.org/english/res_e/statis_e/its2012_e/its12_world_trade_dev_e.htm.

Yonaza, Enock, Tim Kelly, Naomi Halewood, and Colin Blackman, eds. 2012. *The Transformational Use of Information and Communication Technologies in Africa*. Washington, DC: World Bank, African Development Bank, and African Union.

Yoshizawa, Kei. 2013. "Achieving Economic Transformation for Inclusive and Sustained Growth in Africa: Prospects and Challenges." In *For Inclusive and Dynamic Development in Sub-Saharan Africa*, 21-70. Tokyo: JICA Research Institute.

About the Editors and Contributors

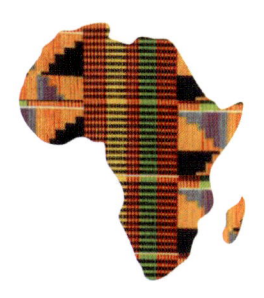

Editors

Theodore Ahlers

Theodore Ahlers is an economist with extensive experience in Europe and Central Asia, the Middle East and North Africa, and Sub-Saharan Africa. He is currently a Senior Associate at the Emerging Markets Forum. Over the last 25 years, he held numerous economist and senior management positions at the World Bank, including Strategy and Operations Director for Europe and Central Asia (2007-12), Maghreb Department Director (2002-07), Strategy and Operations Director for Africa (2000-02), Country Director for Benin, Niger, and Togo (1996-2000), and Lead Economist in West and Central Africa (1994-96). As Strategy and Operations Director he oversaw World Bank analytic and financial support to more than 50 countries in Africa, Europe and Central Asia, formulated regional strategy, and directed the office of the regional vice-president. As Country Director and Lead Economist, he led high-level economic policy dialogue with both middle-income and low-income countries, directed analytic work addressing structural reform issues, and oversaw World Bank lending. He holds a PhD in development economics from the Fletcher School at Tufts University.

Hiroshi Kato

Hiroshi Kato is Vice-President of the Japan International Cooperation Agency (JICA) and Director of the JICA Research Institute. Since joining JICA in 1978, he has served in various positions, including in the General Affairs Department, the Planning Department, and the Southeast Asia Department. He also has experience working at the Ministry of Foreign Affairs of Japan (in Tokyo and in Côte d'Ivoire). He graduated from the University of Tokyo in 1978 majoring in Asian history. He later earned his master's degree in public administration from the John F. Kennedy School of Government, Harvard University in 1988. He is Visiting Lecturer and Professor at Kobe University (Graduate School of International Studies) since 2003. He has been on the board of directors of the Japan Society for International Development since 2002.

Harinder S. Kohli

Harinder S. Kohli is the Founding Director and Chief Executive of Emerging Markets Forum as well as Founding Director, President, and CEO of Centennial Group International, both based in Washington, DC. He is the Editor of *Global Journal of Emerging Markets Economies*. Prior to starting his current ventures, he served over 25 years in various senior managerial positions at the World Bank. He has written extensively on Asia, Latin America, Africa and other emerging market economies, financial development, private capital flows, and infrastructure. He is an author and co-editor of *India 2039: An Affluent Society in One Generation* (2010), *Latin America 2040 — Breaking Away from Complacency: An Agenda for Resurgence* (2010), *A Resilient Asia amidst Global Financial Crisis (2010), and Islamic Finance* (2011), *Asia 2050: Realizing the Asian Century* (2011), and *A New Vision for Mexico 2042: Achieving Prosperity for All* (2012).

Callisto E. Madavo

Callisto Madavo holds a PhD in economics from the University of Notre Dame. He has held senior positions at the World Bank, serving as Program Division Chief for Pakistan, Country Director for East Africa and East Asia respectively, and then Vice President for Africa from 1996 through 2004. Since retiring from the World Bank, he has been a Visiting Professor in the African Studies Program in the School of Foreign Service at Georgetown University. Dr. Madavo has served as a consultant to the World Bank, African Development Bank, the International Fund for Agricultural Development (IFAD), the Global Fund, and the United Nations Office of Evaluation. He has also served on the boards of several not-for-profit organizations dealing with economic and health development issues in Africa.

Anil Sood

Anil Sood is a Principal at Centennial Group International. In his 30-year career at the World Bank, he occupied many senior positions including Vice President, Strategy and Resource Management, and Special Advisor to the Managing Directors. He has since advised chief executives and senior management of a number of development organizations including the African Development Bank, the International Fund for Agricultural Development, the Islamic Development Bank, the United Nations Development Programme, and the United Nations Economic Commission of Africa on matters of strategy and development effectiveness. He is the co-editor of *India 2039: An Affluent Society in One Generation* (2010), *Latin America 2040 — Breaking Away from Complacency: An Agenda for Resurgence* (2010), and *Asia 2050: Realizing the Asian Century* (2011).

Contributors

Mahmood A. Ayub

Mahmood Ayub is a Senior Associate with Centennial International Group in Washington, DC. He is also teaching and undertaking research at the Lahore University of Management Sciences in Pakistan. Prior to this, he worked for 30 years with the World Bank, working on most parts of the world and ending his career there as Director for Operations and Strategy for the Africa Region. He subsequently served as the Resident Coordinator of the United Nations for Turkey, based in Ankara, and as Director of UNDP for Central Asian countries, based in New York. He holds a PhD in economics from Yale University.

Anupam Basu

Anupam Basu is a Senior Associate with Centennial Group International. He joined the Centennial Group after over 30 years at the International Monetary Fund, where he served as Deputy Director of the Africa Department and Senior Advisor in the Policy Development and Review Department. He is an expert in the macroeconomic analysis of developing economies, including the design of fiscal, monetary, exchange rate and structural policies, financial programming, debt management policies and the assessment of debt sustainability. In recent years he has prepared studies on these issues in a number of countries, including Albania, Ghana, Kenya, Uganda, East Timor, Vanuatu, Nigeria, Namibia, and Botswana. He has also worked on the regional integration issues of Sub-Saharan Africa, including issues dealing with monetary and trade integration and the harmonization of various structural policies. Mr. Basu holds a PhD in economics from Stanford University.

James P. Bond

James Bond is an independent financial advisor specializing in energy and infrastructure in emerging economies. He holds several positions in this field including Senior Advisor to the African Development Bank, Senior Advisor to the UNFCCC-sponsored Green Climate Fund, and Non-Executive Director to Helios SE (London), an investment fund specializing in electricity in Africa. He is also member of the Board of Trustees of the Global Heritage Fund (Palo Alto, CA) which conserves and restores heritage sites around the world. James served in numerous managerial positions in the World Bank Group, including Chief Operating Officer of the Multilateral Investment Guarantee Agency (MIGA). Prior to joining MIGA in 2008 James was World Bank Country Director for several francophone countries in West Africa, as well as World Bank Country Director for the Indian Ocean based in Antananarivo, Madagascar. His sectorial responsibilities at the World Bank have included those of Global Director of Energy, Mining and Telecommunications; and Director of Rural Development, Agriculture and Environment for the Africa Region. At the International Finance Corporation (IFC), James was Director of the Mining Department. Before joining the World Bank Group James spent ten years with Total, the international oil and gas company, and has also worked for Gold Fields, a South African mining company. James holds a doctorate in economics from the University of Panthéon-Sorbonne in Paris, a master's degree in energy economics and finance from the French engineering school ENSPM, and a degree in chemical engineering from the University of Witwatersrand in South Africa.

Fantu Cheru
Fantu Cheru is a Distinguished Research Associate at the North-South Institute (Ottawa, Canada), Senior Research Fellow at the Center for African Studies at Leiden University (The Netherlands), and Emeritus Professor of African and Development Studies at American University in Washington, DC. Previously, Dr. Cheru served as a member of UN Secretary-General Kofi Annan's Panel on Mobilizing International Support for the New Partnership for African Development (2005-2007) as well as Convener of the Global Economic Agenda Track of the Helsinki Process on Globalization and Democracy, a joint initiative of the Governments of Finland and Tanzania. Dr. Cheru also served as the UN's Special Rapporteur on Foreign Debt and Structural Adjustment for the UN Commission for Human Rights in Geneva from 1998-2001. Professor Cheru's publications include: *Agricultural Development and Food Security in Africa: The Impact of Chinese, Indian and Brazilian Investments* (2013); *Africa and International Relations in the 21st Century*, co-edited with Scarlett Cornelissen and Timothy M. Shaw (2011); *The Rise of China and India in Africa* (2010). He currently serves on the editorial board of a number of academic journals.

David DeGroot
David DeGroot is a Research Scholar in the New York University Urbanization Project and currently leads, under the direction of Solly Angel, the Urban Expansion Project in Ethiopia. Dave has worked in Ethiopia since 1999 to implement a sequenced program of local government-enabling environment reforms, institutionalized capacity building, and intergovernmental fiscal reforms leading to a system of performance-based grants now being extended to the 44 largest cities in the country. His PhD dissertation focused on the work he and his wife Barbara (an urban planner) did with the World Bank-financed Urban II Slum Upgrading and Resettlement Project (1977) in Davao City. In 1988 he moved to Africa as USAID's regional urban development advisor, moving to South Africa in 1991 to design and implement a large grant program to facilitate the transition to the post-apartheid era. From 1994 to 2002 he worked for the World Bank, designing urban and local government support programs in Zambia, Zimbabwe, Swaziland, and South Africa.

José Fajgenbaum
José Fajgenbaum is the Director of Centennial Group, Latin America. He co-authored *The New Resilience of Emerging Countries: Weathering the Recent Crisis in the Global Economy*, *A New Vision for Mexico 2042: Achieving Prosperity for All*, and has cooperated extensively with the JICA. Previously, he served

at the IMF for some 30 years, progressing from economist to Deputy Director in three departments: African, European, and Western Hemisphere. Key roles included leading missions to countries, such as Brazil, Israel, Peru, Russia, and South Africa. Before joining the IMF, he served as an economist/lecturer in the Economic Development Institute of the World Bank and as a professor in the Economics Department of the National University of Cuyo. He completed studies for PhD in economics at the University of Chicago in 1979 and obtained the degree of Licenciado en Economia from the National University of Cuyo, Argentina in 1972.

Birger Fredriksen

Birger Fredriksen is a consultant on education policies in developing countries. Before retiring, he worked for 20 years in the World Bank including as Director of Human Development for Africa, Macroeconomic Division Chief for West Africa, and Division Chief for Human Development in the Sahel Department. Prior to that, he established and led for three years the Division of International Economics at the Norwegian Institute of Foreign Affairs in Oslo, worked for ten years at UNESCO in Paris, for two years at the Centre for Educational Research and Innovation (CERI) at the OECD in Paris, and for two years at the Institute of Economics at the University of Oslo. Mr. Fredriksen holds a master's degree in economics from the University of Oslo, and a PhD focusing on educational planning in developing countries from the University of Lancaster, UK. He has written extensively on education development, especially in Sub-Saharan Africa, and on effective allocation and use of education aid.

Jean-Pierre Guengant

Jean-Pierre Guengant holds a PhD in development economics and a master's degree in demography. He is Emeritus Director of Research at the Institut de Recherche Pour le Developpement (IRD). He was the resident representative of IRD in Niger and Benin, then Burkina Faso and Côte d'Ivoire until 2009. He is currently associated with The University of Paris I Sorbonne. From October to December 2011, he held the post of Deputy Director of the United Nations Population Division in New York and contributed to the production of a report on youth and adolescents in the world. In 2010 and 2012 he coordinated a series of monographs on 12 West African countries and Chad entitled *How to Capitalize on the Demographic Dividend*, and he is currently working on a similar study for the Democratic Republic of the Congo. He is the author of numerous publications, many on Sub-Saharan Africa and the Caribbean, and is a frequent lecturer on Population and Development, including at the G20 Parliamentary Assembly, the European Union, the African Development Bank, and in many African capitals (Niamey, Ouagadougou, Bamako, Cotonou, N'Djaména, Antananarivo, Kinshasa, Bujumbura, Accra). He was selected by *Le Monde* in its special edition 2010 report as one of 40 scientists and actors who made the news in 2010 for his work and engagement in the field of population in Africa.

Harpaul Alberto Kohli

Harpaul Alberto Kohli is the Manager of Information Analytics at Centennial Group International and the Emerging Markets Forum, where he is responsible for all modeling, statistics, databases, and technology management. He earned a degree with honors in mathematics and philosophy from Harvard University, where he served as co-president of both the Society of Physics Students and the Math Club and was elected a class vice president for life. He earned his MBA at Georgetown University, with emphases on psychology and on financial markets and public policy. He is also a Microsoft Certified Technology Specialist. Prior to joining Centennial, he served as a teacher in prisons in Ecuador and Massachusetts, a researcher at UBS and in the US Congress, a field organizer for the 2004 American general election, and a communications staffer for the Wesley Clark Presidential primary campaign.

Claudio M. Loser

Claudio M. Loser is CEO and President of Centennial Latin America and is Advisor for the Emerging Markets Forum. Loser is also a Senior Fellow at the Inter-American Dialogue. Since 2005 he has been an adjunct professor of economics (Latin American economic development) at George Washington University and has lectured at the Foreign Service Institute of the US Department of State. For 30 years and until November 2002, he was a staff member of the International Monetary Fund. During the last eight years of his tenure he was Director of the Western Hemisphere Department at the IMF. He graduated from the University of Cuyo in Argentina and received his MA and PhD from the University of Chicago. Loser has published extensively, including the book *Enemigos* together with the Argentine journalist Ernesto Tenenbaum, where they discuss the relations of the IMF and Argentina in the 1990s. He also is co-editor of *Latin America 2040 — Breaking Away from Complacency: An Agenda for Resurgence* and *A New Vision for Mexico 2042: Achieving Prosperity for All*.

John F. May

John May, a specialist in population policies and programs, is currently a Visiting Scholar at the Population Reference Bureau (PRB). He also teaches demography at Georgetown University, Washington, DC. For 15 years, he was a Lead Demographer at the World Bank. Prior to coming to the United States in 1987, he worked on population projects around the world for numerous international organizations. He was posted in Haiti and New Caledonia for the United Nations. He also worked for the Futures Group International, a US consulting firm offering services in population policies and programs. In 2012, he published *World Population Policies: Their Origin, Evolution, and Impact (*Springer), which was awarded the Population Institute 2012 Global Media Award for Best Book on population. In March 2013, he was elected an Associate Member of the Royal Academy of Belgium. He earned a BA in modern history (1973) and a MA in demography (1985) from the Catholic University of Louvain (Belgium), and a doctorate in demography (1996), summa cum laude from the University of Paris-V (Sorbonne).

John Murray McIntire

John Murray McIntire is currently Deputy Director General for Integrated Sciences at the International Livestock Research Institute in Nairobi. From 1989 until 2011 he held several senior positions at the World Bank including Country Director for Tanzania, Uganda and Burundi; Country Director for Senegal, the Gambia, Cape Verde, and Guinea; and Director for Agricultural, Environmental, and Social Development in the Africa. Additionally, he developed and managed a National Agricultural Technology Program for Mexico and later worked on Côte d'Ivoire as the country economist. Prior to joining the World Bank, he worked as a Principal Economist in the ICRISAT West Africa Program in Burkina Faso, and eventually he moved with ICRISAT to Niger, where he was one of the scientists involved in establishing the ICRISAT Sahelian Center at Sadore. In 1984 he was appointed Principal Economist at ILCA in Addis Ababa. Based on his work at ILCA and ICRISAT in 1989, he published *Crop Livestock Integration in Sub-Saharan Africa (*1992), with Daniel Bourzat and Prabhu Pingali. He holds a PhD in agricultural economics from the Fletcher School at Tufts University.

Serge Michailof

Serge Michailof is currently an Associate Researcher at the Institut de Relations Internationale et Stratégique (IRIS) in Paris. From 2002 until 2012, he taught at the Sorbonne and then at the Institut National des Sciences Politiques in Paris. He is a regular consultant on fragile states and post-conflict reconstruction. From 2001 to 2004 he was the Director for Operations of the French Development Agency (AFD) and the Vice President of its private sector subsidiary Proparco. Previously he spent 8 years as a country director and senior advisor at the World Bank in Washington and 15 years as regional representative in AFD field offices in various African countries. In 1992/93 he was advisor to the French Minister of Cooperation. Before joining AFD, he spent six years in a French consulting firm, SATEC, where he led the technical department. During a 45-year career dedicated to development, he has worked in 65 different countries. He studied in France (MBA from HEC, PhD in economics, MA in anthropology) and in the United States (MIT). He has published or directed several books. He is a board member of the Conseil des Investisseurs en Afrique (CIAN).

Praful Patel

Praful Patel holds an MA (urban settlements) from the Massachusetts Institute of Technology. He is a former Vice President of the World Bank and currently with Centennial Group International serving as their Vice President for Africa.

Jeffrey Racki

Jeffrey Racki has worked in both the private and public sectors in technical and management positions dealing with housing, urban development, local government, and service delivery. He has also been responsible for developing environmental policies and programs addressing both the consequences of and the opportunities for mitigating the impacts of climate change, and for dealing with the environmental impacts of infrastructure development. He has served in several management positions in the World Bank, including Sector Director, Environment and Social Development. Mr. Racki has an MS in advanced studies in architecture and a master's in city planning from the Massachusetts Institute of Technology.

Graham Stegmann

Graham Stegmann is currently an independent consultant on international development. In a career in the UK Civil Service, principally with DFID, he had a range of positions in London including as Head of Aid Policy and Resources and Head of Human Resources; he served abroad in Bangladesh, in Malawi and South Africa as Head of the Division for Southern Africa. Graham was DFID Director for Africa from 2000-04 and then the Director responsible for the Africa and development input into the UK hosted 2005 G8 Summit and the Africa Commission. After DFID, he moved to Tunis from 2006-11 as Special Advisor to the President of the African Development Bank. Graham was a member of the Board of the British Red Cross for six years to 2012. He was born in Zimbabwe, educated at London and Cambridge University (as a Commonwealth Scholar), and appointed as a CBE in the UK Honours list in 2006.

Tomonori Sudo

Tomonori Sudo is a Senior Research Fellow at the JICA Research Institute currently conducting research on environment and climate change issues. He is also a member of the OECD/DAC Environment and Development Cooperation Network. During his 20 year career at JICA, JBIC and OECF, he has experience in ODA loan operations in Indonesia, Malaysia, Bangladesh, and China, and been seconded to the African Development Bank as a Private Sector Specialist. In addition, he has conducted research on climate policy and capacity building on the Clean Development Mechanism in several Asian countries at the Institute for Global Environmental Strategies (IGES). Before joining JICA, he worked in private sector finance at a Japanese commercial bank. Dr. Sudo received his PhD in international studies from Waseda University, Japan; BA in economics from Osaka University in Osaka, Japan; and MSc in environmental and resource economics from University College London.

Index

2008 financial crisis, 27, 315, 417

Afghanistan, 125, 128-130

aging, 31-33, 98, 225-226

agriculture, 62-64, 118-119, 123, 133, 197, 234-235, 238, 250, 258, 260, 263, 267-308, 387-389, 402, 421-422, 425

aid, 171, 233, 390, 399-409, 418-419, 421, 425

Algeria, 3, 45-46, 62, 85, 92, 119, 140-141, 146, 199, 209, 273, 283, 310, 312, 317, 325, 345, 364, 375, 448

Angola, 3, 80, 88, 116, 142, 144-146, 209, 276-278, 284, 306, 312, 317, 330, 333, 364, 375, 381, 448, 473

Benin, 3, 68, 87, 119, 142-143, 185, 209, 317, 351, 375, 448, 477, 481

Botswana, 3, 15-16, 38, 45, 110, 141, 146, 184, 209, 246, 253, 260, 262, 310, 317, 322-324, 330, 375, 381, 448, 457, 479

Brazil, 44, 46, 143-144, 153, 253, 276, 278, 363, 409, 411, 414, 417

Burkina Faso, 3, 88, 110, 120, 142-143, 146-147, 168, 175, 178, 185, 209, 264, 317, 327, 375, 448, 481, 483

Burundi, 3, 88, 142, 144, 175, 206, 294, 317, 374-375, 448, 483

business, 14, 73, 160, 245, 258, 261, 344, 349, 374

business-as-usual scenario, 15-16, 19-20, 78, 150, 153, 268

Cameroon, 3, 68, 87, 119-121, 141-142, 145-146, 175, 185, 209, 276, 317, 322, 327, 334, 375

Cape Verde, 3, 15-16, 45, 85, 92, 142, 174, 317, 375

Central African Republic, 3, 87, 119, 142, 144-145, 327, 375, 381

Chad, 3, 88, 93, 118-120, 123, 142-147, 175, 273, 283, 312, 317, 330, 375

Chile, 30, 31, 257, 331-333

China, 289, 407, 414

climate change, 34, 268, 283, 289-291, 296, 343, 348, 350, 364, 379-381, 383-384, 386-390, 392-394, 415

Comoros, 3, 87, 142, 206, 317, 375

competition, 13, 59-60, 239-240, 243, 245, 249, 256, 258-259, 438

convergence scenario, 11, 15-20, 69, 150, 153, 159, 168-170, 221, 237, 270, 276, 400, 417

corruption, 2, 30, 38, 73, 76, 112-113, 115, 117-118, 121, 123, 127-129, 131-132, 137, 245-246, 256, 258, 261-262, 313-314, 319-320, 324-330, 416, 418, 420, 423

Côte d'Ivoire, 3, 87, 106, 110, 113, 118, 120, 209

crime, 119-121, 137, 314

    piracy, 120, 415

democracy, 113-116, 118, 122, 125, 127, 250, 404-406, 419

Democratic Republic of the Congo, 3, 38, 58, 75, 88, 107, 109, 120, 125, 127, 129, 138, 141-142, 145, 146, 147, 170, 175, 178, 206, 276, 278, 284, 291, 310, 317, 325, 327, 345, 375

demographic transition, 12, 34, 51, 53-54, 83-85, 90, 99-100, 160, 162, 167, 183, 269-270, 340

dependency ratio, 84, 97, 100

Djibouti, 3, 142, 375

downside scenario, 19-20, 150

Dutch disease, 123, 313-315, 329

economic growth, 2, 12, 14, 27-28, 32, 40-41, 44, 54, 66, 77, 84, 89, 116-117, 131, 138, 150, 160-162, 164, 169-172, 174, 177-178, 184, 189, 196, 208, 222, 224-227, 233-234, 240, 251, 267-269, 271-272, 293, 310, 343-344, 348-349, 352, 361, 366, 381, 384-385, 399, 412, 419, 425

education, 29, 54, 56, 84, 89, 93, 96-97, 143-144, 154, 159-194, 251, 256, 340, 349, 424

    primary school enrollment, 2, 161, 185

Egypt, 3, 22, 46, 53, 78, 92, 140-146, 196, 199, 209, 237, 254, 273, 282-283, 291, 312, 317, 340, 345, 348, 351-353, 361, 363-364, 368, 375

energy, 62, 249, 256-257, 292, 322, 344, 346, 385, 389, 403, 408, 415, 417, 421

entrepreneurship, 28, 44, 60-61, 164, 251, 253-254, 256, 258, 259-261, 263

Equatorial Guinea, 3, 87, 120, 312, 317, 330, 375, 381

Eritrea, 3, 87, 143, 317, 375

Ethiopia, 3, 53, 87-88, 94, 106, 138, 140, 142-143, 146-147, 154, 168-169, 176, 192, 196, 209, 284-285, 290-291, 317, 343, 345, 351-355, 363-364, 375

EU, 182, 369-374, 405-406, 410-412, 414, 417-419

FDI, 14, 28-29, 68-69, 164, 215, 218, 221, 223, 226, 254-258, 260-261, 277, 388, 390, 404, 413-414, 416, 419

fertility rate, 35, 53, 84-90, 92-94, 96, 99, 340

financial crisis, 207-208, 211, 215

Gabon, 3, 87, 142, 209, 312, 317, 327, 375, 381, 386

GDP, 25, 453

    GDP growth, 27, 137, 153

    GDP per capita, 2, 12, 25, 34, 42, 45-46, 97, 120, 197, 340

gender equality, 12, 52, 56, 60-61, 87, 89-90, 92-94, 96, 100, 139-140, 143-144, 153, 160, 162, 167, 171-173, 175, 177-180, 182-183, 236, 253, 258, 262-263, 291, 392-393

Ghana, 3, 87, 91, 106, 113, 120, 141-142, 146-147, 174, 176, 201, 203, 209, 235, 237, 276, 310, 314, 317, 322, 327, 330, 343, 345, 351, 352, 355, 375, 386

Gini coefficient, 41, 140-141, 143, 150

globalization, 5, 78, 161, 165, 190-191, 430

GMOs, 63, 295

governance, 13, 73-76, 109, 112, 124, 165, 191, 242, 292, 351, 416, 418

Guinea, 3, 87, 142-144, 174, 276, 292, 310, 317, 327, 330, 375

Guinea Bissau, 3, 119, 375

Guinea-Bissau, 3, 87, 93, 115, 119, 142-143, 174, 317, 375

health, 85, 89-90, 96-97, 144-145, 153-154, 159, 161, 164-165, 167, 169, 172-174, 177-178, 190, 295, 349

   health care, 168, 178

   HIV/AIDS, 139, 145, 177, 273, 314

   malaria, 55, 139, 144, 175-178, 295, 365, 383

   TB, 139, 177-178, 365

ICT, 33, 164, 171, 190, 249-250, 256-257, 261, 309, 335

inclusive growth, 41, 44, 51, 53, 84, 94, 120, 137, 139, 140, 144-145, 146, 153-154, 159, 165, 170, 313-314, 340, 344, 392, 425

India, 408, 414

infrastructure, 61-62, 64-66, 68, 160, 175, 177, 249, 256-257, 289, 309, 319, 322, 335, 340, 344, 346, 348-350, 352, 355-356, 364, 373-374, 384-386, 388, 390, 400, 402, 421-422, 424

innovation, 33, 60, 127, 161, 164, 189-190, 251, 253, 257-258, 260, 294, 343-344, 349

institutions, 126-127, 129-130, 187, 346, 373, 419, 423

investment, 13, 29, 59, 67, 69, 199, 240, 242, 311, 319, 321, 325, 330-331, 344, 350-352, 354, 356, 375, 388, 390, 394, 399, 401, 403, 408-409, 413, 416-417, 420-421, 437

Japan, 27, 33, 131, 362-363, 379, 406-407, 411-412, 416

JICA, 22, 48, 80, 156, 230, 264, 376, 386, 406

jobs, 11-13, 35, 40, 51, 60-61, 67, 84, 89, 96, 132, 159, 172, 181, 188, 233-234, 238, 251, 258, 262, 314, 340, 343-344, 347, 356, 422, 425

Kenya, 3, 33, 68, 87, 141-143, 145-146, 165, 175, 184, 197, 203, 209, 237, 244, 250, 273, 294-295, 317, 355, 374-375

labor force, 33-35, 84, 124, 133, 162, 164, 181, 183, 233, 236, 256, 453

land, 63-64, 270, 273, 276, 278, 283, 287-288, 339-340, 344-345, 348-349, 352, 354, 356

Lesotho, 3, 142, 144-146, 165, 177, 185, 203, 317, 375

Liberia, 3, 75, 87, 142, 144, 147, 180, 196, 310, 317, 327, 375

Libya, 3, 85, 109, 118, 145-146, 199, 207, 282, 312, 317, 364, 375, 381

life expectancy, 53, 85, 89, 94, 96, 144-145, 153, 177-178

local government, 58, 66-67, 69, 115, 124, 351-356

Madagascar, 3, 87, 138, 142, 147, 184-186, 203, 209, 284, 289, 314, 316-317, 327, 375

Malawi, 3, 88, 141-142, 154, 185-186, 203, 209, 250, 290, 292, 317, 375, 386

Mali, 3, 88, 106-107, 109, 115, 118-120, 122, 125, 130-131, 140, 142-143, 145-147, 169, 175, 178, 185, 203, 209, 238, 250, 273, 285, 317, 327, 351, 375

Mauritania, 3, 87, 118-119, 142, 146, 317, 327, 351, 375

Mauritius, 3, 15, 16, 45, 85, 92, 140-141, 144-146, 197, 209, 239, 246, 253-254, 260, 317, 375

MDGs, 138-139, 146-147, 153, 176, 403, 419

mega-cities, 40, 97, 99, 340, 349

middle class, 12-13, 15, 17, 19, 28, 44, 46, 77, 131, 137, 148, 150, 152-153, 159, 355, 400, 413

middle-income countries, 3, 45

    middle-income trap, 45, 47

middle-income trap, 361-362

Morocco, 3, 61, 62, 68, 75, 92, 141-142, 146, 154, 156, 181, 184, 196, 199, 209, 239, 254, 273, 291, 310, 317, 324, 345, 348, 351, 356, 364, 375

mortality, 84-85, 94, 97, 99, 340

    under-five, 2, 94, 175

Mozambique, 3, 15, 16, 68, 87, 141-144, 146, 178, 185, 209, 277, 284-285, 289-290, 310, 314, 317, 322, 327, 375

multipolar global economy, 31

Namibia, 3, 142, 147, 175, 209, 316-317, 353, 355, 375

natural resources, 30, 32, 35, 38, 64, 65, 123, 207, 228, 233, 309-312, 314, 316-318, 320, 324, 331, 355, 386, 403, 415, 421-422, 424

    gas, 14, 35, 38, 153, 286, 309-311, 314, 316-320, 324, 325, 327-328, 334, 380-381, 399, 407, 415, 425

    minerals, 14, 35, 38

    oil, 14, 35, 123, 309-310, 313, 319, 408-409, 411

Niger, 3, 88, 109, 119-121, 123, 142-143, 147, 168, 185, 203, 209, 273, 289-290, 292, 294, 314, 317, 327, 375

Nigeria, 3, 38, 68, 88, 93, 110, 119-120, 138, 140, 142-143, 146, 154, 177-178, 209, 226, 254, 276, 278, 284, 285, 290-291, 310, 312, 314, 317, 322, 327, 330, 333-334, 345, 361, 363-364, 368, 375

political systems, 41, 113-116, 121, 122, 124-125

population growth, 25, 34, 197, 283, 291, 453

poverty, 12, 15, 42, 119, 137-138, 146, 150, 153, 343, 344, 401

    poverty rate, 2, 41, 139, 150

private sector, 11, 13, 14, 27, 31, 35, 40, 56, 58, 59-65, 69, 117, 131, 189-190, 195, 198, 222, 224, 233-235, 250, 258-263, 292, 309-310, 315, 319, 324-325, 331, 339, 349-350, 388, 390-394, 409, 415, 416, 418-421

productivity, 13, 46, 162, 174, 234-235, 238, 240, 254, 256-257, 269-270, 294, 343, 362, 421-422

public sector, 61, 75-76, 116, 167, 170, 223, 262-263, 315, 349, 393

R&D, 56, 60, 171, 189-190, 251, 253, 295-296, 393, 422

regional cooperation, 3, 14, 55, 67-68, 123, 125, 132-133, 164, 190, 293, 349, 361-378, 421, 424

    regional economic integration, 369-370, 417

Republic of Congo, 3, 142, 327

rural development, 89, 118, 138, 153, 160, 172, 175, 181, 350

Rwanda, 3, 87-88, 94, 130, 140, 142, 146, 169, 175, 178-179, 206, 239, 245, 317, 374, 375

sanitation, 147, 149, 160, 175, 183, 344, 346

Sao Tome and Principe, 3, 87, 317, 375

security, 13, 41, 55, 57-58, 73, 120, 124, 132-133, 414-415, 423

Senegal, 3, 87, 110, 141, 143, 146, 169, 174, 186, 203, 209, 250, 285, 292, 317, 351, 375

Seychelles, 3, 85, 91, 142, 209, 317, 375, 381

Sierra Leone, 3, 38, 75, 87, 142, 145-147, 201, 206, 317, 327, 375

SMEs, 153, 235, 237, 344, 347, 349

Somalia, 3, 88, 102, 106, 127, 132, 146, 175, 317, 375

South Africa, 3, 43, 45-46, 61, 67, 78, 140-146, 153-154, 175, 177, 184, 209-210, 225-227, 237-239, 246, 249, 251, 253, 259-260, 283-284, 290, 295, 310, 317, 321-322, 324, 334, 344-345, 351-352, 353, 355-356, 361, 363-364, 368, 375, 381

South-South cooperation, 389, 403, 408-409

South Sudan, 3, 87, 91, 278, 317, 375

state formation, 106-107, 109-110, 116, 125

Swaziland, 3, 92, 140, 142, 145-146, 177, 184, 206, 209, 317, 351-353, 355, 375

Tanzania, 3, 87, 110, 138, 141-143, 146-147, 154, 165, 175, 180, 184-186, 203, 209, 244, 276-278, 284, 285, 290, 294, 310, 317, 327, 351, 374-375

technology, 33, 63-64, 124, 159, 181-182, 189, 251, 254, 257-258, 260, 277-278, 285, 291, 294-296, 311, 349, 384, 388, 390, 394, 421-422, 424-425

terms of trade, 19, 39, 59, 195, 197, 207, 213, 215-216, 218, 233, 281, 429–452, 430-432, 434, 435-436, 447

TFP, 15-16, 28-30, 221, 223, 235, 237, 240, 242, 251, 253, 257, 260, 268, 274, 362

The Gambia, 3, 87, 142, 146, 203, 375

Togo, 3, 87, 121, 142, 146, 175, 185, 203, 209, 317, 327, 375

trade, 14, 15, 29, 61, 67-69, 245, 256-260, 293, 320, 366-368, 370-371, 373-375, 399, 401, 403, 408-410, 416-417, 421, 423, 430, 438

   terms of trade, 39, 197, 207, 216, 218

trade agreements, 412, 417

trafficking, 107, 118-119, 415

   drugs, 119

Tunisia, 3, 61, 62, 68, 75, 85, 92-93, 120, 140-142, 145-146, 199, 209, 235, 253-254, 260, 273, 291, 312, 317, 347, 351-352, 364, 375

TVSD, 56, 182, 187-188

Uganda, 3, 88, 109, 117, 131, 141-142, 144, 146-147, 154, 175, 180, 184, 201, 209, 230, 244, 290, 294, 343, 351, 374-375

United States, 182, 276, 309, 321, 324, 362-363, 370, 406, 410-414, 417

urbanization, 13, 14, 40, 65-67, 85, 90, 94, 97, 99, 164, 250, 256, 262, 339-340, 343-344, 348, 352, 385

   mega-cities, 40, 97, 99, 340

water, 63-64, 123, 133, 139, 146-148, 154, 160, 175, 183, 257, 273, 283-284, 291-292, 344, 346, 348-390

youth, 84, 96, 99, 162, 263, 324, 340, 400

Zambia, 3, 88, 142, 146, 175, 184, 201, 206, 209, 276-278, 284, 289-290, 295, 310, 317, 327, 351-355, 375

Zimbabwe, 3, 117, 141, 145-146, 276, 285, 317, 321, 352, 355, 375

Photo Credits

xxxii	JICA/Takeshi Kuno	Rwanda
8	Vladyslav Morozov/Shutterstock.com	South Africa
22	JICA/Shinichi Kuno	Egypt
70	U.S. Army Corps of Engineers/Jennifer Schmeltzle	Togo
80	JICA/Koji Sato	Kenya
102	Agata Grzybowska/Agencja Gazeta	Somalia
134	smebeesley/Shutterstock.com	
156	UNHCR / F. Noy / December 2011	Chad
192	Simon Davis/DFID	Ethiopia
230	Simon Davis/DFID	Ethiopia
264	JICA/Akio Iizuka	Burkina Faso
306	Christopher Poe/Shutterstock.com	Angola
337	Nite_Owl/flickr	Kenya
358	Christiaan Triebert/flickr	Kenya
376	Petterik Wiggers/Hollandse Hoogte	Ethiopia
396	donvictorio/Shutterstock.com	South Africa
426	Pete Lewis/Depatment for International Development	Ethiopia
450	JICA/Shinichi Kuno	Egypt
494	UNHCR /F. Noy/ December 2011	Chad

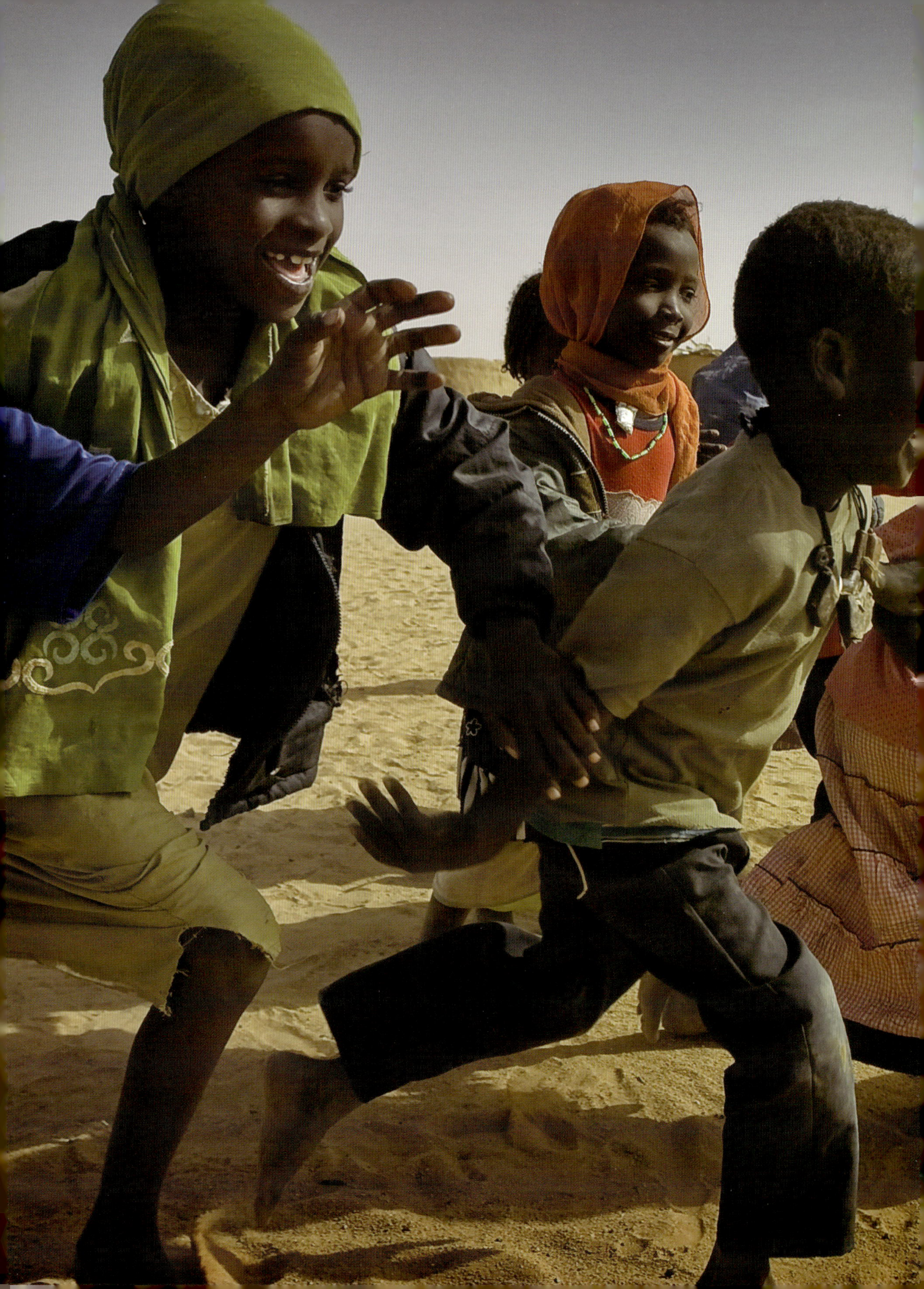

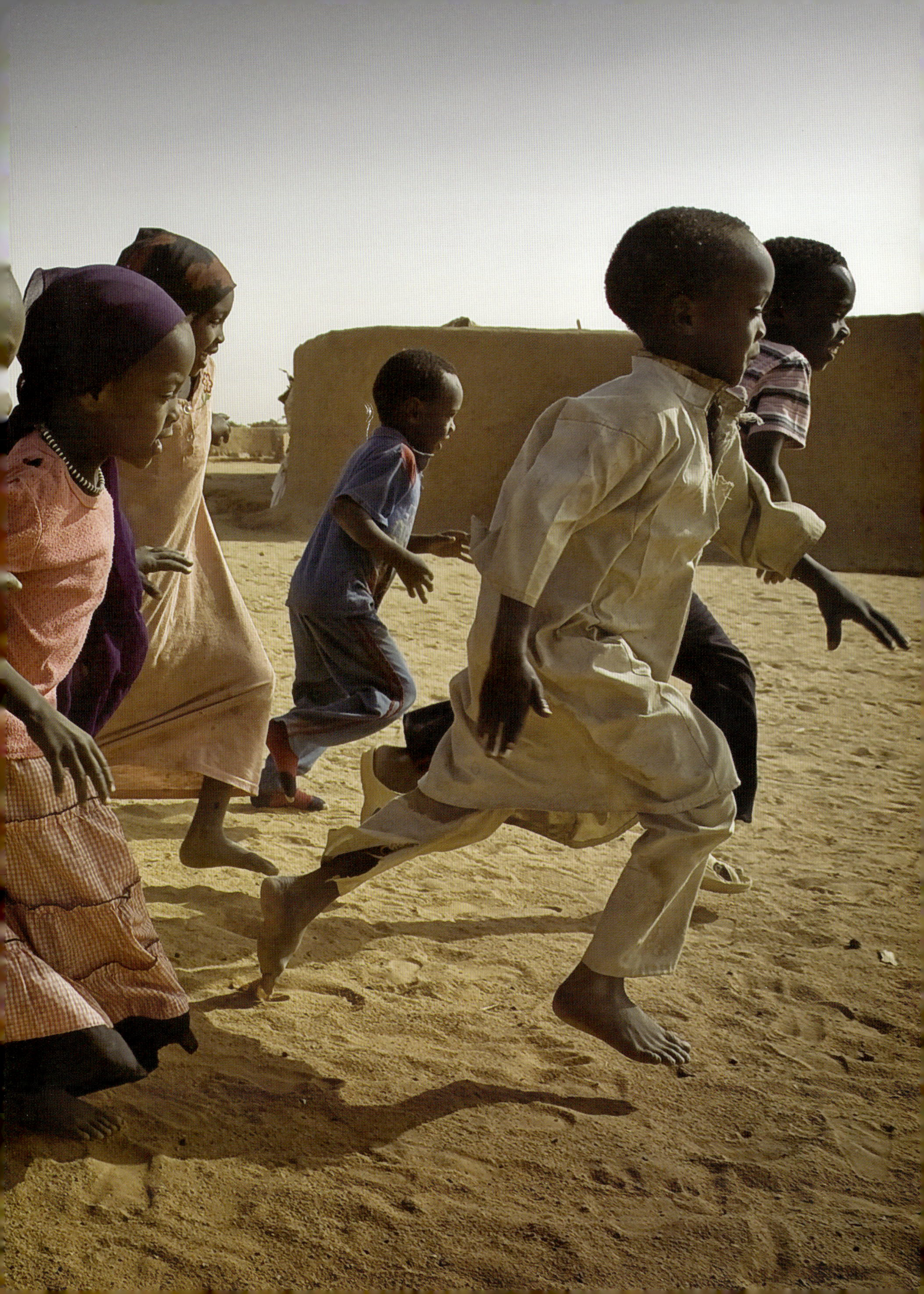